W9-AYL-122

The 20 Greatest Composers

1. Bach
2. Mozart
3. Beethoven
4. Wagner
5. Haydn
6. Brahms
7. Schubert
8. Schumann
9. Handel
10. Tchaikovsky
11. Mendelssohn
12. Dvořák
13. Liszt
14. Chopin
15. Stravinsky
16. Verdi
17. Mahler
18. Prokofiev
19. Shostakovich
20. R. Strauss

To find out why these men are the best of the best, read on. . . .

CLASSICAL MUSIC

The 50 Greatest Composers
and Their 1,000 Greatest Works

PHIL G. GOULDING

FAWCETT COLUMBINE • NEW YORK

Sale of this book without a front cover may be unauthorized. If this
book is coverless, it may have been reported to the publisher as
"unsold or destroyed" and neither the author nor the publisher may
have received payment for it.

A Fawcett Columbine Book
Published by Ballantine Books

Copyright © 1992 by Phil G. Goulding

Orchestra illustrations © 1992 by Random House, Inc.

All rights reserved under International
and Pan-American Copyright Conventions. Published
in the United States by Ballantine Books, a division of Random House,
Inc., New York, and simultaneously in Canada by
Random House of Canada Limited, Toronto.

Grateful acknowledgment is made to the following
for permission to reprint previously published material:
Random House, Inc.: Excerpt from A Working Friendship: The Correspondence
Between Richard Strauss and Hugo von Hofmannsthal, translated by Hanns
Hammelmann and Ewald Osers. Copyright © 1961 by William Collins
Sons & Co. Ltd. Reprinted by permission of Random House, Inc.
Roslyn Targ Literary Agency, Inc.: Excerpts from Letters of Composers
Through Six Centuries, edited by Piero Weiss. Copyright © 1967 by Piero Weiss.
Reprinted by permission of Roslyn Targ Literary Agency, Inc., New York.
Columbia University Press: Excerpt from New Letters of Berlioz, 1830–1868, with
introduction, notes, and English translation by Jacques Barzun. © 1954 by Columbia
University Press, New York. Reprinted by permission of the publisher.

The following illustrations are courtesy
of the Music Division of The New York Public Library
for the Performing Arts, Astor, Lenox and Tilden Foundations:
Johannes Brahms, Gustav Mahler, Dmitri Shostakovich, Giacomo Puccini,
Hector Berlioz, Giovanni da Palestrina, Claudio Monteverdi, Antonio
Vivaldi, Jean-Philippe Rameau, Gabriel Fauré, and Johann Strauss.
The illustrations of Igor Stravinsky and
Sergei Prokofiev are courtesy of Culver Pictures.
Orchestra illustrations by Paul Oxborough.

Library of Congress Catalog Card Number: 95-90301

ISBN: 0-449-91042-3

Cover illustration by Ken Dewey

Manufactured in the United States of America

First Trade Paperback Edition: November 1995
10 9 8 7 6 5 4 3 2

For
Miriam, my life,
And Bob, my brother

Contents

Acknowledgments

At Hamilton College in the late 1930s and early 1940s the student Honor System was practiced. On each paper the student wrote: "This is my own work unless otherwise indicated."

This book on music *is* my own work, in one sense, since I put it together over seven years. But I must also indicate that 95 percent of it comes from used bookstores, new bookstores, and assorted public libraries, including the Library of Congress, and 4.9 percent from interviews with people in the music world.

As stressed throughout the book, I began this project as a total nonexpert—and, in the true sense, I remain a nonexpert. Reporters used to write things called Sunday stories, and perhaps they still do. A Sunday story was a wrap-up, considerably longer than a daily piece and based on picking the brains of the insiders. This book is a long Sunday piece; for the most part the insiders are some two hundred to three hundred authors whose brains and works I have picked—academicians, conductors, composers, critics, and performers. I read no foreign language well enough for this purpose, so all the books I used were written in or translated into English. Most, but not all, were published in this century.

My major acknowledgment, then, goes to all of those who really do know something about music, and on whom I have relied in this research effort. The inevitable mistakes and distortions are, of course, mine and mine alone.

Others include Hannah and Dan Henkin, old and lovely friends who tragically died much too young within a week of one another. Dan and I were reporters together covering the Pentagon and later worked together in the government. Several years ago, he and Hannah took a trip to England with my wife and me. As the trip planner, I used four yellow legal-sized pads. Later, in the early days of this project, when I began to consider it a dumb idea, Dan strongly encouraged me.

But he also wisely warned my wife: "Miriam, dear, this is going to be a hundred-pad thing." His estimate was woefully low.

The indispensable partner was my administrative assistant for fifteen years, Mary Lewis, who put in a few hours of illegal company time on the computer (I had not then gone beyond the manual typewriter) and thousands of hours of her own time, nights, weekends, and holidays. She declined to type if she could not track the meaning. I have no better friend, and without Mary this would not have been.

I am always indebted to my five real children. With them grown and gone, their stepsiblings during these book years were a tiny Pomeranian named Blueberry Muffin (who died at seventeen), a sixty-five-pound Bearded Collie named Angus, and a ninety-five-pound Bernese Mountain Dog named Grindel. All three provided full-time love—and, respectively, warmth and affection, amusement and entertainment, and security against invasion.

Without Miriam, I could not write the alphabet.

From my earliest memory and through this day, in all things of life, the love and support from my older brother Bob has been total.

Although I met some helpful people in the music world, my only two friends from it are Peter Greenough, whose wife, Beverly Sills, is into opera, and Stephen Klein, Executive Director of the National Symphony. I attempted to discuss this project with them, but both looked at me in a peculiar fashion and went away.

My youngest son, in his thirties, summed up the view of many: "Father," he said, "I would not buy a book from a publisher who would publish a book by you on classical music."

Nonetheless, here it is, because of Joëlle Delbourgo, Editor-in-Chief of Ballantine Hardcovers. I am grateful not only for her initial decisions, but also for her insight and professionalism throughout. And I want to give special thanks to Lesley Malin Helm of Ballantine for her day-to-day, line-by-line editing and counsel. Lesley has understood what I have attempted to do, and to the extent that it works she is responsible. To the extent that it does not, neither she, Danny, Miriam, Angus, nor Grindel are to blame.

Introduction

Seven years ago my wife, Miriam, gave me a tape deck for Christmas. We didn't have much in the way of music-making machines, and it was time, Miriam suggested, for me to acquire some music couth. My reading tastes were acceptable, and my professional life had been spent in and around the media and government in Washington, so it was safe to take me out to dinner. Musically speaking, however, I was an embarrassment at age sixty-three.

"We'll buy some good tapes," she said, "and you'll learn about music."

This appeared to be a reasonable idea, and one simple enough to implement. The first decision: What kind of music? Jazz? Opera? Folk, country, or western? The Beatles? Big-band sounds, to which I had not-too-smoothly danced in high school before the last big war our country won?

No, we agreed, let's not be intimidated. Let's go right to classical music—later narrowed to Western classical music of the last three or four hundred years. We would start buying some cassette tapes for my new tape deck and in a few months would have the beginning of a little classical library. We wouldn't worry about long-playing records, since the family turntable was a relic, and compact discs were then new gadgetry beyond the capabilities of my tape machine.

I would like to remember that we chose classical music because of a simmering deep within me since my youth, but that's really not the way it happened. Classical music seemed to offer the greatest mystery and the greatest challenge—and, therefore, maybe the most fun.

Nor were there then plans for this book, even though writing, unlike music, has been a big part of my professional life. My background included fifteen years as a Washington newspaper correspondent, and I had also written a book on the Pentagon, the press, and the public after serving as assistant secretary of defense under Robert

McNamara, Cyrus Vance, and Clark Clifford. Initially, however, I just wanted to play with my new toy and make music a hobby.

But the writing background and the music did merge along the way. That marriage produced this book, an organization primer for:

• those who are just beginning with classical music, know little, and want to know more;

• those who own a few records and tapes and plan to build on them;

• those who have been listening and collecting on a hit-or-miss basis for years, but with little musical background and perhaps even less system;

• those who enjoy an occasional concert and find program notes interesting, but too often condescending and somewhat over their heads;

• and those who know something of Bach and Brahms, but nothing of Bartók or Borodin.

In other words, this is a book for amateurs. Anyone who can tell bake from broil or the League of Women Voters from the National Organization for Women can tell Johannes Brahms from Claude Debussy. Anyone who can tell a wide receiver from a cornerback can tell Johann Sebastian Bach from Wolfgang Amadeus Mozart. And anyone who knows there is little in common between an Eastern Seaboard liberal Democrat and a Mississippi conservative Republican can quickly learn that there is little in common between Béla Bartók and George Frideric Handel.

But I'm getting ahead of my story. I simply wanted to begin a collection of music tapes, and when I went to the nearest record store for the first time, I didn't anticipate a problem. Explaining my amateur status, I asked for the best in classical music. Recalling my single music-appreciation class back in junior high school, I suggested something from the three B's: Bach, Beethoven, and Brahms. That would be enough for openers, and after listening to my new cassettes at home and at work, I would buy another three—perhaps a Chopin, a Liszt, and a Mozart. I was also familiar with at least the names of another dozen composers (over a lifetime I had absorbed a little gentility, owned a few old records, had attended an occasional concert, and had videotaped a few televised symphonies which I would rewatch someday).

Trips to the record stores, however, were disappointing and frustrating. Clerks, generally friendly if a trifle elitist, were interested in sharing their opinions about the most recent treatment of a work by a particular conductor. Mentally, they were not prepared to deal with my primer-level requests and weren't inclined to offer basic advice on which composer to buy, or which of his works. "That," they made clear with noticeable disdain, "is entirely up to you."

Overwhelmed by the thousands of available cassettes, I abandoned the record stores and turned to the classical radio stations for counsel. The men and women airing the music and commenting on it were informed, interesting, and highly professional. But each day they needed to offer listeners different fare, so their programs included music by composers with names such as Milhaud, Tartini, Carissimi, Locatelli, Boccherini, Crumb, Reger, Carter, Delalande, and Viotti. I hadn't heard of even one of them.

Buying a few dozen old copies of the monthly publications from the classical radio stations further confused me. While some of the names in the articles and advertisements were familiar, many more were not. And I had little sense of time-in-history or the various forms of music. Did Mozart come before Beethoven? I wasn't sure. Did it matter? If I liked Dvořák and Borodin, would I also like Prokofiev and Shostakovich? Wasn't one of them still alive? Who in the world was Palestrina? Sibelius and Grieg apparently were both "northerners"; were they from the same northern country?

What is a concerto? How does it differ from a sonata? Is a concerto fifteen or forty-five minutes long? Everyone knows that symphonies are major works, and I knew that both Schubert and Beethoven had written famous ones, but which others were as famous? Did Bach compose symphonies? Why is there always a hush when people say "Bach," as though they were saying Abraham Lincoln or Joe Di- Maggio? Who were the ten best symphonists? And if I collected one symphony composed by each of those ten, would I then have music's ten most famous symphonies? Somewhere I heard that Haydn wrote 104! Which, if any, of those did I want? Besides, Haydn seems to be famous for oratorios. But wasn't that Handel with his *Messiah?* Did those two live at the same time? Why does this thing by Stravinsky sound peculiar while that thing by Stravinsky sounds normal?

To answer these questions, I needed to listen to the best composers, but the total population of highly regarded ones was considerably larger than I had thought. My first goal was to whittle down that number to reasonable size. Ten was too small, one hundred too large. I settled on fifty.

Badly needing help, I turned next to the libraries and bookstores. I bought, borrowed, read, studied, and compared: music dictionaries and encyclopedias; biographies and autobiographies of composers, conductors, performing artists, and critics; music histories; books that specialized in chamber music, in opera, in orchestral music; and books highlighting the piano, the violin, and other individual instruments.

As an ex-reporter and a pad addict, I inevitably began to fill yellow pads with scribbling. My notes ranged from Claudio Monteverdi's contribution to opera to the definition of *continuo*. Out of my stacks of yellow pads came this book.

While some books I was reading, scanning, and studying dealt with as many as four hundred composers and some with as few as twenty, my notes began to show several dozen names appearing over and over again. Not only were Bach, Beethoven, Mozart, and Brahms always there, but also Berlioz, Debussy, and Liszt. So were Chopin, Stravinsky, and Mahler. And Mendelssohn, Tchaikovsky, and Verdi. And Schubert and Schumann, with Haydn and Handel. And Wagner. Everyone wrote about Wagner, the musician and the man. Despite some dramatically different assessments of individual composers between experts writing in 1900 and those writing in the 1980s, the narrowing process to seventy-five pretty much took care of itself. From then on it was more of a coin flip.

The next step was to figure out a pecking order. No second-raters were among my fifty, but though each was a composer of great talent and artistry, surely there were different levels of genius and greatness. Why not start my musical library with the very best?

Bach, Mozart, and Beethoven are the top three on my List. Some would shift the order, but who would violently disagree that those three belong there? And who would argue that the last Listed three, Janáček, Couperin, and Borodin, belong in a less-awesome category?

It is true that little case can be made for selecting Janáček as Number 48 rather than as 46 or 43—no case that would hold up in a court of law. But Liszt and Mendelssohn, Numbers 13 and 11, are unquestionably held in greater esteem than Smetana and Fauré, Numbers 45 and 41—which is not to put down the mastery of the latter two. Anyhow, if you start at Number 1 and collect through Number 30, you win. If you collect only through Number 20, you still win. Nothing is lost because somebody may be outraged that Shostakovich, at Number 19, is ranked higher than Berlioz at Number 21 or Franck at Number 36. Meanwhile, you can learn a little and have a lot of fun.

The ordering process was done in very much the same way as the selection process. Authors of books on music do pay much more attention to some composers than to others. Surveys of listeners of classical radio broadcasts show clearly that some of The 50 are much more popular than others. For instance, in 1950, the Indianapolis Symphony Orchestra published a survey taken of season-ticket holders. One question asked them to name their favorite composers. The top ten were Beethoven, Tchaikovsky, Brahms, Bach, Mozart, Wagner, Debussy, Chopin, Sibelius, and Haydn. (Seven of The List's first ten were thus honored by Indianapolis; three, Schubert, Schumann, and Handel, were not included.) This just goes to show that I'm not the only one who ranks.

As the work of ordering continued, another source emerged as a safety net. The *New Schwann Record and Tape Guide*, a monthly periodical, did not offer anything for sale, but listed available records, compact discs, and cassettes for individual works of each composer. Thousands of classical composers are included in Schwann guides, and tens of thousands of works.*

Schwann became an intimate friend and proved invaluable, not only as a reference source for recorded works but as another check-and-balance tool. The fact that eleven pages of recordings are listed for Beethoven and one line for those of Eugene D'Albert doesn't prove that Mr. Beethoven was a better composer than Mr. D'Albert, but it does suggest that he has made a significantly greater impact on the musical world.

After The List was formulated, I was interested to see how my order compared with the popularity of each of The 50 as reflected in *Schwann* by the numbers of works recorded and the number of recordings of each composition. Beginning at the top of The List, I counted sixteen pages in *Schwann* of Bach works, fourteen and a half of Mozart, and eleven of Beethoven. Continuing with the first ten, there were four pages for Wagner recordings, five of Brahms and of Haydn, four and a half of Tchaikovsky and of Schubert, three and a half of Schumann, and five of Handel.

The "popularity" of a work as measured by the number of recordings obviously doesn't equate to the caliber of the work or the greatness of the composer. Among outstanding composers who aren't on the List—some of whom become more "popular" each year, some of whom don't—are Benjamin Britten, Aaron Copland, Francis Poulenc, Sergei Rachmaninoff, Henry Purcell, and Leonard Bernstein. Others left off the List include Arnold Schoenberg, a big favorite of many music people chiefly because of his influence on composition, and Josquin des Prez and Orlandus Lassus, important Renaissance com-

*In 1991, Schwann Publications was acquired by *Stereophile*, an audio magazine based in Santa Fe, New Mexico, and the catalogue was renamed *Opus*. It continues to be a valuable tool for collectors.

posers. Many assessors would include several—or even all—of these men and, consequently, displace a few of mine.

For instance, my wife, Miriam, will not stop pleading the case of Rachmaninoff. If you feel the same way, wonderful. Substitute his Piano Concerto No. 2 for one of Liszt's piano works. Or go further. Concentrate on forty from The List and then substitute a final ten of your own. This will do you no dishonor. Or, cheat and collect sixty composers instead of fifty. You don't have to tell anybody. If your library contains every recommendation on this List, you will have the best collection on the block!

Having settled on my fifty composers, it was time to start picking out their works. Should I concentrate on four or five compositions by each man (there are no women included) on The List . . . or on forty-five? It soon became obvious that four or five were not enough and that forty-five were too many to handle. By trial and error, I developed a three-phase solution. I sifted through the evidence until I narrowed the field to about twenty compositions for each composer, then continued the research to pick out the ten best known of those, and, finally, further narrowed those ten to a Starter Kit of just five.

It wasn't possible for me to judge the "best" of a composer's works—and it seems uncertain that anyone can, with comfort. But finding the "best known" was readily doable. The works that are most written about, most recorded, most performed, and most sold are best known. For example, it takes little reading about Tchaikovsky to learn that more attention is paid to his Fourth, Fifth, and Sixth Symphonies than his First, Second, and Third. Are the three written later, then, "better" or "greater" than the earlier three? Well, in general, the professionals say they are, although no attack is being made on the first three by earmarking the later three for beginning collectors. I'm simply saying: "These are the three best-known Tchaikovsky symphonies, representing a sound starting point. Maybe you will want to go farther someday with Tchaikovsky symphonies, and maybe not." (In fact, of course, one inevitably *does* go farther; there really is no end to it all. That is the joy of the collecting.)

Another issue was whether to settle entirely on the "best known" works of an individual composer or to be more representative. Listing Beethoven's ten "best-known" compositions, for example, one might come up with five symphonies and five piano sonatas—but this would mean ignoring his string quartets, piano concertos, violin concerto, overtures, his one opera, and scores of other compositions. I decided to be as representative as possible—recognizing that a song and a symphony are different forms of music and perhaps of different "importance."

Anyone with time, patience, and a few years to spend could follow the research paths I have followed in writing this road map. My hope is that readers will have a fraction of the enjoyment using it as I have had producing it.

One of the benefits of becoming more familiar with classical music is that you keep passing Go and collecting another $200. Early on, pleasure comes from recognizing individual compositions. So many are played over and over again on the radio that this was much easier than I had imagined. "Daah, dit-dit-dah, di-di-dump-da" was the beginning of Tchaikovsky's Fifth Symphony. It was impossible to miss; I just had to learn to whom it belonged.

Still more pleasure comes when you begin to recognize some individual composers even though the specific works are not familiar. Some come more easily than others. It doesn't take too long to listen to an orchestral piece and decide: "That's Haydn." And fairly soon you become reasonably confident that something is Mozart, and something else probably Debussy.

A helpful step toward establishing order in my mind was dividing composers into five musical periods: Renaissance, Baroque, Classical, Romantic, and Twentieth Century. It does wonderful things for your ego and interest to hear something and think: "This is Baroque. Maybe Bach, maybe Handel, maybe an unListed composer, but almost certainly Baroque." And then you recognize that strange and initially less pleasant-sounding music as probably Stravinsky or Bartók or one of their Twentieth Century contemporaries. At the beginning I was often wrong, but gradually I improved—and so will you. And don't get uptight about computing precisely *why* the sounds of one fellow's music are so different from the sounds of another's. It would be a nice thing to know, and people (like the late Leonard Bernstein) sometimes appear on television to try to tell us, and you pick up a little as you go along, but it is not essential to your enjoyment. I touch on it just a bit.

I eventually established a few other important ground rules. One lesson is not to be freaked out by the language of the experts, which can overpower the weak at heart. To enjoy classical music, you don't have to know an andante from an allegro. Nor do you have to make the judgment about Mozart that in his piano concertos he consistently showed a "delicate sense of euphony." And for the next ten years you can ignore the expert information that Bach's sonatas in Op. 5 are with one exception either in the Italian keyboard style with tonic-dominant/

dominant-tonic first movements or Mannheim-symphonic with sonata-form first movements, the exception being a prelude and fugue with incongruous rondo finale.

Don't let them do it to you.

Don't blame the writers, who are obviously aiming at a different audience. But don't let them scare you. Shrug your shoulders and go on with your listening. You know a lot of things about your job that they don't know.

Another rule is not to give up on Bach. If his organ music doesn't do much for you, try the orchestral suites. Try just a few minutes of his *St. Matthew Passion*. Try some violin-piano stuff, or Glenn Gould's recordings of the *Goldberg* Variations. But keep trying.

And don't be afraid of string quartets. They are not as formidable as you might think. They certainly should not cause fear or dread. In my case, it helped to ease into string quartets by first listening to the best-known piano quintets—string quartets plus a piano. Perhaps you won't need to do that. And while Borodin is a good starting point for string quartets—you can hear a Broadway musical in his most famous one—don't be afraid of the biggies.

Finally, don't be frightened away from classical music by those kind souls who tell you how much it will enrich your life. While it may be true, this eat-your-spinach approach is lousy public relations. Get into classical music for amusement, pleasure, relaxation, entertainment, kicks. Don't be intimidated by the life-enrichment ploy. Just have fun. In the process of writing this book I discovered some fine music out there by a composer I had never heard of named Fauré. That's what it's all about.

Most of all, good luck!

The book is divided into six sections:

Chapter 1, "The 50 Composers and the Also-Rans": A list of The 50 Greatest Composers of Classical Music, including their nationalities, dates, musical periods, and one-line summaries of what each composer is most noted for. Also included are brief descriptions of the Honorable Mention semifinalists and finalists in each musical period who did not make The List.

Chapter 2, "The Organization of Sound": A few basic musical definitions and a small amount of primer-type information about what music is made of. The purpose is to cast a little flickering light on why some music sounds so different from other music.

Chapter 3, "Setting the Stage": A short description of the several musical periods since 1600, one-paragraph sketches of each of The 50 composers, and brief descriptions of some of the musical forms favored in each period—overture, concerto, sonata, fugue, etc.

Chapter 4, "The Lives and the Works": A longer treatment of each composer, ranked in order and, typically, three separate lists of their compositions—a Starter Kit of five of their most famous works, an expanded list of the Top Ten, and a still longer Master Collection of twenty or twenty-five. (In five special cases, a longer "Library" is offered, and in rare instances the format is slightly modified because that artist created fewer works or less of his work has been recorded.) Additionally, opposite each composition on the Lists is a number tabulated from the *Schwann* catalogue. For popularity comparison purposes, these individual totals show the number of different performances recorded (and available) for each composition.

Chapter 5, "The Orchestra": A brief history and description of the symphony orchestra.

Chapter 6, "Compact Disc Discography": A discography for the 250 Starter Kit selections, recommending specific compact discs.

CHAPTER I

The 50 Composers
and the Also-Rans

My approach to selecting The 50 Greatest Composers of Classical Music was to let the chips fall where they might. The List was not weighted by the composers' countries of origin, the type of music they produced, or their time in history. It might have come out all German or mostly Italian, or mostly opera and a little chamber music, or 70 percent from early Renaissance times and 30 percent from the twentieth century. It didn't, but it might have. I could also have deliberately selected composers most representative of particular periods or types of music, but I didn't choose that route either.

My objectives are to present The 50 in an organized fashion and to provide enough basic information for the amateur listener/collector to make some order of a classical world populated by thousands of artists. Thus, they are not only order-ranked from 1 to 50 but also grouped by date of birth, nationality, and period of music. Here at the outset, they are also given brief "identification bracelets."

The composers are grouped into four levels:

- Immortals
- Demigods
- Composers of Genius
- Artists of a High Order

This is done partly for fun and partly because some readers may find it more convenient to listen, familiarize, and collect by groups instead of one by one. Three Immortals and seven Demigods make up the top ten composers. The next ten are Composers of Genius; the remaining thirty are Artists of a High Order.

A few rules of the road apply in dealing with the four categories:

1. It is not permitted to remove from Immortal status Mr. Bach or Messrs. Mozart and Beethoven.

2. It is exceedingly bad form to lower any of the seven Demigods to the level of Artists of a High Order, the 21-to-50 group. It may be done, but it is bad form.

3. It is not authorized to drop the 11-to-20 Composers of Genius from The List. They may be demoted.

4. Movement of the thirty Artists of a High Order, however, is encouraged. Three types of movement are feasible. An A.H.O. can be elevated to any rank save Immortal; he can be shifted about within the 21-to-50 limits; or he can be cast into darkness and replaced on The List by one of the hundreds of exceptional composers who did not make my final cut.

Many such nonstarters and near-starters, from several countries and several centuries, are mentioned in this chapter to help bring perspective to The List. Each is given five or ten words of identification, far less than he deserves. If you listen carefully to classical-music radio stations in your area, you will hear the music of almost every one of them at some time, but in this book their names will rarely be seen again. This is a conscious decision, made in order to clear the decks for The 50, and with the recognition that these 50 did not make musical history all by themselves. Although this makes things a bit awkward from time to time, and greatly oversimplifies, I believe that oversimplification in pursuit of classical-music outreach is not a vice. Fifty composers spanning four hundred years are quite enough for novices like us to handle.

I will not attempt to deal with the "why" of artistic genius. The professionals say that in the music of the truly great there is something of clarity, something of conciseness, something of intelligence, something of passion, something of substance, something of vitality, something that communicates—something, many would say, of God. Certain music causes something to happen between its creator and the listener that other music fails to spark.

Speaking thirty years ago of Bach, Aaron Copland wrote:

What is it, then, that makes his finest scores so profoundly moving? I have puzzled over that question for a very long time, but have come to doubt whether it is possible for anyone to reach a completely satisfactory answer. One thing is certain; we will never explain Bach's supremacy by the singling out of any one element in his work. Rather it was a combination of perfections, each of which was applied to the common practice of his day; added together they produced the mature perfection of the completed oeuvre. . . . Within the edifice [he

built] is the summation of an entire period with all the grandeur, nobility, and inner depth that one creative soul could
bring to it. It is hopeless, I fear, to attempt to probe further
into why his music creates the impression of spiritual whole-
ness, the sense of his communicating with the deepest vision.
We would only find ourselves groping for words, words that
can never hope to encompass the intangible greatness of
music, least of all the intangible in Bach's greatness.

My feeling is that laymen should not attempt what Aaron Copland
feared to try.

Here, then, is the Master List of The 50 Greatest Composers of
Classical Music:

THE MASTER LIST

Composer	Dates	Period	Nationality
IMMORTALS			
1. Johann Sebastian Bach	1685–1750	Baroque	German
2. Wolfgang Amadeus Mozart	1756–1791	Classical	German
3. Ludwig van Beethoven	1770–1827	Classical	German
DEMIGODS			
4. Richard Wagner	1813–1883	Romantic	German
5. Franz Joseph Haydn	1732–1809	Classical	German
6. Johannes Brahms	1833–1897	Romantic	German
7. Franz Schubert	1797–1828	Classical/ Romantic	German
8. Robert Schumann	1810–1856	Romantic	German
9. George Frideric Handel	1685–1759	Baroque	German
10. Peter Ilyitch Tchaikovsky	1840–1893	Romantic	Russian
COMPOSERS OF GENIUS			
11. Felix Mendelssohn	1809–1847	Romantic	German
12. Antonín Dvořák	1841–1904	Romantic	Czech
13. Franz Liszt	1811–1886	Romantic	Hungarian

Composer	Dates	Period	Nationality
14. Frédéric Chopin	1810–1849	Romantic	Polish
15. Igor Stravinsky	1882–1971	Twentieth Century	Russian
16. Giuseppe Verdi	1813–1901	Romantic	Italian
17. Gustav Mahler	1860–1911	Romantic	German
18. Sergei Prokofiev	1891–1953	Twentieth Century	Russian
19. Dmitri Shostakovich	1906–1975	Twentieth Century	Russian
20. Richard Strauss	1864–1949	Romantic	German

ARTISTS OF A HIGH ORDER

Composer	Dates	Period	Nationality
21. Hector Berlioz	1803–1869	Romantic	French
22. Claude Debussy	1862–1918	Twentieth Century	French
23. Giacomo Puccini	1858–1924	Romantic	Italian
24. Giovanni da Palestrina	1525–1594	Renaissance	Italian
25. Anton Bruckner	1824–1896	Romantic	German
26. Georg Telemann	1681–1767	Baroque	German
27. Camille Saint-Saëns	1835–1921	Romantic	French
28. Jean Sibelius	1865–1957	Twentieth Century	Finnish
29. Maurice Ravel	1875–1937	Twentieth Century	French
30. Gioacchino Rossini	1792–1868	Romantic	Italian
31. Edvard Grieg	1843–1907	Romantic	Norwegian
32. Christoph Gluck	1714–1787	Post-Baroque/ Classical	German
33. Paul Hindemith	1895–1963	Twentieth Century	German
34. Claudio Monteverdi	1567–1643	Baroque	Italian
35. Béla Bartók	1881–1945	Twentieth Century	Hungarian
36. César Franck	1822–1890	Romantic	French
37. Antonio Vivaldi	1678–1741	Baroque	Italian
38. Georges Bizet	1838–1875	Romantic	French
39. Modest Mussorgsky	1839–1881	Romantic	Russian
40. Jean-Philippe Rameau	1683–1764	Baroque	French

Composer	Dates	Period	Nationality
41. Gabriel Fauré	1845–1924	Romantic	French
42. Nikolai Rimsky-Korsakov	1844–1908	Romantic	Russian
43. Gaetano Donizetti	1797–1848	Romantic	Italian
44. Ralph Vaughan Williams	1872–1958	Twentieth Century	English
45. Bedřich Smetana	1824–1884	Romantic	Czech
46. Johann Strauss	1825–1899	Romantic	German
47. Karl Maria von Weber	1786–1826	Pre-Romantic	German
48. Leoš Janáček	1854–1928	Twentieth Century	Czech
49. François Couperin	1668–1733	Baroque	French
50. Alexander Borodin	1833–1887	Romantic	Russian

The next step is to give each of The 50 a special, easy-to-remember identity. Most people have played the word-association game in which one is asked to respond to a name with the first thoughts that come to mind. In chapter 3, I will give a one-paragraph snapshot of each of The 50, and later I will discuss each at some length, but here, at first acquaintance, the description will be limited to such first-thought one-liners.

KEY NOTES FOR THE 50

BACH	A Titan of Western Art
MOZART	The Supreme Natural Musical Genius
BEETHOVEN	Powerful and Passionate Immortal Thunderer
WAGNER	Greatest Dramatic Composer
HAYDN	A Near Immortal; "Father" of the Symphony and the String Quartet
BRAHMS	Purist Romantic Symphonist and a top German Songwriter
SCHUBERT	Classical/Romantic Lyrical Genius of Piano and Melody; German Song King
SCHUMANN	Quintessential Romanticist, Poetic Master of Songs, Piano Music, and Symphonies
HANDEL	Baroque Melodist; Oratorio Genius
TCHAIKOVSKY	Russia's Top Composer; Master of Melody

MENDELSSOHN   Romantic Child Prodigy; Elegant, Melodic
                   Piano Music and Symphonies
DVOŘÁK   Top Czech of Three Listed, and Melodist
LISZT   Best Pianist of all, and Symphonic Poem
                   Inventor
CHOPIN   Mr. Piano
STRAVINSKY   Best Twentieth Century Composer and
                   Avant-Garde Leader
VERDI   Most-Loved Opera Composer
MAHLER   Nine Symphonies, and Songs
PROKOFIEV   Twentieth-Century Dissonant Russian
SHOSTAKOVICH   Top Soviet (as Distinguished from Russian)
                   Composer
R. STRAUSS   Precursor of "New Music"; Creator of
                   Eight Famous Symphonic Poems
BERLIOZ   Radical Romantic; Specialist in Symphonic
                   Spectacles
DEBUSSY   First Impressionist; Songs, Piano, and
                   Orchestral Works
PUCCINI   Post-Verdi Master of Italian Opera
PALESTRINA   Renaissance Master of Catholic Church
                   Music
BRUCKNER   Sixth of Seven Vienna Symphonists
TELEMANN   Baroque Master of 3,000 Works
SAINT-SAËNS   French Grace and Clarity in Opera and
                   Tone Poems
SIBELIUS   Premier Finnish Composer; Nationalist and
                   More
RAVEL   Polished and Precise Frenchman,
                   Commonly Coupled with Impressionist
                   Debussy
ROSSINI   Pre-Verdi Italian Opera Master, with
                   Donizetti
GRIEG   Top Norwegian; Nationalist
GLUCK   Post-Baroque/Classical Opera Reformer
HINDEMITH   One of Five Twentieth-Century "New
                   Music" Dissonants
MONTEVERDI   Baroque "Modernist" of Harmony; First
                   Opera Composer
BARTÓK   Hungarian Twentieth-Century Dissonant
FRANCK   Gentle, Spiritual Beauty; Songs, Oratorio,
                   Symphony, Other Works

VIVALDI	Baroque Violin Music; Prolific
BIZET	Carmen . . . and a little more
MUSSORGSKY	Most Nationalistic and Most Daring Russian Nationalist
RAMEAU	Top Early French Harpsichord Genius, Theorist, and Opera Specialist
FAURÉ	Intimate French Songs and Chamber Music
RIMSKY-KORSAKOV	Most Polished of Russian Nationalists
DONIZETTI	Second to Rossini in Pre-Verdi Italian Opera
VAUGHAN WILLIAMS	Twentieth-Century English Nationalist
SMETANA	Founder of Czech Nationalist Music
J. STRAUSS	Mr. Waltz
WEBER	First True Romantic; German Opera Link Between Gluck and Wagner
JANÁČEK	Twentieth-Century Czech, Most Modern of Three Listed Czechs
COUPERIN	French Baroque Harpsichord Maestro
BORODIN	Melodic Russian Nationalist

These mini-descriptions are obviously oversimplifications. For example, Frédéric Chopin, at Number 14, did a good bit more than is suggested by his two-word tag of "Mr. Piano," and partisans of Franz Liszt may well take exception to Chopin being given that label in preference to him. A fair rebuttal is that Chopin's fame comes entirely from piano works whereas piano virtuoso Liszt was also the father of the symphonic poem and a dominant European force in many areas of music.

In another example, Schumann, Schubert, and Brahms are all hailed as leading songwriters. This ignores one of the great geniuses of German song, a man named Hugo Wolf. But Wolf produced little outside the realm of song and is therefore not on The List.

The next short breakdown, by periods of music, shows the numerical domination by composers of the Romantic era, and the relatively small representation from this century. We begin with the Renaissance, but only by a whisker: The List almost starts in the Middle Ages.

BREAKDOWN BY PERIODS OF MUSIC

Period	Dates	Rank
Renaissance	(1450–1600)	1
Baroque	(1600–1750)	8
Classical	(1750–1825)	4
Romantic	(1825–1910)	
The First True Romantic		1
Two Italian Opera Composers		2
Early Romantic		7
Middle Romantic		13
Late Romantic		4
Twentieth Century	(1910–Present)	10
TOTAL		50

A breakdown by century of birth shows two composers born in the sixteenth century, six in the seventeenth, eight in the eighteenth, thirty-three in the nineteenth, and one in the twentieth.

BREAKDOWN BY CENTURY OF BIRTH

Composer	Dates	Rank	Period
SIXTEENTH CENTURY			
Giovanni da Palestrina	1525–1594	24	Renaissance
Claudio Monteverdi	1567–1643	34	Baroque
SEVENTEENTH CENTURY			
François Couperin	1668–1733	49	Baroque
Antonio Vivaldi	1678–1741	37	Baroque
Georg Telemann	1681–1767	26	Baroque
Jean-Philippe Rameau	1683–1764	40	Baroque
Johann Sebastian Bach	1685–1750	1	Baroque
George Frideric Handel	1685–1759	9	Baroque
EIGHTEENTH CENTURY			
Christoph Gluck	1714–1787	32	Post-Baroque/ Classical
Franz Joseph Haydn	1732–1809	5	Classical
Wolfgang Amadeus Mozart	1756–1791	2	Classical

Composer	Dates	Rank	Period
Ludwig van Beethoven	1770–1827	3	Classical
Franz Schubert	1797–1828	7	Classical/ Romantic
Karl Maria von Weber	1786–1826	47	Pre-Romantic
Gioacchino Rossini	1792–1868	30	Romantic
Gaetano Donizetti	1797–1848	43	Romantic

NINETEENTH CENTURY

Composer	Dates	Rank	Period
Hector Berlioz	1803–1869	21	Romantic
Felix Mendelssohn	1809–1847	11	Romantic
Frédéric Chopin	1810–1849	14	Romantic
Robert Schumann	1810–1856	8	Romantic
Franz Liszt	1811–1886	13	Romantic
Richard Wagner	1813–1883	4	Romantic
Giuseppe Verdi	1813–1901	16	Romantic
César Franck	1822–1890	36	Romantic
Bedřich Smetana	1824–1884	45	Romantic
Anton Bruckner	1824–1896	25	Romantic
Johann Strauss	1825–1899	46	Romantic
Alexander Borodin	1833–1887	50	Romantic
Johannes Brahms	1833–1897	6	Romantic
Camille Saint-Saëns	1835–1921	27	Romantic
Georges Bizet	1838–1875	38	Romantic
Modest Mussorgsky	1839–1881	39	Romantic
Peter Ilyitch Tchaikovsky	1840–1893	10	Romantic
Antonín Dvořák	1841–1904	12	Romantic
Edvard Grieg	1843–1907	31	Romantic
Nikolai Rimsky-Korsakov	1844–1908	42	Romantic
Gabriel Fauré	1845–1924	41	Romantic
Giacomo Puccini	1858–1924	23	Romantic
Gustav Mahler	1860–1911	17	Romantic
Richard Strauss	1864–1949	20	Romantic
Leoš Janáček	1854–1928	48	Twentieth Century
Claude Debussy	1862–1918	22	Twentieth Century
Jean Sibelius	1865–1957	28	Twentieth Century
Ralph Vaughan Williams	1872–1958	44	Twentieth Century

Composer	Dates	Rank	Period
Maurice Ravel	1875–1937	29	Twentieth Century
Béla Bartók	1881–1945	35	Twentieth Century
Igor Stravinsky	1882–1971	15	Twentieth Century
Sergei Prokofiev	1891–1953	18	Twentieth Century
Paul Hindemith	1895–1963	33	Twentieth Century

TWENTIETH CENTURY

Dmitri Shostakovich	1906–1975	19	Twentieth Century

The final breakdown—by nationality—shows the composers' rankings within their own countries (indicated by the order in which they are listed), along with their overall standing on The List (indicated by the number in the left-hand column).

RANK BY NATIONALITY

CZECH
12. Antonín Dvořák
45. Bedřich Smetana
48. Leoš Janáček

ENGLISH
44. Ralph Vaughan Williams

FINNISH
28. Jean Sibelius

FRENCH
21. Hector Berlioz
22. Claude Debussy
27. Camille Saint-Saëns
29. Maurice Ravel
36. César Franck

38. Georges Bizet
40. Jean-Philippe Rameau
41. Gabriel Fauré
49. François Couperin

GERMAN
1. Johann Sebastian Bach
2. Wolfgang Amadeus Mozart
3. Ludwig van Beethoven
4. Richard Wagner
5. Franz Joseph Haydn
6. Johannes Brahms
7. Franz Schubert
8. Robert Schumann
9. George Frideric Handel
11. Felix Mendelssohn
17. Gustav Mahler

GERMAN (continued)
20. Richard Strauss
25. Anton Bruckner
26. Georg Telemann
32. Christoph Gluck
33. Paul Hindemith
46. Johann Strauss
47. Karl Maria von Weber

HUNGARIAN
13. Franz Liszt
35. Béla Bartók

ITALIAN
16. Giuseppe Verdi
23. Giacomo Puccini
24. Giovanni da Palestrina
30. Gioacchino Rossini

34. Claudio Monteverdi
37. Antonio Vivaldi
43. Gaetano Donizetti

NORWEGIAN
31. Edvard Grieg

POLISH
14. Frédéric Chopin

RUSSIAN
10. Peter Ilyitch Tchaikovsky
15. Igor Stravinsky
18. Sergei Prokofiev
19. Dmitri Shostakovich
39. Modest Mussorgsky
42. Nikolai Rimsky-Korsakov
50. Alexander Borodin

Ten countries are represented on The List, with Germany far outranking any other, and Germany, France, Italy, and Russia contributing forty-one of the fifty composers. Those four nations dominated classical music for several centuries, albeit not simultaneously. England's time of music leadership was much earlier—and the United States has not yet emerged as a major player.

Eighteen of the composers on The List are German, nine French, seven Russian, seven Italian, three Czech, and two Hungarian. One each is a Pole, an Englishman, a Norwegian, and a Finn.

The lines defining countries and nationalities are deliberately flexible, to keep things simple. One of the "French" composers, for example, is César Franck, who, while living his entire working life in Paris, was born in Belgium. Frédéric Chopin is listed as a Pole, as he was born of a Polish mother and a French father, reared in Poland, and proud of every Polish drop of blood—even though he lived his adult life in France.

European political and geographical divisions also have changed significantly over the years, one of the troubling places for us being Austria-Germany. I follow *The Harvard Dictionary of Music*, which says:

The development of music in Austria is included under Germany, as is customary and almost inevitable because of the close bonds—political, cultural and musical—between the two countries. Not a few of the most outstanding "Austrian" composers were born in Germany (including Beethoven and Brahms), while on the other hand many of the great "German" masters were actually Austrian by birth.

But the difficulties go beyond that. Germany itself as a political entity was altered significantly during the lives of many composers on The List. When Frederick II (the Great) died in 1786, the Kingdom of Prussia consisted of the electorate of Brandenburg; the duchies of Silesia and Farther Pomerania; the provinces of East Prussia (including Konigsberg, Friedland, and Memel) and West Prussia (seized from Poland in 1772); and various enclaves in western Germany including East Friesland, Munster, and Essen. Later on came Thorn and Danzig in the Second Partition of Poland, Warsaw and the heart of Poland in the Third Partition of Poland, and assorted other regions. Napoleon changed much of that, but a reborn Germany outlasted him. For our purposes, all are "German."

Similarly, all composers from what was to become Czechoslovakia are designated as Czechs, even though the country did not exist by that name until 1918, when it was created from territories which had been part of the Austro-Hungarian Empire. In fact, two composers on The List came from Bohemia, once a kingdom and later a region of western Czechoslovakia, and a third was from Moravia, a region of central Czechoslovakia.

Italians are Italians. Italy has had the same name in both ancient and modern times, since the fall of the Roman Empire, even though for hundreds of years it had no political unity, no independence, and no organized existence as a nation. All composers from Russia are called Russian, whether they lived before or after the revolution of 1917 that created the Soviet Union. The 1991 revolution is not involved.

This next section presents the nominees for The List, period by period and country by country. Particular mention is made of a few near-starters who just missed.

RENAISSANCE

The first-born composer on The List, Giovanni Pierluigi da Palestrina, born c. 1525, is not the first well-known composer of classical music.

At least two strong challengers lived more than a century earlier, and several of his contemporaries were respected contenders.

The Middle Ages began in about the year 500 and ended with the Renaissance, the transitional movement in Europe between the medieval and modern eras, commonly put at 1450 to 1600. Toward the end of the Middle Ages, the dominant school of Western European music was located in northern Europe in the Duchy of Burgundy, under rulers Philip the Good and Charles the Bold. This duchy included what is now the Netherlands, Belgium, and eastern France. From that school the Honorable Mention all-star was the inventive Guillaume Dufay, c. 1400–1474, one of the two earliest strong candidates for The List. Both secular and religious music of Dufay is available in record stores, including a set of ninety-eight secular songs. (An even earlier candidate, although not a Burgundian, was John Dunstable of England, c. 1380–1453, who was important and influential not only in England, where he was the leading composer, but also across the Channel.)

Renaissance nominees for The List came from five countries. Included were six Englishmen, three Spaniards, three Italians, one Frenchman, and four from the "Flemish school," which comprised roughly the same area in Europe as the Burgundian school. While only the Italian Palestrina has been selected, it is easy to become addicted to this kind of music—for many, easier than becoming accustomed to a lot of Twentieth-Century sounds.

ENGLAND

Honorable Mention: The best-known English Renaissance composers were Thomas Tallis, c. 1505–1585, master of the religious motet and the anthem, and important composer of keyboard music; William Byrd, 1543–1623, organ and harpsichord specialist, who is considered by many to be the major figure of English Renaissance music; Thomas Morley, 1557–1602, best known for madrigals, who also set a little Shakespeare to music; John Bull, 1562/63–1628, organ and harpsichord master; John Dowland, 1562–1626, songman and lutist; and finally Orlando Gibbons, 1585–1625, creator of madrigals, keyboard works, and anthems.

SPAIN

Honorable Mention: Three Spanish composers of special note were Luis Milan, c. 1500–1561, master of a guitar/lute instrument called the *vihuela*; Antonio de Cabezon, 1510–1566, blind keyboard artist and composer of both secular and sacred music; and Tomás Luis de Victoria, 1548–1611, another potential challenger of Palestrina as *the* great Renaissance master. Masses and motets of Victoria are available, including couplings with Palestrina, and you may want to cheat on The List just a hair here to listen to them.

ITALY

Winner: Palestrina, *c.* 1525–1594.

Honorable Mention: Two Italian composers of one family, Andrea Gabrieli, *c.* 1510–1586, organist and composer of madrigals, motets, and Masses; and his nephew Giovanni Gabrieli, *c.* 1533–1612, organist and early composer for brass instruments.

FLEMISH SCHOOL

Honorable Mention: From the dominant Flemish school, which consisted of composers living in present-day Belgium, some of Holland, and adjacent northern France, were Johannes Ockeghem, *c.* 1410–1497, the first great master of this school and an early experimenter with simultaneous-melody composition; Josquin des Prez, 1445–1521, the all-time top Flemish composer and an extremely legitimate contender; Jacob Obrecht, *c.* 1450–1505, master of secular and sacred music, including masses; Adrian Willaert, 1490–1562, who greatly influenced Venetian music; and the last of the great Flemish composers, Orlando di Lasso (also known as de Lassus or Lassus), 1532–1594, who married Italian and Flemish styles and is another of the strongest near-starters.

FRANCE

Honorable Mention: There was one French Renaissance finalist, Clement Janequin, *c.* 1485–1558, one of the first writers of what is called "program" music, who composed songs imitating bird calls and other sounds.

BAROQUE

The Baroque period lasted from 1600 to 1750, although the musical giants came toward its end. Thirty composers were in the final pool of nominees: two Englishmen, eleven Italians, four Frenchmen, and thirteen Germans, ten of whom are truly Baroque and three of whom span the period between the Baroque and the Classical. One of the latter made The List, causing minor organizational difficulties about where to put him.

ENGLAND

Honorable Mention: John Blow, 1649–1708, organist and composer of a well-known masque, *Venus and Adonis* (a masque was an elaborate musical performance with costumes and scenery); and Henry Purcell, 1659–1695, a prominent seventeenth-century English composer and a near-starter.

ITALY

Winner: Monteverdi, 1567–1643; and Vivaldi, 1678–1741.

Honorable Mention: Jacobo Peri, 1561–1633, earliest opera composer, who wrote *Dafne* (a work now lost) in 1597 and *Eurydice* in 1600; Giulio Caccini, *c.* 1545–1618, composer of madrigals and early operas; Girolano Frescobaldi, 1583–1643, keyboard composer and top organist of his day; Giacomo Carrissimi, 1605–1674, composer of early oratorios; Arcangelo Corelli, 1653–1717, violinist and composer of violin sonatas and concerti grossi; Guisseppe Torelli, 1658–1709, another Italian violinist and early concerto grosso man; Alessandro Scarlatti, 1660–1725, a founder of *opera seria* (serious opera); Domenico Scarlatti, 1685–1757, harpsichord composer and son of Alessandro.

FRANCE

Winners: Couperin, 1658–1733; and Rameau, 1683–1764.

Honorable Mention: Jacques Champion de Chambonnières, *c.* 1602–1672, founder of the French harpsichord school; Jean-Baptiste Lully, 1632–1687, father of French opera, ballet composer, and near-starter.

GERMANY

Winners: Telemann, 1681–1767; Bach, 1685–1750; Handel, 1685–1759; and Gluck (Baroque/Classical), 1714–1787. Some authorities would place Gluck in the Classical period, by style, but chronologically he is a shade earlier—born a generation before Haydn. His greatest musical triumph, *Iphigenie en Tauride*, came in 1779, nine years after the birth of Beethoven.

Honorable Mention: Heinrich Schütz, 1585–1672, composer of motets, madrigals, psalms, oratorios, and *St. Matthew Passion*; Johann Herman Schein, 1586–1630, best known for suites for strings and sacred songs in both German and Latin; Samuel Scheidt, 1587–1654, composer of magnificats for organ and other religious organ music; Johann Jakob Froberger, 1616–1667, composer and organist who helped develop the suite; Dietrich Buxtehude, 1637–1707, supreme organ composer and organist; Heinrich von Biber, 1644–1704, most famous for sonatas; Johann Pachelbel, 1653–1706, whose now-famous canon is almost as widely known as "White Christmas." From post-Baroque/early-Classical times are the two most famous Bach sons, Wilhelm Friedemann, 1710–1784, and Carl Philipp Emanuel, 1714–1788.

CLASSICAL

The Classical or Classic period lasted for only about fifty years, from 1775 to 1825.

GERMANY

Winners: Mozart, 1756–1791; Haydn, 1732–1809; Beethoven, 1770–1827; and Schubert, 1797–1828.

Honorable Mention: None.

So dominant are Mozart, Haydn, and Beethoven that many regard those three as *being* the Classic school, and certainly they do make up what is sometimes called the "High Vienna Classic school."

That leaves Franz Schubert, 1797–1828, another period-straddler. Some call him a Classicist, some prefer to think of him as a Romantic, and almost everyone considers him a bridge between the Classic and Romantic periods. Here, for convenience, we include him with the Classicists; he is much too good to be left in limbo.

ITALY

Honorable Mention: Luigi Boccherini, 1743–1805, cellist and chamber-music specialist; Muzio Clementi, 1752–1832, best known as a composer of keyboard music; and Giovanni Battista Viotti, 1755–1824, violinist and composer for the violin.

ROMANTIC

The Romantic period in the arts began about 1825, as the Classical period ended, and lasted until shortly before World War I. Musically, it started with the late works of Beethoven and the compositions of Weber and Schubert, and it ended with such Listed composers as Richard Strauss and Jean Sibelius. Twenty-seven Romantic composers made The List—by far the largest number from any period.

FRANCE

Winners: Berlioz, 1803–1869; Belgian-born Franck, 1822–1890; Saint-Saëns, 1835–1921; Bizet, 1838–1875; and Fauré, 1845–1924.

Honorable Mention: Charles François Gounod, 1818–1893, best known for one opera, *Faust*; Edouard Lalo, 1823–1892, inventive creator of the *Symphonie Espagnole*; Emmanuel Chabrier, 1841–1894, who with Lalo foreshadowed Impressionism; Jules Massenet, 1842–1912, famous for the opera *Manon*; and Ernest Chausson, 1855–1899, art-song specialist and creator of one symphony and delicate chamber music.

RUSSIA

Winners: Borodin, 1833–1887; Mussorgsky, 1839–1881; Tchaikovsky, 1840–1893; and Rimsky-Korsakov, 1844–1908.

Honorable Mention: Mikhail Glinka, 1804–1857, father of Russian classical music and creator of the first great Russian national opera, *A Life for the Czar* (1836); and two other members of the Russian nationalist group called the "Mighty Five": César Cui, 1835–1918; and Mily Balakirev, 1837–1910. Alexander Glazunov, 1865–1936, composer of eight symphonies and best known for the ballet *Raymonda*, straddles the two centuries.

ITALY

Winners: Rossini, 1792–1868; Donizetti, 1797–1848; Verdi, 1814–1901; and Puccini, 1858–1924.

Honorable Mention: Vincenzo Bellini, 1801–1835, creator of eleven operas; and Ruggero Leoncavallo, 1858–1919, remembered chiefly for the opera *I Pagliacci*.

GERMANY

Winners: Weber, 1786–1826; Mendelssohn, 1809–1847; Schumann, 1810–1856; Wagner, 1813–1883; Bruckner, 1824–1896; Johann Strauss the Younger, 1825–1899; Brahms, 1833–1897; Mahler, 1860–1911; and Richard Strauss, 1864–1949.

Honorable Mention: Max Bruch, 1838–1920, teacher, symphonist, and composer of one of Germany's four best-known violin concertos (the others were written by Beethoven, Brahms, and Mendelssohn); and Giacomo Meyerbeer, 1791–1864, an influential composer of several grand operas, including *Robert le diable*.

OTHER COUNTRIES

Winners: From countries other than the Big Four are Smetana, 1824–1884, and Dvořák, 1841–1904, from Czechoslovakia; Sibelius, 1865–1957, from Finland; Grieg, 1843–1907, from Norway; Chopin, 1810–1849, from Poland; and Liszt, 1811–1886, from Hungary.

Honorable Mention: One from the United States, Edward MacDowell, 1861–1908, first American to earn an international reputation; one from England, Edward Elgar, 1857–1934, major composer best known for "Pomp and Circumstance"; and one from Spain, Isaac Albéniz, 1860–1909, who spent most of his life outside of Spain but whose music reflected the sound of his country. His most famous piece is a piano suite, "Iberia."

TWENTIETH CENTURY

Our century is a dreadful hodgepodge. More composers are alive today than lived in all previous centuries combined. The term "twentieth-century music" embraces dozens of styles which have developed since 1900. In the first half of the century these included (but were not limited to) leftover Impressionism, Expressionism, atonality, and serial music. Later came "New Age" music, electronic music, *musique concrète*, and even silent music. Experimentation with sounds became a big thing.

Some seventy-five twentieth-century composers were nominees for The List. Twenty-one of these were from the United States; twelve were French, ten German, seven English, seven Russian, six Italian, four Hungarian, and one each Danish, Finnish, Czech, Mexican, Brazilian, Australian, and Greek.

UNITED STATES

Honorable Mention: No native American made The List—but several came very close. Some patriotic flag-waving is not only permissible but praiseworthy, and this is the most appropriate place in the book to spend a minute on classical music in this country.

The greatest American composer before the Civil War was Stephen Foster, who wrote such famous songs as "Old Folks at Home," "My Old Kentucky Home," and "Oh! Susannah." While some would argue that he did not write classical music, he was indisputably a "classic." MacDowell, who specialized in short piano compositions, retains an outstanding reputation. Several modern American composers were born in the 1870s and 1880s. These include Charles Edward Ives, 1874–1954, the first great American composer who worked in the twentieth century, who won a Pulitzer Prize in 1947 for the third of his four numbered symphonies and whose best-known piece may be another orchestral work, "Three Places in New England." Some believe that he is the finest of all American composers. Among contemporaries of Ives were Carl Ruggles, 1876–1971, composer of dissonant and highly individualistic works which include the symphonic suites "Men and Angels" and "Men and Mountains"; and Impressionist Charles Tomlinson Griffes, 1884–1920, a virtuoso pianist who liked to incorporate Asian sounds into his music.

Three Americans a generation later are known for their experimental work during the 1920s and beyond: Wallingford Riegger, 1885–1961, who experimented with the technique called serialism (music based on a series of tones in an arbitrary but fixed pattern without regard for traditional tonality); Henry Cowell, 1897–1965, writer, publisher, pianist, and composer of sixteen symphonies, who introduced new techniques such as plucking the piano strings, and developed something called the "tone cluster"; and Ruth Crawford Seeger, 1901–1953, who anticipated some of the dissonant sounds of later twentieth-century music. Others who were born just before the twentieth century and worked in it include Douglas Moore, 1893–1969, Romantic opera composer whose works include *The Devil and Daniel Webster*; Walter Piston, 1894–1976, teacher, music theorist, and neoclassical composer; Virgil Thomson, 1896–1989, longtime music critic for the *New York Herald Tribune* who composed in and out of twentieth-century styles; Howard Hanson, 1896–1981, for years head of the Eastman School of Music and champion of American classical composers; Roger Sessions, 1896–1985, atonal composer regarded by some as the outstanding American composer of his time (though one critic said his works show genius without charm), whose compositions include nine symphonies, a violin concerto, the opera *Montezuma* and the cantata "When Lilacs Last in the Dooryard Bloom'd"; Roy Harris, 1898–1979, composer of fourteen symphonies, among other works, who said his music was designed to express America's "noisy ribaldry," "sadness" and "groping earnestness"; and Randall Thompson, 1899–1984, known chiefly for choral compositions with a distinctly American sound.

Five other recent American composers represent what came to be called "new sounds." John Cage, born in 1912, said that he was "devoted to the principles of originality." One experimental work that proves his point is "Four Minutes and 33 Seconds," in which the musician sits motionless for that amount of time and then leaves the stage. This is a difficult piece to enjoy on LP, tape, or compact disc, but Cage is a respected artist who has had a considerable influence on other composers. Elliott Carter, born in 1908, went from neoclassicism to dramatic experimentation. William Schuman, 1910–1992, was director of the Juilliard School of Music for sixteen years and is known for concertos, choral works, and ten symphonies; Leonard Bernstein described Schuman's work as filled with "energetic drive and vigorous propulsion." Milton Babbitt, born in 1916, was a professor of mathematics and music, a disciple of Arnold Schoenberg, and an early advocate of electronic music. George Crumb, born in 1929, was a sort of Romantic in his early years. He often wrote in simple forms but has also experimented with new sounds and procedures, such as lowering and raising a gong in a bucket of water and creating mood by having performers wear black masks.

All of these Honorable Mention Americans have been recorded on LPs and cassettes, and some now are on compact discs. By the recording yardstick, Ives is far and away the most popular with the public, followed by Cowell, Cage, and Carter.

Two contemporary Americans who have earned considerable attention in recent years are Philip Glass, born in 1937, and John Adams, born in 1947. Glass has composed several unconventional operas, beginning with *Einstein on the Beach* in 1976, and Adams wrote the opera *Nixon in China*. Both are examples of minimalist music, characterized by a strong beat, a simple tonal structure, and a great deal of repetition of sounds with slight variations. Another well-known minimalist is Steve Reich, born in 1936. The works of these composers were as much a break from Schoenberg-style serial music as his compositions were from Romanticism.

This leaves the three American classical composers best known to the public: George Gershwin, Leonard Bernstein, and Aaron Copland.

Gershwin, 1898–1937, went from musical comedies like *Lady Be Good* to serious compositions like *Rhapsody in Blue*, and from the symphonic poem *An American in Paris* to the opera *Porgy and Bess*, leaving an adoring public at each stop. He combined American popular and "serious" music; we will include him here, sidestepping the debate over whether he was truly a "classical" composer.

Bernstein, 1918–1990, is easily the best-known American classical musician of this century. This is due in part to his international work as a symphonic conductor, in part to his long relationship with television, in part to his showmanlike personality, in part to the spectacular success of his musical *West Side Story*, in part to all of his other compositions for theater and concert hall, and in part to his all-around musical abilities. His works range from the *Jeremiah* Symphony to a Serenade for Violin Solo, Strings and Percussion, and from Broadway musicals to his *Mass* written for the opening of the John F. Kennedy Center in Washington. His *Candide* Overture has been called the most brilliant overture of the century. He wrote in many styles over a long, frenetically paced career, from jazz to twelve-tone, and from Romantic to severe twentieth-century. Milton Babbitt has called him the only American performer-creator to achieve international cultural celebrity. The music world is still working on the question of what his place is today, what it will be in the future—and what it might have been had he managed his genius differently, concentrating on composing pure classical music and paying less attention to the other musical pursuits that occupied him. Had he done so, of course, he would not have been Leonard Bernstein.

The man Ives, Bernstein, and others must challenge as America's all-time top composer of classical music is Aaron Copland, 1900–1990. Copland became an American institution, best known for his "Americana" works and held in esteem (and regarded with affection) for a lifetime of assistance to other American composers. While Schoenberg aficionados will express hostility that their champion is not among The 50, and while academicians will mourn the absence of Josquin and Lassus, and while the Rachmaninoff claque will be heard, the most vocal dissent in the United States is likely to come from the omission of Aaron Copland.

The test, of course, is not listening pleasure. I believe that anyone who would rather listen to Georg Philipp Telemann than to Copland is not playing with a full deck. His or her elevator does not go all the way to the top. Given an eighteenth-century Telemann concerto grosso on the one hand and on the other Copland's *Appalachian Spring, Billy the Kid, Rodeo,* "The Tender Land," "A Lincoln Portrait," or "El Salon Mexico," the choice for most of us is not a difficult one. Over many years he made a conscious effort to write for the many instead of the few. Biographer Arthur Berger has written: "Whatever Copland does has the recognizable virtues of a genuinely creative artist. With the same limitations peculiar to many composers of our time, he can accomplish much more than most of the others. He is at last an American that we may place unapologetically beside the recognized creative figures of any other country. . . . We are not obliged, therefore, to credit Copland merely with what he has done to establish an indigenous style, for his achievements go deeper."

But there are not fifty-one places on a fifty-person list.

Even though no native Americans make The List, both Stravinsky and Hindemith became American citizens. And, as a result of World War II, many other Europeans came to the United States to work, including the Hungarian Béla Bartók and such famous unListed artists as Arnold Schoenberg of Austria, Darius Milhaud of France, Vienna-born Ernst Krenek, and Bohuslav Martinu, 1890–1959, of Czechoslovakia.

GERMANY

Winner: Hindemith, 1895–1963.

Honorable Mention: Max Reger, 1873–1916, dissonant back-to-Bacher; the near-starter Arnold Schoenberg, 1874–1951, originator of twelve-tone serial music, who had a significant influence on the century's music; Ermanno Wolf-Ferrari (Italian-German), 1876–1948, re-creator of the comic opera, including "I quattro rusteghi"; Anton Webern, 1883–1945, one of Schoenberg's two chief disciples; Alban Berg, 1885–1935, the other one; Carl Orff, 1895–1982, who emphasized rhythm more than melody and is best known for the cantata *Carmina burana*; Kurt Weill, 1900–1950, developer of a new art form which he called a *song-play* and composer of the musical *The Three-Penny Opera* and the opera *The Rise and Fall of the City of Mahagonny*; Wolfgang Fortner, 1907–   , composer who shifted from neoclassical music to serial music; Hans Werner Henze, 1926–   , composer of dissonant music and political revolutionary who supported Che Guevara; Karlheinz Stockhausen, 1928–   , pioneer of electronic music also known for his work with serial and aleatory (use-of-chance) techniques.

The Schoenberg case is an interesting one. He and his school of twelve-tone music have had formidable champions throughout the century. Two years before Schoenberg's death in 1951, Copland wrote that no serious musician denied the historical importance of Schoen-berg's contribution nor the fact that all (then) contemporary music owed something, directly or indirectly, to his "daring." But, Copland added, it was hardly possible to arrive at a conclusive judgment as to the merits of Schoenberg's most characteristic compositions—or those of his pupils, Berg and Webern—because their works were performed so infrequently. Although his music is more frequently played and recorded today, it has never enjoyed widespread popular-ity.

Copland went on to comment that "it is one of the ironies of the 12-tone system that its supporters should be so anxious to prove that they are in the main line of music tradition." Early in the century, it was commonly accepted that Schoenberg and his supporters had bro-ken dramatically and radically with the past. Some music people today say that this was a misconception. They argue that he merely followed the logical progression of his style. A layman could consider that he *did* break radically with the past, nonetheless following the logical progression of his style. Try the music and make your own conclu-sions. Radical break or logical progression, it is something different.

FRANCE

Winners: Debussy, 1862–1918; and Ravel, 1875–1937.

Honorable Mention: Paul Dukas, 1865–1935, composer of a fa-mous, delicate orchestral work, *The Sorcerer's Apprentice*; Erik Satie, 1866–1925, rebellious composer who wrote some famous piano works and who influenced a group called *"les Six"* that reacted against both Wagner and Impressionism and supported a return to the simplicity and clarity of classicism; Albert Roussel, 1869–1937, neoclassical composer known for symphonies and two ballets; Edgar Varèse (French-American), 1883–1965, pioneer of electronic music; Nadia Boulanger, 1887–1979, enormously influential teacher of many fa-mous musicians; and four of the members of *"les Six"*—Georges Auric, 1899–1983; Arthur Honegger (Swiss-French), 1892–1955; Dar-ius Milhaud, 1892–1974 (specialist in polytonal music); and Francis Poulenc, 1899–1963. Also André Jolivet, 1905–1974, neoprimitive; Olivier Messiaen, 1908–   , who emphasizes strange rhythms and mysticism in works that include the extremely long opera *Saint Fran-çois d'Assise*; Pierre Boulez, 1925–   , avant-garde representative committed to twelve-tone music in his early compositions and to further experimentation later in his career.

RUSSIA

Winners: Stravinsky, 1882–1971; Prokofiev, 1891–1953; and Shostakovich, 1906–1975.

Honorable Mention: Sergei Rachmaninoff, 1873–1943, superpianist and composer of famous piano concertos who wrote in the melodic, melancholy style of Tchaikovsky; Reinhold Gliere, 1875–1956, symphonic specialist in the conventional Romantic style; and traditionalist Aram Khachaturian, 1903–1978, best known for the "Sabre Dance," which reflects his native Armenia.

ITALY

Winner: Puccini, 1858–1924.

Honorable Mention: Pietro Mascagni, 1863–1945, best known for the opera *Cavalleria rusticana*, a realistic portrayal of life; Ottorino Respighi, 1879–1936, who blended many styles, including Impressionism, in creating the symphonic poems *The Fountains of Rome* and *The Pines of Rome*; and Luigi Dallapiccola, 1904–1975, who married twelve-tone music to outstanding melody.

ENGLAND

Winner: Vaughan Williams, 1872–1958.

Honorable Mention: Frederick Delius, 1862–1934, part Impressionist and part Romantic; Gustav Holst, 1874–1934, admirer of Asia and the occult and best known for the orchestral suite *The Planets*; William Walton, 1902–1983, technical master who wrote in many styles and became a leading composer of symphonies, operas, and concertos, and overtures; Michael Tippett, 1905–   , specialist in vocal music who began as a Romantic and became more eclectic; Benjamin Britten, 1913–1976, best known for operas and other vocal music written in a traditional style, and a near-starter; and Peter Maxwell Davies, 1934–   , a respected composer of extremely dramatic theater music.

OTHER NATIONS

Winners: From Hungary, Bartók, 1881–1945; and from Czechoslovakia, Janáček, 1854–1928.

Honorable Mention: From Hungary, Ernst von Dohnanyi, 1877–1960, Romantic composer much loved in his country; Zoltán Kodály,

1882–1967, colleague of Bartók who married folk music and Romanticism; and Gyorgy Ligeti, 1923–   , who moved on to further experimentation from serial and electronic music. From Mexico, Carlos Chávez, 1899–1978, that country's best-known composer, who founded Mexico's first symphony orchestra; from Romania, Georges Enesco, 1881–1955, violinist, teacher, and leading composer there; from Spain, Manuel de Falla, 1876–1946, all-time leading Spanish composer, who married old Spanish folk music with modern methods; from Australia, its top composer, Percy Grainger, 1882–1961, best known for arranging English folk songs; from Denmark, its leading composer, Carl Nielsen, 1865–1931, who wrote six symphonies; and from Poland, Krzysztof Penderecki, 1933–   , who was influenced by Bartók, Stravinsky, and Schoenberg. Other finalists include Brazil's best-known composer, Heitor Villa-Lobos, 1887–1959, author of more than two thousand compositions, many in folk-music style; and Iannis Xenakis of Greece (and Paris), 1922–   , who has worked with aleatory ("chance") and electronic music and with *musique concrète* (based on "real" sounds such as street noises).

CHAPTER II

The Organization of Sound

Music has been called "the organization of sound toward beauty." For "road map" purposes, this chapter discusses in simple terms six elements composers use to organize their own sounds. A basic familiarity with them helps one understand why music by some composers from some periods sounds so different from music by other composers from other periods—why Mozart, for example, is so unlike Stravinsky.

The six are:

Rhythm	Texture	Form
Melody	Tone color	Tonality

RHYTHM

Webster's defines rhythm as "the aspect of music comprising all the elements (as accent, meter, and tempo) that relate to forward movement." *Movement* is the operative word here; rhythm is the movement in music. Indeed, the word *rhythm* is derived from the Greek *rhein*, "to flow." Breathing is one example of rhythm; the ebb and flow of tides, the tick-tock of a clock, and the clickety-clackety of train wheels are others. Johann Sebastian Bach's *Brandenburg* Concertos have "precise and energetic" rhythm.

Rhythm is what we beat our feet to. It is "the time relationship between tunes." "Tea for Two" has a different footbeat from the longtime favorite of the Democratic party heard at presidential nominating conventions, "Happy Days Are Here Again." Johann Strauss's "Blue Danube" waltz has a different beat from a sea chantey. There are differences in how often the beats are sounded, how regularly, and how long they last. The Gregorian chant had "free rhythm," with the music following the rhythm of the words. Such Baroque pieces as Antonio Vivaldi's *Four Seasons* and Bach's *Brandenburg* Concertos had a steady and precise rhythm. One of the distinguishing features of twentieth-century music is the use of vernacular, far-out "peasant" rhythms in the works of composers such as Béla Bartók of Hungary and Igor Stravinsky of Russia. Bartók's *Miraculous Mandarin* and Stravinsky's *Rite of Spring* have a kind of beat never heard in a Mozart sonata or a Schubert symphony. Impressionist Claude Debussy introduced a floating rhythm in such works as "Clair de lune" because he did not want his music to have a hard, set direction.

One element of rhythm is meter, defined as "a systematically measured and arranged rhythm." A composer chooses double (music people say "duple") or triple or quadruple rhythm, and on up. Professor/author Joseph Machlis, in *The Enjoyment of Music*, offers several common examples: Sing "Twinkle, Twinkle Little Star" and you hear and feel the ONE-two, ONE-two meter in the TWIN-kle, TWIN-kle, LIT-tle, etc. You hear and feel the ONE-two-three, ONE-two-three of triple meter in MY country/'TIS of thee, SWEET land of, etc. "Way Down Upon the Swanee River" is in quadruple meter; "Drink to Me Only with Thine Eyes" in sextuple. You can count it out.

Another element of rhythm is tempo. Meter tells what is accented, but not how slowly or quickly those accents are hit. The composer tells the musician, by scribbling on his score, how rapidly or slowly the music should be played, generally using traditional Italian words and phrases. Among the most common are:

Largo	Very slow
Grave	
Lento	Slow
Adagio	
Andante	Moderate
Andantino	
Moderato	
Allegretto	Fairly fast
Allegro	Fast
Allegro molto	Very fast
Vivace	
Presto	
Prestissimo	

The way in which rhythm is used greatly affects the sound of music.

MELODY

A second building block is melody, or tune, created by a number of musical notes played in succession. With the exception of some twen-tieth-century music, melody is what the piece is "about." Even today, it's still what most people want to hear. Technically one can have a two-note melody, which we learn from the cuckoo and the bob-white—two single tones, one after another, which one can hum, sing, or whistle with no other voices involved, nor any accompaniment. Melodies are traditionally centered on one specific tone that consti-tutes a starting place, a focal point, and a finishing place, and to which other tones in the tune are related. That central tone, chosen by the composer as Square One for his composition, is called a "tonic." (Not as in gin-and-; see "Tonality" later in this chapter.)

It is easier to pick up the melody in some pieces of music than in others. The Romantic melody of a Schumann symphony is more lyrical, more subjective than the Classical melody of a Haydn sym-phony. It is not necessary to have a strong melody in order to have a successful—or even a great—composition, but a lovely, easy-to-hum melody invariably gives conventional lay listeners more enjoyment. Many people who have not studied or analyzed music are most readily attracted to composers specializing in melody—such as Tchaikovsky, one of the most brilliant tune makers on The List. Classical and Romantic composers both make it easier to hear their melody than Baroque and some twentieth-century composers. Long lines of mel-ody are simpler to follow than shorter bursts of melody. Brahms, for example, has much more repetition of melody in his violin concerto than Hindemith has in his.

TEXTURE

Melody is horizontal—one note following another. "Texture" is something added to that line of notes. One way to achieve texture is with harmony. One person cannot "make harmony" with his own voice; he needs a friend to sing with him or a guitar to pluck. If you sing in the shower, you must shower with a friend to have har-mony. Harmony gives music depth, much as perspective gives depth to painting. Whereas melody is a succession of tones, harmony is a combination of tones (historically of related tones and, indeed, of pleasant-sounding related tones) sounded simultaneously.

Chords—three or more notes hit at the same time—play a major role in harmony, which is concerned not only with each chord and its relationship to the melody it supports but also with the movement and relationship of the chords to one another. The impact of a chord is felt as it leads to other chords, as chords "advance and progress." Music dominated by a single melody, supported by chords, is called "homophonic," from the Greek *homophonos*, "being in unison." Much of the music of the Classical and Romantic periods—the music of Beethoven and Liszt—is homophonic. Most of the music of the Renaissance and Baroque periods—the music of Palestrina and Bach—is not.

In music built of melody-plus-chords, the chords often are put together with notes that are "consonant"—that sound agreeable, that are peaceful, that do not jar, that are at rest. But chords can also be made up of combinations that *do* jar, to varying degrees—that are "dissonant," "active," or "restless." The dissonant chord is chosen by the composer to create tension, the consonant chord to ease that tension. The movement back and forth from chord to chord is what harmony is all about.

While the use of harmony in homophonic music is one type of texture, it is not the only way to go. Texture can also be created with the ancient musical device of "counterpoint," also known as "counter-note"—a "note-against-note" technique. In such music, depth is achieved not by adding chords to a melody but by superimposing one melody on another so that both are heard at once. Simple counterpoint is found in a group singing a round such as "Three Blind Mice." The music that results from this technique of using two—or more than two—"voices" at the same time is called "polyphonic," *poly* meaning "many." Bach is unanimously acknowledged as the Crown Prince of counterpoint (no surprise, since he is the Crown Prince of so much else), even though he was not born until 1685, by which time counterpoint had been around for hundreds of years. In fact, by then it was beginning to be supplemented and/or succeeded, first in Italy and then elsewhere in Europe, by single-melody-plus-chords homophonic music. The Italians, forever concentrating on opera, found that a single melody, bolstered by chords, was preferable to multimelody counterpoint for both singer and audience.

The counterpoint technique makes it much harder to find and follow a strong melody in composers such as Bach (or latter-day Bach/Baroque types who keep emerging and who created a back-to-Bach school in the twentieth century) than in the single-melody work of Classical and Romantic composers. In counterpoint music, by listening carefully to one set of instruments carrying one tune and different instruments (or "voices") simultaneously carrying a second and perhaps a third, one *can* identify and track the different tunes. They are there, but for those more accustomed to melody-and-chord harmony, it takes discipline and patience to find them. Counterpoint fans, of course, insist that the tune detection in their kind of music is well worth the effort. (If you devote yourself to Bach alone for a few weeks, you will become a fan for life, regardless of first impressions. His last work, *The Art of the Fugue,* is considered the ultimate example of counterpoint. More fun to listen to, however, are his four orchestral suites.)

Achieving depth by either counterpoint or harmony is called giving "texture" to music. Presumably this is because the weaving together of "horizontal" strands (melody with another simultaneous melody in the case of counterpoint) and "vertical" strands (melody with supporting chords in the case of harmony), duplicates how horizontal and vertical threads are woven together to create the texture of cloth.

A third term describes one-dimensional music as opposed to either polyphonic counterpoint or homophonic melody-plus-chords harmony. It is "monophonic," *mono* meaning "one." This is the simple, one-voiced piece—either you alone in the shower singing a line of notes, or a thousand people singing the same line simultaneously. There are no chords and therefore no harmony; no simultaneous second melody and therefore no counterpoint. All music written up to one thousand years ago was monophonic, including the first thousand or so years of Christian religious music, which culminated in the Gregorian chant.

Nothing in the rule book says that a composer must confine himself in a piece to one of these three techniques. One part of a composition might be written with a homophonic texture, while the next may repeat that melody and intertwine a new one with it, thus moving to a polyphonic texture. And the musical weave may be fine or coarse, just as a fabric weave might be. Counterpoint did not disappear between the time Bach perfected it and its re-emergence with the twentieth-century back-to-Bach movement. Classical and Romantic composers also engaged in counterpoint; it simply did not dominate their music.

TONE COLOR

Each instrument used in classical music has its own tone color, or timbre. The sound—or "color"—of the flute, for example, is very different from the "color" of the tuba, even if both instruments are playing exactly the same note.

Given twenty-odd different kinds of instruments in an orchestra— from violin to bass, from trumpet to tuba, from piccolo to bassoon— the composer has the same variety of colors in front of him that the artist has on his palette. These colors play major roles in orchestration, which is the process of writing music for an orchestra.

One of the finest orchestrators on The List was the Russian Romantic composer Nikolai Rimsky-Korsakov, who said: "Orchestration is part of the very soul of the work. A work is thought out in terms of the orchestra, certain tone-colors being inseparable from it." Orchestration also deals with the volume of various instruments, their ranges, how they sound together, and even such technical things as how quickly they can be played. There is a little more detail on orchestration in the Orchestra chapter.

Music people sometimes like to identify tones with particular colors. The clarinet may give off what sounds like a pastel shade, perhaps of blue, and the trumpet a brilliant red. It is only a small step from there to the suggestion of different emotions that go with those colors. Musicologist Arthur Elson, for example, has come up with the following set of correspondences:

    Violin—All emotions
    Viola—Gloomy melancholy
    Cello—All emotions, but more he-mannish than a violin
    Piccolo—Wild kind of gaiety
    Oboe—Rustic kind of gaiety, also pathos
    Trumpet—Bold, martial, cavalry-is-coming sound
    Tuba—Power, possible brutality
    English horn—Dreamy melancholy
    Clarinet—Eloquence and tenderness, in the middle range

During the Romantic period composers concentrated more on tone color because of a shift in emphasis from "pure" or "absolute" music to "program" music—music that told a story or portrayed a mood or an event that was actually described by the composer in a printed program available to the listener. If the Romantic composer wanted you to hear the sea pounding, ducks quacking, and a "dialogue" between lovers, or to envision a heroic victory over a dragon, he needed to make full use of the different sounds of as many instruments as were available—or might be made available. Thus Berlioz, Liszt, and Richard Strauss, nineteenth-century Romanticists who emphasized program music, were more concerned with tone color than Classicists Haydn or Mozart, who wrote "pure" or "absolute" music—music for music's sake, or "just plain music." Also, as with rhythm, melody, texture, or any other element of music, some composers stressed tone color simply because their talent led them in that direction, or because they tried to break away from past experiences and conventions, or because they were imaginative. Some imagination is required to portray a roaring lion or an opium den in musical terms.

FORM

A fifth element is the "architectural" form chosen by the composer. Some kind of structure obviously is needed; the notes that produce melody, rhythm, and texture cannot float around loose out there, waiting to be summoned in a séance. Each period of music on the "road map" is identified with particular forms of music that reflected the times, the state of musical knowledge, the skills and objectives of the musicians, the development of instruments, and the tastes of the audience.

These structures or molds may be rigid or free. The fact that a mold is rigid, however, does not suggest that the composer is limited in imagination or creativity, as people like Bach, Mozart, and Beethoven have demonstrated. It is not the mold that counts, but what goes into it. Composition in an informal mold, structure, or form may be more difficult for an amateur listener to follow and comprehend, just as free-form sculpture and blank verse may be.

Although the names of major, still-popular forms such as the symphony are commonly known, those of some older forms are not. In the Renaissance era, when vocal music was much more important than instrumental music, the principal forms included motets and madrigals. In Bach's Baroque time, special attention was paid to music constructed around the organ, harpsichord, and clavichord, and to instrumental music with names like the passacaglia, a dance form, and the fugue.

Classical composers were particularly interested in the solo sonata, the symphony, the string quartet, and the concerto. Romanticists developed the symphonic poem and short, lyric piano pieces such as the prelude and the polonaise.

For a moment—but no longer—let's put "form" under a primer microscope.

In a book written in midcentury called *What to Listen For in Music*, Aaron Copland describes musical forms in terms all of us can handle. A long novel, he writes, might be divided into Books I, II, III, and IV. In the music world, these are called *movements*. Each book would have several chapters. The composer calls these *sections*. One chapter could have perhaps a hundred paragraphs as subdivisions, and each musical section has its subdivisions, too, although there is no single term analogous to the writer's paragraph. Paragraphs are made up of sentences; Copland likens these to *musical ideas*. Finally, the novelist uses words, the composer *notes*.

Music people like to say that the basic law of structure in music, whatever the form in question, is repetition and contrast, "unity and variety."

Let's back up to the composer's sections—the equivalent of the author's chapters—and use the letters A and B as names for the sections. The sections may be in two-part form, which the musicians call *binary*, or in three-part, called *ternary*. (That's the last time you'll hear that terminology in this book.)

In a composition written in two-part form, each section might be repeated. A careful listener might hear Section A, then Section A again, followed by Section B, and then B again: A-A-B-B. In this two-part form, Section B often is merely a rearranged version of Section A. This kind of two-part form played a big role in music written between 1650 and 1750, including thousands of short keyboard pieces. The seventeenth-century suite was made up of four or five such works, each in a specific dance form such as the allemande, courante, saraband, or gigue. Among Listed composers, Couperin published four books of two-part clavier pieces.

In three-part form, the composer typically presents Section A, Section B, and then Section A again: A-B-A. Unlike Section B in two-part form, this B contrasts distinctly with A. The second A might then be an exact repetition of the first or a variation of it. Among examples of three-part form are minuets by Haydn and Mozart.

Repetition of one kind or another has dominated classical music from the outset. Copland identifies five different categories of repetition in musical structures: exact repetition, symmetrical repetition, repetition by variation, repetition by fugal treatment, and repetition through development.

Two-part and three-part form are examples of exact and symmetrical repetition, respectively; the passacaglia and the chaconne of repetition by variation; the fugue, concerto grosso, chorale prelude, motet, and madrigal of repetition by fugal treatment; and the sonata of repetition by development.

We will encounter dozens of these "fundamental" forms, from the symphony to something called "theme and variations," as well as "free" forms such as the prelude and the symphonic poem. For our purposes, the term *form* will also include such vocal art forms as the opera, oratorio, mass, and cantata.

TONALITY

A special jargon goes with every occupation. The wine taster speaks of the "authoritative but not aggressive nose," the counterman calls out, "Eighty-six on the hamburgers" (i.e., they're all gone), the football player has "good hands," "quick feet," and a "good read," and the Pentagon general schedules his "weapons system" toward an "initial operational capability." The music world is no different, and our sixth element is "tonality"—which leads us to many destinations, including "dissonance," which was addressed briefly earlier.

"He honors dissonance," we hear about one composer.

"He is rooted in key," we hear about another.

"Polytonality abounds in his work, but despite an occasional leaning toward atonality, he never wholly abandoned the principle of key," it is written about a third.

While this is kindergarten talk for young music students, some of us need a bit of guidance to understand what tonality is all about. Even in a primer such as this, it is mandatory to touch on tonality since it is perhaps *the* major reason why certain composers on The List sound so unlike certain others. The story begins with Pythagoras and his concepts of arithmetical relationships in about 500 B.C. And it has to do with "key," as in Antonin Dvořák's Serenade for Strings in [the key of] E Major.

The best starting place may be a length of string, pulled tight. When twanged, the string produces a tone of a definite pitch—that is, a sound with a specific number of vibrations per second. On a piano the lowest note is about thirty vibrations per second and the highest about four thousand. Whatever the string's length, the tone made by its twang is almost exactly the same as that made by a string either half or twice as long. The sounds made by these shorter and longer strings will be higher and lower, respectively, than the first, but the *tone* of all three will be the same. One note, say C, on a piano keyboard will have the same tone as a higher C up the keyboard or a lower C down the keyboard.

Several hundred years ago Western composers divided each length of string into twelve parts. You can't see them on a violin, but they are represented on a piano keyboard by seven white keys and five black keys for each string length. These represent *the* twelve and the *only* twelve tones of traditional Western music. Each key, white or black, is a half-tone away from its neighbor.

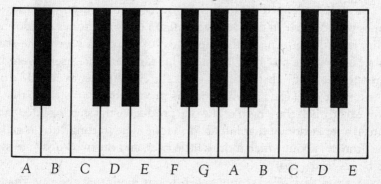

A   B   C   D   E   F   G   A   B   C   D   E

Most readers know that the seven white keys are named for the first seven letters of the alphabet, A through G. Each of the raised black keys has two names. It is called a sharp when it is a step (half-tone) higher than its white namesake, and a flat when it is a step lower. Thus, on the sketch, C-sharp and D-flat are the same black key. There is nothing terribly confusing about this; you are Mr. Smith's neighbor on one side of you and Ms. Jones's neighbor on the other side.

The piano sketch also shows that five of the white keys—A, C, D, F, and G—have a black sharp to their right going up the scale, but that two—B and E—do not. The distance between any two adjacent keys on the piano keyboard is still one-half tone, whether white to white, white to black, or black to white (you can't get from one black directly to another black). Thus there is a whole-tone difference from A (white) to B (white), since there is an intervening black key, but only a half-tone from the white E to the white F, since no black key intervenes.

Every work by every composer on The List consists of some or all of these twelve tones represented on the piano, plus the higher and lower versions of them also represented. Western composers traditionally have had no other tones at their disposal.

There is no law about this; it's simply a matter of custom, just as the length of an American football field is one hundred yards and the distance between baseball bases ninety feet. Canada chooses a different-size football field, and other countries and parts of the world have chosen different types of musical scales. The Arabs have seventeen tones; the Indians' tones are a quarter-step apart instead of a half-step. One can write music in tones one-tenth of a tone apart if one chooses. A violin could play it, but not a piano—unless a special one was constructed to order.

But we don't have one-tenth tones in Western culture. In our musical system we use the tones represented by the seven white keys and the five black ones, period. And we use them in scales.

A scale is defined as an orderly succession of notes; a series of tones put together in consecutive order; a ladder of tones and sound, from the bottom rung to the top. Most of us sang a seven-tone scale in school—do-re-mi-fa-sol-la-ti-do. This familiar scale uses seven different tones, "do" through "ti," plus the eighth note, a second "do," to round it off. (That second "do" is produced by a "string" that is now exactly half the length of the one producing the starting "do," and thus is a repetition of that initial "do" tone. The starting "do" is called the "tonic," about which more a little later, and the two "dos" are said to be an *octave* apart.)

A scale that selects only seven (eight, counting the one that is repeated) of the twelve—the do-re-mi-fa . . . scale—is a "diatonic" scale. (One that goes up and down all twelve tones is called a "chromatic" scale; more on this later.) Most composers on The List built their works around diatonic, rather than chromatic, scales.

In the simplest "road map" explanation, the phenomena of "key" and "tonality" arise from the use of the do-re-mi-fa . . . scale and which seven of the twelve tones a composer chooses. Different combinations of sounds will result if he uses one set of seven as opposed to another set (and still different combinations if, as happened in some late nineteenth- and early twentieth-century music, he uses the twelve-tone chromatic scale).

A pianist running up a scale starting with a white C, hitting only the next seven white keys, will hear the familiar do-re-mi-fa-sol-la-ti-do that each of us can more or less sing. Inasmuch as he chose C as a starting point, if he creates a little tune using only these keys, singly and in chords, that tune will be in the "key of C." Inasmuch as the key of C consists only of white notes (unlike other keys), if he has hit no black notes he has been "wholly loyal to key." He has not "abandoned" or "deserted" key. His work will be centered on that first note of the chosen scale, in this case the C. That C will be the "key note," the common center, the "home tone," the "supreme tone" of the composition. For some three hundred years in Western music, everything was built around the chosen key note and its relationship to other tones.

The term "tonality" refers to this relationship within a group of chords and harmonies which belong to one key. In our composition, having sounded only the chords and harmonies belonging to the key of C, our composer has "established a feeling of tonality."

So much for the key of C. Now let's assume that the composer/pianist wants to write a second piece in another key. He returns to the keyboard and starts this time on a white G. To see how it sounds, he runs up the white keys from that note, hitting all successive white notes through the next G. But the do-re-mi . . . sounds don't quite work this time. One note is sour and "off key." By experimenting, the pianist learns that he must substitute the black F-sharp for the white F in order to achieve the smooth do-re-mi-fa-sol-la-ti-(do) sound. Once this substitution is made, he is functioning in the key of G, and a new tune picked out from this arrangement of notes would not sound like the one created in the key of C. Even though he is now working with six of the same seven tones of the key of C, the seventh is different. And having a new starting place—G instead of C—he now has a new central tone, or "tonic," and the to-and-fro between that new initial note and the other notes on this new scale will produce quite a different tonal sound than the one built around C.

Try it on a piano. By starting on any of the twelve piano notes, white or black, and by experimenting with black notes as substitutes, you can re-create from seven notes the familiar do-re-mi . . . scale. You will find that two black sharps are needed to produce the familiar scale when starting on D, three when starting on A, four when starting on E, and five when starting on B. In each scale-and-key, the composer is working with different combinations of notes—still seven out of twelve, but different starting points and different related other tones.

Actually, it is not necessary to experiment. Achieving the familiar scale is a function of the relationship between the full-tone steps on the keyboard and the half-tone steps. The sketch shows that, starting with a white C, the pattern of rungs on the ladder goes this way: whole tone (from C to D), whole tone (from D to E), half-tone (from E to F), whole tone (from F to G), whole tone (from G to A), whole tone (from A to B), and half-tone (from B to C).

The scale with this arrangement of whole tones and half-tones came down from the Greeks, as one of several in use over the centuries. It is Western culture's "major" scale, the fundamental scale of

Western music since the seventeenth century, and one made permanent by Bach. Instead of trial-and-error experimenting, you could achieve the do-re-mi . . . scale from any starting note simply by following the pattern of whole tone, whole tone, half-tone, whole tone, whole tone, whole tone, half-tone. This "major" scale has the same pattern whether going up the scale or, inversely, down it, as you can hear by trying it on a piano.

But this is only one of the two scales, or *modes*, that dominated Western music in the seventeenth through nineteenth centuries. The other is the "minor" mode (which comprises three different scales), based on the same seven white tones and five black ones, but with a different sequence of tones and half-tones. More specifically, it is distinguished from the major by the number of half-tones between the first and third notes of the scales. In one of the three scales in the minor mode, this sequence is whole tone, half-tone, whole tone (while that of the major, as mentioned above, is whole, whole, half). Traditionally, the major mode was associated with happy or serene music, the minor with sad, gloomy, troubled music.

The key in which a composition is written is called "major" or "minor" depending on whether it is based on a major or minor scale. Prior to the establishment of these two scales as the tonal base, Western music was based on eight scales known as "church modes," which differ in some degree from today's major and minor modes. (Each of the eight scales of the church-mode system consisted of the tones of the C Major scale—the white piano keys—but was limited to the range of one octave and both started and closed on one of four notes: D, E, F, or G.)

The music people make a great deal of the psychological pull between the tonic, the first note of the chosen scale, and the fifth note up from it, called the "dominant." The three-note chord starting on the tonic and including the third and fifth notes up is called the *tonic chord*. Most music written between 1600 and 1900 ends on the tonic chord for the key in which it is written. The relationship between the tonic and the dominant is *the* basic expression of tonality, and thus of agreeable sounds—of "consonance."

In the late 1800s and early 1900s, several composers on The List moved away from this emphasis on one tone, or tonality, and experimented with different combinations of sounds. Some of this music was extremely disagreeable to the ears of the time, even though present-day ears are accustomed to most of it.

When a composer does move away from the concept of total tonality, of building everything around one ultra-important tone, there will be some "dissonance" in his work. For example, should our pianist/composer planning to work in the key of C have strayed, and brought in black notes *not* from the seven that made up the scale that began on C, he would have heard jarring, "off-key" sounds and no longer would have been completely "loyal to key." They might have been only slightly jarring, just a little dissonant, in order to add a little variety, or horribly jarring and "acidly dissonant," just to be original. If, on the other hand, he had stuck with the seven white notes, he would not have been "chromatic." A chromatic tone, or chord, is one that is not in the key of a composition; had he sounded any black note while working in the key of C it would have been a chromatic tone. (The term *chromatic* comes from the Greek word meaning "color.") Composers for hundreds of years have deviated from the chosen key and used such tones to give their works color and variety. Bach and Mozart did it in Baroque and Classical times; Chopin, Schumann, and Wagner in Romantic times. The use of a few chromatic tones does not necessarily change the basic tonality of the piece, nor does some dissonance necessarily disturb the listener.

Webster's defines dissonance as "a mingling of discordant sounds." In music specifically, *Webster's* adds, it is "a clashing musical interval." ("Interval" is the difference in pitch between two tones.) Some tones sound agreeable when played together, and others do not. This is not a matter of personal opinion but of the actual meshing of vibrations-per-second of different tones. The opposite of dissonance is consonance. Some combinations of notes are called "perfect" consonances, some "imperfect" consonances, and some dissonances. And that is the way they sound when played together: perfectly agreeable, less agreeable, and disagreeable. Then there is the full range of disagreeable—disagreeable in a disguised way, mildly disagreeable, acidly or harshly disagreeable, wildly disagreeable, and just plain awful. As noted, composers work some dissonance into their music to give it contrast and tension; melodious Romantic composers, for example, consistently used chords built on tones that were not part of the piece's key. But several twentieth-century composers on The List deliberately chose dissonance; they emphasized dissonance; in music talk, they "honored" dissonance. (Stravinsky of Russia, Bartók of Hungary, and Hindemith of Germany were very good at it for their day.) And, as a result, some of their music screeches on first hearing— or even second or third hearing. A child who grows up hearing it and nothing else, of course, might not consider it screeching at all.

Why do composers of genius try to make unpleasant music? The answer, of course, is that basically, they don't consider it unpleasant.

Rather, they want a little tension and have to go one step farther than their immediate predecessors to get it.

Dissonance was alive and well in Renaissance times, although Palestrina (b. 1525), the first-born Listed composer, was a model for conservative and careful handling of it. Some of his contemporaries were considerably more dissonant. Mozart (b. 1756) was more dissonant than they; Liszt (b. 1811) more dissonant than Mozart; and twentieth-century "new music" composers more dissonant than Liszt. Twentieth-century artists on The List were not simply running amok with dissonance. They had their own game plans, their own ways of organizing harmony and tones, however different the methods and the resultant sounds were from the "norm." Many were, in fact, no more rebellious than Palestrina; they simply were experimenting with an existing system that had come a long way from the system of the 1550s. Dissonance is in the ear of the listener—and is relative. What was rebellious in Palestrina's day was old hat by Schubert's time. Consider, for example, one of Schubert's most famous songs, "The Elf King." The poem, by Johann Wolfgang von Goethe, is a ballad about a father riding with his child through a forest trying to escape from the evil King of the Elves, who kills children by touching them. The father sings in a low voice, the boy in a higher one. The main music is in one key but the King always sings in another, with the key changing from stanza to stanza, to help create tension. Three times in the poem the boy cries out, "My father, my father," and each time his voice is in a higher pitch than the piano, a half-step away. The music people tell us that acute discomfort to the ear is produced by simultaneously sounding two pitches a half-step apart. Schubert consciously used sharp dissonance to show stress. Twentieth-century composers, then, did not invent dissonance or the practice of working in more than one key. But while Schubert changes keys from stanza to stanza, he does not write in two keys at once.

Early twentieth-century experimentation by talented Listed composers is not unlike experimentation by talented contemporary artists creating paintings deemed by some to be unpleasant (or downright silly) or experimentation by great contemporary architects creating magnificent buildings that traditionalists consider eyesores. Creative minds in the late 1800s and the 1900s (or the 1550s) were not satisfied with re-creating the past. They wanted to stretch music in various directions—which, as we have seen, is something composers throughout history have wanted to do. And they did this in many ways.

Some borrowed from folk songs and found "new" (usually very old) scales that had been deep in the countryside for hundreds or thousands of years. Bartók and Stravinsky were among them. Some scales were found close to home in their own countries; some were from Spain or as far away as Bali.

Some experimented with microtones similar to those used in the Far East.

Some tried quarter-tones, as used in India, or one-sixth tones. The piano could not handle these, but other instruments could.

Some stuck with tonality—"loyalty to key"—but broadened it so that their compositions worked in two keys at the same time, the result being termed "bitonality." Ravel, Stravinsky, Bartók, and Prokofiev all tried this.

Some experimented with using more than two keys at once— "polytonality." Prokofiev, Bartók, and Stravinsky were among such experimenters. (Schubert, Wagner, Franck, and others had moved rapidly from key to key for contrast, but had never used more than one key at the same time.)

Some "expanded" tonality by using all twelve semi-tones instead of seven, but nonetheless centering their work on one selected "supreme" tone, say A. The resulting music is not "in A Major" but is still "majorish." The key is still there, but it is not as important. Prokofiev, Bartók, and Hindemith were among this group.

Some used a scale made up only of whole tones. Debussy worked this way as he created Impressionism and veered away from traditional nineteenth-century music.

Some, as discussed in chapter 1, went "atonal," using no key at all. One form of atonality was an entirely new system called "twelve-tone serial music." This used the twelve traditional tones on the piano keyboard but rearranged them in a set order to be used repeatedly. The result was a series of totally different chords and no center at all. Stravinsky worked in this made for a while.

And some of the electronic, aleatory, and *musique concrète* productions of the 1980s make the "shocking" experiments of the first twenty-five years of the century seem pale and not so bold at all.

CHAPTER III

Setting the Stage

No hard lines separate the five periods from which The 50 composers came: Renaissance, Baroque, Classical, Romantic, and Twentieth Century. One movement did not stop in 1599 and another start in 1600. Composers' lives spanned the demarcation points. Some who lived in one period looked backward in their work, some forward. Others served as bridges between the eras. Many artists adhered to certain concepts when young and different ones when old. And history, of course, has created the groupings; a composer living in 1850 was unaware that one hundred years later he would be lumped with others into a Middle Romantic category.

A good many musicians rejected efforts made to categorize them, much as some twentieth-century politicians complain about such labels as "right wing" and "left wing." Some of the most radical composers grumbled about being called "revolutionary," arguing that they were simply taking one or two more steps beyond the norm.

When a good thing has been around long enough, two things generally happen. Some creative, bright people grow weary of it and start working on a successor—any successor (it might be a horseless carriage), just to get out of the rut. In politics, these people are called liberals, and they can come up with some incredibly bad ideas as well as some daring and unconventional good ones. They experiment. They make things happen. Simultaneously, there exists another group of very bright people who respect what has worked before and are reluctant to abandon it, and who devote their efforts to bringing it to its highest level of excellence. They believe in evolution, not revolution, and they employ their intelligence, analytical powers, and technical skills to develop the existing form. Sometimes they resist change for the sake of resisting change, which can be unfortunate. Politically, these are the conservatives. At their best, the two groups can be equally bright, equally courageous, and equally creative—one dedicated to designing anew, the other to perfecting to the ultimate what already exists.

So it is with music. Some of The 50 greatest composers in history were all liberal, some all conservative, most a blend, and the schools of music into which history puts them are also blends. There is no better individual example than Ludwig van Beethoven, a Classical Immortal who developed several musical forms to the ultimate but who was also an innovative experimenter who heralded the long Romantic era and cannot be considered apart from it.

In this chapter you'll find a brief written "snapshot" of each of The 50 composers, era by era, and some scene-setting for each period, including identification of important trends and, as useful on a selective basis, descriptions of the musical elements of each (melody, harmony, rhythm, and so on). Technical descriptions—of the "intervalic bases such as fifths, sevenths, seconds, and others" type—will be scrupulously avoided. But information such as the fact that rhythm dominated the compositions of one era and melody another will be included, in an effort to explain what gives the music of each period its distinctive sound. Of course, it is impossible to describe sounds with words. Professional musicians can communicate with one another because they know what they are doing to make different sounds. They can talk about augmentations, diminutions, retrograde inversions, and other things sometimes indefinite in meaning, sometimes ponderous in terminology, and all totally bewildering to the rest of us.

The bricks-and-mortar differences between one period of music and another are included in the road map in the hope that they will help a little, but the only real way to get a feeling for the music of any given era is to listen. That a Rubens painting differs from a Monet painting is instantly clear to any ten-year-old being taken through a museum as a reward for her good behavior. Similarly, if your collection consists only of Baroque Handel and Impressionist Debussy, a few seconds of listening will enable you to identify which is which. You may not be able to differentiate Bach from Handel that quickly, or Debussy from Ravel, but certainly you'll be able to tell Baroque from Impressionist. If you add Mozart to your collection, identification of the three will be just about as speedy. I will try to describe major trends, new forms, and the like, but the gut fact is that only a limited amount can be accomplished with bricks-and-mortar comparisons, written for the eyes by and for nonprofessionals. Music is for ears.

I've also included here brief descriptions of the main types of musical forms of the periods, both instrumental and vocal, and some examples of compositions in those forms.

LATE RENAISSANCE

Giovanni da Palestrina   1525–1594   No. 24

RENAISSANCE SNAPSHOT

Palestrina is the greatest Italian Renaissance composer and the master of the Catholic mass. A giant in all forms of church music, he composed more than one hundred masses, two hundred motets, and one hundred hymns. His counterpoint mastery set the stage for Bach's counterpoint perfection. Organist, choirmaster, and composer, he was a skillful but conservative user of dissonance.

THE RENAISSANCE SCENE

This was not the Dark Ages. It was the period between ancient and modern times, characterized by a humanistic revitalization that was expressed in the arts, literature, and the beginnings of modern science. This was the era of da Vinci, Michelangelo, and Botticelli in painting, and of Spenser, Shakespeare, Rabelais, Montaigne, and Cervantes in literature. Drake, Magellan, and Balboa were exploring. Copernicus and Galileo were doing their scientific things. The sixteenth century was the time of the Protestant Reformation and the Catholic counter-reformation.

Church music "dominated" the music of the Renaissance, vocal music "dominated" church music, and the mass "dominated" vocal church music. But it is easy to be misled by that kind of talk. Unfortunately, to millions of people in many American cities, the Pittsburgh Steelers "dominated" professional football Super Bowls for a few years. And there was a time when three American automobile companies "dominated" car making and sales. In these cases, a lot of activity took place beyond the "domination." A lot of other football teams were playing games, and a lot of other cars—foreign and domestic— were on the road. In zeroing in on that which "dominates," care must be taken not to overlook the rest of the action.

For musical purposes, the Renaissance ranges from 1425 or 1450 or 1475 to 1600, the starting time depending on whether one assigns the Burgundian school of music in northern France and the Netherlands to the tail end of the Middle Ages or to the beginning of the Renaissance. A compromise date is 1450. For reference, Christopher Columbus was born the next year.

In early Renaissance days, musical genius was centered in northern France and Belgium (unlike painting genius, which was centered in Italy). Eventually the center shifted to Italy. During this period, vocal music was more important than instrumental, and it was centered in the church, chiefly in the form of masses and the short choral compositions called motets. But one of the most significant changes in music during Renaissance times was its movement beyond the church and into the home. Renaissance men sang, joined choral groups, played instruments, and created little informal ensembles. Music became an audience-participation sport.

Renaissance performers were highly skilled on a range of instruments, the most popular of which was the long-necked, string-plucked lute. The major bowed string instrument, a grandfather of the violin, was the viol, which came in bass, tenor, and treble sizes. The recorder, a wooden flute blown through one end, was the favorite woodwind. In the brass category were trumpets and trombones; organs were central to sacred music; string keyboard instruments included the clavichord, whose strings were hit by a piece of metal, and the harpsichord, whose strings were plucked by quills. (In England, the harpsichord was called the spinet or virginal; in Italy, the *clavicembalo*; in France, the *clavecin*. In Germany, any keyboard instrument was known as a *klavier* or *clavier*.) These (and other) instruments are discussed in greater detail in chapter 5.

Religious music was composed for the organ and harpsichord, and dance music for the lute, harpsichord, and ensemble—although there was no standard ensemble such as the later string quartet. In some ways, Renaissance music shares many traits with the Classical music that followed: clarity and balance, with pleasant, sweet sounds.

From the standpoint of influencing others and gaining personal fame, sixteenth-century composers had one big advantage over their predecessors: music printing had been perfected early in the century. As a result, compositions were scattered far beyond the composers' home territories, and distinguished musicians were invited to foreign courts to compose and perform.

The major formal advance of Renaissance music was the development of multivoiced polyphony.

Long before this period, the church had supported and controlled much of Western music. During the Middle Ages, prayers and religious statements were set to more than three thousand melodies and sung in Gregorian chant, aka plainsong, aka plainchant. Lovely and intriguing, Gregorian chant is single-melody, monophonic music (with no harmonic accompaniment), without regularly accented rhythm and without sharp variation in loudness and softness. "Dynamic" it is not.

Somewhere around the year 1000, composers began to develop two-voiced, polyphonic music, with each voice carrying a separate melodic line. This caused European music to break away from the monophonic sounds of the East—that is, of China, Japan, India, and the Arab countries. While both sacred and secular polyphonic music was written during the last part of the Middle Ages, most that has been preserved is from the religious side.

For quite a while, composers gave equal time to high and low voices. Eventually, a tad more emphasis began to be placed on the topmost voice, the lower voice becoming less independent and assuming more of a supporting role. As the Renaissance progressed, composers began to bring in more voices, so that by the time of Palestrina (1525–1594) there were six-part counterpoint choruses.

RENAISSANCE BRICKS-AND-MORTAR

Rhythm: Choral music, the most impressive music composed during the Renaissance, was relatively unaccented, without the regular pulsating rhythm found in later instrumental music.

Melody: Some composers wrote secular songs with a melodious top voice, others with four or five parts of equal interest. When several melodies overlap, with voices singing different words and melodies at the same time, no single, strong melody emerges.

Texture: The dominant feature of Renaissance music is its polyphony.

Orchestral Color: While all instruments played the same parts in early Renaissance days, by the time the period ended small "special assignments" were given to the lute, or sometimes to another instrument.

Tonality: Church modes were much in use as the Renaissance began but were gradually replaced by major and minor scales, with more of the "feeling of key" that was to come, but none of the shifting from key to key that causes dissonance.

Dynamics: There was little variation in loudness and softness.

RENAISSANCE FORMS OF MUSIC: VOCAL

Mass: The mass, the rite of consecration, is the most solemn ritual of the Roman Catholic church, and music written for it includes some of the most beautiful of all Western music. Although the Renaissance was the golden age of the mass, composers have written masses over the centuries and are doing so still. One of America's best-known twentieth-century composers, Leonard Bernstein, wrote a mass for the opening of the Kennedy Center in Washington. Listed composers from Mozart to Vaughan Williams composed masses. The best-known nonoperatic work of Verdi is his *Requiem* Mass, a mass for the dead, and one of the most magnificent compositions ever written is Bach's Mass in B Minor.

In the Roman Catholic church, both the music and the text of the masses used for services are provided by the church. But someone has to write the music. The rite of the mass is divided into two parts, the Ordinary, the text of which is always the same, and the Proper, the text of which varies on different occasions. Composers early on chose the Ordinary for their musical contributions. It consists of several set sections, and for centuries the music for each consisted first of Gregorian-chant melodies and then of a second melody built on them in polyphonic style. In the fifteenth century, composers moved beyond working section-by-section and, instead, composed entire Ordinary masses in polyphonic form—the text, however, remaining constant. Some composers borrowed the music of secular songs, and even of obscene songs. By the time of Palestrina in the sixteenth century, many composers were writing complete masses, but without deviating from the Roman Catholic text.

The five sections of the Ordinary for which this additional music was composed are the Kyrie, Gloria, Credo, Sanctus, and Agnus Dei. The text of the Kyrie is "Lord have mercy upon us," "Christ have mercy upon us," and, again, "Lord have mercy upon us." Then comes the "Gloria in excelsis Deo" ("Glory be to God on high"), known as the hymn of praise. This is followed by the Confession of Faith, "Credo in unum Deum, Patrem omnipotentum" ("I believe in one God, the omnipotent Father"). Next is the Sanctus, actually "Sanctus, sanctus, sanctus" ("Holy, holy, holy"), which ends with "Hosanna in excelsis" ("Praise in the highest") and the Benedictus ("Blessed is He who cometh in the name of the Lord"). The last section is the Agnus Dei ("Lamb of God who taketh away the sins of the world"), which is sung three times. The existing melody around which the new music is written is called the *cantus firmus,* or "fixed song." While initially the cantus firmus was in Gregorian chant, it gradually began to come from other sources, including part of a scale or a nonreligious song. In the fifteenth and sixteenth centuries one such frequently used popular song was "L'Homme arme" ("The Armed Man"). Palestrina was one of many composers who chose it as the basic structure for some masses, before creating the best-known original Renaissance mass, his masterpiece *Missa Papae Marcelli*. (The Latin word for mass is *missa*, meaning "dismissal at the end of the service"; this was the "Marcellus Mass," dedicated to the Pope of that name.)

Motet: Popular in various forms over several centuries, the motet was essentially a song—an unaccompanied choral composition based on Latin text and performed in Catholic services. (In the Middle Ages, secular motets also existed, usually based on such themes as war or love.) The number of parts varied from two to six, with the voices simultaneously singing different text phrases and melodies. Palestrina wrote motets associated with masses, one example being his *Tu es Petrus*.

Madrigal: A secular song, the madrigal was an unaccompanied setting of a poem, usually in five or six parts. It resembled the motet and can be considered its secular counterpart, although it was freer in form. As time passed, the madrigal became longer, more personal, and not unlike a very short opera. (The terms *motet* and *madrigal* existed for centuries, and the structures of each often changed.) A madrigal might have been a happy love song or the story of a man who murdered his wife's lover. Composers in England and Italy wrote madrigals, but Germans preferred a simple four-part song with the melody in the top voice known as a part-song; it was sometimes used by the Lutherans for church services. The eight Petrarch settings in Palestrina's *First Book of Madrigals* are examples of the madrigal.

Chanson: French for "song," the *chanson* was the French equivalent of the Italian madrigal. In Renaissance times, it was a polyphonic secular song, usually dealing with love, and often performed with one voice and several instruments. Since the Italian Palestrina is the only Listed Renaissance composer, no *chanson* examples are offered. If you want to cheat, try one of the French Renaissance composers cited in chapter 1.

RENAISSANCE FORMS OF MUSIC: INSTRUMENTAL

Dances: Instrumental music is as old as vocal music, but it was not as widespread in Renaissance times, although there was more instrumental music elsewhere in Europe—France, Germany, England, and

Spain—than in Italy, home of our only representative. Several dance forms popular in the French court were the *pavane*, a stately, slow, dignified dance; the *galliard*, a more lively dance that frequently followed the *pavane* in court, and the *branle*, a popular round dance usually accompanied by singing. (Later on, composers grouped these dances and others into dance suites.)

Sonata: In the Renaissance, a sonata was simply a composition for instruments rather than voices. The classical sonata, a specific form for solo instrument, did not yet exist. Examples are found in the works of unListed composers identified in chapter 1.

Ricercar: This was an instrumental composition in counterpoint, with several voice-parts imitating the melody in turn. In Renaissance times it was usually written for organ. (Bach includes one in his "Musical Offering.")

BAROQUE

Claudio Monteverdi	1567–1643	No. 34
François Couperin	1668–1733	No. 49
Antonio Vivaldi	1678–1741	No. 37
Georg Telemann	1681–1767	No. 26
Jean-Philippe Rameau	1683–1764	No. 40
Johann Sebastian Bach	1685–1750	No. 1
George Frideric Handel	1685–1759	No. 9

BAROQUE SNAPSHOTS

Monteverdi, the first-born Listed Baroque composer, wrote both secular madrigals and church music in contrapuntal texture. But he is best known as the father of opera reform—for blending music and drama into opera and bringing it to the general public for the first time. He developed the largest orchestra to date and was one of the first to work with single-melody chordal music. He was also among the early users of dissonance—for example, in the "Lament" from his opera *Arianna*.

Couperin was the favorite of a king, the master of the harpsichord, and the patron saint of French keyboard music, as both instrumentalist and composer. His fame has lasted from Baroque times to the present—his works were studied by Bach and Handel in their day and revered by Debussy and Ravel in theirs. One of many musical Couperins in France, he not only did wondrously delicate things with his harpsichord compositions, but also wrote an enduring treatise on the technique of playing that instrument.

Vivaldi wrote masterful violin music (he was one of a long line of Italian violin virtuosos) and remains one of the most prolific composers of all time in several fields, from church music to opera. Although overshadowed in his day by two contemporaries, Handel and Telemann (though not, at that time, by Bach), his advancement of single-melody chordal instrumental music, including four concertos for violin, strings, and continuo—today's popular *Four Seasons*—was a major contribution.

Telemann was considerably better known and more influential than his German colleague Bach while alive, was later rated "superficial" by critics, and now is highly regarded once more. The most prolific composer of his day, he wrote more than three thousand works, including forty operas, forty-four passions, six hundred overtures, two cantatas for every Sunday for many years, and several instructional books on music. He was godfather to one of Bach's sons.

Rameau was the foremost French composer of the eighteenth century, a major figure in French opera (more than one hundred years after Monteverdi's opera work in Italy), a master musical theorist, and one of history's greatest composers of clavier (harpsichord) music. He, too, carried on early experiments in France with single-voiced chordal music.

Bach is Number One.

Handel, a Demigod, born the same year as Bach, is the other Baroque giant, composer of the *Messiah*, and history's most famous oratorio writer. He is the author of many operas, the first successful creator of music designed for the masses, and is also famous for compositions designed for outdoor performances, including *Royal Fireworks Music* and *Water Music*. Born in Germany, he spent most of his creative life in England.

THE BAROQUE SCENE

Perhaps the best way to capture the sense of the Baroque period (1600–1750) is not to listen but to look. Examine a painting by Peter Paul Rubens, jam-packed with color, action, and elaborate figures. Try *The Abduction of the Daughters of Leucippus* or *The Garden of Love* for their controlled energy and decorative splendor. Much was happening in the world. The Thirty Years War took place on the continent of Europe. England experienced a Civil War, a Commonwealth, and a Restoration. Across the ocean the American colonies were being settled and developed. Newton, Kepler, Galileo, and Bacon were revolutionizing the scientific world. Rembrandt, Rubens, Van Dyck, and El Greco were painting. The list of writers was long and distinguished: Milton, Dryden, Defoe, Addison, Swift, Pope, Samuel Johnson, Corneille, Racine, and Molière, among others.

Concepts were grandiose. And in the music world, several developments of far-reaching importance took place. On the one hand, this was the first period in which instrumental music was as important as vocal music. But on the other, it was also the period in which opera emerged. Not only poems but entire dramas were now set to music.

Emerging at the start of the seventeenth century, opera had an impact on all kinds of Baroque music and has remained a major musical form to this day. Everyone knows that operas are performed on stage and that they include not only acting and singing but also scenery, costumes, properties, and lighting. (The point is made in part because the important Baroque oratorio does *not* include all of these things.) The text of the opera is known as the *libretto*; the songs of soloists are *arias*; those sung by two or three singers are *duets* and *trios*, respectively; the speech-type singing dialogue in between arias is *recitative*; the instrumental introduction is the *overture*; a form of dancing sometimes found within operas is *ballet*; and the basic instrumental music comes from the orchestra, arranged in front of the stage in the pit. Instrumental works called *interludes* are sometimes played at different points in the opera.

The merging of music and drama actually began not in the Baroque period but centuries earlier, in Greece. It was revived in the 1590s when a group of noblemen in Florence called the "Camerata" set some Greek plays to music, including one, entitled *Eurydice*, that was performed in 1600 as one of the first operas. The idea quickly spread from Florence to Rome, Venice, and Naples. The second-born Listed composer, Monteverdi, is regarded as the first major opera writer, in part because he pursued and captured what the music people like to call "dramatic truth."

It was the Camerata of Florence who invented the *recitativo* type of single-line vocal music, with that melodic line following the natural intonations of speech, rising and falling with the actor's voice.

As the 1600s continued, in Italy the initial back-to-Greek-mythology concept for opera was gradually replaced by back-to-Roman-history. The operatic stars were the *castrati* (castrated males) with their remarkable, high voices, a temperamental crew but enormously popular. In the late 1600s, France developed its own approach, as the French are wont to do, with opera composers there preferring the plays of good fellow Frenchmen such as Molière and Racine to either Greek mythology or Roman history. The French also introduced ballet to the opera and paid more attention to the orchestra. The first major French operas were written in the 1670s, and they called for huge (forty-piece) orchestras of strings, flutes, oboes, bassoons, trumpets, and drums. Later, French Baroque opera culminated in the work of Rameau, who contributed a new and more sophisticated harmony, new rhythm, and new instrumental color.

Comic opera emerged in the early 1700s as a reaction to the Italian *opera seria*. It was light, humorous, frivolous, and featured commonplace characters rather than heroic historical figures.

BAROQUE BRICKS-AND-MORTAR

Rhythm: In Baroque times, rhythm was typically strong, energetic, steady, and repetitive. There was more emphasis on rhythm than in Renaissance compositions (or in the Classical or Romantic compositions that followed)—although much less emphasis than was coming in twentieth-century music. The terse, pulsating Baroque rhythms are heard in Vivaldi, Handel, and Bach.

Melody: Picture, again, a Rubens painting. The Baroque score was jam-packed with elaborate, energetic, continuously expanding melody. Because it is frequently embellished by trills and other ornamental devices, Baroque melody is not, generally speaking, as tuneful to the ear as either the Classical music that came next or the Romantic music that was to follow.

Texture: While counterpoint—multimelody polyphony—continued to be the basic texture of Baroque music and, indeed, was perfected by Bach, there also was significant development of single-melody-with-chords homophony, particularly in Italian opera. This was logical. Opera quickly became important to the lives of the Italian people. Both singers and their audiences needed a clear understanding of the songs—not easy to achieve in counterpoint, with each singer doing his or her own thing and more than one melody being heard simultaneously. Single-melody chordal music became the favorite medium of composers such as Monteverdi in Italy, Rameau in France, and others in the opera world.

Harmony: A user-friendly gimmick known as the "figured bass" brought about a new approach to harmony. Performing musicians were familiar with chords, and composers therefore developed a musical shorthand for single-melody music. Instead of writing in the notes for the chords to be played by the bass, composers would write simply a numerical figure—a 6, for example—under a given note. The combination of the note and the figure told the performing musician what chord to play. "Figured bass" was also known both as "thorough-bass" (today we would say "through" instead of "thorough") and as "continuous bass" (in Italian, *basso continuo*). In time, *basso continuo* was shortened to *continuo*, a word often seen today in titles of Baroque compositions. At least two musicians were needed to handle the continuo role, the main bass line being carried by the deep sound of a cello, double bass, or bassoon, and that line being supplemented by a friskier lute, guitar, organ, or harpsichord.

Musicians being musicians, it was not long before they began to improvise. After playing the appropriate chord as directed by the number, the continuo chaps would then take off on their own, as jazz musicians were to do several centuries later. As long as they were true to the basic harmony, they were allowed to cut loose, and as a result a piece was rarely played the same way twice. But the single melody was the dominating force, with the continuo harmony lending support. The singers knew what melody to sing and the audience knew what to listen to.

In the simplest terms, this was all a movement toward melody for melody's sake, with the background chords serving as accompaniment. To get a bit more complicated, this separation of melody from harmony led to more detailed attention being paid to each. In one way, the chords were taking a backseat. But in another, they now had a seat of their own, even if in the rear of the bus. This division led composers in later centuries to dwell on each separately—until the time came when the backseat chords/harmony (more complex, structurally) began to receive more emphasis than the front-seat melody.

Tempo and Dynamics: Composers in Baroque days for the first time began to indicate tempo on their scores, using such terms as *adagio* and *allegro*. Very popular were what the music people then called "affections," which we might call mood and emotions. "Terraced dynamics" were also characteristic of Baroque music. This meant that one uniformly soft passage was followed by a uniformly loud one, instead of there being fluctuations within each passage.

Tonality: In the Baroque period, the church modes that had dominated music until this time were, by and large, replaced by the concept of major and minor keys—a concept that endures today, albeit with severe deviations. Pieces first began to have a key identification in their titles—such as Sonata in [the Key of] C—as Baroque composers put more emphasis on the tonal center than had late-Renaissance musicians.

Orchestral and Instrumental Color: Advancement also occurred in the art of orchestration in this period. Bach orchestrated chiefly by designing interchangeable parts for string and wind instruments. Rameau was one of the first to assign separate parts to flutes, oboes, and bassoons, above and beyond what the strings were doing, thus opening the way for the development of tone color in the modern orchestra. The Baroque orchestra—needed for the popular opera—now included these woodwinds as well as strings. "Large" Italian Baroque opera orchestras sometimes had as many as twenty musicians, and the French were to build even bigger ones for opera.

By this time, the violin and its stringed cousins had been perfected. The harpsichord and the smaller boxlike clavichord had been improved, though they were still a long way from their offspring, the piano. The organ had become more versatile. To get a good feel for this era, try the violin music of Vivaldi and other Italians named in chapter 1; the clavier music of Handel, Couperin, Rameau, and Bach; the organ concertos of Handel; and the great fugue and choral preludes of Bach. (No one, in fact, has yet equaled the organ music of Handel and Bach . . . and don't bet the farm that anyone soon will.)

BAROQUE FORMS OF MUSIC: VOCAL

Opera: This was the form that advanced the most in the Baroque period. Despite the great differences between the stilted Baroque opera and the later Classical and Romantic opera (which is so much more popular today), Baroque opera was the starting yeast from which all opera developed. Monteverdi operas are occasionally performed today, as are some by Rameau, Couperin, Vivaldi, and Handel, but they are generally regarded as too stylized and formal for current tastes. However, orchestral excerpts are presented in concert, operatic excerpts appear on singers' programs, and some complete Baroque operas have been shown on television. One can certainly find complete recordings of Monteverdi's *L'incoronazione di Poppea* and other of his operas.

Oratorio: The Baroque oratorio, influenced by the Baroque opera, has had better staying power—especially those by Handel. An oratorio is a major choral composition on a religious subject with solo singers, a chorus, and an orchestra, but without action, costumes, or scenery. It had its origins in early seventeenth-century Italy. Baroque oratorios are still performed, especially Handel's *Messiah*, the most famous ever written. Composed in only twenty-three days, it is on everyone's list of the greatest of the great music. Handel wrote many others which are recorded, and some are still performed today.

Motet: The motet had its heyday during the Renaissance as a form of sacred choral music. Bach, however, wrote six motets, including four for two four-part choruses; one, the famous *Jesu meine Freude*, for five voices; and another for four voices and continuo. Bach's motets were composed in a variety of styles, using both instruments and voices.

Cantata: A shorter choral work than the oratorio, the cantata could be either religious or secular. It was based on a continuous text and had a number of movements, including arias, recitatives, duets, and choruses. Bach wrote two hundred to three hundred cantatas, some of which are among the gems of all music. They differ in length, with some being fairly modest and others nearly as long as oratorios. One of the best known is No. 140, *Wachet Auf*.

Passion: Closer to the oratorio than the average cantata in size and form, the passion is based on the New Testament story of Jesus, from the Last Supper through the Crucifixion, according to one of the four Evangelists: St. Matthew, St. Mark, St. Luke, or St. John. Like the oratorio and the cantata, the passion featured solo singers, chorus, and orchestra. Bach's *Passion According to St. Matthew*, a twenty-four-scene drama, is one of the masterworks of the Baroque period.

Mass: The mass continued as a musical setting for the solemn religious service of the church, although the Protestant Reformation did away with much of the Latin form, shortening it to include only the first two sections, the Kyrie and the Gloria. The Lutheran Bach's Mass in B Minor, however, is a complete Catholic mass. It is a landmark of musical history, regarded by many as his most magnificent work and by some as *the* single greatest composition ever written. (Is *Hamlet the* greatest play? It doesn't matter; what is important is that it constitutes a high peak of culture.) Bach structured it with a Kyrie in three sections, a Gloria in eight, a Credo in eight, a Sanctus in three, and an Agnus in two. It takes some three hours to perform; each movement is broken into sections and each section is complete unto itself. Soloists, chorus, organ, and orchestra participate. Don't be intimidated by the length or by the common notion that Bach may be wonderful but is no fun to hear. It's fair to listen only to individual parts of the B Minor Mass—and, indeed, many recordings of separate sections are available.

Chorale Prelude: This is actually an instrumental form, but with a vocal godfather. The chorale is German in origin, the twin of the Protestant hymn, which was introduced to the church service by Martin Luther (1483–1546) to lure the congregation into the action. A chorale prelude is a short piece that goes with it, written for the organ, to be played as a prelude to the singing. (Some were later arranged for orchestra.) There were four main types: *cantus firmus, coloration chorale, chorale partita,* and *chorale fantasia* (or fantasy). Bach has many in his *Little Organ Book.*

BAROQUE FORMS OF MUSIC: INSTRUMENTAL

Concerto Grosso: The most popular instrumental form of the late seventeenth and early eighteenth centuries was the concerto grosso. Unlike the later concerto—which featured a single instrument supported by a whole orchestra—it was a form of chamber music: ensemble music to be played in rooms with small audiences, with a string orchestra of perhaps no more than four instruments (two violins, a viola, and a cello) in one section and a group of solo instruments in another. It was a major work for those days, consisting of three to five parts (movements). Bach, Handel, Telemann, and Vivaldi composed many. Some people think the concerto grosso loses a lot of its appeal when played on modern instruments and/or by today's large orchestras; others do not. Many recordings are available each way. Examples include any of Bach's famous six *Brandenburg* Concertos, though No. 2 is the one most often performed.

Solo Concerto: An offshoot of the concerto grosso, which it resembles structurally, the solo concerto featured only one instrument rather than a group of them against the larger string ensemble. Bach's Concerto No. 2 in E for Violin and Strings is an example.

Opera Sinfonia: This instrumental form was initially an overture to an opera. In time it became separated from the opera and was played on its own, just as were later overtures.

Passacaglia: The passacaglia began as a slow Spanish dance, then developed into a composition with many variations built around a fixed bass melody. It was usually written for the organ, sometimes for the harpsichord. Bach, Handel, and Couperin composed many passacaglias. The name is used interchangeably with that of another slow processional dance, the *chaconne*—which also consisted of a repeated bass melody with a series of superimposed variations. The best-known chaconne of all appears at the end of Bach's Partita No. 2 for unaccompanied violin. Another of Bach's ultrafamous pieces is his Passacaglia and Fugue in C Minor for Organ.

Prelude, Fantasy, Toccata: These are short, free-style pieces, usually for keyboard instruments, often written to be played with fugues or other longer works, but strong and independent enough to stand alone. Since none of the three has a specific structure or style, there is no architectural distinction among them. Nor are they necessarily related to the compositions with which they may be played. Example: the toccata part of Bach's Toccata and Fugue in D Minor, perhaps the most famous organ work in history.

Suite: A major Baroque instrumental work, the suite at this time was a combination of several different dance forms, usually in a set succession and in the same key. The first three movements often consisted of three separate dances: an *allemande*, a serious piece, moderately fast; a *courante*, which was more rapid; and a *sarabande*, a slow melody from Spain. Following the sarabande were two or three more movements in other dance forms—*minuet, gavotte, bourrée, rigaudon, loure,* or *air*—each of which had a different musical construction. The last movement was usually a *gigue*, a rollicking dance derived from the English and Irish jig. Bach (who else?) is the most famous suite writer. In addition to some single suites, he wrote six "English" and six "French" suites (the "English" and "French" designations are irrelevant) and six "partitas"—the same form as a Baroque suite under a different name—all for the harpsichord. His harpsichord suites are sometimes played today on the modern piano, to the dislike of many traditionalists but not of all Bach scholars—or of all listeners. Try them every which way you can. Someone has said that the harpsichord has the charm of a five-hundred-pound canary, but it's a matter of opinion. Bach's French Suite No. 2 in C Minor is an example of this form.

Orchestral Suite: This had the same structure as the suite but was written for the Baroque orchestra instead of the harpsichord, and it's about as close as Baroque composers came to the not-yet-invented symphony. Bach wrote four, of which the Orchestral Suite No. 2 in B Minor is an example.

Fugue: Born of counterpoint and its interweaving of simultaneous melodies, the fugue is regarded as a musical development of monumental importance. Like the mass (and the sonata form to come), it merits a bit of extra description. The main purpose of the following nontechnical (but rather complex) description is to offer a guide to those who want to listen carefully enough to a fugue to follow the composer at work. The name comes from the Latin *fuga*, meaning "flight"—in this case the flight of a set theme from one human or instrumental voice to another. The cornerstone of the fugue is imitation, with a theme dominating the entire proceedings and being echoed (albeit not identically) by two or three or more voices. A set pattern must be followed: statement of a theme, or "subject," by one voice (soprano, alto, tenor, or bass), then imitation by another voice in what is called the "answer" while the first voice moves on to a "countersubject" or "countertheme." If there are four voices, the subject will then appear in a third and be answered in a fourth, while the first two weave a contrapuntal texture against them. After the initial statement, the composer shifts from key to key in a prescribed manner—one key for the subject, another for the answers—but there is a great deal of leeway within the rules for individual genius. The professionals, talking music-ese, like to say that the main characteristics of fugues are concentration of thought, purity of expression, and organic unity, achieved through ongoing imitation and expansion. Handel and Bach are the acknowledged champions of fugal technique, though Bach really stands alone. One of his best-known fugues is the Fugue in G Minor, called "The Little G Minor." Treat it as a jigsaw puzzle, which can be enjoyable, or just listen without caring that it's a fugue.

Baroque Sonata: Distinctly different from the Classical sonata which was to come, this was a popular form in Baroque days and remains so today. It was usually in four movements, slow-fast-slow-fast. Most Baroque sonatas were written for violin, usually with a harpsichord bass accompaniment. Sonatas were composed for other instruments, however, including the flute, oboe, and viola da gamba. Examples are Handel's Sonata in E for Violin and Continuo (harpsichord bass), his Sonata in G for Flute and Continuo, and Vivaldi's Sonata in A for Violin and Continuo.

POST-BAROQUE/CLASSICAL

Christoph Gluck   1714–1787   No. 32

POST-BAROQUE/CLASSICAL SNAPSHOT

Gluck was a German opera reformer dedicated to combining orchestra, voice, and plot so that the music brought out the dramatic impact of the story—a departure from the Italian "voice-for-voice's-sake" opera with its mellifluous but meaningless tunes. This followed Monteverdi's opera reform work by a century and foreshadowed Wagner's music drama by another.

THE POST-BAROQUE/CLASSICAL SCENE

Considering only List composers, this is a one-man subperiod: Gluck alone. Whatever category one places him in, the important point is that he lived and worked during a time when social conditions were changing in Europe. Louis XIV of France reigned until 1715, Louis XV until 1774, Louis XVI until 1792. Baroque times were giving way to Classical times, with a corresponding cultural trend away from the ornate and embellished toward the more simple. Rousseau was writing about nature and naturalness, and purity and balance were soon to be the goals of music and other forms of art.

The bricks-and-mortar and the vocal and instrumental forms are those of the Baroque period.

CLASSICAL

Franz Joseph Haydn	1732–1809	No. 5
Wolfgang Amadeus Mozart	1756–1791	No. 2
Ludwig van Beethoven	1770–1827	No. 3
Franz Schubert	1797–1828	No. 7

CLASSICAL SNAPSHOTS

Haydn, a Demigod, wrote in every form. He is the soul of Classicism, composer of more than one hundred symphonies, godfather of the string quartet and the modern sonata, teacher of Mozart and Beethoven, a midwife of the orchestra, and the reigning musical figure of his age. He preceded Mozart by a generation and Beethoven by two. He and Mozart were the two great composers of the second half of the eighteenth century.

Mozart is Mozart, Number Two Immortal, history's greatest natural musician.

Beethoven, the Immortal Thunderer, is Number Three.

Schubert, a Demigod, bridges the Classical and Romantic eras. A natural and spontaneous musical genius, he was the first lyric poet of music, the greatest songwriter of them all, and one of the first composers to write in short forms. He also created symphonies of the highest order.

THE CLASSICAL SCENE

It is convenient to think of the Classical period as lasting from 1750, the year of Bach's death, to 1827, when Beethoven died—although it is usually put at 1775 to 1830. (In 1775, Haydn, Mozart, and Beethoven all were alive; 1776 is a useful starting year if that serves as a memory jogger.) One definition of a "classic school" is that it deals in excellence and balance to a greater extent than a previous period. By that definition, a "classic" era would reappear every now and again. *Webster's* says the term "denotes primarily the principles and characteristics of Greek and Roman literature and art; considered as embodying formal elegance, simplicity, dignity and correctness of style."

This was a period of art for art's sake rather than as a statement of the artist; of clear thought, discipline, and self-control; of beauty of form, stability, and order; of logic and precision. These qualities, however, did not preclude experimentation, boldness, creativity, imagination—and, most important, emotion. The perception that this was a period of stodgy, heavy, ultraserious, dreary, inhibited music is a phony one.

You may remember that our chosen symbol for the Baroque age was a painting by Rubens, such as *The Abduction of the Daughters of Leucippus*. The chosen symbol for Classical times is from architecture rather than painting: the Parthenon in Athens. Its order, stability, and balanced simplicity are in marked contrast to the controlled, embellished energy of Rubens.

Comparisons of eras are not quite that simple, of course. One of the major characteristics of the Classical period is clarity of reason—yet no composer ever exhibited the clarity of reason that came from Bach in the Baroque era. What is more, beneath the order and stability of (part of) the Classical era was the rumbling that led to the French Revolution on one continent and the American Revolution on another. And while Haydn was the epitome of genius serving under the patronage of nobility at one end of the Classical period, Beethoven was the independent, passionate thunderer who bowed to no man at the other end.

The Classical period encompassed the eighteenth century of Louis XV in France, Frederick the Great in Prussia, Maria Theresa in Austria, and Catherine the Great in Russia. The nobility superseded the church as the center of music. Noblemen wanted noble music: polished, elegant, beautiful in style, tuneful, pleasant to the ear. But this was also the era of philosophers Immanuel Kant, Denis Diderot, and the French Encyclopedists; writers François Marie Voltaire, Jean Jacques Rousseau, and Adam Smith; and painters such as Thomas Gainsborough, Sir Joshua Reynolds, and Francisco José de Goya. The Industrial Revolution began in England at about the time the Classical era started. This period saw the first vaccine, the steam engine, the spinning jenny, the cotton gin—and electric motors. Scarcely "polished elegance."

CLASSICAL BRICKS-AND-MORTAR

Among Classical composers, Haydn and Mozart had much more in common with each other than either had with Beethoven—and Schubert, with one foot in the Romantic camp, was something else altogether. Also, the manner in which Haydn and Beethoven handled rhythm and the other essential elements of music changed considerably over their long careers. Thus, care must be taken to avoid simple bricks-and-mortar generalities that sweep across the Classical board. What can be safely said is that Classical composers were concerned primarily with the unity of their musical design. Obviously, great attention was paid to rhythm, as to melody, texture, and tone color, but the primary Classical objective was to blend them all together in an orderly, reasoned way.

Rhythm: Perhaps a useful approach here is to compare Classical rhythm with Baroque rhythm. The latter was strong, steady, persistent, relentless, and consistent from beginning to end. Listen to a Baroque piece and you can hear it pounding away. This pounding rhythm is not found in Classical works, where rhythm is handled with what one expert called "the finest nuance and sensitivity," as part of a unified whole.

Melody: Melody has been labeled the "soul" of both Classical and Romantic music. Friedrich Blume, longtime professor of music at Kiel University in Germany and onetime head of the International Musicological Society, has written: "Whatever the importance and the independence of meter and rhythm, of harmony and tonality characterizing the Classic-Romantic work of art, Classic-Romantic music lives by melody, its subtlest and most vital component." Like all things Classical, melody is balanced in works of this period. It is simpler and less turbulent than the elaborate, continuously expanding Baroque melody that came earlier. The music people say it has "balanced phrases and cadences"—a "phrase," in musical terms, being a division of melody that is larger than a "figure" but less than a "period" (defined as a complete musical thought), and a "cadence" being a series of notes that ends a melody. We are not going to bog ourselves down with phrases and/or cadences; the operative word for us here is *balanced*. Aaron Copland, who wrote several good books for the near-amateur, advises us that "only a professional musician is capable of X-raying the melodic spine of a well-constructed melody"—and we'll leave it at that.

Texture: This is the news maker, from a historical standpoint. For the first time in music history, single-melody homophonic texture dominated composition. All classical music since Classical times has been influenced by this turn of events, although in the twentieth century serious efforts have been made to get away from such influence—by some, as far away as possible. Counterpoint, the cornerstone of Baroque music, faded in importance during the Classical years—though it did not disappear entirely from composition that was predominantly homophonic, fugues were occasionally written, and it was to have a big twentieth-century revival. Classical composers used counterpoint as a natural ally of homophonic texture, not as a foreign element. Classical harmony, which pays strict attention to key, is considerably simpler than Baroque harmony.

Tone Color: The most helpful comparison here is with the Romantic music of the future rather than the Baroque of the past. Romantic composers thrived on the relationship of music to painting, literature, and nature, which they sought to express in various ways in their works. To paint musical pictures in their "program" music, they needed to wring as much color as they could from each individual instrument and from instruments playing together. Classical composers were unconcerned with programs, descriptive titles, and story-telling or scene-setting instrumental music. In writing "absolute" music unrelated to extramusical things, they also were less interested in squeezing out maximum color. Some critics of Romanticism charge that Romantic composers at times were so obsessed by tone color as to neglect the composition itself. Classical composers, concentrating on the unity of the whole design, used color to perfect the form.

Dynamics: The "terraced dynamics" technique of Baroque years, consisting of loud passages followed by soft passages, was replaced by more sudden and dramatic changes of loudness and softness within one passage.

CLASSICAL FORMS OF MUSIC: INSTRUMENTAL

What came out of this most-famous era?

One Classical composer (Mozart) wrote perhaps the finest operas of all time, another (Haydn) composed one of the best oratorios in music history, and both made handsome contributions to concerto development. Most significantly, three of music history's most important architectural forms not only arose in this period but also reached their ultimate heights during it.

One was the symphony, created during the Classical years and developed in that era to a level not yet surpassed. A second was the string quartet. Here too, a strong case can be made that many Classical string quartets have not been equaled. The third is the keyboard sonata, an unaccompanied piece for solo instrument (or occasionally two instruments), a form in which Beethoven reigns supreme.

From an architectural standpoint, the three have in common one of the leading compositional developments of the Classical period. This is the *sonata form*—aka "first-movement form," aka "sonata allegro form" (because it was written in fast "allegro" tempo).

Sonata-form: Before discussing the other major forms used by Classical composers, special attention must be paid this one, important not only to the music of this period but also to the music that followed. It merits a fairly detailed semitechnical discussion of the type generally avoided in this primer.

Let's start with a definition of the sonata itself, a form of solo instrumental music that developed gradually from the end of the Baroque period through the Classical. The sonata was written either for the keyboard—piano or organ—or for an instrument such as the oboe, violin, or cello. In the latter case, there was piano accompaniment, so it was not literally a solo performance. Initially the Classical sonata was in three sections, or *movements*, fast-slow-fast, with the first and third movements usually in the same key and the middle one in a different key. (A movement is a major section of a longer work, usually related in some way to the rest of that work. Just how that relationship is forged is up to the composer, and the listener may not always be fully aware of it.)

Each movement customarily had its own key, and each could be identified either by order of appearance—First, Second, or Third—or by the name of the particular form in which it was written. The standard third movement, for example, was a *minuet* or *scherzo*. (A minuet is a French dance in moderate tempo, traditionally danced in court, and was an important musical form for a couple of hundred years. A scherzo, meaning "joke" in Italian, initially was similar in style to a minuet, although it later became a faster piece not appropriate for dancing. Some composers, including Chopin and Brahms in Romantic times, confused the issue a bit by writing stand-alone pieces they called "scherzos." Further, some of these were quite serious, rather than fanciful, as a scherzo was supposed to be.)

In any case, the first movement of the Classical sonata was written according to the rules and regulations of what was called the sonata-form. Classical composers became dedicated to this form, which permitted them to approach a composition on an intellectual basis and provided them with what they considered to be a perfect vehicle for the expression of drama, emotion, mood, and excitement.

The sonata-form has three parts: exposition, development, and recapitulation. In Part I, the exposition, three themes are presented—a first theme, then a supplemental or subsidiary one, usually in a different key, and finally a closing theme. Once offered, these themes might be repeated to complete Part I. In Part II, the development, the composer repeats and combines his themes, selecting and expanding fragments of them, moving to different keys (the music people call that *modulating*), and bringing off some kind of climax. Part III recapitulates, with modification, the themes of Part I. To complete the sonata-form, a composer might or might not add an introduction before Part I and a *coda*—music talk for a concluding segment that is distinct from the main structure.

(The second or "subordinate" theme in the sonata-form is not necessarily really subordinate, despite its name. It might, indeed, be the major theme, more important than the first one. Examples of this can be found in well-known symphonies, because composers so liked the sonata form that they borrowed it from the sonata and used it for the first movements of symphonies, concertos, and string quartets. A good example of a so-called subordinate theme becoming a main theme can be found in Schubert's *Unfinished* Symphony, in which the most familiar theme is not the first but the second.)

As mentioned earlier, the sonata-form had a long life. Not only was it used for the opening movements of symphonies and concertos by Haydn, Mozart, Beethoven, and Schubert, but in Romantic times it served the same purpose for Mendelssohn, Brahms, Tchaikovsky, and others. Some composers, in fact, admired it so much that they used it in all four movements of their symphonies, although that was not common. One example in Romantic times, however, is found in Mendelssohn's Third Symphony, called the *Scotch* Symphony.

Symphony: As noted, among the supreme achievements of the Classical period are the symphonic works of Haydn, Mozart, and Beethoven. While conventional wisdom in the music world holds that new musical forms rarely develop rapidly, the Classical symphony is a counterexample to this rule. Arguably, half or more of the twenty best symphonies of all time were composed by these three men within a relatively short time span—Beethoven's Third, Fifth, Sixth, Seventh, and Ninth; Mozart's 35th, 39th, 40th, and 41st; and Haydn's 92d through 104th are nominees—although the distance between the symphonies of Haydn and those of Beethoven is a long one, with Beethoven building not only on Haydn but on Mozart's advancements from Haydn.

In addition to writing the first movement of the Classical symphony in sonata form, composers also followed a standard format for the second, third, and fourth movements. The second was usually written in a slow tempo, the third as a minuet or scherzo, and the last customarily in a more rapid tempo in something called *rondo* form. (The rondo is another form found in both sonatas and symphonies and sometimes found standing independently. In it, a refrain and contrasting sections are alternated in a sequence such as A-B-A-C-A. Beethoven and Mozart both wrote rondos for the piano; Mozart's Rondo in A Minor is an example.)

The Classical symphony orchestra was considerably larger and more varied than the Baroque orchestra, developed around a body of strings plus flutes, oboes, clarinets, bassoons, horns, trumpets, and timpani (kettledrums). Mozart wrote separate parts for the woodwinds, an advance in orchestration. Beethoven went farther, writing individual parts for the horn, double bass, timpani, and other instruments.

Sonata: Whereas the Baroque sonata was primarily polyphonic in texture, with interwoven melodies, we have seen that the classical version consisted of single-melody-plus-chords harmony. Counterpoint was reserved as a supplemental tool. Mozart wrote many masterful sonatas for piano (and violin), but Beethoven became the all-time El Supremo of piano-sonata writers. Several of Beethoven's piano sonatas are superb examples of this form, including No. 8 in C Minor (*Pathétique*), No. 21 in C (*Waldstein*), and No. 23 in F Minor (*Appassionata*).

Chamber Music: One significant change that occurred in the Classical period was that composers began to write separate parts for each instrument in trios, quartets, quintets, and other instrumental ensembles. While pieces for four stringed instruments had been written earlier, the string quartet as we know it came from Haydn, who wrote more than eighty. Mozart composed more than two dozen, and Beethoven sixteen. The "birth" of the string quartet was a monumental development of the Classical period. Two examples are Haydn's String Quartet in C (*The Emperor*) and Beethoven's String Quartet No. 13 in B-flat, Op. 130.

Divertimento: Also known in Classical times as a serenade, nocturne, or cassation, a divertimento was an instrumental composition in several short, light movements—four to ten—written for a chamber group or small orchestra. Haydn composed more than seventy; Mozart more than thirty. They were considered as important as some early symphonies. A famous Mozart serenade, "Eine kleine Nachtmusik," is an example of a divertimento.

Overture: The overture did not exist as an independent piece in Classical times but was written to open an opera or as incidental music for a play. Not until the Romantic period was the overture produced as a separate thing. Beethoven's *Leonore* Overture and his *Egmont* Overture—now performed independently—are examples of this form.

Concerto: This is a major musical composition, usually in three movements, played by a single instrument accompanied by an orchestra. During the Classical period, the piano replaced the violin as the most frequently used solo instrument, but concertos for violin were also written (and still are today). Beethoven's violin concerto is among the best of the lot. Whereas Beethoven is the Classical—and all-time—piano-sonata king, Mozart is the Classical—and all-time—piano-concerto king. The three movements of the Classical concerto resemble the first, second, and fourth movements of a four-part symphony. In Classical days, the orchestral accompaniment consisted of woodwinds, brass, percussion, and strings. Mozart's Concerto No. 20 in D Minor for Piano and Orchestra is one of many Mozart examples. If limited to the collection of one form of music by one composer, one might want to consider Mozart's piano concertos.

CLASSICAL FORMS OF MUSIC: VOCAL

Opera: Beethoven wrote one esteemed opera, *Fidelio*, that is still performed, and Haydn wrote several that generally are not, but Mozart was the Classical-opera superstar. The term opera encompasses *grand opera*, a serious, usually tragic drama in which the dialogue is sung; *opera buffa*, a comic drama sung throughout; *opera comique* and *opera bouffe*, a combination of singing and speaking; and *singspiel*, a German version of opera comique. Grand opera originally meant opera with a serious subject, set entirely to music. Later the term was used to describe opera involving stage spectacle, historic plots, and ballet, lavishly produced. Classical opera was more lifelike than the Baroque opera of Monteverdi, due in part to the "bridge" work of Gluck, who had stripped the ornamentation, frills, and stilted qualities from Baroque opera. Mozart then took Gluck's form, improved it with his own genius, and created both serious and comic productions which now could truly be called "human theater." A whole lot of experts, and a whole lot of operagoers, hold that no operas surpass those of Mozart—Verdi's Italian masterpieces or Wagner's German music-dramas notwithstanding. *Don Giovanni, The Magic Flute*, and *The Marriage of Figaro* are examples of Mozart's operatic genius.

Oratorio: Handel's magnificent Baroque *Messiah* has never been topped in any musical period, but Haydn, influenced by hearing Handel's work on a London visit, returned home to Vienna to write two famous oratorios of his own, *The Creation* and *The Seasons*. Little difference in form exists between the Baroque and Classical oratorio. With the exception of Haydn's works, and a small number of others, no truly great oratorios have been written since Handel.

Passion: The passion declined in popularity during this era. Little effort was put into it, and there are no outstanding examples.

Mass: The mass was improved at this time, incorporating new developments in both opera and symphony. Haydn, Mozart, and Schubert wrote some of their finest church music in the mass form. An example is Haydn's Mass No. 9 in D Minor, *The Nelson Mass*, which some think is one of his greatest works.

ROMANTIC

Tidy compartments inevitably oversimplify. Putting the composers of nineteenth-century Romanticism into Early, Middle, and Late periods on the basis of their birth years, for example, is problematic. Some lived quite short lives, others very long ones. Some began serious work early in life, and others remarkably late. Chopin and Mendelssohn developed quickly, the latter incredibly quickly. Wagner and Verdi (especially the latter) developed much later. Although they were born Early, they really are more part of Middle Romanticism. And Bruckner, born Middle, flowered Late.

The purpose of all the categories and lists in this book is to construct helpful road signs for the musical traveler. To sort out Romantic composers by peak-of-musical-development would confuse rather than clarify, so we'll hold to the birthday breakdown, consistent with the treatment of other musical periods. But keep the foregoing alert in mind.

THE FIRST TRUE ROMANTIC
Karl Maria von Weber	1786–1826	No. 47

TWO ITALIAN OPERA COMPOSERS
Gioacchino Rossini	1792–1868	No. 30
Gaetano Donizetti	1797–1848	No. 43

EARLY ROMANTICS
1825–1850

Hector Berlioz	1803–1869	No. 21
Felix Mendelssohn	1809–1847	No. 11
Frédéric Chopin	1810–1849	No. 12
Robert Schumann	1810–1856	No. 8
Franz Liszt	1811–1886	No. 13
Richard Wagner	1813–1883	No. 4
Giuseppe Verdi	1813–1901	No. 16

MIDDLE ROMANTICS
1850–1890

César Franck	1822–1890	No. 36
Bedřich Smetana	1824–1884	No. 45
Anton Bruckner	1824–1896	No. 25
Johann Strauss	1825–1899	No. 46
Alexander Borodin	1833–1887	No. 50
Johannes Brahms	1833–1897	No. 6
Camille Saint-Saëns	1835–1921	No. 27
Georges Bizet	1838–1875	No. 38
Modest Mussorgsky	1839–1881	No. 39
Peter Ilyitch Tchaikovsky	1840–1893	No. 10
Antonín Dvořák	1841–1904	No. 12
Edvard Grieg	1843–1907	No. 31
Nikolai Rimsky-Korsakov	1844–1908	No. 42

LATE ROMANTICS
LATE 1800S–EARLY 1900S

Gabriel Fauré	1845–1924	No. 41
Giacomo Puccini	1858–1924	No. 23
Gustav Mahler	1860–1911	No. 17
Richard Strauss	1864–1949	No. 20

SNAPSHOTS: THE FIRST TRUE ROMANTIC AND TWO OPERA COMPOSERS

Weber was the founder of German Romantic opera and a post-Gluck precursor of Wagner. With the overture to his opera *Der Freischütz* he anticipated the Romantic movement even before Schubert. It had all the Romantic characteristics: power, enchantment, imagination, rich tone color, and links with nature, painting, literature, and the supernatural.

Rossini is the next prince of Italian opera on The List (after Monteverdi). One of three composers (with Donizetti and Verdi) who ruled Italian opera during the first half of the nineteenth century, he wrote "bel canto" operas in which singers and singing were all that mattered. Neither spectacles nor psychological creations, these were popular, emotional, formulaic productions designed to show off the voice. Rossini wrote thirty, including *The Barber of Seville* and *William Tell*.

Donizetti, a compatriot of Rossini, composed nearly twice as many operas. Not the equal of Rossini (and not in the same league as the younger Verdi), he nonetheless wrote wondrously melodic music. His most famous works include *Lucia di Lammermoor, Don Pasquale, The Elixir of Love,* and *Daughter of the Regiment.*

EARLY ROMANTIC SNAPSHOTS

Berlioz was one of seven composers who dominated the Romantic movement in the first half of the nineteenth century. He was the first true conscious Romantic: uninhibited, extremist, emotional, a Wild Turk of his time, one of the pioneers of Romantic program music. No composer surpassed him in tone color, and he was one of the godfathers of the modern orchestra. France's top composer, he produced music that is vigorous, passionate, and far more forceful than the "delicate" work of the typical French composer. Melody was not his strength.

Mendelssohn, who composed his first symphony at fifteen and his masterpiece, *A Midsummer Night's Dream,* at seventeen, was the most natural musician of the early Romantics. He was a magnificent pianist, a writer of creative symphonies and overtures, the greatest conductor of his day, and the composer of one of history's best oratorios. Restrained in all things, he produced wonderful, sweet, pure, pleasant-to-the-ear music.

Chopin was the premier composer of piano music, one of the finest pianists in history, an elegant Pole in stylish Paris, the first of the great nationalists with his mazurkas and polonaises, a flawless technician, and an almost perfect musician within the piano-limited boundaries in which he composed.

Schumann, a Demigod, was second only to Schubert as a songwriter. The soul of the fresh Romantic spirit, he wrote four lyrical symphonies and a wealth of piano music. The rebel leader of German Romanticism and founder of a music journal, he championed Brahms and Schubert and yet experimented with less traditional musical forms than they used. Mood, color, beauty, and melody were his loves.

Liszt was the premier keyboard-basher of the Romantic era, its first and greatest piano virtuoso, inventor and developer of the symphonic poem, and composer of piano masterpieces. Still a befriender of young composers across Europe while in his seventies, he became the acknowledged Grand Old Man of Romanticism. An influencer of scores of musical masters, he was one of three (with Berlioz and Wagner) Early Romantic developers of the modern symphony orchestra. You can hear his native Hungary in much of his music.

Wagner, a Demigod who was the dominant figure of the last half of the century, introduced a new kind of opera known as music drama. He was the supreme egotist whose egotism showed in his genius, and for decades was the world's most famous living composer. The Romantic era's link between music and dramatic expression, he created not only continuous and endless melody in opera, but also orchestral work that has rarely been equaled. The Wagner claque would make him an Immortal.

Verdi is the unchallenged master of the four Romantic Italian opera writers on The List, the most beloved and popular of all opera composers, and an Italian national hero to this day. His most famous operas, some highly dramatic, are *Macbeth*, *Rigoletto*, *Il trovatore*, *La traviata*, *La forza del destino*, *Aida*, *Otello*, and *Falstaff*. *Falstaff* is sometimes rated one of Western music's top four comic operas, along with Mozart's *Figaro*, Rossini's *Barber of Seville*, and Wagner's *Meistersinger*.

MIDDLE ROMANTIC SNAPSHOTS

Franck, born in Belgium, was a noble French Classicist among the Romantics, the teacher, the calm presence worshiped by students, upholder of "absolute" music in France as Brahms was in Germany. Composer of masterpieces in many forms, he reestablished instrumental music in France—after decades of domination by opera there—as he blended Romantic choral work with Classical traditions.

Smetana was the founder of the Czech nationalist school, known for opera and many tone poems, his music coming directly out of Bohemian folk music. *The Bartered Bride* (opera), *Ma vlast* (tone poem), and *From My Life* (string quartet) are his best-known works.

Bruckner was a composer of nine long and complex symphonies and a naive, deeply religious writer of masses and sacred choral music. Everything about his music is solemn and slow. A great admirer of Wagner, he himself was not greatly admired by the public until after his death. Most of his major works were written late in life.

Johann Strauss (no relation to Richard) is a special case among The 50. He makes The List only because of his waltz music. He is the only composer of "popular" music on The List, but his genius was such that his popular music has established its own "classical" niche in history.

Borodin was one of a group of Russian nationalists called the "Mighty Five" (two others are on The List: Mussorgsky and Rimsky-Korsakov). His works include the (unfinished) opera *Prince Igor*, one symphony, one string quartet, and one tone poem. Known for incorporating Russian folk motifs into his music, he was also strong in orchestration and rhythm. A chemist by profession, Borodin was only a weekend composer.

Brahms, a Demigod who is just a shade from Immortal status, was a symphonist in the Beethoven tradition, a composer who worked in Classical forms but with Romantic overtones. He shunned Romantic program music and wrote no operas, but composed magnificent and melodious concertos, *lieder* (art songs), piano works, and chamber music.

Saint-Saëns was a leading French musician for seventy years. A pianist, organist, conductor, and teacher, he composed music that was typically more polished than emotional, though he did write rich and colorful orchestral music. Fond of tone poems, he was prolific in many other forms as well. He lived well into the twentieth century (he died in 1921, at age eighty-six) and, mellow in his old age, opposed new sounds such as those of Debussy.

Bizet, French opera composer, is the closest on The List to being a one-work musician. Although he wrote in other forms, Bizet is known chiefly for *Carmen*, one of the most popular operas ever written.

Mussorgsky is the most realistic and nationalistic of all Russians, his music filled with passion and emotion. Another member of the Russian nationalist "Mighty Five," he is best known for his operas, including *Boris Godounov*, a great musical drama and a masterpiece of Russian nationalist music. Powerful and unpolished, he is considered by some to be the greatest Russian composer.

Tchaikovsky is a Demigod and our top Russian composer. Emotional rather than intellectual, and strong on melody, he composed operas, ballets, symphonies, concertos, tone poems, and chamber music. He was another outstanding orchestrator (with Liszt, Berlioz, and Wagner) and a universal artist who nonetheless remained very Russian in his work. He was also a great public favorite.

Dvořák is Czechoslovakia's top composer, another leading Czech nationalist, though more universal than Smetana, and a prolific writer in all branches of music. He is known for his melodies, is most famous for his *New World* Symphony, is the greatest of the central European artists, and mentally was one of the healthiest of all composers.

Grieg is Norway's nationalist, the only Norwegian on The List, and Scandinavia's top composer. He is enormously popular for melodious songs and piano pieces, which are also rich in harmony, and he wrote fine violin sonatas as well. He was fresh, bright, and original.

Rimsky-Korsakov was another (and the most skilled) of the "Mighty Five." A composer of opera, program symphonies, other orchestral works, and piano pieces, he was the most nationalistic Russian except Mussorgsky and the last representative of a great Russian age before a new one began with Stravinsky. His *Scheherazade* is a leading example of the use of orchestral tone color.

LATE ROMANTIC SNAPSHOTS

This is a period of overlap toward the end of the nineteenth century, made up of composers who were born around midcentury and lived into the first years of the 1900s. Some of these represented the final phases of Romanticism throughout their careers; others went through a Romantic phase before moving off the reservation to experiment with different kinds of music.

Fauré was another of the many Frenchmen who worked elegantly and with refinement, concentrating almost exclusively on intimate, small forms and producing no successful operas, symphonies, or other major works. He lived a long life, from the middle of the last century through the first quarter of this one. An outstanding songwriter, he is one of France's great composers despite his self-imposed limits—more lyrical, subjective, and expressive than Saint-Saëns, the last Listed Frenchman before him.

Puccini, second only to Verdi in Italian opera, worked at a time when twentieth-century "Modern Music" was coming into vogue, and he drew upon many of its ideas. But rich, sensuous melodies are what his operas are about. *La Bohème*, *Tosca*, and *Madame Butterfly* are his best-known three; he also wrote *Manon Lescaut* and the unfinished *Turandot*. He stands by himself in post-Verdi Italian opera and ends the long Italian opera dynasty that began with Monteverdi.

Mahler, a German, was the composer of nine symphonies (he was seventh in a long line of Vienna symphonists after Haydn, Mozart, Beethoven, Schubert, Brahms, and Bruckner). Successor to Schubert and Schumann in composing poems set to music (called *song cycles*), he was also a master of orchestration. In his personal life he worried about things like "Life," "Death," and "the Universe."

Richard Strauss, a turn-of-the-century Late Romantic German composer, took the Berlioz-Liszt Romantic tone poem to its highest level, producing in them and in his operas some excruciatingly dissonant music. These then-peculiar sounds—called "shocking modernism" at the time—were forerunners of what came to be known in the early 1900s as "New Music" or "Modern Music." Hailed for his orchestration skills (and for his great talent in general), he was attacked for his strange new harmonies, melodies, rhythms, and indeed a whole strange new style. Thus Richard Strauss, a full-blown Romantic, also was a bridge to the twentieth century—although in 1911 with *Der Rosenkavalier* he began swinging back toward more conventional music. He lived into Nazism, which he found tolerable, and under which he became head of the State Chamber of Music.

THE ROMANTIC SCENE

The Romantic period took up most of the nineteenth century, extending beyond the artistic revolution that ushered in the twentieth, and ending with the disillusionment of World War I. The democratic, individualistic spirit that was loose in the world from the end of the eighteenth century through the nineteenth was inevitably reflected in the arts. Poets, playwrights, painters, dancers, and composers favored subjectivity and expression over objectivity and form.

These were wonderful years for music. It was a time of individual expression, of emotionalism, and of dreams. It was a time of freedom, God, and nature. Man triumphed and Man was liberated in Romantic times. There was a union of the arts, a kinship of literature and music, of poetry and drama. Mood music was in: sad, majestic, joyous, tender, loving. Nationalism was in. Songs and sounds were sensuous. Good won out over Evil every time, or almost every time. Romantic music was a lot kinder and gentler—and more lyrical—than the twentieth-century music that followed.

It was an age of great contrasts for the composers on The List—not unexpectedly, given the prevailing drive for individual expression and emotion. There was the intimacy of Chopin, Fauré, Franck, and many others living and working in Paris, the thundering piano concertos of Liszt, the lyrical love songs of Schumann, the dazzling orchestration of Berlioz, the restraint of Mendelssohn, and the dramatic brooding of Wagner. The period takes its name from the medieval stories and poems called "romances," which centered on heroic figures and were

written not in formal scholars' Latin but in the language of the people—Italian, French, and Spanish. Romantic music appealed to the
broadest audiences thus far in music history.

ROMANTIC BRICKS-AND-MORTAR

Rhythm: Rhythm is regarded as the weak link of Romantic music,
not only in the late move toward Impressionism but in the early years
as well. Romantic composers often used rhythm in stereotypical patterns. Aaron Copland wrote that Romantic composers allowed their
sense of rhythm to be dulled by an overdose of regularly recurring
downbeats. This all changed with Tchaikovsky and others late in the
period who borrowed from strong folk rhythms. In the twentieth
century, Stravinsky and others picked up where Tchaikovsky left off,
and rhythm has never been the same again.

Melody: In contrast to Romantic rhythm, Romantic melody was
extremely strong. In fact, Romantic melody still is the public's idea
of what melody should be. It is songlike and warm. Scores of popular songs are based on Romantic melodies. *Lyrical* is the key word.
In instrumental music, melody was easier to discern in Classical
music than in Baroque, and even easier in Romantic. In vocal music,
opera was big during this era, and in opera melody obviously is all-
important.

Texture: Romantic texture was not unlike Classical texture. It
basically followed single-melody homophonic principles. Polyphony—counterpoint—almost disappeared as a main textural component.

Harmony: Romantic harmony was more dissonant than Classical
harmony, and more complex. There was more modulation (changing
from one key to another within a section of a composition) and more
chromaticism (using notes not part of the seven-note key scale in
which a composition is written).

Orchestration and Tone Color: During the Romantic era the orchestra expanded. Instrument-making advanced. Valves were developed
for horns and trumpets, which enabled them to change their pitch and
produce additional tones. For the first time, orchestration and tone
color were the *primary* goals of some liberal composers, becoming
ends in themselves—to the consternation of the conservatives. Berlioz
thought an ideal concert orchestra should have 121 players, and an
orchestra for giant festivals 465. Romantic composers, fascinated by
the tone-color aspect of composition and by experimentation with
traditional and new orchestral instruments, produced an entirely dif-

ferent kind of music than that of the Renaissance, Baroque, or Classical eras—which is fair enough, since each of those periods produced music different from what had preceded, in part because of the instruments then available.

Berlioz did more than try to enlarge the size of the orchestra. He is accepted as the earliest Romantic innovator in orchestration—the most imaginative, the one most willing to experiment, the most radical, the one who most loved far-out spectacles. Liszt and Wagner took up where Berlioz left off and today are held with Berlioz as the principal godfathers of today's symphony orchestra—and of the art of writing specific parts for individual instruments. But other Romantic composers are famous for their orchestration, including Dvořák and Tchaikovsky. The most complex orchestrator of all was Richard Strauss, who wrung more color out of more instruments for total effect than any other composer on The List—but who, the critics say, did not achieve such magical effects as Wagner in doing it. Mahler is also viewed as an enormously talented orchestral technician; highly skilled musicians are required to perform his symphonies.

All of this helped make the symphony orchestra popular with the public—in much of Europe, almost as popular as opera. And it helped make a new form—the symphonic poem—become one of the three most important outgrowths of Romanticism, along with the new role of piano music and the development of the art song. These three were to the Romantic period what the symphony, the sonata, and the string quartet were to the Classical.

Not that those older forms were abandoned. So great was the shadow of Beethoven throughout the nineteenth century that many Romantic composers could not ignore the three Classical forms he perfected. But most Romantics were less comfortable with them than with their own three new toys.

Tonality: At the peak of Romanticism, music was largely tonal, built around a central key. Classical composers oriented their music around a few key centers, Romantics around many. At the end of the century, a great wave of experimentation began, paving the way for the dramatic atonal and polytonal concepts of the twentieth century.

Dynamics: In Romantic music there was considerably more variation in dynamics than there had been in Classical times. Here, as elsewhere in their music, Romantic composers favored the sudden changes that Classicists avoided.

ROMANTIC FORMS OF MUSIC: INSTRUMENTAL

Symphonic Poem: This architectural structure, also called the tone poem, was the main contribution of Romantics to the large forms of music. "Invented" by Liszt, it is a long orchestral work of program music, written in one movement rather than the four of a Classical symphony. In that one movement, composers wrote contrasting sections, presumably designed to tell a musical story, usually related to nationalist traditions, legends, specific moods, or works of art and literature by the geniuses who were so admired by Romantic composers—Hugo and Byron, Michaelangelo and Raphael, Goethe and Schiller, Petrarch, Dante, and Shakespeare.

Liszt's first (and longest) work in this form was entitled *Ce qu'on entend sur la montagne* (What one hears on a mountaintop) after a poem by Victor Hugo, and he followed it over the years with several others. Other Romantic composers known for their symphonic poems include Smetana and Borodin, whose "programs" related to the "essence" of their countries; Tchaikovsky, Saint-Saëns, and Franck, who took the literary-reference approach initiated by Liszt; Richard Strauss, who brought the symphonic poem to its highest peak; and Debussy and Sibelius, some of whose best-known works, written around the turn of the century, are tone poems. Liszt's *Préludes* is an example of a Romantic symphonic poem.

Piano Works: This was the golden age of the piano. Through the music of such composers as Chopin, Schumann, and Liszt, the instrument's full possibilities were realized. Music people say nothing has been added by later composers to the richness and splendor of Romantic pianistic style. And Romantic composers lead history's piano honor rolls. Chopin, Schumann, and Liszt created both long and short pieces. Mendelssohn concentrated on short compositions. Of them all, the Pole-turned-Parisian, Chopin, is the undisputed piano-composition king. His works offer the best examples of Romantic piano forms, including the following:

• Polonaise—A stately, festive Polish national court dance used for ceremonies. It customarily has a moderate tempo and a steady rhythmic pattern. Some of Chopin's are impassioned and majestic, especially his Polonaise in A-flat, known as the "Heroic."

• Nocturne—A lyrical, usually reflective and melancholy composition, fairly slow in tempo. Such works were known collectively as "character pieces." Chopin wrote nineteen—all sad, some morbid, all beautiful. He did not invent the form, but some of the music people say he perfected it. His No. 3 in E-flat, Op. 9, and No. 2 in G, Op. 37, are examples.

• Waltz—As every reader knows, the waltz is basically a ballroom dance for couples, always in three/four meter. It was considered daring when it first appeared. The tempo ranges from slow to fairly fast. In addition to Chopin, the Romantic composers Schubert, Weber, Liszt, and Brahms all wrote waltzes. In general, these were not designed for dancing, but for the piano and sometimes for orchestra. Chopin wrote nineteen. Like the rest of his music, they are known for unusual harmonies and sweet melodies. His No. 2 in C-sharp Minor is an example.

• Etude—Technically, this was a lesson piece for a student, containing material especially difficult to play. Chopin married this technical difficulty with beauty, producing what have been described as "palpitating music pictures." He wrote two sets of twelve each, plus three others, all designed not only for study but for performance. Examples include two compositions from his Op. 25, No. 9 in G-flat and No. 11 in A Minor.

• Mazurka—Originating as a Polish national dance, the mazurka migrated elsewhere in Europe in the eighteenth and nineteenth centuries. It featured a strong accent on the second or third beat, which the professionals say is usually weak. Chopin wrote more than fifty of them, suggesting it was his favorite form. They were inspired by folk melodies but rarely quoted them. Chopin's were closer to actual dances than his waltzes or polonaises. His No. 3 in C-sharp Minor, Op. 50, is an example.

• Prelude—A very short piece, usually designed to be played as an introduction to something else. Chopin wrote a set of twenty-four, all essentially character pieces based on a short, simple theme and intended to stand alone. His form was later imitated by others, including Debussy. Chopin's No. 15 in D-flat, Op. 28 ("Raindrop"), is an example.

• Ballade—This was a freely constructed dramatic instrumental composition, usually linked to a historical or legendary subject. Chopin's four, inspired by a Polish poet, Adam Mickiewicz, are epics, larger than most of his piano works and combining dramatic and lyrical sections. His No. 1 in G Minor is an example.

• Scherzo—As noted earlier, a scherzo was most commonly the third movement of a sonata, symphony, or quartet—replacing the minuet, which had been Haydn's third-movement choice. Beethoven, Schubert, and Bruckner were accepted masters of that scherzo. However, Chopin and Brahms used the term for some of their independent pieces, in which serious, gloomy, highly dramatic sections alternate with much lighter ones. Chopin's Scherzo in C-sharp Minor is an example.

Orchestral Prelude: Wagner wrote preludes for all of his late operas. These differed from overtures in that they merged into the first scene of the opera rather than being self-contained, but they are recorded and played as individual concert pieces. There is no connection between this type of prelude and the short Baroque keyboard preludes of Bach, which stood alone or went with a fugue; nor between this and the free-style piano character pieces called "preludes" by Chopin. To confuse things even further, Liszt's most famous symphonic poem, noted above, is named *Les préludes*, as it was based on a poem of the same name by Lamartine.

Symphony: This was an AC/DC time for the symphony. The German symphonic stream, principally Viennese, was basically traditional, but there was also a more experimental stream of radical Romanticism, represented by Berlioz, Liszt, and their followers. The German strain was carried on by Schubert (eight symphonies), Mendelssohn (five), Schumann (four), and later by Brahms (four). In the other camp, the rebellious Frenchman Berlioz ignored the rules of the club (paradoxically, as pacesetter Beethoven before him had ignored them in creating his own monumental symphonies) to produce his *Symphonie fantastique*, a work in five movements instead of the traditional Classical four and a major piece of nineteenth-century music. Many Romantic symphonists then followed Berlioz's lead and wrote symphonies that were freer in form, scored for a bigger orchestra, and composed with more experimentation and with much greater emphasis on color.

And some symphonists, not unnaturally, made their own blends. Tchaikovsky combined Berlioz's flair for orchestration and ultra-dramatic approach with his own Russian heritage.

Examples of outstanding Romantic symphonies include Schubert's Symphony No. 8 in B Minor (*Unfinished*), Brahms's No. 4 in E Minor, Tchaikovsky's No. 6 in B Minor, and Berlioz's *Symphonie fantastique*.

Concerto: The concerto continued to be comparable to the symphony in its dimensions, as it had been in Classical days. Since it featured a solo instrument along with the orchestra, and since many Romantic composers were outstanding solo pianists—including Weber, Schumann (until he injured his hand), Mendelssohn, Chopin, Liszt, and Brahms—there was a lot of Romantic piano-concerto activity. And though the piano was the big thing during this era, Mendelssohn and Brahms, among others, also wrote famous violin concertos, and several composers, including Schumann and Dvořák, produced cello concertos. In general, the Romantic concerto was similar to the three-movement Classical concerto established by Mozart. An example is Schumann's Concerto in A Minor for Piano.

Chamber Music: Early Romantic composers such as Mendelssohn and Schumann wrote chamber music in the Classical manner, as Schubert had immediately before them, but it was not the forte of most Romantics. Brahms, always a throwback to the Classical era, was a noteworthy exception. Given their preoccupation with the piano, some Romantics were more interested in writing quintets for a string quartet plus the piano. Toward the end of the century there was a renewed interest in chamber music on the part of Franck, Smetana, Dvořák, and others. Examples of Romantic chamber music are Mendelssohn's Quartet in F Minor and Brahms's Quintet in B Minor for Clarinet and Strings.

Sonata: Several Romantic composers wrote sonatas in the Classical style, but most Romantic solo instrumental music was less rigid in its shapes and forms. Brahms, once again, was an exception, as was the "French Brahms," Franck. And, despite his experimental approach to composition, Liszt wrote a great sonata—the B Minor Piano Sonata—although, typical of free-thinking Liszt, it is in one movement instead of three. Another Romantic sonata is Franck's Sonata in A for Violin and Piano.

Overture: Although the basic form of the overture did not change significantly during the Romantic period, the use did; many Romantic composers wrote orchestral pieces called overtures (or *concert overtures*) which were not connected with any stage performance. An example is the "Tragic Overture" by Brahms. Compared with their Classical cousins, there is more tone color and a greater emphasis on orchestration in Romantic overtures, as there is in most Romantic orchestral works.

Symphonic Variations: This form is made up of a subject and several variations in harmony, melody, texture, rhythm, etc. Some Romantic examples are Brahms's *Variations on a Theme of Haydn* and Franck's *Symphonic Variations* for piano solo and orchestra.

Symphonic Suite: The symphonic suite is a work of program music in several movements, similar to the suites of earlier periods. Examples are Tchaikovsky's *Nutcracker* Suite and incidental music to plays, such as Grieg's *Peer Gynt* Suite.

Dances: The Baroque and Classical periods concentrated on the minuet. But by the end of the eighteenth century, Vienna had established itself as the dance center of Europe and the first dances more familiar to us had appeared. Schubert wrote a slow dance called a "Ländler" which quickly grew into perhaps the most famous dance of

all time, the *waltz*. Between 1830 and 1850, several other dances came
and went in popularity, including the Polish *mazurka*; the *quadrille*,
performed by two or four couples moving in a square; the Bohemian
polka; and a quick-step creation called the *galop*. Liszt was among the
composers who wrote a galop. The mazurka, quadrille, and galop all
were launched in Paris. Some concert music was inspired by folk
dances, examples being Liszt's *Hungarian Rhapsodies* and Brahms's
Hungarian Dances. But the popularity of the waltz was in a class by
itself. The best examples of the waltz, of course, come from Johann
Strauss.

ROMANTIC FORMS OF MUSIC: VOCAL

German *lied* (plural: *lieder*): The *lied* is a merger of a lyric poem, a
vocalist, and a piano accompaniment (although with Mahler orchestral *lieder* became popular). This mixture of poetry and melodic music
was something new and was an essential part of the Romantic movement. In developing and perfecting German *lieder*, such composer
geniuses as Schubert, Schumann, and Brahms set to music the poetry
of such literary geniuses as Goethe, Schiller, and Heine.

Schubert was both the first and the best composer of *lieder*, topping even Listed Schumann and Brahms, who followed him. Others
on The List who wrote beautiful *lieder* include (but are not limited to)
Mendelssohn, Liszt, Wagner, Mahler, and Richard Strauss. (And any
discussion of *lieder* should include the name of unListed Hugo Wolf.)
The birthday of the German *lied* is considered to be October 19, 1814,
the date on which the seventeen-year-old Schubert wrote "Gretchen
am Spinnrade"—which has been called "a miracle of musical art."
Schubert's "Erlkonig" is another example of a *lied*.

Opera: Opera was extremely important to the Romantic period,
with Italians Rossini and Donizetti active at the beginning and two
powerful, vastly different composers dominating the field during the
last half of the nineteenth century—Verdi in Italy and Demigod Wagner in Germany. Wagner's music is accepted as the incarnation of the
Late Romantic period, and his style carried well into the twentieth
century. But while Wagner was the all-powerful musical figure in
Germany and most of Europe with his music-drama, in Italy Verdi's
beloved operas dominated that country's music. In France, long a
country of opera fans, Bizet produced his *Carmen* and many other
French composers made their contributions. And in Russia and other
Eastern European countries, nationalist composers proudly produced
nationalist operas.

Oratorio: Mendelssohn's two oratorios (*Saint Paul* and *Elijah*) are among the top half-dozen in music, a pace behind those of Handel and Haydn. Other well-known Romantic oratorios include Berlioz's *L'enfance du Christ* and Franck's *Béatitudes*.

Mass: While many Romantic composers wrote church music, and some beautiful masses were produced, this was not much of a mass period compared to previous eras. One exception is Verdi's magnificent *Requiem* Mass.

THE TWENTIETH CENTURY

Leoš Janáček	1854–1928	No. 48
Claude Debussy	1862–1918	No. 22
Jean Sibelius	1865–1957	No. 28
Ralph Vaughan Williams	1872–1958	No. 44
Maurice Ravel	1875–1937	No. 29
Béla Bartók	1881–1945	No. 35
Igor Stravinsky	1882–1971	No. 15
Sergei Prokofiev	1891–1953	No. 18
Paul Hindemith	1895–1963	No. 33
Dmitri Shostakovich	1906–1975	No. 19

TWENTIETH-CENTURY SNAPSHOTS

Janáček is the third of the three great Czech composers, after Dvořák and Smetana. While not as gifted as Dvořák, he was a deeper scholar of native music, knowledgeable about Czech speech patterns and their rhythms, which he incorporated into his music as Mussorgsky did in Russia. He was a nationalist, part Romantic, part modern, and decidedly unconventional, and his music is generally cheery to hear—though not without dissonance. His masterpiece is his opera *Jenufa*.

Debussy is "Mr. Impressionist," a rebel against what he viewed as Romantic excesses. A pianist himself, he composed many works for the piano but is also known for orchestral compositions and songs. He was an experimenter who foreshadowed more drastic changes in music color, who hid dissonances, and who kept his music vague and floating, without sharp contrasts. Like the French Impressionist painters, he hinted rather than declared.

Sibelius is Finland's finest composer. Highly nationalistic in his early work, he was a melodious nature poet, a producer of symphonic tone poems based on Finnish legends, a symphonist of note, and the most popular of all composers in the U.S. during the 1930s. Writing everything except operas, he generally ignored the "New Music" seeds germinating around him, although as he grew older he moved away from the lush orchestral aspects of Romanticism toward a more austere style.

Vaughan Williams, the only Englishman on The List, is another who studied and collected folk music as a basis for his work. The burly epitome of There'll-Always-Be-an-England, he scoffed at most musical fashions of the day as he dug several hundred years into English roots. Potentially one of the top symphonists of the twentieth century, he was primarily a melodist, admired melodic Sibelius, and was not untouched by Impressionism.

Ravel was one of the revolutionaries of his day, a blender of new tones, an advocate of charm in music, a creator of immensely popular orchestral works initially written for the piano, a Swiss watchmaker in his composition technique. A lesser genius than Debussy, he was nonetheless France's leading composer after World War I and was another outstanding orchestrator.

Bartók, the leading Hungarian nationalist, married folk rhythms to modern music. A creator of new sounds in his rejection of Romanticism—sounds that were sometimes harsh, dissonant, and severe—he is viewed by a Bartók claque as a challenger of Stravinsky for the title of "the twentieth century's greatest composer." He had a lifetime love affair with the folk songs of Hungary and adjoining nations.

Stravinsky, for fifty years the main force behind what was then avant-garde twentieth-century music, is both the greatest and the most influential composer of the century, and the finest Russian of all except for Tchaikovsky. Trained by Rimsky-Korsakov (of "the Mighty Five") he was nationalistic as a young man but produced music that was exceedingly dissonant—with more "head" than "heart" (the opposite of Tchaikovsky). The strange sounds of his early years came chiefly from powerful rhythms that had never been heard before. In his middle years he returned to Classicism, and in his later work he experimented briefly with (then) ultramodern serial music. His 1913 *Rite of Spring* shocked the music world with its new orchestral sounds, sharp dissonance, and savage rhythm.

Prokofiev, one of two twentieth-century Russians, composed both before and after the Revolution. He began as an aggressive and dissonant anti-Romantic, later produced more "lovable" music, and went in and out of favor with the Kremlin during the last decades of his life. He said his own music was made of jest, laughter, and mockery. A pianist and a prolific writer, he was a prestigious international artist who worked in the near-impossible environment created by the Kremlin. A producer of symphonies, operas, ballets, film music, concertos, and the famous *Peter and the Wolf*, a work for orchestra and narrator, he is one of the twentieth century's most popular composers.

Hindemith is the leading German composer of the twentieth century, a superb craftsman, a musician's musician, and a talented violist, almost Bartók's equal in dissonance in early life but later a back-to-Baroque master of counterpoint. He wrote operas, ballets, song cycles, much chamber music, and solo sonatas for instruments he felt other composers ignored. He lived for a while in Buffalo, N.Y., but didn't like its black snow.

Shostakovich, Prokofiev's younger Russian colleague, was the first prominent "Soviet" musician, is the only Soviet on The List, and is the only one of The 50 born in this century. He wrote more than one hundred compositions, ranging from the dissonant opera *Lady Macbeth of Mtsensk*, which the government condemned for its "quacking and growling," to fifteen symphonies. Denounced by the Kremlin at one time for "modernism," he began to experiment less to satisfy his government masters. In time he became the Soviet Union's official music spokesman. A fair question: What music might he have produced in a different political environment?

THE TWENTIETH-CENTURY SCENE

German musical ascendancy ended with the end of Romanticism at the turn of this century. (Of course, the Germans were soon to engage in and lose a couple of wars.) Of the ten composers in our twentieth-century category, only one, Hindemith (who fled to the U.S. in the thirties), is German. The precursors of the German ascendancy were Bach, Handel, Mozart, and Haydn, followed by a long line of individuals who, in their combined force, overpowered all others: Beethoven, Weber, Schubert, Mendelssohn, Schumann, Brahms, Bruckner, Richard Strauss, Mahler—and, more than anyone since Beethoven, Richard Wagner.

This century is a musical hodgepodge—not surprising for a period that began with man riding horses and was only two-thirds over when man walked on the moon, with two world wars in between. There has been conservatism, radicalism, and absurdism. No century of music has been more diverse. At the beginning, subjectivity, emotionalism, and program music were the watchwords of Romanticism, but before long Romantic program music had been almost completely replaced by a new brand of absolute music. In their flight from Romanticism at and shortly after the turn of the century, composers created many strange new sounds. Impressionism, begun by the French, was largely a reaction against German Romanticism. Expressionism, harshly dissonant and atonal, came from unListed Schoenberg and company. Neoclassicism began about 1920 and for years was a dominant trend. Major neoclassical works included Stravinsky's *Octet for Winds* and *L'histoire du soldat*, Prokofiev's *Classical Symphony*, and Hindemith's *Ludus tonalis*, a piano piece, and his Fourth String Quartet. The neoclassical trend included the revival of counterpoint texture and forms: fugue, toccata, madrigal, and passacaglia.

In both halves of the twentieth century there has been unparalleled musical experimentation. That which at first appeared so novel became tame by comparison with later developments. "Modern" changed to "modernistic." Some experiments have lasted; some have not—but who knows how the twentieth century will be judged in the twenty-first and twenty-second?

In this century different and unusual things have been done to the bricks-and-mortar: to melody, harmony, tonality, rhythm, texture, form, and orchestration. At the beginning of the 1900s Stravinsky-type dissonance shocked the music world. But that was nothing. Before World War II one well-known composer invented a new piano with nails, bolts, screws, rubber, wood, metal, and leather inserted between the strings. Other developments include electronic music; microtonal music, based on such intervals as quarter-tones and one-sixteenth tones; aleatory ("chance") music, written by a throw-of-the-dice technique; and *musique concrète*, based on "real" sounds ranging from thunder in the heavens to a wreck on the freeway. There is serial music and modified serial music, and there is mixed-media music, which combines live electronic sound with taped material with special lighting with dance with film with balloons with audience participation. And there is "New Age" music, which also concerns itself with meditation, ecology, and mysticism.

Only one composer born in the twentieth century has made The List, and he lived from 1906 to 1975. The next two most recently alive died in 1971 and 1963. Only three others lived until the 1950s. So we have representation from great composers who lived and worked in the first half of the century, but none from any born after World War I. This is not because of a prejudice against tape recorders, computers, minitones, electronic music, and ecology, but because the selection system used for The List did not identify masters of sufficient greatness from contemporary times. Attention here is on the music of the Listed twentieth-century composers, not that of the unListed.

Jazz has had a significant impact on classical music in this century, especially but not exclusively on Stravinsky's works. Pre–World War II jazz included ragtime, blues, Dixieland jazz, the big-band sound, and boogie-woogie. After World War II came progressive jazz, cool jazz, soul jazz, and rock.

Two trends emerged in the first half of the century that merit special attention for List composers: nationalism and Impressionism.

As the century began, nationalist composers from Bohemia and Russia, and Impressionist musicians from the French school, helped end the long era of German musical ascendancy. World War I—and later World War II—interrupted whatever German comeback there might have been, although the influence of the twelve-tone technique cannot be overlooked. Composers emerged from many other areas: the ten Listed twentieth-century composers include three Russians, two Frenchmen, and one each from Czechoslovakia, Hungary, England, Finland, and Germany.

Although it would be tidy if a great wall separated the centuries so that we could say that Trend A represented the nineteenth century and Trend B represented the twentieth, obviously it did not work that way. Nationalism was an important part of both the Romantic era and the new century, its influence felt in the late years of the one and the first half of the other. In both centuries, artists from France, Germany, and Italy, with their nations' long traditions of music composition, felt less moved to make patriotic or nationalistic statements than composers from countries and regions that lacked a universal musical tradition, such as Finland, Norway, Bohemia, Hungary, and Poland.

Thus in the Romantic period the most fervent nationalists were Smetana and Dvořák of Czechoslovakia; Borodin, Mussorgsky, and Rimsky-Korsakov of Russia; and Grieg of Norway. In the twentieth century the leading nationalists on the List are Jean Sibelius of Finland and Leoš Janáček of Czechoslovakia. (There is also Ralph Vaughan Williams of England, the exception that proves the rule, inasmuch as England was hardly without a universal musical tradition.)

In both the late years of one century and the earlier years of the next, there were two kinds of nationalist influence. The nineteenth-century boyhood and adult environment of a Russian Tchaikovsky or a Hungarian Liszt inevitably emerges in their music, as the twentieth-century environment emerges in the music of a German Hindemith or a Russian Prokofiev. However international their compositions, no one would dare suggest that Tchaikovsky and Prokofiev are not Russian, nor Liszt not Hungarian and Hindemith not German, any more than one would suggest that Shakespeare and Dickens were not English.

But other composers—like Smetana in the nineteenth century and Sibelius in the twentieth—made conscious and deliberate efforts to absorb, collect, and utilize folk music, to draw on ethnic traits, to speak of their country's history, to dedicate themselves musically in patriotic struggles against those who would control their homelands, and in general to declare their nationalism in strong voices.

As the century opened, some composers, in addition to their emphasis on nationalism, found Impressionism to be a means of breaking away from Romanticism and doing their own thing. They emulated painters of the day who were making the same break—painters such as Monet and Renoir, who put down their impressions of a scene rather than reproducing it "realistically," as a camera would. The first of these composers was Debussy and the second Ravel (although the purists say that Ravel is not truly an Impressionist and note many differences between the work of the two men). Both are precursors of the new sounds of music that were to come. Impressionist music, indirect rather than direct, is more difficult to sing or whistle—but no less beautiful—than other Romantic work.

A third trend emerged at this time, as well: a new kind of music with a whole new sound, known seventy-five years ago as "new" music or "modern" music" or "twentieth-century" music. Of course, the "horrendous" sounds of 1912 no longer seem as peculiar as they once did, and many do not sound peculiar at all. The five Listed representatives of this then-"liberal" music are Stravinsky, Prokofiev, and Shostakovich of Russia; Bartók of Hungary (he also qualifies as a nationalist); and Hindemith of Germany.

A point worth restating is that there has always been liberalism in music. Brahms was not a liberal, and in fact was attacked by contemporaries because he was "reactionary." But more composers on The List were "liberal" than were "conservative," even though some took smaller steps away from the immediate past than others. In music as elsewhere, artistic standards shift; ideals and conventions of ages are modified.

So while Bartók, Stravinsky, and Hindemith triggered protests as a result of the strangeness and dissonance of their music, they were far from the first to do so. The music of Debussy and Ravel was deemed impossibly dissonant. Richard Strauss was attacked for engaging in "daring harmonic extravagances." Beethoven was criticized by some of his contemporaries for being too far out and difficult, as was Wagner a good many years later. Mozart was ahead of his time, and so, most certainly, was the radical Berlioz. Monteverdi was a revolutionary "modernist." So were Rameau, Bach, and Haydn. All of these "liberals" made things happen in the world of music, and not everyone listening at the moment enjoyed the new sounds they created.

All of this notwithstanding, some of the changes brought about early in the century by "Moderns" and "New Music" people were the most radical changes that had taken place in Western classical music since 1600.

TWENTIETH-CENTURY BRICKS-AND-MORTAR

Rhythm: Rhythm has truly come into its own in twentieth-century music. It is more varied, more complex, and more energetic than ever before. Some twentieth-century composers have experimented with "polyrhythm," writing works that feature as many as five different rhythmic patterns at the same time, each fighting the other four. Bartók and Stravinsky are two such Listed composers. In its complexity, twentieth-century rhythm differs greatly from the steady, pulsating, consistent, and persistent rhythm of Baroque music.

Melody: This had always been a solid brick in the foundation. Now, for the first time in hundreds of years, melody was de-emphasized. The "back-to-Bach" composers necessarily wove melody into their polyphonic compositions, but elsewhere melody gave way to rhythm, harmony, and tone color. And twentieth-century melody typically lacks the repetition of earlier melody. It jumps from place to place more than Romantic melody, making it harder to hear (and less frequently a basis for contemporary popular songs). And in the second half of the century, with the emergence of electronic music and its nontonal sounds, there is sometimes no melody at all. But this does not apply to any Listed composers.

Texture: As mentioned above, there was a strong back-to-Bach (i.e., back-to-counterpoint) movement in the first half of the century. This, however, was counterpoint with twentieth-century dissonance, not Bach-sounding counterpoint. It can be heard in Bartók's string quartets and in the chamber music of Hindemith.

Harmony: Dramatic things happened to harmony in the twentieth century. Composers found new and different chord constructions and progressions and new types of dissonance. Not only were chords superimposed on one another, but one strain of harmony was plunked atop another ongoing strain, akin to simultaneous melody in counterpoint music. The sound of "polyharmony" is not at all the sound of the sweeter Romantic music.

Orchestration: Whereas orchestras had become increasingly large as the Romantic movement continued, the trend in the twentieth century was toward a smaller, leaner orchestra, geared to the music being composed. Picture a Picasso painting as opposed to a Romantic canvas: fewer soft tones and more hard ones; fewer light, cheery instruments playing and more dark, heavy ones. The Romantics had gone all out after tone color, and the composition of orchestras reflected this. With the increased emphasis on rhythm in twentieth-century music, percussion instruments became more important. Correspondingly, the works of many twentieth-century composers de-emphasized the stringed instruments.

Tonality: While major things happened across the bricks-and-mortar spectrum in the twentieth century, the most important changes of all were in tonality. We have seen that prior composers on The List traditionally wrote in one key at a time. But this "loyalty to key" began to break down in the Late Romantic era, and in the twentieth century it was to disintegrate completely. Shifts from one key to another within a piece had been commonplace enough with the great masters as far back as Monteverdi, but these composers used only one key at a time. And even the most bold, who strayed from "loyalty to key," did not stray far. Their music was still key-related, despite changes in rhythm, harmony, and other bricks-and-mortar elements.

This all changed in the twentieth century. Some composers were "atonal," writing in no key at all. Others were "bitonal," writing in two keys at once, or "polytonal," writing in a whole bunch of keys at the same time. In some music, the tone center, the foundation of Western music, disappeared.

In summary, the case can be made that *poly*—from Greek and Latin for "many"—is what truly sets twentieth-century music apart from the music of Monteverdi, Bach, Haydn, Mozart, and Beethoven, and even of Liszt, Wagner, Strauss, Debussy, and Ravel. As noted, some composers were polytonal, polyharmonic, and polyrhythmic. As far as the bricks-and-mortar elements are concerned, there was a general drive to experiment as far as possible with any factor neglected or overlooked by the nineteenth-century Romantics. In some cases a return to the 1400s was married to unprecedented new concepts.

Another major difference between some twentieth-century music and what came before involves its "inner core"—emotion and expression. Bach was motivated by religious ecstasy, Beethoven by a passion for individual rights, Brahms by purity, veneration of the past, and loyalty to idea. But what about Stravinsky? He claimed: "I consider that music is by its very nature essentially powerless to express anything at all. . . . I evoke neither human joy nor human sadness."

Defenders of Stravinsky say there is nothing wrong with a composer being coldly logical and brilliantly intellectual. After all, there was no more logical and intellectual a composer than Bach, Number One, Top Immortal of them all. But in contrast to Stravinsky, Bach said: "The aim and final reason of all music should be nothing else but the Glory of God and the refreshment of the spirit."

Some conservatives have complained that too many twentieth-century musicians experimented for the sake of experimentation, ignoring or forgetting that communication was the primary function of art. Adherents of this view argue that even some of The Listed twentieth-century composers—not to mention the early unListed and those in the second half of the century whose work is not covered here—concentrated too much on arranging sounds in a provocative manner and not enough on expressing emotion. Indeed, Stravinsky specifically opposed "expressing" anything.

The music of the Russian Stravinsky, the Hungarian Bartók (at times), and the German Hindemith share several "New Music" elements: greater detachment and objectivity than is found in most Romantic music; a return to Baroque counterpoint; formal order and discipline; a return to absolute (as opposed to program) music; and an emphasis on technique rather than content. With the overlapping rhythms found in Stravinsky's music, there is less to tap one's foot to. And with Hindemith's simultaneous melodies, there is less to hum. While some of this music is back-to-Bach-and-counterpoint, it is dissonant rather than agreeable counterpoint, in part because these composers combined notes and chords that would have distressed Bach and Handel. It is only fair to point out, however, that three hundred years have passed since the birth of those two artists and that one should expect the sounds to change. It is within the ground rules to regret or to applaud.

TWENTIETH-CENTURY FORMS OF MUSIC: INSTRUMENTAL

In contrast to the radical changes in materials and techniques, especially those of the last forty or so years, for the music created by the Listed composers of the twentieth century there have been few dramatic changes in form. Anything goes for some of the music by unListed artists.

Symphonic Suite: An instrumental suite unrelated to the Baroque dance suite and different from the Late Romantic suite, this form, which emerged early in the twentieth century, was more of a cross between a symphony and a tone poem—usually a work with less "program" than the latter and shorter movements than the former. An example of a twentieth-century symphonic suite is the orchestral version of Ravel's *Mother Goose*.

Symphonic Poem: While similar in structure to the Romantic symphonic poem, this was apt to be less noble, more realistic, and sometimes uglier and more brutal than the earlier Romantics would have liked. Richard Strauss's *Eine Alpensinfonie* of 1915, not a success, is an example.

Ballet: An offshoot of opera, modern ballet took off during the first few years of the twentieth century, after the appearance of Tchaikovsky's *Swan Lake*, *Sleeping Beauty*, and *The Nutcracker* toward the end of the nineteenth. Borodin, Stravinsky, Ravel, Richard Strauss, Debussy, Prokofiev, Bartók, and Vaughan Williams all wrote ballets. The best-known pre–World War I "New Music" ballet is Stravinsky's *Rite of Spring*, criticized at the time for its "biting" dissonance, "savage" rhythms, and "primitive" sounds. Try it. And don't give up until you've tried it five times. Then . . .

Concerto: With some exceptions, the Romantic concerto spotlighted the soloist in contrast to earlier concertos, which featured greater equality between the soloist and the orchestra. The twentieth-century concerto tends to go back to this pre-Romantic style, in part because modern orchestras are themselves such star performers that they are not easy to dominate. Twentieth-century concerto writers include Ravel, Stravinsky, Sibelius, Bartók, and Prokofiev. An example is Prokofiev's Piano Concerto No. 3 in C.

Symphony: It is not realistic to try to characterize a "twentieth-century symphony." Some composers at the beginning of the century were writing much the same kind of music they had been writing *before* someone advised them that they were now in a century destined to produce an airplane and two world wars. Others, both then and later in the century, were into entirely different things.

From the standpoint of the listening public, the Classical symphonies of Haydn, Mozart, and Beethoven and the Romantic symphonies of Schubert, Brahms, Tchaikovsky, and Dvořák continued to be the backbone of orchestral programs through most of the century. Twentieth-century composers—at least those interested in writing symphonies—looked for ways to adapt the traditional form of the symphony to changing musical styles, harmonies, and rhythms. The Romantics had kept the conventional format but sometimes almost overwhelmed it with the greater emotional appeal and the additional color of bigger orchestras. What, now, was the next-generation "modern" twentieth-century composer to do?

As we have seen, one major aspect of twentieth-century music which differed from all previous Western music was the obscured tonality—the weakening, or absence, of the concept that music must return to a central note in order to achieve what the music people call a sense of rest and finality. But the structure of a symphony did not accommodate obscured tonality. It demanded the tonal logic from which some "New Music" or "modern" twentieth-century composers were escaping.

Different composers found different ways to handle this problem. Some shrugged their shoulders and went on their radical way without any symphonies in their portfolios. Debussy, who lived until 1918, is one Listed example of this. Some, like Mahler, who lived until 1911, were undisturbed by the new music and wrote big, emotional Romantic symphonies for big, Romantic-sized orchestras, just as they had before the century changed. Some took their symphonies back to Classical times, reduced the size of the nineteenth-century orchestra, and cut down on nineteenth-century emotion and subjectivity. Some went back even farther and restored an emphasis on counterpoint and other musical devices typical of Bach.

In the mid-1900s, by far the most popular symphonist was Jean Sibelius, although many elitists then (as now) insisted that he was merely a fad. The music people say that he had a good, solid tonal foundation, even though his harmony often was dissonant. Writing of his symphonic characteristics nearly a half-century ago, Douglas Moore—professor, composer, and conductor—said:

> Sibelius is perhaps most original in his conception of the symphonic form. Many of the movements are based upon a collection of fragmentary ideas which fuse and coalesce as the music proceeds. This, to the uninitiate, gives them a somewhat chaotic effect. The line is broken, the music is rather desultory, the style seems pictorial and descriptive rather than symphonic. To members of the Sibelius cult, however, these are the manifestations of his subtle genius and, once understood, are the patterns of a master mind. It is an interesting problem for the musical amateur to decide for himself at which point between these conflicting opinions the truth may lie.

We'll simply note the conflict without further pursuit of the truth. Some twentieth-century symphonies that might have been written in the nineteenth are Mahler's Fifth, Sixth, Seventh and Ninth, com-

posed between 1902 and 1910. An example of return-to-Classicism is
Prokofiev's First Symphony, called the *Classical*, written in 1917. It
was a conscious back-to-the-past effort, taken by some to be a parody.

Stravinsky also added to this twentieth-century symphonic stew.
In 1920 he wrote a "severely neoclassical" piece called *Symphonies of
Wind Instruments*, not really a symphony at all, in which, the profes-
sionals tell us, there was no suggestion of emotion or the picturesque.
Ten years later he composed an entirely different kind of thing, his
Symphony of Psalms for chorus and orchestra, based on Latin texts.

In the Soviet Union, Shostakovich in the late 1920s experimented
with two one-movement symphonies, the first dedicated (in good
Communist party style) "to October" and the second called *First of
May*. Critics have described them as unsuccessful attempts to recon-
cile the "contemporary" with the "proletarian."

The critics also note that between the wars, the influence of
Sibelius is evident in Vaughan Williams's Fourth (1934) and Fifth
(1935) Symphonies, the latter dedicated to the Finnish composer.
During World War II, symphonies from Vaughan Williams in England and Shostakovich in Russia were created out of war emotions.

During all of these years, many unListed composers followed the
lead of Schoenberg and his disciples. Symphony was not for them.
Not only did key have no meaning for them, but, the professionals tell
us, they also ignored the centuries-old method of constructing large-
scale architecture by repeating and altering themes. There was no
absence of orchestral music from these twelve-toners, but their approach did not produce works that qualify as symphonies.

The post-World War II avant-garde was not interested in symphony. Large architectural forms were not suitable for its techniques.
In *The Concise Oxford History of Music*, musicologist Gerald Abraham
writes:

> Confronted with "*musique concrète*," aleatory music, elec-
> tronic music, many musicians felt it was not unreasonable to
> deny that this was "music" at all, particularly when shown a
> "score" like that of Stockhausen's "Zyklus" for one percus-
> sion player. It was certainly not music that expressed or com-
> municated anything, but rather a massive exploration of the
> possibilities of organized or random sound on lines only to be
> expected in an age obsessed with technological exploration,
> which might conceivably lead to an art of sound quite different
> from music as we know it, developing its own techniques and
> gradually establishing its own ethos.

In the absence of a typical twentieth-century symphony, there is no example of one for this road map. Nor is it feasible to attempt to describe how a twentieth-century symphony differs from a Romantic one. Sometimes it has a smaller orchestra, and often it is less emotional, and at times it has less tone color, and occasionally it emphasizes counterpoint, and it may have only a single movement. Probably there are newer and different harmonies. Mostly, in the twentieth century, it is every composer for himself.

Chamber Music: Even among Listed composers, chamber music in the first half of the century can be broken down into two camps, traditional and radical. From a twentieth-century perspective, Ravel, Debussy, and Fauré are examples of composers of traditional chamber music. Hindemith and Bartók are examples of the radical side.

It is interesting that some of the twentieth-century radicals (I'm talking about the "radical" first half of the century, not the music-by-chance-and-computer second half) favored chamber music, since this was not the case in the Romantic era. Romantic artists with Classical tendencies—Brahms, Schubert, Schumann, and Mendelssohn—were fond of the string quartet, while the liberals—Liszt, Berlioz, and Wagner—paid little attention to it.

Not so in this century. The radicals and their experimentation jumped into chamber music—no huge symphonic architectural structure here. Some of the music people suggest that the chamber-music audience traditionally has been the intellectual one, the one more interested in thought than emotion, and thus the one more receptive to the atonal (or less tonal) and more dissonant sounds of the radicals. The professionals advise us that one technique of the atonalists was concentration on repetition and on combining rhythmic patterns. The string quartet was deemed to be an ideal medium for this approach.

One of the more traditional twentieth-century chamber-music pieces is Fauré's Quintet No. 1 in D Minor for Piano and Strings. Examples of the more radical works are Bartók's six string quartets.

TWENTIETH-CENTURY FORMS OF MUSIC: VOCAL

Choral Music: Good things happened to choral music in the twentieth century. For most of the period covered in this road map, instrumental music dominated the musical scene. In the Baroque operas and oratorios, large parts were written for instruments; the great religious masses of the Classical and Romantic periods had elaborate orchestral accompaniment; and in Wagner's music-drama opera, more emphasis was put on the orchestra than on the voice. In the twentieth century, however, voice had the opportunity to come into its own.

One route to the twentieth century out of Romanticism and its focus on orchestral tone color was a return to a back-to-Bach contrapuntal style. In taking this route, several twentieth-century Listed composers created choral works designed to show off the voice rather than the instrument. These include Debussy and Ravel, each of whom wrote a set of three *a cappella* (unaccompanied) choruses; Stravinsky, with his *Symphony of Psalms*; and Vaughan Williams, who wrote various choral works.

IN SUMMARY

From the Late Renaissance (the end of the sixteenth century) came the greatest master of Roman Catholic church music; smooth and flowing many-voiced masses, and with them the first deep study of counterpoint; sacred motets and hymns; secular madrigals; and the initial movement toward homophonic music, or single melody supported by chords.

From the Baroque (1600 to 1750) came the beginning of opera and the opera overture, ballet, and the oratorio; the practice of a composer specifying which instruments were to play what music, and thus the start of the orchestra; and many forms of instrumental music—concerto grosso, fugue, dance suite, toccata, passacaglia, chaconne, theme-and-variations, chorale prelude, and early symphony. Further advances were made in both Italy and France in single melody supported by chords, or harmony, while in Germany Bach took simultaneous multimelody music, or counterpoint, as far as it could go.

From the Classical era (about 1750 to 1825) came the string quartet, the sonata as we know it, the symphony as we know it, the piano and violin concerto with solo instruments against the orchestra, absolute music, the establishment of strings as the foundation of the orchestra, the sonata form, and wide-ranging melody arising from single-melody-plus-chords harmony.

From the Romantic period (the rest of the nineteenth century) came lyrical piano music, the lyrical art song, the new symphonic poem, program music, intimate Parisian elegance contrasted with brutal Russian realism, ardent nationalism, unparalleled individual virtuosity, new dimensions for ballet music, Impressionism, magnificent opera, and powerful music-drama.

From the first part of the twentieth century came new sounds, new rhythms, new scales, new harmonies, and acid dissonance—more appropriate to those modern times than lyric poetry or the minuet. Later in the century came neoclassical trends and still later unrest, electronic music, and experimentation of a whole new order, not represented by any composer among The 50. Virtually all types of music are being written today. The bottom line is that it is impossible to determine the eventual importance of many talented twentieth-century composers who are not on The List. And the nice thing is that you can choose any of them in preference to any of The 50—except, of course, Mr. Bach, Mr. Mozart, and Mr. Beethoven.

CHAPTER IV

The Lives and the Works

JOHANN SEBASTIAN BACH (1685–1750)

Number 1

Johann Sebastian Bach, Wolfgang Amadeus Mozart, Ludwig van Beethoven, William Shakespeare, and Michelangelo Buonarroti stand
together at the peak of Western culture.

Comparisons among them are meaningless. But of the three composers, few will argue with putting Bach first.

Robert Schumann said of him: "Music owes as much to Bach as
religion to its founder."

Writers and critics of the twentieth century cannot find superlatives enough in their assessments of him.

They say that his organ music blended science with poetry, technique with emotion, and virtuosity with nobility of thought as has
none other, before or since.

They write that he devoted his entire musical life and talent to
reaching out to mankind.

They tell us that his inspired cantatas give testimony to the fact that music can be both deeply personal and meaningful to the world.

They declare that he vitalized the polyphonic music of the past with the passion and humanity of his own spirit, that he is the culminating figure of Baroque music, that he is a titan in the history of art, that he brought whatever form he touched to its ultimate development, and that his mastery of the techniques of composition has never been equaled.

Then they speak of the incomparable profundity of his thought and feeling.

No other composer, they add, has had the capacity to realize to such an extent all the possibilities in a given musical situation.

They assert that his music is absolute, that it is beyond praise, and that it dwarfs all that precedes and follows with the beauty of perfection, order, and balance.

Bach has excited unique devotion on the part of his colleagues. Among symphony buffs there is a Mahler cult, a Bruckner cult, a Mozart cult, a Beethoven cult, and in France a Berlioz cult. But among composers, the critics say, it is a Bach cult.

FIVE KEYBOARD ARTISTS

Q: What Parisian pianist considered Bach the be-all and end-all of music?

A: Frédéric Chopin, who knew by heart the forty-eight preludes and fugues of The Well-Tempered Clavier.

Q: What Parisian harpsichordist was greatly admired by Bach, who studied his works and made copies of some?

A: François Couperin, born seventeen years before Bach.

Q: Who compared what French organist to Bach?
A: Franz Liszt, speaking of César Franck.

They assert that his artistic powers and insights were on such an immeasurably higher plane than those who preceded him that at his bidding music seems at once to have stepped out of childishness into maturity.

They write that he is the musical bible to all who would be musicians.

Schumann said: "We are all bunglers next to him." Chopin was impressed by only two composers: Mozart and Johann Sebastian Bach.

And so it goes. We have condensed the quotations of the music people but kept their extravagant language. If an anti-Bach school exists, it is hidden in the hills or in the closets, as secret as the circles that worship Satan.

No composer did as much or went as far in perfecting the existing forms of music. All who followed had to seek new mountains.

One of his works, the Mass in B Minor, is frequently called the single greatest musical composition. But even without it, many will argue that no other composer has contributed as much as he to sacred vocal music.

In the instrumental field, his six sonatas for violin and six suites for cello are held among the finest of solo string works.

Many view the *Brandenburg* Concertos as the supreme examples of the concerto grosso.

Bach was the last of the great religious artists and the all-time master of the fugue.

It is clearly the consensus of the experts that his music is the most noble and majestic of all.

Although not an inventor of new musical forms, he did things with existing ones that no one had conceived of, and did them better than anyone since, setting his own agenda and establishing new standards for every musical form of his time except opera—vocal, keyboard, instrumental, orchestral, and chamber.

His techniques and suggestions, developed by Mozart and Haydn and expanded by Beethoven, opened new horizons of music for all time.

Bach is not regarded as a spontaneous creator like Mozart, nor one who fashioned thunder and lightning like Beethoven. Nor did he regard himself that way.

He had a simple enough explanation for what he was: "I work hard," he said—and indeed he did. It took several people many years to pull together his lifework into sixty massive volumes, and at that no one believes that all Bach treasures have been found, or ever will be, since no special value was placed upon them in the marketplace during his life.

But clearly, more than hard work was involved here. In the simplest terms, what made Bach Bach? Perhaps:

- supreme technical mastery,
- a keenly analytical mind,
- a deeply profound mind,
- a consuming belief in God,
- passion and compassion,
- melodic genius,
- just plain genius,
- a conviction that music made by man was meant to be "a harmonious euphony to the Glory of God."

Bach did not starve in the attic, but he was a professional musician—the fifth of seven generations that constituted perhaps the greatest musical family in Western music—and one did not become rich as an organist, a conductor, a musical director of church services, a teacher of boys, and an unpublished composer.

It is not true, as is sometimes written, that he was "forgotten" after his death, especially not by the great composers who followed him, but it is true that for some eighty years thereafter the musical public saw and heard very little of his work. The marketplace breakthrough came in 1829 when young Felix Mendelssohn, long famous already at the age of twenty-seven, revived and conducted in Berlin Bach's *Passion According to St. Matthew*. Four years later the *St. John Passion* was also revived, and by midcentury Bach was widely hailed as a great master. Since then, his reputation has climbed higher and higher.

But it was not as though he had gone unrecognized before this time. In 1802 his first full biographer called him "the greatest musical poet and the greatest musical orator that ever existed and probably ever will exist." And the record shows that Mozart made string transcriptions from several sections of Bach's *Art of the Fugue*, composed preludes for them, and wrote to his father that he had found music from which he could learn something. Beethoven, a piano virtuoso, not only played Bach's *Well-Tempered Clavier* but drew upon its composer for some of the ideas in his late quartets.

World-famous compositions exist in each category of Bach's music: vocal and orchestral, chamber and keyboard. The list is long, and to zero in on just a few is an intimidating task. Still, it needs doing.

Several different kinds of composition make up the foundation for his church music. In the vocal field, the best known include three major works and his astonishing collection of church cantatas.

The so-called major works—"so-called" because one can scarcely consider any of Bach's works minor—are his *St. John Passion*, written in 1724; the *St. Matthew Passion*, written in 1727; and the great Mass in B Minor, a massive work in twenty-four sections including fifteen choruses, six sections for solo voices, and three duets. Created between 1747 and 1749, it is considered Bach's greatest single work—and, as noted, perhaps music's greatest as well.

While the B Minor Mass may well be Bach's masterpiece, his two-hundred-odd cantatas (most of which were written for church services and were based on that Sunday's scripture lesson, although some are secular) make up an extraordinary collection of vocal works. Scores of these are world favorites, the best known including Nos. 4, 51, 80, and 140.

In the orchestral arena, the most frequently performed works are his four suites for orchestra and the famous six *Brandenburg* Concertos. The accompanying outline shows that he also produced many other concertos, some for solo instruments plus orchestra and some for orchestra and combinations of instruments—one or more keyboard instruments; violin; violin and keyboard; violin, flute, and harp; etc. Among the best known are the Concerto No. 1 in D Minor for Piano and Strings (S. 1052) and the Concerto in D Minor for Two Violins (S. 1043).

A CATHOLIC MASS BY A DEVOTED LUTHERAN

Q: Why did Bach, a staunch Lutheran, write the most famous of all Catholic masses—his magnificent Mass in B Minor?

A: It was composed for and offered to his Catholic sovereign, the Elector of Saxony, to make Brownie points with that important ruler.

The outline also shows that Bach's music for the harpsichord includes the French Suites, English Suites, and partitas; the famous *Well-Tempered Clavier* (S. 846–893); and the *Goldberg* Variations (S. 998), an extended series of variations on one melody. Another famous work for keyboard is the Chromatic Fantasy and Fugue (S. 903).

Few families, if any, have been more musical than the one from which the creator of all this came. At one time or another, thirty Bachs held organ posts in Germany. In Eisenach, where Johann Sebastian was born, his father was a respected violinist and violist, and the boy was surrounded by music. After both of his parents died, he moved at age nine or ten to live with a twenty-four-year-old brother thirty miles away in the town of Ohrdruf. The brother did not know he had a world-class genius on his hands; basically he regarded the boy as just one more mouth to feed. He treated him poorly; some biographers say tyrannically. But he was a professional church organist, and young Sebastian, as he was called, learned more about music. What if the brother had been a tax collector, or a shoemaker? Would there have been a Bach?

Five years later, Sebastian made one of the longest trips of his life—two hundred miles—to Luneburg, where he became a paid choir-boy, living in buildings connected with St. Michael's Church. He devoured everything musical he could find, studying organ, clavi-chord, violin, and composition; hiking forty miles to Hamburg to hear an organ master; and once walking sixty miles to Celle to hear French music. (That's what the historians say; one wonders if there were no carts on which a kid could steal rides.)

From 1703 to 1707 he again lived in the district of Thuringia, in Arnstadt, hired now as an organist in St. Boniface's Church. But Sebastian was a restless fellow. Granted a one-month leave of absence to visit the top organist of the times in Lubeck, three hundred miles away, he stayed three months instead, upset the local authorities, was chastised for "making many surprising variations in the chorale," and finally decided to move on. After a short stop en route, in 1708, and after marrying his cousin, Maria Barbara Bach, daughter of an organ-ist, he accepted a major post in the service of the reigning duke of Saxony-Weimar, Wilhelm Ernst, who was seated in Weimar. He played violin in the duke's orchestra, led the chamber musicians, served as court organist, composed music as occasions demanded, and taught. In Weimar, Bach received eighty-five gulden a year plus two trusses of wood, six trusses of faggots, and three measures of corn. In Weimar, too, he had his first exposure to Antonio Vivaldi's music, which the duke liked, and since Vivaldi was Europe's Mr. Concerto during this period, Bach went into the concerto business as well. As noted earlier, in the Bach-Vivaldi concerto, a solo instrument was partner with the orchestra; in later concertos it was the superstar, with the orchestra as accompaniment.

In 1717 Bach became a con and an ex-con. Sulking about lack of promotion, he accepted a job as Kapellmeister to Prince Leopold of Anhalt-Cöthen. But the duke was reluctant to release him, and when Bach got stubborn about it the nobleman tossed him into jail. The duke eased off after a month, however, and the organist-composer made the move to Cothen, where he took over Prince Leopold's musical operation. He worked with the Collegium Musicum, an eighteen-person orchestra, but was not required to play the organ or to compose for religious services. Most of his work here was instrumental and secular.

In 1723, after the prince married a woman who thought little of music or of Bach, he was given a job in Leipzig—but not until the first choice of the local council turned the position down and until Bach had produced the magnificent *St. John Passion* as an employment test. He remained in Leipzig until he died at sixty-five, leaving a second wife, Anna Magdalena Wilcken, and nine surviving children from a total of nineteen. In Leipzig he was in charge of music for four churches, personally leading performances in two; he wrote a cantata for each Sunday and for special festivals, and a passion a year; and he was cantor of St. Thomas's School, where he supervised all musical instruction and did some teaching himself. In 1736 he became court composer to the elector of Saxony, a post he held for the rest of his life.

AN APPEAL

Bach was not easily defeated in his many fights with Leipzig authorities and with officials of the St. Thomas School. When overruled at lower levels, he went right to the top, once addressing his protest to:

His Most Serene Highness, the Mighty Prince and Lord, Frederick Augustus, King in Poland, Grand Duke in Lithuania, Reuss, Prussia, Mazovia, Samogitia, Kyovia, Vollhynia, Podlachia, Lieffland, Smolensk, Severia and Czernienhovia, Duke of Saxony, Julich, Cleve, Berg, Engern and Westphalia, Archmarshal and Elector of the Holy Roman Empire, Landgrave of Thuringia, Margrave of Meissen, also of Upper and Lower Lausiz, Burgrave of Magdeburg, Prince and Count of Henneberg, Count of the Marck, Ravensburg and Barby, Lord of Ravenstein, My Most Gracious King, Elector and Master.

The death of "Old Bach" on July 28, 1750, was not regarded as a big deal. His grave in the St. John churchyard in Leipzig was not identified. No one lined the streets for his funeral procession. There were no headlines or foreign dignitaries. His coffin was not moved inside the church until nearly 150 years later, in 1894. One son, Carl Philipp, became much better known in his lifetime than his father had been. Another, Johann Christian, lived for many years in England and is called the "English Bach."

Musicologists offer several explanations as to why the Great Master was not better known in his own day. One is that most of his works were not published until years after his death and thus were heard only by immediate audiences. A second is that Bach was not a traveling, cosmopolitan, entrepreneurial composer like Handel. He left south-central Germany only two or three times, and even then he did not go far. And a third is that the kind of music Bach created was going out of style during the last twenty or thirty years of his life. The yen for the many-voiced polyphonic music he produced was fading; single-melody-with-chords homophony was becoming the thing.

After all, no one told the people of Weimar and Cothen and Leipzig that this organist and cantata writer was to be one of the half-dozen supreme artists of mankind. "Old Bach" was a good old fellow, a little stern and headstrong and difficult for a musician, probably a little tough on his young pupils, but there had been many Bachs before him in that part of the world and there would be more to come. No one told them a young genius called Mendelssohn was going to dust off this passion in the next century and make "Old Bach" famous. So when he died they put him out in the churchyard.

Connoisseurs divide Bach's work into three periods. His first creative period began during his nine years in Weimar. Here he was recognized as one of the better organists of his day, and these were the years in which he composed most of his works for organ.

The second period, his main instrumental phase, came while he was in Cothen from 1717 to 1723 as Kapellmeister to Prince Leopold. Here he wrote twelve masterworks for violin—six sonatas for violin and piano, three sonatas for unaccompanied violin, and three partitas for unaccompanied violin. The Chaconne from Partita No. 2 in D Minor is regarded by many as the most majestic piece of violin music of all time. This also was the period of the *Brandenburg* Concertos, his orchestral suites, and some of his best-known keyboard works.

During his last period, in Leipzig from 1723 to 1750, he wrote most of his magnificent sacred choral music: motets, cantatas, passions, oratorios, and the Mass in B Minor. And here he died, his eyesight gone—but not his vision.

One way for Bach neophytes to enjoy him is to listen to orchestral transcriptions of his works, especially those performed by the Philadelphia Orchestra under both Eugene Ormandy and Leopold Stokowski. These include several choral preludes; selections from the St. John and St. Matthew Passions; the Fantasia and Fugue in G Minor (S. 542); the "Little" Fugue in G Minor (S. 578); "Jesu, Joy of Man's Desiring" from the cantata Herz and Mund; "Komm Susser Tod"; the Passacaglia and Fugue in C Minor (S. 582); the Prelude in B Minor from The Well-Tempered Clavier; the Prelude and Fugue in E-flat (S. 552); the Prelude and Fugue in F Minor (S. 534); the Prelude from Partita No. 6 in E Minor (S. 830); the Toccata and Fugue in C (S. 564); and the Toccata and Fugue in D Minor (S. 565). While some purists are horrified by the practice of transcribing Bach, the Philadelphia Orchestra thought it was a good idea, and so have many audiences.

My advice is to take him any way you can. "If you should be one of those who consider him the greatest composer of them all," wrote one critic, "you would find yourself in very good company indeed."

THE BACH PRODUCTION

It is not easy to sort out the total Bach musical production without a scorecard. The forms of music are unfamiliar to twentieth-century audiences, and the prolific composer wrote orchestral, chamber, keyboard, and vocal music over a period of many years.

Help comes from a gentleman named Wolfgang Schmieder, who made up a catalogue of Bach works, divided into categories and then numbered continuously from 1 to 1080. The letter S, standing for Schmieder, is used with each number for each work. (Schmieder called his catalogue the Bach-Werke-Verzeichnis, and in some instances the designation BWV is still used instead of the S.)

VOCAL WORKS
Cantatas   —More than two hundred
Motets (six)   —S. 225–230
Masses   —Mass in B Minor; some short masses; a
                  magnificat

Passions and Oratorios	—St. Matthew Passion, St. John Passion, Christmas Oratorio, Easter Oratorio
Arias, Duets, etc.	—Including sixty-nine sacred songs published by Schemelli and songs from Bach's Notebook for Anna Magdalena, his second wife

KEYBOARD WORKS

1. Organ

Sonatas (six)	—S. 525–530
Preludes and Fugues	—S. 531–552. In several cases these might be identified as "Prelude (or Fantasy) and Fugue" or "Prelude (or Toccata) and Fugue"
Little Preludes and Fugues	—S. 553–560
Fantasies, Toccatas, and Fugues; Fugues; Passacaglia and Fugue; the Little Organ Book; chorales; and other miscellaneous organ works	—S. 562–689

2. Clavier (chiefly harpsichord)

Two-Part Inventions	—S. 772–786
English Suites (six)	—S. 806–811
French Suites (six)	—S. 812–817
Partitas (six)	—S. 825–830
The Well-Tempered Clavier	—S. 846–893
Fugues, Fantasies, Toccatas, and other clavier music	—S. 903–922
Concertos (six) after Vivaldi	—S. 972–973; S. 975–976; S. 978; S. 980
Goldberg Variations (aria with thirty variations)	—S. 988

CHAMBER AND ORCHESTRAL WORKS

1. Lute Works

Two Suites, and a Prelude
and Fugue —S. 995–996; S. 998

2. Chamber Music

Sonatas and Partitas for
Unaccompanied Violin —S. 1001–1006

Suites for Unaccompanied Cello —S. 1007–1012

Sonatas for Violin and Clavier —S. 1014–1019

Other Sonatas for Violin
(or Flute) and Clavier —S. 1020–1023

Sonatas for Viola da Gamba and
Clavier —S. 1027–1029

Sonatas for Flute and Clavier —S. 1030–1035

Other Sonatas for Violins,
Flutes, etc. —S. 1036–1038

3. Concertos

Concerto for Violin and Strings;
for Two Violins and Strings;
for Clavier, Violin, Flute,
and Strings —S. 1041–1044

Brandenburg Concertos —S. 1046–1051

Concertos
for Harpsichord and Strings —S. 1052–1057
for Two Harpsichords and
Strings —S. 1060–1062
for Three Harpsichords and
Strings —S. 1063–1064
for Four Harpsichords and
Strings —S. 1065

4. Suites for Orchestra —S. 1066–1069

Musical Offering —S. 1079

Art of the Fugue —S. 1080

STARTER KIT

In one sense, no task is easier than assembling a Bach starter kit: Reach
in and grab almost any five Bach compositions, and start from there.
But this is cheating, and selected for the Bach Starter Kit are five

world-acclaimed works: two orchestral pieces, one organ piece, and two vocal compositions.

The first orchestral piece is his Violin Concerto in D Minor, regarded as one of the best examples of counterpoint in music and one of Bach's most emotional pieces. Both movements are fugue-like, with each of the two violins doing its own thing as an independent voice.

The second orchestral piece is one of the six *Brandenburg* Concertos, written in 1721. (They were named for the Margrave of Brandenburg, who commissioned Bach to write them for his own orchestra.) While all six can be heard on most classical-music radio stations in the course of a week, the most popular is Concerto No. 2 in F (S. 1047), written for solo flute, oboe, trumpet, violin, and string orchestra.

The organ selection is relatively easy. While Bach wrote a dozen world-famous organ works, and many more are often performed, the best known is the Toccata and Fugue in D Minor (S. 565). German organ music is viewed by some experts as Germany's first *real* contribution to the growth of music, and this powerful work is a prime example.

No thought can be given to excluding the Mass in B Minor. Conductor Leopold Stokowski wrote of it:

> While it is cast in a form similar to the great Masses preceding Bach, this form is greatly enlarged and extended. . . . It has cosmic vastness of expression and consciousness. . . . The parts, which are in reality prayers, such as the beginning of the first "Kyrie," have the intensity and simple directness that probably is always one of the chief elements in prayer. . . . In many places, such as the great choruses of the "Gloria in excelcis Deo," the "Credo," the "Sanctus," the "Hosanna," there is a blazing jubilation like radiant sunlight. It is as if all nature, man, the planets, the whole universe were singing together.

The Mass in B Minor, concluded Stokowski, could only have come from the spirit of a man who was moved to the uttermost of his being. That's the kind of language people use about Bach.

Finally, representing all the two-hundred-plus cantatas, the recommended choice is No. 140, *Wachet Auf,* one of his most eloquent and one of the most performed.

Listen to these five—limiting the first hearing of the Mass in B Minor to selected parts and trying both the organ version and an orchestral transcription of the Toccata and Fugue in D Minor—and you will find Johann Sebastian Bach not as formidable or as "untune-ful" as you might have thought him, and certainly not an incomprehensible "technical genius." It is impossible to read Shakespeare—the best of Shakespeare, not the four or five weakest plays—and not (1) recognize his genius, and (2) enjoy the plays. Not by trying to read one in a night, but rather reading it in a week, following footnotes the first time or two, catching up with the language, then reading for pleasure. Similarly, it is impossible not to enjoy Mr. Bach if you start slowly and are willing to devote a little effort at first. The wonderful thing, you will find, is that it will not make any difference what mood you are in. He will fit the mood, however he does it.

BACH: THE STARTER KIT

Composition	Recordings Available*
ORCHESTRAL WORKS:	
Concerto in D Minor for Two Violins [S. 1043]	31
Brandenburg Concerto No. 2 [S. 1047]	20
KEYBOARD WORKS:	
Organ:	
Toccata and Fugue in D Minor [S. 565]	61
VOCAL MUSIC:	
Cantata:	
No. 140, Wachet Auf	C
Mass:	
Mass in B Minor [S. 232]	26

*Represents the number of recorded releases available of each listed composition as found in a recent issue of the Schwann/Opus catalogue. A "C" indicates that a work is only available collected with other compositions.

BACH: A TOP TEN

Composition	Recordings Available*
ORCHESTRAL WORKS:	
Concerto in D Minor for Two Violins [S. 1043]	31
Brandenburg Concerto No. 2 (of six) [S. 1047]	20

Composition	Recordings Available*
Harpsichord Concerto No. 1 in D Minor [S. 1052]	19
Musical Offering [S. 1079]	15
Art of the Fugue [S. 1080]	16

KEYBOARD WORKS:
Organ:
    Toccata and Fugue in D Minor [S. 565]   61
Harpsichord:
    Goldberg Variations [S. 988]   23

VOCAL MUSIC:
Cantata:
    No. 140, Wachet Auf   C
Mass:
    Mass in B Minor [S. 232]   26
Passion:
    St. Matthew Passion [S. 244]   21

BACH: A MASTER COLLECTION

Composition	Recordings Available*

ORCHESTRAL WORKS:

Violin Concerto in A Minor [S. 1041]	22
Violin Concerto in E [S. 1042]	22
Concerto in D Minor for Two Violins [S. 1043]	31
Brandenburg Concerto No. 2 [S. 1047]	20
Harpsichord Concerto No. 1 in D Minor [S. 1052]	19
Concerto for Four Harpsichords in A Minor [S. 1065]	20
Orchestral Suite No. 2 in B Minor [S. 1067]	31
Orchestral Suite No. 3 in D (including Air for the G String) [S. 1068]	18
Musical Offering [S. 1079]	15
Art of the Fugue [S. 1080]	16

CHAMBER MUSIC:

Partita (for violin) No. 2 in D Minor (including the famous Chaconne) [S. 1004]	22

Composition	Recordings Available*
Sonata No. 3 in C (containing one of Bach's most powerful fugues) [S. 1005]	16

KEYBOARD WORKS:

Organ:

Prelude and Fugue in C [S. 531]	39
Prelude and Fugue in D [S. 532]	39
Prelude (or Fantasy) and Fugue in G Minor (The Great G Minor) [S. 542]	15
Toccata and Fugue in D Minor [S. 565]	61
Passacaglia and Fugue in C Minor [S. 582]	33

Harpsichord:

English Suite No. 3 (of six) [S. 808]	11
One of six French Suites [S. 812–817]	18
The Well-Tempered Clavier [S. 846–893]	25
Goldberg Variations [S. 988]	23

VOCAL MUSIC:

Cantata:

No. 140, Wachet Auf	C

Motet:

Jesu Meine Freude [S. 227]	9

Mass:

Mass in B Minor [S. 232]	26

Passion:

St. Matthew Passion [S. 244]	21

A BACH LIBRARY

Because Bach is the Number One Immortal, and because the names of the forms of music in his day are unfamiliar to many new listeners, an outline of most of his works follows. It is built on the listings by Wolfgang Schmieder, who catalogued Bach by categories and then numbered the compositions continuously. The works are not in chronological order.

Schmieder used the categories vocal works; keyboard works, including organ and clavier (we use harpsichord); and chamber/orchestral works. We have rearranged the order to be consistent with the rest of the book.

Composition	Recordings Available*

SYMPHONIES:
None

OTHER ORCHESTRAL WORKS:

Violin Concertos:	
In A Minor [S. 1041]	22
In E [S. 1042]	22
In D Minor (for Two Violins) [S. 1043]	31
Brandenburg Concertos:	
No. 1 [S. 1046]	20
No. 2 [S. 1047]	20
No. 3 [S. 1048]	17
No. 4 [S. 1049]	20
No. 5 [S. 1050]	21
No. 6 [S. 1051]	18
Concertos for Harpsichord and Strings, including: [S. 1052–1065]	
No. 1 in D Minor [S. 1052]	19
No. 2 in E [S. 1053]	5
No. 3 in D [S. 1054]	4
No. 4 in A [S. 1055]	7
No. 5 in F Minor [S. 1056]	11
No. 6 in F [S. 1057]	4
Concertos for Two Harpsichords and Strings:	
No. 1 in C Minor [S. 1060]	6
No. 2 in C [S. 1061]	6
No. 3 in C Minor [S. 1062]	3
Concertos for Three Harpsichords and Strings:	
No. 1 in D Minor [S. 1063]	20
No. 2 in C [S. 1064]	20
Concerto in A Minor for Four Harpsichords and Strings [S. 1065]	20
Orchestral Suites [S. 1066–1069]	
No. 1 in D [S. 1066]	16
No. 2 in B Minor [S. 1067]	31
No. 3 in D [S. 1068]	18
No. 4 in D [S. 1069]	17
Musical Offering [S. 1079]	15
Art of the Fugue [S. 1080]	16

Composition   *Recordings Available**

CHAMBER MUSIC:
Sonatas and Partitas for Solo Violin
  [S. 1001–1006]
    Sonata No. 1 in G Minor [S. 1001]   17
    Sonata No. 2 in A Minor [S. 1003]   22
    Partita No. 2 in D Minor [S. 1004]   22
    Sonata No. 3 in C [S. 1005]   16
    Partita No. 3 in E [S. 1006]   18
Suites for Solo Cello, including: [S. 1007–1012]   20
    No. 2 in D Minor [S. 1008]   20
    No. 3 in C [S. 1009]   20
    No. 4 in E-flat [S. 1010]   20
    No. 5 in C Minor [S. 1011]   20
    No. 6 in D [S. 1012]   20
Sonatas for Violin and Harpsichord, including:
  [S. 1014–1019]
    No. 3 in E [S. 1016]   11
    No. 5 in F Minor [S. 1018]   11
    No. 6 in G [S. 1019]   11
Other Sonatas for Violin (or Flute) and
  Harpsichord [S. 1020–1023]
    In G Minor for Violin and Harpsichord [S. 1020] 18
    In G [S. 1021]   18
    In G Minor [S. 1023]   18
Sonatas for Viola and Harpsichord, including:
  [S. 1027–1029]
    No. 1 in G [S. 1027]   14
    No. 2 in D [S. 1028]   14
Sonatas for Flute and Harpsichord [S. 1030–1035;   26
  S. 1031; S. 1033]
Trio in D Minor for Flute, Oboe, and   3
  Harpsichord [S. 1036]
Sonata in C for Two Violins and Figured Bass   3
  [S. 1037]
Sonata in G for Flute, Violin, and Harpsichord   3
  [S. 1038]

KEYBOARD WORKS:
Organ:
Sonatas [S. 525–530]   C

Composition	Recordings Available*
Preludes (or Toccatas) and Fugues [S. 531–582]	C
Prelude and Fugue in C [S. 531]	39
Prelude and Fugue in D [S. 532]	39
Prelude and Fugue in E Minor [S. 533] (Little E Minor)	39
Prelude and Fugue in F Minor [S. 534]	C
Prelude and Fugue in G Minor [S. 535]	C
Prelude and Fugue in A [S. 536]	C
Prelude and Fugue in C Minor [S. 537]	C
Prelude (or Toccata) and Fugue (Dorian) [S. 538]	14
Prelude and Fugue in D Minor [S. 539]	C
Prelude (or Toccata) and Fugue in F [S. 540]	C
Prelude and Fugue in G [S. 541]	C
Prelude (or Fantasy) and Fugue in G Minor (Great G Minor) [S. 542]	15
Prelude and Fugue in A Minor [S. 543]	C
Prelude and Fugue in B Minor [S. 544]	C
Prelude and Fugue in C [S. 545]	C
Prelude and Fugue in C Minor [S. 546]	C
Prelude and Fugue in C [S. 547]	C
Prelude and Fugue in F Minor [S. 548]	C
Prelude and Fugue in G [S. 550]	C
Prelude and Fugue in A Minor [S. 551]	C
Prelude and Fugue in E-flat (St. Anne) [S. 552]	7
Little Preludes and Fugues [S. 553–560]	C
Fantasy in C Minor [S. 562]	C
Toccata, Allegro, and Fugue in C [S. 564]	C
Toccata and Fugue in D Minor [S. 565]	61
Fantasy in G [S. 572]	C
Fugue in G Minor (Little G Minor) [S. 578]	C
Passacaglia and Fugue in C Minor [S. 582]	33
Also:	
The Little Organ Book, forty-five chorale melodies [S. 599–644]	C
Other Chorales [S. 645–689]	C
Harpsichord:	
Two-part Inventions (miniworks) [S. 772–786]	11
English Suites (six) [S. 806–811]	11
French Suites (six), including: [S. 812–817]	18
No. 2 in C Minor [S. 813]	18

Composition	*Recordings Available**
No. 3 in B Minor [S. 814]	18
No. 4 in E-flat [S. 815]	18
No. 5 in G [S. 816]	18
No. 6 in E [S. 817]	18

Partitas [S. 825–830]

No. 1 in B-flat [S. 825]	29
No. 2 in C Minor [S. 826]	19
No. 3 in A Minor [S. 827]	13
No. 4 in D [S. 828]	17
No. 5 in G [S. 829]	22
No. 6 in E Minor [S. 830]	17

The Well-Tempered Clavier [S. 846–893]   25
Forty-eight preludes and fugues, two each
in all the major and minor keys

Other Fantasies, Fugues and Toccatas,
including: [S. 894–944]

Chromatic Fantasy and Fugue in D Minor   13
[S. 903]

Italian Concerto in F [S. 971]   22

Goldberg Variations (aria with thirty variations)   23
[S. 988]

VOCAL MUSIC:

The Cantatas (more than two hundred), including: C
No. 4, Christ lag in Todesbanden
No. 51, Jauchzet Gott in allen Landen
No. 56, Ich will den Kreuzstab geme tragen
No. 70, Wachet, betet
No. 78, Jesu, der du meine Seele
No. 80, Ein feste Burg ist unser Gott
No. 104, Du Hirte Israel, hore
No. 105, Herr, gehe nicht ins Gericht
No. 140, Wachet Auf
No. 161, Komm, du Suesse Todestunde
No. 202, Weichet nur, Betruebte Schatten
    (Wedding Cantata)
No. 208, Was mir behagt (from it: "Sheep
    May Safely Graze")
No. 211, Coffee Cantata
No. 212, Peasant Cantata

Composition	Recordings Available*
Six Motets, including: [S. 225–230]	
Singet dem Herren Ein Neues Lied [S. 225]	9
Jesu Meine Freude [S. 227]	9
Komm, Jesu, Komm [S. 229]	9
Masses and Magnificat	
Mass in B Minor [S. 232]	26
Four Short Masses	
Missa Brevis No. 1 [S. 233]	2
Missa Brevis No. 2 [S. 234]	2
Missa Brevis No. 3 [S. 235]	2
Missa Brevis No. 4 [S. 236]	2
Magnificat [S. 243]	13
Passions and Oratorios	10
St. Matthew Passion [S. 244]	21
St. John Passion [S. 245]	19
Christmas Oratorio [S. 248]	16
Easter Oratorio [S. 249]	2

WOLFGANG AMADEUS MOZART (1756–1791)

Number 2

Wolfgang Amadeus Mozart is acknowledged as the greatest natural genius of music. The open issue is whether he is the greatest natural genius of all art.

Schumann wrote: "There are things in the world about which nothing can be said, as Mozart's C Major Symphony (No. 41), much of Shakespeare and pages of Beethoven."

Tchaikovsky called him the music Christ.

Don Giovanni is viewed by many connoisseurs as the most perfect opera ever written—while supporters of *The Magic Flute* claim that one is even better.

Haydn described him as the best composer of whom he had knowledge.

Prepare yourself for another round of superlatives:

• Of forty-one symphonies, Mozart's final three are among the top fifteen or twenty greatest symphonic works, and several others, including Nos. 35, 36, and 38, are ranked only a quarter-step behind. Scores of writers put No. 41 with something from Beethoven and something from Brahms in their "top five."

• While he did not invent the piano concerto, he wrote twenty-seven of them, many of which are considered not only among his own best instrumental works but generally unsurpassed (Beethoven challenges) in the piano concerto field. Acknowledged masterpieces include Nos. 14 (K. 449), 15 (K. 450), 17 (K. 453), 19 (K. 459), 20 (K. 466), 21 (K. 467), 23 (K. 488), 24 (K. 491), and 25 (K. 503). (The "K" numbers attached to Mozart's work come from Ludwig von Köchel, who in the 1860s attempted to pull together the composer's production of more than six hundred compositions—few of which actually were published while he was alive, and none of which had opus numbers. Köchel tried to list them in the order in which they were composed.)

• Of more than thirty string quartets, six, dedicated to his friend and admirer Haydn—Nos. 14 (K. 387), 15 (K. 421), 16 (K. 428), 17 (K. 458, *Hunting*), 18 (K. 464), and 19 (K. 465, *Dissonant*)—have been described by critics as sheer beauty and serenity, a supreme contribution to chamber-music literature. These six are generally considered to be Mozart's best—except by those experts who regard No. 21 (K. 575) as being even better. The professionals note a difference in Mozart's quartets as the composer grew older. They say that in the six "Haydn" quartets he built in a daringly experimental fashion upon the foundation created by Haydn—from which Haydn, the older master, then himself learned. Another three, written for the King of Prussia a few years later, including No. 21, are considered less innovative but more graceful and mature. This is all subjective, but the bottom line is evident: Mozart's string quartets, like all of his music, were superb, even if a shade less so than those of Beethoven, Brahms, and Haydn.

• In quintets, Mozart is arguably Number One. The most famous are his Quintet in A for Clarinet and Strings (K. 581), composed in 1789, and two string quintets for two violins, two violas, and cello: a masterpiece in G Minor (K. 516) and a close second in C (K. 515).

THE ASSESSMENTS: NOW AND THEN

The professionals today say that something luminous hovers about the music of Mozart. "For one moment in the history of music," one summarizes, "all opposites were reconciled; all tensions resolved; that luminous moment was Mozart."

Half a century ago, the music gurus wrote that there are things in Beethoven, in Brahms, and in Wagner that some might wish had been written differently, but not in Mozart. "No melody strikes us as too short or too long," one said. "No instrumentation over-refined or overladen; no development too complex or too slight. Everything is in perfect proportion to everything else—everything is just as it should be. . . . For Mozart, besides having genius, had talent; he is one of the few composers in the world who had both, and that one reason is why he is unique."

A quarter of a century before that, Nobel Prize–winner Romain Rolland gave this assessment:

Thus [his] music is a painting of life, but of a refined sort of life. And melodies, though they are the reflection of spirit, must charm the spirit without wounding the flesh or offending the ear. So, according to Mozart, music is the *harmonious* expression of life. This is true not only of Mozart's operas but of all of his work. His music, whatever it may seem to do, is addressed not to the intellect but to the heart, and always expressed feeling or passion. But no unpleasant or offensive passion.

Franz Joseph Haydn, a Demigod composer himself, said to Mozart senior: "Before God, and as an honest man I tell you that your son is the greatest composer known to me, either in person or by name. He has taste and, what is more, the most profound knowledge of composition."

The giant Goethe summed him up: "A phenomenon like Mozart is an inexplicable thing."

• His own favorite instrument was the piano, either in solo or with one or two stringed instruments. The most acclaimed of his solo compositions is the Fantasia in C Minor (K. 475), usually performed with Sonata No. 14 (K. 457). Some believe that this sonata, given its fire and passion, surpassed all others previously composed, foreshadowing the monumental Beethoven sonatas that were to come. (If Mozart is the acknowledged piano concerto king, Beethoven, building on the past, is the master of masters of the piano sonata.) Mozart's Piano Sonata in F for Four Hands (K. 497) is a popular favorite.

• In addition to the unmatched piano concertos, famous Mozart concertos for other instruments include:

  ◦ Violin Concertos No. 3 in G (K. 216), No. 4 in D (K. 218), and No. 5 in A (K. 219);

  ◦ Concerto in B-flat for Bassoon and Orchestra (K. 191);

  ◦ Concertos No. 1 in G (K. 313) and No. 2 in D (K. 314) for Flute and Orchestra;

  ◦ Concerto in C for Flute, Harp, and Orchestra (K. 299);

  ◦ Sinfonia Concertante in E-flat for Violin, Viola, and Orchestra (K. 364).

• Although his forty-two sonatas for violin and piano are not considered his finest compositions, the more mature ones—from No. 20 on—are especially lovely and melodic. Among favorites are an emotional one in E Minor (K. 304), one in D (K. 306), and a tragic-sounding one in B-flat (K. 378).

It is not really possible to dislike Mozart's music. The critics use all the superlatives: he taught the instruments to sing; he had angelic purity; he showed perfection of form. If two words are used more than all others, they are *balance* and *perfection*.

Mozart simply provides more charm, more grace, more of a Fred Astaire touch than any other composer, along with wonderful, singable, seemingly unsophisticated melodies. The experts appreciate Bach even more than Bach-loving amateurs do, but Mozart's appeal is universal.

In his own day his natural genius was recognized, and even his early music was considered charming, graceful, fresh, bright, and free. But some contemporaries believed his compositions lacked the depth needed to be truly great. Unlike Beethoven, who came a little later, Mozart did not overpower. And, indeed, overpowering was not his goal, even when his music was expressing immense sorrow, as in the *Requiem*, or grandeur, as in *The Magic Flute*. Mozart made this clear in his own words. "Passions," he said, "whether violent or not, should never be expressed when they reach an unpleasant stage; and music, even in the most terrible situations, should never offend the ear, but should charm it, and always remain music."

While he produced masterful symphonies, piano concertos, sonatas, and chamber music, Mozart's true love was opera. "Opera to me," he wrote in 1782, "comes before everything else." He composed either eighteen or twenty, depending on one's definition of "opera," with six today held to be among the greatest of the great. They are:

• *Idomeneo* (1781). An *opera seria* (serious opera), more formal than other Mozart operas, it was not as popular in its day as the others but was the first to be composed of those that remain famous today.

• *The Abduction from the Seraglio* (1782). This is a *singspiel*, a German form of comic opera that was popular in the eighteenth century. It was a definite success when first produced. Written in German, it helped pave the way for German national opera.

• *The Marriage of Figaro* (1786). Wagner said about it: "Here the dialogue becomes music and the music itself dialogue." This is melody, from start to finish.

• *Don Giovanni* (1787). A blend of comic and tragic (Mozart was the first to make comic opera much more than entertainment), it caused the experts to debate whether it was technically *opera buffa* (comic opera) or some middle species of *opera semi-seria* (half-serious opera). Some feel that no other opera contains such a range of emotions. It is reported that Rossini, after examining the score, said Mozart was "the only composer who had as much science as genius and as much genius as science" (a description some would apply to Bach).

• *Cosi fan tutte* (1790). An *opera buffa*, it is often nicknamed "Girls Will Be Girls." Much more farcical than *Figaro*, it has also been assessed as less humane.

• *The Magic Flute* (1791). This gigantic fantasy has been described by reviewers as something of beauty, nobility, and grandeur. George Bernard Shaw said that the music for the character Sarastro, a high priest, is the only music that could be put into the mouth of God. It was composed in the last year of Mozart's life.

When considering Mozart, the incredible volume of work produced in so few years must be recognized as well as the individual works of magnificence. He wrote at least forty-one symphonies, twenty-six string quartets, ten instrumental quintets, seventeen piano sonatas, forty-two violin sonatas, twenty-seven piano concertos, forty divertimenti and serenades, nineteen masses, forty-two arias, and many, many songs. And he lived to be only thirty-five years old! One can only imagine what music might have come from a "mature" Mozart, a long-lived Mozart, a Mozart of fifty or sixty. The mind reels with the possibilities, as it is boggled by his far-ranging genius.

In 1788 alone, he wrote his three greatest symphonies, the famous orchestral serenade *Eine kleine Nachtmusik*, several string quartets, and the world-beating clarinet quintet (K. 581); in 1789 three of his finest string quartets, including No. 21 in D; in 1790 the opera *Cosi fan tutte*; and in 1791, his last year, *The Magic Flute*. He then died, apparently of a combination of overwork, kidney disease, and typhus.

THE FACT AND THE FICTION

There was, indeed, an Antonio Salieri in Mozart's life, an esteemed musician favored by Emperor Joseph far more than the young, spirited, playful Mozart. Moviegoers who enjoyed *Amadeus* were not wholly deceived. It is true that Mozart, near death, his mind wandering, believed that Salieri was trying to poison him, although no evidence against Salieri has ever been produced. And it is true that a black-clad stranger appeared at Mozart's door and commissioned him to write a requiem. But in fact the stranger was named Leutgeb, and he was a steward of Count von Wallsegg, who wanted to use Mozart's work as his own and who was not part of a Salieri-led plot to drive Mozart mad. Other stories about Mozart's death are true. He did die in pain while writing the unfinished *Requiem*, only a few people followed his coffin to a pauper's grave in a violent rainstorm, and the grave was unmarked.

If there were a King Arthur and he had a Camelot, the court composer writing for the Round Table, the composer selected to produce pure, clear, knightlike, perfect, natural, flawless music, could only be Wolfgang Amadeus Mozart.

How to condense the musical career of a Mozart? One analytical study divides his life and work into thirty-five different stylistic periods. For road-map purposes, three suffice:

Childhood and Youth (1756–74)
First Masterworks (1774–81)
Vienna (1781–91)

CHILDHOOD AND YOUTH

Mozart was born in Salzburg, then part of Bavaria, now in western Austria. Salzburg had an archbishop; it was a quasi-independent part of the Holy Roman Empire and a center of the arts. Mozart's father, Leopold, was a composer, a fine violinist in the archbishop's orchestra, a music teacher and theorist, and a Hollywood parent. Under his guidance Mozart began playing the piano at the age of four, was a skilled musician at six, and was subsequently propelled through Europe, visiting Vienna at six in 1762, Paris in 1763, London in 1764, and Italy in 1769 at the old age of thirteen. As a young child in Rome, he wrote out the entire score of a nine-voice religious work after hearing it twice. He played the piano brilliantly, he read concertos at sight, he improvised, and he composed from the age of six: his first symphony came at eight, his first oratorio at eleven, his first opera at twelve. At fourteen he conducted twenty performances of that opera. The Pope decorated him; Empress Maria Theresa took note of him. He heard Haydn's string quartets in 1773 and wrote his own first six that same year, at age seventeen.

Mozart is not the only gifted child of music, Felix Mendelssohn being chief among his child-prodigy rivals. But no one did so much, in so many ways, so early.

In 1771, at the age of fifteen, he entered the service of the archbishop in Salzburg in a minor capacity and kept that job for a decade, leaving it temporarily to travel.

The music people say that during these years Mozart began fusing German and Italian music as he created his own. Italian music aimed at entertainment and German at expression; on the whole, Italian music was light and German music serious. The Italians went for vocal music in the form of opera and the cantata; the Germans' bent was instrumental and their natural forms the symphony and the sonata. The natural Italian musical texture was homophony (single melody plus chords), the German polyphony (multivoiced melodies). Italians wanted to charm and please through melody, the Germans to display the science of counterpoint.

FIRST MASTERWORKS

While in Salzburg, Mozart worked for pennies as a court musician and composer in the archbishop's small orchestra, but the court was not particularly impressed by his compositions and, disgruntled, he looked unsuccessfully for better work in Munich. He then tried

Mannheim, with no luck, except that there he fell in love with Aloysia Weber; Paris, with no good musical luck, and also the bad romantic luck of losing Aloysia by long distance to another man; Augsburg, another zero; and back to Salzburg, where he became concertmaster, still at low pay. He ate with the servants; his nickname was "Lump"; and he married Aloysia's sister, Constanza—no great catch, although they were happy.

He described to his father the company he kept at the court dinner table: two valets, the controller, the confectioner, and two cooks. The valets sat at the head, but Mozart rated just above the cooks. (He does not say whether they were good, mediocre, or bad cooks.)

The masterwork phase began when he was still in his teens with two symphonies written in late 1773 and early 1774, No. 25 in G Minor (K. 183) and No. 29 in A (K. 201). During these years he also composed his first thirteen piano sonatas; a famed Flute Quartet in D (K. 285); a popular Oboe Quartet (K. 370); several of the sonatas for violin and piano, most notably the ones in E Minor (K. 304) and in D (K. 306), mentioned above; several divertimenti including No. 10 in F (K. 247) and No. 15 in B-flat (K. 287); a Septet in D (K. 251); several serenades including No. 6 in D (K. 239), No. 9 in D (K. 320), the *Posthorn*, and the most famous of all, the Serenade in G, *Eine kleine Nachtmusik* (K. 525); plus some of his best-known violin concertos including Nos. 3, 4, and 5 cited above; and the Piano Concerto No. 9 in E-flat (K. 271).

Of vocal music, early masterworks include the *Coronation* Mass in C (K. 317), and the Mass in C Minor (K. 427), which is acknowledged as the finest of all his masses. Some consider the C Minor to be in the same mighty class as Bach's Mass in B Minor—or at least as close as any other mass ever created. Finally came the last important composition before Vienna, probably the best of Mozart's serious operas, *Idomeneo*.

This is by no means everything Mozart produced during the pre-Vienna years, but only some of the acknowledged masterpieces. Another list just as long could be offered—and the composer was not yet twenty-five years old! Now, in the words of one biographer, he had left "precocious boyhood" behind him and was "on the threshold of manhood, conscious of enlarged powers and fired with more daring ambitions." Consider that assessment. At twenty-five, with countless masterworks behind him in virtually every form, the greatest natural genius of music was only "on the threshold of manhood." He hadn't begun his "mature" works!

While Mozart was in Salzburg, the archbishop did not permit him to give public concerts or to accept invitations to play at the homes of the local nobility, demanding that he remain on hand to produce special pieces of music at a moment's notice. Much against the wishes of his father, who preferred that his son have a certain—if extremely modest—salary from the archbishop rather than be unemployed and free, Mozart finally broke loose from what he called the *Lichtschirm* (a screen that shuts out sunlight and fresh air from a growing plant) of the archbishop—in short, he quit. He was escorted out of Salzburg by a kick in the rump from Count Arco, the archbishop's steward, and headed for Vienna to try his luck under Emperor Joseph (son of Maria Theresa), whom he knew to be a music lover.

VIENNA

The Vienna years—only ten of them before he died at thirty-five—were disappointing ones, despite a fine beginning.

For a while Mozart enjoyed himself immensely, working as a "free lancer," running with a Bohemian crowd, performing as a pianist, highly regarded as a composer, popular with the public, and generally successful. But after four or five years his popularity fell off, as did his fortunes. In 1787 he achieved a mostly honorary appointment as chamber-music composer to the Emperor—a prestigious enough title, but the pay was only half that of his predecessor, Christoph Gluck.

A BUSY SCHEDULE

Composers in Mozart's time lacked an executive secretariat to make their lives easier. When one gave a concert, he was responsible for organizing it, selling tickets, composing the music, and performing. And he was expected to compose new music for each "academy," or concert. Mozart at one point wrote from Vienna:

These are the academies at which I have to play:
Thursday, Feb. 26th, at the Galitzins
Monday, March 1st, at Joh. Esterhazys
Thursday, March 4th, at the Galitzins
Friday, March 5th, at the Esterhazys
Monday, March 8th, idem.
Thursday, March 11th, at the Galitzins
Wednesday, March 17th, my first private concert.

The Mozart musical production from the Vienna years, however, was astonishing. His four great operas were created here; the last two piano quartets; a piano quintet; the last seven and finest of his symphonies; the last seventeen piano concertos; the clarinet concerto; and the string quintets, including the G Minor (K. 516), which some consider his single best piece of chamber music. His most important solo piano compositions—the Fantasia in C Minor (K. 475) and the Sonata in C Minor (K. 457)—came from this period. So did his great four-handed Sonata in F (K. 497). This also was the period of his finest masterpieces of chamber music, including the Violin Sonata in A (K. 526), the Piano Trios in B-flat (K. 502) and E (K. 542), the Piano Quartets in G Minor (K. 478) and E-flat Major (K. 493), the String Trio (K. 563), and the Clarinet Quintet the *Stadler* (K. 581). The six "Haydn" string quartets—K. 387, 421, 428, 458, 464, and 465—were also from the Vienna period. The list goes on and on. An incredible collection of music can be built from the works of this one composer from this one short period of time.

The speed of his composition is wholly unbelievable, even accepting his own explanation:

Though it be long, the work is complete and finished in my mind. I take out of the bag of my memory what has previously been collected into it. For this reason, the committing to paper is done quickly enough. For everything is already finished, and it rarely differed on paper from what it was in my imagination. At this work I can therefore allow myself to be disturbed. Whatever may be going on about me, I can write and even talk.

Aside from the compositions themselves, however, not much worked for him after the first few years in Vienna.

The music gurus tell us that Vienna never thought as much of Kapellmeister Mozart as Leipzig did of Kapellmeister Bach. While Bach, as a Kapellmeister, was not the social equal of the good solid folk who tanned hides or slaughtered pigs, he was nonetheless respectable. He probably paid his taxes and certainly he went to church regularly. Life was pleasant enough, reasonably tolerable. Clearly he spent a lot of time making children, and that was also respectable. But Mozart was considered more of a servant, a talented fellow who provided amusement for the jet set. If *contempt* is too strong a word to describe the attitude of the Viennese toward Mozart, it is not far off. Someone has written that he got no respect from those he served and was too Bohemian for the respectable citizens he did not serve. While living on the shoulder of the fast lane, he was miserably poor and apparently never paid his taxes, and evidence is lacking that he was a regular churchgoer. He wrote for the theater, scarcely a noble thing to do in those days, and he was not at all a self-assertive fellow like such egotists as Handel, Beethoven, and Wagner—three self-acclaimed geniuses who considered other humans to be lesser creatures.

It is time to set forth one of the few mandatory rules for readers of this road map. While some professionals argue that Beethoven and Haydn may be Mozart's equals in symphonies and at least his peers in string quartets, and while Beethoven is his acknowledged superior in sonatas, in the field of piano concertos, for sheer listening pleasure, Mozart is incomparable. It is not permitted to refuse yourself the joy of Mozart piano concertos before leaving this earthly realm.

STARTER KIT

With Mozart as with Bach, the notion of a Starter Kit limited to five pieces appears not only ridiculous but obscene. But there is a legitimate dissenting view: In these cases, without a selected five where could a neophyte begin?

Two of the three famous last symphonies (all three composed, incredibly, in six weeks) have been chosen, No. 40 (K. 550) and No. 41, *Jupiter* (K. 551); one piano concerto, No. 21 (K. 467); one of his lighter pieces, the famous serenade for strings (K. 525) called *Eine kleine Nachtmusik;* and, inescapably, the *Magic Flute* opera.

From that point on one should move rapidly to collect more symphonies, another half-dozen piano concertos, some piano sonatas, the clarinet quintet, a couple of string quartets, the unfinished *Requiem*, selections from *Don Giovanni*, a violin sonata—and anything else by Mozart that can be bought, taped, or borrowed.

MOZART: THE STARTER KIT

Composition	Recordings Available*
SYMPHONIES:	
No. 40 in G Minor [K. 550]	38
No. 41 in C (Jupiter) [K. 551]	39
OTHER ORCHESTRAL WORKS:	
Piano Concerto No. 21 in C [K. 467]	29
Serenade for Strings in G (Eine kleine Nachtmusik)	39
(chamber music and orchestrated) [K. 525]	

Composition	Recordings Available*

VOCAL MUSIC:
Opera:
   The Magic Flute [K. 620]   11

*Represents the number of recorded releases available of each listed composition as found in a recent issue of the *Schwann/Opus* catalogue. A "C" indicates that a work is only available collected with other compositions.

MOZART: A TOP TEN

Composition	Recordings Available*

SYMPHONIES:
No. 40 in G Minor [K. 550]   38
No. 41 in C (Jupiter) [K. 551]   39

OTHER ORCHESTRAL WORKS:
Piano Concerto No. 20 in D Minor [K. 466]   28
Piano Concerto No. 21 in C [K. 467]   29
Violin Concerto No. 5 in A [K. 219]   18
Serenade for Strings in G (Eine kleine Nachtmusik)   39
   (chamber music and orchestrated) [K. 525]

CHAMBER MUSIC:
Quintet in A for Clarinet and Strings [K. 581]   22
String Quartet No. 21 in D [K. 575]   8

VOCAL MUSIC:
Mass:
   Requiem (unfinished) [K. 626]   18
Opera:
   The Magic Flute [K. 620]   11

MOZART: A MASTER COLLECTION

Composition	Recordings Available*

SYMPHONIES:
No. 35 in D (Haffner) [K. 385]   22
No. 36 in C (Linz) [K. 425]   13

Composition	Recordings Available*
No. 38 in D (Prague) [K. 504]	17
No. 39 in E-flat [K. 543]	27
No. 40 in G Minor [K. 550]	38
No. 41 in C (Jupiter) [K. 551]	39

OTHER ORCHESTRAL WORKS:

Piano Concerto No. 20 in D Minor [K. 466]	28
Piano Concerto No. 21 in C [K. 467]	29
Violin Concerto No. 3 in G [K. 216]	18
Violin Concerto No. 5 in A [K. 219]	18
Clarinet Concerto in A [K. 622]	17
Serenade for Strings in G (Eine kleine Nachtmusik) (chamber music and orchestrated) [K. 525]	39

CHAMBER MUSIC:

Quintet in A for Clarinet and Strings [K. 581]	22
Quintet in E-flat for Horn and Strings [K. 407]	10
Quintet in E-flat for Piano and Winds [K. 452]	13
Quartets:	
No. 17 in B-flat (Hunting) [K. 458]	5
No. 21 in D [K. 575]	8

INSTRUMENTAL MUSIC:

Sonatas for Piano:	
No. 11 in A [K. 331]	11
Other Piano Music:	
Fantasia in C minor [K. 475]	12

VOCAL MUSIC:

Masses:	
Requiem (unfinished) [K. 626]	18
Mass in C (Coronation) [K. 317]	13
Mass in C Minor (The Great) [K. 427]	5
Operas:	
Don Giovanni [K. 527]	7
The Magic Flute [K. 620]	11
The Marriage of Figaro [K. 492]	7

A MOZART LIBRARY

Composition   *Recordings Available**

SYMPHONIES (OF FORTY-ONE):

No. 29 in A [K. 201]   11
No. 35 in D (Haffner) [K. 385]   22
No. 36 in C (Linz) [K. 425]   13
No. 38 in D (Prague) [K. 504]   17
No. 39 in E-flat [K. 543]   27
No. 40 in G Minor [K. 550]   38
No. 41 in C (Jupiter) [K. 551]   39

OTHER ORCHESTRAL WORKS:

Concertos for Piano (of twenty-seven)—piano plus orchestra of wood-winds, brass, percussion, and strings:

No. 9 in E-flat [K. 271]   12
No. 12 in A [K. 414]   13
No. 14 in E-flat [K. 449]   9
No. 15 in B-flat [K. 450]   7
No. 17 in G [K. 453]   12
No. 19 in F [K. 459]   11
No. 20 in D Minor [K. 466]   28
No. 21 in C [K. 467]   29
No. 22 in E-flat [K. 482]   9
No. 23 in A [K. 488]   21
No. 24 in C Minor [K. 491]   16
No. 25 in C [K. 503]   11
No. 26 in D (Coronation) [K. 537]   11
No. 27 in B-flat [K. 595]   12

Concerto No. 10 in E-flat for Two Pianos [K. 365]   10

Concertos for Violin and Orchestra (of seven):

No. 2 in D [K. 211]   8
No. 3 in G [K. 216]   18
No. 4 in D [K. 218]   10
No. 5 in A [K. 219]   18

Concerto in B-flat for Bassoon [K. 191]   11
Concerto in A for Clarinet [K. 622]   17
Concerto No. 1 in G for Flute [K. 313]   6
Concerto in C for Flute and Harp [K. 299]   15
Concerto in C for Oboe [K. 314]   8

Concertos (four) for Horn:

No. 1 in D [K. 412]   34
No. 2 in E-flat [K. 417]   34

Composition   *Recordings Available**

No. 3 in E-flat [K. 447]   36
No. 4 in E-flat [K. 495]   36
Andante in C for Flute and Orchestra [K. 315]   14
Divertimento in D [K. 136]   7
Serenade No. 6 in D (Serenata Notturna) [K. 239] 15
Serenade No. 9 in D (Posthorn) [K. 320]   8
Serenade for Strings in G (Eine kleine Nachtmusik) 39
  (chamber music and orchestrated) [K. 525]
Serenade No. 10 in E-flat for Thirteen Winds   10
  [K. 361]
Sinfonia Concertante in E-flat for Violin and Viola 19
  [K. 364]
Opera Overtures   42

CHAMBER MUSIC:
Adagio and Fugue in C Minor [K. 546]   7
Quintet in G Minor [K. 516]   4
Quintet in A for Clarinet and Strings [K. 581] 22
Quintet in E-flat for Horn and Strings [K. 407] 10
Quintet in E-flat for Piano and Winds [K. 452] 13
String Quartets (his last ten "mature" quartets):
  The six Haydn:
    No. 14 in G [K. 387]   4
    No. 15 in D Minor [K. 421]   5
    No. 16 in E [K. 428]   2
    No. 17 in B-flat (Hunting) [K. 458]   5
    No. 18 in A [K. 464]   3
    No. 19 in C (Dissonant) [K. 465]   5
  No. 20 in D (Hoffmeister) [K. 499]   1
  The Three Prussian:
    No. 21 in D [K. 575]   8
    No. 22 in B-flat [K. 589]   2
    No. 23 in F [K. 590]   3
Quartet in F for Oboe and Strings [K. 370]   18
Divertimento in E-flat for String Trio [K. 563] 3
Piano Trio in E [K. 542]   1

INSTRUMENTAL MUSIC:
Sonatas for Piano (of seventeen):
  No. 8 in A Minor [K. 310]   8
  No. 10 in C [K. 330]   8

Composition	Recordings Available*
No. 11 in A [K. 331]	11
No. 12 in F [K. 332]	5
No. 13 in B-flat [K. 333]	6
No. 14 in C Minor [K. 457]	4
No. 15 in C [K. 545]	8
Other Piano Music:	
Fantasia in C Minor [K. 475]	12
Fantasia in D Minor [K. 397]	12
Sonatas for Violin and Piano (forty-two)	58

VOCAL MUSIC:

Masses etc.:	
Exultate Jubilate [K. 165]	8
Mass in C (Coronation) [K. 317]	10
Mass in C Minor (The Great) [K. 427]	5
Missa Brevis in F [K. 192]	5
Requiem [K. 626]	18
Vesperae Solennes de Confessare in C [K. 339]	7
Operas:	
Abduction from the Seraglio [K. 384]	5
Cosi fan tutte [K. 588]	8
Don Giovanni [K. 527]	7
Idomeneo [K. 366]	3
The Magic Flute [K. 620]	11
The Marriage of Figaro [K. 462]	7
Motet:	
Ave Verum [K. 618]	5

LUDWIG VAN BEETHOVEN (1770–1827)

Number 3

This is Thor—the Thunderer, the Heaven-Stormer, the Prometheus of Music.

Bach is the perfecter of what had come before. Mozart is music's brightest single shining moment. Ludwig van Beethoven is Power, the strangler of fate, who bowed neither to any man nor to lesser gods. He proclaimed his own rules of life and of composition, and he left behind what has been called the mightiest body of music ever created by one composer.

Who, or what, was to dictate to *him* how he should pour his being into music? No one, and nothing, for any reason he could fathom. These were the times of the American and French revolutions, and no government-maker was more committed than Beethoven to the dignity and equality of the individual.

Passion, power, personal pride—and in all things, independence. "I don't want to know anything about your system of ethics," he once wrote. "Strength is the morality of the man who stands out from the rest, and it is mine."

A deathbed anecdote has become part of the Beethoven literature:

On March 26 the Viennese heavens were split with lightning and growled with thunder. It was almost as if the city were giving voice to grief. A peal of thunder rumbled in Beethoven's death room. Ever the rebel, Beethoven feebly raised a defiant fist toward the heavens. Then he fell back, and died.

It is the kind of story that should be true, and it is nobler to report than quotes from the composer's letters complaining of his diarrhea, or historians' speculation as to whether at one time he was suicidal because of his deafness.

His religion, the literature tells us, was freedom—the right of the creative ego to assert itself.

"With whom need I be afraid of measuring my strength?" he asked.

And again: "With men who do not believe in me . . . I cannot and will not associate."

Another well-known story concerns the two great German contemporaries Beethoven and Johann Wolfgang von Goethe. It is told in a letter from Elisabeth (Bettina) Brentano, a German author who knew both men well, and is said to have taken place on one of the walks the two men took together:

> There came towards them the whole court, the Empress [of Austria] and the dukes. Beethoven said: "Keep hold of my arm, they must make room for us, not we for them." Goethe was of a different opinion, and the situation became awkward for him; he let go of Beethoven's arm and took a stand at the side with his hat off, while Beethoven with folded arms walked right through the dukes and only tilted his hat slightly while the dukes stepped aside to make room for him, and all greeted him pleasantly; on the other side he stopped and waited for Goethe, who had permitted the company to pass by him where he stood with bowed head. "Well," Beethoven said, "I've waited for you because I honor and respect you as you deserve, but you did those yonder too much honor."

Romain Rolland, Nobel Prize–winner for literature, wrote in *Beethoven, the Creator* (1927):

> He is not the shepherd driving his flock before him; he is the bull marching at the head of his herd. . . . In painting his portrait, I paint that of his stock—our century, our dream, ourselves . . . Joy. Not the gross joy of the soul that gorges itself in its stable, but the joy of ordeal, of pain, of battle, of suffering overcome, of victory over one's self, the joy of destiny subdued, espoused. . . . And the great bull with its fierce eye, its head raised, its four hooves planted on the summit, at the edge of the abyss, whose roar is heard above the time . . .

BEETHOVEN, HOMER, AND MOSES

Georges Bizet on Titans: "Like you, I place Beethoven above the greatest, the most renowned. The symphony with chorus is for me the culmination of our art. Dante, Michelangelo, Shakespeare, Homer, Beethoven, Moses!—Neither Mozart, with his divine form, nor Weber, with his powerful, colossal originality, nor Meyerbeer, with his overwhelming dramatic genius, can, in my opinion, contend for the crown of the 'Titan,' the 'Prometheus' of music."

No composer was more committed to the struggle of mankind. Bach wrote for the Glory of God, Mozart because genius must out (and because he had to eat), Beethoven to impose his will on the world.

He was far from a perfect fellow. His disposition was absolutely horrible—in biographer language, there was a "want of much that passed for conventional good manners." Throughout his life he lied about his age. He mistrusted almost everyone in almost every relationship, professional and personal. As a pianist-composer, he deliberately put trills at the ends of compositions because of his "desire to embarrass those Viennese pianists, some of whom are my sworn enemies." He predicted that when the fellow pianists encountered his variations, "they would cut a sorry figure with them."

Sort of a cheap shot.

DEBUSSY ON MOZART VERSUS BEETHOVEN

"Genius can, of course, dispense with taste: of this Beethoven is an example. Mozart on the other hand, his equal in genius, has, in addition, the most delicate taste."

He was proud. The gold snuffbox given him by the King of Prussia was "such a one as might have been customary to give an ambassador."

In 1801, only thirty years old and knowing that he was going deaf, he wrote: "I must confess that I am living a miserable life." He wallowed in self-pity. And later: "You can scarcely believe what an empty, sad life I have had for the last two years."

But yet:

"I will seize Fate by the Throat; it shall certainly not crush me completely."

STRAVINSKY ON SEIZING DESTINY

"Beethoven is the friend and contemporary of the French Revolution, and he remained faithful to it even when, during the Jacobin dictatorship, humanitarians with weak nerves of the Schiller type turned from it, preferring to destroy tyrants on the theatrical stage with the help of cardboard swords. Beethoven, that plebeian genius, who proudly turned his back on emperors, princes and magnates—that is the Beethoven we love for his unassailable optimism, his virile sadness, for the inspired pathos of his struggle, and for his iron will which enabled him to seize destiny by the throat."

What did he produce?

Nine symphonies, of which five are among the dozen greatest in history; five heralded piano concertos; one violin concerto commonly acknowledged as music's best; sixteen string quartets, some of which are considered music's finest (Brahms and Haydn are the main challengers); thirty-two piano sonatas (another form he perfected); two masses, of which one stands at or near the level of Bach's Mass in B Minor; ten overtures; ten sonatas for violin and piano; five sonatas for cello and piano; much miscellaneous instrumental music; and one opera, an acknowledged masterpiece.

One approach divides Beethoven's lifework into three periods: Imitation (1792–1803), Externalization (1803–1817), and Reflection (1817–1827). The more commonly used designations are early, middle, and late, or youthful, middle, and final.

EARLY

From this period came his first twenty-one piano sonatas, two symphonies, eight violin sonatas, the famous six string quartets of Op. 18

(Nos. 1 through 6), and three of his five piano concertos. Among the piano sonatas were at least two ultrafamous ones: No. 8 in C Minor (*Pathètique*) and No. 14 in C-sharp Minor (*Moonlight*—not his title, and not written for romance). During these years he built on the work of Bach, Haydn, and Mozart.

MIDDLE

This was the time when he grew deaf, first mildly and, gradually, totally. These were experimental, iconoclastic years, when Beethoven was breaking the established rules of composition in "length, intensity and originality." In 1804 came the *Eroica*, his Third Symphony, which the experts say shattered the ground rules of symphonic writing for all time. These also were the years of the three famous *Rasumovsky* string quartets of Op. 59, Nos. 7, 8, and 9; of the Fourth and Fifth Piano Concertos; of the magnificent violin concerto; and of Symphonies Nos. 4 through 8. During these years came several more famous piano sonatas, including No. 21 in C (*Waldstein*) and No. 23 in F Minor (*Appassionata*); his only opera, *Fidelio*; and his famous sonata for violin and piano, the *Kreutzer*, Op. 47.

LATE

This was the time of the far-out Beethoven, the time in which his compositions were said to "transcend all previous music, soaring to the loftiest planes the human imagination can reach." That's pretty lofty. In this period he wrote his two most massive works, the Ninth Symphony (the *Choral*) and the *Missa Solemnis*, and the last piano sonatas, including No. 29 in B-flat, the famous, emotional *Hammer-klavier*, which has been called "herculean" and "gargantuan." The last string quartets, Nos. 12 through 16, also date from these years. They are widely considered to be in the same profound class as the piano sonatas (some believe so profound as to be beyond understanding). Included among them is No. 14 in C-sharp Minor, which some critics regard as the greatest string quartet ever written, as the *Hammerklavier* is perhaps the greatest piano sonata, the Ninth the greatest symphony, and the *Missa Solemnis* one of the two or three greatest masses.

With all of this, why is not Beethoven Number One, rather than third after Bach and Mozart?

Perhaps he is.

The professionals agree that there is significant musical development between early Beethoven and final Beethoven—which, however, does not gainsay the value of the work of early Beethoven. Out of the changes in form and style, the music people say, and out of the independence and originality, came a personal expressiveness not previously heard in music—what one expert has called the "complete emancipation of human emotion and mind."

Beethoven's own favorite work was his only opera, *Fidelio*. Written in 1805 and based on a play called *Leonore*, it was extensively revised in 1814 and is regarded (not surprisingly, this being Beethoven) as more symphonic than vocal in character. He wrote four overtures for this opera, three known as the *Leonore* Overtures 1, 2, and 3 and the fourth as the *Fidelio* Overture. When the opera is performed today, the *Fidelio* Overture usually opens the work and the *Leonore* 3 is played between the two acts.

TCHAIKOVSKY ON MUSIC'S GOD AND CHRIST

"I bow before the greatness of his works—but I do not love Beethoven. My attitude toward him reminds me of what I experienced in childhood toward the God Jehovah. . . . And if Beethoven occupies a place in my heart analogous to the God Jehovah, then Mozart I love as the musical Christ. . . .

"I cannot discourse on music and shall not go into details. However, I shall mention that in Beethoven I love the middle period, at times the first, but I fundamentally detest the last, especially the last quartets. Here there are glimmers—nothing more. The rest is chaos, over which, surrounded by an impenetrable fog, hovers the spirit of this musical Jehovah."

In his fifty-six years, he wrote five piano concertos to Mozart's twenty-five; thirty-two piano sonatas to Mozart's seventeen; nine symphonies to Mozart's forty-one; one opera to Mozart's eighteen; one violin concerto to Mozart's seven; seventeen string quartets to Mozart's twenty-six.

Germany was not a nation when Beethoven was born, but a loose group of some 250 states, each with its own laws, taxes, army, and customs. The Holy Roman Empire still existed, with an emperor chosen by "electors" from the nine most important states: Austria, Prussia, Bavaria, Saxony, Brunswick-Lüneburg, Cologne, Mainz, Hanover, and Trier. The seat of the electorate of Cologne was in Bonn, where Beethoven was born and spent his early years. The composer's grandfather Ludwig (Louis) van Beethoven was a trained musician who, in 1733, became a bass in the electoral chapel in Bonn, and later was named Kapellmeister. His son, much less skilled, was a tenor and a mediocre piano and violin teacher married to the daughter of a cook at the electoral summer palace. Their second child, born in 1770, was another Louis, or Ludwig. He made it big.

Musical instruction began early for young Ludwig, forced harshly on him from age four by a tyrannical, alcoholic, sometimes violent father. The child's best instrument was the piano.

Before his twelfth birthday he had begun his first real lessons from the court organist. At twelve or thirteen (the date is uncertain) his teacher got him a job as cembalist (harpsichordist) in the court orchestra; at thirteen or fourteen he became assistant organist and received, for the first time, a yearly salary—150 florins, equivalent to about $1,000 today. He met Mozart on a quick trip to Vienna in 1787. The story is that Mozart was impressed by Beethoven's improvisatory skills and said, "Watch this young man; he will yet make a noise in the world." No one seems able to prove it, but no one can disprove it, either; it is a good story, and Mozart should have said it if he didn't. Beethoven returned to Bonn, played viola in a reorganized court orchestra, and went back to live in Vienna after his father's death in 1792.

A befriender of Beethoven in those Bonn years was Count Ferdinand von Waldstein, a talented musician and a good friend of the new elector, Maximilian Francis, Maria Theresa's youngest son and brother of Hapsburg Emperor Joseph II. Beethoven later dedicated to Waldstein what was to become one of his most famous piano sonatas, No. 21 in C, Op. 53.

The count wished him well as he left for Vienna: "Dear Beethoven, you are traveling to Vienna in fulfillment of your long-cherished wish. The genius of Mozart [who had died December 5, 1791] is still weeping and bewailing the death of her favorite. . . . Labor assiduously and receive Mozart's spirit from the hands of Haydn. Your true friend Waldstein."

Historians Will and Ariel Durant describe Beethoven's arrival in Vienna, where he was to live for the rest of his life, studying for a time under Haydn and then Salieri, when Mozart's least-favorite Italian came from Bonn:

Arrived in Vienna, he found the city alive with musicians competing for patrons, audiences and publishers, looking askance at every newcomer, and finding no disarming beauty in the youth from Bonn. He was short, stocky, dark-complexioned (Anton Esterhazy called him "The Moor"), pockmarked, front upper teeth overlapping the lower, nose broad and flat, eyes deepset and challenging, and head "like a bullet," wearing a wig and a "van." He was not designed for popularity, with either the public or his competitors, but he was rarely without rescuing a friend.

(There is not general agreement on that latter point.)

Beethoven didn't think much of his face either. "Oh God," he cried in 1819, "what a plague it is to one when he has so fatal a face as mine."

At this time in Vienna the old harpsichord and the new pianoforte were battling, and the pianoforte won. First one of Bach's sons, then Mozart, then Haydn turned to it. Beethoven became famous as a pianist in Vienna, giving concerts at the homes of musical patrons.

Basically, the Beethoven disposition was not a monumental improvement over the Beethoven appearance. Though an undisputed genius, he was perhaps the most disagreeable composer on the list— not the tenth-rate human being Wagner was, but thoroughly disagreeable nonetheless.

But this has never prevented the gridlock of superlatives about his spirit and his work.

The New Grove Dictionary of Music and Musicians says:

> Beethoven's heroism was seen in his force of character, his independence and libertarianism, his deafness and conspicuous suffering and failure to find a woman's love, and his manifest (as it seemed) ability to transform lonely adversity into a series of affirmative artistic visions.

The historian Durant:

> In February, 1824, he completed the Ninth Symphony. Here his struggle to express his final philosophy—the joyful acceptance of man's fate—broke through all the trammels of classic order, and the impetuous monarch let the pride of his power carry him to massive exultations that sacrificed the old god order to the young god liberty. In the profusion of shattered altars the themes that should have stood out as pillars to the edifice disappeared from all but esoteric view, the phrases seemed unduly insistent and repeated; an occasional moment

of tenderness or calm was overwhelmed by a sudden fortissimo flung as if in rage at a mad and unresponsive world. Not
so, a great scholar (D. F. Tovey) replies; there is, in this apparent embarrassment of riches, "an extreme simplicity of form,
underlying an elaboration of detail which may at first seem
bewildering until we realize that it is purely the working out,
to its logical conclusions, of some ideas as simple and natural
as the form itself."

You have to believe in the tooth fairy to accept the ending of one
music duel. By 1823 Rossini's operas had captured Vienna, as they had
the rest of Europe. To counter melodious Rossini, Beethoven supporters had only a long, serious *Missa Solemnis* and a long, rule-
destroying *Choral* Symphony to offer. Who would produce a concert
of these serious works when Rossini opera was the competition? An
offer came from Berlin, but the loyal Viennese rejected it, insisting that
the supreme works of their Master should be performed at home, not
in some distant Super Bowl. Instead, a Vienna concert was held on
May 7, 1824; on the program was an overture, four parts of the *Missa
Solemnis*, and the Ninth Symphony. At the end, the deaf composer
stood on the platform, his back to the audience, unaware of its reaction. Not until he turned did he see the hands clapping in enthusiastic
applause.

The public response to this concert (and to Beethoven's music in
general) was not unanimously positive, however. One Providence,
Rhode Island, critic wrote: "The general impression it left on me is
that of a concert made up of Indian warwhoops and angry wildcats."
And the English essayist John Ruskin has written: "Beethoven always
sounds to me like the upsetting of a bag of nails, with here and there
an also dropped hammer."

DEBUSSY ON THE SIXTH SYMPHONY

"It would be absurd to think that I am wanting in respect to
Beethoven, but a musician of his genius could err more blindly
than another. . . . No man is expected to write only masterpieces; and if the Pastoral Symphony is classed as such, the
term loses force when applied to his other works. That is all
I mean to say."

An earlier dissenter was Felix Mendelssohn's father, Abraham: "Your endless Beethoven," he said to his son, "is nothing but a bore and an imposter, and his compositions rank gibberish." But Abraham was a banker and so should be regarded with tolerance on sensitive matters.

Beethoven died on March 26, 1827, after three months of final suffering. Pneumonia was one diagnosed cause; a postmortem examination showed a good many other internal problems. Thirty thousand people came to his funeral. Schubert was a torchbearer. On his tombstone were the dates of his birth and death and one word: *Beethoven.*

Would Beethoven have been Beethoven without the deafness? Did the colossal struggle—the genius composer against total deafness—provide something that would not otherwise have been part of his music? One need not be a learned musicologist or psychologist to know that the torment must have had immeasurable impact. But how? In what direction? And with what results? This is not a new subject, of course, and volumes have been written for those interested.

STARTER KIT

For the musical Jehovah's Starter Kit, one approach is to suggest Symphonies Nos. 3, 5, 6, 7, and 9. And who could argue? To be more representative, however, I have chosen Symphony No. 5; the Piano Concerto No. 5 (*Emperor*); the Violin Concerto in D; the String Quartet No. 13 in B-flat, Op. 130; and the Piano Sonata No. 23 in F Minor (*Appassionata*).

One might then move very quickly to Symphonies Nos. 3, 6, 7, and 9; the *Hammerklavier* Sonata No. 29; the String Quartet No. 14, Op. 131; any other of the five piano concertos; and both the overture and excerpts from *Fidelio*. Or . . .

BEETHOVEN: THE STARTER KIT

Composition	Recordings Available*
SYMPHONIES:	
No. 5 in C Minor	38
OTHER ORCHESTRAL WORKS:	
Piano Concerto No. 5 in E-flat (Emperor)	44
Violin Concerto in D	36

Composition   Recordings Available*

CHAMBER MUSIC:
String Quartets:
   No. 13 in B-flat, Op. 130   8

SOLO INSTRUMENTAL MUSIC:
Piano Sonatas:
   No. 23 in F Minor (Appassionata)   43

*Represents the number of recorded releases available of each listed composi-
tion as found in a recent issue of the *Schwann/Opus* catalogue. A "C" indicates that a work is only available collected with other compositions.

BEETHOVEN: A TOP TEN

Composition   Recordings Available*

SYMPHONIES:
No. 3 in E-flat (Eroica)   29
No. 5 in C Minor   38
No. 7 in A   26
No. 9 in D Minor   42

OTHER ORCHESTRAL WORKS:
Piano Concerto No. 5 in E-flat (Emperor)   44
Violin Concerto in D   36

CHAMBER MUSIC:
String Quartet:
   No. 13 in B-flat, Op. 130   8

SOLO INSTRUMENTAL MUSIC:
Piano Sonatas:
   No. 14 in C-sharp Minor (Moonlight)   46
   No. 23 in F Minor (Appassionata)   43

VOCAL MUSIC:
Opera:
   Fidelio   3

BEETHOVEN: A MASTER COLLECTION

Composition	Recordings Available*
SYMPHONIES:	
No. 3 in E-flat (Eroica)	29
No. 5 in C Minor	38
No. 6 in F (Pastorale)	29
No. 7 in A	26
No. 8 in F	15
No. 9 in D Minor	42
OTHER ORCHESTRAL WORKS:	
Piano Concerto No. 4 in G	27
Piano Concerto No. 5 in E-flat (Emperor)	44
Violin Concerto in D	36
Leonore Overture 3	C
CHAMBER MUSIC:	
String Quartets:	
No. 13 in B-flat, Op. 130	8
No. 14 in C-sharp Minor, Op. 131	5
Great Fugue (written as last movement of No. 13)	22
Trio No. 6 in B-flat, Op. 97 (Archduke)	17
SOLO INSTRUMENTAL MUSIC:	
Piano Sonatas:	
No. 8 in C Minor (Pathétique)	38
No. 14 in C-sharp Minor (Moonlight)	46
No. 21 in C (Waldstein)	28
No. 23 in F Minor (Appassionata)	43
No. 26 in E-flat (Les Adieux)	17
No. 29 in B-flat (Hammerklavier)	17
No. 31 in A-flat	18
No. 32 in C Minor	19
Sonata No. 9 in A for Violin and Piano (Kreutzer)	14
VOCAL MUSIC:	
Opera:	
Fidelio	3
Mass:	
Missa Solemnis in D	4

A BEETHOVEN LIBRARY

Composition   *Recordings Available**

SYMPHONIES:

No. 1 in C	9
No. 2 in D	9
No. 3 in E-flat (Eroica)	29
No. 4 in B-flat	10
No. 5 in C Minor	38
No. 6 in F (Pastorale)	29
No. 7 in A	26
No. 8 in F	15
No. 9 in D Minor	42

OTHER ORCHESTRAL WORKS:

Piano Concerto No. 1 in C	15
Piano Concerto No. 2 in B-flat	18
Piano Concerto No. 3 in C Minor	17
Piano Concerto No. 4 in G	27
Piano Concerto No. 5 in E-flat (Emperor)	44
Violin Concerto in D	36
Romances for Violin and Orchestra (two)	13
Overtures:	
Egmont	C
Coriolan	C
Fidelio	C
Leonore 1	C
Leonore 2	C
Leonore 3	C

CHAMBER MUSIC:

Septet in E-flat for Strings and Winds	11
String Quartets:	
Op. 18 (six):	
No. 1 in F	3
No. 2 in G	3
No. 3 in D	3
No. 4 in C Minor	2
No. 5 in A	4
No. 6 in B-flat	4
Op. 59 (three) (Rasmovsky):	
No. 7 in F	3
No. 8 in E Minor	4

Composition	*Recordings Available**
No. 9 in C	5
No. 10 in E flat, Op. 74 (Harp)	4
No. 11 in F Minor, Op. 95 (Quartetto serioso)	3
No. 12 in E-flat, Op. 127	3
No. 13 in B-flat, Op. 130	8
No. 14 in C-sharp Minor, Op. 131	5
No. 15 in A Minor, Op. 132	5
No. 16 in F, Op. 135 (his last work)	3
Great Fugue (written as last movement of No. 13)	22
Trio No. 6 in B-flat, Op. 97 (Archduke)	17
Trio No. 7 for Violin, Cello, and Piano in B-flat, Op. 11	7

SOLO INSTRUMENTAL MUSIC:

Piano Sonatas:

No. 1 in F Minor	5
No. 2 in A	4
No. 3 in C	6
No. 4 in E-flat	3
No. 5 in C Minor	2
No. 6 in F	5
No. 7 in D	10
No. 8 in C Minor (Pathétique)	38
No. 9 in E	3
No. 10 in G	2
No. 11 in B-flat	3
No. 12 in A-flat (Funeral March)	3
No. 13 in E-flat	5
No. 14 in C-sharp Minor (Moonlight)	46
No. 15 in D (Pastorale)	8
No. 16 in G	2
No. 17 in D Minor (Tempest)	11
No. 18 in E-flat	7
No. 19 in G Minor	3
No. 20 in G	4
No. 21 in C (Waldstein)	28
No. 22 in F	3
No. 23 in F Minor (Appassionata)	43
No. 24 in F-sharp	8
No. 25 in G	7

Composition	Recordings Available*
No. 26 in E-flat (Les Adieux)	17
No. 27 in E Minor	9
No. 28 in A	10
No. 29 in B-flat (Hammerklavier)	17
No. 30 in E	12
No. 31 in A-flat	18
No. 32 in C Minor	19
Sonata for Horn and Piano	10
Sonatas for Violin and Piano (of ten):	
No. 5 in F, Op. 24 (Spring)	10
No. 9 in A, Op. 47 (Kreutzer)	13

VOCAL MUSIC:

Opera:	
Fidelio	3
Masses:	
Mass in C	2
Missa Solemnis in D	4
Choral Fantasy in C Minor for Piano, Chorus, and Orchestra	6

RICHARD WAGNER (1813–1883)

Number 4

Richard Wagner was a dreadful human being. He was a liar, a cheat, a wife-stealer, a home-wrecker, and a betrayer of friends. He was anti-Semitic, anti-Catholic, and anti-French. He was immoral and dishonorable. No one in music had a bigger ego, and he properly belongs high on a list of the World's Most Unpleasant Men.

He was also, of course, an incredible musical genius. It is impossible to like Wagner, but almost equally impossible to deny his genius. True, some operagoers become woefully weary watching Siegfried, Brunnhilde, and their relatives, friends, and foes stalk through the four *Ring* operas, but one need not attend any opera to hear the beautiful orchestral music that is part of the Wagner mastery.

And, experts almost unanimously agree, he had one vital redeeming feature: belief in himself and the music he would create, whatever the odds, obstacles, opinions, and objections.

Authors Milton Cross and David Ewen write:

> Here, at any rate, was the one religion which he could worship with honesty and humility, here was the one truth to which he could remain unswervingly faithful. He doubted if the "Ring" cycle (the four operas making up *The Ring of the Nibelungen*] to which he was giving so much of himself for so many years, would ever be performed in his time, because of the vastness of the scheme, the prodigious demands it made upon singers, musicians, and the stage, and finally the fabulous expense it would involve. But the belief that the supreme artistic effort of his life would not be performed did not deter him from bringing it into existence. . . . Where his art was concerned, he was incapable of opportunism or compromise.

Certainly he occupies a special place in opera with what he called his "music dramas." One legitimate question is whether Verdi "opera" equals in magnificence Wagner "music drama." A second is where Wagner and the Immortal Mozart rank among opera composers. Dedicated Wagnerites believe their man to be not only the greatest opera composer who has ever lived but also the greatest composer. He is Number One, the Elvis Presley, the Olivier, the Pelé, the King. Some true disciples who travel thousands of miles to Wagner festivals rank him not only first but also second and third among all composers, with such lesser artists as Bach, Mozart, and Beethoven to follow, respectfully in arrears, as numbers four, five, and six.

On one point there is no dissent: Wagner exerted enormous influence on the music world in the second half of the nineteenth century. Singlehandedly, the professionals say, Wagner changed the destiny of opera.

More essays, treatises, and books have been written about Wagner than about any other composer, and he, in turn, wrote more than almost any other musician—essays, books, poems, and librettos for his own operas. Among his books outlining his own point of view are *Art and Revolution*, the two-volume *Opera and Drama*, and *The Artwork of the Future*.

If the critical component of Romanticism is emotionalism, Wagner qualifies. If it is experimentation, he qualifies. If it is preoccupation with legends and mythology, he qualifies. If it is tone color, he qualifies.

Who else would write an opera that required four evenings to perform—four *long* evenings? And expect that the public would attend? And observe that the public *did* attend! And, in the end, see a great music center established in the city of Bayreuth to which Wagnerians flock to see the master's work performed in a fan-shaped theater built especially for it?

Other composers—including Mozart, who can scarcely be considered an opera specialist—wrote "operas." Wagner wrote "music dramas"—his own term. "Every bar of dramatic music," he said, "is justified only by the fact that it explains something in the action or in the character of the actor."

For those who admire melody, Wagner offers continuous melody in his operas. But—unlike traditional Italian opera, which is dominated by voice—in Wagner's music drama the orchestra dominates. The professionals tell us that this orchestral domination is the unifying principle of music drama. It is the orchestral music that recalls the past and predicts the future, and that rules over the action and the characters.

In midlife Wagner became involved with the revolutions that were bubbling in Europe in 1848. He fled his home in Dresden to visit Franz Liszt in Weimar and then moved on to safety in Zurich. By this time, at thirty-six, he had written his "Romantic" operas, but not the "music dramas."

One of the most famous Wagner biographers is Ernest Newman, who wrote that he was "packed with a vitality too superabundant for the moral sense always to control it, but always believing in himself with a faith that moves mountains, and finally achieving a roundness and completeness of life and a mastery of mankind that makes this record read more like a romance than reality."

Well, that's OK if he hasn't stolen your wife.

Wagner's Romantic operas include:

Rienzi, 1840

The Flying Dutchman, 1841

THREE VIEWS OF THE GENIUS EGOTIST

Music critic Harold C. Schonberg:

"Such was Wagner's ego it is not stretching a point to suggest that he secretly regarded himself as a god. He was sent to earth by mysterious forces. He gathered disciples unto himself. He wrote holy scriptures in word and music (the Sacred writings eventually to be gathered in ten large volumes of prose and twenty more of letters). He caused a temple at Bayreuth to be created, in which his works could be celebrated and He Himself worshiped. He cast out all those who did not agree with his divinity. But his egomania was supported by genius; and, after him, music was not the same."

Pulitzer Prize–winning composer Virgil Thomson:

"There is no sounder proof of Shakespeare's central position in English literature, or of Dante's in Italian, than the fact that nobody objects to it. Such a position in music is occupied, by common consent, by a triumvirate—Bach, Beethoven and Mozart. Wagner's pretensions to universal authority are inadmissible from the very fact that the music world is not unanimous about admitting them. Mozart is a great composer, a clear value to humanity, because no responsible musician denies that he is. But Wagner is not an absolute value from the very fact that Rossini denied it and Nietzsche denied it and Brahms denied it and, in our own time, Debussy and Stravinsky have denied it."

Pianist/conductor Bruno Walter, on hearing *Tristan and Isolde*:

"So there I sat in the topmost gallery of the Berlin Opera House, and from the first sound of the cellos my heart contracted spasmodically. . . . Never before had my soul been so deluged with floods of sound and passion, never had my heart been consumed by such yearning and sublime bliss, never had I been transported from reality by such heavenly glory. I was no longer in this world. . . . My ecstasy kept singing within me through half the night, and when I awoke on the following morning, I knew that my life was changed. A new epoch had begun: Wagner was my god, and I wanted to become his prophet."

Tannhäuser, 1845

Lohengrin, 1848 (probably his most popular)

Then came the music-dramas, beginning with:

The Ring of the Nibelungen, consisting of a prologue:

The Rhinegold, 1854

And the trilogy:

The Valkyrie, 1856

Siegfried, 1871

The Twilight of the Gods, 1874

His other music-dramas which were not part of the *Ring* cycle include:

Tristan and Isolde, 1859

The Mastersingers of Nuremberg, 1867

Parsifal, 1882

No operas exceed his music dramas in power and intensity. Wagner believed not only that serious drama could be presented in opera form but that the music could raise that drama to even greater heights—not only vocal music but orchestral music as well. One of twelve-year-old Wagner's favorites was Weber's opera *Der Freischütz*, and the music people say that from it he developed the "leitmotif" concept that helps make his music enjoyable for the amateur. This is the idea of having different main characters, important inanimate objects, or abstract principles represented by sets of notes or musical phrases called *leitmotifs* ("leading motives"). Wagner described them as "basic themes," which is a simpler way to think about them. Professor Joseph Machlis explains what they mean to a drama:

> They have an uncanny power of suggesting in a few strokes a person, an emotion, or an idea; an object—the gold, the ring, the sword; or a landscape—The Rhine, Valhalla, the lonely shore of Tristan's home. Through a process of continual transformation the leitmotifs trace the course of the drama, the changes in the characters, their experiences and memories, their thoughts and hidden desires. As the leitmotifs accumulate layer upon layer of meaning, they themselves become characters in the drama, symbols of the relentless process of growth and decay that rules the destinies of gods and heroes.

Wagner was very much into gods and heroes. Born in Leipzig, the son of a police-court clerk, he was strongly influenced by a scholarly uncle and as a boy liked Shakespeare, Goethe, Dante, and the Greek myths. At fourteen he wrote a tragic drama packed with violence, love, ghosts, and witchcraft. After a few organ lessons, he began devising his own music theory to turn his drama into an opera. As a musician he was largely self-taught (he devoted particular attention to Beethoven), although he took a course in music theory while studying philosophy at the University of Leipzig.

HIS FRIEND LUDWIG

While technically an opera composer—or more specifically a creator of "music drama"—Wagner was also one of the nineteenth century's great masters of orchestral writing and influenced virtually all of Romantic music. Liszt was a close friend; Richard Strauss, Bruckner, and Mahler were disciples; Debussy, Ravel, and others tried to shake off his powerful influence and move in other directions. Another disciple, and an important one, was the great pianist and conductor Hans von Bülow. And still another was the philosopher Nietzsche.

But to Wagner the most important of all he influenced was a young man named Ludwig. At eighteen this young man became King of Bavaria, and one of his first acts was to invite a rejected and dejected Wagner to come to Bavaria to finish the last two parts of *The Ring of the Nibelungen*. The first two parts, at that time, were interesting very few people. Wagner closes his own autobiography: "I was never again to feel the weight of everyday hardships of existence under the protection of my exalted friend."

At nineteen he wrote his only symphony, the Symphony in C, and at twenty completed his first opera, *Die Feen* (The Fairies). By this time he had read enough and learned enough in his job as a theater choirmaster to start conducting—and to start a five-year effort on *Rienzi*, a five-act spectacle with a large cast and a big orchestra. Its performance, followed by *The Flying Dutchman*, made his reputation.

Then came *Tannhäuser*, a medieval German story of a poet-musician who had a thing with Venus; the beautiful *Lohengrin*, based on another medieval German legend involving a knight who defends the Holy Grail; and, finally, the monumental *Ring* cycle. Wagner began the latter by writing a series of poems that were to become the libretto—poems based on old German and Scandinavian legends and which led to the four music-dramas constituting what he called *The Ring of the Nibelungen*. It took twenty-six years to complete all four, with *Tristan and Isolde* and Wagner's one happy opera, *Die Meistersinger*, composed in the interim. *Parsifal*, which Wagner called "a consecrational festival play" and which is perhaps the most interpreted opera ever written, was his last.

A LIFELINE

Franz Liszt wrote a sensitive appraisal of Wagner's *Lohengrin* after the first performance. Wagner, having problems with his music and his life at the time, sent back his thanks in a letter:

"For the first and only time you give me the joy of being understood. See, in you I have unfolded completely. Not a tiny fiber, not a smallest heartbeat remains which you have not felt with me."

One enlightening appraisal of *The Ring* came in 1898 from George Bernard Shaw, a big fan:

First, "The Ring," with all its gods and giants and dwarfs, its water-maidens and Valkyries, its wishing-cap, enchanted sword and miraculous treasure, is a drama of today, and not of a remote and fabulous antiquity. It could not have been written before the second half of the Nineteenth Century, because it deals with events which were only then consummating themselves. Unless the spectator recognizes in it an image of the life he is himself fighting his way through, it must needs appear to him a monstrous development of the Christmas pantomimes, spun out here and there into intolerable lengths of dull conversations by the principal baritone. "The Ring" is full of extraordinarily attractive episodes, both orchestral and dramatic. The nature music alone—music of river and rainbow, fire and forest—is enough to bribe people with any love of the country in them to endure the passages of political philosophy in the sure hope of a prettier page to come.

Everybody, too, can enjoy the love music, the hammer and anvil music, the clumping of the giants, the tune of the young woodsman's horn, the trilling of the bird, the dragon music and nightmare music and thunder and lightning music, the profusion of simple melody, the sensuous charm of the orchestration: in short, the vast extent of common ground between "The Ring" and the ordinary music we use for play and pleasure. . . .

My second encouragement is addressed to modest citizens who may suppose themselves to be disqualified from enjoying "The Ring" by their technical ignorance of music. They may dismiss all such misgivings speedily and confidently. If the sound of music has any power to move them, then they will find that Wagner exacts nothing more. There is not a single bar of "classical music" in "The Ring"—not a note in it that has any other point than the single direct point of giving musical expression in drama.

Psychologist; conductor; orchestrator extraordinaire; creator of passionately emotional music and intense drama; controversial in music, political beliefs, and personal life (he had a long relationship that led to marriage with Liszt's illegitimate daughter, Cosima); exile; builder of a temple for his music—Wagner was one of a kind. Psychologists and philosophers still study him and his work.

Some would lift him a notch into Immortality—as some would lift Brahms, the other giant of German music in the second half of the nineteenth century, and some Haydn. But by no means is everyone pro-Wagner, which is one reason we have decided on only three Immortals. Debussy, an original admirer and a rebel in his own right, later wrote: "Don't you see that Wagner, with all his formidable power—yes, in spite of his power, has led music astray into sterile and pernicious paths."

Wagner would scarcely agree. "I am not made like other people," he said. "I must have brilliance and beauty and light. The world owes me what I need. I can't live on a miserable organist's pittance like your master, Bach."

It is rather outrageous that he produced such music.

Beethoven's Ninth Symphony was Wagner's ideal. He wrote that it brought music into the "realm of universal art." "Beyond it," he

KEEPER OF THE KINGDOM

The writer Ernest Newman, one of music's accepted authorities, sums up the composer's life in a biography, *Wagner as Man and Artist*:

"He lived, indeed, to see himself victor everywhere, in possession of everything for which he had struggled his whole feverish life through. He completed and saw upon the stage every one of the great works he had planned. He found the one woman in the world who was fitted to share his throne with him when alive and to govern his kingdom after his death with something of his own overbearing, inconsiderate strength. He achieved the miracle of building in a tiny Bavarian town a theater to which, for more than a generation after his death, musicians would still flock from all the ends of the earth."

added, "no further step is possible, for upon it the perfect art world of the future alone can follow: The universal drama for which Beethoven forged the key."

Naturally, the writer nominated himself as the producer of that universal drama.

Wagner's universally dramatic productions divided much of the musical Europe of the mid-1800s. On the one side was the Classical, absolute music of Brahms, championed both by conservatives and by musicians such as Schumann. On the other side were Wagner's colorful and dramatic extravaganzas, championed by Liszt and his cohorts. Not surprisingly, the battle between the conservative and liberal opposites of music continues to this day.

STARTER KIT

There are several different ways to go. One is to ignore non-opera music and concentrate on five complete operas. Another is to choose five orchestral works from one opera, or one each from five operas. You can concentrate exclusively on the *Ring* cycle, steeping yourself in these great works, or sample scenes from some Romantic operas and some music dramas.

My Starter Kit selection consists of one non-operatic piece, the "Siegfried Idyll," written for orchestra in 1870 in honor of Wagner's and Cosima's young son, named Siegfried, and the four complete *Ring* operas.

This is, in a sense, illogical, since the interminable hours of music that make up the *Ring* four—*The Rhinegold*, *The Valkyrie*, *Siegfried*, and *The Twilight of the Gods*—constitute more of a postgraduate course than a Starter Kit. But the *Ring* is so much "Wagner" that there's really no way around it. One excellent way to cheat, and to enjoy Wagner enormously, is to begin with just orchestral music from the four *Ring* operas and some of the others and then follow up with a few selected scenes identified in the expanded recommendations.

WAGNER: THE STARTER KIT

Composition	Recordings Available*
ORCHESTRAL WORKS:	
Siegfried Idyll	15
VOCAL MUSIC:	
Operas:	
The Ring of the Nibelungen (Der Ring des Nibelungen)	5
The Rhinegold (Das Rheingold)	5
The Valkyrie (Die Walküre)	6
Siegfried	5
Twilight of the Gods (Götterdämmerung)	5

*Represents the number of recorded releases available of each listed composition as found in a recent issue of the *Schwann/Opus* catalogue. A "C" indicates that a work is only available collected with other compositions.

WAGNER: A TOP TEN

Composition	Recordings Available*
ORCHESTRAL WORKS:	
Siegfried Idyll	15
Opera Selections:	
From Tristan and Isolde	
Love Death	30
From The Valkyrie (Die Walküre)	
The Ride of the Valkyries	22

Composition	Recordings Available*
From Tannhäuser	
Venusberg Music	16
Opera Overtures and Preludes:	
From The Mastersingers of Nuremberg	
(Die Meistersinger von Nürnberg)	
Overture and Prelude to Act III	16
From Lohengrin	
Preludes to Acts I and III	15

VOCAL MUSIC:
Operas:

The Ring of The Nibelungen	
The Rhinegold	5
The Twilight of the Gods	5
Siegfried	6
The Valkyrie	5

WAGNER: A MASTER COLLECTION

Composition	Recordings Available*
SYMPHONIES:	
Symphony in C	2
OTHER ORCHESTRAL WORKS:	
Siegfried Idyll	15
Opera Selections:	
From Tristan and Isolde	
Love Death	30
From Tannhäuser	
Venusberg Music	16
From Parsifal	
Good Friday Music	4
From the operas of the Ring Cycle:	
The Valkyrie	
Magic Fire Music	12
The Ride of the Valkyries	22
The Twilight of the Gods	
Siegfried's Rhine Journey	4
Siegfried's Funeral Music	6

Composition	Recordings Available*
Opera Overtures and Preludes:	
From Tristan and Isolde	
Preludes to Acts I and II	30
From The Mastersingers of Nuremberg	
Overture and Prelude to Act III	16
From Tannhäuser	
Overture and Prelude to Act III	16
From Parsifal	
Prelude to Act I	4
From Lohengrin	
Preludes to Acts I and III	15

VOCAL MUSIC:

Operas:

The Flying Dutchman (Der fliegende Höllander)	4
Lohengrin	4
Tristan and Isolde	5
The Mastersingers of Nuremberg	3
Tannhäuser	4
Parsifal	5
The Ring of the Nibelungen (Der Ring des Nibelungen)	
The Rhinegold	5
The Twilight of the Gods	5
Siegfried	6
The Valkyrie	5

Songs:

Five Wesendonck Songs	7

FRANZ JOSEPH HAYDN (1732–1809)

Number 5

Haydn wrote the happiest symphonic music of all, the most cheerful, the most buoyant. If things aren't going well and you want a symphony—a reasonably short symphony, as that's how Haydn created them—go for Franz Joseph Haydn. His own words tell a lot about the compositions and the composer: "Since God has given me a cheerful heart, he will forgive me for serving him cheerfully." He was actually a lonely man (perhaps the closest friend of his life was a youngster twenty-four years his junior named Mozart), but his spirit and music were all upbeat.

It does "Papa" Haydn a great disservice, however, to conclude that his happy, bouncy symphonies reflect a cheerful lightweight. There are no lightweights among the Demigods of the Top Ten—nor, indeed, among The 50 on The List—and if there were one, it would assuredly not be this great genius. Haydn, a deeply religious man, could and did write tragic and intensely powerful music, and his contribution to classical composition and its continued development was immeasurable.

He is called the father of the symphony, of which he wrote 104, although he is actually its prime developer rather than its creator. He is also the near-inventor—certainly the crystallizer—of the string quartet. And he is at least the godfather of both the sonata and the sonataform.

Haydn did not start writing symphonies until he was twenty-seven, and it was not until his forty-fifth symphony, composed in 1772, that the experts began applying the word "masterpiece." At that time he was forty years old and serving, as he did for so much of his life, as Kapellmeister for Count Esterhazy. Symphony No. 45 in F-sharp Minor, called the *Farewell*, is one of the earliest Haydn sym-

THE ESTERHAZY CONNECTION

Prince Nikolaus Esterhazy was Haydn's patron and employer for nearly thirty years, beginning in 1762, after Haydn had been for one year in the service of the prince's brother, Paul Anton Esterhazy. The family was one of the richest and most influential of Hungarian nobility. Haydn was based first in a palace in Eisenstadt and then for most of his service in a new palace called Eszterhaza. Vienna was not far away, but for most of his later life Haydn was at either Eisenstadt, in the winter months, or Eszterhaza. This was a vastly different existence from the Paris of Chopin, Berlioz, and Liszt, or the Leipzig of Schumann and Mendelssohn.

phonies that are still regularly performed, although all 104 have been recorded and even the earlier ones are often heard on classical-music radio stations. A long string of masterpieces began in 1784 when Haydn was commissioned to write two sets of symphonies from Paris, three in each set (Nos. 82 through 87). Then came the London symphonies of 1791 to 1795 (Nos. 93 to 104), his most famous, in two sets of six, each set written for one of Haydn's two visits to London. Along with Mozart's best, these are considered to be the peak of symphonic writing before Beethoven. In the London twelve, Haydn brought many instruments together—strings, oboes, bassoons, horns, trumpets, flutes, timpani, and clarinets. Ten of the twelve were scored for two flutes, and five of the twelve for clarinets.

But Haydn is far more than symphonies.

Melvin Berger, in his informative and detailed book on chamber music, includes thirty-six Haydn string quartets as worthy of mention—composed from the early 1760s to 1799. Haydn's chamber-music output included eighty-three string quartets, sixty-seven string trios, thirty-one piano trios, and a good bit more.

The experts speak of the "perfection of form" in his quartets, of their "transparency, neatness, and clarity," of the individualization yet unification of the four instruments. They say that Mozart learned much about string quartets from Haydn—and that Haydn, in turn, later learned much from the younger man. They describe Haydn's quartets as tender, playful, fresh, graceful, charming, neat, and witty—and nearly flawless.

TWO FRIENDS

Haydn on Mozart: "Friends often flatter me that I have some genius, but he stood far above me."

Mozart on Haydn: "It was from Haydn that I first learned the true way to compose quartets."

Haydn on an unusual passage of Mozart's: "If Mozart wrote it so, he must have had good reason."

Mozart on dedicating quartets to Haydn: "Your approval above all encourages me to offer them to you and leads me to hope that you will not consider them wholly unworthy of your favor."

Haydn was born in the village of Rohrau in Austria, the son of a wheelwright, and educated in a Vienna cathedral where he sang in the choir—until his voice changed, whereupon he began to make his living playing a broken-down clavier and singing in the streets. Then the aristocracy found him, and he spent most of his life near Vienna, at a time when music still belonged chiefly to the nobility and there was little in the way of public concerts. It was a patronage system.

A CONTRACT FOR A GENIUS

Haydn's contract with the noble Esterhazy family read, in part:

"The said Haydn . . . must be temperate, not showing himself overbearing toward his musicians, but mild and lenient, straightforward and composed. . . . The said Joseph Haydn shall take care that he . . . appears in white stockings and white linen, powdered, and with either a pigtail or a tiewig. . . . He should conduct himself in an exemplary manner, abstaining from undue familiarity, and from vulgarity in eating, drinking and conversation."

If you wanted to be a European musician in George Washington's time, and wanted to eat regularly—either vulgarly or in a dainty manner—this was the way to go.

Haydn lived by a simple code: "Be good and industrious, and serve God continually." He matured slowly as a composer, not writing Demigod music until he was forty or so. Schubert died at thirty-one, Mozart at thirty-five. There would have been no Haydn in history had he too died young; he was not a spontaneous genius like Mozart, Schubert, or Mendelssohn. Nor, of course, was anyone else, although many came a lot closer than Papa Haydn.

In the concerto field, his most popular works include a Trumpet Concerto in E-flat and concertos for cello, horn, and harpsichord.

But with all of the symphonies, all of the string quartets and trios, more than forty piano sonatas, twenty-odd operas, and many masses and songs, some of Haydn's most beautiful music came from still another musical form.

Haydn died in 1809 at seventy-seven, and it was not until his late sixties that he produced what is generally regarded as his greatest single composition, the oratorio *The Creation*. His oratorios were motivated in part by his respect for Handel, whose *Messiah* is still the undisputed champion of all oratorios, and who produced several others nearly as sublime. Handel, who died in 1759 when Haydn was twenty-seven, had turned down the text for *The Creation*. Haydn later accepted it, as a mission in music and a mission for God. He wrote in his diary of this experience: "Daily I fell on my knees and begged God to vouchsafe me strength for the fortunate outcome of my work. . . . I felt so penetrated with religious feeling that before I sat down to the pianoforte I prayed to God with earnestness that he would enable me to praise Him worthily."

The Creation is viewed by some as being almost in the same league as the *Messiah* as a medium of religious worship. It has been called a work of rare inspiration and religious majesty, reflecting the voice of a genius who, nearing death, had glimpsed other and greater worlds. One critic described it as a masterwork in that it has no weak point, nothing that could be changed or omitted, although a more accepted view is that it is sublime in some parts and stilted in others.

So successful was *The Creation* that Haydn almost inevitably went to *Rocky II*, composing another masterful oratorio, *The Seasons*.

Senior citizens should be encouraged by the late-blooming Haydn, and even more by the continuing-to-bloom Haydn. In 1792, at the age of sixty-three, he was the world's greatest living composer. Mozart had been dead for a year; Beethoven was only twenty-two and had not yet produced his first symphony. Yet not only Haydn's two oratorios, but also his best piano music, his most acclaimed masses, and his greatest chamber music had not yet been written. Consider only the string

A MUSICIAN'S LIFE

Haydn on his wife: "She was continually inviting the clergy to dinner, had many Masses said, and was freer with charitable contributions than her situation warranted."

Haydn on influential people: "I have associated with emperors, kings and many great people, and I have heard many flattering things from them, but I would not live in familiar relations with such persons; I prefer to be close to people of my own standing."

Haydn on his Esterhazy arrangement: "My prince was content with all my works, I received approval, I could, as head of an orchestra, make experiments, observe what created an impression and what weakened it, thus improving, adding to, cutting away, and running risks. I was set apart from the world, there was nobody in my vicinity to confuse and annoy me in my course, and so I had to become original."

quartets, for example. His supreme string quartets are recognized today as the six of Op. 76, completed in 1797 and 1798 when he was approaching seventy. The professionals shift back and forth for their favorite among No. 2 in D Minor, the *Quinten*; No. 3 in C, the *Emperor*; and No. 5 in D, often called the *Largo*, whose slow (largo) movement ranks with the most beautiful music in quartet literature. There also are votes for No. 4 in B-flat, the *Sunrise*. But many other beautiful Haydn quartets exist, and extra credit is given for not passing over the earlier ones en route to Op. 76.

Road maps such as this one are frustrating in that they leave little time for users to go down the small roads. For example, Haydn produced two horn concertos, the first of which is judged by the music people to be at the level of Mozart's four famous concertos for horn. Every composer on The List, and scores who are not, have such individual triumphs that are largely overlooked as we concentrate on even greater achievements.

A great deal happened in the music world between Bach's death in 1750, when Haydn was a youth of eighteen, and Beethoven's First Symphony, written in 1800, nine years before Haydn's death. Musical style changed enormously. As we have seen, homophony, the style of single melody plus harmony, became the "in" thing in place of counterpoint, the simultaneous interweaving of different melodies. The symphony, the sonata, the string quartet, and the instrumental concerto replaced the mass, the oratorio, the suite, the fugue, and the concerto grosso. The center of music had been the church; now it shifted to the palace, and later the "public" concert platform. The experts say that musical values changed as well—there was now more of an emphasis on individualism, more independence, less formality, less rigidity. Unorthodox techniques were replacing traditional ways of doing things. Haydn is considered the first major force in bringing about this evolution—which was to be continued by Beethoven and then Schubert and inherited by the Romantic age still ahead. The difference between the uncluttered music of Haydn and the music that came before was significant.

STARTER KIT

The Creation, first performed in Vienna in 1798 with Haydn conducting, is the first Starter Kit selection, even though it is a bit monumental for the beginner. After an overture, designed to depict order emerging out of chaos and light out of darkness, comes the full story of the Creation through the six days, told in three parts. "One moment I was as cold as ice, and next I seemed on fire," the composer wrote about this work. "More than once I thought I should have a fit." Perhaps the thing to do is collect it early on but to start actual listening with a few short symphonies.

On the other hand, listening to parts is fun—and especially easy to do on compact discs. There is no reason to take on the entire *Creation* at one time. It is available in both German and English, although there is something of an unwritten rule that it is supposed to be recorded in German only.

In Starter Kit recommendations, a constant issue is whether to go with the greatest masterpieces or to lure the listener along with shorter works that are presumably easier to handle. Two of Haydn's finest symphonies, both fun to listen to, are an appropriate middle ground. One is No. 94 in G, called the *Surprise*, and the second is No. 104 in D, called the *London* (confusing in that all of these last symphonies, commissioned by an impresario named Johann Peter Salomon for Haydn's two visits to England, are called the London symphonies). The older Haydn had by this time been greatly influenced by his young friend Mozart, which helped make these twelve Haydn's greatest symphonic works. Few guarantees are offered in this road map, but one is that you will enjoy this group of symphonies.

There is additional promise of enjoyment from his Concerto in E-flat for Trumpet and Orchestra. While the professionals appear to be more taken by his Concerto in D for Cello and Orchestra and another Concerto in D (Op. 21) for Harpsichord and Orchestra, the trumpet concerto is one of Haydn's most recorded—and most popular—works. Its slow movement is particularly famous. (Incidentally, another cello concerto, this one in C, was discovered in Prague in the early 1960s and was hailed by music lovers as a wonderful addition to the rather limited cello repertory.)

The last choice is a toss-up among the six Op. 76 quartets. The Austrian national anthem can be heard in the second movement of No. 3, the *Emperor*; No. 5, the *Largo*, is the favorite of many; the critics consider No. 2, the *Quinten*, to be the most unified. Our selection is No. 4 in B-flat, the *Sunrise*.

"UBER ALLES"

Haydn wrote his first string quartet in 1750 at age twenty-eight, was captivated by the form, and composed another eighty-two in his lifetime. After forty of them he adopted the four-movement approach that has persisted.

If you want to hear a familiar theme in one of his greatest quartet sets, try the third of six in Op. 76, in C, called the *Kaiserquartett* (Emperor quartet). Haydn builds into it, as the second movement, the Austrian national anthem he had written earlier at the request of the kaiser. World War II veterans, fewer in number every day, may just as soon pass over this *Deutschland über Alles* theme, which will remind them of wartime Germany—but in a Haydn framework it is lovely music.

This set of six quartets was Haydn's last complete opus.

HAYDN: THE STARTER KIT

Composition	Recordings Available*
SYMPHONIES:	
No. 94 in G (Surprise)	13
No. 104 in D (London)	12

Composition   *Recordings Available**

OTHER ORCHESTRAL WORKS:
Concerto in E-flat for Trumpet and Orchestra   15

CHAMBER MUSIC:
String Quartet:
    Op. 76, No. 4 in B-flat (Sunrise)   7

VOCAL MUSIC:
Oratorio:
    The Creation   8

*Represents the number of recorded releases available of each listed composition as found in a recent issue of the *Schwann/Opus* catalogue. A "C" indicates that a work is only available collected with other compositions.

HAYDN: A TOP TEN

Composition   *Recordings Available**

SYMPHONIES:
No. 94 in G (Surprise)   13
No. 100 in G (Military)   8
No. 101 in D (Clock)   9
No. 103 in E-flat (Drum Roll)   12
No. 104 in D (London)   12

OTHER ORCHESTRAL WORKS:
Concerto in E-flat for Trumpet and Orchestra   15

CHAMBER MUSIC:
String Quartets:
    Op. 76:
        No. 3 in C (Emperor)   8
        No. 4 in B-flat (Sunrise)   7

VOCAL MUSIC:
Oratorio:
    The Creation   8
Church Music:
    Mass No. 7, Missa in Tempore belli   5
    (Paukenmesse)

HAYDN: A MASTER COLLECTION

Composition   *Recordings Available**

SYMPHONIES:

No. 45 in F-sharp Minor (Farewell)   7
No. 92 in G (Oxford)   5
No. 94 in G (Surprise)   13
No. 96 in D (Miracle)   5
No. 100 in G (Military)   8
No. 101 in D (Clock)   9
No. 103 in E-flat (Drum Roll)   12
No. 104 in D (London)   12

OTHER ORCHESTRAL WORKS:

Concerto in E-flat for Trumpet and Orchestra   15
Concerto in D for Harpsichord   7
Concerto No. 1 in D for Horn   5
Concerto in D for Cello and Orchestra   5

CHAMBER MUSIC:

String Quartets:
   Op. 20:
      No. 4 in D   6
      No. 5 in F Minor   6
   Op. 64:
      No. 5 in D (Lark)   1
   Op. 76:
      No. 2 in D Minor (Quinten)   5
      No. 3 in C (Emperor)   8
      No. 4 in B-flat (Sunrise)   7
      No. 5 in D (Largo)   7

SOLO INSTRUMENTAL MUSIC:

Sonatas for Piano (fifty-two)   41

VOCAL MUSIC:

Oratorios:
   The Creation   8
   The Seasons   8
Church Music:
   Mass No. 1 in F, Missa Brevis   3
   Mass No. 7, Missa in Tempore belli   5
      (Paukenmesse)
   Stabat Mater in G Minor   2

A HAYDN LIBRARY

Composition	Recordings Available*

SYMPHONIES:

No. 45 in F-sharp Minor (Farewell)	7
No. 49 in F Minor (La Passione)	7
No. 82 in C (L'Ours)	5
No. 83 in G Minor (Poule)	5
No. 85 in B-flat (La Reine)	5
No. 88 in G	10
No. 92 in G (Oxford)	5
No. 94 in G (Surprise)	13
No. 95 in C Minor	4
No. 96 in D (Miracle)	5
No. 99 in E-flat	6
No. 100 in G (Military)	8
No. 101 in D (Clock)	9
No. 103 in E-flat (Drum Roll)	12
No. 104 in D (London)	12
Toy Symphony	7

OTHER ORCHESTRAL WORKS:

Concerto in E-flat for Trumpet and Orchestra	15
Concerto in D for Cello and Orchestra	5
Concerto in D for Harpsichord	7
Concerto No. 1 in D for Horn	5
Concerto in C for Oboe and Orchestra	5
Concerto No. 1 in C for Violin	6
Sinfonia Concertante in B-flat	7

CHAMBER MUSIC:

String Quartets (of eighty-odd):	
Op. 3, No. 5 in F (Serenade)	2
Op. 20:	
No. 4 in D (Sun)	6
No. 5 in F Minor	6
No. 6 in A	6
Op. 33, No. 3 in C (Birds)	1
Op. 50:	
No. 3 in E-flat	2
No. 6 in D (Frog)	1
Op. 64, No. 5 in D (Lark)	1

Composition	Recordings Available*
Op. 74, No. 3 in G Minor (Rider or Horseman)	3
Op. 76:	
No. 2 in D Minor (Quinten)	5
No. 3 in C (Emperor)	8
No. 4 in B-flat (Sunrise)	7
No. 5 in D (Largo)	7
Op. 77:	
No. 1 in G	3
No. 2 in F	3
Seven Last Words of Christ	7

SOLO INSTRUMENTAL MUSIC:

Sonatas for Piano (fifty-two)	41

VOCAL MUSIC:

Oratorios:

The Creation	8
The Seasons	8

Church Music:

Mass No. 1 in F, Missa Brevis	3
Mass No. 5 in B-Flat (Little Organ)	3
Mass No. 7, Missa in Tempore belli (Paukenmesse)	5
Mass No. 9 in D, Missa Solemnis (Nelson Mass)	4
Mass No. 12 in B-flat (Harmoniemesse)	3
Stabat Mater in G Minor	2

JOHANNES BRAHMS (1833–1897)

Number 6

Though there are only three Immortals on The List, a strong case can be made for two or three or four more. One ever-active cult would instantly nominate Richard Wagner, and for years there has been on-again, off-again sentiment about Johannes Brahms: Demigod today, Immortal tomorrow, lesser artist next month, then back to Demigod. Fifty years ago, the older generation will recall, schoolchildren learned in music-appreciation class that the three B's were at the top of the ladder—Bach, Beethoven, and Brahms. Mozart has since streaked up, of course, and Brahms slipped in public favor for a while before climbing again. It is interesting and perhaps meaningful that not many other names are mentioned as legitimate candidates at the highest level. One other is Haydn. Some would say Schubert.

While significant differences of opinion about Brahms are found in music criticism of the last hundred years, today there is general agreement that he was a superstar.

The last of the great Romantics, he was also a quintessential Classicist, oriented toward the past. He worshiped Beethoven and Bach. He believed in conventional form and structure and was a stalwart opponent of the rebelliousness of Wagner, Liszt, and what these two called the "music of the future." One critic has called him the Keeper of the Classic Flame. Two words often used in speaking of him are *nobility* and *integrity*. His music was gentle, mellow, and flowing.

Brahms wrote a good deal, and much of what he wrote remains as popular today as it was nearly a century ago. He composed four famous symphonies. Along with Schumann, he was a direct successor to Schubert as a writer of German *lieder*, of which he composed some two hundred. And he was a master of short, lyric piano music, in a class with Schubert, Chopin, Liszt, Mendelssohn, and Schumann. But not all of his nonsymphonic work was short. He wrote two monumental piano concertos, a violin concerto of the highest caliber, and a superb concerto for violin and cello. He was Romanticism's greatest writer of chamber music, exceeded by few from any era—one exception being Beethoven. Chamber-music masterpieces include a Quartet in A Minor, a Piano Quintet in F Minor, a Clarinet Quintet in B Minor, piano trios, and piano-violin sonatas. His choral music includes the *German Requiem*, acknowledged as the greatest Protestant religious music of his day.

JUST AN EXPERIMENT

The first performance of Brahms's Piano Concerto No. 1 in D Minor was a failure. This was in Hanover. The second, in Leipzig a few days later, was also a failure. Brahms had this reaction, in a letter about the Leipzig performance:

"The first rehearsal excited no kind of feeling either in the performance or the audience; no audience came at all to the second, and no performer moved a muscle of his face. In the evening, the first and second movements were listened to without the slightest display of feeling. At the conclusion three pairs of hands were brought together very slowly, whereupon a perfectly distinct hissing from all sides forbade any such demonstration. . . .

"The failure has made no impression upon me whatever. After all, I am only experimenting and feeling my way. But the hissing was too much."

He wrote no opera, and not a line of the program music that was so much a part of Romantic times. He would have been comfortable being born with Beethoven fifty years earlier—indeed, he might have preferred it, for he was a late symphonic bloomer and was worried about the shadow of Beethoven until the music world's acceptance of his "early" works—composed in his late thirties and forties. Some believe he is the most legitimate challenger of Beethoven for symphonic supremacy—or, at least, that his best should be included in the same symphony Hall of Fame.

One opinion of Brahms comes from a friend and colleague, the great violinist Joseph Joachim, who wrote:

> All he cares is to write music without interference; and his faith in a more sublime world of fantasy, and his manner of keeping all the unhealthy sensations and imaginary sufferings of others at arm's length borders on genius. . . . His compositions, so rich and ruthlessly rejecting all earthly woes, are such an effortless game in the most complex disguise. Never have I encountered such talent.

His *German Requiem*—the monumental choral work of 1868 inspired by the death of his mother and (scandalously, at the time) written not in Latin but in German—made him famous. This was followed by his first symphony in 1876, his second in 1877, his famous violin concerto in 1878, the B-flat Piano Concerto in 1881, his third symphony in 1883, his fourth in 1885, and his Concerto for Violin and Cello in 1887.

This was the era when the shocking, sensational tone poems of Richard Strauss were the rage of Europe. But while Strauss was heralding the future with dissonant sounds, Brahms was becoming more mellow than ever with his Violin Sonata in D Minor, a clarinet quintet, and his piano intermezzi.

Brahms was born in Hamburg in 1833, twenty-odd years after Liszt, Wagner, and Schumann, who were to play important parts in his life; a decade after Bruckner; about the same time as Borodin of Russia and Saint-Saëns of France; and a decade before Rimsky-Korsakov. His childhood was not ideal. He lived in a tenement, or near-tenement, in a grubby part of Hamburg; his parents fought; he hated school (and particularly French); he was bullied by other students. His father played poor double bass in a poor ensemble, but he did teach the boy to play the piano, and at ten and eleven Johannes was picking up a little money playing in waterfront bars where the sailors hung out. Hamburg being Hamburg, one assumes various social activities took place in the buildings. This was scarcely the boyhood of a Bach or a Mozart.

Still, money was found for some early piano lessons. He held a recital at fifteen and then tried a little composing before stopping to teach piano full time in order to live. In 1853, at twenty, he met a drifting Hungarian violinist named Eduard Remenyi, a meeting that triggered a series of events that led him to violinist Joseph Joachim and on to Liszt, Schumann, and overnight fame. Stories vary as to how he met Joachim, a key player in this action. One is that Remenyi took Brahms to Joachim's house, where the renowned artist was impressed by the young man's piano playing. A second is that Brahms was accompanying Remenyi's violin performance of Beethoven's *Kreutzer* Sonata and Joachim, sitting in the audience, was enraptured. (That one is more fun.)

Whichever is accurate, Joachim pronounced him "pure as a diamond, soft as snow" and gave him letters of introduction to Liszt in Weimar and Schumann in Düsseldorf. The violinist and the two composers were three of the major musical figures of Germany and in fact all of Europe, and connections with them—especially with Schumann—had an enormous impact on Brahms's life.

THE DOZING GUEST

Johannes Brahms accomplished the near-impossible, a feat few—if any—achieved in the nineteenth century. Somehow, while sitting in a small room, among a small audience, and while the incomparable Franz Liszt was playing the piano . . . Brahms fell asleep. Worse yet, he was a young and unknown pianist-composer, a first-time guest at a party in the great virtuoso's home.

Brahms did visit Liszt in Weimar, with unhappy results, and then moved on to see Schumann and his piano-virtuoso wife, Clara, in Düsseldorf. There he played for the Schumanns, who were thrilled by his work. Robert Schumann, who was publishing a critical magazine, the *Neue Zeitschrift für Musik*, wrote that the young Brahms was a "genius" and predicted that the youngster would "give the highest and most ideal expression to the tendencies of the times." Brahms lived with the Schumanns for several months, became fond of both, and rushed back to be with them not long after his departure when a depressed Schumann tried to drown himself in the Rhine (before spending his last two years in an asylum). For the rest of his life Brahms loved Clara Schumann and carried on a long correspondence with her. She was fourteen years his senior, they never married, and it is unclear just what kind of love they had for each other. Brahms, in fact, lived until his mid-sixties and never married, although there were other women in his life. Perhaps as an outgrowth of his adolescent days around the docks, he was not unfriendly with prostitutes later in life.

As a result of the Schumann connection, the young itinerant pianist-composer became famous very quickly, at a much earlier age than had Beethoven, whom he admired enormously, and to a much greater degree than Bach, whom he adored. He once wrote Clara Schumann about Bach: "On a system for a small instrument, a man writes a whole world of the deepest thoughts and the most strenuous emotions."

Mellow, noble, and classic in his music, Brahms was a rude fellow, not easy to get along with, sloppy in his dress, stingy, often mean, uncompromising, prickly. He liked Dvořák and Grieg and tried to help them; he was unmoved by the music of Liszt and Wagner, and he was only lukewarm about Mahler, Bruckner, Tchaikovsky, Verdi, and Richard Strauss. He was outspoken about his feelings; one story has it that he left a party saying, "If there is anybody here I have not insulted, I apologize." Musicologists say that while the story should be true, it isn't.

It is not surprising that a chap with this kind of personality made enemies.

"Brahms will never become a star of the first magnitude," wrote one critic.

Another said Brahms's patrons were "overenthusiastic" about him.

A third said he "had not the intellect of an antelope," and a fourth called his work "musical small talk; meaningless twaddle."

Mahler, who greatly admired Bruckner, who in turn greatly admired Wagner, called Brahms "a mannequin with a somewhat narrow heart."

But when Brahms's First Symphony appeared in 1876, Hans von Bülow called it "the Tenth," suggesting equality with Beethoven (who stopped at nine).

Critic Arthur Elson, only eighteen years after Brahms's death, wrote:

The appreciation of Brahms is still growing; and the next generation will probably admit that Hans von Bülow's ranking him with Beethoven was practically justified. In the wild chaos of modern radicalism (Richard Strauss, Stravinsky, Bartók), Brahms stands as a model of all that is sane and well-balanced in music. If others do not follow his lead, it is because they do not possess his genius.

HANSLICK ON SYMPHONY NO. 1

It is still said that no one in the history of music has been as powerful as Eduard Hanslick, a writer for the Vienna *Neue Freie Presse* in the second half of the nineteenth century. Hanslick was the leading champion of Schumann and Brahms and the leading opponent of Wagner and Liszt—and of their musical heirs, Richard Strauss and Anton Bruckner.

His comments on Brahms's First Symphony:

"Seldom, if ever, has the entire musical world awaited a composer's first symphony with such tense anticipation—testimony that the unusual was expected of Brahms in this supreme and ultimately difficult form. But the greater the public expectation and the more importunate the demand for a new symphony, the more deliberate and scrupulous was Brahms. Inexorable conscientiousness and stern self-criticism are among his most outstanding characteristics. He always demands the best of himself and dedicates his whole strength to its achievement. He cannot and will not take it easy. . . .

"The new symphony of Brahms is a possession of which the nation may be proud, an inexhaustible fountain of sincere pleasure and fruitful study."

These were also times when Vienna was split into two armies, those heralding the "music of the future," who worshiped Liszt and Wagner, and those who opposed this camp and their music. Although the controversy was far more complex than a black-and-white choosing of sides, feelings were so intense that not many in the music world were able to remain neutral. And, as is so often the case, the supporters of the great tended to be more vocal and bitter than the great themselves. Brahms made it clear that he was not a proponent of Wagner's music, and he actively despised the vehement Wagnerians who fell to their knees as they revered the Master.

Felix Mendelssohn was the Romantic conservative in the first phase of nineteenth-century Romanticism, Brahms in the second. Liszt (1811–1886) and Wagner (1813–1883) were the champions of the spectacular in European music from midcentury on; Brahms was not. Some of his contemporaries were Romantics looking toward the twentieth century; Brahms was a Romantic looking back to Classical days.

STARTER KIT

For Brahms, as for Bach, Mozart, Beethoven, and Haydn, recommended selections include a basic library as well as a selected twenty-five, a top ten, and a Starter Kit of five. For the Starter Kit, the choices for orchestral works include one symphony, the famous violin concerto, and a piano concerto. For chamber music, the recommendation is a masterwork produced late in his life, the clarinet quintet. And there must be some solo piano music, much of it played regularly by pianists today.

Any of his four symphonies might be chosen. The first, which took four to five years to write and which was completed when Brahms was forty-three, after he had been composing for more than twenty years, is the one most frequently recorded. Many consider his fourth to be his finest, although it is harder to listen to than the first. Some critics hold out for the third; literature from the 1930s and 1940s suggests that it was not only Brahms's best but also the best since Beethoven—and, some even said back then, perhaps the best ever written. The second, not as popular as the others today, is the most melodious. It's a take-your-pick situation. My choice is Symphony No. 1 in C Minor—but all four are included in the Brahms top-ten list.

His only violin concerto is a must. It is one of the two or three rivals to Beethoven's as the greatest ever composed, and some believe that it is surpassed neither by Beethoven nor by anyone else. Critics have called it one of the supreme musical inspirations of the world.

Brahms's two piano concertos are both reasonable choices. They are equally popular today, although the first was written in his younger days, in 1856, and the second in 1881. The second, more mellow, is the Starter Kit selection.

The Clarinet Quintet in B Minor, which premiered in Berlin in 1891, is one of his most personal works. In it the composer seems to be looking back over his life in a clarinet-mellow mood. It is soft, gay, resigned, and filled with melody.

Piano options include his Piano Sonata in F Minor, Variations on a Theme by Handel, and a whole repertory of caprices, intermezzi, and other small-scale piano pieces. These are well represented by twenty lovely miniatures—the professionals say his most finely polished miniatures—of Op. 116 through Op. 119. These were written in 1891 to 1893, when Brahms was nearing (or at) sixty.

My recommendation, then, is to cheat and add some songs.

HANSLICK ON SYMPHONY NO. 4

"What symphony of the last thirty or forty years is even remotely comparable with those of Brahms? And yet more symphonies are being composed these days than is generally appreciated. The Leipzig 'Signale' lists no fewer than 19 symphonies performed for the first time last year. It looks as though Brahms's successes had stimulated production, following the long silence which set in after Mendelssohn and Schumann. . . . Brahms is unique in his resources of genuine symphonic invention; in his sovereign mastery of all the secrets of counterpoint, harmony, and instrumentation; in the logic of development combined with the most beautiful freedom of fantasy. . . .

"All these virtues are abundantly present in his Fourth Symphony; they even seemed to have gained in stature—not in melodic invention, perhaps, but certainly in executive craftsmanship. Individual preference may favor one or the other of Brahms's symphonies; my particular favorite is the third. But I do not want to exclude the possibility that my opinion may change when I have become equally familiar with this latest work. Neither its treasure of ideas nor its chaste beauty is apparent at first glance; its charms are not democratic."

BRAHMS: THE STARTER KIT

Composition	Recordings Available*
SYMPHONIES:	
No. 1 in C Minor	22
OTHER ORCHESTRAL WORKS:	
Piano Concerto No. 2 in B-flat	23
Violin Concerto in D	24
CHAMBER MUSIC:	
Clarinet Quintet in B Minor, Op. 115	10

Composition	Recordings Available*
OTHER INSTRUMENTAL MUSIC:	
Twenty Piano Miniatures, Op. 116 to Op. 119	16

*Represents the number of recorded releases available of each listed composition as found in a recent issue of the *Schwann/Opus* catalogue. A "C" indicates that a work is only available collected with other compositions.

BRAHMS: A TOP TEN

Composition	Recordings Available*
SYMPHONIES:	
No. 1 in C Minor	22
No. 2 in D	8
No. 3 in F	13
No. 4 in E Minor	18
OTHER ORCHESTRAL WORKS:	
Piano Concerto No. 2 in B-flat	23
Violin Concerto in D	24
CHAMBER MUSIC:	
Clarinet Quintet in B Minor, Op. 115	10
OTHER INSTRUMENTAL MUSIC:	
Twenty Piano Miniatures, Op. 116 to Op. 119	16
VOCAL MUSIC:	
German Requiem	14
Songs	C

BRAHMS: A MASTER COLLECTION

Composition	Recordings Available*
SYMPHONIES:	
No. 1 in C Minor	22
No. 2 in D	8
No. 3 in F	13
No. 4 in E Minor	18

Composition	Recordings Available*
OTHER ORCHESTRAL WORKS:	
Piano Concertos:	
No. 1 in D Minor	22
No. 2 in B-flat	23
Violin Concerto in D	24
Violin and Cello Concerto in A Minor	11
Overtures:	
Academic Festival	23
Tragic	25
Hungarian Dances (Nos. 1, 5, 6, 7, 17)	18
(also with chamber orchestra)	
Variations on a Theme by Haydn	23
CHAMBER MUSIC:	
Sextet in G, Op. 36 (Agathe)	6
Piano Quintet in F Minor, Op. 34	6
Clarinet Quintet in B Minor, Op. 115	10
Horn Trio in E-flat, Op. 40 (horn, violin, piano)	9
Clarinet Trio in A Minor, Op. 114 (clarinet, cello, piano)	8
OTHER INSTRUMENTAL MUSIC:	
Sonatas (two) for Clarinet and Piano	13
Sonata for Cello and Piano in F, Op. 39	9
Four Ballades, Op. 10	10
Twenty Piano Miniatures, Op. 116 to Op. 119	16
Variations on a Theme by Handel	11
VOCAL MUSIC:	
German Requiem	14
Liebeslieder Waltzes	9
Songs	C

A BRAHMS LIBRARY

Composition	Recordings Available*
SYMPHONIES:	
No. 1 in C Minor	22
No. 2 in D	8

Composition	*Recordings Available**
No. 3 in F	13
No. 4 in E Minor	18

OTHER ORCHESTRAL WORKS:
Piano Concertos:

No. 1 in D Minor	22
No. 2 in B-flat	23
Violin Concerto in D	24
Violin and Cello Concerto in A Minor	11

Overtures:

Academic Festival	23
Tragic	25
Serenade No. 1 in D	6
Serenade No. 2 in A	6
Hungarian Dances (Nos. 1, 5, 6, 7, 17)	18
(also with chamber orchestra)	
Variations on a Theme by Haydn	23

CHAMBER MUSIC:

Sextet in B-flat, Op. 16	6
Sextet in G, Op. 36 (Agathe)	6
Piano Quintet in F Minor, Op. 34	6
Viola Quintet in F, Op. 88	6
Clarinet Quintet in B Minor, Op. 115	10
String Quartet in C Minor, Op. 51, No. 1	6
String Quartet in A Minor, Op. 51, No. 2	6
String Quartet in B-flat, Op. 67	6
Piano Quartet in G Minor, Op. 25	2
Piano Quartet in A, Op. 26	4
Piano Quartet in C Minor, Op. 60	4
Piano Trio in B-flat, Op. 8	4
Piano Trio in C, Op. 87	4
Piano Trio in C Minor, Op. 101	4
Horn Trio in E-flat, Op. 40 (horn, violin, piano)	9
Clarinet Trio in A Minor, Op. 114 (clarinet, cello, piano)	8

OTHER INSTRUMENTAL MUSIC:

Sonatas (two) for Clarinet and Piano	13
Sonatas for Violin and Piano:	
No. 1 in G	3

Composition	Recordings Available*
No. 2 in A	2
No. 3 in D Minor	6
Sonatas for Cello and Piano:	
In E Minor, Op. 38	9
In F, Op. 39	9
Sonata for Piano No. 3 in F Minor	5
Variations on a Theme by Handel	11
Four Ballades, Op. 10	10
Twenty Piano Miniatures, Op. 116 to Op. 119	16

VOCAL MUSIC:

German Requiem	14
Liebeslieder Waltzes	9
Songs	C

FRANZ SCHUBERT (1797–1828)

Number 7

"Gretchen at the Spinning Wheel" was written in one afternoon, October 11, 1814, when Franz Schubert was seventeen.

The "Erlkonig" was composed in several minutes on another afternoon the next year. There was no pianoforte in Schubert's father's house, and the young artist and his friends rushed to a nearby seminary to hear it for the first time.

This is genius. And these are two of the best-known songs in classical music, written by the man Franz Liszt called "the most poetic of them all."

SCHUBERT ON MOZART

A June 15, 1816, diary entry gives us a glimpse of the nineteen-year-old Schubert:

"A brilliant, beautiful day, the memory of which will remain with me for my whole life. From distant space echo still within me the magic tones of Mozart's music. How wonderfully powerful and yet gentle and soft, played in Schlesinger's masterly style, penetrating deeply into my heart. No time or circumstances can efface these beautiful sounds from my memory, sounds which will everlastingly affect our inner existence. Oh! Mozart, how many and endless are the impressions of a brighter and better life that you have imprinted on our souls! This quartet is certainly one of his finest works; I felt that I, too, must contribute something, and so played some of Beethoven's variations and sang my settings of Goethe's 'Rastlose Liebe' and Schiller's 'Amalia.' Although I can congratulate myself on 'Amalia' being a success, I can't deny that Goethe's poetic genius had the lion's share of the applause."

By his death at age thirty-one, Schubert had composed more than five hundred songs, among them the world-famous "Ave Maria." His greatest gift was song—song coupled with melody: simple melody, soaring melody, soft melody, magic melody, melancholy melody. Schubert was a poet, not a mass designer. Nor was he either conductor or virtuoso instrumentalist (he was one of the few great composers not skilled at one or both of those arts).

He did write symphonies, most of which are criticized by design-conscious professionals for their structure—but never for their poetry, melody, and beauty. The bean counters say there are nine in all, although the Seventh exists only in sketches. The first three are early works, composed in 1813 and 1815 when Schubert was still in his teens. Critics call them "classical," "light," "sparkling," and "good examples of his early freshness and spirit," but none is considered monumental. The Fourth (the *Tragic*), written when Schubert was not yet twenty, was, the experts say, influenced by Beethoven's work—was, in fact, an attempt to produce his own version of Beethoven's powerful *Eroica* Symphony. In the Fifth, composed the same year as the Fourth, Schubert stopped trying to emulate someone else and returned to being himself. This was a wise decision; the Fifth is regarded as the masterpiece of his early years—and is known colloquially as the symphony without trumpets or drums. It is a cheerful, sunny, happy work, without a dark thought in it.

The Sixth (called the *Little C Major*) is regarded as a series of setbacks and fresh starts, sort of a prologue to his last, the Ninth (the *Great C Major*). Then came the *Unfinished* Eighth, begun in 1822, the favorite of most listeners—although many professionals lean more toward the Ninth as *the* Schubert masterwork. Some put the *Unfinished* with Mozart's final three symphonies and selected Beethoven offerings as the greatest of Vienna classical symphonies. This assessment overlooks Papa Haydn and, in fact, to laymen Schubert symphonies generally sound more like Mozart and Haydn than like Beethoven. They neither have the dramatic intensity of Beethoven nor, apparently, were designed to have it.

The Ninth is seen as the realization of what Schubert was trying to accomplish in his Fourth and Sixth: the composer as himself, but having been influenced by Beethoven. It was completed in Schubert's last year, in his final burst of energy, along with the song cycle *Schwanengesang*, the C Major String Quintet, an oratorio, a mass, and many songs. After one performance in 1828, a month after Schubert's death, the Ninth was lost—or put aside—for some ten years until Robert Schumann came upon it at the home of Schubert's brother in a bundle of Schubert manuscripts.

Marcel Schneider, a Schubert biographer, wrote of the Ninth: "This time Schubert aspires to meet Beethoven on the plane of the Choral Symphony (No. 9). He was successful; the tradition was to be continued by Brahms, and brought to its peak by Bruckner and Mahler. We do not know whether Schubert had heard Beethoven's Ninth Symphony, or whether he had simply read the score, but he obviously knew of it and knew of its magnitude, and it is evident that he planned his work on Beethoven's huge scale."

(Beethoven had died in 1827; his own world-famous Ninth had been completed in 1824 and performed for the first time that year.)

The pint-sized (five-foot one-inch) Schubert is usually characterized as the main bridge between the Classical period of Mozart, Haydn, and Beethoven and the Romantic era of Chopin, Schumann, and Liszt. The basic forms in which he composed included the older ones—symphonies, string quartets, and sonatas—but he fashioned

NO ARMS

The Venus de Milo of music is Schubert's *Unfinished* Symphony, No. 8 in B Minor, which has only two movements instead of the usual four of Classical times. One might suspect that the composer died before he had time to complete it, but that is not the case. In 1822, when Schubert was twenty-five, he was elected an honorary member of a musical club in Austria and submitted these two movements as his official membership-initiation fee. They were neither published nor performed at that time. Although Schubert lived for another six years, he made no known effort to complete the work. He did, of course, write one more outstanding symphony, No. 9 in C.

It was once thought that Schubert felt he could not equal the first two movements and did not want to "spoil" the masterpiece he had created. Schubert biographers now lean toward the view that he had said all that he had to say in this particular work, had done his thing and saw no valid reason to continue. There was much other work to be done; it was better to turn to it.

In 1928 a record company in the United States, commemorating the composer's death, offered a prize to the living composer who would do the best job of completing the symphony. Happily, the musicians of the world screamed in protest, and the ridiculous idea was dropped.

them in his own way, and more lyrically than any predecessor.

Lyricism is a word the music people like a lot. *Webster's* defines it as "songfulness" and as "a personal direct intense style or quality in an art, as poetry or music."

SCHUBERT: SELF-DESCRIPTION

Schubert explained his work in these words: "My music is the production of my genius and my misery."

Schubert is one of the two or three natural geniuses of classical music (along with Mendelssohn), rated only a hair behind the incomparable Mozart in spontaneous creativity, although more than a hair behind for the depth of his work. (No one equals Mozart in the combination of sheer genius and depth; Bach adds his extraordinary intellect and his spiritual passion to help him achieve his Number One position.)

It is difficult, although perhaps not quite impossible, to be a solid part of the Romantic movement without being oriented toward piano and song, and Schubert, as the Classical-Romantic link, was heavily involved in both. By consensus, he was the top classical songwriter of all time, with Schumann (born 1810), Brahms (born 1833), and un-Listed Hugo Wolf as his chief competitors. Mahler (born 1860) is in the next breath. Schubert is credited with bringing the German art song—or *lied*—to its highest point of perfection. A nice definition of a song—popular, folk, or art song—is "the musical setting for a poem." Schubert almost flawlessly combined melody, structural beauty, the meaning and emotion of the original poem, and the subtle touch from his piano accompaniments. With Schubert, the professionals say, a song becomes a complete artwork.

He wrapped some of his most famous songs into packages called *song cycles*—groups of integrated songs, perhaps fourteen or twenty or twenty-four, usually built exclusively from the lyrics of one poet. Schubert's two best-known song cycles are *Die schöne Müllerin* (The fair maid of the mill) and *Die Winterreise* (Winter's journey), both written to poems by Wilhelm Müller. Some consider these to be the finest series of songs in literature.

Another famous series of Schubert songs, although not integrated by one poet, is the *Schwanengesang* (The swan song), in which the first seven songs are by Rellstab, the next six by Heine, and the last by Seidl. In these, too, the critics talk about "perfect balance of beauty" and "emotional force."

Of individual *lieder*, the best-known are "Gretchen am Spinnrade" (Gretchen at the spinning wheel); the "Erlkonig," Goethe's tragic poem of a father on horseback trying to outride death; "Ave Maria"; and "Who Is Sylvia." Schubert *lieder* have been called "the maximum of artistic creation in the minimum of space." The professionals describe these songs as natural, never overemphasized, always simple, never forced—and yet dramatically powerful.

Despite his tragically short life—shorter than any other composer on The List—Schubert was extremely productive. Although he composed no concertos, he did write—in addition to the songs and symphonies, for which he is best known—some other famous orchestral pieces, including lovely incidental music to *Rosamunde* (it will sound familiar), a great deal of chamber music, countless piano works of various lengths, six church masses, and several operas (none of which is performed regularly today). Some suggest, however, that the famous song cycles, such as *Die schöne Müllerin*, were, in essence, short tragic operas in themselves.

In the realm of chamber music, Schubert wrote more than twenty quartets, several trios, and several piano trios. The best known of the latter is his Piano Trio in B-flat, Op. 99, about which his admirer Schumann wrote: "One glance . . . and the troubles of our human existence disappear and all the world is fresh and bright again."

Two string quartets are especially well known, one in D minor, called *Death and the Maiden* (one of its themes is borrowed from his song of that name, based on a poem by Matthias Claudius), and an unfinished one in C minor (one movement-plus), called "Quartett-satz" (Quartet movement).

Another often-played piece of chamber music is his Cello Quintet in C, Op. 163, considered by some music professionals as Schubert's greatest work. Most string quintets add a second viola to the basic string-quartet mix, but Schubert chose (in his only string quintet) to add an extra cello instead. This was another work not published until after his death.

While the Cello Quintet is perhaps the chamber work most respected by professionals, the one most enjoyed by the public is the *Trout,* a quintet for piano and strings, composed when Schubert was twenty and based on a theme from another of his songs, called "Die Forelle" (The trout). The strings consist of the usual violin, viola, and cello, but with a double bass substituted for the customary second violin. The first important piece of chamber music that combines the piano with four strings, the *Trout* is a fine chamber-music starting point for neophytes because it is lighthearted and happy, filled with gay, melodious tunes. One need not be at all stuffy or knowledgeable to like it; indeed, it is good to be antistuffy. And the music people also are high on it, which is not always the case with fun compositions. Parts of it come from popular dance rhythms of the countryside.

Of piano music, most of Schubert's sonatas are held by the connoisseurs to be in a lesser class than those of Mozart or Beethoven, although one, No. 21 in B-flat, published posthumously, is regarded as a masterpiece by any standard. Most of his piano music was in small form, similar to the miniature piano compositions that came later from Schumann and Mendelssohn.

Although Schubertians claim that no one has ever written melody as Schubert did, the experts emphasize that he was also a genius at harmony, an astonishing orchestrator (given that he never had an orchestra to orchestrate), and a "master of the subliminal." (It is not true that the subliminal is an early Romantic instrument favored by small musicians because of its lighter weight.)

Concerning the bricks-and-mortar elements of music, Schubert sometimes shifted from major to minor key and back again, not a characteristic of Classical music, and was considerably more dissonant in his harmonies than Mozart and Beethoven. These are the kinds of things that cause the musicologists to consider him a bridge between the Classical and Romantic eras.

Biographers are inclined to have their subjects begin life in abject poverty, and Schubert's first biographer, Sir George Grove, said the composer was "born in the lowest ranks." Maybe so, by Sir George's standards, but in fact his father was a hardworking schoolmaster in a Vienna suburb. Young Franz, his father, and his two older brothers had their own little family quartet. Franz learned piano and violin; he also had a good voice, and at twelve he entered the Imperial Court Choir School. While there he studied Latin, Greek, mathematics, history, and natural science—far more education than Mozart, Beethoven, or Brahms received—and at seventeen he was teaching Vienna youngsters himself.

By the time he completed his Third Symphony, at eighteen, he had given up teaching, and he spent the rest of his life composing and socializing with his Bohemian friends in Vienna—poets, artists, composers, and actors, a wholly different gang from the ones with which Beethoven and Haydn ran—and perhaps one reason why Schubert is Schubert. It was not all wine, women, and song; the group met at "Schubertiades" at different houses, where each club member did his or her own artistic thing. It was not an affluent environment; some music historians use the term *poverty*.

Schubert never married. He did catch a venereal disease. There is disagreement on whether he died from it, as was believed years ago, or from typhus, which was another theory, or from typhoid fever, which was still another. The most respected authorities today blame syphilis. He lived what biographers call "an uneventful life," almost unknown publicly as a composer, with much of his work not discovered until years after his death. There is debate in the music world as to what kind of music a mature Schubert might have produced. Would his genius, which many regard as resulting from his glorious spontaneity and freshness, have endured?

SCHUMANN WEPT

Robert Schumann was a devoted Schubert admirer, once writing of him: "He has strains for the most subtle thoughts and feelings, nay even for the events and conditions of life; and innumerable as are the shakes of human thought and action, so various is his music." On hearing of Schubert's death, the sensitive Schumann spent the night in tears.

STARTER KIT

To be representative, the Starter Kit needs at least one symphony, one piece of chamber music, one piano work, and, since Schubert is the foremost songwriter on The List, one song cycle. In each case there are legitimate alternates for the ones selected. I've chosen the following:

• Symphony No. 8 in B Minor, the *Unfinished*, his most popular symphony and one we cannot bypass despite some heavy professional sentiment for the *Great C Major*.

• The *Trout* Quintet in A for Piano and Strings, chiefly because it is such fun to hear but also for its historical significance. Experts might lean toward the Cello Quintet.

• Two solo piano compositions, because the piano was such a part of Schubert's work and of the Romantic era. One is his Sonata in B-flat, one of three published after his death, and today one of the most frequently played of all piano sonatas—if you don't count Beethoven, and when piano sonatas are the issue it is wise not to get into a head-to-head competition with him. *Poignancy* is the word used by the experts to describe this composition; some of them think it Schubert's most poignant work. The second-chosen piano composition is a much longer one, the *Wanderer Fantasy*, a set of variations that gets its name (and some of its music) from his song "The Wanderer," written several years earlier. Schumann said of it: "Schubert would like, in this work, to condense the whole orchestra into two hands." Liszt later arranged it for piano and orchestra, thus making it into sort of a piano concerto. It was extremely popular when published in 1823 and remains so. (More typical of the composer are his impromptus [two volumes of them] and his "Moments Musicaux," short lyrical masterpieces that typify Schubert's poetry-in-music. The most famous of the latter is "Moment Musical in F Minor," Op. 94, No. 3.)

• Finally, for the greatest of all art-song writers, a song cycle. *Die schöne Müllerin*, composed in 1823 when Schubert was twenty-six, is a cycle of hope, love, and tragedy in which a young miller finds death while seeking the love of a young maiden.

SCHUBERT: THE STARTER KIT

Composition	Recordings Available*
SYMPHONIES: (OF NINE)	
No. 8 in B Minor (Unfinished)	28
CHAMBER MUSIC:	
Quintet in A (Trout) for Piano and Strings	23
PIANO MUSIC:	
Piano Sonata No. 21 in B-flat (posth.)	18
Wanderer Fantasy	12
VOCAL MUSIC:	
Song Cycle:	
Die schöne Müllerin	8

*Represents the number of recorded releases available of each listed composition as found in a recent issue of the *Schwann/Opus* catalogue. A "C" indicates that a work is only available collected with other compositions.

SCHUBERT: A TOP TEN

Composition	Recordings Available*
SYMPHONIES: (OF NINE)	
No. 8 in B Minor (Unfinished)	28
No. 9 in C (The Great)	21
CHAMBER MUSIC:	
Quintet in A (Trout) for Piano and Strings	23
Cello Quintet in C	9
Quartet No. 14 in D Minor (Death and the Maiden)	14
Piano Trio No. 1 in B-flat	14

Composition	Recordings Available*

PIANO MUSIC:

Sonata No. 21 in B-flat (posth.)	18
Wanderer Fantasy	12
Impromptus (two volumes of four each)	23

VOCAL MUSIC:
Song Cycle:

Die schöne Müllerin	8

SCHUBERT: A MASTER COLLECTION

Composition	Recordings Available*

SYMPHONIES: (OF NINE)

No. 5 in B-flat	11
No. 8 in B Minor (Unfinished)	28
No. 9 in C (The Great)	21

OTHER ORCHESTRAL WORKS:

Rosamunde, Incidental Music	11

CHAMBER MUSIC:

Octet in F for Strings and Winds	4
Quintet in A (Trout) for Piano and Strings	23
Cello Quintet in C	9
Quartets:	
No. 12 in C Minor (Quartettsatz)	14
No. 14 in D Minor (Death and the Maiden)	14
No. 15 in G	4
Piano Trio No. 1 in B-flat	14
Piano Trio No. 2 in E-flat	9
Sonata for Arpeggione and Piano	13

PIANO MUSIC:

Sonatas (of twenty-two):	
No. 10 in A	9
No. 19 in C Minor	5
No. 20 in A (posth.)	8
No. 21 in B-flat (posth.)	18

Composition	Recordings Available*
Wanderer Fantasy	12
Moments Musicaux	16
Fantasia in F Minor (duet)	4
Impromptus (two volumes of four each)	23

VOCAL MUSIC:
Song Cycles:
    Die schöne Müllerin   8
    Die Winterreise   9
Songs:
    Gretchen am Spinnrade   17
    Erlkonig   18

ROBERT SCHUMANN (1810–1856)

Number 8

It is not difficult for the true neophyte to confuse Franz Schubert and Robert Schumann. In addition to their sound-alike names, they were alive at the same time, born thirteen years apart. Both were German (as used here; actually Schubert was Austrian and Schumann German). The former, born when Beethoven was only twenty-seven, was an initiator of Romanticism and passed that spirit on; the latter received it and took it to its zenith. Although both wrote symphonies and chamber music, both also specialized in magnificent *lieder*, and both composed for the piano at a level reached by few others in music history. Both are Demigods, among the Top Ten on The List.

Schubert was much more of a natural musical genius, and his total work is more highly regarded than Schumann's. But in music poetry and songwriting, only Schubert—whom Schumann worshiped—is Schumann's better.

Few dispute that Schumann was the most romantic of the Romantics. "What I really am," he wrote, "I do not know myself. . . . If I am a poet—for no one can become one—destiny will decide one day." Destiny aside, history has decided: definitely a poet of music.

The musicologists talk about the new "hero" born of the Romantic movement. Instead of taking on life with the assured, confident step of the Classical hero, the Romantic hero gropes his way forward, faltering and staggering. He sees an abyss ahead but knows he is not capable of filling it. One critic wrote of this hero: "With all his energies reinforced by the desperate consciousness of the uselessness of his effort, he strives toward those heights whose attainment has been forbidden."

As the quintessential Romantic, with that view of life, it is not surprising that Schumann was melancholy even during his productive years. He later suffered a nervous breakdown, once attempted suicide, and died in an asylum at forty-six.

Biographer Andre Boucourechliev said of him: "He was one of those hallucinated spirits, ripe for an early death because of their rejection of an imperfect world in which the clocks could not be turned back. He was, in fact, one of that unhappy race who, in their search for the infinite, ventured not only their work, but even their lives and their reason."

In his approach to composition Schumann was the first complete musical dissenter of his time. He saw no reason to honor the Classical structure and what he considered to be its binding limitations. "As if all mental pictures must be shaped to fit one or two forms," he declared. "As if each idea did not come into existence with its own form ready-made! As if each work of art had not its own meaning and consequently its own form!"

That was to become Romantic doctrine—but it was heresy when first asserted by Schumann. Out of the marriage of his own genius and this rule-breaking approach came the lyrical beauty, the many different moods, and the wide-ranging emotions of his music—not strange, given that the composer himself was a man of many different moods and wide-ranging emotions. The words most commonly used to describe his compositions are "impetuous," "whimsical," "lyrical," "poetic," and "melodious."

"Works are needed for every level of culture," he wrote. "The only things which must be excluded from art are hypocrisy and ugliness, which disguises itself with seductive veils. It is these polygraphs to whom creation is only a question of money (and there are distinguished names among them), these vagrants, these poor and poverty-stricken simulators who clothe their need in tawdry finery, whom we must fight with all our strength."

He was not slow to attack the unworthy. On the publication of the 302d work of a contemporary (unListed) composer, he wrote: "However diligent the critic may be, it is quite impossible for him to catch up with Herr _____. If I had enemies and wanted to destroy them, I would condemn them to listening to nothing but music like this."

Schumann's music has been called an expression of states and conditions of the soul, never spectacular and never objective. "No composer," wrote one critic, "has whispered such secrets of subtle and ravishing beauty to a receptive listener. The hearer of Schumann's music must in turn be imaginative and a dreamer. He must often anticipate the composer's thought." Well, maybe we amateur listeners don't have to anticipate the composer's thought, but just remember that the music began in a poet's dream world.

While regarded as a consummate master of smaller forms, especially for piano and for voice, Schumann did not restrict himself to those forms. Although the critics find him "less at ease" with symphonies, concertos, and string quartets, he was wholly prepared to tackle them.

Works in the larger forms include four symphonies, a cello concerto, a piano concerto, and in the chamber-music arena, an acclaimed piano quartet, a popular piano quintet, and some string quartets, although they are not regarded by the experts as among his finest works.

The first of his piano masterpieces, written at age twenty-three, a set of twelve variations on a theme, was called *Etudes Symphoniques*. Like so many masterworks, it was largely ignored for fifty years or so until piano virtuoso Anton Rubinstein began performing it for concert audiences. Another early piano masterpiece was the *Carnaval*, composed in 1834–1835, which consists of twenty-one movements. Biographer Andre Boucourechliev says it is the first piece in which Schumann "gave his genius full rein." Two more recognized masterworks were *Fantasiestücke*, written in 1837, made up of eight small "fantasy pieces," and *Kreisleriana*, composed of another eight piano sketches.

Two albums for children also are well known: *Kinderscenen* (Scenes from childhood) and *Album für die Jugend* (Album for the

THE TRUE APOSTLE

Schumann had his opinions about Schubert, Brahms, Mendelssohn, Bach, Rossini, Wagner, and Liszt.

On Schubert: "I did not speak freely about Schubert. Or, rather, I only spoke of him to the trees and the stars."

On Brahms: "I am convinced that he will create the greatest sensation in the musical world. . . . I believe that Johannes is the true apostle who will also write revelations which hordes of Pharisees will be unable to decipher even after centuries."

On Mendelssohn: "Mendelssohn told me just as he was saying good-bye that he had had no opportunity to express how much my music (the Quartets) pleased him. I was very happy to hear it, since his opinion is the one which counts most with me."

On Bach: "That genius who purifies and gives strength" (and whom, throughout his life, he considered his true master).

Rossini and the other Italian composers: "Those canaries!"

On Wagner: "Without doubt Wagner is a clever Fellow, full of mad ideas and bold to a degree, but he does not know how to write out four consecutive bars which are beautiful or even correct."

On Liszt: "Most of all he gives me the impression of being a spoilt child. He is good, over-bearing, amiable, arrogant, noble and generous, often hard with others. . . . Liszt can play as he likes, and the result is always full of interest even if one can often find faults of taste, particularly in his compositions which I cannot qualify in any other term than 'awful'. . . . I am very near to detesting him as a composer, but as virtuoso he has sent me into a transport of admiration."

young). The former has thirteen pieces, the latter forty-three simple ones.

Although some of these works are fairly "big," the professionals note that even here Schumann's preference was to string together a lot of smaller individual pieces rather than play architect and attempt to unify them.

The most famous of his piano compositions is probably the monumental Fantasy in C. In 1838 Schumann wrote about it to his beloved Clara Wieck, a piano virtuoso whom he pursued and won despite vehement opposition from her music-instructor father. Although Schumann was not yet married at the time of the letter, the father had already lost the war after winning a battle or two. "I have just finished a Fantasy in three movements which I sketched down to its details in June, 1836," Schumann wrote. "I do not think I ever wrote anything more impassioned than the first movement. It is a profound lament about you. You can understand the Fantasy only if you transport yourself back to the unhappy summer of 1836, when I had to give you up. Now I have no reason to compose in so miserable and melancholy a way!"

Some professionals believe that this Fantasy is one of the three major pieces of solo piano music from the Romantic era, the other two being Chopin's Sonata in B-flat Minor and Liszt's Sonata in B Minor. No survey of musicologists has been undertaken to validate that belief, but all three are among our Starter Kit choices and merit attention.

The move from pure piano music to German art songs is a natural one, and no more beautiful love songs exist than those Schumann wrote in 1840, at age thirty, immediately after marrying his Clara. In that year alone he composed some 140 songs, among the most famous of which are "Im wunderschönen Monat Mai," "Mondnacht," "Lied der Zuleika," "Ich grolle nicht," "Frühlingsnacht," "Widmung," "Die Lowenbraut," "Schöne Wiege," "Du bist wie eine Blume," "Die Lotusblume," "Wanderlied," "Der Nussbaum," and "An meinem Herzen." For many years one of his most popular songs was a ballad, "Die beiden Grenadiere" (The two grenadiers). Today the two favorites are perhaps "Widmung" and "Der Nussbaum."

He also composed several song cycles, the two best known being the *Dichterliebe* (Poet's love) and *Frauenliebe und Leben* (Woman's love and life). *Dichterliebe* includes sixteen songs to lyrics by Heine, and *Frauenliebe und Leben* eight songs to lyrics by Chamisso.

As a composer, Schumann concentrated on one form at a time—writing nothing but piano music for several years, for example, and then turning to something else entirely, with chamber music and symphonies coming late in his life. His four symphonies, readily available today, are No. 1 in B-flat (*Spring*), a joyous work; No. 2 in C, which is more like an upstate New York winter than a spring; No. 3 in B-flat, the *Rhenish*, presumably reflecting Rhenish life and generally considered by the professionals to be the most "interesting" of the four; and No. 4 in D Minor, the most "mature and unified."

DRAMATIC MICROCOSMS

Beethoven wrote some eighty songs with piano accompaniment, nineteen of them with texts by Goethe. Weber helped introduce the Romantic movement in his hundred-plus songs. But it was Schubert who made the German *lied* what the professionals call a "complex and profound piece of music," a "dramatic microcosm." Schumann inherited this perfect—or near-perfect—art form and worked to bring about an even more intimate unity of voice, poetry, and piano accompaniment. He composed 248 songs, using texts by many poets of the day, great and unknown—and even including one text from Shakespeare. (Byron, as readers of Romantic poetry might suspect, was the Englishman closest to his heart.) His greatest inspiration, however, came from German poets, particularly Ruckert, Eichendorff, and Heine. (Most of the love poems used in the many *lieder* written by the composer for his Clara were by Ruckert.)

There is no set form in which *lieder* must be composed. Some consist of a number of stanzas with a refrain repeated after each; sometimes the music differs from stanza to stanza and sometimes it is the same; some *lieder* are in three-part form; and sometimes the music follows the poetry without any established repetition.

The composer did not take his symphonies lightly. Biographers say he felt an urge and an obligation to follow in the wake of symphonists Beethoven, Schubert, and Mendelssohn. Early on, needing new universe-penetrating experiences and creations, he wrote: "I am tempted to smash my piano as it is becoming too narrow to contain my ideas. I really have very little practical experience of writing for the orchestra, but I don't despair of acquiring it."

THE SCHUMANN LIST

His List of the truly great: Bach, Mozart, Beethoven, Schubert, Chopin, Mendelssohn, and Berlioz.

When his first symphony was almost completed, he wrote (on February 14, 1841): "The Symphony has given me many happy hours and is now almost finished. I often give thanks to the beneficent spirit for allowing me to bring a work of this importance to a successful issue, in so little time and with such facility. The sketch of the entire Symphony was completed in four days. Exhaustion followed after the many sleepless nights."

His chamber-music output included three string quartets and, more important from the standpoint of music development, the first serious piano quintet (in E-flat, Op. 44), scored for a piano and the standard string quartet. (Recall that Schubert's piano quintet, the *Trout*, was the first major work involving the piano and four strings, but he substituted a double bass for one of the usual two violins. It takes only a little listening to ascertain that a double-bass sound comes from one but not the other.)

Schumann wrote a violin concerto that is not often played and a cello concerto that gets considerably more attention—in part because it is deemed to be better music and in part because there is much less cello music on the market than violin music. The professionals say that the violin concerto is not Schumann at his most inspired, but they point to an impressive second subject, and there is a fun slow movement.

But the goalposts are moved when it comes to the piano music. His Piano Concerto in A Minor, his most-recorded composition, is unquestionably one of the best known of the species. In fact, not surprisingly for nonarchitect Schumann, it did not begin life as a concerto but rather as a one-movement piece he called a "Fantasia," composed for his adored—and adoring—wife. Several years later he added two more movements, an intermezzo and a finale, to turn it into a three-part concerto.

Schumann, one might say, was destined to be a Romantic. His father owned a bookshop in the small Saxon town of Zwickau, where Robert was born. The senior Schumann spent more time writing in his study, creating gloomy tales about knights of old, than selling books. Schumann's mother called the boy *Lichter Punkt*: point of light. That's 999 short for 1990-era American politics, perhaps, but indicative of Robert's spirit. At age twelve he formed a small orchestra, composed a psalm, and studied Mozart, Haydn, and Weber, the first true Romantic. But music was second in his heart to literature in his early years. He was particularly fond of Byron, as well as of Goethe, Schiller, and Jean-Paul Richter. His biographers claim that he knew Goethe's *Faust* by heart (this probably means he knew quotations from it, not the entire play) and that he recited so much of it that school friends nicknamed him both "Faust" (the aging scholar) and "Mephistopheles" (the Devil, who takes Faust's soul). Young Robert founded a literary society, wrote a dissertation on art and poetry, and was a happy youth until age fifteen, when he became withdrawn, indifferent, and melancholy—beginning, perhaps, to seek a universe beyond his reach. A computer could not program a more appropriate childhood for a great—*the* great—German Romantic.

At seventeen he wrote: "Earliest youth experienced these moments when the heart could not find what it desired, for, darkened by an inexpressible nostalgia, and by tears, it knew not what it sought. It was something silent and sacred in which the soul could feel its rapture, when the youth made dreamy question of the stars."

That isn't Stravinsky, Bartók, or Hindemith speaking from the twentieth century. Romantics were driven to penetrate the universe by creative acts. For the sensitive youth, universe penetration is not a weekend chore.

POET-MUSICIAN

Many have called Robert Schumann the incarnation of the spirit of Romanticism. One gets a vivid glimpse of that spirit in this excerpt from a letter to his mother, written in 1828:

"And so it is throughout human life—the goal we have attained is no longer a goal, and we yearn and strive and aim ever higher and higher, until the eyes close in death and the storm-tossed body and soul lie slumbering in the grave."

When his father died, his mother led Schumann into law. After devoting several years to faithful but uninterested legal study, he made the decision to pursue music, as a concert pianist. Tragically, he permanently paralyzed one finger while experimenting with exercises to make his fingers more flexible. The consensus in academia today is that his hand had probably already been weakened by a mercury-based medicine he had been taking to treat syphilis. Whatever the medical cause, the finger was paralyzed, and Schumann the young virtuoso pianist thus became Schumann the Romantic composer—and the music journalist. He devoted enormous efforts in Leipzig to a critical music review, the *Neue Zeitschrift für Musik*, which he founded when he was twenty-four.

He was at his most creative for several years after marrying Clara. Their love affair lasted until his death after several unhealthy last years.

STARTER KIT

Four of the Starter Kit choices are almost automatic. There must be songs (*lieder*), and they are most available in the famous song cycles. Of these, the *Dichterliebe* cycle includes several famous *lieder* and is easy to find in the record stores. Little or nothing would be lost, however, by shifting to *Frauenliebe und Leben*. There also must be solo piano music, and it is impossible to leave out the popular Fantasy in C, written with Clara in mind and dedicated to the greatest of all pianists, Franz Liszt.

Schumann's oft-recorded Piano Concerto in A Minor was completed in 1845 during his biggest creative period, before nervous disorders took control of him. One critic has written that in it he "has left an imperishable trace of his genius," although when it was first performed, by Clara Schumann, a critic on the scene praised her loyal but futile efforts "to make her husband's curious rhapsody pass for music."

In the chamber-music category the favorite and acknowledged masterpiece is his Quintet in E-flat, composed in 1842 (when he wrote nearly all of his chamber music). The same critic who attacked the piano concerto wrote that the quintet would always keep its place in the first rank of musical masterpieces.

Which symphony to choose? That is more of a challenge, given the experts' consensus that there is no mighty Schumann symphony. One might be overly influenced by the experts and select another piano solo work, say *Kinderscenen*, as the fifth Starter Kit choice. But the goal of the Starter Kit is to offer a smorgasbord when feasible. The happy First Symphony is the most fun, but the Third has the most variety, and some professionals say it is his most important, while others settle on the Fourth as the "finest work, overall." Presumably we should go with the finest overall, so the recommendation is Symphony No. 4 in D Minor, composed in 1841 but not published until a decade later because Schumann wasn't happy with it. After revision, it was finally introduced in Düsseldorf in 1853, conducted by the composer. (Some time when you are blue, sneak in when no one is around and turn on the First. Say to yourself, "This obviously is not really a great symphony; it is poorly constructed." And then listen and start feeling better.)

SCHUMANN: THE STARTER KIT

Composition	Recordings Available*
SYMPHONIES:	
No. 4 in D Minor	8
OTHER ORCHESTRAL WORKS:	
Piano Concerto in A Minor	27
CHAMBER MUSIC:	
Quintet in E-flat for Piano and Strings	9
PIANO MUSIC:	
Fantasia in C	21
VOCAL MUSIC:	
Song Cycle:	
Dichterliebe	7

*Represents the number of recorded releases available of each listed composition as found in a recent issue of the *Schwann/Opus* catalogue. A "C" indicates that a work is only available collected with other compositions.

SCHUMANN: A TOP TEN

Composition	Recordings Available*
SYMPHONIES:	
No. 3 in E-flat (Rhenish)	8
No. 4 in D Minor	8
OTHER ORCHESTRAL WORKS:	
Piano Concerto in A Minor	27
Overture to Manfred	13
CHAMBER MUSIC:	
Quintet in E-flat for Piano and Strings	9
PIANO MUSIC:	
Fantasia in C	21
Kinderscenen	20
Carnaval	17
Fantasiestücke	11

Composition   Recordings Available*

VOCAL MUSIC:
Song Cycle:
  Dichterliebe   7

SCHUMANN: A MASTER COLLECTION

Composition   Recordings Available*

SYMPHONIES:
No. 1 in B-flat (Spring)   7
No. 2 in C   5
No. 3 in E-flat (Rhenish)   8
No. 4 in D Minor   8

OTHER ORCHESTRAL WORKS:
Piano Concerto in A Minor   27
Violin Concerto in D Minor   3
Cello Concerto in A Minor   7
Overture to Manfred   13
Konzertstück in F for Four Horns and Orchestra   6

CHAMBER MUSIC:
Quintet in E-flat for Piano and Strings   9
Quartet in E-flat for Piano and Strings   6

PIANO MUSIC:
Fantasia in C   21
Kinderscenen   20
Arabeske (for piano)   15
Carnaval   17
Fantasiestücke   11
Kreisleriana   11
Humoreske   7
Papillons   7
Sonata for Piano in G Minor   6
Etudes Symphoniques   11

OTHER INSTRUMENTAL MUSIC:
Fantasiestücke for Clarinet and Piano   13
Romances for Oboe (three)   11

Composition   *Recordings Available**

VOCAL MUSIC:
Song Cycles:
    Dichterliebe   7
    Frauenliebe und Leben   9

GEORGE FRIDERIC HANDEL (1685–1759)

Number 9

Beethoven called him "the greatest of us all." That would have included not only Vivaldi and Palestrina from earlier times but also
Bach, Mozart, Haydn, and Beethoven himself. On our List he is Number 9, trailing those four and another four who came later. It is of no
matter; George Frideric Handel is one of the most powerful figures in
music history. He is also one who gave the public what it wanted—
joyous and bright melody, song, and grand choral music.

Like the Romantic composer Georges Bizet, Handel is best known
for one work, *Messiah*, considered the greatest oratorio ever written,
and one of the most famous pieces of music of any category. Unlike
Bizet, however, Handel was tremendously productive and highly respected in his day for many other compositions—nearly fifty operas,
music's second-best-known set of concerti grossi, some highly popular
orchestral works, and, most important, more than twenty oratorios.

He was born in Halle, Saxony (Germany) and was baptized Georg
Friederich Handel. But he lived in England from 1712 to his death in
1759, became an English citizen, and was buried—at his request—in
Westminster Abbey. Tour guides today claim him as an Englishman,
pointing out his monument and grave in the Poet's Corner of the

Abbey, guarded by a stone tablet bearing a portion of the *Messiah* score. And he held a dominant position in music for a hundred or more years in his adopted England, not in Germany.

Few seriously question that *Messiah* is the greatest oratorio, or that Handel is the all-time master in the composing of the choral music of which an oratorio is made. The question is whether the next-best oratorio is another of Handel's, or one of Haydn's two, or possibly Mendelssohn's *Elijah*. *Messiah* was first produced in 1742, more or less in the middle of Handel's oratorio period, which followed many earlier years during which his fame came almost entirely from Italian-type opera. During that time he had become England's premier musician. Like other operas of their era, Handel's sound stilted and artificial to the modern ear.

Messiah, while based on the coming of Christ, His suffering and Crucifixion, and the Resurrection, was intended not as a church or religious work but as an "entertainment" and was composed in twenty-five days for the Lord Lieutenant of Dublin, Ireland. Yet this "entertainment" by Handel—musician/impresario/theater-owner/worldly figure of London—is far better known to the general public today as a religious work than are Bach's spiritual Mass in B Minor or *St. Matthew Passion*, the many magnificent mystical masses of Palestrina, or any requiem, including Mozart's.

Upon completing the "Hallelujah Chorus" in Part II of *Messiah*, Handel—not a religious man in the sense of Bach—is reported by biographers to have said to his servant: "I did think I saw all Heaven before me, and the great God himself." And, later: "I think God has visited me." This is precisely what any good public-relations man would have advised this entrepreneur-musician to say, but that is no reason to doubt the story, and the glory of the music is indeed Godlike.

Handel began as an organist in his native Halle, settled in Hamburg as a member of the opera orchestra in 1703, traveled for three years, became Kapellmeister in Hanover, studied Italian opera in Italy, visited England first in 1711, and returned at age twenty-seven in 1712 to live, initially as an opera composer. In the opera field he was not a reformer like Monteverdi, Gluck, or Wagner, but rather a man of his time who took the ready-made forms he found and filled them with all the beauty he was capable of producing—which, the professionals say, far surpassed the operatic efforts of his contemporaries. After many years of acclaim and fortune, however, the bottom dropped out of Italian opera, and things did not go well for the transplanted German. He was out of favor and broke when he turned to oratorios.

In part because Handel's genius was music, not theater, his operas

FOR THE RELIEF OF PRISONERS

The "Hallelujah Chorus" from *Messiah* has been called the single greatest cry of musical triumph ever written. A work proclaiming the King of Kings, the Lord of Lords, it was created by a musical entrepreneur then down on his luck and fortune. The first *Messiah* performance was for charity in Dublin—"for the relief of the prisoners in the several gaols, and for the support of Mercer's Hospital in Stephen's-street and of the Charitable Infirmary on the Inn's Quay."

have nearly disappeared—but not completely, and several are available in complete versions as recordings, including *Alcina*, *Allesandro*, *Atalanta*, *Hercules*, and *Julius Caesar*. Many excerpts from his operas are performed, one of the most famous being the Largo (the aria "Ombra mai fu") from the opening of the opera *Serse* (Xerxes), first performed in 1738. Two suites of popular orchestral music have come from *Alcina*, and Sir Thomas Beecham devised an orchestral suite that is still played from *Il Pastor Fido* (The faithful shepherd). Beautiful individual arias are recorded from *Atalanta* ("Care selve"), *Floriante* ("Alma mia" and "Caro amore"), and *Rinaldo* ("Lascia ch' io pianga" and "Cara sposa").

While Baroque operas followed set forms and rules, oratorios were without costumes, scenery, action, or acting and were an ideal form for Handel's musical genius. His oratorio fame began with *Haman and Mordecai* in 1732 and continued with *Saul* (1738), *Israel in Egypt* (1739), *Messiah* (1741), *Samson* (1741), *Judas Maccabaeus* (1747), and *Joshua* (1751). *Israel in Egypt*, overshadowed for centuries by *Messiah*, was called by critic Romain Rolland "the most gigantic effort ever made in oratorio."

In *Israel in Egypt* Handel produced some great pictures and imitations of natural happenings. In his double chorus, "And there came all manner of flies and lice in all their quarters," he produced from the instruments the buzzing of flies. "He gave them hailstones" has been called one of the greatest replicas of a storm in the history of music. In "He sent a great darkness" one can imagine the heaviness of night, and in "He led them through the deep" one can hear and see the rolling of great waters.

Israel in Egypt is not a greater masterpiece than *Messiah*, but if you enjoy oratorios, its music is fascinating—even though it initially lasted

EARLY TONE COLOR

Although later Romantic composers were better known for orchestration and tone color, Handel wrote for the theater and knew how to turn on an audience. In *Saul* he used trombones to build up the presence of the king and two bassoons to provide the right atmosphere for the prophet's ghost. And his *Royal Fireworks Music* is scored for forty trumpets, twenty horns, sixteen oboes, sixteen bassoons, eight kettledrums, and—long predating Tchaikovsky's *1812* Overture—a cannon.

for only three performances. The second part is called "Song of Moses," and one number in it, "The Lord Is a Man of War," a duet for two basses, is one of the most famous of Handel's songs.

Handel, like Bach, was a highly talented organist. Both were geniuses and both counterpoint masters. Born the same year in Germany, both are among the top ten composers of history—giving us two Baroque artists among those Immortals and Demigods.

Bach, while often difficult to get along with, was retiring, basically a homebody with many children, reasonably humble, dedicated to satisfying his perfectionist self, ultrareligious, possessor of a deep faith. Handel was proud, a man of the world, part of the in-group of London, a portly bear of a figure, a presence to be reckoned with, arrogant, blustery, rude, subservient to no one. Handel's music is more melodic, easier to understand, and, on first hearing, easier to enjoy; Bach's is deeper, coming from the soul, and, on fourth hearing, something very special.

Handel was a public figure in England, worshiped by many and, not surprisingly given his imperious manner, disliked by some. One who did not like him was another musician, Battista Buononcini, who has rather disappeared, but in the days when the two were competing, one humorist wrote:

"Some say, as compared to Buononcini
That Mynheer Handel's but a ninny
Others aver that he to Handel
Is scarcely fit to hold a candle
Strange all this difference should be
Twixt tweedledum and tweedledee."

The Handel-Bach comparison is aided by the opinions of the professionals. Professor Joseph Machlis offers his expert view, noting that Bach and Handel complement each other as the representative figures of the late Baroque. Bach's art, he writes, is introspective, while Handel is a man of action. "Bach rhapsodizes in the organ loft; Handel is the courtier. Bach is the meticulous artist who brings to perfection every form he touches; Handel, tossing off his scores for the theater, is a magnificent improviser. Bach is a master of detail; Handel works with sweeping brush strokes. Bach's mystic gaze is turned upon the world to come; Handel hymns the pomp and power of this world." Both men, Machlis adds, were inspired by an ethical ideal; but Bach was a Lutheran, while Handel was a man of the Enlightenment whose moral sense was bound to no creed or dogma.

MASTER OF MASTERS

Ludwig van Beethoven had no reservations about Handel's genius, once commenting: "Handel is the unattained master of all masters. Go to him and learn how to produce great effects with scant deploy of means." Shortly before he died, Beethoven received as a present a complete set of Handel's works, about which he said: "I have wished to own them for a long time because Handel is the greatest, the most solid of composers; from him I still can learn something. Fetch the books over to me!" And again: "In the future I shall write after the manner of my grand master Handel."

The two were not quite contemporaries, Handel living from 1685 to 1759 and Beethoven born in 1770.

Aside from oratorios, Handel's most respected works include a group of twelve orchestral concerti grossi. It is easy to get confused about Handel and concerti (or concertos, if you wish). Six concerti grossi were published in 1734 as Op. 3. Better known and more esteemed by the experts are twelve for strings appearing as Op. 6, called the *Grand* Concertos. The official announcement of these concerti grossi in the *London Daily Post* of October 29, 1729, read: "This day are published proposals for printing by subscription, with His Majesty's royal license and protection, Twelve Grand Concertos, in

Seven Parts, for Four Violins, a Tenor, a Violoncello, with a thorough-bass for the Harpsichord. Composed by Mr. Handel. Price to subscribers, two guineas. Ready to be delivered by April next."

Handel borrowed the concerto grosso form from the Italians, appreciating the idea of contrasting two to four solo instruments (such as two violins and a cello) against the rest of the orchestra, which consisted mainly of strings. The twelve of Op. 6 stand with Bach's famous *Brandenburg* set as the finest Baroque concertos. The music people point out that the emotional range is great: majesty in No. 1, tragedy in No. 3, a haunting feeling in No. 6, and serenity in No. 12. They go from lighthearted dances to ungainly fugue subjects. They have been called the "apotheosis of improvisation . . . integrated by the sheer force of Handel's creative personality." Beyond that, they make pleasant listening, once you get into Baroque sounds.

There are also three volumes of organ concertos, as opposed to orchestral concerti grossi. Six of these were published as Op. 4, another six without an opus number, and a third six as Op. 7. In most of these, a harpsichord is used in place of an organ at times. It is a little confusing that four of the middle set are transcriptions for organ of four Op. 6 *Grand* Concertos.

Outside of the concerto field, the two best-known Handel orchestral works are the *Royal Fireworks Music* and the lively, cheerful *Water Music*. The *Royal Fireworks Music* was composed in 1749 and the *Water Music* in 1717, for a July 17 concert on the river given by George I, elector of Hanover, who had been proclaimed king of England.

Handel's lack of humility did not prevent him from being humorous, and he could take a joke on himself—especially if he was the giver. When a friend commented on the poor music being heard at Vauxhall Gardens, he replied: "You are right, sir; it is very poor stuff. I thought so myself when I wrote it." When friends tried to console him on an empty house for one of his oratorios, he replied: "Never mind; the music will sound the better." To explain its lack of popularity, he said: "The Jews will not come to it because it is a Christian story; and the Ladies will not come because it is a virtuous one." His English was never good, despite the many years spent in London, and biographers tell of one loud exclamation, heard through the theater, when a violinist finally concluded a long and rambling cadenza: "You are welcome home, Mr. Doubourg!"

He worked hard, composed rapidly, never married, had no public love life, had an evil temper, swore in several languages, was aggressively independent, avoided politics, loved to eat and drink—and dominated music in England for years.

THE BLACKSMITH

The music world is full of wonderful stories, many more legend than fact. One well-known Handel piece is "The Harmonious Blacksmith," actually one movement from his Fifth Harpsichord Suite. An oft-told story has it that the composer ducked into a blacksmith's shop during a thunderstorm, was inspired by the even beat of the hammer on the anvil, and wrote the music.

It never happened. The truth seems to be that a blacksmith in Bath, England, was particularly fond of the music and sang it so often that his friends began calling him the "harmonious blacksmith." A publisher with a Madison Avenue bent printed the work independently of the suite and gave it that title.

The tune is catchy, although the music people consider it more pleasure-giving than great composition.

STARTER KIT

Messiah belongs among the first ten pieces in anyone's music collection. It is not necessary to listen to all two and a half hours and fifty-odd musical numbers composed for the entire production—overture, recitatives, arias, and chorales. Most performances are of condensed versions. Two orchestral works are included in the score: the overture, and the Pastoral Symphony, in Part I. Part I also contains one of the work's most beautiful arias, "He shall feed his flock like a shepherd," found in most abridged versions.

Other famous passages include "I know that my Redeemer liveth," "How beautiful are the feet," "Behold and see," "Lift up your heads," and "Why do the nations so furiously rage together?" And, of course, most famous of all is the "Hallelujah Chorus." The literature says that King George II began the practice of rising to his feet in his box when he first heard the chorus, a tradition that continues in many places today.

Two orchestral choices are the popular Water Music and the Royal Fireworks Music, the latter written to celebrate the peace treaty signed at Aix-la-Chapelle ending the war between the British and the French.

Years ago some historians said that Handel regained favor with King George I, and received a life pension, by composing Water Music and surprising the monarch with an orchestral concert while floating down the Thames alongside the royal barge. This story has been discredited, but some of the music, at least, *was* played during a boat trip down the Thames.

No one knows any longer exactly how many *Water Music* pieces there were originally, but it seems there were about twenty. These are now put together into three suites, one of nine movements and two of five each. But the "suite" that is still best known is in six movements: Allegro, Air, Bouree, Hornpipe, Andante, and Allegro deciso. Our recommendation is to collect that basic "Water Music Suite," which will sound familiar.

The fourth selection is any one of the twelve *Grand* Concertos of Op. 6, the most popular of Handel's concerto works and highly respected by the experts, even if less widely known than Bach's *Brandenburg* Concertos. No. 6 in G Minor is an example, although others of the twelve are valid substitutes.

To complete the Starter Kit we have chosen, for variety, Handel's Trio Sonatas—Op. 2, Nos. 1 through 6, or Op. 5, Nos. 1 through 7. This passes up the "Coronation Anthems," the *Alexander's Feast* Concerto, and the famous Largo, the aria "Ombra mai fu" (Never was there a shadow) from the opera *Xerxes*, but any such substitutions are acceptable. The bottom line, though, is that Handel is Mr. Oratorio, and the true Handel fan would insist at least on *Israel in Egypt* in addition to *Messiah*—and probably on *Saul* and *Jeptha*, his last. It is fair with any Demigod to collect ten works instead of five.

HANDEL: THE STARTER KIT

Composition	Recordings Available*
ORCHESTRAL WORKS:	
Water Music (complete or suite)	19/30
Royal Fireworks Music	30
Concerto Grosso (from Op. 6):	
No. 7 in B-flat	7
Trio Sonatas, Op. 2 or Op. 5	19
VOCAL MUSIC:	
Oratorio:	
Messiah	25

*Represents the number of recorded releases available of each listed composition as found in a recent issue of the *Schwann/Opus* catalogue. A "C" indicates that a work is only available collected with other compositions.

HANDEL: A TOP TEN

Composition	Recordings Available*
ORCHESTRAL WORKS:	
Water Music (complete or suite)	19/30
Royal Fireworks Music	30
Concerti Grossi (from Op. 6):	
No. 6 in G Minor	10
No. 7 in B-flat	7
Concerto in C (Alexander's Feast)	6
Concerto in B-flat for Harp and Orchestra,	5
Op. 4, No. 6	
CHAMBER AND SOLO INSTRUMENTAL MUSIC:	
Trio Sonatas, Op. 2 or Op. 5	19
VOCAL MUSIC:	
Oratorio:	
Messiah	25
Opera:	
Serse (Xerxes) (including the famous Largo)	2
Coronation Anthems (four, including Zadok	2
the Priest)	

HANDEL: A MASTER COLLECTION

Composition	Recordings Available*
ORCHESTRAL WORKS:	
Water Music (complete):	19
Suite No. 1 in F with Horns	
Suite No. 2 in D with Trumpets	
Suite No. 3 in G with Flutes	
Water Music Suite (excerpts from above)	30
Royal Fireworks Music	30
Concerti Grossi (twelve orchestral concertos,	
Op. 6) including:	
No. 6 in G Minor	10
No. 7 in B-flat	7
Concerto in C (Alexander's Feast)	6
Concertos for Organ:	
Op. 4, No. 2 in B-flat	C

Composition	Recordings Available*
Op. 7, No. 4 in D Minor	C
Op. 7, No. 5 in G Minor	C
London in F (The Cuckoo and the Nightingale)	C
Concerto for Harp, Op. 4, No. 6 in B-flat	C
Concerto for Wind Choirs and Strings, No. 2 in F	C

CHAMBER AND SOLO INSTRUMENTAL MUSIC:

Suite No. 5 in E for Harpsichord (including the famous Harmonious Blacksmith)	10
Sonatas, Op. 1 (fifteen):	
No. 4 for Flute (of seven)	19
No. 6 for Oboe and Continuo (of two)	7
No. 12 and No. 13 for Violin (of six)	7
Trio Sonatas	14

VOCAL MUSIC:

Oratorios:	
Saul	3
Israel in Egypt	1
Messiah	25
Operas (complete and excerpts):	
Giulio Cesare (Julius Caesar)	3
Serse (Xerxes) (including the famous Largo)	2
Other:	
Coronation Anthems (4, including Zadok the Priest)	2
Cantatas	C

PETER ILYITCH TCHAIKOVSKY (1840–1893)

Number 10

This is a sentimental, theatrical, melodious, pessimistic composer. Some of the most respected music people gave him short shrift as recently as twenty-five years ago, deeming him too emotional. Wonderful orchestrator, unquestioned talent, eloquent, but too emotional.

Well, Peter Ilyitch Tchaikovsky was a Russian—and the unemotional Russian is rare. He was an arch-Romantic—and emotionalism was the lifeblood of the Romantic era. His greatest genius was in creating melody. So what we get is an ultra-emotional, ultramelodious Russian composer—with a flair for the dramatic and a tormented soul.

Given that combination, it is easier for the neophyte to love an emotional Tchaikovsky, even if the emotion is anguish or despair, than an intellectual Bach. (But don't give up on Bach.)

Tchaikovsky is the only non-German among the first ten on The List (but three more Russians are in the next ten). He is unquestionably the most loved and most popular Russian composer. Whether he also is the "greatest" Russian composer would be disputed by the Stravinsky claque, who would certainly want to regard influence on other composers for decades to come as part of the assessment. The safe way out is to assert that Stravinsky *is* the greatest composer of his century and Tchaikovsky is *not* the greatest composer of his. But then, Stravinsky did not face the same competition. Our system posts the emotional Tchaikovsky several points higher. If you choose to reverse the positions of the two, some contemporary critics will be pleased and these pages will not self-destruct.

Tchaikovsky was another great composer who lived a tragic and relatively short life—he died at the age of fifty-three, having once attempted suicide after a foolhardy nine-day marriage he undertook despite his homosexuality.

TCHAIKOVSKY ON RIMSKY-KORSAKOV AND LISZT

On Rimsky-Korsakov: "I know the variations, by Rimsky-Korsakov & Co. (The "Mighty Five"). Of its kind, the work is certainly unusual and displays remarkable harmonic virtuosity. However, I don't like it. Even as a tour de force it is heavy, bulky and difficult to digest, with all those tiresome thematic repetitions. As an artistic creation it is nul."

On Liszt: "As for Liszt, he is an old hypocrite who replies to any piece submitted to his august judgment with the most exaggerated flattery. By nature he is kind; indeed he is one of the few famous artists who has never been touched by jealousy or the temptation to impede the success of his fellow man. Wagner and—in part—Anton Rubinstein owe their success to him, and he has done a great deal for Berlioz. But he is too much the hypocrite to be trusted for sincere criticism."

The son of a government mine inspector, he studied law and clerked in the Ministry of Justice before shifting to music and studying at the St. Petersburg Conservatory. Later he taught at the Moscow Conservatory for several years en route to becoming a world-famous composer. He is one of four Russians among the thirteen Middle Romantic composers on The List, most of whom were born before 1850 and died before 1900. The other three were Rimsky-Korsakov, Borodin, and Mussorgsky, three of the nationalist "Mighty Five." Tchaikovsky was a much more cosmopolitan and international composer than they (and was attacked by them because of it); his work, the experts say, shows the influence of Italian opera, French ballet, and German symphony and song. Notwithstanding these influences—he lived in both Italy and Paris and traveled and performed in the United States—he also drew on Russian folk music, and he wrote one of the best known of all Russian nationalist works, his *1812* Overture, which is still immensely popular with the public although not highly regarded by the critics. (It was not highly regarded by the composer, either, who said his heart was not in it.) It *is* a little schmaltzy, but it works pretty well played outdoors by the National Symphony Orchestra under Maestro Rostropovich on the Fourth of July with some 300,000 summer visitors from fifty states standing between the Capitol and the Washington Monument. A lot of people clap. Some cheer and cry and yell, as millions of viewers all across the country see on television each year. So enjoy it anyhow, recognizing deep down that you are not sophisticated. That's okay. Look at yourself in the mirror afterwards and say, "I was a little gauche today. I enjoyed the *1812 Overture*."

The work is often cited as an example of the use of "musical quotations," two of its main themes being the French national anthem and the Imperial Russian national anthem, fighting each other musically. With Russian Tchaikovsky writing of French Napoleon's unsuccessful invasion of Russia in 1812, one can predict the outcome of this contest.

Russian culture in those days was itself a blend of French and German influences, and musicologists say that Tchaikovsky simply absorbed more of this than did ultranationalists Rimsky-Korsakov, Borodin, and Mussorgsky. Unlike them, he did not deliberately turn his back on extra-Russian influence. But this is a far cry from making him "anti-Russia."

TCHAIKOVSKY ON BERLIOZ AND BEETHOVEN

On Berlioz: "The French are a queer people. Whatever appears under the name of Berlioz is received with uniform rapture. In truth 'The Siege of Troy' is a weak, tedious piece, revealing the principal defects of its composer; namely, poverty of melody, overharmonization and an imagination too rich for its owner's musical invention. Berlioz was a high-minded man who conceived beautiful things but lacked the power to fill his conceptions."

On Beethoven: "The work [Tchaikovsky's own Fourth Symphony] is patterned after Beethoven's Fifth Symphony—not as to musical content but as to the basic idea. Don't you see a program in the Fifth? Not only does such a program exist, but there is no question as to what it means. My symphony has much the same basic idea, and if it does not appear clearly, it only means that I am not a Beethoven—which is no news to me."

Tchaikovsky described his own love for Russia in a letter to his longtime pen pal Nadejda von Meck, which is quoted in the book *Beloved Friend* by Catherine Drinker Bowen:

Why is it that the simple Russian landscape, a walk in summer through Russian fields and forest or on the steppes at evening, can affect me so that I have lain on the ground numb, overcome by a wave of love for nature, by the indescribably sweet and intoxicating atmosphere that drifted over me from the forest, the steppe, the little river, the faraway village, the modest little church—in short, all that makes the poor Russian landscape.

Igor Stravinsky, second-rated Russian on The List and the leading twentieth-century composer, helped resolve the issue of whether Tchaikovsky was "sufficiently" in love with his country, in a flat declaration: "He was the most Russian of us all."

While Tchaikovsky produced outstanding work in virtually all fields of music, he was known primarily for orchestral works in many forms, most of which were composed in melancholy minor keys. Romantic in his feeling and his approach to composition, he was one of the greatest melodists of The 50, a creator of flowing, lyrical, Romantic melodies. The persistent professional criticism that he is too sentimental has done nothing over the years to lessen his continuing popularity with the public. Out there with the real people, sentimental melody remains a winner.

Three of his "emotional" symphonies—the Fourth (1878), Fifth (1888), and Sixth (1893)—are often performed today. Much less frequently produced are two of some ten operas, *Eugene Onegin* and *Pique Dame* (Queen of spades). He made ballet-writing respectable for serious and great composers with *Swan Lake* (1876), *The Sleeping Beauty* (1889), and *The Nutcracker* (1892)—although none of the three, now among the most honored and performed of all ballets, was an immediate success.

Other popular Tchaikovsky works include three well-known pieces of program music: *Romeo and Juliet* (1870), his first masterwork; *Francesca da Rimini* (1876), inspired by Dante's *Inferno*; and *Capriccio Italien* (1880); the passionate Piano Concerto No. 1 in B-flat Minor (1875); the now-triumphant Violin Concerto in D (1878); more than one hundred songs; and the *1812* Overture. The piano concerto is on everybody's list of the best works in that form, and his melody-filled violin concerto is also ranked close to the top, along with those of Beethoven, Brahms, and Mendelssohn, and probably favored by most over those of Dvořák, Bartók, Sibelius, Saint-Saëns, and Prokofiev. (Bach's violin works from the Baroque era are judged separately.)

Tchaikovsky wrote little chamber music, but respected works include a Quartet in B, Op. 11, and a Piano Trio in A Minor, Op. 50.

THE TRIUMPH OF "SAVAGERY"

This was Viennese critic Eduard Hanslick's unfavorable view of Tchaikovsky's violin concerto, expressed in 1881:

"For a while the concerto has proportion, is musical, and is not without genius, but soon savagery gains the upper hand and lords it to the end of the first movement. The violin is no longer played. It is yanked about. It is torn asunder. It is beaten black and blue. I do not know whether it is possible for anyone to conquer these hair-raising difficulties, but I do know that Mr. [Adolf] Brodsky martyrized his hearers as well as himself. The Adagio, with its tender national melody, almost conciliates, almost wins us. But it breaks off abruptly to make way for a Finale that puts us in the midst of the brutal and wretched jollity of a Russian kermess. We see wild and vulgar faces, we hear curses, we smell bad brandy. Friedrich Vischer once asserted in reference to lascivious paintings that there are pictures which 'stink in the eye.' Tchaikovsky's violin concerto brings to us for the first time the horrid idea that there may be music that stinks in the ear."

Of his more than one hundred songs, perhaps the best known is the setting of a Goethe poem, "None But the Lonely Heart." As is so often the case, the critics believe that many others—less sentimental, less melancholy, and less well liked by the public—are more representative of his better work.

The critics point out that in their art the Russians have never been content with mere statement, that they have always exaggerated, that the basic Russian spirit gave Tchaikovsky his emotion, his peculiar alternation of melancholy mood and almost hysterical gaiety, of grief and joy. They say that the whole idea of suffering and atonement that flavors his works was part of the ethos of the time. That gets us back to an emotional Russian at the peak of Romanticism.

A good example of how perceptions of a composition change is provided by Tchaikovsky's piano concerto, so often heard in today's concert halls. The composer himself was proud of it back in 1874, so much so that he dedicated it to his friend Nicholas Rubinstein, a pianist and conductor and the brother of the then-famous composer Anton Rubinstein.

TCHAIKOVSKY ON MOZART

"You say that my worship for Mozart is quite contrary to my musical nature. But perhaps it is just because—being a child of my day—I feel broken and spiritually out of joint, that I find consolation and rest in Mozart's music, wherein he gives expression to that joy of life which was part of his sane and wholesome temperament, not yet undermined by reflection. It seems to me that an artist's creative power is something quite apart from his sympathy with this or that great master. . . . Dissimilarity of temperament between two artists is no hindrance to their mutual sympathy."

Tchaikovsky wrote about it to his friend von Meck:

On Christmas eve, 1874, we were all invited to Albrecht's and Nicholas [Rubinstein] asked me . . . to play the concerto in a classroom of the Conservatory. . . . I took my manuscript, and Nicholas and Hubert came. . . . I played through the first movement. Not a criticism, not a word. Rubinstein was silent. He was preparing his thunderstorm. . . . The silence of Rubinstein said much. It said to me at once: "Dear friend, how can I talk about details when I dislike your composition as a whole?" But I kept my temper and played the concerto thoroughly. Again silence.

"Well," I said, and stood up. Then burst forth from Rubinstein's mouth a mighty torrent of words. . . . It appeared that my concerto was utterly worthless, absolutely unplayable; passages were so commonplace and awkward that they could not be improved; the piece as a whole was bad, trivial, vulgar. . . . [Rubinstein] pointed out many passages which needed thorough revision, and added that he would play the concerto in public if these changes were ready at a certain time. "I shall not change a single note," I answered, "and I shall publish the concerto exactly as it is now." And this, indeed, I did.

Teed off, Tchaikovsky scratched Rubinstein's name from the dedication page and substituted that of Hans von Bülow, an esteemed musician and conductor, who introduced the concerto in Boston the following year. Eventually, both Tchaikovsky and Rubinstein yielded: the composer did make some revisions, and the pianist did perform the piece in Russia and Paris. A couple of years later, after Rubinstein's death, the sensitive Tchaikovsky also dedicated to him his Piano Trio in A, Op. 50, signed "To the memory of a great artist." Hundreds of such examples exist (that is, of a composition's reception-at-birth differing radically from its reception-by-history)—and, of course, today's assessments will no doubt change as well.

TCHAIKOVSKY ON BRAHMS AND WAGNER

On Brahms: "Yesterday . . . I studied the new symphony of Brahms—a composer who is praised to heaven in Germany. I don't understand his attraction. In my opinion he is dark, cold and full of pretense, of obscurity, without true depth."

On Wagner: "What a Don Quixote Wagner is! Why does he strain himself in pursuing the impossible when in his hands is a great gift from which, if he would only submit to its natural direction, he could extract a whole ocean of musical beauty? In my opinion, Wagner is a symphonist by nature. The man has a glorious talent, but affectation ruins him, his inspiration is always paralyzed by some new theory that he desires to put in practice and for which he would sacrifice anything. Pursuing realism, truth and rationalism in opera he has quite lost music, which in his last four operas is most conspicuous by its absence. . . . But that he is a wonderful symphonist is beyond all question."

The world has room enough both for engineers and mathematicians and for sensitive poet-composers—especially if the latter are emotionally supercharged individuals who love making melody and who, in their work, are not looking for rules to break or experiments to launch or dragons to slay. Still, world opinion of this genius goes in cycles. If the intellectual music of a Stravinsky or the structural perfection of a Bach does the most for you, Tchaikovsky may not be your bag. If you like apple pie, hot dogs, and baseball games, and if you like beauty, color, personality, melody, and fairy tales, and if you are not sophisticated enough to recognize the architectural flaws the professionals find, and if you love your spouse, children, and mother, Peter Ilyitch Tchaikovsky should appeal.

STARTER KIT

For the Starter Kit, all of the Top Ten works are worthy of inclusion, since all are great public favorites, frequently performed. But holding to five, we begin with the last of Tchaikovsky's symphonies, No. 6 in B Minor, subtitled *Pathétique* (meaning *pathos* rather than *pathetic*). It has been called the most dramatic piece in modern symphonic literature and clearly has one of the most dramatic contrasts, involving a triumphant march in the third movement (you will recognize the tune, although you may not have known it as part of a Tchaikovsky symphony) and then what sounds like deep despair in the conclusion of the fourth. Tchaikovsky did a very unusual thing by making the fourth (and last) movement a slow one, thus ending the symphony on a gloomy note. (For listening fun, there is a beautiful theme sounded by a clarinet in the first movement.)

The Violin Concerto in D and the Piano Concerto No. 1 in B-flat Minor—the latter viewed by many as *the* Tchaikovsky masterpiece—are mandatory recommendations. While the best-known overture is the *1812*, almost as popular and rated much higher by the critics is *Romeo and Juliet*, which Tchaikovsky called an "overture fantasy" and which others call a tone poem. The musicologists cite this as one of the two best-known treatments of Shakespeare's play, the other being Berlioz's *Romeo and Juliet* Symphony. Finally, a Tchaikovsky Starter Kit should include one of the three famous ballets. Any one will do; we have selected his first, *Swan Lake,* either complete or in the form of a ballet suite (a selection of excerpts, strung together to make a concert piece).

Many will recognize the popular song "Our Love" from *Romeo and Juliet* and other popular tunes from the violin concerto. The Fifth Symphony provides "Moon Love," another hit tune the older generations will remember, and String Quartet No. 1 still another. And from the Piano Concerto in B-flat Minor comes "Tonight We Love."

TCHAIKOVSKY: THE STARTER KIT

Composition   *Recordings Available**

SYMPHONIES:

No. 6 in B Minor (Pathétique)   32

Composition	Recordings Available*
OTHER ORCHESTRAL WORKS:	
Piano Concerto No. 1 in B-flat Minor	37
Violin Concerto in D	26
Romeo and Juliet (overture fantasy)	39
Ballet Music:	
Swan Lake (complete or excerpts)	33

*Represents the number of recorded releases available of each listed composition as found in a recent issue of the *Schwann/Opus* catalogue. A "C" indicates that a work is only available collected with other compositions.

TCHAIKOVSKY: A TOP TEN

Composition	Recordings Available*
SYMPHONIES:	
No. 4 in F Minor	22
No. 5 in E Minor	28
No. 6 in B Minor (Pathétique)	32
OTHER ORCHESTRAL WORKS:	
1812 Overture	44
Capriccio Italien	32
Piano Concerto No. 1 in B-flat Minor	37
Violin Concerto in D	26
Romeo and Juliet (overture fantasy)	39
Ballet Music:	
Nutcracker (complete, excerpts, or suite)	31
Swan Lake (complete or excerpts)	33

TCHAIKOVSKY: A MASTER COLLECTION

Composition	Recordings Available*
SYMPHONIES:	
No. 1 in G Minor	9
No. 2 in C Minor	9
No. 3 in D	10
No. 4 in F Minor	22
No. 5 in E Minor	28

Composition	Recordings Available*
No. 6 in B Minor (Pathétique)	32
Manfred Symphony	5

OTHER ORCHESTRAL WORKS:

1812 Overture	44
Capriccio Italien	32
Marche Slave	28
Piano Concerto No. 1 in B-flat Minor	37
Piano Concerto No. 2 in G	4
Piano Concerto No. 3 in E-flat	4
Violin Concerto in D	26
Francesca da Rimini (symphonic fantasy)	10
Romeo and Juliet (overture fantasy)	39
Ballet Music:	
Nutcracker (complete, excerpts, or suite)	31
Swan Lake (complete or excerpts)	33
Sleeping Beauty (complete or excerpts)	23
Serenade for Strings in C	22
Variations on a Rococo Theme for Cello	12

CHAMBER MUSIC:

String Quartets (three):	
Andante cantabile from Quartet No. 1 in D	11
Trio in A Minor	9

VOCAL MUSIC:

Opera:	
Eugene Onegin	3
Queen of Spades	0
Songs	C

FELIX MENDELSSOHN (1809–1847)

Number 11

This is refined, comfortable, controlled, melodious, flawless music, not as deep and inspired as the Immortals offer, not violent with passionate emotion, but nonetheless the product of genius. You cannot feel depressed after listening to Mendelssohn's melodies—and nothing has clashed in your ears. Neophyte listeners know that they are hearing graceful and beautiful music; the professionals acknowledge magnificent skill even though the naysayers among them are disappointed that the composer did not reach the still-greater heights of which they think he was capable. But one can be original and outstanding without being deeply fervent or rebellious.

No attic-starver, Mendelssohn was the child of a rich German Jewish banker who passed on to his son all the conservatism and restraint that bankers are supposed to have. Critics say that the major fault with Mendelssohn's music is that he never let himself go completely; one does not picture a Mendelssohn challenging God on the playing fields of Olympus as Beethoven would, nor pouring out his emotion in an uninhibited way as did Schumann, the most romantic of Romantics. Usually lighthearted, when sad he is gracefully sad, with reserve.

Much more than just a methodical and highly talented musician, he had an incredible amount of natural ability going for him—hence his rating of Number 11 in the world, topping the Composers of Genius, and just a breath below the Demigods who make up Numbers 3 to 10. This is not a ranking to be taken lightly; directly beneath him are Antonin Dvořák, Franz Liszt, Frédéric Chopin, Igor Stravinsky, and Giuseppe Verdi. It is not an embarrassment to trail Bach, Mozart, Beethoven, and a handful of others.

His grandfather was Moses Mendelssohn, a famous philosopher, his banker father an art lover, and his wealthy mother a reader of Homer in the original Greek. He was the most natural musician of all the Romantics and comes as close as any in history to equaling Mozart's astonishing natural gifts. A magnificent pianist, he also was *the* conductor of his day, a superb organist, an esteemed educator, and a world-class composer.

Mendelssohn was born in Hamburg, where he spent his earliest years surrounded by the comfort and culture of his parents. He moved with the family to Berlin at the age of three when Hamburg became occupied by the French army. Soon after, he began taking piano lessons from his artistic mother. His exceptional talent demanded top-level professional music tutors (they were of course provided) and his first public piano concert was held in Berlin when he was only nine. Among guests in the Mendelssohn home for whom he and his siblings performed in 1821 was Karl Maria von Weber. Another admirer that year of the boy genius was Goethe, who in earlier years had heard Mozart as a child and, struck by the new prodigy, invited young Mendelssohn to his home in nearby Weimar.

"I am Saul and you are David," Goethe later wrote to the young composer. "Come to me when I am sad and discouraged and quiet my soul with your sweet harmonies."

One expects and finds proportion, balance, and a wholly proper approach from the young Mendelssohn, who, educated at the equivalent of the best New England prep schools and the top Ivy League colleges, and surrounded by wealth and love, could sit down at seventeen to compose his Overture to *A Midsummer Night's Dream*. Most fairy-tale music, almost by definition, is light, fun, happy music, and this fairy-tale composition is a unanimous choice of the critics as a musical work that far transcends the abilities of the ordinary master of any age. And, while not Mendelssohn's best work, both he and it would still be rated highly had he written nothing else. The music people say that no one before or after—not even Mozart—produced a composition of such magnitude at so young an age.

Felix Mendelssohn was a student of the works of all three Immortals, Bach, Mozart, and Beethoven. In 1829, at twenty, already a virtuoso pianist, composer, and conductor, he put together a performance of Bach's *St. Matthew Passion*—one of the great Bach's greatest works—and thus triggered a new interest in Bach's music. To say that this rescued Bach from obscurity would be an overstatement, but it did draw fresh attention to the Great One, who has never again needed a revival presentation. One contemporary is reported to have said, "There is no God but Bach, and Mendelssohn is his prophet."

Mendelssohn, like Brahms, did not rebel against the Classical traditions as did most Romantics. He was never boisterous. By osmosis he *was* a Romantic, given the times in which he lived, but he was not as unorthodox as a Berlioz or a Liszt, or as active as a Schumann or a Chopin, all contemporaries. If Schubert was the Romantic Classicist, Mendelssohn was the Classical Romantic.

In 1833, not long after returning home from a Grand Tour of Italy, France, England and Scotland, he was appointed musical director in Düsseldorf, in charge of church music, opera and a couple of choral groups—his first professional music "employment." Six months later he quit, reportedly unchallenged by his duties, but in short order he accepted the more prestigious post of musical director of the famous Gewandhaus Orchestra in Leipzig. The musical Mendelssohn and the musical Leipzig were a perfect fit. He stayed for five happy years before reluctantly leaving to return to Berlin as head of the musical department of a projected Academy of Arts. Although the academy never quite got off the ground, after another trip to England, he was so solidly established in the musical world that he was given the honorary post of Kappellmeister to the King of Prussia. This was a portfolio-without-residence, and he was able to return to his beloved Leipzig to conduct the Gewandhaus Orchestra and to compose. With the king's encouragement and financial support, he was also the main founder in 1843 of the Leipzig Conservatory. Additional, fabulously successful trips to England in 1846 and 1847 were part of his workaholic career. But his health soon weakened and he was not to live past age thirty-eight.

Nevertheless, he was quite prolific. His works include five symphonies, three sonatas, a violin concerto, two piano concertos, several very well-known overtures, two highly praised oratorios, much incidental music, and a great many chamber works. His last major effort was *Elijah*, generally regarded as one of the top oratorios, after Handel's *Messiah* and along with Haydn's *Creation*. It was Mendelssohn's finest public triumph and won him a note from Prince Consort Albert of England: "To the noble artist who has weaned our ears from the senseless confusion of mere sound and won them to comprehension of all that is harmonious and pure." A second oratorio, *St. Paul*, while not as popular as *Elijah*, is another finalist on the Ten Best Oratorios list.

In his orchestral work, the Romantic side of Mendelssohn is heard most clearly in three overtures: *Fingal's Cave*, a poetic, "delicately balanced" tone poem in true Romantic style; *Calm Sea and Prosperous*

THE LEIPZIG AGENDA

If we classify Schubert as a Classicist, Mendelssohn is the fifth-ranking Romantic on The List. He could scarcely have been more different from his friend Schumann, but he was a Very Important Person in the music world of his time—probably the foremost music authority of his day, a man who had great influence over European orchestral playing and programming by virtue of his conducting prowess, a man to whom Chopin and Schumann turned for advice and leadership, and a focal point of musical activity in England and Germany. At twenty-six he became director of the Leipzig Gewandhaus Orchestra, which by itself made him the central musical figure in one of Germany's central cities—a Germany that was the musical center of Europe. (In a small churchyard in Leipzig was buried Johann Sebastian Bach.)

Leipzig was not the kind of city for his showmanlike virtuoso contemporary, Liszt. Not enough "countesses and princes," complained Liszt. Hearing this comment, Schumann replied: "Let him take care. We have our own aristocracy: 150 bookshops, fifty printing plants, and over thirty periodicals."

As music director in Leipzig, Mendelssohn was a smash hit. Almost everything he did was right, from attracting the great performers of the times to doubling and tripling the salaries of his musicians.

His own compositions were only tenth among those he chose to conduct during his Leipzig tenure. Who were the leaders? Mozart, Beethoven, Haydn, Bach, and Handel—and he presented the first performance of Schubert's Symphony in C, the *Great C Major*, the one discovered in the custody of the composer's brother by Schumann. Having already revived Bach's *St. Matthew Passion*, Mendelssohn now also introduced this other masterwork to Leipzig.

Voyage; and *Beautiful Melusine*. If you listen carefully, you can hear the washing waves in *Fingal's Cave*.

The five symphonies are numbered in order of publication rather than order of composition. They are:

• No. 1 in C Minor, 1824, written when Mendelssohn was fifteen, considered respectable;

• No. 2 in B-flat, *Lobgesang* (Hymn of praise), 1840, a choral symphony in the manner of Beethoven's Ninth and panned by many critics—but praised by those who say it need not be compared with the greatest of all choral symphonies;

• No. 3 in A Minor, *Scotch*, 1842, deemed by the professionals to be inferior to the *Fingal's Cave* overture, also written in Scotland;

A SCOTTISH INSPIRATION

Mendelssohn described the origins of the *Scotch* Symphony in a letter written from Scotland to his two sisters in 1829: "We went in the deep twilight to the Palace of Holyrood where Queen Mary lived and loved. . . . The chapel is roofless; grass and ivy grow abundantly on it; and before the altar, now in ruins, Mary was crowned Queen of Scotland. Everything around is broken and mouldering, and the bright sky shines through. I believe I found today in that old chapel the beginning of my Scotch symphony." (The consensus of the experts is that it is a little difficult to find very much in the work on, from, or about Scotland, despite the composer's thoughts.)

• No. 4 in A, *Italian*, 1833, the almost unanimous favorite;

• No. 5 in D Minor, *Reformation*, with the familiar hymn "Ein' fest Burg" in the finale, 1832. It was published twenty years after the composer's death, and he had wanted to burn it.

Mendelssohn had composed twelve symphonies for string orchestra between ages twelve and fourteen, all relatively short and all in three movements, before he wrote the numbered First. These early twelve, as well as the main five, are all available, are all performed, and are all heard on classical radio stations. The *Italian*, No. 4, is by far the most frequently performed today, with No. 3, the *Scotch*, next, and No. 5, *Reformation*, also popular, despite the weaker critical assessments of it.

Mendelssohn's well-known piano works include *Songs without Words*, *Rondo Capriccioso in E*, and his Prelude and Fugue.

While some consider his masterpiece to be the oratorio *Elijah* (others consider it brilliant but uneven), one of his most popular compositions is his lyrical Violin Concerto in E Minor, generally placed among the top half-dozen in music, and another work you will recognize upon hearing, whether or not you had earlier identified it with Mendelssohn. It was requested of Mendelssohn in 1838 (when the composer was twenty-nine) by a famous violinist, Ferdinand David, but was not written for another several years. Mendelssohn replied to the request: "It is nice of you to urge me. I have the liveliest desire to write one for you, and if I have a few propitious days here I'll bring you something. But the task is not an easy one. You demand that it should be brilliant, and how is such a one as I to do this?" The music people say that this is not a "profound" work ("profound" is a big favorite of expert critics in many important fields: literature, political theory, wine), but they say also that it is eloquent, melodious, and consistently beautiful. Ethan Mordden, a helpful author who knows how to write for the lay reader, describes the first movement as "passionate," the second as "tender," and the third as "chipper"— words that mean something to a listener. It does not take you long to know it is a violin concerto; the violin is talking to you almost from the opening notes.

And let's not forget Mendelssohn's exuberant exit "Wedding March," perhaps better known by more people than any other single piece of classical music, written as part of the incidental music for *A Midsummer Night's Dream*.

Unlike many Listed composers, Mendelssohn was popular during his life. Biographer Herbert Kupferberg writes: "Possibly no other composer's music had ever spread through the world so quickly. It took the Philharmonic Society of New York until 1846, 22 years after its composition, to perform Beethoven's Ninth Symphony (and then it was a failure); but within a few years of Mendelssohn's death the Philharmonic had presented the 'Midsummer Night's Dream' and 'Hebrides' Overtures, the G Minor Piano Concerto, the 'Scotch' Symphony, the 'Italian' Symphony, and other works."

Not everyone was a Mendelssohn fan. Among his most severe detractors was George Bernard Shaw, a music critic for the *London Star* from 1888 to 1894 under the pseudonym Corno di Bassetto. He wrote: "Mendelssohn, though he expresses himself in music with touching tenderness and refinement, and sometimes with a nobility and pure fire that makes us forget all his kid glove gentility, his conventional sentimentality, and his despicable oratorio mongering, was not in the foremost rank of great composers. He was more intelligent than Schumann, as Tennyson is more intelligent than Browning: he is, indeed, the great composer of the century for all those to whom Tennyson is the great poet of the century. He was more vigorous, more inventive,

KISSES FROM GOETHE

Four Mendelssohn quotes:

On *Elijah:* "No work of mine ever went so admirably at first performance or was received with such enthusiasm both by musicians and the public as this. . . . It appears to me that the dramatic should predominate—the personages should be introduced as acting and speaking with fervor; not however to become mere musical pictures, but inhabitants of a positive practical world."

On the comment by violinist Ferdinand David that there had been only one great violin concerto but that now there would be two: "No, no! If I finish this concerto it will be with no wish of competing with Beethoven." (Yet another musician asserted: "He [Beethoven] has made the Adam of concertos, and you have mated it with Eve.")

On Leipzig: "When I first came to Leipzig, I thought I was in paradise."

At age sixteen, Mendelssohn wrote: "Every morning I get a kiss from the author of 'Faust' and 'Werther,' and every afternoon two kisses from the father and friend Goethe. Think of that! In the afternoon, I play to Goethe for about two hours, partly Bach fugues and partly improvisations."

more inspired than Spohr, and a much abler and better educated man than Schubert. But compare him with Bach, Handel, Haydn, Mozart, Beethoven, or Wagner, and then settle, if you can, what ought to be done to the fanatic who proclaims him a 'master.' "

One of the nice things about Mendelssohn is that while his stock has gone up and down with the critics at various times over the 140 years or so since his death, the public—during his lifetime and since—has always thought he was absolutely outstanding. And it still does.

Mendelssohn enthusiasts make the case that he might have been the most "total" musician of them all, considering his youthful precocity, great natural ability, and versatility: he was a gifted composer, educator, arranger, performer, and conductor. Not "the greatest," but the most "total." In a sense he was sort of an all-around runner-up—which does enable one to collect a lot of second-place votes for a total score, but denies one Immortality.

Although Mendelssohn and Schumann worked together in Leipzig and were the same age, the differences between them were many. Schumann let it all hang out; Mendelssohn was restrained in nearly all things. Schumann rejected the dedication to traditional forms; as we have seen, he wrote things called *Carnaval* and *Kinderscenen*, *Arabesque* and *Kreisleriana*. What kinds of names were those for musical compositions? Composers were supposed to write madrigals, motets, and fugues, and, later, sonatas, symphonies, and concertos. That was the proper thing to do, and that is what Mendelssohn did. Author-critic Harold Schonberg offers the perfect quote to illustrate Mendelssohn's approach to life. In correspondence with his sister, the composer wrote: "Do not commend what is new until it has made some progress in the world and acquired a name, for until then it is a mere matter of taste." One cannot imagine a Schumann cautioning a sister in this way.

The differences obviously carry over into the music. Schumann—and Chopin, Liszt, Berlioz, and Wagner—were Romantic experimenters with the bricks-and-mortar of music: with rhythm and key relationships and chords; with dissonance and contrast and conflict. This was not Mendelssohn's way. But his music was flawless, or nearly flawless. Was that why he so admired Bach? Not necessarily; all musicians admired Bach. But it is one reason fellow musicians admired him during his life, even though he was less adventuresome than many of them.

Mendelssohn died after several weeks of a then-unexplained illness on November 4, 1847, at thirty-eight years, eight months. Modern physicians believe he suffered a series of small strokes preceding some larger ones. He was far from the shortest-lived of the composers on The List—Schubert was only thirty-one when he died—but with him, as with the others, one cannot help thinking, "What if . . . ?"

STARTER KIT

The Starter Kit includes one symphony, No. 4 in A, the *Italian*, the critics' choice and the most popular with the public. By Mendelssohn's own orders, it was not published during his lifetime, although he conducted the first performance of it in London in 1833. Two years earlier, he had written in a letter from Rome: "I am making great progress with the Italian Symphony. It will be the most mature thing I have done, especially the last movement, Presto agitato." The last movement, indeed, is still the one most favored by the experts today.

There is no question about the inclusion of the Violin Concerto

GO REDSKINS!!

While Mendelssohn and Berlioz wrote very different kinds of music, one story suggests the admiration of the latter for the conducting talents of the former. While in Leipzig for a musical performance, Berlioz asked Mendelssohn for his baton as a keepsake. Mendelssohn agreed, but only on condition that he be given Berlioz's baton in exchange.

"I shall be giving copper for gold, but never mind, I consent," said Berlioz. With his baton the Frenchman, who had been reading James Fenimore Cooper, sent this note:

"To the Chief Mendelssohn: Great chief! We have promised to exchange tomahawks. Mine is a rough one—yours is plain. Only squaws and pale-faces are fond of ornate weapons. Be my brother! And when the Great Spirit shall have sent us to hunt in the land of souls, may our warriors hang up our tomahawks together at the door of the council chamber."

in E Minor, perhaps Mendelssohn's most lyrical work, whose melody alone puts it in the same league as the major violin concertos of Beethoven and Brahms. Nor can a Starter Kit ignore the Overture to *A Midsummer Night's Dream*, everyone's favorite. In addition to the overture, Mendelssohn wrote a dozen or so numbers for the play—including, of course, the exit "Wedding March." The overture was written in 1826, the other music, commissioned by King Frederick William of Prussia, not until 1842.

The fourth choice is a piece of chamber music, his Octet in E-flat, selected in part because he composed it at sixteen, even before the *Midsummer Night's Dream* Overture, and because it established him as not merely a fine young composer but a truly great one. It is typical early Mendelssohn, light-as-air and tender, and many experts call it the equal of his more mature quartets.

Finally, there is one of the composer's most popular works and one much respected by the music people—the overture *Fingal's Cave*, also called the *Hebrides*. (Geography chaps have long since pointed out that Fingal's Cave is a natural phenomenon on a small island west of Mull, which is not really in the Hebrides anyhow.) It is a seascape; author-critic David Ewen quotes this description: "Certainly it gives a wonderfully vivid impression of the surging sea, of waves resounding in rocky caves, of the harsh cry of the sea gulls, the odor of the salt air, the sharp flavor of seaweed, and the melancholy sound of this northern scene. What a masterpiece of romantic imagination and romantic tone painting!''

MENDELSSOHN: THE STARTER KIT

Composition   *Recordings Available**

SYMPHONIES:

No. 4 in A (Italian)   24

OTHER ORCHESTRAL WORKS:

Violin Concerto in E Minor   30
Hebrides Overture (Fingal's Cave)   11
A Midsummer Night's Dream (Overture and   19
    Incidental Music)

CHAMBER MUSIC:

Octet in E-flat for Strings   9

*Represents the number of recorded releases available of each listed composition as found in a recent issue of the *Schwann/Opus* catalogue. A "C" indicates that a work is only available collected with other compositions.

MENDELSSOHN: A TOP TEN

Composition   *Recordings Available**

SYMPHONIES:

No. 3 in A Minor (Scotch)   16
No. 4 in A (Italian)   24
No. 5 in D Minor (Reformation)   10

OTHER ORCHESTRAL WORKS:

Concerto No. 1 in G Minor for Piano and   9
    Orchestra
Violin Concerto in E Minor   30
Hebrides Overture (Fingal's Cave)   11
A Midsummer Night's Dream (Overture and   19
    Incidental Music)

Composition   *Recordings Available**

CHAMBER MUSIC:
Octet in E-flat for Strings   9
Piano Trio No. 1 in D Minor, Op. 66   10

VOCAL MUSIC:
Oratorio:
  Elijah   4

MENDELSSOHN: A MASTER COLLECTION

Composition   *Recordings Available**

SYMPHONIES:
No. 1 in D   5
No. 2 in B (Lobgesang)   3
No. 3 in A Minor (Scotch)   16
No. 4 in A (Italian)   24
No. 5 in D Minor (Reformation)   10

OTHER ORCHESTRAL WORKS:
Concerto No. 1 in G Minor for Piano and   9
  Orchestra
Concerto No. 2 in D Minor for Piano and   7
  Orchestra
Violin Concerto in E Minor   30
Hebrides Overture (Fingal's Cave)   11
A Midsummer Night's Dream (Overture and   19
  Incidental Music)
Overture to Ruy Blas   4
Overture to the Fair Melusine   5
Capriccio Brillant for Piano and Orchestra   2

CHAMBER MUSIC:
Octet in E-flat for Strings   9
String Quartet in D, Op. 44, No. 1   4
String Quartet in E-flat, Op. 44, No. 3   4
String Quartet in F Minor, Op. 80   4
Piano Trio No. 1 in D Minor, Op. 49   10
Piano Trio No. 2 in C Minor, Op. 66   6

Composition	Recordings Available*
OTHER INSTRUMENTAL MUSIC:	
Sonatas for Organ (six)	10
Songs without Words, for Piano	6
Variations Sérieuses, for Piano	6
Sonata No. 2 for Cello and Piano	4
VOCAL MUSIC:	
Oratorios:	
Elijah	4
St. Paul	0

ANTONÍN DVOŘÁK (1841–1904)

Number 12

Antonín Dvořák challenges a lot of myths. Everyone knows that classical music is an acquired taste and that in acquiring this taste there is a normal progression from popular music to Victor Herbert to light works of the not-quite-geniuses to the real thing—but first only to carefully chosen, easy-on-the-ears works of the real thing. Then, finally, the listener is ready for the masters' masterpieces.

Nonsense. Certainly that is one way to go, but it isn't the only way. For virtually every composer on The List there are fun, entry-level masterworks (or entry-level movements or excerpts, if length is a consideration). And for Dvořák there is a slew of such material. Author Ethan Mordden, as he often does, puts it well: "How can anything that catchy be any good?" But Dvořák *is* good, as well as catchy, with music right out of Bohemia, created by a Bohemian violinist, violist, organist, and conductor.

One game to play as you listen to some of Dvořák is to form your own conclusions as to whether you are hearing Bohemian sounds, as some argue, or American Indian/cowboy/Negro spiritual (it *was* "Negro" back then) sounds, as others argue. We'll settle for "Bohemian-American," and the truth is that there are a lot of similarities between folk music from different parts of the world.

FIVE EASY QUESTIONS

Questions:

What famous European composer most admired Stephen Foster?

What composer slipped a little of "Yankee Doodle" into one of his most famous works?

What composer wrote a cantata for the American flag?

What composer offered to write a new national anthem for the United States?

What does Spillville, Iowa, have in common with Nelahozeves, Bohemia?

Answer: Antonín Dvořák.

At Number 12, Dvořák is only the second non-German thus far on The List, Tchaikovsky having been the first. He is one of three Listed Czechs. Chronologically they are Smetana, Dvořák, and Janáček; in List ranking, Dvořák, Smetana (Number 45), and Janáček (Number 48). He was one of the last of the Middle Romantic composers, born within four or five years of Saint-Saëns and Bizet of France, Rimsky-Korsakov and Mussorgsky of Russia, and Grieg of Norway. The Magnificent Seven of earlier Romantic days were in their thirties at that time. And he is the highest-rated of the nineteen on The List who lived into the twentieth century (although he admittedly didn't do so by much).

Dvořák's father was a butcher and innkeeper in Nelahozeves, Bohemia, who liked music and song and played a lot of zither and a little violin. This was, after all, rural Bohemia. But there was no question about Antonín's future; he was to go into the innkeeping business. As a boy, he fiddled as good Czechs do; he heard folk songs, folk dances, ceremonial tunes, and occasional Gypsy music, and he absorbed this type of melody and brisk rhythm into his Bohemian being. But as a future innkeeper, at fourteen he was sent by his father to an uncle in nearby Zlonice to learn German. (A man could not keep a successful inn in Bohemia in those days without knowing German.) In Zlonice, however, the boy encountered a friend of his uncle's who saw and heard a talent of a different nature than is required to be a Master of the House. The friend taught him the viola, piano, and organ, and argued with Father Dvořák—at first unsuccessfully—that the boy should go to Prague for further study. The ending was a happy one for the world: Uncle and teacher finally won, stubborn father who needed his son's help lost, and at sixteen Antonín went off to the well-known Organ School in Prague. Inasmuch as Antonín rather than his father is the hero of this story, the available literature does not tell us what happened to the inn. (It is clear that the Nelahozeves inn was shut down and that one opened in Zlonice. Ask the next time you are in Zlonice; certainly the facts are well known there.)

Dvořák's music is the essence of Bohemia. While rarely using existing folk themes, he wrote his own in their fashion. But his genius was such that today his works are deemed far more universal than those of the earlier Smetana, usually called the "founder" of Czech music (although "classical-music spokesperson" might be more appropriate for Smetana, since the folk part of Czech music obviously had been around for a long time and was not "founded" by anyone).

Some of the phrases frequently used to describe Schubert, including "spontaneous original melody," apply as well to Dvořák. Other words from the critics for Dvořák are "simple," "sincere," "unsophisticated," "sweet," and "sad." He wrote music from the heart for the heart, easy-to-hear music, and—always—beautifully melodic music. During a three-year stint in the United States late in his life he became entranced by black American folk music and fond of American Indian and cowboy music. Their sounds can be heard in his most famous symphony, in his best-known quartet, and elsewhere in his works. At least they probably can be. As mentioned above, there is some dispute about that.

Dvořák worked hard over his sixty-two years, producing nine operas; nine symphonies; overtures and other orchestral pieces; concertos for piano, cello, and violin; songs; solo piano music; chamber works, including fourteen string quartets; a ballad; an oratorio; cantatas; and a *Stabat Mater*.

DVOŘÁK ON THE CELLO

"High up it sounds nasal, and low down it growls," he said of the cello. Nonetheless, Dvořák wrote one long cello concerto as a young man and another in 1895 at age fifty-three, just before ending his three-year trip to the New World.

But Dvořák's comments on the cello pale alongside George Bernard Shaw's—scarcely a fair comparison, because most things most people say pale before Shaw, who was not fond of the cello. "Ordinarily," he said, "I had just as soon hear a bee buzzing in a stone jug."

More of a fan was Rimsky-Korsakov. In his *Principles of Orchestration* he wrote: "The combination of horns and cellos, frequently employed, produces a beautifully blended, soft quality of tone."

After going to Prague at age sixteen, he led the life of a young student away from home at the Organ School, and then spent eleven years playing violin and viola in Prague's National Opera Orchestra. He was thirty-one when his composition of a patriotic cantata drew some attention to him, and thirty-two when his Symphony in E-flat, rarely heard in the United States today, won him a national prize. Smetana, seventeen years his senior, was conducting the National Opera during these years, and over time he helped interest Dvořák in concentrating on writing Bohemian national music. One such composition, "Airs from Moravia," won him a $250-a-year pension, which enabled him to spend more time composing—encouraged and assisted by Johannes Brahms, by then one of Vienna's most influential musicians, only eight years Dvořák's senior but far advanced musically. Dvořák said later that he spent his time "in hard study, occasional composition, much revision, a great deal of thinking and little eating." After his marriage he said he ate less and thought more.

Dvořák's most famous work is his *Symphony from the New World*, commonly called simply the *New World* Symphony, No. 9 in E Minor. It was written chiefly in New York City at 827 East Seventeenth Street and polished in the small Bohemian-settled town of Spillville, Iowa, where he spent summers in the 1890s after he had been lured from Prague to become director of Manhattan's National Conservatory of Music. Not only is it Dvořák's best-known work, it is also one of the two or three most-recorded and performed symphonies in the United States. Lay listeners will find melodies in it with which they are wholly familiar. The second, Largo, movement is one of the three or four best known of all single symphonic movements, along with the first from Schubert's *Unfinished* Symphony and the fourth movement of Beethoven's Ninth. It is sort of shameful not to enjoy the *New World* Symphony, one of the classics of symphonic literature despite the onetime debate over how much of it sprang from Bohemian folk music, how much from what was called Negro spiritual music, and how much from American Indian sounds.

VOICE OF AMERICA

Dvořák was brought to the United States in 1892 by a Mrs. Jeanette Thurber, who had helped found the National Conservatory of Music in New York, wanted him to head it, paid him extremely well to do so, and was interested in building a national American school of composition. The composer was eager to go along, telling the *New York Herald Tribune*: "In the Negro songs I have found a secure basis for a new national music school. . . . America can have her own music, a fine music growing up from her own soul and having its own special character—the natural voice of a free and great nation."

The discussion over whether Dvořák's made-in-America music is "American" or "Bohemian" has taken many forms over the years. Three different views have been expressed about the haunting song of the English horn in the second movement of the *New World* Symphony. One is that it is based on a Negro spiritual. Another is that the composer was writing of Hiawatha's betrothal. And a third is that he was just plain homesick for his native land, to which he returned to spend the rest of his life, dying in 1904 not long after his opera *Armida* had failed in the Prague that loved him.

Though he was terribly homesick for his beloved Prague and returned home after three years in New York, Dvořák and the United States had a love affair. When he died in Prague in 1904, many American newspapers ran editorials mourning him, and national figures paid him tribute. A case can be made that he is the closest to an "American" composer on The List. (Paul Hindemith became a citizen after fleeing Germany for the United States, but he also returned to Europe. His music doesn't sound very American, anyhow, but he was, after all, a professor at Yale, which is not truly representative of much of America such as Cleveland, Milwaukee, and Brainardsville, New York.)

Of Dvořák's symphonies, significant attention is paid today to two others: No. 7 in D Minor, 1885, and No. 8 in G, 1889. The professionals, or at least some of the professionals, believe No. 7 is the most complete as a symphonic work, but it is played much less often than No. 8 and not nearly as frequently as No. 9.

Even more familiar to listeners is one of the eight piano pieces by Dvořák in a set called *Humoresques,* all of which are charming. No. 7 is the one around which many playful lyrics have been written, including what fifty years ago was the familiar "Passengers will please refrain/ From flushing toilets while the train/Is standing in the station, I love you." (Some of us still don't flush toilets in the station, despite modern sanitary engineering.)

With Brahms's help, Dvořák was commissioned to write a set of *Slavonic Dances* in the manner of the older composer's own successful *Hungarian Dances.* Published in 1878 when he was thirty-seven as Op. 46, they gave Dvořák a touch of fame throughout Europe and are today among the most frequently played of his works. They consist of eight authentic Bohemian folk melodies, adapted as piano duets and later orchestrated. Eight years later he wrote another set, Op. 72, these drawn from Yugoslavian and Russian music.

Dvořák was the first Czech to produce concertos, which he wrote for the piano, violin, and cello. All survive, the violin effort belonging on the "best-known" violin concerto list and the cello work, written during his stay in America, recognized today as one of the most popular of the cello species—of which there are not all that many.

His chamber music includes a Quartet in F, called the *American,* written after three Iroquois Indians visited him in Iowa; a Piano Quintet in A, and a Piano Trio in E Minor known as *Dumky,* from a Russian word taken by the composer to mean "a fleeting but emotional thought." The *Dumky* Trio, for violin, cello, and piano, is made up of six short movements combining, the critics say, "melancholy and joy of life."

Another highly praised work is his *Stabat Mater;* still another very popular one his Serenade in E for Strings. (The Stabat Mater is a Latin

DON'T TOUCH IT

Dvořák was very fussy about his Cello Concerto in B Minor, worried that soloists would foul it up while trying to show off. He wrote to his publisher: "I give you my work only if you will promise me that no one—not even my friend Wihan [cellist Hans Wihan, founder of the Bohemian String Quartet] shall make any alteration in it without my knowledge and permission, also that there be no cadenza such as Wihan has made in the last movement. . . . The finale closes 'like a breath' . . . ; the solo dies away to a pianissimo, then there is a crescendo, and the last measures are taken up by the orchestra, ending stormily. That was my idea, and from it I cannot recede."

The professionals say that it is extremely tough to write any kind of extended work for the cello because it is primarily a "singing" instrument without the violin's "variety of vocabulary." The virtuoso can do very complicated, swift, and varied things with the cello, but even the most expert, according to the music people, have trouble making those complicated results sound like music.

Other Listed composers who have written successful cello concertos include Schumann, Saint-Saëns, Prokofiev, and Shostakovich, plus Hindemith for chamber orchestra.

poem from about 1300 that was officially made part of the Catholic liturgy in the eighteenth century. Several Listed composers have written music for it, including Palestrina, Haydn, Rossini, Schubert, and Verdi. Dvořák's is regarded as a particularly good one.)

Smetana was the patriotic Czech, the nationalist Czech, but Dvořák's music sounds more Czech, at least to the unsophisticated ears of those of us who are mostly a blend of English, Irish, French, and other non-Czech ancestry.

Dvořák was one of the least neurotic of the great composers, along with Haydn and Handel; it is clear, from listening to his music, that his was not a tortured soul. It is not a bit necessary to be any kind of an expert to like him. But if you are a beginner and do like him, be comforted by the fact that a good many elitists like him, too. He has been called a natural, an heir of Schubert in his seemingly spontaneous melodic creation, and one of the most inventive of the nationalist composers.

STARTER KIT

If a reader were to choose only ten works from the thousand or so mentioned in this book, one of them should be Dvořák's *New World* Symphony. As mentioned earlier, the composer became captivated by black American melodies during his tour as director of the National Conservatory of Music in New York in the 1890s, and he was particularly taken by "Swing Low, Sweet Chariot," which can be heard from the flute in the first movement of the symphony. In a statement released to the United States public after the symphony was performed, he said: "These beautiful and varied themes are the product of the soil. They are American. They are the folk songs of America and your composers must turn to them. In the Negro melodies of America I discover all that is needed for a great and noble school of music."

A second Starter Kit choice for chauvinistic Americans is Dvořák's Quartet in F, called the *American*, with a first movement that sounds just the way music about the great open West is supposed to sound and with an Indian-like theme opening the second. (His Quintet in E-Flat, composed immediately thereafter, also has an Indian sound to it. Or a Bohemian sound, if you prefer.)

A third choice is his Cello Concerto in B Minor, also written while the composer was in the United States. Listen to the second theme in the first movement for more Bohemian/American music. A fourth selection, for variety, is an orchestral work, the *Carnival* Overture, Op. 92, one of a trilogy initially titled *Nature*, *Life*, and *Love*. What is now called the *Carnival* began life as *Life*. Dvořák's written program for it states: "The lonely, contemplative wanderer reaches the city at night fall, where a carnival of pleasure reigns supreme. On every side is heard the clangor of instruments, mingled with shouts of joy and the unrestrained hilarity of people giving vent to their feelings in their songs and dance tunes."

The *New World* Symphony is heard so frequently that Dvořák's other works are easily overlooked. A logical choice for the final Starter Kit selection could be Symphony No. 8 in G or the Violin Concerto in A Minor. Recommended instead, however, to give Bohemia its due, are his *Slavonic Dances*, which brought him international renown. They originally were composed for two pianos, but Dvořák later orchestrated them.

DVOŘÁK: THE STARTER KIT

Composition   *Recordings Available**

SYMPHONIES (OF NINE):
No. 9 in E Minor (New World)   45

OTHER ORCHESTRAL WORKS:
Cello Concerto in B Minor   17
Carnival Overture   16
Slavonic Dances (piano-duet and orchestral   21
   versions)

CHAMBER MUSIC:
Quartet No. 12 in F (American)   12

*Represents the number of recorded releases available of each listed composition as found in a recent issue of the *Schwann/Opus* catalogue. A "C" indicates that a work is only available collected with other compositions.

DVOŘÁK: A TOP TEN

Composition   *Recordings Available**

SYMPHONIES (OF NINE):
No. 7 in D Minor   9
No. 8 in G   18
No. 9 in E Minor (New World)   45

OTHER ORCHESTRAL WORKS:
Violin Concerto in A Minor   8
Cello Concerto in B Minor   17
Carnival Overture   16
Serenade in E for Strings   15
Slavonic Dances (piano-duet and orchestral   21
   versions)
Romance for Violin and Orchestra   9

CHAMBER MUSIC:
Quartet No. 12 in F (American)   12

DVOŘÁK: A MASTER COLLECTION

Composition	Recordings Available*

SYMPHONIES (OF NINE):

No. 7 in D Minor	9
No. 8 in G	18
No. 9 in E Minor (New World)	45

OTHER ORCHESTRAL WORKS:

Piano Concerto in G Minor	4
Violin Concerto in A Minor	8
Cello Concerto in B Minor	17
Rondo in G Minor for Cello and Orchestra	4
Silent Woods for Cello and Orchestra	6
Carnival Overture	16
Othello Overture	3
Serenade in E for Strings	15
Slavonic Dances (piano-duet and orchestral versions)	21
Romance for Violin and Orchestra	9
Symphonic Variations	2
Scherzo Capriccioso	5
The Garland Tone Poems:	0
Water Goblin	
Mid-Day Witch	
Golden Spinning Wheel	
Wood Dove	

CHAMBER MUSIC:

Piano Quintet in A	7
Viola Quintet No. 3 in E-flat	4
Quartet No. 12 in F (American)	12
Quartet No. 13 in G	2
Quartet No. 14 in A-flat	2
Piano Trio in E Minor (Dumky)	7
Czech Suite (also for full orchestra)	4

PIANO MUSIC:

Humoresque in G-flat	0

VOCAL MUSIC:

Stabat Mater	3

FRANZ LISZT (1811–1886)

Number 13

Franz Liszt, the first of two Hungarians on The List, was a mover and shaker, a rebel, a womanizer, a man of strong personality and enormous talent who exerted a major influence on nineteenth-century music. Some say *the* major influence. He also was perhaps the greatest pianist in history and unquestionably the greatest piano showman of all time.

While not a Demigod composer and certainly not an Immortal, Liszt holds a secure place in the history of music as the piano virtuoso who brought music to the adoring masses, and as a conductor, critic, essayist, city music director, and generous champion of dozens of other artists—especially Wagner. He created modern piano-playing technique and pioneered in harmony and form of piano composition. On the orchestral side, his great innovation was the symphonic poem. One of the most expert of the experts, musicologist Alfred Einstein, says his historical significance "cannot be exaggerated."

The professionals say he was not genius enough (except where the piano was involved) to carry his innovative ideas to the very highest level. Realization did not match intention. If he were judged only on his compositions, rather than on his total place and influence as a musician in the nineteenth century, most critics would move him down a few notches. (This is another case where the composer's works most loved by the public are not, in the critics' opinion, that artist's top works.)

It is perhaps curious, although indicative of the range of his talents, that it is not through the piano that piano virtuoso Liszt exerted his greatest influence on music, but rather through his invention (or near-invention) of the symphonic poem, which changed the direction of Romantic orchestral music across Europe. Saint-Saëns once wrote about Liszt and the symphonic poem: "This brilliant and fertile creation will be his best title to glory with posterity."

The symphonic—or tone—poem was defined earlier as a piece of orchestral music based on a pictorial, literary, or other "nonmusical" idea. Unlike the symphony, which consists of three or four frequently unrelated movements, the symphonic poem is a one-movement composition unified within itself, a free form with ideas linked together in various ways moving freely throughout it. And unlike "absolute" music, it requires a "program"; it attempts to tell a story or to set a scene. It gave a lot of nineteenth-century composers an opportunity to do their thing in ways that were different from the music of Haydn, Beethoven, and Mozart of Classical times or of Handel and Bach of Baroque days. Liszt wrote thirteen symphonic poems, the most famous of which are *Les préludes*, *Tasso*, and *Mazeppa*. Some symphonic poems were nationalistic in orientation, and composers influenced by Hungary's Liszt who followed this pattern include Smetana of Czechoslovakia, Borodin of Russia, Saint-Saëns of France, Sibelius of Finland, and Vaughan Williams of England. Another approach followed by Liszt was to draw on such literary sources as the writings of Hugo, Goethe, Schiller, Lamartine, and Shakespeare for the program of the music. Other composers who followed this literary model include Tchaikovsky of Russia and Saint-Saëns and Franck of France. If Liszt invented the tone poem, Richard Strauss perfected it near the end of the century. And Debussy used a similar format for his most important Impressionist works.

In the orchestral realm, Liszt also wrote two concertos for piano and orchestra, with No. 1 in E-flat the much better known. (A third was discovered fairly recently, but as of this writing it has not been added to the official list of his works.) The famous No. 1 in E-flat, written in 1849, was first performed in 1855 in Weimar with Liszt playing the piano and the famous Hans von Bülow conducting. While it is technically in four movements, Liszt runs the movements together, so it is considered a one-movement work. It is one of his most popular compositions.

He also composed two vast symphonies, neither of which is performed often today. He and his friend and colleague Berlioz shared respect and admiration for Johann Wolfgang von Goethe, Germany's literary giant, and both wrote works inspired by Goethe's masterpiece, *Faust*. Berlioz dedicated his *Damnation of Faust* to Liszt, and Liszt his seventy-minute *Faust* Symphony to Berlioz. His other, equally long symphony, the *Dante* Symphony, was dedicated to Wagner. Both are program works; the three movements of *Faust* are called "Faust,"

"Gretchen," and "Mephistopheles," and the movements of *Dante* are "Inferno," "Purgatory," and "Vision of Paradise." Not many professionals accept either symphony as the work of a master symphonist.

While his work in developing the form of the symphonic poem was Liszt's major contribution to music, his best compositions were for the piano. Saint-Saëns, a virtuoso organist and pianist himself, wrote: "We owe to him the invention of picturesque musical notation, thanks to which, by an ingenious disposition of notes and an extraordinary variety in presenting them to the eye, the composer contrived to indicate the character of the passage and the exact way it should be executed. Today, these refined methods are in general use. But above all, we owe to Liszt the introduction on the piano of orchestral effects and sonority."

If Liszt did not create a masterful symphony, he knew the piano so well and could make it do so many things that he could transcribe the great symphonies of a Beethoven for the piano alone. No one, the musicologists say, had ever successfully done that before.

The best known of his piano works are his nineteen *Hungarian Rhapsodies*, all written between 1846 and 1885. The best known of these is No. 2, and the other most popular ones include Nos. 9, 12, 13, 14, and 15. All are heard on classical radio stations from time to time. All are available both in solo-piano and orchestral versions. All are filled with legitimate Hungarian Gypsy melodies that have been turned, twisted, and developed by Liszt, and all include his own melodies in the Gypsy fashion. All also contrast slow and fast pace.

HUNGARIAN MUSIC?

Over time, there was quite a to-do in Hungary about the *Hungarian Rhapsodies*. Many people, including some high in the government, were upset by the title and by the fact that the world was accepting Gypsy music (on which the rhapsodies are based) as typical of all valid "national Hungarian" music. Those who objected argued that there was a great deal to their country, its history, its customs, and its values beyond that represented by the nomadic Gypsies.

Later, the second Hungarian on The List, Béla Bartók, went far beyond the Gypsies in studying true Hungarian folk song, found in remote villages and utterly unconnected to Gypsy music.

Liszt also wrote an extremely popular Piano Sonata in B Minor and three pieces called *Liebesträume* (Love's dreams), created first as songs and then adapted for piano. The third is universally loved and has become one of the most frequently played piano compositions. Another piano favorite is the "Sonetto del Petrarca" No. 104. His piano works also include three books of *Années de pèlerinage* (Years of pilgrimage), "Valse impromptu," *Valses caprices*, twelve *Grandes études de paganini*, the "Mephisto Waltz," and the *Transcendental Etudes*.

One reason Liszt was so influential is that he lived so long, generously encouraging other artists throughout his life. Of the "Magnificent Seven," Mendelssohn died in 1847, Chopin in 1849, Schumann in 1856, and Berlioz in 1869. Of the two opera writers among the Seven, Wagner died in 1883. But Liszt lived to 1886 (to age seventy-five) and at the time of his death was considered the Grand Old Man of European music. Something of an egomaniac himself, and a lonely man who kept losing longtime friends, he was apparently so secure in his own genius that he was not jealous of or threatened by the success of others. The Frenchman Berlioz, perhaps the strongest of all early Romantic revolutionaries, was for years a devoted Lisztian, although their styles differed and Berlioz was not a piano man. Liszt gave a great deal of support to Smetana in Czechoslovakia and Grieg in Norway, and the literature tells us he also influenced the Russian composers, including two of the "Mighty Five," Borodin and Rimsky-Korsakov, as well as Tchaikovsky.

But perhaps his most significant involvement in the music of others was in the career of Wagner. Until his death, Liszt loved Wagner's music, but his personal relationship with Wagner suffered considerably after The Unprincipled One broke up the marriage of Cosima, the illegitimate daughter of Liszt and the infamous Countess d' Agoult (she called herself Daniel Stern in her writings), and started living with her (he was later to marry her).

Liszt was born in Hungary in 1811, Berlioz in France in 1803, and Wagner in Germany in 1813. Of the seven Early Romantics on The List, these Big Three were the strong rebel leaders of their day—and their day took up most of a century. They were the heart and soul of what Wagner called "the music of the future." And, while their talents differed, they did much to bring the modern orchestra into existence.

Liszt was a radical, an experimenter, an activist, building on the past but, the experts say, totally unafraid to seek new directions. He made things happen, seizing from Beethoven, Schubert, Schumann, and Mendelssohn, pushing Wagner, preparing for Debussy and post-

---

EVERYONE WAS DOING IT

The influential nineteenth-century Viennese critic Eduard Hanslick was a proponent of the "pure" music of Brahms and a bitter enemy of Liszt and Wagner. One of Liszt's most popular songs was called "Es muss ein Wunderbares sein" (It must be a wonderful thing). Commenting on its popularity, Liszt said, "Everyone in Vienna sings it—even Mrs. Hanslick."

Debussy modernism. He was not afraid of dissonance, and some of his work, based on Gypsy scales, helped lay the groundwork for twentieth-century atonality. It is generally agreed that he was inferior to the flamboyant Berlioz in originality but far surpassed him in intellectual power.

As a pianist, his chief rival was Sigismond Thalberg, born in Switzerland in 1812, a supreme virtuoso with his own camp of supporters. Their rivalry culminated in a "shoot-out" at the Paris salon of Princess Cristina Belgiojoso on March 31, 1837, an event billed as "Rome versus Carthage." Biographer Alan Walker reports the princess's diplomatic verdict: "Thalberg is the first pianist in the world. Liszt is the only one."

Walker adds: "Liszt's career remains the model which is still followed by pianists today. The modern piano recital was invented by Liszt. He was the first to play entire programmes from memory. He was the first to play the whole keyboard repertory (as it then existed) from Bach to Chopin. He was the first consistently to place the piano at right angles to the platform, its open lid reflecting the sound across the auditorium."

Walker also points out that Liszt was the first to tour Europe from the Pyrenees to the Urals. In Milan and St. Petersburg he played before audiences of three thousand or more, the first time a solo pianist had appeared before such crowds. In Berlin he gave twenty-one concerts in ten weeks, playing eighty works—fifty of them from memory.

Liszt smashed the barriers. He put performing artists on a different social plateau. Whereas Haydn and Mozart entered through the back door, and whereas Beethoven forced recognition for himself because he hurled lightning, Liszt sold the notion that performing artists,

PAGANINI OF THE PIANO

Franz Liszt would have put the twentieth-century Liberace to shame. He would appear for piano concerts before an adoring public in Hungarian Magyar costume, with bejeweled sword and medal-covered chest—music's first box-office virtuoso. Showmanship aside, he is generally accepted as the greatest pianist in history. Some music people consider Chopin more of the "pianist's pianist" and Liszt more of the "public's pianist," but none gainsay his great technical brilliance and the impact of his modern piano technique on all who followed. One writer said he "raised a generation of giants of the keyboard"; no one has raged and ranged up and down that keyboard as he did. It was exciting to have him around; the ladies would swoon as they watched him remove his velvet gloves before playing, and they envied the women who appeared on the stage with a basin to wash his hands in advance of the great event. He was a ladies' man of the highest order in his personal life, a fact known to female admirers who fought for his snuffbox and tore apart his handkerchiefs.

divinely gifted, were superior by definition and thus were owed not only respect but homage.

"This view of the artist who walks with God and brings fires down from heaven with which to kindle the hearts of mankind became so deeply entrenched in the Romantic consciousness that today we regard it as a cliché," biographer Walker wrote.

Liszt came from a comfortable background; his father was a steward for a sheep-breeding station in Raiding, Hungary, on the estate of the Esterhazys. (Haydn, who served the Esterhazys, died in 1809, two years before Liszt was born.) The senior Liszt was a fine amateur musician, and young Franz was taught the piano early at home. Friendly noblemen became interested in him; he was perceived as brilliant, schooled in Vienna, further trained in Paris, and toured Europe as a prodigy virtuoso at fourteen. By sixteen he had started a long series of love affairs for which he was as famous, throughout his life, as he was for hitting the piano keys.

In 1848 Liszt was named Kapellmeister to the grand duke of Weimar, a post he held for ten years. In this capacity he encouraged more budding composers than perhaps any master in music history—and in doing so made Weimar a music center of Europe. After this period he turned to religion, becoming an abbé. There is evidence that his romantic liaisons continued even under these circumstances. His life was one of contradictions: he had both intimate friends and loneliness; he was devoted to both women and religion; and he loved both Hungary and Paris.

In addition to Liszt's roles as virtuoso, composer, public hero, and transcriber, he was also a devourer of literature, at one time writing:

> Here is a whole fortnight that my mind and fingers have been working like two lost spirits—Homer, the Bible, Plato, Locke, Byron, Hugo, Lamartine, Chateaubriand, Beethoven, Bach, Hummel, Mozart, Weber are all around me. I study them, meditate on them, devour them with fury. Besides this, I practice four to five hours. . . . Ah! Provided I don't go mad you will find an artist in me! Yes, an artist such as you desire.

STARTER KIT

For Liszt, we bypass the symphonies and begin with a piece that is far more of a concert favorite, his Piano Concerto No. 1 in E-flat, written around 1849. Like so many masterpieces, it almost died at birth, and it was some twenty years before its revival—now known to be a lasting revival.

Even more popular is the third of his thirteen symphonic poems, *Les Préludes,* composed in 1848 and revised a few years later. Its program is taken from the French poet Alphonse de Lamartine's "Meditations poetiques," which begins: "What is our life but a series of Preludes to that unknown song of which death strikes the first solemn note?" Man's soul, Lamartine proposed, seeks out love until "he hastens to the post of peril, whatever may be the strife which calls him to his ranks, in order to regain in combat the full consciousness of himself and the complete command of his powers."

Liszt's only piano sonata, a long one, the Sonata in B Minor, is included. The critics say it has grandeur, eloquence, and power on the one hand but shallow dramatics and disorganization on the other. Nonetheless, there is general agreement that it includes some of the most brilliant passages in what the music people call "the piano literature."

For pianist Liszt, devoted Hungarian, the Starter Kit appropriately includes the nineteen *Hungarian Rhapsodies* for piano, published first in 1840, after Liszt visited a Gypsy encampment in Hungary, under the title *Magyar dallok* (Hungarian national melodies) and republished after revisions, in 1851–1853.

Because of the importance of the symphonic poem and Liszt's role in its development, a second one, *Tasso*, is also included in the Starter Kit. However, you may want to exchange it for one of the orchestrated versions of the *Hungarian Rhapsodies*.

FRANZ LISZT: THE STARTER KIT

Composition	Recordings Available*
ORCHESTRAL WORKS:	
Piano Concerto No. 1 in E-flat	19
Symphonic Poems:	
No. 2, Tasso	8
No. 3, Les Préludes	23
PIANO MUSIC:	
Hungarian Rhapsodies for Piano (nineteen)	25
Sonata in B Minor for Piano	19

*Represents the number of recorded releases available of each listed composition as found in a recent issue of the *Schwann/Opus* catalogue. A "C" indicates that a work is only available collected with other compositions.

FRANZ LISZT: A TOP TEN

Composition	Recordings Available*
SYMPHONIES:	
Faust Symphony (with voice)	6
OTHER ORCHESTRAL WORKS:	
Piano Concerto No. 1 in E-flat	19
Totentanz (Dance of Death) for Piano and Orchestra	8
Symphonic Poems:	
No. 2, Tasso—Lament and Triumph	8
No. 3, Les Préludes	23
Hungarian Rhapsodies:	
Nos. 2, 5, 6, 9, 12, 14 (orchestral versions)	20

Composition	Recordings Available*

PIANO MUSIC:

Hungarian Rhapsodies for Piano (nineteen)	25
Mephisto Waltz No. 1	15
Sonata in B Minor for Piano	19
Liebesträume (Love's Dreams)	C

FRANZ LISZT: A MASTER COLLECTION

Composition	Recordings Available*

SYMPHONIES:

Faust Symphony (with voice)	6
Dante Symphony	3

OTHER ORCHESTRAL WORKS:

Piano Concerto No. 1 in E-flat	19
Piano Concerto No. 2 in A	4
Hungarian Fantasia for Piano and Orchestra	12
Totentanz (Dance of Death) for Piano and Orchestra	8
Symphonic Poems:	
No. 2, Tasso—Lament and Triumph	8
No. 3, Les Préludes	23
No. 4, Orpheus	3
No. 6, Mazeppa	6
Hungarian Rhapsodies:	
Nos. 2, 5, 9, 6, 12, 14 (orchestral versions)	20

PIANO MUSIC:

Hungarian Rhapsodies for Piano (nineteen)	25
Mephisto Waltz No. 1	15
Transcendental Etudes After Paganini for Piano (six)	7
Sonata in B Minor for Piano	19
Sonetti del Petrarca (three)	10
Rhapsodie Espagnole	7
Liebesträume (Love's Dreams)	C
Harmonies poétiques et religieuses	9
Ballades for Piano (two)	8

FRÉDÉRIC CHOPIN (1810–1849)

Number 14

Paris in the 1830s. Victor Hugo, Honoré de Balzac, Comte Alfred
Victor Vigny, Ferdinand Delacroix, Alphonse de Lamartine, Heinrich
Heine. The artistic elite; the intellectuals; painters, poets, critics; the
literati. Among them the talented George Sand—cigar-smoker, famous novelist, wearer of men's suits, mistress of a succession of
literary greats. What a setting for a slim, frail, elegant, soft-spoken,
aristocratic-looking Polish exile who was a composer of genius, one of
the finest pianists in history—and recipient of a diamond ring from the
czar of Russia.

One drools.

Liszt was there. So were Berlioz and Rossini. Mendelssohn came
and went.

For the NFL fans among our amateur audience, it wasn't quite
Cleveland when Jim Brown was running or Pittsburgh at the height of
Bradshaw, but it was something special.

Frédéric Chopin was another of the "Magnificent Seven," the
seven early Romantics born within ten years of one another in the
early 1800s, all of whom are in the top one-third of The List. He was
the all-around piano man in a piano age: one of the finest pianists in
history (some critics prefer him to the thundering Liszt), and the only
one of the superstar composers who wrote virtually nothing but piano
music—no symphonies, operas, or oratorios, and very little orchestral
work. He did compose two piano concertos, but even those are centered on the piano, with the orchestra as a backdrop, rather than being
works in which the piano and the orchestra have equal parts.

Pianist Glenn Gould once said of him that the "worthy Frédéric
scarcely ever kept a large-scale structure going with the impetus" given
by other leading composers.

Chopin was a master of the small form. Chopin gives us no *Eroica* Symphony or *Marriage of Figaro* or Mass in B Minor on which to concentrate as a manifestation of genius. The piano pieces he wrote were called *preludes, scherzos, mazurkas, nocturnes, polonaises, fantasies, rondos, impromptus,* and the like. Most of them are intense, poetic, and filled with feeling—and many are delicate, as is to be expected of a Parisian, though some are fervently patriotic, as is to be expected of a Pole. (His father was a French émigré; his mother was Polish.)

His work includes seventeen polonaises, fifty-seven mazurkas, four scherzos, four ballades, twenty-six preludes, twenty-seven études, nineteen nocturnes, fourteen waltzes, two piano concertos written when he was young, two famous piano sonatas, and nineteen songs. (The Piano Sonata No. 2 in B-flat Minor contains one of music's most famous funeral marches; a second can be found in Beethoven's Third Symphony and a third in Wagner's *Götterdämmerung*.) Curiously, for a Romantic he was not much of a songwriter.

Liszt, an artist generous with praise for many colleagues, said of Chopin's polonaises: "They exhale the courage and worth that distinguish this warrior nation [Author's note: Poland, certainly not France] from others. Resolution, courtesy, pompous pride, honor, concern with trivial matters, scorn for haste, slow bows, sudden straightenings, a dance begun by the master of the house and followed by others according to rank, dedicated to the most valiant and the most beautiful, a single line of all society made a circle and took pleasure admiring itself."

The polonaise, which has its origins in Poland, is more conventionally defined as a proud, stately, processional ballroom dance. Chopin's most famous include the "Military" in A, Op. 40; the F-sharp Minor, Op. 44, and the "Heroic" in A-flat, Op. 53.

The mazurka is a uniquely Polish dance, native to Chopin's home territory. Liszt, no master of understatement, as evidenced by his comment on the polonaises, offers a similarly effusive description of Chopin's mazurkas: "Almost all the mazurkas are full of that amorous mist which floats like an ambient fluid around his preludes, nocturnes, and impromptus, where the turns of passion are traced one by one, resembling a fairy world, and reveal the indiscreet confidences of the Peris, the Titanias, the Ariels, the Queen Mabs, of all the genii of the air, the water, the fire."

Well, the artistic Liszt was something of a charlatan, and maybe the turns of passion are not traced all that easily. What is clear even to amateur ears is that neither these mazurkas nor any other of Chopin's compositions have anything in common with the powerful German music that was influential in Europe at this time. In fact, nothing about Chopin is very much like anything German; he has been called the most non-German of all great composers.

Of Chopin's mazurkas, biographer Bernard Gavoty writes: "The[y] occupy a privileged position in the total output of Chopin. They only briefly express the sentiments of heroism, grandeur and revenge produced by the sonatas, scherzos, ballades and polonaises. But as music per se, they are perhaps Chopin's most refined, most personal and most prodigiously original creations."

Whether or not they are his "most original" works (critical opinions differ on this), the mazurkas *are* quintessential Chopin—more emotional than intellectual, and alternating between happy and sad. Sample a couple; some are no more than two minutes long.

The nocturnes—dreamlike, melodic night music, as their name suggests—include melodies so beautiful that some professionals consider them the most beautiful in all music. Although Chopin did not invent the nocturne—it came from Ireland—he is credited with having made both the name and the style famous. Fauré was to write thirteen of them after Chopin's death.

The scherzos were another set that covered a whole emotional range, from passion to light fantasy. Normally a scherzo is the third movement of a sonata, symphony, or quartet, but Chopin's scherzos are dramatic pieces that stand on their own, as are Brahms's.

The preludes, nearly all very short, are not preludes in the sense of being the beginning of something; rather, they too stand alone. Chopin-fan Liszt said they "have the free and great features that characterize the works of genius." Schumann added: "I must declare them very remarkable. I confess that I expected something quite different, carried off in a grand style like the etudes. . . . But in each piece we find his refined, peace-studded writing. . . . His is the boldest and proudest poetic soul of today." Like Bach's forty-eight preludes, Chopin's twenty-four use a single theme, and each is in a different key.

An étude is generally the name for a study for piano students. But Chopin's études are accepted masterpieces in their own right. The other piano études of greatest fame are Liszt's.

It has been said that there should be a special niche in musical history for the works of Bach, the thirty-two piano sonatas of Beethoven, and the piano music of Chopin, with its sweeping melodies and pure beauty of sound. His lyricism—the personal, very emotional quality of his music—played a major role in the development of the Romantic movement. Although not as radical as Berlioz, nor as oblivious to rules as Liszt, who tried to turn the piano into an entire symphony orchestra, Chopin was an experimenter. The experts say he

THE FEELING WAS NOT MUTUAL

Schumann had great respect for Chopin, and in an article in his music journal he wrote about the young Pole, "Hats off, gentlemen, a genius." Chopin graciously thanked Schumann for the article by dedicating the second of his four ballades to him. Schumann dedicated his *Kreisleriana* to Chopin. But Chopin was not, in fact, a great admirer of Schumann's work. In a letter to his publisher, A. M. Schlesinger, he wrote, "Schumann's 'Carnaval' [one of Schumann's better-known piano compositions] is not music at all."

was deep into dissonances which, while not the "biting" or "wild" ones that came in twentieth-century/new/modern music, were "star-tling." The professionals refer to them as "disguised" dissonances that don't spoil the beauty of his works.

As for Chopin's playing, the words from the critics duplicate those used for his compositions. It was precise, without excess or sloppiness, with nothing uncontrolled; at all times it showed good manners, high breeding, and poetic warmth.

Chopin was born at Zelazowa Wola, near Warsaw, and when he first played the piano in public, at age nine, a biased Warsaw (not unexpectedly) called him "the new Mozart." That he was not; he was the new boy, named Chopin—which was quite good enough. In 1830, after much musical study and scattered public appearances, he gave three great farewell concerts in Warsaw, visited various German cities, considered visiting the United States, rejected the idea because things were a little too primitive there, and settled in Paris. He was welcomed there by the in-group and shortly gave up public piano performances for composition and other good things. In all, he gave no more than thirty public concerts as an adult.

One of the other good things was author George Sand, aka Mme. Aurore Dudevant, with whom he lived "in close connection," as the biographers used to say in more guarded days, for ten years. They met when he was twenty-eight and she thirty-four, spent one famous win-ter in Majorca (described in one of her books), and were together much of the time either in Paris or Nohant at her château. Sand was a political activist, opposed to monarchy, tradition, and convention; he was a musician, not deeply concerned with social injustice. Hers was the dominant personality. His objective was to "create a new era in art"; hers was to remake an unfair world.

She ended the relationship in 1847 (later portraying Chopin as Prince Karol in a novel, *Lucrezia Floriani*), and he returned to his Paris quarters and to composition. Authors and music historians have devoted enormous effort to delving into the relationship of the two, with some claiming that the physical aspect may have been nonexistent after a promising beginning—but we'll leave it as one of the great and intriguing romances of music, despite a bitter ending.

GEORGE SAND ON HER LOVER

"His creative power was spontaneous, miraculous. It came to him without effort or warning. . . . But then began the most heart-rending labor I have ever witnessed. It was a series of attempts, of fits of irresolution and impatience to recover certain details. He conceived a melody as a whole, but when he tried to write it down he analyzed it too much, and his regret at not recovering it in clear-cut form plunged him—by his own account—into a sort of despair. He would shut himself in his room for days, pacing up and down, breaking his pens, repeating and modifying one bar a hundred times. . . . He would spend six weeks over a page, only to end by writing it out finally just as he had sketched it in the original draft."

Chopin died of tuberculosis in Paris at thirty-nine in 1849, two years after the affair ended, his creative energies depleted. In a letter from Scotland written not long before his death, he lamented: "What has become of my art? And my heart, where have I wasted it? I scarce remember any more how they sing at home. That world slips away from me somehow. I forget. I have no strength. If I rise a little, I fall again, lower than ever."

Despite Liszt's sometimes enthusiastic praise of his work, Chopin, the private pianist, was not fond of Liszt, the ultimate virtuoso showman. Arthur Hedley writes in *The Chopin Companion*:

Liszt's public pianistic career, which ended "officially" just before Chopin's death, was founded on the grandiose, the astounding, the dazzlingly effective both in composition and performance, coupled with an equally effective pathos and the heart frankly worn on the sleeve. It was these very elements that caused Chopin's revulsion, especially when he saw, as he did on occasions, Liszt tampering with his music and encouraging others to do so.

Everyone agrees Paris never got the Polish out of the pianist. Author Georges Jean-Aubrey wrote: "Poland, Poland, how many nights has he held her to his heart. Yes, in the Majorca evenings, and the nights in Paris, amongst the ocean breezes which blew over the old convent in the Baleares, amidst drawing room talks and elegant women and all the little refinements dear to his sensitive taste, he thought but of Poland."

Well, let us hope that he had an occasional moment with George Sand in which he thought of something other than Poland. But the Poles have never stopped thinking of Frédéric Chopin; indeed, the last music heard over Warsaw radio before the city surrendered to the Nazis was music familiar to all Poles—the first eleven notes of the Polonaise in A.

The music people differ somewhat on how much "great" music Chopin wrote, but there is common agreement that he wrote little or no "bad" music. And there is near-unanimous agreement that there is beauty, subtlety, magnificence, and power in his compositions. There is also prejudice within the music community against using "genius" for anyone lacking a significant body of orchestral pieces.

STARTER KIT

Chopin's Piano Concerto No. 1 in E Minor is not viewed as a masterpiece; the orchestra really was not his thing. It is nonetheless included in the Starter Kit since there should be some representation of other-than-solo-piano work. And he was only twenty when he wrote it, which makes it relatively special in any event. At this time in musical history, the thing to do, for a virtuoso performer-composer, was to write a concerto or two for his instrument. That's what Chopin did; he composed two, both frequently recorded, even if the experts don't consider them extra-special.

Of the two best-known polonaises—Op. 40, No. 1 in A, the "Military," and Op. 53, in A-flat, the "Heroic"—the arbitrary Starter Kit selection is the more familiar "Heroic." But the "Military" is a wholly acceptable substitute. There is nothing of Parisian eloquence in these; this is good, strong Polish music.

Chopin wrote only three works that he called sonatas, of which by

YOU CAN'T TAKE THE COUNTRY
OUT OF THE BOY

Chopin was born in Poland of a Polish mother, lived there the first twenty years of his life, and is still hailed by Poland as its premier composer. His father was French, however, and he spent his adult life in sophisticated Paris. Polish roots are deep in his work, but Parisian culture and atmosphere played a greater role in developing his genius. Biographer Bernard Gavoty has him eternally homesick on the one hand and a vigorous Paris-lover on the other—a combination many would find tolerable. Polish intensity, French delicacy—"a Polish poet of a Parisian piano."

For a less-than-objective view of Chopin's true heritage, here are the words of Ignace Paderewski, the legendary pianist and former president of the Republic of Poland:

Familiar dances of the Mazovian countryside, melancholy nocturnes, lively "Krakowiaks," mysterious preludes, roaring polonaises, titanic fabulous etudes, epic ballades in which tempests howl, heroic sonatas—he understands everything, he feels everything, because everything belongs to him, everything is Polish. Chopin has embellished and ennobled everything. In the depths of Polish soil he has found gems and he left us a treasure. He was the first to confer the highest nobility on the Polish peasant—that of the beautiful. . . . Poet, magician, monarch by the force of his spirit, he has made all classes equal, not in the lower depths of daily life, but above, on the lofty summit of feeling. This is how the Poles listen to Chopin. The Poles listen, and like the poet, dissolve in tears. This is how we all listen to him—how else can we listen to this bard of the Polish people!

far the best known is Sonata No. 2 in B-flat Minor, composed in 1838 when he was seriously ill. Schumann wrote of the Finale: "This great movement is perhaps the boldest page which has ever been written in the whole of music. Death appears here in all the cruel realism of its brute force, which destroys and ruins all things." This Finale follows the third movement, which includes the famous funeral march known to tens of millions (most of whom do not realize it is Chopin). A biographer calls this "incontestably the most imaginative of all Chopin's music."

While Schumann-the-musician was excited about the quality of the Finale, Schumann-the-journalist didn't think much of the composition as a sonata. "To have called this a sonata must be reckoned a freak, if not a piece of pride," he wrote. "For he has simply linked together four of his maddest children in order to introduce them by fraud under this name into a place which otherwise they would perhaps never have entered."

The other two works chosen are his Fantaisie in F Minor, still one of his most-performed pieces, and one of his four ballades, No. 1 in G Minor, the single most recorded of all Chopin piano compositions. The ballades were inspired by poems of the Polish poet Adam Mickiewicz, who had been arrested by the Russians. Some of the experts prefer No. 3 in A-flat and No. 4 in F Minor.

CHOPIN: THE STARTER KIT

Composition	Recordings Available*
ORCHESTRAL WORKS:	
Piano Concerto No. 1 in E Minor	21
PIANO MUSIC:	
Ballade No. 1 in G Minor	42
Fantaisie in F Minor	21
Polonaise:	
Op. 53, in A flat (Heroic)	18
Sonata No. 2 in B-flat Minor for Piano	19

*Represents the number of recorded releases available of each listed composition as found in a recent issue of the *Schwann/Opus* catalogue. A "C" indicates that a work is only available collected with other compositions.

CHOPIN: A TOP TEN

Composition	Recordings Available*
ORCHESTRAL WORKS:	
Piano Concerto No. 1 in E Minor	21
Piano Concerto No. 2 in F Minor	19

Composition	Recordings Available*
PIANO MUSIC:	
Andante Spinato and Grande Polonaise	23
Ballade:	
No. 1 in G Minor	42
Fantaisie in F Minor	21
Polonaises:	
Op. 40, No. 1 in A (Military)	7
Op. 53, in A-flat (Heroic)	18
Nocturne:	
Op. 9, No. 3 in E-flat	12
Sonata No. 2 in B-flat Minor for Piano	19
Sonata No. 3 in B Minor for Piano	18

CHOPIN: A MASTER COLLECTION

Composition	Recordings Available*
ORCHESTRAL WORKS:	
Piano Concerto No. 1 in E Minor	21
Piano Concerto No. 2 in F Minor	19
PIANO MUSIC:	
Andante Spinato and Grande Polonaise	23
Ballades (of four):	42
No. 1 in G Minor	
No. 3 in A-flat	
No. 4 in F Minor	
Fantaisie in F Minor	21
Etudes (of twenty-four):	26
Op. 25, No. 9 in G-flat	
No. 11 in A Minor	
Preludes (of thirty):	26
Op. 28, No. 4 in E Minor	
No. 15 in D-flat (Raindrop)	
Waltzes (of fifteen):	26
Op. 64, No. 1 in E-flat (Grande valse brillante)	
No. 2 in C-sharp Minor	
Polonaises (of eleven):	
Op. 40, No. 1 in A (Military)	7
Op. 61, in A-flat	13
Op. 53, in A-flat (Heroic)	18

Composition	Recordings Available*
Nocturnes (of twenty-one):	15
Op. 9, No. 3 in E-flat	
Op. 37, No. 2 in G	
Mazurkas (of fifty-one):	11
Op. 30, No. 4	
Op. 50, No. 3 in C-sharp Minor	
Op. 56, No. 2	
Impromptus:	
Fantaisie impromptu	C
Sonata No. 2 in B-flat Minor for Piano	19
Sonata No. 3 in B Minor for Piano	18
Barcarolle in F-sharp	12

IGOR STRAVINSKY (1882–1971)

Number 15

Who wrote this fiendish "Rite of Spring"
What right had he to write the thing,
Against our helpless ears to fling
Its crash, clash, cling, clang, bing, bang, bing?

And then to call it "Rite of Spring"
The season when on joyous wing
The birds harmonious carols sing
And harmony's in everything!

He who could write the "Rite of Spring"
If I be right, by right should swing!

Igor Stravinsky, *Rite of Spring* composer, is the second-ranked Russian on The List, after Tchaikovsky, and the highest rated of composers who lived and worked deep into the twentieth century, surviving until Richard Nixon was president of the United States. Generally considered to be the century's leading composer, he is so recognized here. He was a dominant force in music, the top-rated composer on The List to have been involved with the clash-cling-clang noises that once were called "new" or "modern" music. An intellectual, he liked to experiment with strange and different sounds, and as a young man he created some music that sounded astonishingly peculiar in its day. So, as we have seen, did many others, but not at his level. Not surprisingly, given his long (eighty-nine-year) life, he went through various composing evolutions, at one time spending several years in a neoclassical phase and at the end embracing twelve-tone (serial) music, which he had previously rejected. It is difficult to choose music from one part of his long career and say, "This is the typical sound of Stravinsky," although the connoisseurs say that anything composed by Stravinsky is recognizable as such.

He wrote: ballets that shocked the music world as it rarely had been shocked before; works that he called *symphonies*, but not all of them were what one expects symphonies to be; choral music disguised as symphony; a very well-known work that is a cross between an opera and an oratorio; a famous opera; a violin concerto; and a couple of works that are sort of piano concertos.

Stravinsky was born in Oranienbaum, Russia, the son of a bass singer in the St. Petersburg Opera. He attended the university there to study law, also studied the piano, worked under Rimsky-Korsakov, and gave up law to compose. He became known overnight in 1910 at the young age of twenty-eight after the publication of one ballet, *The Firebird*, and even better known a year later after the publication of another, *Petrushka*. But the real thermonuclear explosion came with a third ballet, *Le sacre du printemps* (The rite of spring) in 1913, when he was only thirty. Some music people say that it was to the first half of the twentieth century what Beethoven's Ninth Symphony and Wagner's *Tristan und Isolde* were to the nineteenth. But a common 1913 reaction of a less flattering nature is typified in the poem cited above, published in the *Boston Herald*, which has since been widely reprinted.

This was true dissonance for its time; these were new rhythms, melodies, and harmonies; this was grunt and growl; this was 1913 "modern," "new," "twentieth-century." It made Stravinsky the *enfant terrible* of music, the shock-you genius.

The experts note that although he did not (for the most part) go the atonal route of some dissonance-driven twentieth-century

HE HISSED AND SHE SPAT

Few single pieces of music have caused such a furor as *The Rite of Spring*, and many of the same stories are reported in various sources about the work's premiere. Saint-Saëns rose from his seat early in the performance, made a sarcastic remark, and left the theater in anger. One critic yelled out that the music was a fraud. The Austrian ambassador laughed aloud. One man, hissing, was slapped in the face by an irate female neighbor. A society woman spat in the face of one of the demonstrators. While Saint-Saëns was stalking out, fellow Frenchman Ravel was shouting "genius" and Impressionist Claude Debussy was pleading for silence. Milton Cross reports one description from Carl van Vechten's book *Music after the War*: "A certain part of the audience, thrilled by what it considered to be a blasphemous attempt to destroy music as an art, and swept away with wrath, began very soon after the rise of the curtain to whistle, to make catcalls, and to offer audible suggestions as to how the performance should proceed. Others of us, who liked the music, and felt the principles of free speech were at stake, bellowed defiance. The orchestra played on unheard." Television viewers in presidential-election years may be reminded of a Democratic National Convention.

composers, the things he did with rhythm and other basic musical elements were extreme. The opening night of *The Rite of Spring* was one of the most riotous in modern musical history, a rock concert gone wild, with people hooting, screaming, hissing, and slapping one another—and presumably with no controlled substances involved.

Writing in midcentury, Milton Cross summed it up this way:

"The Rite of Spring" shook the world of music to its very foundation. Stravinsky's growing boldness in dispensing with traditional harmonic, rhythmic, and melodic concepts—evident first in "The Firebird" and increasingly apparent in "Petrushka"—had grown in his latest score into outright anarchy, or so it appeared in 1913. With "The Rite of Spring," Stravinsky became the most provocative, publicized and fiercely discussed figure in music.

One doesn't need to take a music-appreciation course to know that *The Rite of Spring* is, indeed, something different. As with the dissonant music of Bartók, Hindemith, and, in some cases, Prokofiev and Shostakovich, one need only listen. We *hear* that these are different-sounding sounds; we don't need the experts to tell us so—although after nearly a century of listening the strange has become relatively familiar. As is so often the case with progressives, Stravinsky did not view himself as a bomb-throwing radical. "I hold that it was a mistake to consider me a revolutionary," he once wrote. "If one only need break habit in order to be labeled a revolutionary, then every artist who has something to say and who in order to say it steps outside the bounds of established convention could be considered revolutionary."

DANCING TO DEATH

The composer wrote of how *The Rite of Spring* began: "One day when I was finishing the last pages of 'L'oiseau de feu' in St. Petersburg, I had a fleeting vision which came to me as a complete surprise. . . . I saw in imagination a solemn pagan rite; sage elders seated in a circle, watched a young girl dance herself to death. They were sacrificing her to propitiate the god of spring. Such was the theme of the 'Le sacre du printemps'!"

Erik Satie, Honorable Mention French composer and leader of young rebels in the arts in the early twentieth century, took that a step or two further. "He is a liberator," said Satie. "More than anyone else, he has freed the musical thought of today."

But Stravinsky did not follow one approach to composition for the rest of his long life. The musicologists divide his work into several periods. The earliest one is traditional; these were his youngest days, when he was the "soul of Russia" as a student of nationalist Rimsky-Korsakov, a time when he wrote his Symphony in E-flat. The next was the period that included the three ballets plus "The Song of the Nightingale" and *Les noces* (The wedding), a ballet/dance cantata of a Russian peasant wedding. This was the period of complicated rhythms, dissonance, polytonality, and severe melodies. While the sounds he made were very different from the more traditional earlier ones, the experts say that his work in both of these two periods was basically "Russian," drawn from his native background. After World War I he broke with the Soviet Union and moved to Paris, where he lived for fifteen years (and applied for French citizenship). Among his best-known works written there over the next dozen years are a charming ballet-type piece, *L'histoire du soldat*, 1918 (The story of a soldier); *Symphonies of Wind Instruments*, 1921; a suite, *Pulcinella*; various concertos; the opera-oratorio *Oedipus Rex*, 1927; the ballet *Apollo*; and the choral piece *Symphony of Psalms*, 1930, considered a major mature work.

Stravinsky realized early in this period that these works would not be as popular as the three famous ballets. Commenting on *Symphonies of Wind Instruments*—"symphonies" in this case meaning "instruments sounded together," not an orchestral symphony in the traditional sense—he said in a 1935 autobiography: "It lacks all those elements that infallibly appeal to the ordinary listener, or to which he is accustomed. It is futile to look in it for passionate impulse or dynamic brilliance. The music is not meant to 'please' an audience, nor to arouse its passions. Nevertheless, I had hoped that it would appeal to some of those persons in whom a purely musical receptivity outweighed the desire to satisfy their sentimental cravings."

STRAVINSKY ON THE PRESS AND PUBLIC

Stravinsky, like Verdi and many other composers, did not think much of music critics and was not overly friendly toward the public. "They cannot and will not follow me in the progress of my musical thought," he said. "What moves and delights me leaves them indifferent, and what still continues to interest them holds no further attraction for me. For that matter, I believe that there was seldom any real communion of spirit between us. If it happened—and it still happens—that we liked the same things, I very much doubt whether it was for the same reasons."

That appears to be another way of saying that the days of Romanticism in music were—or, in his opinion certainly should have been—days of the past.

Stravinsky first came to the United States in 1925, made many visits thereafter, and, in 1939, with another war coming to Europe, moved to this country. He married in Boston (we have no record of whether he subscribed to the *Boston Herald*) and, in 1941, settled in California after applying for American citizenship. The year before he had written the Symphony in C, in honor of Classicists Haydn and Mozart. In 1945 came the *Symphony in Three Movements*, a major work; in 1947 the ballet *Orpheus*; in 1948 a *Mass*; and, most important, in 1951 his opera *The Rake's Progress*—called by critics the quintessence of neoclassicism. The early revolutionary primitivism was far behind him now. His writing, the music people say, was clear, lucid, and economical.

AN APPLE PIE AMERICAN

Stravinsky moved to the United States in 1939 and thereafter did all sorts of American-type things. He bought a house in Hollywood, became an American citizen, wrote a polka for the Ringling Brothers' elephants to dance to, produced some ballet music for a Broadway show, composed a piece ("Ebony Concerto") for Woody Herman's big dance band, wrote some music for television—and even produced a new arrangement of "The Star-Spangled Banner" (which no one liked).

In the final years of his composing career he entered still another phase, creating some of the more extreme twelve-tone serial music he had previously opposed. The most important works of this period include "Sacred Song to Honor the Name of St. Mark" (1955) and "A Sermon, a Narrative and a Prayer" (1960–1961).

In 1961 he was invited to return to the Soviet Union to conduct a concert of his own music on the occasion of his eightieth birthday. He did so and while there was asked by Chairman Nikita Khrushchev to come back permanently and live in a beautiful *dacha* (country house) in the Crimea. Although he had been deeply moved by the reception given him by the Russian people, he declined. He died in New York in 1971, shortly before his eighty-ninth birthday, and was buried in Venice.

It is widely agreed that Stravinsky was the most inventive pupil of Rimsky-Korsakov and that his ballet music, from *The Firebird* to *The Rite of Spring*, did more to enrich orchestral sounds than the works of any Listed composer of his time, including orchestra-minded Richard Strauss, who was born eighteen years earlier than Stravinsky. This enrichment ranged from the most sophisticated to the most barbaric— or, at least, to that which then seemed to be the most barbaric. Blanket comparisons don't work well with the giant musicians. Stravinsky could create sounds as delicate as those of Impressionist Debussy, but he was also capable of writing music with a brutality and a power that Debussy either could not or did not want to produce.

An intellectual composer who created intellectual works for a sophisticated and (musically) intellectual audience, Stravinsky is still not a concert-hall favorite. But he is held in high esteem today by the professionals, and there should be few objections for placing him this high on The List.

STRAVINSKY ON HIS MUSIC

"I live neither in the past nor in the future. I am in the present. I cannot know what tomorrow will bring forth. I can only know what the truth is for me today."

STARTER KIT

Aside from *The Rite of Spring*, the next best known of Stravinsky's works are the other two ballets from the same prewar period, *The Firebird* (L'oiseau de feu) and *Petrushka*. All three were commissioned by the Ballets Russes, which had been organized in the early 1900s. *The Firebird* is based on an old Russian legend and involves thirteen beautiful young girls, a magic Firebird, and Death emerging from a crushed eggshell. Completed in St. Petersburg, it was first presented in 1910 in Paris, where Debussy is reported to have rushed backstage to congratulate the twenty-eight-year-old composer.

One negative reaction to *The Firebird* came from fellow Russian Prokofiev, nine years Stravinsky's junior. After seeing it several times in London, Prokofiev said: "What vivid, almost blinding colors in the score, what inventiveness in all these grimaces and how sincere is the creation. But I could not for a moment be captivated by the music. Where is the music? Nothing but deadwood."

Petrushka, with Vaslav Nijinsky as the principal dancer, was even more successful a year later. It is built around three carnival puppets— Petrushka, a shy clown; the beautiful ballerina he loves; and a brutal blackamoor who crushes Petrushka to death on stage.

All three ballets could be included here, but the Starter Kit rules demand representative selections, so I've limited the recommendation to the historic *Rite of Spring*—the complete ballet or the orchestral suite from it, which is the piece most frequently played. To that is added the *Symphony of Psalms*, (Nos. 39, 40, and 60), a vocal work rather than a true symphony, composed in 1930 for chorus and orchestra; the *Symphony in Three Movements*, the third of his three real symphonies, written in 1945; and, mostly for fun, the earlier *L'histoire du soldat*, a dance piece based on an old folktale about a soldier meeting the Devil in his hometown after returning from a war.

Years later, Stravinsky had this to say about *L'histoire du soldat*, which included a little tango, a little march, a little waltz, a little hymn music, and a touch of jazz. "My knowledge of jazz was derived exclusively from copies of sheet music, and as I had never actually heard any of the music performed, I borrowed its rhythmic style not as played but as written. I could imagine jazz sound, however, or so I like to think. Jazz meant, in any case, a wholly new sound in my music, and 'L'histoire' marks my final break with the Russian orchestral school in which I had been fostered."

He had composed the work at the end of World War I, when he was thirty-six and still had a long life of creative music in front of him.

The final Starter Kit selection is the heavy *Oedipus Rex*, which the composer called an opera-oratorio, part of his neo-Classical period, written for chorus, vocal soloists, and orchestra and first performed in Paris in 1927. "I had in mind," wrote Stravinsky, "an opera or an oratorio on some universally familiar subject. My idea was that I could thus concentrate the whole attention of the audience, undistracted by the story, on the music itself, which would thus become both word and action." It was presented in concert form, Stravinsky adds, because potential producers "were too short both of time and funds" to present it in a stage setting.

(For lighter listening, assume we have not mentioned *Oedipus Rex* and try the *Dumbarton Oaks* Concerto, for chamber orchestra, and the Capriccio for Piano and Orchestra. And for fun, if not for history, substitute *The Firebird* for the earth-moving *Rite of Spring*.)

STRAVINSKY: THE STARTER KIT

Composition	Recordings Available*
SYMPHONIES:	
Symphony of Psalms	5
Symphony in Three Movements	7
OTHER ORCHESTRAL WORKS:	
Ballet:	
The Rite of Spring	30
ASSORTED MUSIC:	
L'histoire du soldat	8
VOCAL MUSIC:	
Opera-Oratorio:	
Oedipus Rex	2

*Represents the number of recorded releases available of each listed composition as found in a recent issue of the *Schwann/Opus* catalogue. A "C" indicates that a work is only available collected with other compositions.

STRAVINSKY: A TOP TEN

Composition	Recordings Available*
SYMPHONIES:	
Symphony of Psalms	5
Symphony in C	5
Symphony in Three Movements	7
OTHER ORCHESTRAL WORKS:	
Ballets:	
The Firebird	21
Petrushka	22
The Rite of Spring	30
Dumbarton Oaks Concerto in E-flat (for chamber orchestra)	5
ASSORTED MUSIC:	
L'histoire du soldat	8
Symphonies of Wind Instruments	2

Composition   *Recordings Available**

VOCAL MUSIC:
Opera-Oratorio:
   Oedipus Rex   2

STRAVINSKY: A MASTER COLLECTION

Composition   *Recordings Available**

SYMPHONIES:
Symphony of Psalms   5
Symphony in C   5
Symphony in Three Movements   7

OTHER ORCHESTRAL WORKS:
Early Nationalist Period
Ballets:
   The Firebird   21
   Petrushka   22
   The Rite of Spring   30

Neo-Classical and Neo-Baroque Period
   Pulcinella Suite   5
   Ballet Suite:
      The Fairy's Kiss   1
   Apollo (for string orchestra, from ballet)   2
   Capriccio for Piano and Orchestra   1
   Violin Concerto in D   6
   Dumbarton Oaks Concerto in E-flat   5
      (for chamber orchestra)
   Danses Concertantes   4
   Ballet:
      Orpheus   2

Serial-Music Period
   Ballet:
      Agon   2
   Movements for Piano and Orchestra   2

CHAMBER MUSIC:
Three Pieces for String Quartet   5
Concertino for String Quartet   2
Octet for Wind Instruments   2

Composition	Recordings Available*
ASSORTED MUSIC:	
L'histoire du soldat	8
Ballet/Dance Cantata:	
Les noces	4
Symphonies of Wind Instruments	2
Ebony Concerto	2
VOCAL MUSIC:	
Opera:	
The Rake's Progress	2
Opera-Oratorio:	
Oedipus Rex	2
Sacred Song to Honor the Memory of St. Mark	C

GIUSEPPE VERDI (1813–1901)

Number 16

Privo di talento musicale. That was the verdict on Giuseppe Verdi. Lacking in musical talent.

Notwithstanding this rejection of one of them by the Milan Conservatory, music's greatest opera composers may be whittled down to two men: Giuseppe Verdi and Richard Wagner.

There are other composers of high artistry who dedicated themselves chiefly to opera and produced both magnificent music and fierce drama, but basically these two, the Italian and the German, stand alone. They do not, of course, stand alone *together*. The orchestral supremacy, psychological insight, and deep intellect of Wagner that are manifested in his music drama are acknowledged by almost all music people—but so are the melodic beauty, theatrical genius, dramatic truth, and human passion of Verdi. You leave Wagner's five-hour *Die Walküre* knowing you have witnessed an epochal happening; you leave Verdi's *La traviata* having personally experienced tragedy and beauty. (Some of us also leave five hours of *Die Walküre* exhausted and mildly bored. With all respect for his insight into the human condition, Herr Wagner needed a good editor.) The two composers were born the same year; one dominated all of Europe . . . except Italy, where the other reigned as a god.

The third opera composer of first rank is named Wolfgang Amadeus Mozart. But he was so much more than opera, such a total musical genius, creator of so many different kinds of music, that he is excluded from a head-to-head assessment of the opera specialists.

VERDI ON IMITATING WAGNER

"If the Germans, setting out from Bach and arriving at Wagner, write good German operas, well and good. But we descendants of Palestrina commit a musical crime when we imitate Wagner. We write useless, even trivial music. . . . We cannot compose like the Germans, or at least we ought not to; nor they like us."

Down-to-earth, peasant-stock, commonsense Verdi and intellectual Wagner never met, although both lived for much of the nineteenth century. There is no evidence that either considered their nonmeeting a tragic event. "Opera is opera," Verdi once said, referring to his works versus Wagner's music-drama, which emphasized orchestral music. "Symphony is symphony." Aaron Copland pointed out that for years Verdi's name was not mentioned in symphonic company in the same breath as Wagner's. Some of the music people found him a fairly trite and ordinary composer who wrote too many weak operas. The public never seemed to care about the bad ones; it devoured the good ones.

Chronologically, relative to the other three Listed nineteenth- and early twentieth-century Italian opera artists, Verdi comes after Donizetti (1797–1848) and Rossini (1792–1868) and before Puccini (1858–1924)—after *The Barber of Seville/William Tell* and *Lucia di Lammermoor/Elixir of Love*, and before *La Bohème*, *Tosca*, and *Madame Butterfly*.

DONIZETTI ON PASSING THE BATON

Speaking of Verdi, his Italian opera successor, Donizetti said: "The world wants new things. Others, after all, have yielded the place to us, so we must yield it to others."

Verdi wrote some thirty operas over a career that began with *Oberto* in 1839 and ended with one of the greatest of all comic operas, *Falstaff*, in 1893, when he was just shy of his eightieth birthday. Three of his Big Four were produced over a very short period of time when he was fortyish: *Rigoletto*, 1851; *Il trovatore*, 1853; and *La traviata*, 1853. The fourth, *Aida*, was written almost twenty years later, in 1871.

The other two Verdi operas of greatest fame are the last two of his life, deemed by many professional assessors to be not only his two finest but also the ones that changed the evaluation of him among the pro-Verdi group from "brilliant operatic composer" to "one of the greatest dramatic geniuses of all time." Both of these works were based, appropriately, on plays written by another genius, William Shakespeare—*Otello* in 1887 and *Falstaff* in 1893.

The best known of his many other operas include: *Nabucco*, 1842; *Ernani*, 1844; *Joan of Arc*, 1845; *Macbeth*, 1847; *Simon Boccanegra*, 1857; *Un ballo in maschera* (A masked ball), 1859; *La forza del destino* (The force of destiny), 1862; and *Don Carlo*, 1867.

A particularly helpful description of Verdi comes from Paul Henry Lang, longtime professor of musicology at Columbia University:

> Verdi was the last great figure of Italian opera, and with him ends the lineage that started with Monteverdi. Over and above all restrictions of time and environment he once more solved the three-hundred-year-old problem of the lyric drama of opera. . . . Aided by Shakespeare's spirit, Verdi tore out live

threads from life, lacing them anew in his own manner, through music. Being more human than Wagner, he is much nearer to us and to our faculty of understanding and enjoyment. Wagner drew ideals; Verdi men. . . . Verdi builds up not the hero but the passions of which he is hero and victor; his men are like ourselves, fundamentally weak and self-deceiving, of consequence only in their passions and not in their acts. . . . Verdi's men and women can be divested of their exterior, of their sixteenth-century ruffs, Egyptian tunics, Venetian armor, and Gypsy robes, but Rigoletto's pathetic impotence, Aida's unflinching love, Iago's diabolic cunning, Othello's consuming, senseless jealousy, and Azucena's half-demented vengefulness will still remain. These constant elements in man Verdi has given us in music, in opera, which exemplifies the essence of the lyric drama: the transliteration of human emotions from a literary sketch into pure music.

SMASH HITS

The popularity of *La traviata*, *Il trovatore*, and *Rigoletto* in the mid-1800s was incredible. Of eighty-seven performances in a Paris opera house in 1856, fifty-four were of these three Verdi operas. The same thing was happening in London, where the magazine *Punch* published this:

> Three Traviatas in three different quarters,
> Three Rigolettos murdering their daughters,
> Three Trovatori beheading their brothers,
> By the artful contrivance of three gypsy mothers.

Verdi was born in Le Roncole, Parma, Italy, on October 10, 1813, only five months after Wagner's birth in Leipzig. His father was the local innkeeper and grocer; this was a peasant family of modest means. His father sent him to live with a cobbler's family in nearby Busseto, where he studied the organ, worked with the town orchestra, and was sent by the townspeople to study at the Milan Conservatory. But he was rejected: too old (over fourteen), too untrained, too untalented—*privo di talento musicale.* (In fairness to the conservatory, the youth *was* four years over the maximum age and untrained for his age. A special waiver would have been needed to accept him. Still, his application had been accepted rather than returned on the grounds of age, and there was examination enough of him to conclude that his piano playing was too weak, so Milan is not completely off the hook.) He returned to Busseto and later began working on his first opera, *Oberto*, produced at La Scala in 1839 when he was twenty-six. Unlike the first efforts of many on The List, it was a success, and he won a contract for three new operas.

The first of these was a comic opera, *Un giorno di regno* (King for a day), produced in 1840—and booed and hissed by the audience. It was a traumatic experience for the composer, already severely dejected because he had tragically lost his wife and two children not long before. He almost stopped writing opera, then changed his mind, but vowed never to try comic opera again (a vow he kept until *Falstaff*). Perhaps in response to the negative reception of *Un giorno di regno*, Verdi developed a rather peculiar relationship with the public—one that lasted from that point on. "It may be that it is a bad opera," he wrote, "though many no better are tolerated and even applauded. Had the public not applauded, but merely endured my opera in silence, I should have had no words enough to thank them! . . . I do not mean to blame the public, but I accept their criticism and jeers only on condition that I do not have to be grateful for their applause."

He did, of course, continue to write . . . and write . . . and write. And his fame grew . . . and grew . . . and grew. The operas most frequently performed today, the Big Four—*Rigoletto*, *Il trovatore*, *La traviata*, and *Aida*—were midcareer productions. For sixteen years after *Aida* he wrote no operas, and then he amazed the music world with the final two, the tragic *Otello* and the comic *Falstaff*.

REPULSIVE IMMORALITY

Venice was controlled by Austria in the mid-1800s, and the Austrian censors did not like the libretto for *Rigoletto*. It was, they said, "rampant with the most repulsive kind of immorality and obscene vulgarity."

But Verdi had a contract, this was his seventeenth opera, he fought for it, threatened to make a big ruckus, and won.

In *Otello*, we are advised by the critics, Verdi refined and intensified his earlier operatic technique and further developed his orchestration, but without either losing his superb melodies or overriding the singers' voices.

The best-known arias from *Otello* include the "Drinking Song" from Act I; Iago's "Credo" (Credo in un Dio crudel) from Act II; Otello's soliloquy on Desdemona's infidelity, "Dio! mi potevi scagliar" from Act III; and the "Willow Song" (Salce, salce), the majestic "Ave Maria" for soprano, and "Otello's Death" (Nium mi tema) from Act IV.

From *Falstaff* the "Oberon Song" demonstrates that Verdi still was the same lord of melody. *Falstaff* is one of the rare Verdi operas without several "big numbers"—and without spectacular scenes or overpowering dramatic climaxes. The critics have called it one of the greatest of all lyric comedies, containing the finest qualities of the three great comic operas that preceded it: Wagner's *Die Meistersinger*, Mozart's *Marriage of Figaro*, and Rossini's *Barber of Seville*. One professional wrote that its integrated musical texture, a "miracle of workmanship," is Wagnerian; its musical characterization Mozartian, and its gaiety and laughter Rossinian.

RICHARD STRAUSS ON FALSTAFF

" 'Falstaff' is the greatest masterpiece of modern Italian music. It is a work in which Verdi attained real artistic perfection. If I could only bring my own comic opera up to such exalted beauty."

Verdi did write some nonoperatic music: a beautiful Requiem Mass in memory of the Italian writer Alessandro Manzoni, composed in 1873; and, after *Falstaff*, four sacred choral works and some other miscellaneous numbers.

When Verdi died on January 17, 1901, not only all of Italy but all of the music world mourned. In addition to opera, he had been much into politics, a fervent nationalist who worked for (and saw) a united Italy. From 1860 to 1865 he had been a deputy in the part of Italy that was then united. On his death, the Italian senate was called into special session; hundreds of thousands lined the streets of Milan; the schools were closed. Nearly a century later, he remains a national Italian hero, and nothing suggests that this will not be the case in 2101.

Of all who applaud Verdi, Tchaikovsky perhaps put it most simply, saying, "A very gifted man."

STARTER KIT

The only real decision here is whether to go with the Big Four operas or to substitute one of the last two Shakespearean works, *Otello* or *Falstaff*. The argument for the latter is that they show the most mature Verdi in all of his dramatic genius. The case for the former is that they are the best known, the most widely and frequently performed, and the operas that made Verdi Verdi. It is not easy to leave behind a work which, as the experts say, combines the best of Rossini, Mozart, and Wagner, but our choice is to stay with the four: *La traviata*, *Rigoletto*, *Il trovatore*, and *Aida*.

Rigoletto is based on a play by Victor Hugo, *Le roi s'amuse*, and was the first of Verdi's super-operas, following several earlier popular successes. Although it was a smash hit, conservative critics were offended by its misshapen humpback moving across the stage. The next opera was *Il trovatore* (The troubador), two years later, which may have more famous melodies than any single opera in history—although the critics at the time did not like it either, in part because it was not melodic enough! (And some critics still do not like it.) The next effort, *La traviata*, from Dumas's famous novel *La dame aux camélias*, is still another that initially was not well received. It was considered immoral, the costumes were deemed in poor taste, and the buxom, big-boned soprano looked much too healthy to be dying. The proper *London Times* spoke of its "foul and hideous horrors." The last of the Big Four, *Aida*, came nearly two decades later, commissioned by the Khedive Ismail Pasha of Egypt to help Cairo celebrate the opening of the Suez Canal. While the local Egyptian audience was ecstatic, the reception back in Italy was once again apathetic, in part because the Italians were not keen about their incomparable home melodist venturing into such exotic themes. But, as with the others of the Big Four, this initial coolness toward the work quickly vanished. Not only in Italy but in France, England, and other nations, the public could not get enough of the first three.

The best-known arias from the four include:

Rigoletto: The aria of the opera is "La donna e mobile," one of the most popular of all tenor arias, from Act III. Other famous numbers are Rigoletto's monologue, "Pari siamo," and the soprano aria "Caro nome," from Act I; and the duet between Rigoletto and Gilda from Act II, "Piangi, piangi, fanciulla."

La traviata: From Act I, the drinking song, "Libiamo no' lieti calici," and the soprano aria "Ah! fors e lui"; from Act II, the baritone aria "Di provenza, il mar, il suol"; and from Act III, the soprano aria "Addio del passato." The orchestral preludes to Acts I and III are also well known.

Il trovatore, which one writer calls a "veritable cornucopia" of well-loved arias: From Act II, "Strida la vampa," Azucena's story of how her mother was burned at the stake; the Anvil Chorus; "Chi del gitano"; and the "Il balen del suo sorriso." Also, from Act III, the Soldiers' Chorus and "Di quella pira"; and from Act IV, the chant of the "Misere" and the "Ai nostri monti" (Home to our mountains).

Aida: From Act I, "Celeste Aida" (Heavenly Aida), "Ritorna vincitor!" (Return victoriously!), and the Temple Scene; from Act II, the Grand March and the Ballet music; from Act III, the soprano Nile air.

The fifth Starter Kit recommendation is not an opera, although it is operalike in many ways. It is the *Requiem* Mass composed by Verdi in 1873 after the death of a friend, the Italian novelist Alessandro Manzoni. To honor him, Verdi told the mayor of Milan that he was willing to write a Requiem. The offer was accepted and the result was generally well received—although, again, some critics called it tawdry and cheap. It is usually played in a concert hall, not in a church, although the premiere performance was in St. Mark's Cathedral in Milan, directed by the composer. Given the makeup of the composer, it is necessarily theater, and some picky critics have faulted its theatrical elements.

(A Requiem mass is generally shorter than a regular mass, omitting the "Gloria" and including instead a "Requiem aeternam," "Lux aeterna," and "Dies irae," a thirteenth-century poem describing the Day of Judgment.)

VERDI: THE STARTER KIT

Composition	Recordings Available*
OPERAS (COMPLETE AND EXCERPTS):	
Aida	8
Rigoletto	10
La traviata	12
Il trovatore	9

Composition   *Recordings Available**

OTHER VOCAL MUSIC:
Requiem Mass   13

*Represents the number of recorded releases available of each listed composition as found in a recent issue of the *Schwann/Opus* catalogue. A "C" indicates that a work is only available collected with other compositions.

VERDI: A TOP TEN

Composition   *Recordings Available**

OPERAS (COMPLETE AND EXCERPTS):

Aida	8
Ernani	4
Falstaff	4
La forza del destino	4
Macbeth	5
Otello	7
Rigoletto	10
La traviata	12
Il trovatore	9

OTHER VOCAL MUSIC:
Requiem Mass   13

VERDI: A MASTER COLLECTION

Composition   *Recordings Available**

ORCHESTRAL WORKS:
Overtures and Preludes from operas:

La forzo del destino	11
La traviata	11
Il trovatore	11
Nabucco	11
Aida	11
Vespri Siciliani	11
Giovanna d'Arco	11

CHAMBER MUSIC:
String Quartet in E Minor   4

Composition	Recordings Available*
VOCAL MUSIC:	
Operas:	
Aida	8
Un ballo in maschera	4
Don Carlos	5
Ernani	4
Falstaff	5
La forza del destino	4
Un giorno di regno	1
Luisa Miller	1
Macbeth	5
Nabucco	3
Oberto, conte di San Bonifacio	2
Otello	7
Rigoletto	11
Simon Boccanegra	2
La traviata	12
Il trovatore	9
Church:	
Requiem Mass	13

GUSTAV MAHLER (1860–1911)

Number 17

Meine Zeit wird noch kommen, predicted Gustav Mahler. "My time will yet come." And indeed it did, although not with full force until the last forty years or so. When Dwight David Eisenhower was president,

Mahler might have missed The List, or barely made it toward the bottom. One reasonable theory for his latter-day popularity is that the world has needed a little escapism in recent years.

Mahler is one of four Listed Late Romantics, along with Puccini, Fauré, and Richard Strauss, all born shortly before or after the middle of the nineteenth century. He is symphonies and songs—seventh in the long line of Vienna symphonists and, with Brahms, one of the great successors to Schubert and Schumann in *lieder*. His life overlapped that of Bruckner (1824–1896), and the two are sometimes considered in the same breath, both overshadowed in Germany during their later years by Richard Strauss (born in 1864). Since the end of World War II, professional opinions of both Mahler and Bruckner, and most recently Mahler in particular, have risen sharply. Different views doubtless will prevail in the next century, and while Mahler is ranked Number 17, Strauss Number 20, and Bruckner Number 25, it is likely that the Japanese cherry blossoms in Washington will continue to bloom each spring when a future list-maker switches them around a little.

As in the case of Schubert and Schumann, it is not difficult for new listeners to confuse Mahler and Bruckner. Both have two-syllable, Germanic, –er names. Both composed nine long symphonies—some of them very, very long. Both were Austrians. Both studied and worked in Vienna. Both were intense worshipers of Wagner. Both were natural Romantics. In *Music for the Millions*, published nearly fifty years ago, David Ewen writes of the two:

> Like Mahler, Bruckner has been since his death a controversial figure in music. There are those who consider him one of the greatest symphonists of all time; and there are others who look upon him as a charlatan. The truth is that he was neither, and he was both. . . . Like Bruckner, Mahler has been a provocative and controversial figure in music. There are those who feel that Mahler's symphonies represent the apotheosis of that form, that his was a prophetic voice in music—that, in short, he was one of music's great masters, a worthy successor of Beethoven and Brahms. . . . Others, however, condemn Mahler for his garrulousness, his habit of using a paragraph to do the work of a sentence, his tendency to yield to hysteria, bombast, pompousness. The truth lies somewhere midway between these two poles of critical opinion.

Some of the experts used to say that it was difficult, after hearing a Bruckner or Mahler symphony, to decide whether it was good stuff in spite of some bad moments or bad stuff in spite of some good moments.

There is agreement that the personality and nature of the two were extremely different: Mahler was a complex doubter concerned about the question What Is Man? And Bruckner a simple, devout person who accepted without question the concept of a good God and all that follows from it. Mahler once wrote: "Whence do we come? Whither does our road take us? Have I really willed this life, as Schopenhauer thinks, before I was even conceived? Why am I made to feel that I am free while yet I am constrained within my character, as in a prison? What is the object of toil and sorrow? How am I to understand the cruelty and malice in the creations of a kind God? Will the meaning of life be finally revealed by death?"

Jeepers. Mr. Bach did not mix himself up that way, and neither did Papa Haydn.

A FRIGHTFUL JOKE?

Some of Mahler's doubts as to the meaning of life were expressed in a letter he wrote describing his Symphony No. 2 in C Minor, *Resurrection*: "I have called the first movement 'Celebration of the Dead.' If you wish to know, it is the Hero of my first symphony whom I bear to the grave. Immediately arise the great questions: Why have you lived? Why have you suffered? Has it all been only a huge, frightful joke? We must all somehow answer these questions, if we are to continue living, yes, even if we are only to continue dying. Whoever hears this call must give a reply. And this reply I give in my last movement."

Mahler was born in Kalischt, Bohemia, studied at the Vienna Conservatory, became conductor of the Prague Opera, and conducted later in Budapest, Hamburg, and Vienna, becoming accepted as—and still considered—one of the great conductors in music history. He came to New York to conduct the Metropolitan Opera in 1908 and the New York Philharmonic in 1909. Those were not happy times; he had been a mini-emperor at home, but boorish New York respects no one; before long he collapsed in New York, then returned to Europe and died in Vienna in 1911.

"To write a symphony is, for me, to construct a world," he said. He composed almost no chamber music (one known early work), no concertos, no music for solo instruments, no operas, no masses. Just symphonies and songs. All nine of his complete symphonies and an unfinished tenth are played today, and his other orchestral work, *Das Lied von der Erde* (The song of the earth), is a blend of orchestral music and a cycle of six songs based on old Chinese poems adapted into German.

Another assessment from fifty years ago comes from professors Howard D. McKinney and W. R. Anderson:

> The future of Mahler's music is uncertain. In the world-turned-anti-Romantic of the past decades, there is no question but that it has fared badly; there is also no question but that a reaction will come in favor of Romanticism. The particular difficulty of this specific manifestation of its spirit is that for its effect it depends so largely upon an interpreter imbued with the same intuitive and almost psychic spirit that inspired its creation. In the hands of a conductor like Bruno Walter, the composer's great disciple, this music is safe: we can almost be persuaded that it is the work of a genius. When interpreted by others, it can sound merely platitudinous and sentimental, a fact which can never make for the sort of universal admiration given to such composers as Brahms, Wagner, or even Tchaikovsky. . . . Perhaps [Ernest] Newman has summed it up as well as anyone: Mahler's music has too many faults to be designated a success; but if it's a failure, it is a noble one. The composer's grasp may not have been equal to his span, but the span itself commands our admiration; if somewhat flawed, he is still a genius.

How does that play today? As Casey Stengel used to say, you could look it up. One recent record catalogue showed twenty-three recordings of Symphony No. 1 in D, *Titan*, 1888; twelve of No. 2 in C Minor, *Resurrection*, 1894; five of No. 3 in D Minor, 1896; twenty-two of No. 4 in G, 1900; thirteen of No. 5 in C-sharp Minor, 1902; seven of No. 6 in A Minor, 1904; six of No. 7 in E Minor, *Song of the Night*, 1905; five of No. 8 in E-flat, 1906; twelve of No. 9 in D, 1909; nine of No. 10 in F-sharp, 1910, unfinished.

This adds up not simply to recognition, but to smashing recognition. Certainly the existence of twenty-odd recordings by the world's greatest orchestras and conductors does not prove that a work is musically distinguished, but it does suggest that the composer today is considered more than a "noble failure."

Comments from more contemporary professionals refer to the lyricism of the nine symphonies, their long lines of melody, and their rich harmonies. In his sense of tone color, Mahler is ranked with the great masters of orchestration.

The music gurus say that Mahler's nine symphonies are put together differently from "normal" classical symphonies, so much so that some critics fifty years ago questioned whether they really should be called symphonies at all. But nowadays that debate appears to be over, whatever the blend of genius and banality, and however the compositions depart from the classical norm.

A WAY TO THE COUCH

Mahler was a neurotic fellow, often on the verge of nervous collapse. Typical of his mind-stressing approach to life are two oft-quoted remarks:

"Tradition is just slovenliness," and "The symphony should be like the world; it must contain everything."

Some of the music people suggest that Mahler was a lyricist at heart and that his symphonies were basically great big symphonic songs. But, they note, a symphony is supposed to be an epic dramatic form, not a mammoth song. Professor Joseph Machlis writes: "He never solved the nineteenth century conflict between classic form and romantic content, betwen symphonic tightness and lyric diffuseness . . . His nine symphonies dissolve in a stream of fervid strong lyricism, and look nostalgically to the past."

The relationship between his symphonies and songs is a close one. The First Symphony uses melodies from his *Songs of a Wayfarer* song cycle. His Second Symphony has five movements, of which the last two use voices. His Third has six movements, with voices in the fourth and fifth. There is a soprano song in the Finale of his Fourth Symphony. And although his Fifth, Sixth, and Seventh Symphonies are entirely orchestral, the professionals point out that instrumental echoes of his songs are heard in each of them. The Eighth, which consists of two long sections, uses such a big combination of vocal and orchestral forces that it is called the *Symphony of a Thousand*. Although the cast is actually somewhat shy of a thousand, the work does call for a boys' choir, an adult chorus, eight solo vocalists, and a very large orchestra. Among other attractions, the final scene is from Goethe's *Faust*. (It may not be your favorite, but, again, the purpose of a road map is not to suggest the favorite visiting spots of either map user or map maker.) Leopold Stokowski gave nine straight performances of the Eighth in Philadelphia and New York and said that it made more of an impression on the audiences than anything he had ever done.

THE PERFECTIONIST

Mahler on conducting:

"There are frightful habits, or rather inadequacies, which I have encountered in every orchestra. They cannot read the score markings, and thus sin against the holy law of dynamics and of the inner hidden rhythms of a work. When they see a crescendo they immediately play *forte* and speed up; at a diminuendo they become *piano* and retard the tempo. . . . And should one ask them to play something that is not written down—as is so necessary a hundred times when one accompanies singers in opera—then one is lost with every orchestra."

The most famous Mahler work of all is not one of his symphonies, however, but rather *Das Lied von der Erde*, written in 1908, toward the end of his life. Some musicologists suggest he poured into it his own disappointments stemming from the failure of the world to accept his music. Though he died before hearing it performed, he had referred to it as a "symphony for tenor and contralto (or baritone) and orchestra."

Mahler's most famous pure song cycles are *Lieder eines fahrenden Gesellen* (Songs of a wayfarer), 1885; *Des Knaben Wunderhorn* (The youth's magic horn), 1892–1898; and *Kindertotenlieder* (Songs on the death of children), 1904. The first is a set of four songs, with the texts written by Mahler himself, about a rejected lover wandering the world. The magic horn cycle is from a famous collection of German folk poetry, and the children cycle from poems by Friedrich Ruckert, who had lost two of his own children and then written more than one hundred elegies. The composer chose five to set to music: "Once More the Sun Would Gild the Morn," "Ah, Now I Know Why Oft I Caught You Gazing," "When My Mother Dear," "I Think Oft They've Only Gone Abroad," and "In Such a Tempest." Quoting the composer's friend, disciple, and admirer, conductor Bruno Walter: "Mahler created a soul-stirring specimen of lyric art. Just as the poems are in no sense popular poetry, so his music, too, is entirely removed from the popular mood of his former songs. Noble symphonic melodies form their musical substance."

One of Mahler's own two children died shortly after he completed this composition, and, understandably, he always felt guilty that somehow he was in part or in whole responsible because he had undertaken a work on the death of children.

Mahler was not a cheery soul. "I am thrice homeless," he once said. "As a Bohemian born in Austria. As an Austrian among Germans. As a Jew throughout the world." But his Zeit has komm.

EINSTEIN ON MAHLER AND STRAUSS

There is no more respected a musicologist than Alfred Einstein, who was born in Munich in 1880 and died in the United States in 1952. In a book published first in 1920, he said about Mahler:

"His music, torn between ecstasy and despair, faithfully reflects the inner dissonance of the times—the period that led to the [First] World War—and in this respect contains much greater artistic truth than the aesthetic veneer of Richard Strauss. And his posthumous Ninth Symphony is already on the borderline between late Romanticism and contemporary New Music."

STARTER KIT

The question is: Which and how many symphonies should be chosen, relative to which and how many songs? For balance, the recommendation is: Try two symphonies, two song cycles, and the song/orchestral composition *The Song of the Earth.*

The latter work, composed in 1908, started out as a ninth symphony, but the "Beethoven ghost" (one is permitted only nine symphonies) that wrapped itself around so many composers influenced Mahler as well. He feared he would die after the nine—after all, both Beethoven and Schubert had—so he turned this into a nonsymphony (but later went back to symphonies anyhow). *The Song of the Earth* is an hour long, with the first song, "The Drinking Song of Earthly Woe," for tenor; the next, "The Lonely One in Autumn," for contralto; "Of Youth" for tenor; "Of Beauty" for contralto; "The Drunken One in Spring" for tenor, and the finale, "Farewell," for contralto. The connoisseurs suggest it is one work that may be made more enjoyable by following a translated text, but that need not be for everyone.

The recommended symphonies are No. 1 in D, praised by the professionals for its "mastery of form," and No. 4 in G, a sunny, joyous work, which may be the most enjoyable for the amateur. Although admired today, it had a horrible reception when first performed in Budapest in 1889. Reports are that the critics were "vitriolic." Whereas Mahler saw it as "an adventure of the soul," they saw it as "overpretentious," "pompous," and "windy." Conceivably these are not mutually exclusive sentiments; all of us have encountered some pompous souls.

And while not many people thought very good thoughts about Mahler's Fourth Symphony back at the turn of the century, not many people thought good thoughts about *any* Mahler symphony back then. Master conductor, supreme conductor, despotic conductor, yes. Symphonist, no. And books on music written only forty-five years ago pass over the Fourth pretty quickly, after acknowledging that it is, indeed, joyous. Today, however, it is regarded as the least uptight of Mahler's symphonies—less drama, less psychology, more lightness, and, praise the Lord, the shortest of them all. For the longest, try No. 3 in D Minor, written four years earlier, which has no apparent end. Still going strong after considerably more than sixty minutes, it probably is the longest symphony played with any regularity today.

The Starter Kit choices for song cycles were a toss-up; the arbitrary recommendations are *Songs of a Wayfarer* and *The Youth's Magic Horn.*

MAHLER: THE STARTER KIT

Composition	Recordings Available*
SYMPHONIES (OF TEN):	
No. 1 in D	23
No. 4 in G	22

Composition   *Recordings Available**

OTHER ORCHESTRAL WORKS:
Das Lied von der Erde (The song of the earth)   13

VOCAL MUSIC:
Song Cycles:
    Lieder eines fahrenden Gesellen (Songs of   11
        a wayfarer)
    Des Knaben Wunderhorn (The youth's   7
        magic horn)

*Represents the number of recorded releases available of each listed composition as found in a recent issue of the *Schwann/Opus* catalogue. A "C" indicates that a work is only available collected with other compositions.

MAHLER: A TOP TEN

Composition   *Recordings Available**

SYMPHONIES (OF TEN):
No. 1 in D   23
No. 2 in C Minor (Resurrection)   12
No. 4 in G   22
No. 5 in C-sharp   13
No. 6 in A Minor   7
No. 9 in D   12

OTHER ORCHESTRAL WORKS:
Das Lied von der Erde (The song of the earth)   13

VOCAL MUSIC:
Song Cycles:
    Lieder eines fahrenden Gesellen (Songs of   11
        a wayfarer)
    Des Knaben Wunderhorn (The youth's   7
        magic horn)
    Kindertotenlieder (Songs on the death of   7
        children)

MAHLER: A MASTER COLLECTION

Composition	Recordings Available*
SYMPHONIES (OF TEN):	
No. 1 in D	23
No. 2 in C Minor (Resurrection)	12
No. 3 in D Minor	5
No. 4 in G	22
No. 5 in C-sharp	13
No. 6 in A Minor	7
No. 7 in E Minor	6
No. 8 in E-flat (Symphony of a Thousand)	5
No. 9 in D	12
No. 10 (Unfinished)	9
OTHER ORCHESTRAL WORKS:	
Das Lied von der Erde (The song of the earth)	13
Suite from the Orchestral Works of Bach	2
CHAMBER MUSIC:	
Piano Quartet	2
VOCAL MUSIC:	
Song Cycles:	
Lieder eines fahrenden Gesellen (Songs of a wayfarer)	11
Des Knaben Wunderhorn (The youth's magic horn)	7
Kindertotenlieder (Songs on the death of children)	7
Ruckert Lieder (Songs from Ruckert)	3
Das Klagende Lied	1
Lieder und Gesänge aus der Jugendzeit	2
Other Songs	C

SERGEI PROKOFIEV (1891–1953)

Number 18

If you were charged by your government with writing "useless and harmful garbage," how would you respond? Sergei Prokofiev of the Soviet Union accepted the allegations, blamed his "infection" on "Western ideas," and promised to be good in the future, using only "lucid melody" and "a simple harmonic language."

That he did. He was fifty-seven at the time, lived another five years, composed a harmless vocal symphonic suite and an oratorio condemning "Western warmongers," and, not surprisingly, was rewarded with the Stalin Prize for music.

Tragically, the criticism of the State in those days was not something to be taken lightly. It did not pay to argue and object. Some who did were arrested and died in gulags. Comrade Prokofiev need not be quickly censured for having followed orders when necessary.

Born in what now is Ukraine, Prokofiev was a child prodigy who composed his first opera at twelve. He was educated at the St. Petersburg Conservatory, where he was a student of Rimsky-Korsakov. A virtuoso pianist as well as a composer, he left the Soviet Union at the time of the 1917 Revolution and lived abroad until 1932, visiting the United States during those years but chiefly living (and composing anti-Romantic music) in Paris. Then he returned home to Russia for the rest of his life, initially welcomed as a musical genius and hero and later falling in and out of favor with the Communist party, along with many other Soviet artists. Although a giant figure in the music world everywhere, and although honored off and on as a giant at home, he still was not immune to the dictates of the party.

Along with Shostakovich, he was a leader of the Soviet proletarian school of composers. He was always pro-worker, pro-Russia, pro-

COMPOSING UNDER COMMUNISM

Being born and reared in Moscow in the twentieth century was not the same as being born and reared in Chateaugay, New York, or Bowman, North Dakota. American composer and critic Virgil Thomson wrote years ago: "Soviet music is the kind of music it is because the Soviet composers have formally and long ago decided to write it that way, because the Communist party accepts it that way, and because the people apparently take it. Russians, mostly, I imagine, believe in their government and their country. Certainly these great, official public figures do. They could not, in so severe and censored a period, have become national composers by mere chicanery."

State, and pro-Soviet—which does not mean that he necessarily welcomed government intervention in how and what he composed. At the beginning of his career he was one of the most dissonant composers on The List. Later he also was the creator of a different kind of music: monumental spirit-of-Russia war music written as his country fought off the Nazi invaders, and tragedy-of-war music composed both during and after the great struggle.

Aside from the war works, his music expresses satire, whimsy, comedy, and laughter. He considered melody the most important aspect of music, but not what he called "cheap, saccharine, imitation melody." Sometimes his melody is more difficult to find than that of nineteenth-century composers. For decades the prevailing figure in Soviet music, Prokofiev is one of the most interesting examples of genius and art under the Central Committee.

Few twentieth-century composers produced more works that became concert-hall favorites. His best-known orchestral creations include his First, Fifth, and Sixth Symphonies, his Piano Concerto No. 3, his Violin Concerto No. 1, and film music for a Russian movie, *Lieutenant Kijé*. Other popular compositions include the *Alexander Nevsky* Cantata written for a film by the same name; two operas, *Love for Three Oranges* and *War and Peace*; and several ballets, including *The Age of Steel*, *The Child Prodigy*, *Romeo and Juliet*, and *Cinderella*. There are also four more symphonies, four more piano concertos, a second violin concerto, a cello concerto, the dissonant *Scythian Suite*, three violin and piano sonatas, two string quartets, ten piano sonatas, an "Overture on Hebrew Themes," and a good bit more.

With all of this he is perhaps best known to the public for his narrated symphonic fairy tale for orchestra, *Peter and the Wolf*, presumably for children. If you have no children or grandchildren, give it to yourself for Christmas. Each character is illustrated by a different musical instrument to teach children the timbres of the orchestra— Peter by the strings, his grandfather by the bassoon, the bird by a flute, the duck by an oboe, the cat by a clarinet, and the wolf by three horns. Whether or not one enjoys all of Prokofiev, it is not permitted to dislike *Peter and the Wolf*. Eleanor Roosevelt loved it and narrated a classic version. So did William F. Buckley and Peter Ustinov, among many others.

The music people speak of the "deliberate primitivism" in Prokofiev's music, hard to miss in such early works as the 1914 *Scythian Suite* for orchestra and the 1919 opera, *Love for Three Oranges*. "Unorthodox" was a key word for him, both in those early days before the Revolution and later when he was living abroad—unorthodox harmony, unorthodox tonality, and unorthodox melody.

While at the conservatory in St. Petersburg, he rocked the faculty with what the professors considered the rawest dissonance ever produced by a student of talent. These early works included a piano sonata, piano études, a piano concerto, and an opera. This was Prokofiev, rebellious youth, at his most dissonant. After ten years of study, he graduated with honors in 1914 at age twenty-three. Rimsky-Korsakov wrote on Prokofiev's conservatory graduation paper, "Talented but completely immature."

Anatol Lyadov, professor of music at the conservatory, would say to students who angered him: "Perhaps you should be teaching me, and not I you. I don't understand why you come to me. Go to Richard Strauss or Debussy." Given the common Russian view of those two at that time, it was as though he was saying, "Go to the Devil." Of Prokofiev, the learned professor would add: "He'll write himself out of this nonsense." That he did, but not for many years, and we do not know how much of the "calmer" Prokofiev resulted from maturity and change of heart and how much from the Central Committee.

Prokofiev was not dragged back to the Soviet Union in the early 1930s. He chose to return, making it clear that he believed in the Communist system, and later writing: "I did not realize that the events there demanded the collaboration of all citizens, not only men of politics but art as well."

Stravinsky, in his memoirs, offers a harsh view of why Prokofiev

CATS ON A ROOF

In 1913, after attending Prokofiev's pregraduation performance of the young composer's Piano Concerto No. 2, one critic wrote: "He takes his place at the piano and seems to be either dusting the keys or striking high or low notes at random. He has a sharp, dry touch. The public is bewildered. Some indignant murmurs are audible. One couple gets up and stalks toward the exit: 'This music is enough to drive you mad!' The hall empties. The young artist concludes his concerto with a relentlessly discordant combination of brasses. The audience is scandalized. The majority hiss. With a mocking bow, Prokofiev resumes his seat and plays an encore. The audience flees to the exits, exclaiming: 'To hell with all this futuristic music! We came here for enjoyment. The cats on our roof make better music than this!' Meanwhile, the enchanted progressivists try to drown them out with: 'This is the work of a genius!' . . . 'How fresh, how new!' . . . 'What temperament! What originality!' "

Another critic, commenting on the same performance, took a long-range view: "The audience booed. This means nothing. Some ten years hence the same audience will pay for this booing with unanimous applause for the then famous composer who will be recognized in all of Europe."

decided to go home: "It was a sacrifice to the bitch goddess and nothing else. He had no success in the United States and Europe for several reasons, while his visit to Russia had been a triumph. When I saw him for the last time in 1937, he was despondent about his material and artistic fate in France. He was politically naive, however. . . . He returned to Russia, and when finally he understood his position there, it was too late."

In 1948, after many years at home, Prokofiev was attacked, along with his younger colleague Shostakovich and several others, by the Central Committee's "resolution" that composers "must reject as useless and harmful garbage all the relics of bourgeois formalism in musical art." Although some have reported comments by Prokofiev to the effect that his heart was not in his words, he wisely and pragmatically—and probably with no real choice—acknowledged that he had sinned and joined the other chastised artists in a joint and abject apology.

During his life he was called "the Bolshevik Pianist" and "the Age-of-Steel Man" and his work "the Peak of Polyphonic Dissonance." But despite the dissonance, he won the Stalin Prize for the first time in 1943 for his Piano Sonata No. 7, called the *Stalingrad*, written for the war effort as the Nazis (having learned nothing from Napoleon) were invading Mother Russia. This, of course, was before he fell out of favor. After becoming a post-revolution good boy, he earned a second Stalin Prize in 1951 before his death of a cerebral hemorrhage in 1953.

Prokofiev's music sounded different from the music of Romanticism because he ignored the older rules governing melody, rhythm, and harmony and because he aimed for various degrees of discord and dissonance. He knew that some of his work would be considered barbaric by contemporaries. He, of course, did not consider it barbaric at all. Just different. A *New York Times* critic called him the "psychologist of all the uglier emotions—hatred, contempt, rage, disgust, despair, mockery, defiance." He was also "primitive" and "grotesque." That's sort of strong stuff from the sober *New York Times*. It was not that an artist of his talent could not write in other ways; this was the way in which he *wanted* to write.

It is perhaps useful for those of us on this side of the ocean, living in a different society, to keep in mind that Prokofiev and Shostakovich *were* the leaders of Soviet proletarian music—music for the working class. As indicated, in Prokofiev's case, his proletarian work began many years before he returned to Russia. His ballet *The Age of Steel*, written in 1925–1926, glorifies industrial development in Russia, the urban life, and the mechanized society, presenting factory noises and machinery rhythms. This was a long way from the poetic emotion of the Romantics, and it is inevitable that the sounds were different. Once he returned home, some of his best music was for two Soviet motion pictures, *Lieutenant Kijé* and *Alexander Nevsky*. Needless to say, movies produced under the Soviet government in the 1930s were consistent with the government's goals. *Lieutenant Kijé* is a satire on Czarist stupidity; *Alexander Nevsky* portrays the triumph of the Russian people over erstwhile invading forces.

World War II in the Soviet Union was not a time for Prokofiev's wit and satire. Among the war-oriented music he wrote, in addition to his *Leningrad* Piano Sonata, was his Fifth Symphony, considered by some critics to be not only his finest symphony but one of the century's best. It presents two pictures: one of the tragedy and destruction of war, and, later, one of faith and hope. There is no absence of melody here, and the experts point to its intensity of expression and rhythm. He dedicated it, *à la* Beethoven, to "the spirit of man," and the music people say that one of his objectives was to return symphonic music to the Beethoven approach.

DIAGHILEV ON PROKOFIEV AND STRAVINSKY

Serge Diaghilev, famous director of the Ballets Russes, said of Prokofiev: "Serge is certainly very talented, a fountain of melody—which Igor [Stravinsky] is not—but Igor is intelligent whereas Prokofiev is an utter imbecile." He also said that Prokofiev had great charm. "Yes, charm . . . That's something impossible to acquire. Stravinsky is the only Slav musician who lacks Slavic charm."

Another point should be made in connection with both Prokofiev and Shostakovich. Neither the 1917 Revolution nor the Communist party under which they worked negated their Russian heritage—the yen and talent for orchestral coloring, the use of folk songs and dances, the unusual peasant rhythms, and the link to Asiatic Russia. Nor can anything eliminate the love of her people for Mother Russia. After his years of self-exile spent wandering outside his native country, Prokofiev wrote: "I've got to live myself back into the atmosphere of my native soil. I've got to see real winters again, and spring that bursts into being from one moment to the next. I've got to hear the Russian language echoing in my ears. I've got to talk to people who are of my own flesh and blood, so that they can give me back something I lack here—their songs, my songs. Here I'm becoming enervated. I risk dying of academicism. Yes, my friend—I'm going back!"

And, as suggested earlier, there were pluses of another kind once he got home—as there were for Shostakovich, who never left. Compositions were published. Works were performed. There was no competitive market system. The music-loving Russian people, ready-made audiences, came by the thousands to listen. Automobiles, houses, and other good things were available for the artists of talent who pleased. These composers were bemedaled national heroes—unless they went astray.

This was not the world found by Prokofiev on an unsuccessful tour of the United States, peddling his own music as a virtuoso pianist in the days before he returned to Russia. He wrote of those days: "I wandered through the enormous park in the center of New York, and looking up at the skyscrapers that bordered it, thought with cold fury of the marvelous American orchestras that cared nothing for my music, of the critics who balked so violently at anything new, of the managers who arranged long tours for artists playing the same old hackneyed programs fifty times over." (America was not completely indifferent to his music, however. *Love for Three Oranges* was long a favorite of the New York City Opera, which gave several perform- ances of it each year. And millions of Americans were more famil- iar with it than they knew: From 1944 to 1958, the march from this opera was the theme for the CBS radio program *Your FBI in Peace and War*.)

Better to come home a hero. For Shostakovich, better to stay home a hero than to go out into that uncivilized, market-oriented chaos.

Also, without reference to harsh orders from headquarters, there was the basic philosophical issue of whether art is supposed to be the truest form of self-expression or is meant to serve the State. Prokofiev wrote: "Can the true artist stand aloof from life and confine his art within the narrow bounds of subjective emotion? Or should he be where he is needed most, where his words, his music, his chisel can help the people live a better, finer life?"

And, a year before his death: "When I was in the United States and England I often heard discussions on the subject of whom music ought to serve, for whom a composer ought to write, and to whom his music should be addressed. In my view, the composer, just as the poet, the sculptor, or the painter, is in duty bound to serve man, the people. He must beautify human life and defend it. He must be a citizen first and foremost, so that his art may consciously extol human life and lead man to a radiant future. Such, as I see it, is the immutable goal of art."

STARTER KIT

Certainly *Peter and the Wolf* must be included; to ignore it would be to choose Liza Minnelli's best songs and to leave out "Cabaret." It shows the whimsical side of the artist, but beyond that is a necessary part of life, such as watching *Casablanca*.

Of seven symphonies up for consideration, the most popular are the *Classical*, Symphony No. 1 in D, composed in 1916–1917 before Prokofiev left Russia, and No. 5 in B-flat, his wartime work and the favorite of the critics. I have selected those two. In the First, Prokofiev deliberately chose to write in Classical style. He later said he had attempted to "catch the spirit of Mozart and put down that which, if he were living now, Mozart might put into his scores."

The Fifth was his first symphonic effort in some fifteen years, his Fourth having failed in Paris. He had changed his own approach by this time, writing: "Music has definitely reached and passed the greatest degree of dissonance and of complexity that it is practicable for it to attain. Therefore I think the desire which I and many of my fellow composers feel, to achieve a more simple and melodic expression, is the inevitable direction for the musical art of the future."

Piano Concerto No. 3 in C is that rarity, a favorite of both critics and the public. Written between 1917 and 1921 in Russia, the United States, and Paris, it is one of the most frequently played twentieth-century piano concertos.

The choice for the fifth Starter Kit work was between two orchestral suites—from the opera *Love for Three Oranges* of 1924, written in Paris, or from the score of the film *Lieutenant Kijé*, composed in the Soviet Union in 1934. The film music, which comprises five sections, is our selection, but no penalties are imposed if you go for the *Three Oranges*. As noted, *Lieutenant Kijé* is a satire about a stupid czar, and that was very much permitted in a 1934 Soviet Union.

(A personal favorite is the seven-movement cantata from the twenty-one-segment music for the film *Alexander Nevsky*. If you want Russia, a great battle on the ice, and a magnificent lament for the dead, try it—even with American musicians and voices.)

HOW TO DO PROKOFIEV

A strong case can be made that the way to do Prokofiev is to start out with his strong, dissonant, and different early works: the *Scythian Suite*, Piano Concerto No. 1, Violin Concerto No. 1, and Piano Concerto No. 3. Then move to 1928 and the *Prodigal Son* ballet. And wind up in 1944 with Symphony No. 5. You then will have tasted of youthful freshness, midlife experience, and developed maturity. Add Symphony No. 1 because everybody does.

PROKOFIEV: THE STARTER KIT

Composition	Recordings Available*
SYMPHONIES:	
No. 1 (Classical)	25
No. 5	9
OTHER ORCHESTRAL WORKS:	
Piano Concerto No. 3 in C	10
Lieutenant Kijé Suite	14
Peter and the Wolf	20

*Represents the number of recorded releases available of each listed composition as found in a recent issue of the *Schwann/Opus* catalogue. A "C" indicates that a work is only available collected with other compositions.

PROKOFIEV: A TOP TEN

Composition	Recordings Available*
SYMPHONIES:	
No. 1 (Classical)	25
No. 5	9
OTHER ORCHESTRAL WORKS:	
Piano Concerto No. 3 in C	10
Violin Concerto No. 1 in D	2
Violin Concerto No. 2 in G Minor	5
Love for Three Oranges Suite	13
Lieutenant Kijé Suite	14
Ballet:	
Cinderella	1
Peter and the Wolf	20
CHAMBER MUSIC:	
String Quartet No. 1 in B Minor	1

PROKOFIEV: A MASTER COLLECTION

Composition	Recordings Available*
SYMPHONIES:	
No. 1 (Classical)	25
No. 2	2
No. 5	9

Composition	Recordings Available*
No. 6 in E-flat Minor	3
No. 7	4

OTHER ORCHESTRAL WORKS:

Piano Concerto No. 1 in D-flat	5
Piano Concerto No. 2 in G Minor	4
Piano Concerto No. 3 in C	10
Violin Concerto No. 1 in D	2
Violin Concerto No. 2 in G Minor	5
Sinfonia Concertante for Cello and Orchestra	2
Love for Three Oranges Suite	13
Lieutenant Kijé Suite	14
Ballets:	
Romeo and Juliet	5
Cinderella	1
L'enfant prodigue (The prodigal son)	1
Peter and the Wolf	20

CHAMBER MUSIC:

String Quartet No. 1 in B Minor	1
String Quartet No. 2 in F	1

OTHER INSTRUMENTAL MUSIC:

Seven Sonatas for Piano, including:	
No. 6 in A	14
No. 7 in B-flat	15
No. 8 in B-flat	7
Sonata for Flute and Piano, Op. 94	6
Sonata for Cello and Piano	5

FILM MUSIC:

Lieutenant Kijé, incidental music	2
Alexander Nevsky	6

DMITRI SHOSTAKOVICH (1906–1975)

Number 19

The Prokofiev experience (see the preceding chapter) demonstrates that it was difficult being a creative artist in what was the Soviet Union—which would have been no news to the many Russians who deeply loved their country but found that artistic genius, artistic freedom, and the Will of the State were not easily reconcilable.

Consider the added complexities if your face was featured on the cover of *Time* magazine, topped by a firefighter's helmet, a heroic symbol of your country's resistance to Hitler's World War II invasion. *Time*'s cover story reflected this country's appreciation for the wartime value of Dmitri Shostakovich's Seventh Symphony, composed to inspire his countrymen to hold out against Germany's siege of Leningrad. The music was adopted by the United States in support of our ally and played by every major orchestra in this country, after a premiere performance by Arturo Toscanini over NBC radio.

Shostakovich is the only completely Soviet composer on The List—that is, the only one who lived his entire adult life after the

---

THE LENINGRAD

Alexei Tolstoy's comment on Shostakovich's Seventh Symphony, composed when Leningrad was holding out against the Nazi army:

"He rested his ear against the heart of his country and heard its mighty song."

Russian Revolution. A pocket calculator and a calendar are needed to trace his musical career, for he went in and out of periods of creative genius and in and out of favor with the fellows in the Kremlin. The wonder is that an artist functioning in such a repressive environment could create at all—unless he was sympathetic to the objectives of that society, even if opposed to the means used to move toward those objectives.

Some background:

Immediately after the 1917 Revolution, an avant-garde disciple of France's Debussy was named head of music in the Soviet Union, and pupils of Rimsky-Korsakov were put in charge of the conservatories. Things were good. But after a few years two groups formed: The Association of Proletarian Musicians (APM) and the Association for Contemporary Music (ASM). As the names suggest, the APM opposed "contemporary" works and any other music not geared to the worker and the peasant. The ASM view was that music should not be ideological.

During the 1920s the "contemporary" school was dominant. Such works as Prokofiev's *Love for Three Oranges* were applauded; Mahler's symphonies were performed and were popular. But as the 1930s began, the ASM collapsed and the proletarians took power. Their musical know-how was limited, and they made such a mess of things that the Central Committee of the Communist party stepped in to straighten it all out. The party put a plague on both houses, suppressing contemporary "formalism"—art for art's sake—on the one hand and crude "proletarian" art aimed at the peasant and the worker on the other. It advised composers that their music should fall under the rubric of "socialist realism." Music was to serve a purpose; it was to be strong, optimistic, and true to the country's heritage.

The music gurus point out that the music written by Prokofiev and Shostakovich in the 1920s thus differs from their music of the early 1930s. No one knew just how a particular composition would be received. In the later decade, lyrical parts were in, vulgar parts out. Melody was in, crude rhythms out. One year Shostakovich's opera *Lady Macbeth of Mtsensk* was called a "most significant landmark in the development of Soviet musical art"—but two years later it was a "deliberately discordant, confused stream of sounds." A Prokofiev civil-war opera was bad, but Prokofiev string quartets were good. (Instrumental music was more difficult to weigh on the party scales than operas and songs.)

Then came the probability of World War II, the actual war, and the defense of Leningrad. The government paid less attention to individual works. The composers, dedicated and patriotic Russians, wrote to inspire their countrymen and were applauded.

Shostakovich wrote a "monumental" Eighth Symphony in 1943 and, as we have seen, Prokofiev a Sixth in 1947. But government postwar reassessment later condemned both.

Shostakovich is the only composer on The List born in the twentieth century. He is also the most recently living of The 50, having died in 1975. Like Prokofiev, Shostakovich is a "modern" of what was, in his day, the "new" school. Like the music of Prokofiev, fifteen years his senior, some of his work shocked the music world—and, more important from a personal standpoint, shocked the State. It isn't nice to fool Mother Nature, but it was downright dangerous for even country-loving Soviet citizens to challenge the party.

EXPERT OPINION

A fascinating phenomenon encountered consistently is the inconsistency in expert critical opinion in the music world. One school admires greatly the earlier Shostakovich—the Shostakovich of the First Symphony (1925), the satirical opera *The Nose* (1928), an early piano concerto (1933), and the infamous opera *Lady Macbeth of Mtsensk* (1934)—but argues that after Stalin's attack in 1936 the composer never wrote another note of genius. Prokofiev took over, says this school, and was alone the dominant force in Soviet music.

Another school hails Shostakovich's Fifth Symphony (1937) as brilliant, recognizes some powerful pluses in the *Leningrad* Seventh, and declares that his fifteen string quartets, begun after the attack on *Lady Macbeth* and continued until a year before his death, constitute one of the peaks of twentieth-century music.

Criticism written fifteen years ago predicted a great revival of Shostakovich's music by "1990 or so." Well, it is 1990 or so, and acclaim for the fifteen quartets, especially, is high and contagious. They have been called among the most "inward-looking and uncompromising works of the century." All have been recorded, although the choices are limited. One assessment comes from the *Penguin Guide*: "The Shostakovich Quartets thread through his creative life like some inner odyssey and inhabit terrain of increasing spiritual desolation."

Whereas Prokofiev's maturity predated the Russian Revolution of 1917, Shostakovich was a child of the Revolution. The résumé for his yo-yo career inside the Soviet Union would look something like this:

Born: St. Petersburg, 1906

Revolution: October 1917

Entered Leningrad Conservatory: 1919 (at thirteen).

Graduated Leningrad Conservatory: 1925. Family poor. Played piano in movie theater for a while.

Symphony No. 1: 1925. Written by nineteen-year-old as graduation exercise. Emotional. Honest. No political dogma. Regarded by many—but not by the majority—as his best symphony. Composer became world-famous when it was performed in Berlin and elsewhere. Stravinsky had defected, Prokofiev was abroad, and Shostakovich was *the* Soviet star.

Manifestations of Dogma: 1927, at age twenty-one: "I cannot conceive of my future creative program outside of our socialist enterprise, and the aim which I assign to my work is that of helping every way to enlighten our remarkable country. . . . There can be no music without an ideology. . . . Lenin himself said 'music is a means of unifying broad masses of people.' . . . Even the symphonic form . . . can be said to have a bearing on politics. . . . Good music . . . is no longer an end in itself but a vital weapon in the struggle."

Symphony No. 2: 1927. Called the *October*, it was written to celebrate tenth anniversary of October Revolution. Not musically successful.

Symphony No. 3: 1929. Written to honor May Day, it included choral movement. Also unsuccessful. Shostakovich called both the Second and Third Symphonies "Soviet tracts."

The Nose: Opera. Late 1920s. Satirized the government. Government was not amused.

Three ballets: Late 1920s and early 1930s. *The Age of Gold, The Bolt*, and *The Limpid Stream* (or Brook), all satirizing something. Modestly successful. *The Age of Gold* is still performed.

Lady Macbeth of Mtsensk: 1934. Opera, performed in Moscow and Leningrad. Murder and adultery. Dissonant music. Peculiar sounds. Smash hit in Russia for a couple of years and popular around the world. Performed in both Cleveland and New York in 1935. (In both cities, much larger audiences were watching the Yankees murder the Indians.)

Delayed government reaction: 1936. *Lady Macbeth* severely attacked by Kremlin. *Pravda* called it "pandemonium instead of music . . . crude, primitive, vulgar. . . . The composer apparently does not set himself the task of listening to the desires and expectations of the

Soviet public. He scrambles sounds to make them interesting to formalist-aesthetes, who have lost all good taste." And: "The music cracks, grunts and growls, and suffocates itself." Critics today dissent from *Pravda*'s evaluation, of course, praising the composer's dynamic rhythmic forces and lyricism. But presumably they are "formalist-aesthetes" themselves. Along with this after-the-fact second evaluation of *Lady Macbeth*, *Pravda* now attacked *The Limpid Stream* as well. "The composer," it said, "apparently has only contempt for our national songs." For Shostakovich, one plus was that at only thirty-one he was receiving an enormous amount of top-level attention.

Nonperson: 1936–1937. Sat out the criticism.

Symphony No. 5: Late 1937. Performed during twentieth-anniversary celebration of Revolution. Soviet critics heard "work of great depth," of "emotional wealth," of "great importance." Critics of our time agree. Generally held now as his masterpiece. Also now the most popular of his symphonies, although some prefer his First.

Symphony No. 6: 1939. Less popular, then and now, than the Fifth.

Stalin Prize: 1940. Awarded to the hero-composer for his Piano Quintet of that year. Considered today a first-rate work.

Symphony No. 7: 1941–1942. The famous *Leningrad*. The Nazi army was overrunning Mother Russia. Leningrad was fighting for survival. The composer dedicated the symphony "to our struggle against Fascism, to our future victory, to my native city." It won another Stalin Prize for Shostakovich and was played—and hailed—across the non-Nazi world. Even today, many World War II veterans are thrilled by the first movement.

Symphony No. 8: 1943. "Monumental" by today's assessment. The war was still on, and it was written to portray the suffering of the people. Some critics consider it the most intense of all Shostakovich symphonies. After the war, it was suppressed for ten years.

Symphony No. 9: 1945. The hero was charged by the government with "ideological weakness." His symphony, though happy in mood, did not properly reflect life in the Soviet Union. Yesterday's hero; today's bum.

The Great Party Proclamation against "formalism" in music: 1948. Music being produced in the Soviet Union was too modernist. Too intellectual. Shostakovich had "decadent tendencies." (So, as we saw, did Prokofiev, and so did others not on The List.) In "modern" music there was "the negation of the basic principles of classical music." "Modern" music, too, constituted "a sermon for atonality, dissonance, and disharmony." From now on the objective was "to condemn the formalistic movement in Soviet music as anti-national and leading to the liquidation of music." The party said it was necessary for "Soviet composers to realize fully the lofty requirements of the Soviet people upon musical art, to sweep from their path all that weakens our music and hinders its development, and assure an upsurge of creative work that will advance Soviet musical culture." Shostakovich got the message, as did Prokofiev, and publicly acknowledged that he had erred. While a product of the system, he was far from the first who wanted to create music close to the spirit of the people.

"THE PARTY IS RIGHT"

This was Shostakovich's response to the 1948 Communist party proclamation against "formalism" in music:

"As we look back on the road traversed by our art, it becomes quite clear to us that every time the Party corrects errors of a creative artist and points out the deviation in his work, or else severely condemns a certain tendency in Soviet art, it invariably brings beneficial results for Soviet art and for individual artists. . . . I can now clearly see that I overestimated the thoroughness of my artistic reconstruction; certain negative characteristics peculiar to my musical thought prevented me from making the turn that seemed to be indicated in a number of my works of recent years. . . . I know that the Party is right. . . . The absence in my works of the interpretation of folk art, that great spirit by which our people live, has been with utmost clarity and definiteness pointed out by the Central Committee. . . . I shall try again and again to create symphonic works close to the spirit of the people from the standpoint of ideological subject matter, musical language and form."

Song of the Forests: 1949. An oratorio, appropriately praising Stalin's reforestation plan. Now that was more like it.

Fall of Berlin: 1949. Music for a film of that name. Back on the right track.

Honored member of Soviet delegation at Cultural and Scientific

Conference for World Peace in New York: 1949. The cold war was on, and his speech, delivered while in the United States, attacked Western democracies. *Time* magazine cover story was forgotten. Difficult for public to tell which is the real Dmitri Shostakovich.

Third Stalin Prize: 1950.

Symphony No. 10 in E Minor: 1953. Symphonic version of *Song of the Forest.*

Hero of the Soviet Union: 1966. Highest honor of them all; he was first musician to receive it.

Death in Russia: 1975.

As was the case with many other composers, Shostakovich did not produce "scrambled sounds" and "quacks and growls" throughout his career. Some critics believe that his most beautiful work, quackless and growl-less, is found in his chamber music, including fifteen string quartets and the 1940 Classical-style Piano Quintet in G Minor.

Not much is heard these days of *Lady Macbeth of Mtsensk*. Of symphonies, the critics lean to the Ninth and Tenth as well as the First and Fifth. His ballet *The Age of Gold*, a satire on decadent capitalism, was once regarded as energy-packed but blatant and vulgar. But that was 1930 Shostakovich. Different sounds are heard in the earlier First and later Tenth Symphonies, and in the piano quintet. The latter is somewhat dissonant, because it is Shostakovich, but less sharply dissonant than some of his other works. For easy listening, his Piano Concerto No. 1 (1933) is light and charming.

The gurus say that twentieth-century composers on The List did not abandon melody with their "modern" music but merely found different ways to make it. While modern melody is not the same as Romantic or Classical melody, it is by no means nonexistent. But it takes more work. Listen to Shostakovich's Symphony No. 10 a half-dozen times running, and you'll agree.

STARTER KIT

While some professionals consider Symphony No. 10 in E Minor, composed in 1953, to be Shostakovich's symphonic masterpiece, we have selected No. 1 in F (1925) and No. 5 in D Minor (1937). The First, written before his twentieth birthday, was performed first in Leningrad, then in Moscow, then in Berlin by Bruno Walter, and eventually in the United States under Leopold Stokowski. The Soviet government liked it, Moscow Radio saying, "It is a symphony which reflects all that a composition can give of the most important in the artist." For years it was his most-performed work.

Later it was pre-empted by the Fifth, which drew rave reviews not only in Russia but in the West as well. It is by far his most popular symphony today. Shostakovich called it "a Soviet artist's practical, creative reply to just criticism," and it's still difficult for outsiders to know whether that was sincerity, sarcasm, or acceptance of inevitability speaking. It is the most melodic of his symphonies.

In 1930 the composer produced a satirical ballet, *The Age of Gold*, which followed a satirical opera, *The Nose*. As a ballet *The Age of Gold* was a failure, but as music it has survived—especially a popular polka, which satirized the Geneva Peace Conference, and a Russian dance. It is included, rather than another symphony, to broaden the list.

The fourth recommended orchestral piece is the Concerto for Piano and Trumpet (plus string orchestra), written in 1933, interesting to professionals in that not too many great works feature a single trumpet and strings, and good listening for the rest of us.

For chamber music, I've chosen his Piano Quintet in G Minor (1940), which won the Stalin Prize of 100,000 rubles—more than anyone had ever received for one chamber-music composition. Other well-known Shostakovich chamber music includes fifteen esteemed string quartets and some piano trios.

SHOSTAKOVICH: THE STARTER KIT

Composition	Recordings Available*
SYMPHONIES (OF FIFTEEN):	
No. 1 in F	5
No. 5 in D Minor	11
OTHER ORCHESTRAL WORKS:	
Concerto No. 1 in C Minor for Piano and Trumpet	5
Ballet:	
The Age of Gold (suite or complete)	3
CHAMBER MUSIC:	
Piano Quintet in G Minor, Op. 57	2

*Represents the number of recorded releases available of each listed composition as found in a recent issue of the *Schwann/Opus* catalogue. A "C" indicates that a work is only available collected with other compositions.

SHOSTAKOVICH: A TOP TEN

Composition	Recordings Available*
SYMPHONIES (OF FIFTEEN):	
No. 1 in F	5
No. 5 in D Minor	11
No. 10 in E Minor	4
OTHER ORCHESTRAL WORKS:	
Concerto No. 1 in C Minor for Piano and Trumpet	5
Concerto No. 1 in A Minor for Violin	3
Concerto in E-flat for Cello	4
Ballet:	
The Age of Gold (suite or complete)	3
CHAMBER MUSIC:	
Piano Quintet in G Minor, Op. 57	2
OTHER INSTRUMENTAL MUSIC:	
Sonata for Cello and Piano	4
VOCAL MUSIC:	
Opera:	
Lady Macbeth of Mtsensk	1

SHOSTAKOVICH: A MASTER COLLECTION

Composition	Recordings Available*
SYMPHONIES (OF FIFTEEN):	
No. 1 in F	5
No. 5 in D Minor	11
No. 6	4
No. 7 in C (Leningrad)	2
No. 9 in E-flat	4
No. 10 in E Minor	4
No. 12 (Lenin)	2
No. 14	3
OTHER ORCHESTRAL WORKS:	
Concerto No. 1 in C Minor for Piano and Trumpet	5

Composition	Recordings Available*
Concerto No. 2 for Piano and Orchestra	3
Concerto No. 1 in A Minor for Violin	3
Concerto in E-flat for Cello	4
Ballet:	
The Age of Gold (suite or complete)	3

CHAMBER MUSIC:

Chamber Symphony for String Orchestra	2
String Quartet No. 8	1
String Quartet No. 10	1
String Quartet No. 15	1
Piano Quintet in G Minor, Op. 57	2
Piano Trio No. 2 in E Minor	2

PIANO MUSIC:

Three Fantastic Dances for Piano	3

OTHER INSTRUMENTAL MUSIC:

Sonata for Cello and Piano	4
Sonata for Viola and Piano	4
Sonata for Violin and Piano	3

VOCAL MUSIC:

Opera:

Lady Macbeth of Mtsensk	1
The Nose	0

RICHARD STRAUSS (1864–1949)

Number 20

Richard Wagner lived from 1813 to 1883, worshiped himself, and was the dominant figure of his time in German music. Richard Strauss lived from 1864 to 1949, worshiped Wagner, and was the dominant figure of *his* time in German music.

Both were masters of the orchestra—masterful orchestrators of big orchestras.

Both were masters of theater and drama.

Both were masters of combining orchestra, drama, and voice.

Both made music that triggered hostility and controversy during their lives and both achieved great fame. It is a fascinating musical fact that the musician in Munich more hostile to Wagner during the latter's lifetime than any other was a virtuoso first-horn player in the court orchestra named Franz Strauss, father of Richard.

Young Richard was influenced by his father's anti-Wagner teaching. He was brought up in a strictly classical way—playing the piano at four, composing a polka at six, and writing chamber music, a concerto, and a symphony in his teens. His genius was recognized; this was a budding Brahms, another young creator of absolute music. His youthful works included a Quartet in A, a Symphony in D Minor, an Overture in C Minor, a Serenade for Thirteen Wind Instruments, a Concerto for Horn and Orchestra—and later (at twenty) a Symphony in F Minor and a piano quartet. Some of these works are still performed today, but not often.

Musicologists say that the Symphony in F Minor was modeled after works of Beethoven, Mendelssohn, and Schumann, and it won the approval of the prestigious Brahms.

Then all hell broke loose.

OPUS 1

As a sixteen-year-old, Richard Strauss wrote to a publishing firm in Leipzig and tried to persuade them to publish his music:

"Dear Mr. Breitkopf: Since, as a total stranger, I am about to trouble you with a request, I shall first take the liberty of introducing myself to you. My name is Richard Strauss and I was born on the eleventh of June '64, the son of Franz Strauss, chamber musician and teacher at the Music School in this city. At the moment I am attending the gymnasium, the lower sixth form to be precise, but shall wholly dedicate myself to music, in fact specifically to composition. . . . The enclosed Festival March is dedicated to my uncle, Brewery Owner Georg Pschorr, whose wish it is that the same appear from the presses of one of the top music-publishing concerns, the printing costs to be borne by him. I therefore address myself to you with the request that you will be so good as to undertake the publication of the Festival March, since your name, well-known in every respect to the musical world, is, after all, of the greatest influence in spreading the name of a young aspiring musician. The March, as well as some other larger compositions of mine, has occasioned very favorable comments on the part of General [Music] Director Franz Lachner, who has granted me gracious permission to submit to him one of my compositions from time to time. I commend myself to your goodwill and remain

Yours respectfully,
Richard Strauss"

For one thing, Strauss became close friends with a man named Alexander Ritter, a member of the Meiningen Orchestra, of which Strauss was assistant conductor under the famed Hans von Bülow. Ritter, married to Wagner's niece, was an all-out Wagner supporter. For another thing, young Strauss began listening to Wagner's music instead of his father's words. Ritter pushed not only Wagner, but program music, music-drama, Liszt, symphonic poems, the whole bag.

"His influence was in the nature of a stormwind," Strauss said later. "He urged me to the development of the poetic, the expressive in music, as exemplified in the works of Liszt, Berlioz and Wagner."

The real Richard Strauss now stood up: In 1886, after a visit to Italy, came a symphonic fantasy called *Aus Italien*, so dissonant for its time that almost everyone hated it. Strauss called it "the connecting link between the old and the new." And then began a decade of tone poems that made him internationally famous, internationally controversial, an artist to be hated and reckoned with. Some of these were grim, some humorous, some light. The first was *Macbeth* in 1888, later twice revised; the next *Don Juan* in 1889; the third *Death and Transfiguration* in 1889; the fourth *Till Eulenspiegel's Merry Pranks* in 1895; the fifth *Thus Spake Zarathustra* in 1896; the sixth *Don Quixote* in 1897; and the last *Ein Heldenleben* in 1898. Some critics believe Strauss declined as a composer from *Till Eulenspiegel* on, but others strongly dissent.

The series of tone poems drew all sorts of responses from the contemporary critics: "rambling," "incoherent," "noisy," "outlandish," "blatant," "vulgar," "story-and-picture music taken to the extreme," "sound-and-fury," "daring," "sensational," "vividly descriptive," "imaginative," "unequal," and "a jumble of instrumental cackles."

OTHER COMPOSERS' VIEWS

An unListed member of Russian's ultranationalist "Mighty Five" said of some Strauss music: "This is not music, but a mockery of music." Impressionist Claude Debussy of France, an innovator and progressive in his own right, said that listening to a Strauss tone poem was like spending an hour in an asylum. While Debussy's Impressionism was at the other end of the pole from Strauss's realism, one must always be a little suspect of what the French and Germans say about one another.

In the midst of producing these works (all frequently heard today on classical-music radio stations), this Wagner-worshiper turned to a new form: opera. His first, which premiered in 1894, was called *Guntram* and was a dreadful failure. Neither audience nor critics liked it, and it had only one performance. The second, *Feuersnot*, in 1901, did no better. By 1905 a good number of years had passed since Strauss had shaken up the music world with his first tone poem, but he did it all over again with the opera *Salome,* introduced in Dresden. Drawn from an Oscar Wilde text, it told of the Princess of Judea's sensual love for John the Baptist. It was bad enough to have sensual love for John the Baptist, but to dance lasciviously before Herod and then to kiss the lips of John's severed head resting on a silver platter was a bit much for 1905.

But it was not only the Wilde plot that distressed the world. There also was a strong reaction to Strauss's music, considered by many to be just as sensual and decadent as the story line. Milton Cross and David Ewen say that "with his lavish orchestration, the erotic suggestions of his tortuous melodies and impulsive rhythms, and his suggestive characterizations, Strauss was, in his own way, as offensive to his contemporaries as was Wilde to his." It sounds like a dissonant *Deep Throat.* Strauss was consciously courting the sensational with wild rhythms and unorthodox music, convinced that his music would in time be accepted—as it was.

The music world hadn't yet recovered from the lust-in-her-dance of Salome before Strauss tried again with another one-act opera, *Elektra,* based on the Sophocles drama from ancient Greece. Elektra, no Mary Worth, has only one reason for living: to see her mother killed for having plotted, with her lover, the death of her husband the King, Elektra's father. Elektra is ecstatic when her missing brother returns to kill both mother and lover, and she celebrates in another far-out dance ending in her death.

These were evil and frightening productions—and, the critics today say, superb theater. *Elektra* drew this comment from the *New York Times* reviewer: "It is a prodigious orchestral orgy, with nothing that can be called music in the score, and makes superhuman demands upon the physical and mental powers of the singers and players. The marvelous imitative effects of the orchestra are blood-curdling, drastic and gruesome to the last degree. It is fortunate for hearers the piece is no longer for it would be too nerve-racking."

That Richard Strauss then faded away, although this was 1909 and he lived for another forty years.

One masterwork of a wholly different nature came two years later: *Der Rosenkavalier* (The knight of the rose), a comic opera, light and gay, applauded by the critics then and now. It is considered by some to be Strauss's most inspired music and by all to be his most lovely. The composer is reported to have said, "I always wanted to write an opera like Mozart's," and this was his attempt to do so. No one writes operas like Mozart's, including Strauss, but in *Der Rosenkavalier* he nonetheless does graceful and delightful things with music, characters, romance, sophistication, and fun. Some consider the music in the final scene as beautiful as any in opera. The whole work is tender, compassionate, and charming.

Though Strauss was alive and well in Germany and Switzerland through World War II, no later music equaled that of his early years.

2001

Millions are far more familiar with Richard Strauss's music than they might think. The first movement of *Thus Spake Zarathustra* is the theme music for the film *2001*.

Liszt has been identified as the creator of tone poems, and Strauss is accepted as their perfector. As noted earlier, the tone poem, without actors, narrators, singers, or words, is supposed to tell a story or communicate a message. For this program music the composer provides an actual written AAA trip-ticket for the listener. An example is Strauss's own words for his tone poem *Thus Spake Zarathustra*, taken from the philosopher Nietzsche's work: "First movement: Sunrise. Man feels the power of God. Andante religioso. But man still longs. He plunges with passion (second movement) and finds no peace. He turns toward science and tries in vain to solve life's problems in a fugue (third movement). Then agreeable dance tunes sound and he becomes an individual and his soul soars upward while the work sinks far beneath him."

It is unlikely that many of us would receive this message merely by listening to the music, especially the vain attempt to solve life's problems, but the idea is to read the program and then see how the composer has put those thoughts into music. It can be fun, but it's not at all necessary to enjoyment of the music.

David Ewen, author of some fifty books on music, writes that Strauss threw off his early post-Romantic, Brahmsian manner and then created "a new kind of music—realistic, descriptive, utilizing the fullest modern resources of orchestration, adventurous in its use of structure, skillful in counterpoint, and magnetizing for its power and passion."

There is general agreement among the gurus that Strauss's genius is in orchestration, in his magical use of orchestral color, his imaginative use of each instrument—and in the to-hell-with-it spirit of his use of the orchestra. Once advised what to look for, the amateur can catch some of that.

SHEEP

No composer on The List produced more realistic, descriptive sounds than Strauss did in his tone poems: sheep bleating, wind blowing, geese gabbling, horses' hoofbeats, pot and pans clanging, storms thundering. Mozart did not try to do that.

Why, then, the "strange" sounds? This is the question arising again and again about early twentieth-century music. The answer is: Because the composers were up to their navels in sweet, euphonious music and wanted a change. *Webster's* defines *euphony* this way: "Pleasing or sweet sound; the acoustic effect produced by words so formed and combined as to please the ear. The opposite of cacophony." But cacophony—of its time—was precisely what Strauss—and, even more so, unListed others who followed—chose to write.

There is more to Strauss as a musician than the tone poems and operas. He was a renowned conductor, one of the finest of his time. For twelve years he was director of the prestigious Berlin Royal Opera, one of the better musical posts in Europe. And he was a songwriter, considered by many critics to be only a hair behind Schubert, Schumann, and Brahms (and some unListed colleagues). He wrote more than 150 songs, beginning when he was in his teens and ending late in his life. The professionals prefer his early ones, written before 1900. Among the best-known are "Allerseelen," "Zueignung," "Morgen," "Wiegenlied," "Traum durch die Dammerung," "Standchen," and "Cacilie."

Strauss was born in Munich and lived most of his life in Germany, cozying up to Adolf Hitler and the Third Reich in the early 1930s, but later being put under house arrest for a time and finally spending the last war years in Switzerland. A de-Nazification court in Munich in 1948 cleared him of Nazi collaboration charges, which did not impress those of his critics who believed he continued working with the Hitler thugs far too long. He died in the Bavarian Alps in 1949 at eighty-five, an accepted giant.

To sum up:

Richard Strauss was a conventional Late Romantic composer who turned radical in his midtwenties for a decade or so, shocked the music world during that period with a series of symphonic tone poems and two avant-garde operas, and then slowly returned to more conventional work during the last half of his long eighty-five-year life. His fame and his place high on The List, at Number 20, come chiefly from the relatively busy experimental period. While some, such as Mahler, who described him as "the great opportunist," are less than impressed by him, Strauss, as a result of his experimental works, is today regarded as one of the top three or four composers of the twentieth century.

STARTER KIT

Dare one leave off the Starter Kit both *Elektra* and *Salome* when they play such a vital role in the Strauss musical oeuvre? Yes, provided that one crucial number from *Salome*, the "Dance of the Seven Veils," is included as one recommendation to represent both operas.

Der Rosenkavalier is included, in part simply because it is so much more pleasant than either of the aforementioned. Among the best-known selections are: from Act I, "Di rigori armato il seno," for tenor, and "Was erzurn' ich mich denn?" sung by the princess; from Act II, the duet "Mit ihren augen voll thranen" and the waltz "Ohne mich, ohne mich, jeder tag dir so bang"; and from Act III, "Hab' mirs gelobt, ihn lieb zu haben," sung by the princess, and the duet "Ist ein traum, kann nicht wirklich sein."

Three tone poems complete the Starter Kit: *Death and Transfiguration, Till Eulenspiegel's Merry Pranks,* and *Ein Heldenleben.*

Strauss's friend Alexander Ritter wrote the program for *Death and Transfiguration* (Tod und Verklarung), offered here to give a sense of what programs are like:

> In the little room, dimly lighted by only a candle end, lies the sick man on his bed. He has wrestled despairingly with Death. Now he has sunk exhausted in sleep. . . . But Death does not long grant sleep and dreams to his victim. Cruelly he shakes him awake, and the fight begins afresh. Will to live and power of Death! What a frightful wrestling! Neither bears off the victory, and all is silence once more! Sunk back, tired of

STRAUSS ON DISCORDANT TONE POEMS

In a letter of August 24, 1888, to the conductor Hans von Bülow, Strauss wrote:

"I have found myself in a gradually ever-increasing contradiction between the musical-poetic content that I want to convey and the ternary sonata-form that has come down to us from the classical composers. . . . If you want to create a work of art that is unified in its mood and consistent in its structure, and if it is to give the listener a clear and definite impression, then what the author wants to say must have been just as clear and definite in his own mind. This is only possible through a program. I consider it a legitimate artistic method to create a correspondingly new form for every subject, to shape which neatly and perfectly is a very difficult task, but for that reason the more attractive."

battle, sleepless, as in fever-frenzy the sick man sees his life pass before his inner eye. . . . First the morning red of childhood. . . . Then the youth's saucier play—exerting and trying his strength—till he ripens to the man's fight, and now burns with hot lust after the higher prizes of life. The one high purpose that has led him through life was to shape all he saw transfigured into a still more transfigured form. Cold and sneering, the world set barrier upon barrier in the way of his achievement. . . . And so he pushes forward, so he climbs, desists not from his sacred purpose. What he has ever sought with his heart's deep yearning, he still seeks in his death sweat. . . . Then clangs the last stroke of Death's iron hammer, breaks the earthly body in twain, covers the eye with the night of death. But from the heavenly spaces sounds mightily to greet him what he yearningly sought here: deliverance from the world, transfiguration of the word.

The peculiar thing about this program is that it was written *after* the music. A good game might be to play some music by someone and have everyone in the room write their own program. A better game might be to sit back and enjoy.

Till Eulenspiegel, based on an old German legend, is considered by some to be the greatest of the tone poems. The character Till was a prankster, a sort of continental Robin Hood, who had a wonderful time until the world caught up with him. But he is finally brought to justice and, in the Strauss version, hanged by the neck until he is quite dead. The legendary Till made out considerably better; he was a rogue but not a to-be-hanged criminal.

The last of the successful tone poems was *Ein Heldenleben* (A hero's life), about a chap who overcomes all enemies and obstacles and improves the state of the world. It is biographical and repeats fragments from several other Strauss works, including three other tone poems, some songs, and an opera. It is in six sections: the Hero, the Hero's Antagonists, the Hero's Helpmate, the Hero's Battlefield, the Hero's Mission of Peace, and the Hero's Escape from the World. A favorite of lovers is the Hero's Helpmate section, in which a violin plays the part of Ms. Hero.

STRAUSS: A STARTER KIT

Composition	*Recordings Available**
ORCHESTRAL WORKS:	
Tone Poems:	
Death and Transfiguration	14
Till Eulenspiegel's Merry Pranks	23
Ein Heldenleben	17
Dance of the Seven Veils (from Salome)	5
VOCAL MUSIC:	
Opera:	
Der Rosenkavalier	5

*Represents the number of recorded releases available of each listed composition as found in a recent issue of the *Schwann/Opus* catalogue. A "C" indicates that a work is only available collected with other compositions.

STRAUSS: A TOP TEN

Composition	*Recordings Available**
ORCHESTRAL WORKS:	
Tone Poems:	
Don Juan	21
Death and Transfiguration	14

Composition	Recordings Available*
Till Eulenspiegel's Merry Pranks	23
Thus Spake Zarathustra	27
Ein Heldenleben	17
Horn Concerto No. 2 in E-flat	3
Dance of the Seven Veils (from Salome)	5

VOCAL MUSIC:
Operas:

Der Rosenkavalier	5
Salome	3
Elektra	2

STRAUSS: A MASTER COLLECTION

Composition	Recordings Available*

SYMPHONIES:

Aus Italien	2

OTHER ORCHESTRAL WORKS:
Tone Poems:

Don Juan	21
Death and Transfiguration	14
Till Eulenspiegel's Merry Pranks	23
Thus Spake Zarathustra	27
Don Quixote	7
Ein Heldenleben	17
Symphonia domestica	2
An Alpine Symphony	5
Dance of the Seven Veils (from Salome)	5
Der Rosenkavalier Suite	5
Le bourgeois gentilhomme Suite	4
Horn Concerto No. 1 in E-flat	3
Horn Concerto No. 2 in E-flat	3
Oboe Concerto in D	3
Burleske in D Minor for Piano and Orchestra	3

OTHER INSTRUMENTAL MUSIC:

Sonata for Cello and Piano	5
Sonata in E-flat for Violin and Piano	5
Metamorphosen for Twenty-three Solo Strings	4

Composition	Recordings Available*
VOCAL MUSIC:	
Operas:	
Der Rosenkavalier	5
Salome	3
Elektra	2
Arabella	1
Ariadne auf Naxos	1
Songs (150)	C

HECTOR BERLIOZ (1803–1869)

Number 21

Anyone who was ever in the same room with Lyndon Baines Johnson knows he was Bigger than Life. It had nothing to do with sound or weak national policy, Republicans or Democrats, foes or friends, conservatives or liberals, civil rights or Vietnam. It didn't even have anything to do with being president of the United States; it was just the same when he was majority leader of the Senate. Lyndon Johnson filled any room the moment he entered it. The sense of power was undeniable—and oftentimes scary. Lyndon Johnson, in person, was a happening. Lyndon Johnson on television was dishwater.

Something of the same feeling is experienced in a concert hall listening to Hector Berlioz's *Symphonie fantastique*. It overwhelms. Whether or not it's your favorite symphony, whether or not you've heard it before, and regardless of the rating it receives from today's professionals, it is a happening. But for the full effect you must hear it live; the feeling isn't captured on recordings. Maybe not dishwater, but the power just isn't there.

Hector Berlioz was the greatest French composer, the finest French symphonist, the first true French Romantic, and a loner leader of the radical side of the Romantic movement. He was also a godfather of the modern orchestra, the epitome of Romantic music-literary synergism, and an early prince of program music—music that tells a story. Beyond that, he was a self-proclaimed heir to Beethoven, a masterful conductor, and, above all, a fiery-tempered rule-breaker and innovator.

PLEASURE AND PARALYSIS

The music people take Berlioz's autobiography with a grain of salt. One writer says the accuracy of this work is not to be trusted since Berlioz had the artistic instinct for lying, which makes a good storyteller. This flamboyance is found in his own description of his reaction to music:

"When I hear certain pieces of music, my vital forces seem at first to be doubled. I feel a delicious pleasure, in which reason has no part; the habit of analysis comes afterwards to give birth to the admiration; the emotion, increasing in proportion to the energy or the grandeur of the ideas of the composer, soon produces a strange agitation in the circulation of the blood; tears, which generally indicate the end of the paroxysm, often indicate only a progressive state of it, leading to something still more intense. In this case I have spasmodic contractions of the muscles, a trembling in all my limbs, a complete torpor of the feet and the hands, a partial paralysis of the nerves of sight and hearing; I no longer see, I scarcely hear; vertigo . . . a semiswoon."

If you believe that, cheap waterfront real-estate plots are available for you.

Berlioz was born in Isère, a mountainous part of France southwest of Geneva. His father was a well-to-do doctor and something of a scholar, who taught his son Latin and interested him in Virgil, the author of the *Aeneid*. He also gave him a flute, a guitar, and piano

lessons. Young Hector liked the flute and became reasonably proficient with it, but—surprisingly for a Romantic composer—was not
much of a pianist.

Although he tried a little composing in his youth, the family game
plan was for him to have a medical career like his father. At age
eighteen he was sent to Paris to study. But this was Paris, and his time
was divided, he later said, between "hideous corpses and enchanting
dances." Put that way, his choice was rather obviously music. His
family was horrified, and not financially supportive, but he entered the
Paris Conservatory anyhow. As time passed he gave music lessons,
sang in a theater chorus, and picked up a few francs here and there by
performing various musical chores. By 1825 he had managed to put on
a church performance of his *Solemn Mass*, a work written for an
orchestra of more than 150 performers—three or four times normal
size. One newspaper commented: "The young and seething composer
pays more attention to his own inspiration than to the narrow rules of
counterpoint and fugue."

His career breakthrough came in 1830, at age twenty-seven, when
he was awarded the Prix de Rome, which gave him a stipend and a
chance to live and work in that city.

However, for much of the rest of his life his main income came
from music journalism—criticism, reviews, and articles. A good bit of
his writing related to his own compositions as he attempted to drum
up an audience capable of understanding and appreciating his own
radical works. As the years passed he became recognized as perhaps
the greatest music critic of his time, and as a solid conductor, but
not—during his life—as an outstanding composer.

Toward the end of his life Berlioz conducted his music in the
capitals of Europe (in part because it was difficult to get anyone else to
do so) while continuing to make his living reviewing music by other
composers who were relative nonentities. He composed nothing in his
last seven years.

It is sometimes said that three men represented the core of Romanticism: the writer Victor Hugo, the painter Eugène Delacroix, and
Berlioz. Berlioz was an experimenter from early on. This is not surprising since both the mighty Beethoven and the great Haydn were alive
and flourishing when he was born. Beethoven, in fact, not only lived
until Berlioz was in his midtwenties but was still busily composing
until the last. Rebellion must have come easily for composers who
looked up at those giant figures and whose choice was to better them
at their game or to find a new playing field not yet occupied. Like
another nonconformist musical artist one hundred years later, Berlioz
wanted to do it his way.

One who placed him in the most rarefied company was Mussorgsky of Russia, who wrote: "In poetry there are two giants: coarse Homer and refined Shakespeare. In music there are two giants: the thinker, Beethoven, and the superthinker, Berlioz." The prestigious critic Ernest Newman wrote of him: "All modern programmists [composers of program music] have built upon him—Liszt, Richard Strauss and Tchaikovsky. Wagner felt his influence, though he belittled it. . . . [Berlioz's] own words, 'I have taken up music where Beethoven left it,' indicates his position. He is the real beginner of that interpretation of music and the poetic idea which has transformed modern art."

It was not until after World War II that the music of Berlioz was rediscovered—one might even say discovered—by the general music world. Earlier, even among the avant-garde, it was Wagner who had the audience, the attention, and the disciples, not lone-wolf Berlioz. Wagner appreciated him; in 1860 the German composer said openly that there were only three living composers worthy of note: himself, Liszt, and Berlioz. (Wagner omitted Verdi, and by this time Schumann, Mendelssohn, and Chopin were dead). But a hundred years or so were to pass before Berlioz and his far-out music received the appreciation they now have.

WAGNER ON BERLIOZ, LISZT, AND HIMSELF

Pleased by an article Berlioz published on one of his compositions, Richard Wagner wrote Liszt about the genius he, Liszt, and Berlioz shared:

"Berlioz's article, especially, had once more clearly shown me how lonely the unfortunate man is; and that he too has such sensitive and deep feelings that the world can only hurt him and misuse his wounded irritability; that the world and the influences of his environment lead him wonderfully astray, and can so estrange him from himself that, unknowingly, he deals himself blows. But exactly because of this queer phenomenon, I realized that great talents must, to be properly recognized, have only very great talents for their friends; and this afforded me the insight that, in the present period, we alone are on a par; that is—You—He—and I!—But this is the last thing one can tell him: he'll lash out, if he hears it. Poor devil: such a plagued god!"

In his biography of Wagner, professor Ronald Taylor notes that Wagner probably envied Berlioz's superior skill in orchestration and was perhaps put out because Berlioz was just as much a nonconformist as he and had equally bitter fights with the musical establishment.

Taylor continues: "Both were iconoclasts, *enfants terribles* to their contemporaries; both were drawn to Goethe and wrote works on his Faust, and both shared an enthusiasm for Shakespeare; and although they were both active as conductors for their own and other composers' works, neither of them was an instrumentalist. Above all, both, in a way easier to sense than to define, have something of the uncut diamond about them."

Berlioz did not write symphonies numbered one, two, and three. He wrote symphonies called *Fantastic*, *Harold in Italy*, and *Romeo and Juliet*. The volcanic *Symphonie fantastique* (the composer called it the "immense symphony"), composed in 1830 when he was twenty-six, is his most famous work. His last major composition was the opera *Beatrice and Benedict*, patterned after Shakespeare's *Much Ado about Nothing* and held by the music people to be a lesser work than his earlier compositions. Like Schubert and many others, he was not considered a supercomposer during his life and died lonely and disappointed, as revealed in his memoirs: "I have neither hopes nor illusions nor great thoughts left. My son is nearly always absent. I am alone. My contempt for the stupidity and meanness of men, my hatred of their detestable ferocity are at their height. And I say hourly to death, 'When you will.' Why does he delay?"

This was not a happy camper. The program he wrote for *Symphonie fantastique* reads, in part: "A young musician of morbid sensibility and ardent imagination in a paroxysm of love-sick despair has poisoned himself with opium. The drug, too weak to kill, plunges him into a heavy sleep accompanied by strange visions. His sensations, feelings, and memories are translated in his sick brain into musical images and ideas. The beloved one herself becomes for him a melody, a recurrent theme that haunts him everywhere."

The "recurrent theme" Berlioz referred to is one he had written to tie together the five movements, the theme changing according to the mood and atmosphere of the movements. The idea of recurrent themes was not new to Berlioz; Classical masters had done the same thing. What was new, however, was tying the themes to specific characters or recurring environments in a "literary" sense, tracking the program of the music. This was a real groundbreaker. Wagner, as we have seen, was to carry this to new heights with his use of leitmotifs.

VIVIDNESS AND REALISM

Esteemed musicologist Ernest Newman has written:

"All Berlioz' music, whether that of the painting of a scene or that of psychological probe—and he has achieved some marvels in the latter field—has the quality of controlled objectivity that is the antithesis of the northern ecstatic mystical swoon; it is the seeing of things as they appear and are, not as one would fain persuade oneself they are by calling in speculation and metaphysic to supplement the evidence of the eye."

The grim program of *Symphonie fantastique* was born out of Berlioz's despair because of the unreturned love he had for an English Shakespearean actress named Henrietta Smithson. A rumor that she had become engaged threw him into a wild rage and caused him to revise the symphony to symbolize the treachery of his beloved. A mild problem was that he was not her beloved. He had instantly fallen in love with her upon seeing her as Ophelia in Paris in 1827. They did not speak the same language, and he tried unsuccessfully as a Stage Door Johnny to see her and deluged her with love letters that disturbed and terrified her. Finally he even arranged a special concert of his own works to impress her. He was so smitten that he failed to realize she was not even aware that the concert had taken place.

Five years later, after other love affairs, Berlioz found that Henrietta had returned to Paris, and he became emotionally involved again, arranging another special performance of the *Symphonie fantastique* for her. This time she did attend, with a sister. Berlioz later wrote in his memoirs:

On entering her box in front of the stage, she found herself in the midst of an immense orchestra, and an object of interest to the whole room. So astonished was she at the unprecedented murmur of conversation of which she was plainly the object, that without being able to account to herself for it, she was filled with a kind of instinctive terror, which moved her powerfully. . . . When I came in panting and sat down beside [the conductor], Miss Smithson, who until then had doubted whether she were not mistaken in the name at the head of the program, saw and recognized me. "It is the same," she said to herself. "Poor young man. No doubt he has forgotten me. I hope that he has." The symphony began and created a tremendous effect. This success and the passionate character of the work were bound to produce, and did in fact produce, an impression as profound as it was unlooked for upon her.

Miss Smithson was not doing well financially at the time, Berlioz did woo and win her (at one point trying to commit suicide in front of her to show his love), they were married in 1833 at the British Embassy in Paris—and they did not live happily ever after. After many emotional brawls they separated, and he found a new lover. Years later, after she had become an invalid, he treated her tenderly, but upon her death in 1853 he married the woman he had been seeing in the interim. Sadly, that marriage was a failure as well.

As an innovator, Berlioz did things with orchestration that had never been done before. One twentieth-century master has pointed out that until Berlioz's time composers used instruments in order to make them sound like themselves, whereas Berlioz mixed the instrumental tones and colors to produce new results. The critics say that he was daringly original, that he defied convention, that he had boundless audacity—that, in fact, he was one of music's most original figures. And he was always on the lookout for literary properties he could turn into music.

BERLIOZ: CAST OF THOUSANDS

In 1845 Berlioz agreed to a concert in Lyons. He described his demands in a letter to the concert arranger:

"I should want to give a concert in Lyons only if we can do something unusual: by raising the prices, by scattering posters in neighboring towns, such as Chalons, Macon, Vienne, Bourgoin, Nantua, Bellay, etc., and by placarding all the steamboats on the Rhone and the Saone, we should take in nine or ten thousand francs; if this is utopian, let us forget the whole thing; it is not worth stirring up all your musical world of Lyons to obtain only average results. Besides, I am so weary of rehearsals, this drill-sergeant life has wrecked me so at Marseilles that it will require a great effort to take it up again.

"For the program I should like to present I shall need: 34 violins at least; 10 violas; 11 cellos; 9 double basses; 2 flutes; 2 oboes; 1 English horn; 2 clarinets; 4 bassoons; 4 horns; 2 natural trumpets; 2 cornets; 3 trombones; 1 ophicleide in C; 2 tympanists; 1 cymbal player; 1 bass drum; 1 triangle; 1 tambourine.

"Plus, for a piece for 2 orchestras: 4 first clarinets in B flat; 4 second clarinets in B flat; 1 small clarinet in E flat; 1 third flute; 1 piccolo in D flat; 2 horns; 2 trumpets; 2 ophicleides, 1 in C, 1 in B flat; 3 trombones; 2 oboes; 4 drummers.

"And lastly, a chorus of 80 men (or 70) and 20 women (or 30).

"A singer (basso cantante) and some other, a woman soloist to complete the program, offering one or two arias of her choice. For each performer of the large orchestra there should be one section rehearsal and two general: for the Military band one would be enough, two at the most. The choruses would have to work in proportion to their lack of facility or the reverse.

"Please find out, my dear Mr. Hainl, whether this is possible and at the same time whether the poor will agree to collect only a tenth, as they did at Marseilles and as they invariably do at my concerts in Paris.

"Curiosity will no doubt be lively enough among my fellow townsmen (as I am almost from Lyons) for a rather full house to be plausibly counted on. Let us take advantage of this as well as we can and give the concert soon, for my time is limited."

There are many examples of the wide-ranging literary interests that began with his exposure to Virgil: The overtures *Waverly* and *Rob Roy* were from Walter Scott; the dramatic legend *The Damnation of Faust* from Goethe; *Harold in Italy*, a program symphony, and *The Corsair*, an overture, from Byron; the overture *King Lear*, the dramatic symphony *Romeo and Juliet*, and the opera *Beatrice and Benedict* from Shakespeare; and the opera *Les troyens* from Virgil.

Berlioz, who really should have been a Texan, thought big. His *Requiem* (mass for the dead), written in 1837, and his *Te Deum* (hymn of praise), written in 1849, were both scored for giant instrumental assemblies. To depict Judgment Day in the *Requiem*, he ordered up a huge orchestra plus four brass bands, one facing east, one west, one south, and one north. And, though it never came to pass, he envisioned an orchestra of 450 with a chorus of 350. He wanted 242 strings, 30 pianos, 30 harps, and a couple of hundred wind and percussion instruments. This was an original fellow.

Although he lived until age sixty-five, most of his best-known works were created by the time he was forty. One exception, which he wrote at age fifty-one, is the oratorio *L'enfance du Christ*, not generally put at the level of Handel, Haydn, and Mendelssohn oratorios, but still on the best-of-oratorios lists.

During his most productive, younger years, Berlioz created:

Symphonie fantastique, 1830;
Harold in Italy, a symphony for viola, 1834
Romeo and Juliet, a symphony, 1839;
Symphonie funèbre et triomphale, 1840;
Roman Carnival Overture, 1844;
Corsair Overture, 1844;
The Damnation of Faust, a "dramatic legend," 1845;
Marche funèbre pour la dernière scene d'Hamlet, 1848.

The *Symphonie fantastique* sums up the composer and his musical life. In addition to having a recurring theme to unite the movements, it differed from symphonic convention by having five movements instead of the usual four. It had a program, a story told through music, which also flouted symphonic tradition. The tone qualities of the orchestral instruments were explored in new ways that, the experts say, helped make this symphony an original work of historic importance.

Mr. Originality. Not Mr. Perfection, but Mr. Originality.

Berlioz's popularity, like that of most composers on The List, has risen and fallen over the years. But his originality has never been questioned. As he often has done, professor Joseph Machlis put it in perspective: "There is some dispute among musicians as to the ultimate value of what he heard, but none can gainsay that it had never been heard before."

STARTER KIT

The first choice is *Symphonie fantastique* (subtitled "An Episode from the Life of an Artist"). Its five movements are called: "Revery and Passion," "The Ball," "Scenes in the Country," "March to the Gallows," and "Witches' Sabbath." Berlioz's program for the last movement reads:

> He [the hero] sees himself at a witches' sabbath, surrounded by a host of fearsome specters who have gathered for his funeral. Unearthly sounds, groans, shrieks of laughter . . . The melody of his beloved is heard, but it has lost its noble and reserved character. It has become a vulgar tune, trivial and grotesque. It is she who comes to the infernal orgy. A howl of joy greets her arrival. She joins the diabolical dance. Bells toll for the dead. A burlesque of the Dies Irae [the Judgment Day prayer/hymn in a requiem mass]. Dance of the witches. The dance and the Dies Irae combined.

A second choice is *Romeo and Juliet*, 1839, a dramatic symphony for orchestra, soloists, and chorus. Of it the critic B. H. Haggin has written: "The stimulation of Shakespeare's poetry gives us . . . a work whose central sections are the supreme, the incandescent achievements of his [Berlioz's] powers." Toscanini once called the Love Scene in Part 2 the most beautiful piece of music in the world. Berlioz himself considered it his greatest music. And Ernest Newman wrote of the whole work: "His spirit touched to finer issues, he sings, not Berlioz, but humanity as a whole. He is now what every great artist is instinctively—a philosopher as well as a singer."

A third choice, one of his most frequently played pieces nowadays, is the *Roman Carnival* Overture, 1844, originally written as a prelude to the second act of his opera *Benvenuto Cellini*. English-horn freaks love it for one of music's most beautiful passages for their instrument.

A fourth choice is a work for orchestra, soloists, and chorus, *The Damnation of Faust*, written in 1829 and revised in 1846. (Berlioz was not the only Listed composer who was motivated to write music about the legendary Dr. Faust, popularized—though not originated—in 1593 by dramatist Christopher Marlowe in England. Others include the Hungarian Liszt in 1857 with his *Faust* Symphony, Schumann in 1849 with *Scenes from Goethe's Faust*, Wagner in 1844/1855 with a *Faust* Overture, Donizetti in 1832 with a not-too-successful opera, and

Prokofiev in 1923 (revised 1927) with *The Fiery Angel*.) Three popular orchestral selections from *The Damnation of Faust* are "Minuet of the Will-o'-the-Wisps," "Dance of the Sylphs," and the "Rakoczy March," of which Berlioz wrote: "I begin the March with a trumpet passage in the rhythm of the melody, after which the theme itself appears pianissimo in the flutes and clarinets, accompanied by the strings pizzicato. . . . When the crescendo arrived, and fragments of the March were heard amidst the thunder of cannon from the big drum, they woke up; and when the final explosion burst upon them in all the fury of the orchestra, the shrieks and cries which bent the hall were positively terrific, and so extraordinary as fairly to frighten me."

In contrast to the typically volcanic Berlioz work is the fifth Starter Kit choice, the song cycle *Les nuits d'été* (Summer nights). Among the beautiful songs in the cycle are "Au cimetière" and "Surs les lagunes." Critics of Berlioz complain that he was too obsessed with gigantic orchestras, dramatic orchestral color, extravagant flamboyance—the whole Big-Is-Best syndrome. Berlioz buffs cite the loveliness of the songs as evidence of his tremendous originality and his great genius, and as absolute proof that as a musician he could be about anything he wanted to be.

BERLIOZ: THE STARTER KIT

Composition	Recordings Available*
SYMPHONIES:	
Symphonie fantastique	29
Romeo and Juliet	7
OTHER ORCHESTRAL WORKS:	
The Damnation of Faust	4
Overture:	
Roman Carnival	9
VOCAL MUSIC:	
Song Cycle:	
Les nuits d'été	15

*Represents the number of recorded releases available of each listed composition as found in a recent issue of the *Schwann/Opus* catalogue. A "C" indicates that a work is only available collected with other compositions.

BERLIOZ: A TOP TEN

Composition	Recordings Available*
SYMPHONIES:	
Symphonie fantastique	29
Symphonie funèbre et triomphe	3
Harold in Italy	6
Romeo and Juliet	7
OTHER ORCHESTRAL WORKS:	
The Damnation of Faust	4
Overture:	
Roman Carnival	9
VOCAL MUSIC:	
Opera:	
Béatrice et Bénédict	2
Oratorio:	
L'enfance du Christ	3
Church Music:	
Requiem	8
Song Cycle:	
Les nuits d'été	15

BERLIOZ: A MASTER COLLECTION

Composition	Recordings Available*
SYMPHONIES:	
Symphonie fantastique	29
Symphonie funèbre et triomphe	3
Harold in Italy	6
Romeo and Juliet	7
OTHER ORCHESTRAL WORKS:	
The Damnation of Faust	4
Reverie and Caprice for Violin and Orchestra	4
Lelio	3
Overtures:	
Roman Carnival	9
Rob Roy	2
Waverly	2

Composition	Recordings Available*
Corsair	2
King Lear	2

VOCAL MUSIC:

Operas:

Béatrice et Bénédict	2
Les Troyens (including ballet music)	2
Benvenuto Cellini	2

Oratorio:

L'enfance du Christ	3

Church Music:

Requiem	8
Te Deum	3

Song Cycle:

Les nuits d'été	15

CLAUDE DEBUSSY (1862–1918)

Number 22

The Old Order can be changed by revolution or evolution. Revolutions can be violent or, in skilled hands, peaceful. The truly talented revolutionary can bring one off so smoothly that significant changes take place with few people suffering intolerable pain. Igor Stravinsky and his wildly dissonant *Rite of Spring* jammed a musical revolution down people's throats. Claude Debussy kept people calm and peaceful as he dealt in colors and shadows and mist. If Debussy had been in the swimming-pool business, he would have built a freeform pool, never a twenty-by-forty-foot rectangle.

Commonly considered to be the founder of Impressionist music, he was France's second-greatest composer and one of the top creators of piano music. One of the most creative of artists, he represented a major transition from Romanticism to twentieth-century music.

Some would argue that Debussy, rather than Berlioz, is France's all-time finest, and you can still pass Go and collect $200 if you reverse their positions on The List.

Within academia, it has become sort of trendy to walk away from the term *Impressionism* in music. Impressionism was the name of a movement of nineteenth-century French painters, but Debussy himself felt that his work was more influenced by such Symbolist poets as Paul Verlaine and Stephane Mallarmé than by the Impressionist artists. His own favorite painters, in fact, were not Impressionists, and he specifically rejected the use of the term to describe his music. Musicologists today also dislike talking about an Impressionist school, for while Debussy influenced Ravel and several other Listed and unListed composers, none of these considered himself part of a special Debussy-led group.

Hence, despite his new theories of light and color in music, the only true musical Impressionist denied that he was one. Still, for a century now, the notion has persisted that an Impressionist school of music was created by Debussy to parallel the school of painting, so we won't quibble too much about it.

Debussy's objective was to liberate music from past conventions and traditions. "Is it not our duty," he asked, "to find the symphonic formula which fits our time, one which progress, daring and modern victory demand? The century of airplanes has a right to its own music."

Just what kind of music did Debussy create? Verlaine described it this way: "Music before everything else, and to obtain the effect of music choose the asymmetrical rather than the symmetrical, the odd rather than the even, vaguer and more evanescent, unweighted and unresting." Mallarmé, a friend of Debussy's, wrote of this concept of art: "I think there should be nothing but illusion. The contemplation of objects, the fleeting images of the daydreams they excite—these are the song; the Parnassians [a school of French poets more concerned with meter than emotion and imagery] take the thing as a whole and show it to you; hence they are wanting in mystery; they deprive the mind of that delicious job of believing that it is creating."

Verlaine and Mallarmé used words to produce color—choice of words, flow of words, arrangement of words. Monet used paint; Debussy musical tones. Listeners "feel" different tone colors as different instruments play. They "feel" or "sense" most effectively when the artists creating the tones work most expertly. Among composers, none surpassed Debussy in tone-color expertise.

Of the several on The List involved in the transition from Romanticism to twentieth-century music, few were more important than Debussy, who was born a few years before Berlioz died (there was no overlap in their working lives). It has been said that Debussy killed the symphony. While this is something of an overstatement, he did inflict severe wounds upon it. While he wrote famous orchestral works, none was in symphonic form. If Haydn "invented" the symphony, if

Mozart developed it, if Beethoven perfected it, if Schubert and Berlioz experimented with it—still working within its boundaries—Debussy simply turned his back on it, and on its orchestral cousins. He composed no symphonies, concertos, or overtures, having little affinity with or interest in the symmetry they demanded. Other post-Romantic composers maintained symmetry while experimenting with new sounds within the boundaries. Debussy discarded the boundaries.

Debussy was born near Paris, entered the Paris Conservatory at eleven, was a child prodigy at composition, and won (on his third try, at twenty-two) the cherished Prix de Rome. He was most productive in his thirties and early forties, became world famous as the founder of Impressionism in music, and was the hero of a cult of "Debussyists." He suffered from cancer, composed little during World War I, and died in 1918.

The expert view is that Debussy effected a complete revolution in musical art, inventing new ways of associating chords hitherto regarded as "dischords" and using them to produce exquisite harmonies. He broke most conventional rules, making new ones designed to express fleeting sensations and delicate, drifting emotions.

DEBUSSY ON TRADITION

Debussy summed up his own musical approach this way:

"I am more and more convinced that music, by its very nature, is something that cannot be cast into a traditional and fixed form. It is made up of colors and rhythms. The rest is a lot of humbug, invented by frigid imbeciles riding on the backs of the Masters—who, for the most part, wrote almost nothing but period music. Bach alone had an idea of the truth."

One of the wonderful things about listening to Debussy is that one need know nothing about music to find his beautiful. Indeed, for us amateurs, the absence of rule-following is perhaps a blessing. Since he made up his own rules, we are not required to know which are being broken and can just sit back and enjoy.

Several experts who write about Debussy cite this summary description from Henri Prunières, French musicologist (1886–1942):

"He was the incomparable painter of mystery, silence and the infinite, of the passing cloud, and the sunlit shimmer of the waves—subtleties which none before him had been capable of suggesting."

Compared with other greats, Debussy did not write a lot of music. He began producing masterpieces after he had hobnobbed in the cafés of Paris with the Impressionist painters and the Symbolist poets toward the end of the nineteenth century. The works that launched Impressionism began in 1893 with his Quartet in G Minor; the next year brought his single most famous composition, the orchestral prelude he called *L'après-midi d'un faune* (The afternoon of a faun). Its subject is not a *fawn*, fleeing through the woods away from Bambi-killers with their rifles and their bows and arrows, but a *faun*, a mythical figure similar to a satyr, part man and part horse or goat or the like. Among compositions he completed over the next several years were the song cycle *Chansons de Bilitis* and three nocturnes for orchestra, all well known today. The nocturnes, finished in 1899, are entitled "Nuages" (Clouds), "Fêtes" (Festivals), and "Sirènes" (Sirens). Of the first two the composer wrote: " 'Nuages' portrays the unchangeable appearance of the sky, with the slow and solemn march of clouds dissolving in a gray agony tinted with white," and "Festivals" are "rich with movement, rhythm, dancing . . . the festival and its blended music." And of "Sirènes": "The sea and its innumerable rhythms; then amid the billows silvered by the moon the mysterious song of the Sirens is heard; they laugh, and the song passes on." These Sirens belonged to Greek mythology, by the way, not to police cars, and sang to charm mariners to their destruction.

In this period, too, Debussy began writing his only opera, *Pelléas et Mélisande*, by far his most ambitious undertaking. Ten years passed before he completed it—and when produced it created another of music's pro-and-con brawls, with severe reactions on both sides. The liberals shouted that it was French opera "genius," and the traditionalists maintained that it was (a) not opera and (b) not much of anything.

The controversy came from the fact that the French Debussy, in direct reaction against the operas of the German Wagner, consciously avoided drama, pathos, and emotional pitch. This was an Impressionist opera, filled with symbolism, mysticism, and what the experts have called "incorporeal transparency." As one might expect from incorporeal transparency, the plot is a wee bit difficult to find and follow.

His largest orchestral work is *La Mer* (The sea), written in three "sketches" (Debussy did not use the term *movement*) and completed in 1905. Over the next few years came three more orchestral pieces called *Images* (not to be confused with another set of *Images* composed for

SKINS AND HELMETS

A good Frenchman, Debussy disliked Germans, as Frenchmen are wont to do, and complained loudly that the French
were too easily influenced by "the tedious and ponderous
Teuton." One colorful quotation illustrates his reaction to
Wagner's *Ring* cycle: "The idea of spreading one drama over
four evenings! Is this admissible, especially when in these four
evenings you always hear the same thing? . . . My God! how
unbearable these people in skins and helmets are by the fourth
night." Dismissing the *Ring* cycle, however, was not quite the
same as dismissing its creator, and Debussy acknowledged
Wagner's genius and influence.

the piano): "Iberia" (the best known of the three), "Gigues," and
"Rondes de Printemps."

The music people say that Debussy's contribution to twentieth-
century piano music compares with Chopin's contribution to nineteenth-century piano music. Just before World War I he wrote two
sets of preludes, twelve in each set, which came to be regarded as
landmarks of piano composition. One critic said of them in midcentury: "No one since Chopin so changed the character and technique
of piano writing as did Debussy. . . . The new colors, nuances, effects,
atmosphere created by Debussy—largely through his harmonic writing and a new approach to resonance—brought an expressiveness of
the keyboard it did not know even with Chopin and Liszt."

Other piano music includes *Suite bergamasque*, known chiefly for
the next-to-last movement, the famous Impressionistic picture of night
"Clair de lune."

Debussy was a melodist, but a different kind of melodist. The
experts note that his melodies are not the phrase-long melodies of
Classical music and that he does not repeat and develop the short
motives of Romantic composers. Instead, Debussy used short melodic
fragments that fit together like pieces of stained glass.

He is considered one of the finer songwriters, though his songs are
totally different from German *lieder*, showing instead the same sort of
vague, shimmering, elusive quality typical of the rest of his music.
Among his better-known songs are "Beau soir," "Mandoline," "Ro-

MUSICIANS, IMAGES, AND COWS

Among Debussy's best-known works are two sets of *Images* for the piano, the first dating from 1905. When he and his publisher were corresponding between different rural vacation sites, Debussy commented on these works and on musicians as contrasted with cows:

"Have you played the 'Images' . . . ? Without false vanity, I believe that these three pieces carry themselves well and that they will take their place in the piano literature . . . to the left of Schumann, or to the right of Chopin . . . as you like it.

"All my compliments for the admirable cows at the Bel-Ebat estate, and what a fine house in the background. How much more agreeable it must be to associate with all this than with musicians!

"Give me your news very soon and believe in the affection of

Claude Debussy."

mance," "Fantoches," "Les cloches," "Harmonies du soir," and "La chevelure." The song cycle *Chansons de Bilitis* is set to words by Pierre Louÿs.

Debussy was a gentleman who liked the ladies, without grave concern as to their marital status. For several years he adored Madame Vasnier, an older married woman, wife of a friend; for a decade or so he lived with Gabrielle Dupont, whom he called "Gaby of the green eyes"; and later he was married to a dressmaker he called "Lily-Lilo," whom he abandoned for Emma Bardac, the wife of a wealthy banker. Heartbroken Lily-Lilo then tried to commit suicide; Debussy's friends turned away from him and, curiously, he could not quite understand why. "I have never seen so many desertions around me!" he wrote. "Enough to be forever disgusted by anything that bears the name of man. . . . I have suffered greatly morally." After a double divorce, the poor sufferer did marry Emma, to whom he was apparently devoted, and remained with her for the rest of his life. Various of his works are dedicated to one or another of his lady loves. *The Afternoon of a Faun* and the three lovely Nocturnes came during the "Gaby of the green eyes" period.

STARTER KIT

Since Debussy wrote no symphonies, concertos, or overtures and only one opera (which some say is not really an opera at all, however well done), the Starter Kit includes some orchestral things, some pianistic things, and some song things.

On the orchestral side, a mandatory choice is the *Prelude to the Afternoon of a Faun*, a dreamy piece set to a poem by the composer's close friend Mallarmé. It was totally different, stylistically, from any piece heretofore composed, so much so that some experts give it a place in history comparable to Beethoven's *Eroica* Symphony and Monteverdi's *L'Orfeo*. It is hard to think of music more different from this misty piece than the work coming out of Germany at this time by the two Richards, Wagner and Strauss. Some years later the famous Russian dancer, Vaslav Nijinsky, used the music for a scandal-causing ballet.

The poet Camille Mauclair recalled the initial reception to the original composition:

> I was present near Mallarmé, who was my initiator and my teacher, and whose indulgent affection and infinite kindness toward me in the beginnings of my career will remain the honor of my life. And we returned struck with consternation by the hisses of a public which denounced this music as lacerating the ears, this music so volatile that one scarcely hears its adorable murmuring!
>
> And what a revenge, afterwards when the ovations given "L'après-midi" in all the concerts of the world are numberless. Through them the name of Mallarmé will remain inseparable from that of the musician who so marvelously understood his mystic and sensuous vision of the Ancient World.

Another choice is the composer's biggest orchestral work, the three-part *La mer* (The sea), not quite as popular as the much shorter *Faun* but also frequently performed. And a third is the set of three works that make up the orchestral Nocturnes—"Nuages," "Fêtes," and "Sirènes." Either think about musical impressions of drifting clouds, festival merrymakers, and enchantresses luring sailors to their death, or else just listen to the beautiful music.

For the piano, a "must" recommendation is "Clair de lune," from *Suite bergamasque*, and for vocal music the song cycle *Chansons de Bilitis*.

DEBUSSY: THE STARTER KIT

Composition	Recordings Available*
ORCHESTRAL WORKS:	
Three Nocturnes for Orchestra:	25
Nuages	
Fêtes	
Sirènes	
Prelude to the Afternoon of a Faun	35
La Mer	31
PIANO MUSIC:	
Clair de lune (from Suite bergamasque)	21
VOCAL MUSIC:	
Song Cycle:	
Chansons de Bilitis	8

*Represents the number of recorded releases available of each listed composition as found in a recent issue of the *Schwann/Opus* catalogue. A "C" indicates that a work is only available collected with other compositions.

DEBUSSY: A TOP TEN

Composition	Recordings Available*
ORCHESTRAL WORKS:	
Three Images for Orchestra:	9
Gigues	
Iberia	
Rondes de printemps	
Three Nocturnes for Orchestra:	25
Nuages	
Fêtes	
Sirènes	
Prelude to the Afternoon of a Faun	35
La Mer	31
Danses Sacrée et Profane for Harp and Orchestra	16
CHAMBER MUSIC:	
Quartet in G Minor	11

Composition   *Recordings Available**

PIANO MUSIC:
Preludes (two books)   13
Clair de lune (from Suite bergamasque)   21

VOCAL MUSIC:
Opera:
    Pelléas et Mélisande   4
Song Cycle:
    Chansons de Bilitis   8

DEBUSSY: A MASTER COLLECTION

Composition   *Recordings Available**

ORCHESTRAL WORKS:
Three Images for Orchestra: 9
    Gigues
    Iberia
    Rondes de Printemps
Three Nocturnes for Orchestra: 25
    Nuages
    Fêtes
    Sirènes
Ballet:
    Jeux   5
Prelude to the Afternoon of a Faun   35
Danses Sacrée et Profane for Harp and Orchestra   16
La Mer   31

CHAMBER MUSIC:
Cello Sonata in D Minor   12
Quartet in G Minor   11

PIANO MUSIC:
Reverie   5
Preludes (two books)   13
The Children's Corner   6
Clair de lune (from Suite bergamasque)   21
Arabesques   8
Images for Piano, Books 1 and 2   10
Estampes   11

Composition	Recordings Available*
OTHER INSTRUMENTAL MUSIC:	
Syrinx for Flute	11
Sonata No. 1 in D Minor for Cello and Piano	8
Sonata No. 3 in G Minor for Violin and Piano	8
VOCAL MUSIC:	
Opera:	
Pelléas et Mélisande	4
Song Cycle:	
Chansons de Bilitis	8

GIACOMO PUCCINI (1858–1924)

Number 23

" 'La Bohème,' even as it leaves little impression on the minds of the audience, will leave no great trace upon the history of our lyric theater," wrote an Italian critic in February 1896, after attending the premiere performance, conducted by Arturo Toscanini.

The Italian writer was not alone in this sentiment, and even today a good many music gurus are not impressed by Giacomo Puccini. He writes tearjerkers. He is much too sentimental, too sweet. His tunes are too obvious. His last acts are weak. He is, they feel, icky.

Not, however, in the eyes of the public. Not *La Bohème* or *Madame Butterfly* or *Tosca*. Those are Puccini's Big Three, with his first huge success, *Manon Lescaut*, and his last, the not-quite-completed *Turandot*, also in the "something special" category. One would need a tabulation of box-office receipts the world over for the past hundred years or so to prove the case, but a strong one could be made that Puccini is the most *popular* opera composer of them all.

He is, basically, a song man and a theater man—a combination that makes him a man born for the opera house, not the symphonic concert hall. Wagner frequently is heard in the concert hall (the personal preference of the author for Wagner *is* there, rather than the opera house, but the author is a declared amateur), and so are Rossini's overtures and Verdi's magnificent *Requiem* . . . but not Puccini. Puccini is theater and sensuous song; melodic melodrama. He is also warm, lucious melody, harmony, and orchestration.

"I love small things," he said. "And the only music I can or will make is the music of small things, so long as they are true and full of passion and humanity and touch the heart."

Puccini is the last-born of the opera composers on The List (Stravinsky, born in 1882, wrote *The Rake's Progress* some twenty-five years after *Turandot*, but he does not qualify as an "opera composer" in the same sense), the last of the Italians, the designated successor to the great master, Verdi, who himself followed famous Italians Rossini and Donizetti, and, as noted, the composer of three of the most popular operas ever written. Puccini ends one long line as Mahler ends another. Much twentieth-century opera has been written and performed, of course, and no one can predict with certainty where Puccini and even Verdi will stand a hundred years from now. (The same statement, of course, could be made about Messrs. Bach, Mozart, and Beethoven—but will not be made here.) Puccini lived and worked through the first quarter of the twentieth century, with his greatest triumph, *La Bohème*, coming just four years before the 1900s began and *Turandot* still incomplete when he died at sixty-five in 1924.

VERDI ON PUCCINI

"I have heard the musician Puccini very well spoken of. I have seen a letter that praises him very much. He follows the modern tendencies, and that is natural, but he remains attached to melody, which is neither modern nor ancient. But it appears that the symphonic element is predominant in him! No harm. Only, one ought to be cautious here. Opera is opera: symphony is symphony, and I don't believe that it is beautiful to write a symphonic fragment in an opera, simply for the pleasure of putting the orchestra through its paces."

Unlike Rossini and Donizetti, Puccini did not dash off operas casually and did not choose, as they did, almost any libretto near at hand, with the primary objective—almost the sole objective—of making lovely, singable music. Instead, he was serious about the text. He worked slowly. Four of his biggest five operas came at about four-year intervals: *Manon Lescaut* was first performed in 1893; *La Bohème* in 1896; *Tosca* in 1900; and *Madame Butterfly* in 1904. Six years later came *The Girl of the Golden West*; eight years thereafter a successful trio of one-act operas, *Il trittico*; and finally *Turandot*.

For a view put forth some thirty years ago, I turn to *David Ewen Introduces Modern Music*, in which the author writes of Puccini: "But though he worked with miniatures, his creations are integrated masterworks—unforgettable for their sweet and personal lyricism; for their gentle and tender moods; for their subtlety of harmonic and orchestral writing; for their elegance of style and wonderful sense of the theater; and for their remarkable capacity to project three-dimensional female characters."

Puccini was part of the late-nineteenth-century *verismo* school—he dealt with today's real world in today's real settings, rather than with history, legend, or traditional heroes. *La Bohème* is concerned with starving young artists on Paris's Left Bank in the 1830s; *Tosca* with a brutal Roman police chief, torture, and attempted rape in 1800; *Madame Butterfly* with a Japanese woman who falls in love with and marries an American naval lieutenant in 1900. There are none of Wagner's giants or gods here—and there is little similarity between the tender, feminine melodies of Puccini and the Teutonic sound of Wagner.

The critics note that Puccini's music is "theater" that goes directly to the dramatic point, using whatever style of harmony and melody the composer felt was appropriate. They point out that he sometimes used leitmotifs (see Wagner) to bind the musical framework together, but didn't become carried away by them.

Author Arthur Elson provides a 1915 evaluation, writing of *La Bohème*: "The music has a haunting sweetness, and the plot seems to give the touch of nature that makes the whole world kin."

Puccini was born in Lucca, Italy, on December 23, 1858, the son of a choirmaster and organist, grandson and great-grandson of musicians, none of whom had left Lucca. At seventeen (or maybe eighteen—there is a difference of opinion), he walked thirteen miles to Pisa to attend Verdi's *Aida*. It is said that Puccini the opera composer was then born. A great-uncle helped send him to the Milan Conservatory (which had rejected Verdi) in 1880. His first opera was *Le Villi*, performed in Milan in 1884 and accepted by La Scala, which then com-

THE TOP SEVEN OPERAS

Puccini, Verdi, and Bizet are the composers of the top seven operas that have been performed by New York's Metropolitan Opera. They are:
1. Verdi's *Aida*
2. Puccini's *La Bohème*
3. Bizet's *Carmen*
4. Verdi's *La traviata*
5. Puccini's *Tosca*
6. Puccini's *Madame Butterfly*
7. Verdi's *Rigoletto*

Wagner does not come in until tenth, with *Lohengrin*.

missioned him to write a second opera, *Edgar*, a failure. For a time he lived on beans and onions, in 1890 writing to his brother: "I am sick of this eternal struggle with poverty."

But, beans or not, three years later he wrote *Manon Lescaut*, and the press reported: " 'Manon' is the work of the genius, conscious of his powers, master of his art, a creator and perfector of it. 'Manon' can be ranked among the classical operas. Puccini's genius is truly Italian. His song is the song of our paganism, of our artistic sensualism. It caresses us and becomes part of us."

One Puccini story is rather disturbing. When *Madame Butterfly* was produced in Milan in 1904, Puccini's rivals, jealous of his success, hired a bunch of hooters, hissers, and groaners to attend and disrupt the performance. They did, but the opera survived anyhow. In these civilized times we are fortunate that nothing like this takes place in this country, especially in national political campaigns for the presidency.

Juicy Puccini quotations are not hard to find. He wrote to one friend: "Almighty God touched me with his little finger and said, write for the theater—mind, only for the theater. And I have obeyed that supreme command." With—or despite—God's touch, this was a man who loved gambling and who described himself as "a mighty hunter of wild fowl, opera librettos and attractive women." Puccini once also said for the record: "Just think of it! If I hadn't hit on music I should never have been able to do anything in the world."

In any event, Touched or not, he made several million dollars and lived the Good Life until 1924, dying in Brussels while being treated

LIFE AND TRUTH

Madame Butterfly premiered at La Scala in Milan on February 17, 1900. It was not well received, and Puccini withdrew the score after that first performance. But he wrote to two friends of his continued faith in it as an opera.

"It is I who am right," he told one. "It is the finest opera I have written."

And to the other: "You must have been dismayed at the vile remarks of an envious press. But never fear! 'Madame Butterfly' is full of life and truth, and soon she will rise from the dead. I say it, and stick to it, with unwavering conviction.'"

The next performance was four years later in Brescia, this time to a more appreciative audience.

for throat cancer. Music aside, he was a fairly lazy fellow who had never exhibited talent for anything substantive until he began writing successful operas. But he was not casual in his work. Once he zeroed in on an opera subject, he paid great attention to detail for the sake of authenticity, be it Japanese music for Butterfly or the appropriate church-bell tones for Tosca. And perhaps his greatest genius was his blending of arias, dialogue, action, and orchestral continuity, to produce "theater."

STARTER KIT

Puccini's five best-known operas make up the Starter Kit: Tosca, La Bohème, Madame Butterfly, Manon Lescaut, and Turandot. Some of the most popular arias from the Big Three are:

LA BOHÈME

Act I   "Che gelida manina" (Your tiny hand is frozen), tenor;
           "Mi chiamano Mimi" (My name is Mimi), soprano;
           "O soave fanciulla" (Oh lovely maiden), love duet;
Act II   "Quando m'en vo soletta per la via" (Musetta's waltz song);
Act III   "Donde lieta usci" (Mimi's farewell), soprano;
           "Addio, dolce svegliare," quartet;

Act IV   "O Mimi, tu piu" (Mimi, false one), duet;
            "Sono andati" (the Death Scene), duet.

MADAME BUTTERFLY
Act I   "Amore o grillo," tenor;
            "Spira sui mare" (Cio-Cio San's love song);
            "Viene la sera," duet;
Act II   "Un bel di vedremo" (One fine day), one of the great
                soprano arias;
            "Tutti i fior" (Flower Duet);
Act III   "Addio fiorito asil," tenor's farewell to the house;
            "Tu, tu piccolo Iddio," soprano's farewell to her son.

TOSCA
Act I   "Recondita armonia" (Mario's hymn), tenor;
            "Non la sospiri la nostra casetta," soprano;
            Utterances of Scarpia against Te Deum background
                music;
Act II   "Vissi d'arte" (Visions of art), great soprano aria;
            the Torture Scene;
Act III   "E lucevan le stelle" (The stars shone), tenor;
            Mario's farewell.

Our suggestion for Starter Kit purposes is to try highlights and
collections of arias rather than complete operas, except for videotaped
versions. Operas are show biz and should be seen. Memory-jogging
recordings can then be fun.

PUCCINI: THE STARTER KIT

Composition   *Recordings Available**

VOCAL MUSIC:
Operas:

Tosca	8
Madame Butterfly	6
La Bohème	8
Manon Lescaut	2
Turandot	5

*Represents the number of recorded releases available of each listed composi-
tion as found in a recent issue of the *Schwann/Opus* catalogue. A "C" indicates that a work is only available collected with other compositions.

PUCCINI: A TOP TEN/A MASTER COLLECTION

Composition   *Recordings Available**

VOCAL MUSIC:

Operas:

Tosca	8
Madame Butterfly	6
La Bohème	8
Manon Lescaut	2
The Girl of the Golden West	1
La Rondine	5
Turandot	1
Trio of one-act operas:	
Il Tabarro	1
Suor Angelica	2
Gianni Schicchi	3

GIOVANNI DA PALESTRINA (1525–1594)

Number 24

When Palestrina died, his coffin was placed in a side chapel in the old Church of St. Peter in Rome. On the coffin were the words "Princeps Musicae" (The Prince of Music). In fact, Palestrina was not really Palestrina at all, but Giovanni Pierluigi, born in the Italian town of Palestrina and known by that name. (George Washington, St. Francis, and Cincinnatus sort of did it the other way around.) Few composers have had so many aliases; he was also known as the "Homer of Music" because of the "nobility and stateliness" of his compositions, "the

Catholic composer," "the Upholder of the Sacred Standard," "the High Priest of Sacred Art," and "the Legendary Saint of Music."

In music before Bach, the major figures selected are Palestrina and Monteverdi. There are other famous early composers, near-starters for The List, Honorable Mention challengers, but none of more creative genius than these two Italians.

(To reset the Renaissance time clock: Palestrina is the first-born on The List (c. 1525), preceding by forty-two years the only other sixteenth-century figure who makes it, Monteverdi (1567), and by about 150 years the third earliest, still another Italian, Vivaldi (1678). By Vivaldi's time, however, we are out of the Renaissance and into the Baroque era of Telemann, Handel, Bach, Couperin, and Rameau.)

Except for a few madrigals, Palestrina's whole output was sacred music—and even most of the madrigals were spiritual compositions. Secular music had almost no place in his art. Palestrina's work grew out of the church; it was what one writer called "the flowering of a new religiosity . . . creating a sacred art based on the Catholic principles of universality." Fifty years ago, professor Paul Henry Lang wrote: "In the eyes of many, church music ended with Palestrina and became history . . . . [He] remains one of the greatest geniuses who have graced the arts and letters of all time."

Stories circulated for centuries about how Palestrina alone "saved" music for the Catholic church service. Due in part to Flemish influence, music sung in church was becoming too secular for many Renaissance church figures, and a reform movement undertook to clean up the act. Pope Pius IV summoned cardinals to the Council of Trent in 1562 to see what should be done, with a minority suggesting the possibility of removing from the church all music except the old Gregorian chant. The legend is that Palestrina was commissioned to write a mass as a kind of test case and that the result—*Missa Papae Marcelli* (The Mass of Pope Marcellus)—was so beautiful that it influenced the cardinals to vote in favor of retaining music. According to latter-day musicologists, Palestrina wrote not one mass on this occasion but three, and he was only one of several invited to do so. In any event, *Missa Papae Marcelli* is still regarded as exquisitely beautiful and as the best of Palestrina's works. It is also recognized as the supreme model for polyphonic (counterpoint) settings of the Liturgy—the public rites and services of the Christian church.

Like several others, he makes The List in part for his contribution to music development—in this case, of religious music—as well as for the enduring popularity of his individual compositions.

Palestrina wrote several hundred known works in thirty-three books (published in Germany in the late 1800s) and undoubtedly much more that has not survived. We know of some thirteen volumes of masses, seven of motets, four of madrigals, and others of hymns, lamentations, offertories, magnificats, litanies, etc.

The critics' words for his religious music: "contemplative beauty," "universality," "mysticism," "spiritualism," "aloofness," "serenity."

A CHOIRMASTER'S VIEW

Richard Runciman Terry, a famous choirmaster for thirty years, wrote a profile on Palestrina for Volume I of *The Music Masters*, published some forty years ago. He said:

"It is this fundamental 'rightness' that characterizes Palestrina and gives him unchallenged right to the title with which his contemporaries invested him—'Princeps Musicae.' His personal rectitude is reflected in his music with its crystal clarity and singleness of aim. If we keep that in view we shall see how everything he wrote falls into place as part of one great scheme. His fertility was amazing, as the 33 volumes of his known works testify. Yet amongst the 95 Masses [modern-day scholarship attributes 104 masses to Palestrina], nearly 400 Motets and an almost equal amount of other music, it would be difficult to lay a finger on any single one and say it gave evidence of being thrown off in the mood of the moment. He did not write capriciously or at haphazard. From his great works—such as the Stabat Mater, the Masses 'Ecce Ego Joannes' or 'Dum Complerentur' down to his smallest motet—we see but one aim, the presentation of the liturgical ideal and the subordination of everything else in life to that end."

Giovanni Pierluigi was born about 1525 in the cathedral town of Palestrina, twenty miles from Rome. As a youth he went to Rome to join the choir of the Roman Basilica Santa Maria Maggiore, returning to Palestrina for seven years and serving as choirmaster and organist at the cathedral. His bishop there became Pope Julius III, who brought Palestrina back to Rome as choirmaster of the Julian Choir, a choral body attached to "the person of the Pope," a training ground for the Sistine Choir. In 1554 he dedicated his first book of masses—five in all—to Pope Julius, who honored him by making him a member of the Sistine Choir in the Vatican. This was not quite kosher, since Palestrina was married, and the next pope, appropriately, removed him from it. But he held various other posts in Rome for the rest of his life, as maestro di capella at the Basilica of St. John Lateran (the Cathedral Church of the Pope in his capacity as Bishop of Rome), at St. Maria Maggiore, and, finally, at the Papal Choir.

According to the professionals, Palestrina perfected a style of choral writing that had its origins in the Netherlands in the fifteenth century. While many younger Italian composers were filling their madrigals with dissonances and "anguished outcries" (they were the New Music grunt-and-growl chaps of their day), the voices in Palestrina's music moved "serenely and almost angelically." Palestrina's melodies, the experts say, show his genius at its height—long and flowing, at times floating gently down from high to low and at other times soaring gradually upward.

THE LOVE OF MONEY

Palestrina is known for his incredible output of vocal music, most of it religious. He was also a priest. However neither the production of sacred music nor the priesthood interfered with his fondness for money.

The record tells us that he demanded a prohibitively high salary from two would-be employers, the Emperor Maximilian and the duke of Mantua—both of whom, it is true, were in a position to pay without tapping the public coffers. It also shows us that after taking only minor orders he suddenly married a wealthy widow—having lost his first wife, two sons, and two brothers to an epidemic. After his second marriage he spent a good bit of time managing—and managing well—her financial affairs.

After Palestrina's death, music went in different directions—opera, symphony, chamber music—but his church music continued to be sung. Perhaps more important, according to the experts, it became the basis for the study of counterpoint. It has now lasted for four centuries.

One ardent twentieth-century fan of Palestrina's was Aaron Copland. The great American artist spoke at length about the Renaissance composer in a lecture series at the University of New Hampshire in 1959, comparing him with Beethoven:

> Beethoven seems to be exhorting us to Be Noble, Be Strong, Be Great in Heart, yes, and Be Compassionate. The core of Beethoven's music seems indestructible. What a contrast it is to turn from the starkness of Beethoven to the very different world of a composer like Palestrina. Palestrina's music is heard more rarely than that of the German master; possibly because of that it seems more special and remote. In Palestrina's time, it was choral music that held the center of the stage, and many composers lived their lives, as Palestrina did, attached to the service of the church. Without knowing the details of his life story, and from the evidence of the music alone, it is clear that the purity and serenity of his work reflects a profound inner peace. Whatever the stress and strain of living in sixteenth-century Rome might have been, his music breathes quietly in some place apart . . . . Its homogeneity of style, composed, as much of it was, for ecclesiastical devotions, gives it a pervading mood of impassivity and otherworldliness. Such music, when it is merely routine, can be pale and dull. But at its best, Palestrina's masses and motets create an ethereal loveliness that only the world of tones can embody."

Copland went on to express a point that should be re-emphasized in this road map: "My concern here with composers of the first rank like Bach and Beethoven and Palestrina is not meant to suggest that only the greatest names and the greatest masterpieces are worth our attention."

Few Italian artists are insensitive to the human voice, and Palestrina was certainly no exception. "I have held nothing more desirable," he said, "than that what is sung throughout the year, according to the season, should be agreeable to the ear by virtue of its vocal beauty."

STARTER KIT

The single most famous work of the sixteenth century is the *Missa Papae Marcelli*. One expert wrote that in it "the utmost sensuous beauty is united to a great wealth and subtlety of technical resource, without, however, detracting from the profoundly devotional character of the music."

Our selected Palestrina authority, choirmaster Richard Terry, calls the *Missa Papae Marcelli* "immortal." He says the *Improperia* has appealed to musicians of every generation and every country (including Mendelssohn). He also praises especially the "delightful" *Missa inviolata* and the *Missa ad fugam*, as well as the *Missa sine nomine*, the famous *Missa brevis*, and two other masses published at the same time in 1570, the *Missa ut re mi* and the *Missa l'homme arme*. He speaks of the "perfection" of the brief *Bone pastor* motet, gives a special recommendation for *Tu es Petrus*, and also includes among Palestrina's "great works" the *Stabat Mater* (a stabat mater is music for the sorrows of Mary, mother of Jesus, following him to the Crucifixion) and the masses *Ecce ego Joannes* and *Dum complerentur*.

In addition to the *Missa Papae Marcelli*, the Starter Kit recommendations are the *Missa brevis*, the eight-part *Stabat Mater*, the eight-part *Magnificat* (a magnificat is the Latin version of the Song of the Virgin), and the motet and mass *Tu es Petrus*. There are not scads of Palestrina recordings, however, and aside from *Missa Papae Marcelli*, the best idea is to sample what is readily available, including any madrigals and other masses.

PALESTRINA: THE STARTER KIT

Composition	Recordings Available*
VOCAL MUSIC:	
Masses:	
Missa Papae Marcelli	4
Missa brevis	2
Missa Tu es Petrus	2
Stabat Mater	2
Magnificat	2

*Represents the number of recorded releases available of each listed composition as found in a recent issue of the *Schwann/Opus* catalogue. A "C" indicates that a work is only available collected with other compositions.

PALESTRINA: A TOP TEN

Composition	Recordings Available*
VOCAL MUSIC:	
Masses:	
Missa Papae Marcelli	4
Missa brevis	2
Missa ut re mi	1
Missa l'homme arme	1
Missa tu es Petrus	2
Stabat Mater	2
Litaniae de Beata Virgine Maria	1
Magnificat	2
Motet:	
Bone pastor	1
Jesu Rex admirabilis (hymn)	1

PALESTRINA: A MASTER COLLECTION

Composition	Recordings Available*

VOCAL MUSIC:
(examples from some three to four hundred motets, about one hundred masses, seventy-five offertories, forty-five hymns, and scores of magnificats, litanies, and other pieces of church music):

Masses:	
Missa Papae Marcelli	4
Missa inviolata	1
Missa ad fugam	1
Missa sine nomine	1
Missa brevis	2
Missa ut re mi	1
Missa l'homme arme	1
Missa tu es Petrus	2
Missa ave Maria	1
Missa nascelagioia mia	1
Missa hodie Christus natus est	1
Stabat Mater	2
Improperia	1
Exsultate Deo	1
Litaniae de Beata Virgine Maria	1

Composition	Recordings Available*
Magnificat	2
Hymnus in adventu Dei	1
Hodie Beata Virgo	1
Motets:	
Quam pulchri sunt	1
Peccantem me quotide	1
Bone pastor	1
Ave Maria	1
Hodie Christus natus est	1
Jubilate Deo	1
Jesu Rex admirabilis (hymn)	1

ANTON BRUCKNER (1824–1896)

Number 25

For a country bumpkin at large in sophisticated Vienna, a humble man whose clothes never fit, a composer who proudly conducted his own treasured symphony and turned in humiliation and shock to an emptied hall, a fellow so naive that he tipped the great conductor who had successfully led one of his symphonies, an artist ignored by most of the public and ridiculed by many of the critics for much of his life, Anton Bruckner finally made it big.

Today he is the sixth of the "Magnificent Seven" of Vienna symphonists—the others being Haydn, Mozart, Beethoven, Schubert, Brahms, and Mahler. On our List he is the thirteenth German of the top twenty-five artists.

Today some of the critics' words for Bruckner's late nineteenth-century symphonies are "peaceful," "poignant," "serene," and "noble." While he lived, and for many years thereafter, the more common words were "dull," "pompous," "uneven," and "second-rate."

Like Mahler's, most of Bruckner's acclaim as a composer has come in the last twenty-five or thirty years. But while Mahler was recognized when alive as one of the world's top conductors, Bruckner, in his lifetime, went from disappointment to disappointment. Like Mahler, too, Bruckner was largely a symphonist. But where Mahler's other interest was song, Bruckner's was religious choral work—and he might have concentrated exclusively on vocal music had he not encountered the music of Wagner. Once under the influence of Wagner—and of Liszt—he turned to symphonic orchestral music. And he found a few champions. One was his Vienna disciple, twenty-six years his junior, Mahler himself. Another was Wagner, the composer of Europe (everywhere, at least, but in Verdi's Italy) at the time, who called Bruckner the only symphonist comparable to Beethoven. But Wagner was the object of Bruckner's worship—not too strong a word—and the Wagner claque was feuding with the Brahms claque (deemed by his supporters as comparable to Beethoven), so Wagner's objectivity is suspect.

Wagner was only eleven years older than Bruckner, but music historians tell us that the younger man would stare for hours at the older one in silent worship before screwing up enough courage to approach him. And after hearing Wagner's Parsifal—not as an impressionable, hero-worshiping youth but rather as a mature fifty-seven-year-old—Bruckner is said to have fallen on his knees before Wagner, murmuring, "Master, I adore you." (Wagner, being Wagner, undoubtedly felt this was precisely what he was due, and it can be assumed that he responded with the German equivalent of "So what else is new?")

The son of village schoolteachers, born in Ansfelden, Austria, Bruckner was trained as a schoolteacher himself, attended a music school at thirteen, later began teaching in a mountain village, left to join the faculty of his own music school at twenty-one, and soon thereafter started composing. His first important work was a Requiem in D Minor. After a few years he moved to Vienna and devoted the rest of his life to music. For twelve years he was organist at Linz Cathedral in Vienna, and he eventually became a professor at the Vienna Conservatory.

As a young man he wrote two unnumbered symphonies. His numbered First and Second Symphonies are not often played. Assigning specific dates to many of the symphonies is problematic, since they were often revised and some exist in two versions. The Third, in D Minor, dedicated to Wagner, was first performed in Vienna in 1877—when Bruckner was fifty-three! There are three versions of Symphony No. 4 in E-flat, the Romantic, from 1874, 1880, and 1886. No. 5 in B-flat was written in 1875–1876; No. 6 in A in 1881; No. 7 in E in 1883; No. 8 in C Minor in 1887–1890; and No. 9 in D Minor between 1891 and 1896. Considering all the revisions, it is safe to say that Bruckner's nine symphonies were produced between the ages of forty-two and seventy-two.

The most popular ones today are No. 4, the first to be received reasonably favorably and therefore a very important work for the composer, and No. 8, written a decade later. The competition in Vienna in those years was tough. Wagner was at his peak: *Das Rheingold* was introduced in 1869, *Die Walküre* in 1870, *Siegfried* and *Götterdämmerung* in 1876. And over in the other camp, Brahms's First Symphony appeared in 1876, his Second a year later, his Third six years later, and his Fourth in 1885.

COSMIC SYMPHONIES

A strong Bruckner supporter is Alfred Einstein, internationally renowned musicologist, who called Bruckner "a Romantic of the first order," adding:

"A romantic in so far as he made pure sound the basis of his symphonies, and thereby produced his most harmonious work in his Fourth Symphony, which depends almost entirely on beauty of sound; a symphonist also, whose nine symphonies, in contradistinction to those of Brahms (which are really rooted in chamber music), once more attained the monumental stature of true symphony. Of the four sources of his musical expression—Bach, Beethoven, Schubert, Wagner—the Schubertian certainly flows most abundantly in his symphonies. He had the same spring of primal melodic invention, the same breadth of form. . . . His symphonies breathe once more a cosmic spirit. . . . The simple, rustic 'uneducated' musician was not a great thinker, but a great and sensitive human being, whose battles had been fought within himself, who had known both doubt and joy, despair and exultation, and who had the divine capacity to express what he had suffered in compositions rich in invention and primitive creative power."

Bruckner's lack of sophistication is legendary. Seven years after he completed his Fourth Symphony, on February 20, 1881, the famous Hans Richter conducted its premiere at a Philharmonic concert in Vienna. Later, Richter told this story:

"The thaler [a coin worth a few pennies] is the memento of a day when I wept. For the first time I conducted a Bruckner symphony, at rehearsal. Bruckner was an old man then. His works were hardly performed anywhere. When the symphony was over, Bruckner came to me. He was radiant with enthusiasm and happiness. I felt him put something in my hand. 'Take it, and drink a mug of beer to my health.' It was a thaler."

The story of the country bumpkin and the world-famous conductor has a happy ending. Richter, not wanting to offend the composer, kept the coin and later fastened it to his watch chain. [Editor's note: In 1881 Bruckner was fifty-seven. Some of us who have seen seventy would not consider that to be the age of "an old man." Ripe middle age, perhaps.]

The story is repeated over and over in the music literature, presumably because it offers a miniportrait of the composer always described as simple, awkward, unassuming, pious, half-yokel and half-seer, a villager of peasant stock. He was a superb organist; he was a teacher; he was naive, lonely, and sensitive. Given his temperament, his adoration of Wagner was not a good thing for him, since musical Vienna was an armed camp between the Wagnerites and the anti-Wagnerites, and the most powerful anti-Wagner figure on the scene was Eduard Hanslick, critic for the *Neue freie Presse*. For Hanslick, all who opposed Wagner were friends and all who supported him were enemies. Bruckner was not the kind of man who wanted to take on a Hanslick, nor was he capable of doing so. Robert Bagar and Louis Biancolli report in *The Concert Companion* (1947): "Disciples of Bruckner affirmed that Hanslick lay awake nights 'plotting his [Bruckner's] destruction,' that he tried to have him ejected from the Vienna Conservatory, that he intrigued to prevent performances of his work." Perhaps this was an overstatement, but it is a fact that in the Vienna music world Hanslick was rather a combination of Sam Donaldson, John McEnroe, and a Doberman pinscher.

There is a story that Emperor Francis Joseph once told Bruckner to name any wish and the composer asked the monarch to stop Hanslick from insulting him in print. Musicologists do report one late-in-life Bruckner comment: "I guess Hanslick understands as little about Brahms as about Wagner, me and others. And the Doctor Hanslick knows as much about counterpoint as a chimney sweep about astronomy." Not terribly sharp, not a devastating salvo, but at least one arrow fired in return by the country bumpkin.

One strong defense of Bruckner came after his death from the famous conductor Felix Weingartner, reported by Bagar and Biancolli:

> Think of this schoolmaster and organist, risen from the poorest surroundings and totally lacking in education, but steadily composing symphonies of dimensions hitherto unheard of,

UNPERFORMED AND BROKE: 1875

In a letter written in Vienna in January 1875, Bruckner tells
of his music, his financial woes, and the antics of the anti-
Wagnerian Hanslick:

"My 4th Symphony is finished. I have still improved the
Wagner Symphony (D minor) considerably. Wagner's conductor 'Hans Richter' was in Vienna and told in several circles
how splendidly Wagner speaks of it. Performed it is not.
. . . Brahms appears to have suppressed my C minor Symphony No. 2 in Leipzig. . . . What Hanslick has done to
me. . . .

"I have only the Conservatorium, on which it is impossible to live. Had to borrow money already in September, and
again later, if I did not choose to starve. (700 fl.) No man is
helping me. . . . Fortunately there have come some foreigners
who are taking lessons from me—; otherwise, I should have to
go begging.

"Hear me further: I asked all the chief piano professors for
lessons; they all promised; but except for some few theory
lessons, I got nothing. . . . I would gladly go abroad if only I
could get a sustaining position. Where shall I turn to! . . . My
life has lost all joy and pleasure—in vain and for nothing.
. . . What ought I to do?"

crowded with difficulties and solecisms of all kinds, which
were the horror of conductors, performers, listeners, and critics, because they interfered sadly with their comfort.

Think of him thus going unswervingly along his way
toward the goal he had set himself, in the most absolute certainty of not being noticed and of attaining nothing but failure—and then compare him with our fashionable composers
borne on by daily success and advertisement, who puzzle out
their trifles with the utmost 'raffinerie.' And then bow in
homage to this man, great and pathetic in his naivete and his
honesty. I confess that scarcely anything in the new symphonic music can weave itself about me with such wonderful
magic as can a single theme or a few measures of Bruckner.

Although Symphonies No. 4 and No. 8 are probably the most popular, some of the music people consider No. 7 in E to be Bruckner's masterpiece—his most consistent, his most inspired, the one in which "his aspirations come closest to being met."

Bruckner wrote one of its movements, a funeral march "blending majesty and sorrow," as a tribute to Wagner—not in memory, since Wagner was still alive, but nonetheless as a tribute. "At one time," he said, "I came home and was very sad; I thought to myself, it is impossible that the Master can live long, and then the adagio came into my head."

By the time Bruckner died, he had become an honorary doctor of the University of Vienna and had been honored by Emperor Francis Joseph. But applause was a long time coming, and few stories in music are sadder than the account of the premiere of his Third Symphony, under his direction. Most of the audience, including a director of the Vienna Conservatory, first laughed and then departed during the performance, until only a dozen or so remained. One was Mahler, devoted disciple. The composer's shock at turning to await applause, but instead finding an emptied room, is heart-tearing. With tears streaming down his cheeks, he brushed off his few supporters, saying, "Let me go. The people don't want to know anything about me." (After such experiences, he sort of rates today's fine recognition, as something of a revenge of the nerds.)

But he kept working, despite his defeats, in large part because he was deeply religious and knew that God expected him to do his best. Once he said: "When God calls me to Him and asks me: 'Where is the talent which I have given you?' Then I shall hold out the rolled-up manuscript of my 'Te Deum' and I know He will be a compassionate judge."

The Te Deum was only one of his choral works that are much praised today; others include his Mass in E Minor and Mass in F Minor. He also composed several other masses, some motets, a requiem, and some psalms. He wrote almost no chamber work, one example being a viola quintet begun in 1878 and completed the next year—just sixteen years after he had been asked to compose it by a director of the Vienna Conservatory!

The professionals indicate that there is too much of the organist in nearly all of his work, especially the symphonies. His melodies can be lovely; his structure, according to the music people, often leaves a good bit to be desired if compared with the supergreat. It is pointed out in the literature that his last wish was to be buried beneath the organ that he had played so long at the St. Florian monastery chapel,

PERFORMED AND JUBILANT: 1886

In a letter to a noble patron, Bruckner shows his joy at some success and his feelings toward Wagner:

"High-born Lord!
"Most Noble High Patron!
"A thousand thanks for Your Lordship's gracious visit; it grieved me deeply that I did not know of it and that I could not return the visit but, especially, that I had to miss Your Lordship's excellent speech.

"The highly ingenious letter, so flattering to me, made me very happy! My deepfelt thanks! The poem is splendid! Unhappily, I am buried in the 8th Symphony now and have hardly any time to compose. On the 14th inst. I was in Graz, at the performance of my 7th Symph. The performance, under the ingenious Dr. Muck from Würzburg, [was] excellent (14 rehearsals), the reception magnificent beyond all description. After the finale they welcomed me with trumpets and kettledrums.

"On the 21st inst. the same performance [sic] in Vienna by the Philharmonic, under Richter's direction, was quite excellent: the success—indescribable jubilation; 5 or 6 curtain calls, already after the first movement, and tempestuous ones at that. At the conclusion, endless enthusiasm and curtain calls; laurel wreath from the Wagner Society and banquet. The Sublime, immortal unequaled Master's picture was hung round my neck with the wreath. Very thoughtful indeed; I made it the starting point of my speech and could not help weeping bitterly; next morning too, when I received from Dresden, through my pupil Dr. Behn who is here from Germany, my dearly beloved Master's and Ideal's bust, which I smothered with kisses, weeping.

"Still, the 'five hostile papers' will see to the annihilation of this success with the distant public, at Hanslick's request!

"With gratitude and the deepest respect,

"Your High-born
"Lordship's most obliged"

with "some cynics maintaining that he was buried under this instrument long before he was dead."

Author-critic Harold C. Schonberg wrote of him:

> The scherzo movements of the Bruckner symphonies often use Austrian dances, and these too involve [religious] belief. Mozart's third movements evoke the court; Haydn's the peasants; Beethoven's the gods at play. But Bruckner's evoke some kind of religious ideal involving nature. The religiosity of Bruckner's nine symphonies (and, of course, of his Masses and other religious choral music) suggests to his admirers a kind of message that is allied to the Infinite. Even unbelievers can find themselves carried away by the simple conviction of the man.

STARTER KIT

For a composer whose fame rests almost entirely on symphonies, it is fitting that the Bruckner Starter Kit consist almost entirely of symphonic works. Apart from symphonies, he largely wrote religious work, and the fifth choice is representative of this.

The best-known symphony, and the one most praised by the most critics, is No. 4 in E-flat, called *Romantic* for no apparent reason except that some Bruckner colleagues were urging him to give it that name. This is a happy work, and an enjoyable one.

A second recommendation is Symphony No. 7 in E, written in 1883, inspired by Wagner's imminent death, and one of the most melodious of the nine symphonies (or the eleven, counting the first two, which Bruckner did not number). A third choice is No. 8 in C Minor, 1887–1890, a massive creation, longer than any but the Fifth; and the other symphonic selection is the last, No. 9 in D Minor, not finished, without a fourth and final movement—but with a gigantic, solemn third.

Bruckner himself, dying, may have suggested that the final Starter Kit choice, his *Te Deum,* was supposed to be used as the fourth movement of the Ninth Symphony, and sometimes conductors go that route—but not usually. The theory arises because he includes some opening music of the *Te Deum,* composed first in 1881, in sketches for a final movement of the Ninth. Most critics consider it an improbable theory, but given the choral conclusion of Beethoven's Ninth, it persists. The massive *Te Deum* itself is scored for soloists, chorus, orchestra, and organ.

BRUCKNER: THE STARTER KIT

Composition	Recordings Available*
SYMPHONIES (OF NINE):	
No. 4 in E-flat	16
No. 7 in E	9
No. 8 in C Minor	12
No. 9 in D Minor	10
VOCAL MUSIC:	
Sacred:	
Te Deum	9

*Represents the number of recorded releases available of each listed composition as found in a recent issue of the *Schwann/Opus* catalogue. A "C" indicates that a work is only available collected with other compositions.

BRUCKNER: A TOP TEN/A MASTER COLLECTION

Composition	Recordings Available*
SYMPHONIES (OF NINE):	
No. 4 in E-flat	16
No. 7 in E	9
No. 8 in C Minor	12
No. 9 in D Minor	10
CHAMBER MUSIC:	
Viola Quintet in F	1
VOCAL MUSIC:	
Sacred:	
Te Deum	9
Masses:	
No. 1 in D Minor	1
No. 2 in E Minor	2
No. 3 in F Minor	2
Motets/Songs	C

GEORG TELEMANN (1681–1767)

Number 26

Question: "Who was the best-known and most respected composer of the early 1700s?"

Answer: "Mr. Bach."

Wrong.

Next answer?

"George Frideric Handel."

Wrong again.

New Question: "Who was the first choice to be cantor of St. Thomas Church in Leipzig, who turned it down, forcing the administration to turn to a 'mediocre' second choice, Johann Sebastian Bach?"

Answer: "I don't want to play this game any longer."

Georg Philipp Telemann is not the most familiar name on The List—and, indeed, a short time ago may have vied with Gluck and perhaps Couperin, Rameau, and one or two others as among the least familiar. Despite an increased recent popularity, the odds are still good that he is less well known to the public than other composers of the top thirty on The List. But nearly three hundred years ago he was the most respected musician of his time—far more so, in fact, than his now-illustrious contemporaries, Bach and Handel.

It may be comforting for amateurs to know that many professionals say it takes an expert to identify the composers of much Baroque music. Distinguishing Baroque from Romantic music is one thing; distinguishing among individual Baroque composers to identify the creator of a specific concerto grosso is quite another. After a few listenings, one learns to recognize individual Bach *Brandenburg* Concertos, perhaps especially No. 2 and No. 3. But to listen to a more obscure Bach composition and declare with confidence, "Ah! That is

Bach!'' is another thing altogether. I cannot, and it's nice to know that neither can many semipros.

Telemann was an incredibly prolific composer, with more than three thousand works to his name. Known in his day as "the Father of Sacred Music" (Palestrina held a similar title 150 years earlier), he was the first composer to produce complete cycles of cantatas for all Sundays and feast days of the year. Because we have to rely on record keeping of 250 to 300 years ago, no one is certain exactly how many compositions of what types he created; reports vary from twelve to twenty complete cantata cycles; nineteen to forty passions; twenty to forty operas; forty serenades; more than six hundred miscellaneous instrumental pieces; seventy to one hundred arias—and much more.

THE PROLIFIC RADICAL

The professionals admire Telemann because they see him as a major link between Baroque and Classical music. Some see him as a radical, looking for the new and different, ready to experiment, bringing fresh ideas to the stodgy German style. As one example, he did away with the basso continuo—the practice of using an organ or harpsichord to play chords to fill in the harmonies suggested by the cello. He also is admired because he wrote so much for so long, beginning at age ten and not stopping until he was eighty-six in 1767.

He was born in Magdeburg, Germany, was largely a self-taught musician, attended Leipzig University, organized a music society, and in 1721 became music director of five churches in Hamburg, where he stayed for the rest of his life, with occasional trips to Paris and Berlin. In 1722 he turned down an offer to be cantor at St. Thomas Church, thus opening the door for the second choice, a capable albeit slightly younger man named J. S. Bach. "Since the best man could not be obtained," said a city councilor, "mediocre ones would have to be accepted." Oh well. A United States Senator from Nebraska said not too many years ago that mediocrity had a right to be represented on the Supreme Court, so why not settle for a Bach in Leipzig?

An eighteenth-century editor, surveying the field, had this to say in comparing Telemann with other composers:

"A Lulli fame has won; Corelli may be praised,
"But Telemann alone above all else is raised."

Not Shakespearean, perhaps, but it makes the point.

Romain Rolland, in *A Musical Tour through the Land of the Past*, wrote of Telemann:

"But who is this old man, who with his nimble pen, full of a pious enthusiasm, enchants the Eternal Temple? Listen! How the waves of the sea are roaring! How the mountains cry aloud with joy and sing hymns unto the Lord. How harmonious an 'Amen' fills the devout heart with a sacred awe! How the temples tremble with the pious shout of Alleluia! Telemann, it is thou, thou father of sacred music."

That's pretty strong stuff. Trembling temples are not an everyday occurrence, at least not off the San Andreas Fault—especially when the composer causing them to tremble was a lawyer by training, having studied law at the University of Leipzig before turning to music. According to the professionals, his music is characterized by simple harmonies and highly ornamented melodies, and he brought fresh air to the music of Germany at the time. He was a friend of Mr. Bach, indeed, a godfather to one of the many Bach children, as well as a correspondent of Handel.

In the early years of the eighteenth century, Telemann served as Kapellmeister to a count in Poland, and the folk music he heard there impressed him greatly. Writing about that time, he later said: "An attentive observer could gather from these folk musicians enough ideas in eight days to last a lifetime."

His music is usually described as intelligent and delightful. Some of us would add boring. He is one of three or four composers on The List who would be unListed quickly if these were personal favorites of the author rather than representatives of a research effort. One Telemann concerto grosso a month just about does it for me. For readers who have the same reaction to Telemann, my advice is to strike him from The List and substitute Sergei Rachmaninoff.

In contrast to the high esteem in which Telemann was held in his lifetime and a significant revival of that opinion of his worth over the last few decades, a music book published in 1925 disposed of him in one line, lumping him with two unListed composers and saying, " . . . but without Handel's genius for melody and sublimity, their music was rarely heard after their own generation had passed away." But now a *Schwann/Opus* recordings guide lists some three and a half pages of Telemann works—not neccessarily a measure of the composer's excellence, but a sound indication of his popularity.

SUGGESTED SUBSTITUTE: RACHMANINOFF

Born in Russia in 1873, Sergei Rachmaninoff studied at the Moscow Conservatory, became famous within Russia by the turn of the century as a composer, conductor, and virtuoso pianist and toured the United States for the first time in 1909. He didn't like the Russian Revolution of 1917 and from then on he lived in Switzerland and the United States. He died in California in 1943.

If you like emotional, moving, sentimental Tchaikovsky, it is probable that you'll like Rachmaninoff, one of the most important men of Russian music before World War I. He was general manager and conductor of the Grand Theater in Moscow for several years before going into seclusion in Dresden to devote himself to composition.

His music has not gone away, although he has been dead half a century and the critics are not excited by his work. Neither were most of his contemporary critics. He was viewed as an ill-tempered, self-indulging, self-pitying melancholic—technically adroit and melodic, but without true musical substance. But some others saw him as a connecting link between Impressionism and "futurism" and praised his imaginative creativity.

We surely would have him on a list of the next 50, and we offer him as an acceptable substitute for Telemann—or, farther down the List, for Vivaldi.

For his Starter Kit: His Piano Concerto No. 2 in C Minor, Piano Concerto No. 3 in D Minor, Piano Preludes in C-sharp Minor (Op. 3, No. 2) and G Minor (Op. 28, No. 5), the Symphony No. 2 in E Minor, and his fifteen-movement *Vespers*, written in 1915. To these could be added a Cello Sonata in G Minor, Piano Sonatas No. 12 in D Minor and No. 2 in B-flat Minor, the *Symphonic Dances*, and his Piano Concerto No. 4 in G Minor.

Telemann wrote three autobiographies, in addition to his composing and his other musical work. He was a rebel of his time, open to new ideas from Italy, France, or wherever, and a student of the past as well, picking the brains of other composers and developing their ideas.

"One should never say to art: 'Thou shalt go no farther,' " he wrote. "One is always going farther and one should always go farther."

Those who thought otherwise, he said, were "fossils."

The music people point out that, unlike Bach's music, a great deal of Telemann's cantata work was published in his lifetime. It was extremely popular because it was smooth, transparent, uncluttered, lively, and gracious. This fit beautifully with the prevailing taste of both connoisseurs and the general public.

Some of Bach's compositions circulated in manuscript copies, and some people recognized his genius, but he was a church musician, with the great majority of his works being vocal compositions for the church. Telemann's style was the popular one of the times; Bach's vocal church style was considered peculiar and entirely opposed to the Italian models that were most admired. Bach was an organist performer, a highly admired technician, an acknowledged master of counterpoint. Telemann was beloved.

STARTER KIT

The wise approach to Telemann, as to a few others, is to familiarize yourself with his *kind* of composition rather than to zero in on specific selections. Some of the distinctions between orchestral works and chamber music are a bit arbitrary in any case, since the sizes and combinations of the orchestra and the chamber ensemble varied so in those days.

Sticking to the Starter Kit regulations, however, one choice is his Suite in A Minor for Flute and Strings, probably his single most popular work today—although in part this is due as much to the popularity of the flute and individual flutists as to supporters of Telemann. Other recommendations are for the Concerto in D for Trumpet and Strings; Concerto in G for Viola; Concerto in D for Three Trumpets, Two Oboes, and Orchestra; and Concerto in F for Three Violins and Orchestra. (Telemann played the oboe skillfully and wrote a good deal of music for it.)

But if you have difficulty tracking down these works, try some others. Better (probably) to do that than to ignore this artist—and maybe, if you're interested enough, one day you can begin to say to the car radio, "This is a Telemann, not a Bach or a Handel." It is not, however, at all necessary to acquire this skill.

The professionals tell us that his keyboard music, especially, was written in the "gallant" style, which was the musical version of rococo painting and sculpture. Couperin, the French composer who comes later on The List, was one of the leading proponents of this kind of music, which made its way to Germany and captured Telemann and his godson, Carl Philipp Emanuel Bach. Our Mr. Bach perfected good, solid counterpoint. "Gallant" music was—as the name suggests— lighter, more graceful, and more elaborate.

TELEMANN: THE STARTER KIT

Composition	Recordings Available*
CONCERTOS AND CHAMBER MUSIC:	
Concerto in D for Three Trumpets, Two Oboes, and Orchestra	4
Concerto in F for Three Violins and Orchestra	4
Concerto in D for Trumpet and Strings	8
Concerto in G for Viola	6
Suite in A Minor for Flute and Strings	15

*Represents the number of recorded releases available of each listed composition as found in a recent issue of the *Schwann/Opus* catalogue. A "C" indicates that a work is only available collected with other compositions.

TELEMANN: A TOP TEN

Composition	Recordings Available*
CONCERTOS AND CHAMBER MUSIC:	
Concerto in D for Three Trumpets, Two Oboes, and Orchestra	4
Concerto in F for Three Violins and Orchestra	4
Overture in D	4
Concerto in D for Trumpet and Strings	8
Concerto in G for Viola	6
Concerto in G for Two Solo Violas and Strings	3
Concerto in E-flat for Two Horns and Strings	4
Suite in A Minor for Flute and Strings	15
Trio Sonatas	11
Fantasies for Flute (twelve)	15

TELEMANN: A MASTER COLLECTION

Composition   *Recordings Available**

CONCERTOS AND CHAMBER MUSIC:

Concerto in D for Horn and Orchestra	3
Concerto in D for Three Trumpets, Two Oboes, and Orchestra	4
Concerto in F for Three Violins and Orchestra	4
Concertos for Flute and Orchestra	5
Overture in D	4
Concerto in D for Trumpet and Strings	8
Concerto in G for Viola	6
Concerto in G for Two Solo Violas and Strings	3
Concerto in E-flat for Two Horns and Strings	4
Musique de Table (suites)	7
Suite in A Minor for Flute and Strings	15
Trio Sonatas	11
Fantasies for Flute (twelve)	15
Concerto in D for Trumpet, Two Oboes, and Continuo	3
Concerto in B-flat for Two Flutes, Two Oboes, and Strings	C
Concerto in E-flat for Oboe	C
Concerto in D for Oboe d'amore	C
Double Concerto in E Minor for Recorder, Flute, and Strings	C
Triple Concerto in D for Trumpet	C
Oboe Concerto in C Minor	C
Concerto in C for Four Violins	C
Concerto in D for Four Violins	C
Concerto in G for Viola	C
Suite in A Minor for Recorder and Strings	C

VOCAL MUSIC:

Cantatas, including:	
Du aber, Daniel, gehe hin (funeral cantata)	C

CAMILLE SAINT-SAËNS (1835–1921)

Number 27

The nice thing about Camille Saint-Saëns's music is that it sounds the way classical music is supposed to sound. It is "correct"—many say "impeccable"—but never stuffy. Saint-Saëns was an intellectual and something of a Renaissance man: child genius, writing music at age three and analyzing it at seven; piano prodigy; premier organist (arguably the finest of his time); author of books on painting, philosophy, literature, and the theater; revered conductor; and incredibly prolific and talented composer.

He was not explosive, like Berlioz, nor spiritual, like Franck, nor "profound," like his German contemporaries. Liszt, a friend and colleague in early years, said he was the world's greatest organist—no small compliment from the world's finest pianist. His works include four tone poems, influenced by the Liszt-Wagner cabal, but he also has been called "the High Priest of Absolute Music." Though not the only composer to have had an AC/DC relationship with program/absolute music, he was one of the few who excelled in both.

At the outset he was, like Liszt, a progressive. He was an experimenter, pro-Wagner and later an early admirer of Impressionist Debussy. But he lived to be eighty-six, grew more conservative as the years passed, continued to produce a great deal of music, and eventually found Debussy too modern.

What he lacked most was fire in the belly. The critics note that his works show the most characteristic qualities of the best French music: logical construction, lucidity, frankness, euphony, masterful workmanship. He knew exactly what he wanted and how to express himself to achieve it.

His best-known piano concerto is No. 2 in G Minor, composed in 1868. Saint-Saëns sent it to Liszt for criticism, and the great pianist replied: "The form of it is new and very happy. . . . Pardon me this detailed remark, dear Monsieur Saint-Saëns, which I venture to make only while assuring you in all sincerity that the totality of your work pleases me singularly."

Berlioz was not an admirer, once saying of Saint-Saëns: "He knows everything, but he lacks in experience."

Often not the most courteous of composers, Saint-Saëns was outspoken about his disregard for Franck's music. And when yet another contemporary was elected before him to membership in the Institut in Paris and sent him a gracious telegram saying, "My dear colleague, the Institut has made a terrible mistake," Saint-Saëns immediately responded, "I entirely agree with you."

He has been called a French Mendelssohn, a composer who never lived up to his genius, skilled but not passionate, elegant but not volcanic, witty but not inspired, a perfectionist but not an emotional perfectionist. One critic wrote that he did not have the rugged power of a Berlioz nor the mystic fervor of a Franck, but that he did have an incredible blend of remarkable, hard-to-describe elements that made him very special.

One of Saint-Saëns's best-known works is the spectacular grand opera *Samson et Dalila*, a melodic and charming three-act production first performed in 1877. It took him some nine years to write and was poorly received at first, but later it became popular and is still praised by some professionals—although other critics prefer his operas that the public has not liked.

Saint-Saëns wrote five symphonies; four orchestral tone poems; a dozen operas; five piano, three violin, and two cello concertos; oratorios; piano fantasies; much chamber music; and more than one hundred songs, none highly acclaimed. His best-known program music is *Danse macabre*, his third symphonic poem, in which skeletons leave their graves at midnight and dance about, bones rattling, until the cock crows at dawn. Its main melody is a morbid march. Another famous orchestral piece—and a much more cheerful one—is *Carnival of the Animals*, for two pianos and orchestra, which features elephants, kangaroos, and a cuckoo, and which contains perhaps the best-known melody written for solo cello, "The Swan." In it he also takes on music critics, which must have been refreshing to a thousand other composers who would have liked to. Another frequently played Saint-Saëns piece is the *Introduction and Rondo Capriccio* for violin and orchestra.

By founding the Société Nationale de Musique in Paris, and through his own compositions, Saint-Saëns was a big player in reviving French orchestral music after the 1870 Franco-Prussian War. All

CREATIVE CRUMB

One composer who was not impressed by the miniatures created by Saint-Saëns was Modest Mussorgsky.

"Who is this M. de Saint-Saëns?" asked that powerful and unpolished artist in 1875, when Saint-Saëns was coming to Russia to conduct some of his works. "One knows of him partly from the papers, partly from conversations. What does M. de Saint-Saëns do?—he utilizes a miniature chamber orchestra and attains with it such solidity that he shows in rich orchestral powers tiny little thoughts inspired by a tiny versifier, and calls this crumb 'Danse macabre.' . . . This is no matter for brains. And why did these brains throw themselves into symphonic program music? One hears that the brains have brewed an opera entitled 'Samson': evidently propaganda for female labor ('coupe de cheveux')—and will have to be forbidden in Russia. I don't trust M. de Saint-Saëns' 'Samson' any more than I do 'his innovator's toys.' It's not merely music, words, palette, and chisel that we need—no devil take you, you liars and dissemblers 'e tutti quanti'—give us living thoughts, having living talks with people, whatever 'subject' you've chosen! You can't fool us with sweetish sounds: the lady luxuriously passes the box of bonbons to her 'dear friend,' and that's all. You, master of orchestral powers, M. de Saint-Saëns, you—creative crumb, you are so omnivorous that you derive pleasure from various trios, quartetti, quintetti, etc., arithmetically. M. de Saint-Saëns, innovator! With every bit of brain in my skull—I deny him; with all the strength in the beating of my heart—I push him aside! A utilizer of miniatures, what business of ours is he!"

four of his symphonic poems—*Danse macabre, Le rouet d'Omphale, Phaeton,* and *La jeunesse d'Hercule*—were written for concerts of the Société. Other composers associated with it included Franck and Ravel. And among Saint-Saëns's many pupils was Fauré. Romain Rolland wrote that Saint-Saëns's Société Nationale de Musique was "the cradle and sanctuary of French art. All that has been great in French music from 1870 to 1900 came out of it."

The critics agree that Saint-Saëns is very good indeed and rates high, even though they seem to have problems deciding quite why.

Nearly everything he did in music was done well, with honor and integrity, although he produced no single sensational masterpiece.

MATA HARI

Saint-Saëns was a friend of the seductive Dutch dancer shot by the French as a spy, Mata Hari. Our research does not indicate how good a friend.

The son of a French government employee, he was born in Paris, did all of his astounding prodigy things, entered the Paris Conservatory at thirteen, won prizes for organ and composition, became organist of a small church in Paris, and, at twenty-two, was named organist at the Madeleine Church, one of Paris's most famous. He remained there for more than twenty years, was elected to the Institut at forty-six, and lived on for many years, acquiring honors, writing music, enjoying respect, being liked and admired, teaching, working hard, editing music of other masters, and touring as a concert pianist. Aside from music, he studied astronomy and physics; he wrote poetry and a play; he devoured literature; and he spoke several languages. Saint-Saëns had a high-class mind. He suffered tragedy, losing two children within weeks and later walking out of his marriage, and his disposition was less than ideal, but he was a musician of considerable talent.

He once wrote: "The artist who does not feel completely satisfied by elegant lines, by harmonious colors, and by a beautiful succession of chords, does not understand the art of music." That wouldn't fly today.

STARTER KIT

The two most performed works of Saint-Saëns are his Symphony No. 3 in C Minor, called the *Organ* Symphony, and the symphonic poem *Danse macabre*. The symphony was written in 1886, the symphonic poem in 1874.

A brief quote from Saint-Saëns about his symphony gives us a glimpse into the composer's creative process: "The second movement begins with an energetic theme which is followed immediately by a third transformation of the initial theme in the first movement, more agitated than it was before, introducing a fantastic mood that is frankly

SAINT-SAËNS ON DEBUSSY

A Debussy biographer, Oscar Thompson, tells of an article written in 1911 by Saint-Saëns and aimed particularly at Debussy. "He noted ironically how under the new dispensation everyone was to be free to make his own rules, how there was no such thing as a dissonant chord, or even a common chord, much less a wrong chord; how any combination was legitimate . . . and this . . . is what they call developing one's sensibility!"

disclosed in the presto. . . . The phrase rises to orchestral heights and rests there as in the blue of a clear sky. . . . The initial theme of the first movement, completely transformed, is now played by divided strings and the pianoforte (four hands) and repeated *by the organ* (emphasis mine) with the full orchestra."

The *Danse macabre*, with Death tuning his fiddle and bones rattling (played by the xylophone), turned off some prudes at the time, but it is scarcely in today's heavy-metal category.

The *Carnival of the Animals*, a work for two pianos and orchestra, is one of the most fun and most popular pieces of music (although Saint-Saëns did not like it and refused to have it performed during his lifetime). Included also in the Starter Kit, for variety, is the most popular of his five piano concertos, No. 2 in G Minor, written in less than three weeks in 1868 and dedicated to Liszt. The final recommendation is for one of his two cello concertos, in part because there are not all that many respected cello concertos in the literature. The more popular of the two is No. 1 in A Minor, first performed in 1873. (The professionals consider his Violin Concerto No. 3 in B Minor to be the best of his concertos, although it is not the most frequently performed—perhaps because of the considerable competition in the violin concerto field.)

The choices would not please some critics who complain that Saint-Saëns is best known for his "weaker" music—*Samson et Dalila*, "The Swan," *Danse macabre*—and not for his Septet for Piano, Trumpet, and Strings; his Violin Sonata in D Minor; and his Piano Quartet in B-flat. All of these are on our Master Collection list, so you can substitute the favorites of the experts for the most popular—or collect both. The violin sonata is, indeed, beautiful. Opera lovers should sample music from *Samson et Dalila* in any case.

SAINT-SAËNS: THE STARTER KIT

Composition	Recordings Available*
SYMPHONIES:	
No. 3 in C Minor (Organ)	20
OTHER ORCHESTRAL MUSIC:	
Danse macabre (symphonic poem)	19
Carnival of the Animals (including "The Swan" for solo cello)	13
Cello Concerto No. 1 in A Minor	10
Piano Concerto No. 2 in G Minor	10

*Represents the number of recorded releases available of each listed composition as found in a recent issue of the *Schwann/Opus* catalogue. A "C" indicates that a work is only available collected with other compositions.

SAINT-SAËNS: A TOP TEN

Composition	Recordings Available*
SYMPHONIES:	
No. 3 in C Minor (Organ)	20
OTHER ORCHESTRAL MUSIC:	
Danse macabre (symphonic poem)	19
Le rouet d'Omphale (symphonic poem)	8
Carnival of the Animals (including "The Swan" for solo cello)	13
Introduction and Rondo Capriccioso for Violin and Orchestra	13
Cello Concerto No. 1 in A Minor	10
Piano Concerto No. 2 in G Minor	10
Havanaise for Violin and Orchestra	9
KEYBOARD, CHAMBER, AND SOLO INSTRUMENTAL MUSIC:	
Piano Quartet in B-flat	1
VOCAL MUSIC:	
Opera:	
Samson et Dalila (complete or excerpts)	1

SAINT-SAËNS: A MASTER COLLECTION

Composition	*Recordings Available**
SYMPHONIES:	
No. 3 in C Minor (Organ)	20
OTHER ORCHESTRAL MUSIC:	
Danse macabre (symphonic poem)	19
Carnival of the Animals (including "The Swan" for solo cello)	13
Introduction and Rondo Capriccioso for Violin and Orchestra	13
Cello Concerto No. 1 in A Minor	10
Violin Concerto No. 3 in B Minor	7
Piano Concerto No. 2 in G Minor	10
Piano Concerto No. 4 in C Minor	7
Piano Concerto No. 5 in F	2
Le rouet d'Omphale (symphonic poem)	8
Havanaise for Violin and Orchestra	9
Allegro appassionato	5
CHAMBER MUSIC:	
Piano Quartet in B-flat	1
Septet in E-flat for Piano, Trumpet, and Strings	2
OTHER INSTRUMENTAL MUSIC:	
Sonata No. 1 in D Minor for Violin	4
Sonata No. 1 in C Minor for Cello and Piano	2
Sonata for Clarinet and Piano	3
Sonata for Oboe and Piano	5
Sonata for Bassoon and Piano	6
VOCAL MUSIC:	
Opera:	
Samson et Dalila	1

JEAN SIBELIUS (1865–1957)

Number 28

"How," asked one critic, "could the composer of 'Valse Triste' be taken seriously?"

First, even San Francisco's Joe Montana and Virginia's Thomas Jefferson had some bad days.

Second, the same composer is Finland's greatest symphonist, assessed as sometimes heroic, sometimes majestic, often "pure in spirit," sometimes subtle, usually original.

Third, a symphonist need not have the dimension of a Brahms or a Beethoven to be taken very seriously indeed. Even Byron wasn't Milton.

The only Finn on The List and one of two northerners, along with Grieg of Norway, Jean Sibelius is a twentieth-century composer who does not fit easily into one niche. He was an intense nationalist and an ardent patriot, but not a user of folk music in the sense of a Rimsky-Korsakov, a Borodin, a Mussorgsky, a Smetana, a Janaček, or a Vaughan Williams, all of whom borrowed folk rhythms and worked from folk scales. Sibelius just made his music *sound* like original folk pieces. Though he lived until midcentury, he is not in the "New Music" category of Stravinsky, Prokofiev, Shostakovich, Bartók, and Hindemith. Though he was a nationalist, his later works are not nearly as heart-of-Finland as his more famous earlier ones. And, though most of his compositions are far from New Music, one symphony displays some early twentieth-century modernist tendencies. One of the most peculiar things about him is that he did not write a note after 1929 even though he lived until 1957.

He was, and is, unquestionably a Finnish national hero—perhaps *the* Finnish national hero, with his own postage stamp, a special government pension, and other rewards befitting national stardom. The issue of whether Sibelius was a genius is not raised by a wise visitor to Finland. Outside of Finland, however, critics have never known quite what to make of him. Indeed, "Valse Triste," *the* hit tune of its day many decades ago, is considered mawkish and sentimental nowadays, and there is general agreement among professionals that it is not outstanding music. (It was originally sold to two Leipzig publishers for 300 marks as incidental music for a play, *Kuolema,* written by Sibelius's brother-in-law.) One current assessment suggests that Sibelius "deserves an honorable place among the minor composers." On this List, twenty-seven composers are ahead of him. Whether that constitutes high-among-minor or low-among-major is uncertain.

BRAHMS SAID NO

Sibelius was a big fan of Tchaikovsky's—although not all Finns love all Russians—and an admirer of the orchestration genius of Richard Strauss. Strauss was only a year older than Sibelius but became known and respected as a musician several years before Sibelius did. At one point Sibelius, armed with strong letters of recommendation, attempted to study under Johannes Brahms in Vienna. The crusty Brahms, however—no Liszt as an encourager of fellow artists, although he did help Dvořák and some others—would have none of it. Sibelius had to settle for his Finnish countryside and his love of Finnish mythology.

In any event, today's appraisal is much better than the one the composer received from some earlier critics. One compared him to "a spare, knotted barbarian from the world of the sagas . . . one who might have been comrade to pelted warriors who fought with clubs and hammers, who might have beaten out a rude music by black smoking hearthsides."

Fortunately, not everyone over the years has shared that elitist opinion of epic Finnish music.

Another rather negative view came in 1940 from Virgil Thomson, composer and music critic for the *New York Herald Tribune,* who called Sibelius's Second Symphony "vulgar, self-indulgent and provincial beyond description." Be that as it may, one does note that Mr. Sibelius's symphony has lasted very well indeed into the later years of the century—which cannot be said of Mr. Thomson's newspaper, however excellent it once was. In the 1940s the American radio audience, responding to a CBS poll, voted Sibelius its favorite classical composer. Whether these were the same people who later gave *Dallas* its high television ratings is unknown, but classical music on radio is not really akin to soap opera on television.

More important, there are those who believe that the seven Sibelius symphonies, all different from one another, give him a fair claim on the title of this century's greatest symphonist, perhaps sharing that honor with Vaughan Williams of England, and not overlooking Prokofiev and Shostakovich. Each decade seems to produce a different view of Sibelius, which is fair enough. And, as in any assessment, each assessor looks for different things and approaches the judgment with his or her own prejudices.

Notwithstanding the public's admiration of his symphonies, and particularly its support of the First and Second, Sibelius became world famous not from these works but from his tone poems, which are made of Finnish legends and heroes—and of pine trees, fire, ice, snow, and winds. The most famous of these, at one time more beloved in Finland than was its national anthem, is *Finlandia*, written in 1899 when czarist Russia was prohibiting free speech in Finland and ruling it with the czarist foot of a General Bobrikov. Conceived as a musical symbol of freedom, the work not only swept Europe but got the Finns so charged up when they heard it at home that Russia banned it. Later, as the Finns fought for and gained independence, it became the national rallying point for Finnish freedom. It is in the same category as Tchaikovsky's *1812* Overture—hailed by the public but not accepted as magnificent by the professionals (although not deemed as unmagnificent as "Valse Triste").

Other nationalist tone poems include his first, *En Saga*, written in 1892, and the famous and lovely *Four Legends*, inspired by a famous Finnish epic called the *Kalevalá* and bearing wonderful names: *The Swan of Tuonela, Lemminkäinen's Return, Lemminkäinen and the Maidens*, and *Lemminkäinen in Tuonela*. Sibelius described the color of *The Swan of Tuonela* in these words: "Tuonela, the Kingdom of Death, the Hall of Finnish mythology, is surrounded by a broad river of black water and rapid currents, in which the Swan of Tuonela glides in majestic fashion and sings." The experts note that it is virtually a concerto for English horn, and even if your name is Callaghan or McTavish you will feel Finland when you hear the *Four Legends*. Or

WILL IT PLAY IN PEORIA?

Sibelius's first important work, and the one in which Finnish national music first emerged, was his tone poem *En Saga*. The composer explained how it came about:

"Robert Kojanus [unListed Finnish composer] once pointed out to me how desirable it would be to have a piece by me in the regular repertory of the orchestra, written for the general public and not making too great demands on their powers of concentration and comprehension. This would be an advantage both for the orchestra and for my popularity as a composer, Kojanus said. I was not at all disinclined to write a piece in a more popular style. When I got to work, I found that some notes I had made in Vienna were suitable for adaptation. In this way, 'En Saga' appeared."

when you hear *Tapiola*, another tone poem, to which Sibelius attached these words: "Wide-spread they stand, the Northland's dusky forest; ancient, mysterious, brooding savage dreams. Within them dwells the forest's mighty god, and wood-sprites in the gloom weave magic secrets." This music offered sounds in the mid-1890s that no one had ever heard before.

Sibelius was born in Tavastehus, Finland, the son of an army doctor. His interest in music began early; he enrolled in the Finnish Model School at eleven, began studying violin at fourteen, went to Helsingfors University to learn law, shifted entirely to music within the year, attended the Musical Academy, and then traveled to both Berlin and Vienna for further study. Returning to Helsingfors, he taught music and played the violin in a string quartet.

The case has been made that Sibelius belongs more to the nineteenth century than the twentieth. His melodies and harmonies are largely traditional; for the most part his work ignored the new concepts of melody, harmony, and tonality that were developing around him. The music people say that his early style echoed nineteenth-century German composition, with some Tchaikovsky thrown in. Later he was pure Sibelius, with a particular mastery of tone color, including the dark colors that seemed to come from his native land. Sibelius was generally conservative compared with such contemporaries as Bartók, Stravinsky, Debussy, and the unListed Schoenberg, although some of his symphonies, especially the Fourth, break a rule or two. Nonetheless, Sibelius is not a quack-and-growl composer.

DOLEFUL MUTTERINGS

While not the most popular with concert audiences, the most acclaimed Sibelius symphony today may be the "bold" (a favorite word of record reviewers) Fourth in A Minor. When it was published, a Boston critic called it an assembly of "dissonant, doleful mutterings, generally leading nowhere."

Seven Listed composers lived to be at least eighty-five, with Sibelius the most long-lived of all. Vaughan Williams and Richard Strauss died at eighty-five, Telemann and Saint-Saëns at eighty-six, Verdi at eighty-seven, and Stravinsky at eighty-eight. Several of the others kept composing actively until very late along. Not so Sibelius, who lived until he was ninety-one.

In the last third of his life, he did not compose a note. This was in spite of the fact that at age thirty-two he had been granted 3,000 Finnmarks a year by the Finnish Senate, allowing him to spend as much time writing music as he chose. He did compose for another three decades, but then stopped completely while still in his sixties. Some critics say he was just tired, or worn out. Others believe he simply was not willing to cope with the twentieth-century atonal music of his contemporaries. Maybe he just had more fun doing other things. In any case, despite his silence of thirty years, he had a long and creative career.

STARTER KIT

The problem here is deciding which and how many of the seven symphonies to include. Two have been selected, plus two tone poems and, for variety, a lovely violin concerto. The symphonies are No. 1 in E Minor and No. 2 in D, composed in 1899 and 1901–1902, respectively. This is the pair that is most popular with the public, although some critics have considered them too indulgent, dramatic, and emotional—basically the same criticisms leveled at Tchaikovsky, another heart-on-his-sleeve symphonist of greater genius. Sibelius himself acknowledged the Tchaikovsky influence. The first symphony is classified as solidly Romantic, the second as fervently nationalistic. Many professionals say that the two early symphonies do not begin to equal the maturity and development of Symphony No. 4, which is more "restrained" and less "stirring," more "introspective," "severe," "bleak," and "compact"—and much more unconventional in harmony, nodding toward turn-of-the-century "New Music." Symphony No. 7, his last, is considered the most majestic by some critics, and more experimental in form than his others. Interestingly, some connoisseurs favor the Fifth, and some the Sixth. It's a grab-bag.

SIBELIUS ON THE PIANO

"I dislike the piano: it is an unsatisfactory, ungrateful instrument, an instrument for which only one composer, Chopin, has succeeded in writing perfectly, and of which only two others, Debussy and Schumann, have had an intimate understanding."

Finlandia is, of course, a must, as quintessential Sibelius. While there were allegations that the composer had borrowed Finnish folk melodies for this work, he denied this to a biographer, Rosa Newmarch, saying: "There is a mistaken impression among the press abroad that my themes are often folk melodies. So far I have never used a theme that was not of my own invention. The thematic material of 'Finlandia' and 'En Saga' is entirely my own."

The second tone poem in the Starter Kit is one of the *Four Legends: The Swan of Tuonela*, written in 1893, twice revised, and inspired by the Finnish epic *Kalevalá*. It is the third in the four-part cycle. Actually, the tone poems are short enough so that all four should be collected and counted as one entry. The fifth recommendation is the Violin Concerto in D Minor, published in 1905. One commentator heard in it "the settled melancholy of a Finland of Northern darkness, where the sea heaves blindly to the shore and human lives blossom only briefly and precariously to the job of melody." It is romantic, melodious, and sentimental, whether or not one realizes life is blossoming only briefly. Not one of the three or four top-rated violin concertos, it is nonetheless wonderful to listen to.

SIBELIUS: THE STARTER KIT

Composition	Recordings Available*
SYMPHONIES:	
No. 1 in E Minor	7
No. 2 in D	16
OTHER ORCHESTRAL WORKS:	
Violin Concerto in D Minor	12
Tone Poems:	
Finlandia	19
Swan of Tuonela (from the Four Legends)	12

*Represents the number of recorded releases available of each listed composition as found in a recent issue of the *Schwann/Opus* catalogue. A "C" indicates that a work is only available collected with other compositions.

SIBELIUS: A TOP TEN

Composition	Recordings Available*
SYMPHONIES:	
No. 1 in E Minor	7
No. 2 in D	16
No. 5 in E-flat	11
OTHER ORCHESTRAL WORKS:	
Violin Concerto in D Minor	12
Tone Poems:	
Finlandia	19
Swan of Tuonela (from the Four Legends)	12
Tapiola	7
Karelia Suite	13
Valse Triste (from Kuolema)	12
CHAMBER MUSIC:	
String Quartet in D Minor	4

SIBELIUS: A MASTER COLLECTION

Composition	Recordings Available*
SYMPHONIES:	
No. 1 in E Minor	7
No. 2 in D	16
No. 3 in C	5
No. 4 in A Minor	9
No. 5 in E-flat	11
No. 6 in D Minor	5
No. 7 in C	6
OTHER ORCHESTRAL WORKS:	
Violin Concerto in D Minor	12
Tone Poems:	
Finlandia	19
En Saga	4
Four Legends:	3
Lemminkainen and the Maidens	2
Lemminkainen in Tuoenela	2
Swan of Tuonela	12
Return of Lemminkainen	5
Tapiola	7
Pohjola's Daughter	6
Karelia Suite	13
Valse Triste (from Kuolema)	12
Pelléas et Mélisande (incidental music)	5
Night Ride and Sunrise	2
CHAMBER MUSIC:	
String Quartet in D Minor	4
String Quartet in A Minor	2
VOCAL MUSIC:	
Songs	C
Kullervo Symphony (for two soloists, male choir, and orchestra)	1

MAURICE RAVEL (1875–1937)

Number 29

" 'Boléro'," said its composer, "is 17 minutes of orchestra without any music."

And so it is: one of the most popular pieces of music of any period consists of two short themes of a single melody repeated over and over for seventeen minutes, with different instrumental "colors." Scarcely your typical composition, but representative of its meticulous creator and his acknowledged orchestral mastery.

The critics protested that Maurice Ravel was too artificial.

"Has it occurred to them," retorted the composer, "that one may be artificial by nature?"

It was not the allegation of artificiality that most bothered Ravel but the widespread impression in the music world that he was an imitator of the Impressionism of his French colleague, Debussy. Even years after Debussy's death, the younger Ravel was still gnawing on that bone:

> For Debussy the musician and the man, I have had profound admiration, but by nature I am different from Debussy, and while I consider that Debussy may not have been altogether alien to my personal inheritance, I should identify also with the earliest phases of my evolution Gabriel Fauré, Emmanuel Chabrier and Erik Satie. . . . I believe that I myself have always followed a direction opposite to that of Debussy's symbolism. . . . It has been claimed with some insistence that the earlier appearance of my "Jeux d'eau" possibly influenced Debussy in the composition of his "Jardins sous la pluie," while a coincidence even more striking has been suggested in the case of my "Habanera"; but comments of this sort I must leave to others. It could very well be, however, that conceptions apparently similar in character should mature in the consciousness of two different composers at almost the same time without implying direct influence of either one upon the other.

Ravel was a "post-Impressionist" by consensus, whether he wanted to be or not, and even though academics today quarrel with the term. And, with Debussy, he was one of the two leading turn-of-the-century French composers. He was much more precise and less emotional than Debussy—Stravinsky called him a "Swiss watchmaker"—and considerably more dissonant. He favored the exotic rhythms of Spanish music, smaller works rather than larger ones, and larger orchestras rather than smaller ones. Like Berlioz, Rimsky-Korsakov, and Richard Strauss, he was a master of orchestral color, working with his own compositions and those of others, and also was one of the twentieth century's top piano composers. And he loved to listen to jazz in Harlem nightclubs.

The fourth-ranked of ten Frenchmen on The List, Ravel was born in the small town of Cibure in southwestern France near Spain, of a Basque mother and Swiss father. From age six on he lived in Paris. Despite the early charges that he was plagiarizing Debussy, thirteen years his senior, he became regarded as successor rather than imitator. One critic described the difference between the two composers this way: "Where Debussy's music is wrapped in a kind of sensuous haze, Ravel's outlines are hard and clear-cut; where one shimmers, the other glitters."

Webster's says that a *shimmer* is "a subdued sparkle or sheen, or a wavering, sometimes distorted visual image." To *glitter* is "to shine by reflection with brilliant or metallic luster, or to sparkle." That suggests a subdued sparkle for Debussy and an outright sparkle for Ravel. In any case, Ravel suggests rather than reproduces. He created veiled, mystical music rather than black-and-white photographs. Whatever the sparkle factor, Ravel follows Debussy as the main exponent of what was called the French Impressionist school—a style that led the way to the different (and then less pleasant) sounds of "new" (twentieth-century) music.

CATS

Maurice Ravel and Claude Debussy had more in common than their French nationality and their Impressionist music. Both were cat lovers, Ravel an extraordinary one. His cats sat on his lap, invaded his work table, and consumed a good bit of his unmarried life. He spoke to them in cat language, played with them incessantly, and wrote about them to his friends. He regarded his mother as the most important love of his life, followed by his villa, "Belvedere," and then his cats.

Ravel sort of asked for trouble on the Debussy copycat issue. Debussy wrote *Ibéria*, Ravel *Rapsodie Espagnole*; Debussy wrote a piano set called *Images*, Ravel *Miroirs*; Debussy wrote *Reflets dans l'eau*, Ravel *Jeux d'eau*. There was a scandal in Paris in the early 1900s as musicians chose sides as to whether Ravel was for real or a carbon copy. But Paris loves scandals and, wisely, most of the rest of the world ignores them, as the wise Americans in Des Moines and Pascagoula ignore Washington's inside-the-Beltway political tempests and a good bit of what interests provincial New York.

An earlier scandal, of somewhat greater musical significance, developed when the young Ravel was turned down for the fourth time for the cherished Prix de Rome, despite the fact that he had submitted his Quartet in F and his piano piece *Pavane pour une infante défunte* (Pavane for a dead princess). The prestigious Romain Rolland wrote to the conservatory director: "I cannot understand why one should persist in keeping a school in Rome if it is to close its doors to those rare artists who have originality . . . to a man like Ravel."

The director was forced to resign, but Ravel still did not get his honored award. As a result of both scandals, however, he became famous, a Parisian personality, someone to be seen with and to reckon.

In Ravel's music there is:
- something of Spain;
- something of Austria;
- something of children;
- something of jazz;
- something of—or akin to—Impressionism.

A DEPRESSED ARTIST

Ravel entered a period of depression at about the same time much of the world did in the late 1920s and early 1930s—although for none of the same reasons. He was in his mid-fifties, he was a perfectionist, and composing was extremely difficult for him.

"I have failed all my life," he wrote. "I am not one of the great composers. All the great ones produced enormously. But I have written relatively very little, and with a great deal of hardship. And now I cannot do any more, and it does not give me any pleasure."

He was to live another several years, restless and unhappy, before contracting a brain disease and dying after surgery without regaining consciousness.

In the realm of orchestral music, Ravel's first success was the *Rapsodie Espagnole*, 1907–1908, regarded by some as *the* Ravel orchestral masterpiece. Another famous orchestral piece—one of many Ravel transcriptions from a piano work—is *Alborado del gracioso*, written in 1905 and transcribed in 1918. (*Alborado* is Spanish for "a serenade or song in the morning"; *gracioso* is "jester.") Initially, the piece was the fourth of five piano pieces jointly entitled *Miroirs*.

Despite the popularity of *Rapsodie Espagnole* (and, of course, *Boléro*), the critical consensus is that the orchestral music from *Daphnis et Chloé*, a ballet, constitutes Ravel's masterpiece. The composer divided the music into two "series," or suites, with Suite No. 1 performed considerably more often than No. 2.

Another well-known piece, *Mother Goose* (Ma mère l'oye), went through several typically Ravelian configurations. It was written as a piano duet for two children in 1908–1910, converted into a ballet that was first performed in 1912, and from that score later made into an orchestral suite.

Most people who watched the magnificent English ice-skating team of Torvil and Dean on television a few years back became entranced by Ravel's *Boléro*, which he described as "a dance in a very modern movement, completely uniform in melody as well as harmony and rhythm, the latter marked without interruption by the drum. The only element of diversity is brought into play by an orchestral crescendo." While some critics remain a little "up-nosed" about it, the public—over the years—has made it a great favorite.

RAVEL ON BOLÉRO

"I am particularly desirous that there should be no misunderstanding about this work. It is an experiment in a very special and limited direction . . . consisting wholly of orchestral tissue without music—of one very long, gradual crescendo . . . no contrasts and practically no invention except in the plan and the manner of the execution."

Another of Ravel's more popular orchestral pieces is *La valse*, written in 1920, long after Vienna's peak waltz time had passed, and with none of the happy-old-times sound to it. The composer called it a "choreographic poem" and published with it this text: "Whirling clouds give glimpses, through rifts, of couples waltzing. The clouds scatter, little by little. One sees an immense hall peopled with [a] twirling crowd. The scene is gradually illuminated. The light of chandeliers bursts forth fortissimo. An imperial court, about 1855.''

His last two orchestral pieces were his two piano concertos, a Concerto in D for the Left Hand and a Concerto in G for Piano and Orchestra, both published in 1931.

Among his best-known piano pieces are these four:

• *Pavane pour une infante défunte*, an elegy for a dead princess. This was completed in 1899 and is heard both in the original piano version and in Ravel's own orchestrated version. Readers old enough may recognize in it a popular 1939 song, "The Lamp Is Low."

• *Jeux d'eau* (Fountains), composed in 1901. Ravel said it came from "the sound of water and the music of fountains, cascades and streams."

• *Valses nobles et sentimentales*, written in 1911 for the piano and transcribed a couple of years later by Ravel for orchestra.

• *Le tombeau de Couperin*, also transcribed by Ravel for orchestra, in 1920. It was written in honor of François Couperin, Number 49 on The List, France's greatest composer of harpsichord music.

A declared experimenter, Ravel was part of a group of artists in Paris called the "Société des apaches," an "apache" being a member of the French underground—and thus an outcast. One of the other members was a Russian only seven years younger, Igor Stravinsky, who took new/modern/twentieth-century music into even more distant and discordant fields.

Professor Paul Henry Lang, one of my favorite experts, is cool about Ravel, writing: "In his later years [he] became a mere orchestrator, handling his many-headed orchestra with supreme skill but without much spiritual conviction, and ended by orchestrating other composers' works (Mussorgsky, 'Pictures at an Exhibition') or writing stunts appropriate for the modern cinema orchestra ('Boléro')."

With respect for professor Lang's awesome musical knowledge, his is not a unanimous view. What is unanimous is the professor's opinion of Ravel's skill at orchestration. And while Ravel did not create *Pictures*, his orchestrated version is performed and recorded far more often than Mussorgsky's piano original—which speaks to public taste but not to professor Lang's expert opinion.

STARTER KIT

For the Starter Kit, two choices are mandatory since they are among the most recorded and performed of all music. One is *Boléro*, written in 1928, which won more quick success than almost any composition of the twentieth century, winding up not only as part of a Broadway musical but also as the name of a motion picture starring George Raft. Written for a ballet company, it is one-of-a-kind music that justifiably fascinates the public.

His next best-known music is the piano work *Pavane pour une infante défunte*. A pavane is a slow, stately court dance. As mentioned above, the "infante" (*infanta* in Spanish) is not an infant but a Spanish princess, and this is a poignant, haunting elegy on her death.

Two other orchestral works were chosen for the Starter Kit: *Rapsodie Espagnole*, written in 1907–1908, a four-movement suite that sounds as Spanish as its name suggests; and either *La Valse*, one of his few works written directly for orchestra, with music that evokes the dancing of a mid-1800's Vienna court, or *Valses nobles et sentimentales*. The latter, composed in 1910, began life as a piano suite but was later orchestrated. It consists of seven "noble and sentimental" waltzes.

For variety, the fifth recommendation is a piece for violin and piano, *Pièce en forme de Habanera*, a habanera being a Cuban dance. This bypasses his String Quartet in F, *Daphnis et Chloé* (my favorite), and his one-act comic opera, *L'heure Espagnole*, all valid substitutes.

RAVEL: THE STARTER KIT

Composition	*Recordings Available**
ORCHESTRAL WORKS:	
Boléro	47
Rapsodie Espagnole (suite for orchestra)	21
La Valse	14
PIANO MUSIC:	
Pavane pour une infante défunte (piano or orchestrated version)	47
OTHER INSTRUMENTAL MUSIC:	
Pièce en forme de Habanera for Violin and Piano	12

*Represents the number of recorded releases available of each listed composition as found in a recent issue of the *Schwann/Opus* catalogue. A "C" indicates that a work is only available collected with other compositions.

RAVEL: A TOP TEN

Composition	Recordings Available*
ORCHESTRAL WORKS:	
Boléro	47
Rapsodie Espagnole (suite for orchestra)	21
Ma mère l'oye (suite from ballet)	15
Alborado del gracioso	16
La Valse (choreographic poem for orchestra)	14
Daphnis et Chloé (suites from ballet):	
Suite No. 2	16
Valses nobles et sentimentales	17
PIANO MUSIC:	
Le tombeau de Couperin (suite for piano)	15
Pavane pour une infante défunte (piano or orchestrated version)	47
OTHER INSTRUMENTAL MUSIC:	
Pièce en forme de Habanera for Violin and Piano	12

RAVEL: A MASTER COLLECTION

Composition	Recordings Available*
ORCHESTRAL WORKS:	
Piano Concerto in D for the Left Hand	9
Piano Concerto in G	9
Boléro	47
Rapsodie Espagnole	21
Ma mère l'oye (suite from ballet)	21
Alborado del gracioso	16
La Valse	14
Daphnis et Chloé (suites from ballet):	
Suite No. 2	16
Tzigane for Violin and Orchestra	12
Valses nobles et sentimentales	17
Ballets:	
Ma mère l'oye	19
Daphnis et Chloé	10

Composition	Recordings Available*
CHAMBER MUSIC:	
String Quartet in F	11
PIANO MUSIC:	
Rapsodie Espagnole (for two pianos)	10
Le tombeau de Couperin (suite for piano)	15
Pavane pour une infante défunte (piano or orchestrated version)	47
OTHER INSTRUMENTAL MUSIC:	
Pièce en forme de Habanera for Violin and Piano	12
Sonata for Violin and Cello	6
VOCAL MUSIC:	
Opera:	
L'enfant et les sortilèges	3
SONGS:	
Chansons madécasses (songs for voice, flute, cello, and piano)	8

GIOACCHINO ROSSINI (1792–1868)

Number 30

"Give me a laundry list," said Gioacchino Rossini, "and I will set it to music."

And so he could, and almost did, turning out thirty-eight operas by the time he was thirty-seven—and then, strangely, not another one even though he lived another thirty-nine years.

These were the days (the early decades of the nineteenth century) when Italian opera composers traveled across the country, dashing off new operas on a formula basis for new impresarios in different cities visited. Two composers on The List were superstars of Italian opera in the first half of the century, both then succeeded and surpassed by the great master, Verdi. The better one was Rossini; the lesser (albeit a melody and voice master in his own right) was Donizetti (1797–1848), who comes later on The List as Number 43.

Both Rossini and Donizetti specialized in what was called *bel canto* ("beautiful singing") opera—opera for the voice. Never mind the depth of the plot, the development of the characters, or an equal-opportunity musical share for the orchestra. Bel canto opera was for singers and singing, as described in the words of Berlioz: "Music for the Italians is a sensual pleasure and nothing more. For this noble expression of the mind they have hardly more respect than for the art of cooking. They want a score that, like a plate of macaroni, can be assimilated immediately, without their having to think about it or even pay attention to it."

Many people who enjoy music (and life) find nothing second-rate about a fine plate of macaroni, which may account for Rossini's enormous popularity.

Rossini was born in Pesaro, Italy, the son of the municipal trum-

MELODY MAGIC

Rossini's inexhaustible fount of melody changed the operatic world. Before Rossini, Parisian national opera was Parisian-like—elegance was the thing, with Parisian wit and Parisian sophistication. Although it contained what the professionals describe as a "tinge of romantic color," it was basically as unromantic as elitist Parisians could make it. Rossini had his initial successes in his native Italy, but then the force of his magical melodies overpowered not only Vienna but Paris itself. "Grand opera" in Europe became Rossini opera: ridiculous but sensational situations, wonderful historical costumes, and handsome, exceptional singers of both sexes. All of it was worked into a package which the impresarios could—and did—peddle far afield of Italy.

peter, sort of a musically inclined town crier. Apparently the father
sometimes reported the facts with no more objectivity than some of
his twentieth-century successors on television news. Although not a
boy genius of the Mozart-Mendelssohn variety, the son showed a
significant amount of musical talent. At fourteen he played both the
horn and the viola with competence and was good enough on the
cembalo (harpsichord) to perform with local theater companies. He
was even more skilled as a boy singer and by age thirteen had already
written a fair amount of music. All of this was without any serious
training or instruction.

He was something of a latchkey kid. The senior Rossini had fierce
republican views and often made as much noise with his vocal opinions of government as he did with his trumpet. The government was
not pleased—presumably he was supposed to be kind of a civil servant—and he was fired. He was able to earn some money from trumpet gigs in local theaters around Bologna, and his wife worked as
a seamstress in people's homes. While his parents worked, young
Gioacchino stayed home in the charge of his grandmother and aunt.
The records suggest that this did very little for his reading, writing, and
arithmetic, and not much more for his music. One writer offers the
following rather gentle description of his juvenile delinquency: "An
uncommonly high-spirited boy, he had a vitality that manifested itself
in a naughtiness probably unique in the annals of great masters of
music."

All of this was before his voice changed. In 1804 his parents settled
in Bologna. Now twelve, Gioacchino had begun to reform, and at
fourteen he began to study cello seriously and to learn counterpoint
at a music school. The counterpoint did not "take" at first, despite
strenuous efforts by his masters, and he said later that he learned much
more from studying the scores of Mozart and Haydn. But he stuck
with counterpoint, eventually won a medal for his knowledge of it,
and at age sixteen, in 1808, he wrote a cantata that was played at the
school's annual ceremonies.

Two years later he left school, mostly because his parents needed
his financial help. But not long thereafter he was asked to write a
one-act opera in Venice. He accepted and composed *La cambiale di
matrimonio*; it was a success, and he was commissioned to write several
more operas.

Those were the appetizers. The main course came shortly thereafter in 1813 with the production of his first full-scale opera, *Tancredi*,
based on Voltaire's romantic tragedy. The Venetians loved it; Rossini

was now a success although still a very young man, and before the year was out he had an even bigger hit with a comic opera, *L'Italiana in Algeri* (The Italian girl in Algiers). The composer was only twenty-one, he was good-looking, everyone who was anyone in Venice was talking about him and singing his songs, he liked the girls, the girls liked him—and the moral seems to be that juvenile high jinks don't destroy you if you are one of history's great opera composers.

Later he moved to Naples, making it his headquarters while he wrote operas for producers in Naples, Rome, Milan, and other cities. Still later came commissions in Vienna, Paris, and London (where he quickly made $20,000, an incredible feat in those days). There followed a short period back in Italy, after which he returned to Paris, where he spent the last half of his life. No one really knows why he wrote no operas after composing one of his two most famous, *William Tell*, in Paris in 1829. He was rich, fat, happy, a consumer of gourmet foods, famous, and seemingly altogether content—which are perhaps reasons enough not to work.

ROSSINI VERSUS VERDI

Eduard Hanslick, Viennese music-critic-and-czar in the last half of the nineteenth century, compared the music of Rossini and Verdi this way:

"We prefer to see nations, as well as individual artists, effective through those virtues which are their natural endowment; thus, the Italians through fresh and fulsome melody. Even in Verdi's operas feeling has always come to the surface in the form of melody. Who is not acquainted with the many Verdian melodies which express real feeling with compelling forcefulness, unlike the 'buffo' music in Rossini's tragedies which exercises a certain sensual charm quite independent of its relation, or want of relation, to the dramatic situation?"

Rossini's greatest supporters—and there are many, so sparkling and melodious is his music—do not speak of his "nobility," "depth," or "grandeur," words commonly applied to the great Verdi. But for *opera buffa*—opera based on real people who could be made fun of, rather than on serious themes—many professionals consider him incomparable. He also had a hard-nosed attitude about the temperamental singers who, until his time, had run with the written notes in whatever direction most suited them. Rossini had the audacity to insist that the performers sing his notes the way they were written.

The accepted Rossini masterpiece is *The Barber of Seville*, a gay comedy first performed in Rome in 1816, written (not untypically) in fifteen days when the composer was twenty-four and based on the play by Beaumarchais. (Mozart had earlier produced *The Marriage of Figaro* from the same comedy, in collaboration with librettist Lorenzo da Ponte, who wound up peddling booze illegally in New York City.) Notwithstanding a very unsuccessful first performance, Rossini's version brought him widespread fame, and he wrote sixteen more operas in the next six years—good ones and poor ones, triumphs and fiascos, all making him Italy's Number One opera composer. *The Barber of Seville* was the first opera sung in Italian in New York, long before Fiorello La Guardia was mayor or Mario Cuomo governor.

STAR-CROSSED PREMIERE

Popular though Rossini's *Barber of Seville* became, and esteemed masterpiece of satirical comic opera though it is, opening night was a disaster.

In the first place, Rome's operagoers in 1816 were unhappy that another opera had been written on the theme of Beaumarchais's famous work. In the second, a lead tenor couldn't get his guitar properly tuned on stage. In the third, a cat stalked across the stage in the midst of the performance—a cat without a proper part. In the fourth, one singer suffered a nosebleed in midsong.

But the second performance went much better, and soon the composer was a European hero.

Rossini's other great work was his last, *William Tell*, first performed in Paris in 1829, thirteen years after *The Barber of Seville*. It is based on Schiller's play about the Swiss father who shoots an apple from his son's head. It is serious, much deeper than anything else he wrote, totally different from *The Barber of Seville* (and indeed from all other Rossini works), and runs six hours long when uncut (his longest opera by far, and never performed in full). Like *The Barber of Seville*, *William Tell* had an unsuccessful initial performance; unlike *Barber*, it was still not widely acclaimed after a second and third performance. The critics differed in their appraisals, as critics are wont to do, one of them writing: "The tunefulness and brilliance are here in abundance, but they strike a deeper and more modern note. . . . There is dignity, and a loftiness of expression, a picturesqueness and a feeling for the portrayal of true patriotism which are entirely different from and on a far higher level than anything else he ever wrote." Other observers felt that Rossini had tried to undertake something that was beyond his reach and that he could not bring off, despite the quality of the music itself.

Tens of millions of people who have never been to an opera recognize the *William Tell* Overture, one of classical music's best-known melodies, brought into nearly every home in America by radio and television as the Lone Ranger heigh-hoed Silver across the West with it as a theme.

Among the other best-known Rossini operas are *L'Italiana in Algeri* (The Italian girl in Algiers), 1813; *La Cenerentola* (Cinderella), 1817; and *Semiramide* (Semiramis), 1823.

In addition to the Lone Ranger's favorite, the overtures to *L'Italiana in Algeri*, *Semiramide*, and another opera, *La gazza ladra* (The thieving magpie), are frequently heard.

Rossini's last famous piece of music was his choral work *Stabat Mater*, presented in 1842, thirteen years after *William Tell* and still twenty-six years before his death. Some experts of the day called it the greatest choral music since Haydn's *Creation*, and it is still highly regarded. In dealing with a religious text, Rossini does not lose what the critics call his "natural jauntiness."

Milton Cross and David Ewen perhaps best sum up the composer: "There was so much of the hack in Rossini that it is sometimes difficult to remember that he was also a genius."

STARTER KIT

Despite the sound reputation of his *Stabat Mater*, for an opera composer of Rossini's type and caliber it seems to make sense to restrict the Starter Kit to opera material. Good recordings of the religious piece are available, and it may be worthwhile to make a mental note that it exists.

"BLESS YOU"

Heinrich Laube was a nineteenth-century German playwright who, after watching a performance of Wagner's *Die Meistersinger*—presumably a comic opera—exclaimed:

"Bless you, lighthearted Rossini!"

Wagner was many things and a composer of much beautiful music, but he is not famed as a master of the light touch. His archfoe, Vienna supercritic Eduard Hanslick, had this to say about Wagner's attempts at humor: "In comedy, Wagner's music is even less successful; it is stilted, profuse, even repulsive."

Not everyone agrees that *Die Meistersinger* is stilted, profuse, and repulsive, but it is fair to say that Rossini brought something to the special field of comic opera that is not found in Herr Wagner's music.

One reasonable way to handle the operas is to include just the overtures for three of them and the complete versions of the two most famous ones. The overture selections are *William Tell, L'Italiana in Algeri*, and *Semiramide* or *La gazza ladra*; the complete operas are *William Tell* and *The Barber of Seville*.

Best-known passages of *The Barber of Seville* include the overture, the "Largo al factotum" aria for baritone, "Una voce poco fa" for soprano, and "La calumnia" for bass. *William Tell* arias most frequently recorded include "Selva opaca" from Act II, "Tirolese" and the ballet music in Act III, and the tenor aria "O muto asil del pianto" in Act IV. Complete operas are available, as well as highlights of some, collections of arias and scenes, and selected overtures.

ROSSINI: THE STARTER KIT

Composition	Recordings Available*
ORCHESTRAL WORKS:	
Overtures:	
William Tell	23
L'Italiana in Algeri	11
Semiramide	13

Composition	Recordings Available*
VOCAL MUSIC:	
Operas:	
William Tell	2
The Barber of Seville	7

*Represents the number of recorded releases available of each listed composition as found in a recent issue of the *Schwann/Opus* catalogue. A "C" indicates that a work is only available collected with other compositions.

ROSSINI: A TOP TEN

Composition	Recordings Available*
ORCHESTRAL WORKS:	
Overtures:	
William Tell	23
L'Italiana in Algeri	11
Semiramide	13
La gazza ladra	11
VOCAL MUSIC:	
Operas:	
William Tell	2
The Barber of Seville	7
Otello	0
The Siege of Corinth	1
L'Italiana in Algeri	2
Sacred:	
Stabat Mater	3

ROSSINI: A MASTER COLLECTION

Composition	Recordings Available*
ORCHESTRAL WORKS:	
Overtures:	
William Tell	23
L'Italiana in Algeri	11
Semiramide	13
La gazza ladra	11

Composition	Recordings Available*
VOCAL MUSIC:	
Operas:	
William Tell	2
The Barber of Seville	7
Otello	0
The Siege of Corinth	1
L'Italiana in Algeri	2
Semiramide	1
La gazza ladra	1
Tancredi	2
La Cenerentola	2
Sacred:	
Petite Messe Solennelle	2
Stabat Mater	3

EDVARD GRIEG (1843–1907)

Number 31

Notwithstanding Debussy's opinion that he was a "pink bon bon wrapped in snow," Edvard Grieg is generally considered a pretty fair composer. Not an Immortal, certainly, but The List has only three Immortals and seven Demigods. It has been fashionable over the years to put down Grieg as not much more than a supranationalist. (Debussy, a contemporary, always sharp-tongued, also wrote that apart from being a gifted interpreter of his country's folk music, Grieg was only a "clever musician," "more concerned with effects than with genuine art.'') George Bernard Shaw called him "the infinitesimal Grieg.''

But his honors were many while he was alive, and his music keeps coming back. He is the only Norwegian on The List and the only representative of the North Country besides Sebelius.

In time he won appointments to the Swedish Academy and the Leyden Academy, was elected to the French Academy of Arts, received honorary degrees from Cambridge and Oxford, and was honored around the world in many other ways. Among laureates honored with him at Cambridge were a couple of other musicians of some reputation, Tchaikovsky and Saint-Saëns. Unconvinced, Debussy described Grieg's songs this way: "Very sweet and innocent, music to rock the convalescents of rich neighborhoods.'' There was a lot of TV anchorman and congressional-committee arrogance in Monsieur Debussy.

But Grieg is a national hero in Norway, not only its finest composer but also one whose work incorporates everything that is Norway—history, tradition, geography, customs, people, folk dances, peasant songs, village carnivals, fjords, church bells, forests, and mountain streams—the whole bit.

GRIEG ON IBSEN

Ibsen's *Peer Gynt* did not paint a happy picture of Norway and Norwegians, portraying the people as basically apathetic. After Ibsen's death, Grieg wrote:

"Many Norwegians formerly believed, as I myself did, that Peer Gynt represents only an exceptional type. Unhappily it has been shown in the last years how shockingly true to life the poet sketched that national character. Ibsen exposed a dangerous side of our whole people mercilessly. For that reason it is that he stands in such bad odor in our country politically.''

If you have been to Norway you know that the wise visitor says nothing unkind about living World War II resistance fighters—men and women whom Norwegian police traditionally have driven home if they have been caught drinking and driving, despite the fact that all other drunken drivers are hit with some of the toughest DWI penalties in the world—or about Edvard Grieg. The resistance fighters are growing fewer every year, but Grieg's popularity lives on.

The critics' words for Grieg's music: stylish and graceful; tasteful and charming; tuneful, colorful, and intimate; and, always, Norway nationalistic. Hans von Bülow, famous nineteenth-century conductor (and husband of Liszt's daughter, Cosima, until Wagner stole her away), once called him "the Chopin of the North"—because he excelled at smaller compositions, because his best writing was for the piano, and because his music was poetry. He has not been regarded as a North Country Chopin in the eighty years since his death, however; the experts don't find him "profound" enough to rank with the supreme masters, but he is called a "minor master" at worst (which is hardly shameful) and a good bit more than that at best—regardless of the Debussyites and dedicated putter-downers. Everyone isn't a Mozart or an Abraham Lincoln.

Critics in the early years of the century were kinder to Grieg than were those in midcentury. Arthur Elson wrote in *The Book of Musical Knowledge*, first published in 1915: "The richness of melodic and harmonic beauty in Grieg's works of course goes beyond the popular style, but is nevertheless a very definite idealization of it. Grieg's melodies are lyrical and full of a sweetness that is never commonplace, but always remarkable for its joyous enthusiasm or plaintive sadness. There is in his works a melting tenderness, a warmth of sentiment that seems perennially charming." No one says "earth shaking." People say short, exquisite compositions.

Several music historians quote Lawrence Gilman, a supporter. "Grieg," he wrote, "has individuality—individuality that is seizing and indisputable. That, one feels, is his distinguishing possession. His accent is unmistakable. His speech may sway one, or it may not; but always it is the voice of Grieg. . . . Grieg is thrice admirable in this: he wears no man's mantle; he borrows no man's speech."

Grieg was born in Bergen, Norway, and studied at the Leipzig Conservatory. From early on he was a nationalist composer, eager to bring Norwegian music to the attention of the world, to free it from dominating German influence, to capture folk sources and from them to create authentic Norwegian sounds. With a friend he founded a music society called Euterpe, whose members discussed (and exclusively played) Norwegian music. This music was Grieg's lifework.

In time Grieg found a powerful ally in Liszt, who, as mentioned earlier, helped almost every worthy musician within reach in the course of his long life. After hearing Grieg's Sonata in F for Violin and

EARLY IMPRESSIONISM

Grieg studied for several years at the Leipzig Conservatory. Some of the music people say the musical language he learned there was not right for expressing his feelings about his beloved pine and fir skylines, mountain vistas, vast forests, and rushing waterfalls at home in Norway.

In his *Impressionism in Music*, Christopher Palmer writes of Grieg: "For an alternative he turned to the virtually untapped resources of his native folk-music, instinct as it was with the life-spirit of the Norwegian countryside and its peasantry. He glimpsed in the rhythmic, melodic and (potentially) harmonic unfamiliarities of folk-song a whole new dimension of expressive power—the means whereby music could become a vehicle for colour and atmosphere rather than for form and logic. Grieg became in effect the first mystic in music."

In expressing the "lyrical essence" of his fatherland, Palmer says, Grieg found new concepts of harmony and timbre which anticipated the Impressionist style.

Piano, Liszt wrote to the composer: "It evidences a powerful, logically creative, ingenious and excellent constructive talent for a position, which needs only to follow its natural development to attain high rank. I could hope that you are finding in your own country the success and encouragement you deserve; you will not fail of them elsewhere." The two met in time; the Hungarian master continued to encourage the Norwegian and to push his work, and he helped make a success of Grieg's only acclaimed large composition, his Concerto in A Minor for Piano and Orchestra, written in 1868 when the composer was twenty-five. It is not only his most popular work today but one of the most frequently played of all piano concertos. This absence of many major works is one reason professionals do not elevate Grieg to a higher status. (On the other hand, Chopin is so elevated, and he also wrote little of magnitude.)

The best known of his orchestral works are two suites he developed from twenty-two pieces of incidental music for Henrik Ibsen's play *Peer Gynt*, first performed in 1876.

Grieg's wife later wrote of the composition of that music:

For several days he went about in a nervous, restless state, in great doubt and anxiety as to the heavy task. The more he saturated his mind with the powerful poem the more clearly he saw that he was the right man for a work of such wild witchery and so permeated with the Norwegian spirit. In the suburb of Sandviken, outside Bergen, he found a pavilion, with windows on every side, high up on a hill . . . with a magnificent view of the sea on one side and the mountains on the other. "Solveig's Song" was the first number to see the light. Then "Ase's Death." I shall never forget the bright summer evening on the mountains, as we sang and played together "Solveig's Song." For the first time, Grieg himself smiled, well-pleased with the song, and called it a "public lamp." Grieg himself considered "Ase's Death" and "Solveig's Song" to be his best work.

The first of the two *Peer Gynt* Suites, by far the more famous, has four movements: "Morning," which depicts a beautiful rising sun; "Ase's Death," melancholy and gloomy; "Anitra's Dance," gay and rhythmic, and "In the Hall of the Mountain King," in which gnomes, goblins, and elves cavort in their cavern. The final movement of the second suite is "Solveig's Song," pathos-filled and a favorite.

While Grieg is best known for the first *Peer Gynt* Suite—years ago every suburban schoolchild heard "In the Hall of the Mountain King" in seventh-grade music-appreciation class—the critics are not all that fond of it. Some, indeed, argue that another reason Grieg is not more highly regarded is that people listen too much to this piece and not enough to his other works. Grieg himself apparently felt about "Hall of the Mountain King" much as Judy Garland grew to feel about "Over the Rainbow," Ms. Garland publicly declaring at one time that she felt "up to my ass in rainbows." Grieg's less colorful comment: "As for the piece I wrote for the Hall of the Mountain King, I can tolerate it no longer."

Another of his well-known compositions is the *Holberg* Suite, composed for piano and later transcribed by Grieg himself for string orchestra. It honored the two hundredth birthday of Ludvig Holberg, a famous Scandinavian writer.

His works for piano include a Sonata in E Minor and his major piano composition, *Lyric Pieces*, comprising sixty-six works in ten volumes, written over thirty years. Some are rated higher than others, and, as one might suspect, those drawn directly from Norwegian folklore are deemed the best.

GRIEG ON HIS PEER GYNT SUITES

"Peer Gynt, the only son of poor peasants, is drawn by the poet as a character of a morbidly developed fancy and a prey to megalomania. In his youth he has many wild adventures—comes, for instance, to a peasants' wedding where he carries off the bride up to the mountain peaks. Here he leaves her to roam about with wild cowherd girls. He then enters the kingdom of the mountain king, whose daughter falls in love with him and dances to him. But he laughs at the dance and the droll music, whereupon the enraged mountain folk wish to kill him. But he succeeds in escaping and wanders to foreign countries, among others to Morocco, where he appears as a prophet and is greeted by Arab girls. After many wonderful guidings of Fate, he at last returns as an old man, after suffering shipwreck on his way to his home as poor as he left it. Here the sweetheart of his youth, Solveig, who has stayed true to him all these years, meets him, and his weary head at last finds rest in her lap."

Grieg wrote many songs and adapted two of the most famous for string orchestra in a piece called *Two Elegiac Melodies*—"The Wounded Heart" and "The Last Spring." His best-known individual song, however, is "Ich liebe Dich," written for his wife.

One praised piece of chamber music is his String Quartet in G Minor, completed in 1878. He also composed three beautiful violin sonatas, which are often performed today, as well as his occasionally heard Symphony in C Minor.

In 1885 Grieg moved to a villa called Troldhaugen (Hill of mountain men), six miles from Bergen, overlooking a fjord. The Norwegian equivalent of modern tour buses paid so much attention to him that he posted a sign, "Edvard Grieg does not desire to receive callers earlier than four in the afternoon." He was honored around the world on his sixtieth birthday and was nearly mobbed by joyous English music-lovers at two London concerts in 1906. After he died of a heart attack in 1907, his body lay in state, dozens of foreign governments participated in his funeral, and some 400,000 Norwegians are reported to have lined the streets in tribute. That crowd counts in those days were more accurate than current estimates of United States twentieth-century presidential campaigns, pro-or-con abortion rallies, or outdoor rock concerts is unlikely, but anyhow, there were a lot of people. For a "minor master," even a very good one, Mr. Grieg did himself proud.

STARTER KIT

Despite the critics, and because of the public's general familiarity with "In the Hall of the Mountain King," *Peer Gynt* Suite No. 1 is included, and with it Suite No. 2, chiefly because of "Solveig's Song." And there can be no question about including the Piano Concerto in A Minor, Grieg's most successful large work.

For another orchestral work, it was a toss-up between the *Holberg* Suite and *Norwegian Dances*, with the latter selected. In the realm of piano music, the *Lyric Pieces* are most representative. The best known of them include "Papillons," "Lonely Wanderer," and "To Spring" from Op. 43; "Melodie" from Op. 47; "Cradle Song" from Op. 68; and "Puck" from Op. 71. As in other cases where several short and very short compositions are recommended, the best idea is simply to listen to a few *Lyric Pieces* and decide whether they appeal to you.

Songs were important to Grieg and are a major part of his work, nationalist miniaturist that he was. "The Herder's Call" is one example; there are dozens more. You cannot buy one song, so sample any song collection.

GRIEG: THE STARTER KIT

Composition	Recordings Available*
ORCHESTRAL WORKS:	
Concerto in A Minor for Piano	31
Peer Gynt Suites No. 1 and No. 2 (incidental music)	19
Norwegian Dances (four)	9
PIANO MUSIC:	
Lyric Pieces	6
VOCAL MUSIC:	
Songs:	C
Ich liebe Dich	

*Represents the number of recorded releases available of each listed composition as found in a recent issue of the *Schwann/Opus* catalogue. A "C" indicates that a work is only available collected with other compositions.

GRIEG: A TOP TEN

Composition	Recordings Available*
ORCHESTRAL WORKS:	
Concerto in A Minor for Piano	31
Peer Gynt Suites No. 1 and No. 2 (incidental music)	19
Holberg Suite	15
Two Elegiac Melodies (for string orchestra)	9
Norwegian Dances (four)	9
CHAMBER MUSIC:	
String Quartet in G Minor	2
PIANO MUSIC:	
Lyric Pieces	6
OTHER INSTRUMENTAL MUSIC:	
Sonatas for Violin and Piano (three)	5
Sonata in A Minor for Cello	4
VOCAL MUSIC:	
Songs:	C
Ich liebe Dich	

GRIEG: A MASTER COLLECTION

Composition	Recordings Available*
SYMPHONIES:	
Symphony in C Minor	2
OTHER ORCHESTRAL WORKS:	
Concerto in A Minor for Piano	31
Peer Gynt Suites No. 1 and No. 2 (incidental music)	19
Holberg Suite	15
Two Elegiac Melodies (for string orchestra)	9
Norwegian Dances (four)	9
Lyric Suite	6
CHAMBER MUSIC:	
String Quartet in G Minor	2

Composition	Recordings Available*
PIANO MUSIC:	
Piano Sonata in E Minor	5
Lyric Pieces	6
OTHER INSTRUMENTAL MUSIC:	
Sonatas for Violin and Piano (three)	5
Sonata in A Minor for Cello	4
VOCAL MUSIC:	
Songs:	
Solveig's Song	C
The Nightingale	C
Ich liebe Dich	C

CHRISTOPH GLUCK (1714–1787)

Number 32

"He," said Handel, "knows no more counterpoint than my cook."

The cook's name was Gustavus Waltz, and he *was* something of a musician—a trained bass singer—but even so it was not a kindly remark for one German to make of another, even if the speaker was making his fortune in London and the other his opera reputation in Paris.

The fellow who knew so little counterpoint was Christoph Willibald Gluck, and he was to change the nature of opera forevermore.

Gluck was not the first opera reformer, however. One who came before him was Monteverdi, born almost 150 years earlier, due up on The List in just a moment, and generally acclaimed as the first opera genius. Some of Monteverdi's contemporaries had "invented" Italian opera in an attempt to revive the "music drama" the Greeks had established some two thousand years earlier. Monteverdi made a legitimate stab at creating music-drama. During the next 150 years, however, opera went in another direction, becoming stilted, ornamented, ostentatious "entertainment" built chiefly for and around singers. The productions existed chiefly for the sake of vocal display. Gluck's mission, in very basic terms, was to return to Monteverdi's conception of music-drama, to recapture it, and to move forward with it. The opera experts say that he succeeded astonishingly well, leaving a baton to be picked up by Weber and handed by Weber along to Wagner. It certainly didn't hurt his cause that he found a friend in a woman named Marie Antoinette. It was a good thing to please Marie Antoinette if you were producing an opera in Paris in the 1770s, especially if you had been rather unsuccessful with several earlier attempts. Gluck did please her, and it helped him considerably with his new kind of opera.

AN EXCITED MARIE ANTOINETTE

"At last, a great triumph," wrote the queen. "On the nineteenth we had the first performance of Gluck's 'Iphigénie.' I was carried away by it. We can find nothing else to talk about. You can scarcely imagine what excitement reigns in all minds in regard to this event. It is incredible."

Gluck, who earns his place on The List more from his contribution to opera development than from the quality of his actual compositions, described his mission this way:

When I undertook to set the opera of "Alceste" to music, I resolved to avoid all those abuses which had crept into Italian Opera through the mistaken vanity of singers and the unwise compliance of composers, and which had rendered it wearisome and ridiculous instead of being, as it once was, the grandest and most important stage of modern times. I have

tried to restrict music to its proper function, serving the poetry by strengthening the expression of the sentiment and the
interest of the situations without interrupting the action or
weakening it with useless ornamentation. . . . I also thought
that my chief endeavor should be to attain a grand simplicity,
and consequently have avoided making a parade of difficulties
at the cost of clearness."

This was a German approach, designed to counter the pageantry
and vocal fireworks of the Italian opera style with a different technique: a blending of drama and music, with the songs sung more
naturally and the whole show produced more simply. The singers
were to remain singers, doing their thing, but not dominating both
orchestra and drama.

One writer said Gluck opened the doors to allow "human naturalness" to become part of the opera world. The characters and the story
were meant to be more important than the music, singing, and dancing.

In the simplest terms, here is what Gluck did to take opera out of
the hands of singers and put it into the hands of the composer:

• demanded that the temperamental and show-off superstars sing
what was written

• shortened their arias

• cut down on the number of arias in favor of more recitative
(heightened speech, or sung speech)

• built up the instrumental accompaniment behind the *recitative*

With these changes, the singers no longer ran the show. Additionally, Gluck:

• made the overture part of the drama

• chose librettos that demonstrated emotional realism and development of the characters

• wrote music that reinforced the meaning of the poetry in the
libretto

Before Gluck's reforms, one Italian satirist had written: "In working with singers, especially castratos, the composer will always place
himself on the left and keep one step behind, hat in hand."

Gluck was the son of a forester on the private summer estate of
Prince Lobkowitz in Erasbach, Upper Palatinate. He studied music
under the Jesuits, became a wandering minstrel at eighteen, sang in
church choirs, played the violin at village fairs, and eventually settled
in Vienna, where he was hired by Prince Lobkowitz to play in his
private orchestra. He toured Italy with another prince, studied and

GLUCK ON HIS REFORMS

"I flattered myself that the others would be eager to follow the road I had broken for them, in order to destroy the evil practices which have crept into Italian opera and have dishonored it. I am not convinced that my hopes were in vain. The half-learned, the judges and legislators of art—a class of persons unfortunately too numerous, and at the same time of greater disadvantage to art than ignoramuses—rage against a method which, if established, would obviously endanger their criteria. . . . No obstacles will deter me from making new attempts to achieve my purpose; 'sufficit mihi unus Plato per cuncto populo'; I would rather have one Plato on my side than all the populace."

wrote Italian opera in Milan, visited other European countries (including England, where he did not impress Handel), and returned to Vienna, having been gone twelve years all told.

His first opera, *Artaserse*, was produced in Italy in 1741, followed by several others in the Italian style.

After writing for a while in the so-called French style (i.e., with more "economy of means" than the Italians liked), Gluck was influenced by the writings of a ballet master which asserted that in both ballet and opera the basic elements were the plot and the feelings—emotions—of the characters. Music, singing, and dancing were to be subordinate to the story and to the characters' behavior. In 1762, Gluck used this approach to create a new kind of opera, *Orfeo ed Euridice*. There were only three characters, plus a chorus; it was a simple, poignant production, with deep feeling. Of some fifty Gluck operas, this is the only real survivor.

A couple of dozen or more operas have been written about Orpheus, Greek hero and fabulous musician who sings his way to the Underworld to rescue his dead wife, Eurydice; does so; and loses her when he breaks the rules and looks back at her to reassure her of his love. The most famous versions are Gluck's and Monteverdi's (written in 1607) both of which changed the original story to provide happier endings. In Monteverdi's, Eurydice does not return to earth with Orpheus, but the Gods do take pity on the couple and bring her up into the heavens. In Gluck's the two stay together.

After *Orfeo*, Gluck wrote a series of operas based on various legends. They included *Iphigénie en Aulide*, *Alceste*, *Armide*, *Iphigénie en Tauride*, and *Echo et Narcisse*. *Iphigénie en Aulide* was first performed in 1774, after the failure of *Alceste* and of another opera, *Paride ed Elena*. This was Gluck's first French venture, introduced at the Paris Opera. There were a great many production problems, but it had one great champion—Marie Antoinette, a onetime pupil of Gluck and wife of Louis XVI. In part because of her support, the opera was a smash hit, bringing record receipts to the Paris Opera.

Gluck's operas are among the oldest still performed. And while one reason is his successful approach to expressive drama, another is the fact that he was a highly skilled, daring, and resourceful orchestrator. Critics have written that in the use of instruments he often made his orchestra sound like that of Weber, Berlioz, or even Wagner.

BENJAMIN FRANKLIN'S MUSICAL GLASSES

Not everyone knows that in the 1740s Benjamin Franklin developed a musical instrument consisting of a set of thirty-five circular glasses arranged on a central rod, tuned to play three octaves. For a long time one could be seen in New York City at the Metropolitan Museum of Art. In Goldsmith's *Vicar of Wakefield*, "fashionable ladies spoke of nothing but pictures, taste, Shakespeare and musical glasses."

The inventor was Gluck, who once played a concerto on twenty-six drinking glasses and claimed he could play on them anything that could be performed by violin or harpsichord. Franklin first heard them in London and went on to refine the instrument.

A question for the musicologists seems to be: Did Gluck's opera reform really catch on and lead to permanent changes, or was he forgotten until later historians revived him? Some say his influence was evident on "large-scale, heroic" opera centered in Paris, which in turn led to the "grand opera" of the next century. That debate aside, there is agreement that his operas were a departure from tradition and that they were to have a strong influence on Wagner years later.

STARTER KIT

Not a great deal of Gluck's work survives on record, tape, or compact disc. *Orfeo ed Euridice* is available, complete and in excerpts. The opera's best-known numbers include "Dance of the Furies," "Dance of the Blessed Spirits," and the aria "Che faro senza Euridice?" (What shall I do without Eurydice?).

Other recommendations are the overture to *Iphigénie en Aulide*, the overture to *Alceste*, the "Suite du divertissement" from *Iphigénie en Aulide*, and, for non-opera variety, the Concerto in G for Flute. The two overtures are said by musicologists to be the first examples of the overture as we know it today.

Alceste was the immediate successor to *Orfeo*, first performed in Vienna in 1767. One critic has said that its music faced even more bravely toward the new world Gluck had previously explored in his earlier opera, sounding a new dramatic note in operatic music.

The opera was written in Italian, and Gluck revised it a few years later in French. Among the best-known numbers are "Divinités du Styx," "Ah, malgré moi," and "Non, ce n'est pas un sacrifice." (Saint-Saëns later turned ballet music from *Alceste* into a well-known piano piece.)

GLUCK: THE STARTER KIT

Composition	*Recordings Available**
ORCHESTRAL (AND CHAMBER ORCHESTRA) WORKS:	
Overture: Iphigénie en Aulide	2
Concerto in G for Flute	1
Suite du Divertissement, from Iphigénie en Aulide	1
Overture: Alceste	1
VOCAL MUSIC:	
Opera:	
Orfeo ed Euridice	6

*Represents the number of recorded releases available of each listed composition as found in a recent issue of the *Schwann/Opus* catalogue. A "C" indicates that a work is only available collected with other compositions.

GLUCK: A TOP TEN

Composition   *Recordings Available**

ORCHESTRAL (AND CHAMBER ORCHESTRA)
   WORKS:

Overture: Iphigénie en Aulide	2
Suite du Divertissement, from Iphigénie en Aulide (chamber orchestra)	1
Concerto in G for Flute (chamber orchestra)	1
Overture: Alceste	1
Don Juan (ballet)	1

VOCAL MUSIC:
Operas:

Orfeo ed Euridice	6
Iphigénie en Tauride	5
Iphigénie en Aulide	2
Alceste	1
La Corona	1

GLUCK: A MASTER COLLECTION

Composition   *Recordings Available**

ORCHESTRAL (AND CHAMBER ORCHESTRA)
   WORKS:

Overture: Iphigénie en Aulide	2
Suite du Divertissement, from Iphigénie en Aulide (chamber orchestra)	1
Concerto in G for Flute (chamber orchestra)	1
Overture: Alceste	1
Don Juan (ballet)	1

VOCAL MUSIC:
Operas:

Orfeo ed Euridice	6
Iphigénie en Tauride	5
Iphigénie en Aulide	2
Alceste	1
La Corona	1
Echo et Narcisse	1
Paride ed Elena	1

Composition	Recordings Available*
Contessa de numi	0
L'isle de Merlin	0
La recontre Imprévue	0
Parnaso confuse	0
Telemacco	0
Trionfo di Clelia	0
La Danza (dramatic pastoral)	1
Armide (arias)	C

PAUL HINDEMITH (1895–1963)

Number 33

No native-born Americans made The List, although some came close and several would be among a second fifty. But there are several naturalized citizens, one of whom is Paul Hindemith, a leading composer of the twentieth century. German-born, German-reared, German-educated, and a onetime professor of music in Berlin, he came to the United States in early 1940, a few months after Germany's September 1939 invasion of Poland that began World War II. While the trip was disguised as his fourth musical tour of America, the actual purpose was for him to settle here. For a short time he taught music at the University of Buffalo, but he disliked the weather, which he described as "slush, ice, and snow," and worse yet, "black snow." Before long he joined the School of Music at Yale, where there was less snow and it was more often white. He was named head of the school in 1942; became a United States citizen in 1946; and after the war, in 1953, returned to Europe to live in Switzerland.

Of the twenty latest-born composers on The List, only three are German: Mahler, born in 1860; Richard Strauss, born in 1864; and Hindemith, born in 1895. Mahler lived only eleven years into this century, but Strauss was alive until 1949 and Hindemith until 1963. With the exception of Shostakovich, he is the most recent composer on The List. Appropriately, he was into what earlier in the century was called New Music.

In 1925 he wrote: "I am firmly convinced that a big battle over New Music will start in the next few years—the signs are already there. It will have to be shown whether or not the music of our day, including my own, is capable of survival. I, of course, believe firmly in it, but I also believe that the reproaches made against most modern music are only too well deserved. . . . I am of the opinion that in the next few years the utmost orderliness will be called for, and I myself shall do all I can to achieve it."

Hindemith is not only one of the core group of the five New Music composers on The List (along with Bartók, Stravinsky, and [sometimes] Prokofiev and Shostakovich), he is also the twentieth century's leading throwback to Bach. He is acknowledged as the prime twentieth-century producer of Bach-type music, a master of counterpoint and of "unity, logic, and clean construction." He was a musician's musician; *the* musician's musician of this century as Bach was of his times—and some critics say the most complete, technically proficient musician of the century. In his early work he was also "the last word in acid dissonance," a quack-and-growl composer of the first magnitude. Author-critic Harold Schonberg wrote of those sounds: "Well known is Richard Strauss' complaint to Hindemith: 'Why do you have to write this way? You have talent.' Less well known is the cocky Hindemith's answer to the distinguished composer thirty-one years his senior: 'Herr professor, you make your music and I'll make mine.' "

There is no real contradiction in composers producing peculiar new sounds and putting them in familiar neoclassical or neo-Baroque forms. The music they write sounds nothing like the music of Bach or Haydn, but the architecture they use recalls those pre-Romantic days.

Hindemith, the experts say, did not formally adopt atonality; nonetheless, he did things with dissonance that make his music sound severe and brutal—as distant from Bach or Haydn as it could be.

Hindemith went through one phase committed to music with mass appeal, called *Gebrauchsmusik* ("functional music," "workaday music"), for radio, films, and the like. This was part of a movement devoted to *Zeitkunst* (contemporary art). In his own words, an opera could be set "in a factory, in the streets of a large city, in a railway train or anywhere you like. All I am trying to say is that I don't think a good opera has to contain a heavy shot of romance, it doesn't have to be naturalistic, veristic or symbolic. The main thing is that one should be able to write some real music for it." One product of this approach in 1929 was an opera called *Neues vom Tage* (News of the day), a farce about marital problems.

When the Nazis seized power in 1933 Hindemith was second only to Strauss as Germany's most respected musician—famous as a composer, a professor of composition, a theorist, a chamber-music performer, and a virtuoso violist. But the Nazis didn't like his modern

---

MAD AS A HEN

Although Hindemith chose to leave the United States and spend his last years in Europe, at one time American citizenship was very important to him. He applied shortly after arriving in the States and, five years later, spent considerable time studying the required booklets before presenting himself for his test. The judge decided that one of the world's top music figures should not be interrogated in public and invited him to a private room, then issued the oath without subjecting him to any questions whatever about the Constitution, Joe DiMaggio, or other important bits of Americana. This special treatment, his friends said, made him "mad as a red hen."

---

music—and they didn't like the fact that his wife was Jewish, that he welcomed Jews in his orchestra, and, Hitler forbid, that he even had Jews for friends! To Hindemith's credit, he did not change his ways—and, as the world learned to its horror, the Nazis did not change theirs.

One rather typical Nazi comment about his work: "The foulest perversion of German music." Dr. Goebbels, Hitler's monstrous minister of propaganda, said of Hindemith: "Technical mastery is not an excuse but an obligation. To misuse it for meaningless music trifles is to besmirch true genius." Such assessments are reason enough for those of us not easily captured by Hindemith to reexamine our positions and clutch him to our hearts.

While in Germany, Hindemith spent several years composing an opera, *Mathis der Maler* (Mathis the painter), named for a famous Renaissance painter, Matthias Grünewald, one of the great figures in German art. Grünewald appealed to Hindemith because he fought for the peasants in the Peasants' War against tyranny. The musicologists say it was Hindemith's way of protesting against Nazism. But the Nazis would not allow the opera to be performed, which led to one of the best art-versus-state showdowns of the century. From the opera music Hindemith developed a three-movement symphony, also called *Mathis der Maler*, one of his masterpieces, if not *the* masterpiece of his life. The conductor of the Berlin Philharmonic Orchestra at the time was Wilhelm Furtwängler, a Good Guy and a magnificent conductor, who was so highly regarded by the nation that he felt the Hitler gang would not take him on. The concert was held in 1934, and Hindemith's music was denounced as "unbearable to the Third Reich." Good Guy Furtwängler fought for Hindemith but inevitably lost, and Hindemith found it convenient to go teach music to the Turks, before coming to Buffalo. Anyone who has been in both Istanbul and Buffalo might wonder at that second move, but by then World War II had begun. Strauss, incidentally, was a Bad Guy and sided with the Nazis against Hindemith.

Hindemith's first big success was an opera, *Cardillac*, introduced in Dresden in 1926, based upon the novel by E. T. A. Hoffman *Das Fraulein von Scuderi*. It is a not-too-cheerful story about a goldsmith, Cardillac, who gets his kicks from murdering people by dousing his gold works with poison. The orchestral music in *Cardillac* is considered to be as fine as any Hindemith produced.

In the same general time period he composed a series of well-known pieces of chamber music for various instruments, including *Kammermusik* No. 2 for Piano and Twelve Instruments, 1924; No. 3 for Cello and Ten Instruments, 1925; No. 5 for Viola and Chamber Orchestra, 1927; and No. 6 for Viola D'Amore and Chamber Orchestra, 1927. These, the professionals say, combine Bach's counterpoint with the harmonic, rhythmic, and melodic innovations of the twentieth century.

Most of Hindemith's most serious work came a little later: *Konzertmusik*, for string orchestra and brass instruments, 1930; *Der Schwanendreher* (The swan turner), a viola concerto, 1935; Violin Concerto, 1939; *Nobilissima visione*, both a ballet and an orchestral suite, 1938; Symphony in E-flat, a conventional symphony, 1940; and *Symphonic Metamorphosis of Themes by Karl Maria von Weber*, 1943. Other later works include *Ludus Tonalis*, consisting of twelve fugues, one in each key, a twentieth-century version of Bach's *Well-Tempered Clavier*; *Symphonia Serena*, in two movements for full orchestra, one scored for woodwinds and one for strings; and Symphony in B-flat for Concert Band.

Hindemith is also known for his sonatas, string quartets, and song cycles. Two of his ballets are still heard, and so is the song cycle *Das Marienleben* for piano and soprano vocalist, based on fifteen poems describing the life of the Virgin Mary.

In his final years, a mellower Hindemith produced music with a distinctly Romantic sound—just the kind of sound, in fact, that he had once so vigorously rejected.

The story is told of how he composed funeral music for King George V of England in one day for a 1936 London concert, causing

---

BLOOMING LILACS

The Robert Shaw Chorale is well known, but less so the fact that Robert Shaw commissioned Hindemith to write a requiem mass for loved ones who died in World War II. Hindemith called the piece *When Lilacs Last in the Dooryard Bloom'd*. The composer had just become an American citizen and based the requiem on Walt Whitman's poem about Abraham Lincoln. Typical of Hindemith's craftsmanship, it includes marches, passacaglias, and a fugue. It is one of Hindemith's most emotional compositions, and one of his best.

English critic Walter Leigh to write: "Such a feat can rarely have been accomplished since Handel's day in the sphere of serious music. Only a composer with a complete mastery of technique and an exceptionally fertile invention could perform it successfully. It is the more remarkable because the work bears no trace of speed, and this very simplicity is one of its great merits."

Hindemith is perhaps the greatest teacher on The List. Aaron Copland once complained that Hindemith was so forceful at Yale that all young American composers seemed to be writing Hindemith-like music. In addition, he wrote many books about music which have played an important role in music education in this country. One, *The Craft of Musical Composition*, describes his own approach to composing. Two others on traditional harmony have been published in several languages. Also, his series of Harvard lectures in 1949–1950, published as *A Composer's World*, are highly regarded. These days, in fact, the music people pay much more attention to his teachings than the public does to his compositions; he was considerably more popular at his death in 1963 than he is today. But no one questions his prowess as virtuoso performer on both violin and viola, and as author, conductor, teacher, and music scholar.

STARTER KIT

Mathis der Maler, the symphony, is a mandatory selection, both because it is a major orchestral work and because of the role it played in Hindemith's future under Nazism, leading in part to a plot (of which Hindemith apparently was not fully aware) to spirit him in and out of the United States several times in order to set up his eventual emigration.

Perhaps his most frequently played music today is his Sonata for Trumpet and Piano, composed in 1939 in the Alps just before he came to the United States. Among other sonatas composed at the same time were those for clarinet, horn, and harp. His publisher had written, "I am willing, as a spur to your imagination, to send you a list of instruments which have perhaps escaped your eagle eye." These sonatas are a nearly universal part of the student repertoire for virtually all instruments.

The biggest work composed that year was his Violin Concerto. After a U.S. performance of it, he wrote his publisher, "Last Friday Violin Concerto—excellently done, huge success." An optional orchestral choice is the rousing *Symphonic Metamorphosis of Themes by Weber*, of which there are many recordings. But my recommendation is his *Concert Music for Strings and Brass*.

The chamber-music selection is *Kleine Kammermusik* No. 2 for Wind Quintet, written much earlier (in 1922), and the vocal-music choice is *Das Marienleben* (The life of Mary), a song cycle for piano and soprano, composed in 1922–1923. Geoffrey Skelton, Hindemith's biographer, says that in it "Hindemith first fully discovered his true roots in the polyphonic style of the early eighteenth century." Hindemith told his publishers, "I definitely think they are the best things I have yet written." And they agreed, saying, "It is a really wonderful work." He later orchestrated some of the songs. If it is not available, try the requiem *When Lilacs Last in the Dooryard Bloom'd*.

HINDEMITH: THE STARTER KIT

Composition	Recordings Available*
SYMPHONIES:	
Mathis der Maler	3
OTHER ORCHESTRAL WORKS:	
Concert Music for Strings and Brass	3
CHAMBER MUSIC:	
Kleine Kammermusik No. 2 for Wind Quintet	4
OTHER INSTRUMENTAL MUSIC:	
Sonata for Trumpet and Piano	6

Composition   Recordings Available*

VOCAL MUSIC:

Das Marienleben (song cycle for piano and   3
  soprano)

*Represents the number of recorded releases available of each listed composi-
tion as found in a recent issue of the *Schwann/Opus* catalogue. A "C" indicates that a work is only available collected with other compositions.

HINDEMITH: A TOP TEN

Composition   Recordings Available*

SYMPHONIES:
Mathis der Maler   3

OTHER ORCHESTRAL WORKS:
Violin Concerto   4
Symphonic Metamorphosis of Themes by   5
  Weber
Symphony in B-flat for Band (ensemble)   5
Ballet:
  Nobilissima Visione   5
Concert Music for Strings and Brass   3

CHAMBER MUSIC:
Kleine Kammermusik No. 2 for Wind Quintet   4

OTHER INSTRUMENTAL MUSIC:
Sonata for Trumpet and Piano   6
Sonata for Oboe and Piano   5

VOCAL MUSIC:
Das Marienleben (song cycle for piano and   3
  soprano)

HINDEMITH: A MASTER COLLECTION

Composition	*Recordings Available**
SYMPHONIES:	
Mathis der Maler	3
Symphony in E-flat	1
OTHER ORCHESTRAL WORKS:	
Violin Concerto	4
Symphonic Metamorphosis of Themes by Weber	5
Der Schwanendreher, for Viola and Small Orchestra	3
Symphony in B-flat for Band (ensemble)	5
Concert Music for Strings and Brass	3
Ballets:	
Nobilissima Visione	1
The Four Temperaments	1
Concert Music for Strings and Brass	2
CHAMBER MUSIC:	
Kleine Kammermusik No. 2 for Wind Quintet	4
String Quartet No. 3	1
OTHER INSTRUMENTAL MUSIC:	
Sonata for Trumpet and Piano	6
Sonata for Oboe and Piano	5
Sonata for Alto Horn	6
Sonata for Bassoon	6
Sonata for Unaccompanied Cello	4
Sonata for Clarinet and Piano	5
VOCAL MUSIC:	
Das Marienleben (song cycle for piano and soprano)	3
Requiem Mass:	
When Lilacs Last in the Dooryard Bloom'd	

CLAUDIO MONTEVERDI (1567–1643)

Number 34

German domination of The List begins with Bach and his colleagues, Handel and Telemann, all of whom composed in the first half of the 1700s. Before them Italian music, especially Italian vocal music, dominated. With the exception of Vivaldi, whose specialty was string concertos, all Italians on The List, from whatever time period, made their major contributions (and earned their reputations) creating music for people to sing.

The first-born of these vocal-music artists was Giovanni da Palestrina, the father of Catholic church music. The second-born, some fifty years later, was Claudio Monteverdi, the father of Opera. Palestrina did not "invent" Catholic sacred music, of course, and Monteverdi did not "invent" the concept of opera. Both forms evolved, as jazz, baseball, and the environmental movement have evolved. But Monteverdi played a major role—or *the* major role, if you will—in bringing opera out of the closet. In large part due to his efforts, opera not only emerged from the shadows but quickly found itself immensely popular—in his lifetime there were sixteen *public* opera houses in Venice alone.

But Monteverdi was much more than opera. The finest composer of the seventeenth century, in his day he was to music what Shakespeare, born three years earlier, was to play writing. As well as being the major early proponent of drama in music, he was the perfector of the madrigal; the first important orchestral-color specialist, foreshadowing Berlioz and Richard Strauss; and the major transitional figure between the sixteenth and seventeenth centuries—that is, between Renaissance and Baroque music.

In all things, Claudio Monteverdi was a mighty musical experimenter.

DISSONANT FOOLS

Monteverdi is considered by some gurus to be the first composer to whom lovers of eighteenth- and nineteenth-century music can listen with real pleasure and understanding. Whatever the style, his music is viewed as dramatic, romantic, and adventurous. But many of his more traditional contemporaries were not turned on. One, Giovanni Artusi (c. 1545–1613), wrote:

"These new composers believe that they have done everything when they satisfy the ear. Day and night they spend their time at their instruments, that they may try out the effects of pieces interlarded with dissonances—the fools. They never realize that these instruments betray them. They seem to be satisfied if they can produce the greatest possible tonal disturbance by bringing together altogether unrelated elements and mountainous collections of cacophonies."

Opponents of dissonant twentieth-century sounds would not have enjoyed Monteverdi in his day. He was an innovator of the highest order, using dissonance for tension and dramatic effect, the musicologists tell us, and orchestral color for atmosphere. He did compose with scales more like major and minor keys than church modes (the earlier church scales), but he liked sudden "daring" changes from one key to another—although he never got into using two or three keys at the same time, as experimenters did three hundred years later. Still, he was revolutionary for his time, with one prime example of this then-dissonance being the "Lament" from his opera *Arianna*.

Monteverdi was born in Cremona, Italy. He was a young choir singer, composed one book of religious madrigals at sixteen and a second book at twenty-one, and was a violinist and singer for the duke of Mantua, who took his court musicians with him to war and elsewhere on his travels. After leaving the duke, he was choirmaster of the famed St. Mark's Cathedral in Venice from 1613 until his death in 1643. In a third, fourth, and fifth book of madrigals—essentially mini-operas, with up to nine singers participating—Monteverdi put more and more passion into his work, more drama, more of his personal feelings.

One of his most famous compositions, from his eighth book of

UNION ORGANIZERS NEEDED

Monteverdi had long wished to be *maestro di cappella* for the duke of Mantua, but when the appointment finally came, in 1601, he found the work a little hard to take. Then his health began to deteriorate. He asked his patron to ease up, writing in 1604:

"I do most heartily pray your most Serene Highness, for the love of God, no longer to put so much work upon me; and to give me more time, for my great desire to serve you, and the excess of my fatigue will not fail to shorten my life; and if I live longer, I may yet be of service to your Serene Highness, and of use to my poor children."

In fact, he lasted another thirty-nine years. And he produced his famous opera, *L'Orfeo*, three years later, while still under the patronage of the duke.

madrigals, written in 1638, is called *Madrigali guerrieri et amorosi* (Madrigals of war and love). Of these, the best known is a mini-chamber-opera, "Il combattimento di Tancredi et Clorinda" (The combat of Tancredi and Clorinda). Two lovers dressed in armor meet and duel, not recognizing each other, and one dies. The orchestral music helps set the mood, going beyond its (then) usual function of just accompanying the singers. This was a significant move in music and opera development, a clear step toward opera as we know it.

The Monteverdi opera most often heard today is *L'Orfeo* (Orpheus), which is all about the legendary chap who followed his dead wife to the underground regions, trying to rescue her from the King of Shadows. The "huge" orchestra Monteverdi gathered for *L'Orfeo* consisted of "two harpsichords, two bass viols, ten tenor viols, one double harp, two small French violins, two large guitars, two wooden organs, three viole da gamba, four trombones, one regal, two (wooden) cornetti, one treble flute, one clarion and three trumpets with mutes." This was considerably bigger than any orchestra had ever been—and larger than a lot of orchestras to follow for some time to come.

L'Orfeo is still performed, appears and reappears on public television, and is still regarded as the first real beginning of drama in music, combining solo songs, choruses, dances, laments, an opening overture (another first), and a closing ballet with the big orchestra.

"Rarely in the history of music," writes one critic, "has any composer in one work shown so many paths to the future as did Monteverdi in 'Orfeo.' "

Monteverdi's last opera was *L'incoronazione di Poppea* ("The coronation of Poppa"), based on Roman history as opposed to the Greek legend of *L'Orfeo*. It too has been broadcast on public television.

As one of the great experimenters of music, Monteverdi helped with the transition from the Renaissance simultaneous-melodies style to the melody-plus-chords approach that developed in the Baroque era. Among other things, he pushed *recitative*, a type of dramatic writing for voice, a cross between ordinary speech and pure singing, usually sung/spoken in opera by one performer or used as a form of communication among several solo voices.

Monteverdi was not the first to use the recitative technique, which had been invented a few years earlier by a group in Florence called the Camerata as they broke from the long technique of polyphonic, simultaneous-melodies music—the style made near-perfect by Palestrina and totally perfect by Bach. But Monteverdi's use of recitative forced a separation of melody and harmony, thus helping advance the notion of a single melody supported by chords.

Musicologist Alfred Einstein writes:

> The general structure of early opera was based on an entirely false conception, the engineer, the scene-painter, and the dancer being considered more important than the poet or the musician. In his "Orfeo," produced at Mantua in 1607, Monteverdi showed for the first time that within this framework it was possible to create a living, passionate, intensely dramatic music. For the first time he allowed the instruments to speak a language of their own—though it is a mistake to assert that he already used them in the modern manner. He won a place in the drama for instrumental music, which it was to lose all too soon. . . .
>
> In his lifetime Monteverdi drew upon himself that hatred of the reactionaries which is the lot of genius. . . . He is the greatest representative of a period of revolution in which the very foundations of tradition were shaken.

STARTER KIT

Vocal music is what Monteverdi is about, even though what he did with instruments in connection with vocal music was part of his special genius.

Complete recordings and excerpts are available for two of the recommended operas: *L'Orfeo* and *L'incoronazione di Poppea*. The only surviving music from *Arianna* is the "Lament."

His single choral masterpiece is *Vespro della Beata Vergine*, composed in 1610.

And try any masses and madrigals you can find. Collections from his many books of them are available. It is not expected that many readers will devote themselves to Monteverdi rather than Mozart, but it's not difficult to become entranced by Monteverdi's vocal music. The music people are very high on his madrigal work. Professor Donald Jay Grout describes Monteverdi's madrigals as: "flexible, animated, vivid and variegated . . . rich in musical invention, humorous and sensitive, audacious yet perfectly logical in harmonies. . . ."

THE FLOWERS OF SPRING

Monteverdi published his first book of madrigals for five voices in 1587 and dedicated it to Count Marco Verita. He wrote in the preface:

"I beseech my Lord, accept these madrigals as a simple testimony of my gratitude for the favors I have received at your hands . . . and I can expect for compositions so youthful no other praise than that which is accorded to the flowers of spring."

Monteverdi was only twenty at the time. He went on to publish eight books of madrigals in his lifetime—all this *before* getting into the opera composition for which he is best known.

MONTEVERDI: THE STARTER KIT

Composition	Recordings Available*
VOCAL MUSIC:	
Operas:	
L'Orfeo	4
Lament, from Arianna	3
L'incoronazione di Poppea	5
Madrigals: any collection	C

Composition   Recordings Available*

SACRED MUSIC:
Vespro della Beata Vergine   8

*Represents the number of recorded releases available of each listed composition as found in a recent issue of the *Schwann/Opus* catalogue. A "C" indicates that a work is only available collected with other compositions.

MONTEVERDI: A TOP TEN

Composition   Recordings Available*

VOCAL MUSIC:
Operas:
   L'Orfeo   4
   Lament, from Arianna   3
   L'incoronazione di Poppea   5
   Il ballo delle ingrate (opera-ballet)   3
   Il combattimento di Tancredi e Clorinda   7
     (opera-ballet)
   Il ritorno d'Ulisse in patria   1
Madrigals:
   Lagrime d'Armante   C
Sacred Music:
   Vespro della Beata Vergine   8
   Motets, including:
     Cantate domino a six   C
     Domine ne in furore a six   C

MONTEVERDI: A MASTER COLLECTION

Composition   Recordings Available*

VOCAL MUSIC:
Operas:
   L'Orfeo   4
   Lament, from Arianna   3
   L'incoronazione di Poppea   5
   Il ballo delle ingrate (opera-ballet)   3
   Il combattimento di Tancredi e Clorinda   7
     (opera-ballet)
   Il ritorno d'Ulisse in patria   1

Composition   *Recordings Available**

Madrigals:
    Lagrime d'Armante   C
    Chiome d'oro   C
    Hor ch'el cied e la terra   C
    Amor che deggio far   C
    Gira il nemico insidioso   C
    Lamento della ninfa   C

BALLET MUSIC (COMPLETE)   1

SACRED MUSIC:
    Magnificat a six voci (from Vespro)   2
    Vespro della Beata Vergine   8
    Confitebor Tibi (Psalm 110)   1
    Missa de cappella a four   C
    Missa de cappella a six   C
    Motets, including:
        Cantate domino a six   C
        Domine ne in furore a six   C

BÉLA BARTÓK (1881–1945)

Number 35

The greatest folk-music expert on The List is Béla Bartók. No one is really in second place.

• He spent years combing through remote mountains and villages of Eastern Europe;

• He published some two thousand folk tunes, chiefly, but not entirely, from Hungary and Romania;

• He wrote five books and scores of articles on folk music;

• His own compositional style, while wholly original, incorporated the fundamental elements of folk music as no classical composer ever had before. His music involved powerful, irregular folk rhythms, melodies based on old folk-music scales, and unusual—some say "brutal"—folk-music orchestration.

Like Hindemith, Bartók is one of the leading twentieth-century "New Music" composers, and many present-day critics would put him considerably higher than I have. (Some listeners not accustomed

to his kind of music would unList him, but they would be sorry about
that if they persevered and became more accustomed to his no-longer
"new" sounds.) His lifework was to honor the real folk music of
Hungary, in part by bringing its harmonies and rhythms to his own
twentieth-century compositions.

Bartók is unquestionably one of the more dissonant composers on
The List, and his sounds are peculiar for ears accustomed to Brahms,
Beethoven, Mozart, and Mendelssohn. Along with Stravinsky, Hindemith, Prokofiev, and Shostakovich (all to varying degrees), he "honored dissonance." Recall the *Webster's* definition of dissonance: "A
mingling of discordant sounds . . . want of agreement . . . incongruity."
Of consonance, *Webster's* says: "Agreement or congruity. . . . Loosely,
a pleasing combination of sounds."

To dismiss Bartók cavalierly, however, is wholly unfair to our
century, since "honoring dissonance" became a badge of merit for
young turn-of-the-century composers fed up with a century of Romanticism. Escaping from Romanticism became the natural thing to do; as
we have seen, one escape route open to composers was investigation
of nationalist music and the use of unfamiliar scales and rhythms
found in the back country; another choice was working in more than
one key simultaneously, or in no key at all.

Bartók was born in Nagyszentmiklos, a small town in Hungary,
just five years before the death of the other Hungarian on The List,
keyboard-thunderer Liszt. His father was the director of an agricul-
tural school, his mother a piano teacher. He studied in Budapest at the
Royal Academy of Music, became a brilliant pianist, and, early on
(after hearing a young peasant girl singing), seriously began to investi-
gate and collect Hungarian folk music. He became a world authority
on folk songs, not only from Hungary but from Romania, Bulgaria,
and other Eastern European countries, from the Carpathian Mountains to the Black Sea. A true musicologist, he was an acclaimed
research scientist.

He wrote of his folk study: "The genuine Hungarian peasant
music was all but unknown at the time. In the most valuable part of
it, the oldest Hungarian peasant melodies, the material was at last
discovered that was destined to serve as the foundation for a renaissance of Hungarian art music."

Bartók is one of several composers sometimes described as part
Classicist, part Romantic, and part turn-of-the-century modernist—
classically traditional in the forms he chose, Romantic in his use of
orchestral color, "modern" in his use of primitive rhythms, and ultra-
imaginative in scales and harmony.

BARTÓK ON FOLK MUSIC

On exploring peasant music: "The excesses of the romantics began to be unbearable to many."

On folk harmony: "It may sound odd, but I do not hesitate to say that the simpler the melody, the more complex and strange may be the harmonizations and accompaniments that go well with it."

On composers finding anti-Romantic hope only in atonal music: "Far be it from me to maintain that the only way to salvation for a composer in our day is for him to base his opinion on folk music. But I wish that our opponents had an equally liberal opinion of the significance of folk music."

The seeds of his dissonant music came from the thousands of Hungarian folk songs he collected, which were themselves discordant as well as rhythmically complex. The professionals say that in some works he has as many as four keys going at the same time. Yet he put this strange-sounding, stark, Hungarian folk music (for which he invented new harmonies) into familiar Classical structures—no symphonies, but sonatas for piano and for violin, six string quartets, three piano concertos, and one concerto for orchestra. He also wrote one opera, *Bluebeard's Castle*, two large ballets, *The Wooden Prince* and *The Miraculous Mandarin*, and a well-known six-volume set of 153 piano pieces called *Mikrokosmos*.

Before getting into folk songs, Bartók learned from the music of Richard Strauss and Debussy as those two veered off from the nineteenth-century music that people were accustomed to hearing— Strauss being one of the first turn-of-the-century composers to emphasize discords, and Debussy creating new Impressionistic sounds replete with mists, colors, nuances, moods, shadows, sensations, and atmospheres.

In 1927 Bartók toured the United States for ten weeks, assisting in performances of his important works. He was greeted respectfully but not enthusiastically, and the attitude toward him was similar when he returned to live here thirteen years later. The critics agreed that he was the best Hungarian composer; the music gurus applauded him for his monumental contributions to musical folklore; and the Bartók claque argued that he was one of the most original and forceful musical figures of our generation. But the concertgoers were not turned on, and his works were not performed frequently.

Bartók spent the last five years of his life in the United States, dying in 1945, out of work, unfamous, and basically broke.

One way to become exposed to Bartók and his new twentieth-century music is to listen to the first two minutes of *The Miraculous Mandarin,* a one-act "danced pantomime"/orchestral suite. It tells more about "strange musical progressions" and "unusual melodies" than a dozen pages of commentary.

YEHUDI MENUHIN ON BARTÓK

When Bartók was still alive, one of his strongest supporters was the virtuoso violinist Yehudi Menuhin. In his autobiography, *Unfinished Journey,* Menuhin wrote:

"Deriving from the East, Bartók's music could not but appeal to me, but in his greatness a local heritage had been absorbed, interpreted and recast as a universal message, speaking to our age and culture and to every other. As he elevated folk music to universal validity, so he gave noble dimensions to human emotion. Strong with the earthy, primeval strength of its origins, his music has also the cultivated strength of a steely, ruthless discipline which refuses all indulgence. Here, in the twentieth century, was a composer to bear comparison with the giants of the past.

"So, at [conductor Antal] Dorati's urging, I came to love above any other contemporary works the compositions of Bartók, and more particularly the Second Violin Concerto and the First Sonata for Piano and Violin (Bartók's own instrument was the piano, but like all Hungarians, he understood the violin)."

But pause before returning immediately to lush, melodic Tchaikovsky. One suggestion is to concentrate *only* on cassette tapes of Bartók, Stravinsky, and Hindemith for a few weeks while driving to and from work, avoiding all other music. Give each composer a week, listening carefully to two long tapes of his work. It is a fairly safe bet that you'll get hooked on two of the three—not necessarily to the point of preferring this music over any other, but almost certainly to the point of enjoying it. It is unlikely to happen at first hearing, despite the insistence of the professionals that Bartók is clear, simple, and beautiful.

Esteemed musicologist Alfred Einstein, one of Bartók's special supporters, wrote in midcentury: "That it is not impossible to produce New Music without resorting to negation, to program, or to compromise—a music, that is, which is not stamped by the crises of the war-torn Twentieth Century and its postwar aftermath—can be seen in the work of the Hungarian Béla Bartók. He has his roots in the true—as distinct from the gypsy—folklore of his country, while at the same time retaining his individuality. He restores balance to the future elements in music. He demonstrates that the future of music does not lie in imitation, in parody of the past, or in a vain return to the past, nor in this school or that clique, nor in any particular system, but in the great and creative personality of the individual—that is, in the human."

STARTER KIT

Since the ears of most of us are not accustomed to Hungarian music, and the ears of some of us are still not accustomed to all of the savage things Bartók did to Hungarian music, it may take a little more work than usual to enjoy the Starter Kit selections.

Recommended as representatives are three orchestral pieces, one string quartet, and some Hungarian peasant instrumental music. Orchestral pieces include his Concerto for Orchestra, written in 1944, which is neither a Baroque-period concerto grosso with one small group of instruments playing against a larger group, nor a nineteenth- or twentieth-century solo concerto featuring a soloist pitted against the orchestra. Bartók's concerto has small group against large group, like the old concerto grosso, but the instruments making up the small group constantly change.

The composer said of it: "The general mood of the work represents, apart from the jesting second movement, a gradual transition from the sternness of the first movement and the lugubrious death song of the third, to the life assertion of the last one."

In 1936 he wrote a four-movement piece that he called simply *Music for Strings, Percussion, and Celesta*. It has been selected, as well as the ballet suite *The Miraculous Mandarin*—which, as indicated, is as "New Music"-sounding as any composition in this book.

Bartók's six string quartets, ridiculed when produced, have

become greatly admired by the professionals, and several performers have recorded all six of them. They are a mixture of "piercing and agonizing chords," atonal music, and reasonably conventional and pleasant sounds. We have selected No. 4, but any of the others will do. Whichever you choose, play it several times running. A strange thing might happen to your "hearing buds."

For a bonus, try the solo violin sonata commissioned by Yehudi Menuhin.

BARTÓK: THE STARTER KIT

Composition	Recordings Available*
ORCHESTRAL MUSIC:	
Concerto for Orchestra	17
Music for Strings, Percussion and Celesta	10
The Miraculous Mandarin (ballet and suite)	9
CHAMBER MUSIC:	
String Quartet No. 4	9
OTHER INSTRUMENTAL MUSIC:	
Hungarian Folk Songs and Peasant Songs	14

*Represents the number of recorded releases available of each listed composition as found in a recent issue of the *Schwann/Opus* catalogue. A "C" indicates that a work is only available collected with other compositions.

BARTÓK: A TOP TEN

Composition	Recordings Available*
ORCHESTRAL MUSIC:	
Concerto for Orchestra	17
Violin Concerto No. 2	9
Music for Strings, Percussion and Celesta	10
Dance Suite	14
The Miraculous Mandarin (ballet and suite)	9
Romanian Folk Dances	17
CHAMBER MUSIC:	
String Quartet No. 4	9

Composition	Recordings Available*

OTHER INSTRUMENTAL MUSIC:
Solo Violin Sonata	3
Hungarian Folk Songs and Peasant Songs	14

VOCAL MUSIC:
Opera:
Bluebeard's Castle	6

BARTÓK: A MASTER COLLECTION

Composition	Recordings Available*

ORCHESTRAL MUSIC:
Concerto for Orchestra	17
Piano Concerto No. 1	6
Piano Concerto No. 2	5
Piano Concerto No. 3	4
Violin Concerto No. 2 (1938)	9
Concerto for Viola and Orchestra	5
Divertimento for String Orchestra	5
Romanian Folk Dances	17
Music for Strings, Percussion and Celesta	10
Dance Suite	14
The Miraculous Mandarin (ballet and suite)	9

CHAMBER MUSIC:
String Quartet No. 4	9
String Quartet No. 5	11

OTHER INSTRUMENTAL MUSIC:
Mikrokósmos	9
Sonata for Piano	7
Sonata for Two Pianos and Percussion	6
Sonata No. 2 for Violin and Piano	7
Solo Violin Sonata	3
Hungarian Folk Songs and Peasant Songs	14

VOCAL MUSIC:
Opera:
Bluebeard's Castle	6

CÉSAR FRANCK (1822–1890)

Number 36

César Franck was Mr. Integrity, Mr. Serenity, and something of Mr. Dangerfield, except that Rodney makes a big thing of his condition and Franck did not. And, unlike Rodney, Franck was not totally denied respect; he had pupils who adored him. One admirer wrote near the close of the century: "He stands out from his contemporaries as one of another age. They are scoffers, he was a believer; they vaunt themselves, he worked in silence; they seek glory, he let it seek him. . . . They shrink from nothing—concession, compromise, meanness even; he performed his mission faithfully, and without counting the cost, leaving us the noblest example of uprightness." As this tribute suggests, he was a simple, humble man: a teacher and for nearly thirty years the organist at Sainte-Clotilde Church in Paris. Sharp-tongued Debussy, who so ridiculed Grieg, had soft feelings about this fellow Frenchman, saying of him: "He was a man without guile. The discovery of a beautiful harmony was sufficient to make him as happy as the day is long. . . . This man who was unfortunate, unrecognized, possessed the soul of a child, and one so good that neither contradictory circumstances nor the wickedness of others could ever make him feel bitter."

These tributes notwithstanding, during his lifetime Franck was one of the least acclaimed of composers—though much admired as an organist and a teacher. He worked for a decade on *Les Béatitudes*, an oratorio, and in 1879 invited the music bigwigs of Paris to his home to hear him play it. All but two declined, many at the last minute with phony excuses. The introduction of his Symphony in D Minor in 1889 was another disaster. And so was the first performance of his Piano Quintet in F Minor, his first significant chamber work. The pianist was Saint-Saëns, who was so displeased by it that he walked off the stage at the conclusion, refusing to return for applause and leaving behind the score—even though it had been dedicated to him. This sort of thing kept happening to "Father Franck," as his students called him, throughout most of his life. And when, finally, his String Quartet in D *was* strongly applauded, he said mildly, "There, you see, the public is beginning to understand me." This was in 1890, the year of his death.

SPECIAL TALENT

At sixteen Franck competed in the finals of the piano competition at the Paris Conservatory. His performance wowed the judges, as reported in a Paris musical publication on August 5, 1838:

"First of all the jury awarded with one voice the first prize to M. Franck. But after that, the jury decided to look into the matter again. After some discussion, M. Cherubini announced with his customary grace: 'The jury has now decided that M. Franck stands so incomparably far ahead of his fellow competitors that it is impossible to nominate another to share the prize with him. Accordingly, a second first prize will be given to those who would in ordinary circumstances have deserved the senior award.' "

Franck was born in Liège, Belgium, of an old family descended from famous painters. His father was a bank clerk, but one who appreciated the musical leanings of both César and his brother, Joseph. After César had completed part of a course at the Paris Conservatory, his father took him on a concert tour in the manner of Leopold Mozart and *his* young son. The senior Franck hoped he had a young virtuoso and also hoped to make some money, part of which was to go for further musical study. César turned out not to be a Mozart, but he did return to the conservatory and eventually became a professor of organ there, and master of the organ at Sainte-Clotilde. That was his life: teaching, playing, and composing—quietly, mostly in obscurity. The consensus of the music historians is that he was incapable of passion, of intensity, of spiritual or emotional conflicts. The hallmarks of his music are serenity, peace, and brotherly love.

The music people tell us that Franck's aim was to write Romantic music within Classical structures. They say also that he brought to his compositions an organ-oriented style characterized by a good deal of improvisation and contrasting timbres. He is known, too, for his shifting harmonies and his frequent and sudden modulations—moves from one key to another.

Franck is the fifth Frenchman (he became a French citizen and lived nearly all his life in Paris) on The List. Through his teaching and his attention to instrumental music (rather than opera, which had been dominating French musical interests), he became an extremely influential musical force in France in the latter part of the nineteenth century. But it is unlikely that he would have been recognized as a composer of merit by the music world outside of Paris had he died a half-dozen years earlier. Other composers on The List were late bloomers, but none more so than César Franck. He wrote one work now recognized as a major piece in each of several forms, all of which came very late in life:

Les Béatitudes, his Sermon on the Mount, an oratorio in eight parts for solo voices, chorus, and orchestra, completed in 1879 when he was fifty-six;

Piano Quintet in F Minor, his first significant chamber work, also 1879;

Le chasseur maudit, a tone poem, 1882;

Variations symphoniques, for piano and orchestra, 1885;

String Quartet in D, the one success he enjoyed while alive, 1890;

Violin Sonata in A, his most popular work today, 1886;

Symphony in D Minor, now an accepted masterwork, and his only symphony, 1888, at age sixty-five.

Without these works, there would have been organ compositions much admired by the organ world—many of them often performed today—but there would be no "Father Franck, the Master." According to critic-composer Virgil Thomson, Franck's compositions for the organ are better than those of almost any other major composer—but his own best organ compositions are not as commanding as his half-dozen best chamber and orchestral works. The best-known organ pieces include Cinq pièces, forty-four Petites pièces, Offertoire on a Breton Air, and L'organiste, which contains eighty-eight works.

Even now, Franck is one of those on The List whose name is unfamiliar to a lot of beginning listeners, and the professionals debate whether he should be called a "major" composer. As a teacher he was the most important and influential figure in French instrumental music in the late 1800s, even though he was not recognized as a strong composer by the rest of the music world during his lifetime. He also receives a lot of Brownie Points for having helped pave the way for a school of French symphonists. My view, of course, is that all of The 50 are "major" composers, as well as another fifty and more identified in the Honorable Mention lists.

If the pro-Franck words are "purity," "serenity," "mysticism," and "simple eloquence," the anti-Franck words are "cloying," "self-indulgent," and "lacking power."

The fact is that composers on the second half of The List are, by definition, not perceived to be on the same level as those on the first half. Nowhere is there a suggestion that Franck is a Bach—although Liszt, who had something good to say about so many composers, did drift into the church where Franck was playing the organ one day and say that Bach had been brought back to life. "Not hardly," as John Wayne kept declaring in the movie Big Jake, as villain after villain who fell before him sighed in despair, "I thought you was dead." But one need not be another Bach to be a fine composer.

In France a hundred years ago, as now, who you knew was often as important as what you knew. Liszt may have summed up Franck's Rodney Dangerfield life well. "I fancy," he said, "he is lacking in that convenient social sense that opens all doors." However, Franck may have had something better than social sense in the affection and respect of his pupils, one of whom described his master as "a man of shining genius, loyal of heart and strong of soul, who seemed to have known the angels."

STARTER KIT

Franck's one symphony, his three-movement Symphony in D Minor, was written in 1888. It contains examples of what the music people call the "cyclical form," which others of us would describe as repetition of earlier themes later in the work. The criticism of Charles Gounod (unListed composer of one of France's most famous operas, Faust) that the work was "incompetence pushed to . . . dogma" notwithstanding, it is now regarded as one of the finest symphonies of his times. In the slow movement is a long, lovely line of melody played by English horn and harp. It seems to say everything there is to say about Franck's "serenity." The connoisseurs point out that Franck was not afraid to use a harp in a symphony, whereas Dvořák and Brahms never would have done so—but it's okay to like the composition without picking out the harp.

The most frequently performed Franck work is his Sonata in A for Violin and Piano, which the experts say sounds Bach-like, not surprising since Franck—professor and master of organ—worshiped Bach, the greatest organ master of them all. Now rated alongside the violin sonatas of Beethoven and Brahms, it, too, was poorly received.

What *was* well received was his only String Quartet, written in the key of D, one of his last works, with a third movement considered to be perhaps Franck's most beautiful music. More frequently performed today is the recommendation here, his Piano Quintet in F Minor, composed ten years earlier, when Franck was in his late fifties. This was the work treated in such a boorish fashion by Saint-Saëns (a musician not known for his generous disposition).

A GOOD PLACE TO CHEAT

It is good for the soul to ignore Starter Kit recommendations occasionally, and an excellent substitute in Franck's case is his String Quartet in D.

The *Penguin Guide*, an invaluable tool for anyone buying recordings, says of it:

"Franck's Quartet is highly ambitious in its scale; its almost orchestral textures and its complex use of cyclic form always seems on the point of bursting the seams of the intimate genre of the string quartet. Yet as a very late inspiration it contains some of the composer's most profound and most compelling thought. In every sense this is a work which seeks to take up the challenge presented by the late Beethoven in a way that few nineteenth-century composers attempted, not even Brahms."

Another extremely popular Franck work is *Variations symphoniques* for piano and orchestra, the closest the composer came to a piano concerto. As the name indicates, it offers a lovely piano melody and a half-dozen variations of it.

To treat Franck appropriately, some organ compositions should be included in the Starter Kit. One could choose the *Pièce héroïque* or the *Grand pièce symphonique* or his Chorales, all very popular with organists today. I've selected the Chorales as they are the easiest to find in the record stores.

FRANCK: THE STARTER KIT

Composition	Recordings Available*
SYMPHONIES:	
Symphony in D Minor	18
OTHER ORCHESTRAL WORKS:	
Variations symphoniques, for piano and orchestra	20
CHAMBER MUSIC:	
Piano Quintet in F Minor	4
ORGAN MUSIC:	
Chorales for Organ (three)	13
PIANO (AND OTHER) MUSIC:	
Sonata in A for Violin and Piano	22

*Represents the number of recorded releases available of each listed composition as found in a recent issue of the *Schwann/Opus* catalogue. A "C" indicates that a work is only available collected with other compositions.

FRANCK: A TOP TEN

Composition	Recordings Available*
SYMPHONIES:	
Symphony in D Minor	18
OTHER ORCHESTRAL WORKS:	
Variations symphoniques, for piano and orchestra	20
Les eolides (symphonic poem)	2
CHAMBER MUSIC:	
Piano Quintet in F Minor	4
ORGAN MUSIC:	
Pièce héroïque	12
Grand pièce symphonique	6
Chorales for organ (three)	13

Composition	Recordings Available*

PIANO MUSIC:

Prelude, chorale, and fugue for solo piano	5
Sonata in A for Violin and Piano	22

VOCAL MUSIC:

Les Béatitudes (oratorio)	2

FRANCK: A MASTER COLLECTION

Composition	Recordings Available*

SYMPHONIES:

Symphony in D Minor	18

OTHER ORCHESTRAL WORKS:

Variations symphoniques, for piano and orchestra	20
Symphonic Poems:	
Les djinns (The demons), with solo piano	2
Le chasseur maudit (The damned hunter)	3
Psyche	3
Les eolides	2

CHAMBER MUSIC:

Quartet in D	2
Piano Quintet in F Minor	4

ORGAN MUSIC:

Pièce héroïque	12
Grand pièce symphonique	6
Chorales for organ (three)	13
Pastorale	5
Prière (Op. 20) for Organ	5
Fantaisie in A	7
Fantaisie in C	3
Final in B-flat	4

PIANO (AND OTHER) MUSIC:

Prelude, aria, and final	2
Prelude, chorale, and fugue for solo piano	5
Sonata in A for Violin and Piano	22

VOCAL MUSIC:

Les Béatitudes (oratorio)	2

ANTONIO VIVALDI (1675–1741)

Number 37

Bach was expected to provide a new cantata each Sunday in Leipzig; Handel a new opera each year in London. That's the way it was in the eighteenth century; the practice of falling back on earlier "classics" was not yet in vogue.

Consistent with the times, Antonio Vivaldi's job was to furnish new oratorios and concertos for every recurring festival in Venice, where for nearly forty years he was employed at the Conservatory of the Pietà. This made for a lot of music.

To reset the European Baroque stage:

Couperin of France (b. 1668) was the outstanding creator of harpsichord works.

Telemann of Germany (b. 1681), Rameau of France (b. 1683), and Vivaldi of Italy (b. 1675) were noble artists and great musicians.

Handel of Germany (b. 1685) was a Presiding Genius.

Mr. Bach of Germany (b. 1685) was Immortal.

And to position Vivaldi in Italian music:

He came to prominence 100 years after one Italian colleague, the opera master Monteverdi, and 150 years after the other early Italian on The List, the prince of religious music, Palestrina. But where Palestrina's fame comes from vocal masses and motets, and Monteverdi's from his vocal opera work, Vivaldi is best remembered today for instrumental music—mainly for concertos constructed around violins. The demand was strong for concertos, which were played weekly during church services. Vivaldi, however, was not a specialist. He also composed forty-nine operas, on one occasion turning one out in five days, and countless cantatas, motets, and oratorios, all of which influenced the vocal music of his time. Still, he was Baroque Italy's master composer of concertos, creating some 450 of them, including

ALL-GIRL ORCHESTRA

The conservatory in which Vivaldi worked was one of many of its kind in Naples and Venice in the eighteenth century. Their purpose was to shelter orphans and illegitimate children, and music was an important part of the curriculum. One traveler wrote of the unusual sight of a choir and orchestra composed almost entirely of teenaged girls:

"They are reared at public expense and trained solely to excel in music. And so they sing like angels and play the violin, the flute, the organ, the violoncello, the bassoon. . . . Each concert is given by about 40 girls. I assure you there is nothing so charming as to see a young and pretty nun [they weren't really nuns] in her white robe, with a bouquet of pomegranate flowers in her hair, leading the orchestra and beating time with all the precision imaginable."

Such was the domain of Maestro Vivaldi.

his most famous work, *The Four Seasons*, a four-concerto set that was to become one of the most frequently played classical compositions in the United States a little more than three hundred years after the composer's death.

STRAVINSKY ON VIVALDI

Stravinsky said that Vivaldi wrote the same concerto a hundred times. But don't tell that to your Yuppie friends, unless you're also prepared to tell them you don't like cappuccino.

The term *concerto* was not clearly defined in Baroque times, when composers put their own labels on works and when even the composer could not be sure how many performers would be involved when those works were played. Writing for today's symphony orchestra, an artist can count on a standard group of instruments, layered in a standard way. Not so in Europe in the 1700s:

• The *orchestral concerto* was a work for orchestra or ensemble that gave some special attention to the first violin but did not feature it.

• The *solo concerto* was a composition in which the solo instrument—usually a violin, but sometimes another instrument, such as a bassoon, cello, or flute—had much more of a virtuoso role, playing in contrast to the rest of the group. Sometimes there were two or three or even four solo virtuoso parts.

• The *concerto grosso* (grand concerto) pitted a small group of instruments against the larger part of the ensemble—usually two violins with a bass continuo, although other individual instruments could be substituted for or added to the two violins. (A *continuo*, as we have seen, is not a Baroque instrument that has gone out of fashion, but rather the backup music designed to give the composition continuity in harmony and rhythm. The term is a shortening of *basso continuo*, meaning "continuous bass." It was generally played by harpsichord or organ and usually assisted by a bass instrument such as cello or bassoon.) Vivaldi, Bach, Handel, and unListed Arcangelo Corelli were the main architects of the concerto grosso, with Corelli deserving perhaps the chief credit.

BAGPIPES

The stronghold of bagpipes on the Continent is Brittany, but their use has not been confined to that region of France. Vivaldi was fond of a delicate orchestral version of the bagpipe called the *musette* and included it in some of his compositions.

In all cases, the orchestra itself was usually a string ensemble consisting of first and second violins, viola, violoncello, violone, and bass continuo. Here and there, a composer might add a few brasses or woodwinds.

This listener has a good bit of trouble distinguishing one Baroque concerto from another and falls back upon a major principle: Be Not Intimidated. Just listen, and after giving one a fair chance, move on. It is not obligatory to recognize just what kind of concerto one is hearing. It's also fair for admirers of the concerto grosso who are not into football to remark that the passing of Mark Rypien and Randall

Cunningham looks very much alike to them, a comment some would consider incredible.

Vivaldi was born in Venice, the son of a violinist of St. Mark's Chapel, and educated as both a clergyman and a musician. He was ordained but, because of his poor health, chose music as a career, and he spent the years 1704 to 1740 at the Pietà Conservatory as conductor, composer, teacher, and general music boss.

In this capacity he wrote an enormous amount of vocal music, and while many of these compositions still exist in manuscript form, what has chiefly survived is the instrumental music for which he is famous—and which, for some of us, is overplayed today.

MUSICAL PRIEST

Music histories tell a story, true or false, that illustrates Vivaldi's dual life as musician and priest: As an old man, he was summoned before the Inquisition on the charge that when conducting mass he suddenly stopped the ceremony, left the church, and rushed to his office to write down a musical idea before it got away from him. The Inquisition found him mentally unfit to celebrate mass.

Known as "the Red Priest"—not for prescient leanings toward the unborn Communist party but because of his red beard—Vivaldi wrote some twenty-three sinfonias, seventy-five solo or trio sonatas, and many other instrumental pieces, in addition to his four-hundred-odd concertos. (A *sinfonia* was something of a minisymphony—or, more accurately, a precursor of a symphony, since the symphony did not then exist.) The authoritative professor Donald J. Grout credits Vivaldi with playing an important role in the development of the symphony, writing of him:

"As usual in this period, the terminology is imprecise, but the music, especially that of the sinfonias, clearly demonstrates that its composer is entitled to be reckoned among the earliest forerunners of the pre-Classic symphony. The conciseness of form, the markedly homophonic texture, the melodically neutral themes, the minuet finale . . . all are found in Vivaldi."

Vivaldi's music is hailed by its supporters for its fresh melodies, zesty rhythms, instrumental and orchestral color, and clarity.

One Baroque-era admirer of Vivaldi was Mr. Bach across the mountains over in Germany, who worked over at least ten of Vivaldi's concertos, arranging six for harpsichord, three for organ, and one for four violins (and later for four harpsichords) and string orchestra. In so doing, Bach helped move music away from the forms most popular in Baroque times and toward the violin and piano concertos that followed in Classical times and have persisted to this day.

Of Vivaldi's hundreds of concertos for orchestra, three sets became particularly well known. One consists of the twelve works of *L'estro armonico* (Harmonic inspiration), of which the eleventh, in D minor, is the most popular today. A second is *La stravaganza,* another set of twelve concertos. And a third set of twelve was *Il cimento dell'armonica e dell'inventioni* (The trial of harmony and invention). The first four works of this third set are *Le quattro stagione* (The four seasons), by far the best known of all Vivaldi's works and in the United States a composition that sometimes seems to threaten the popularity of "White Christmas." This set of four is scored for solo violin, small string orchestra, and harpsichord.

Each of the four is accompanied by a poem written by Vivaldi, with the lines printed on the score. While the Romantic period is the one best known for program music, *The Four Seasons* is pretty programmatic itself. "Spring," for example, is accompanied by this text:

"Spring is here and the birds salute it festively with their joyous song. . . . Meanwhile the streams and springs at the breath of gentle breezes, run their course with a sweet murmur. . . . Thunder and Lightning come to announce the season, covering the air with a black mantle. . . . When things have quieted down, the little birds return to their melodious warbling."

The poem goes on to talk about such things as a storm and a sleeping shepherd in the summer, a hunt and a peasant celebration in the fall, and cold winds and a walk on the ice in the winter.

Trendy today, Vivaldi's music slipped into obscurity after his death until fairly recently. Whether you enjoy his music or not, Vivaldi holds a place in music history as a premier violinist, a master of the concerto, and a key transitional figure between the Baroque and early Classical eras.

STARTER KIT

As noted, the four violin concertos that make up *The Four Seasons* are among the most frequently played compositions on many classical-music stations today and stand near the top in audience surveys in some areas of the country. In the late 1980s it became the in thing to mention them in polite dinner-table conversation on Manhattan's Upper East Side or in Washington's Georgetown.

In fact, an unofficial survey of a dozen New York and Connecticut residents dining in Greenwich, Connecticut, in the early 1990s produced unanimous agreement that Vivaldi was played more than any other composer on New York's classical-music stations. Less is heard of him in Grand Forks, North Dakota, according to family members there, or in Chateaugay, New York, near the Canadian border. But the temperature never dips to thirty below zero in Georgetown, and rarely in Manhattan, and perhaps that accounts for the difference. At those temperatures, Bach, Mozart, and Beethoven are required to keep life in perspective. Vivaldi and Telemann won't hack it.

Whatever the merits of Manhattan versus upstate New York, a Vivaldi Starter Kit must include *The Four Seasons*, Op. 8, for solo violin, strings, and harpsichord continuo—"Spring" in E, "Summer" in G Minor, "Autumn" in F, and "Winter" in F Minor. If you consider these to be only one selection, the kit should include four more works.

A sound second choice is the Gloria in D. (The Gloria—"Glory to God in the highest"—is the second of five sections of the Ordinary of the Roman Catholic mass. Some composers created an independent Gloria, and Vivaldi's is one of the most famous.) For the final three choices, sample collections of Vivaldi concertos for mandolin, lute, viola d'amore, cello, trumpet, bassoon, etc.

VIVALDI: THE STARTER KIT

Composition	Recordings Available*
ORCHESTRAL WORKS:	
Four Violin Concertos (The Four Seasons):	62
Concerto in E (Spring)	
Concerto in G Minor (Summer)	
Concerto in F (Autumn)	
Concerto in F Minor (Winter)	
Collections of Concertos for other instruments, such as:	
Concerto in D for Guitar and Orchestra [R. 93]	C
Concerto in C for Mandolin and Orchestra [R. 425]	C
Concerto in C for Two Trumpets and Strings [R. 537]	10

Composition   *Recordings Available**

VOCAL MUSIC:
Gloria in D   14

*Represents the number of recorded releases available of each listed composition as found in a recent issue of the *Schwann/Opus* catalogue. A "C" indicates that a work is only available collected with other compositions.

VIVALDI: A TOP TEN

Composition   *Recordings Available**

ORCHESTRAL WORKS:
Four Violin Concertos (The Four Seasons):   62
   Concerto in E (Spring)
   Concerto in G Minor (Summer)
   Concerto in F (Autumn)
   Concerto in F Minor (Winter)
Concertos for Flute and Orchestra, Op. 10   25
Concerto in D for Guitar and Orchestra [R. 93]   C
Concerto in C for Mandolin and Orchestra   C
   [R. 425]
L'estro armonico (collection of violin concertos),   15
   Op. 3
Bassoon Concertos   C
Cello Concertos   C
Trumpet Concertos   C

VOCAL MUSIC:
Gloria in D   14
Credo   5

VIVALDI: A MASTER COLLECTION

Composition   *Recordings Available**

ORCHESTRAL WORKS:
The Trial between Harmony and Invention   6 (and C)
   (Il cimento dell'armonia e dell'invenzione)
   (twelve violin concertos), Op. 8
   The first four of these: The Four Seasons: 62
      Concerto in E (Spring)
      Concerto in G Minor (Summer)

Composition   *Recordings Available**

      Concerto in F (Autumn)
      Concerto in F Minor (Winter)
La cetra (The lyre) (twelve violin concertos),   13 (and C)
    Op. 9
La stravaganza (twelve violin concertos),   5
    Op. 4
L'estro armonico (twelve violin concertos),   15 (and C)
    Op. 3, including:
        Double Violin Concerto in A Minor,
          No. 8
        Quadruple Violin Concerto in B Minor,
          No. 10
        Triple Concerto in D Minor for Two
          Violins and Cello, No. 11
Triple Violin Concerto in F [R. 551]   6
Six Flute Concertos, Op. 10   C
Bassoon Concertos, including:
    in C [R. 466]   C
    in C [R. 467]   C
    in C [R. 469]   C
    in C [R. 470]   C
    in C [R. 474]   C
Flute Concertos, including:
    in D [R. 84 and 89]   C
    in G [R. 102]   C
Concertos for Flute and Strings, including:
    in G [R. 435]   C
    in F [R. 442]   C
Guitar Concertos, including:
    in D [R. 93]   C
    in A Minor (from Op. 3, No. 6)   C
Cello Concertos, including: C
    in G [R. 413]   C
    in B Minor [R. 424]   C
Double Cello Concerto in G Minor, R 531   2
Concertos for mandolin, oboe, trumpet,   C
    recorder, etc.

CHAMBER WORKS:
Sonatas for Cello and Harpsichord   C
Sonatas for Two Violins and Continuo   C

Composition	Recordings Available*
VOCAL MUSIC:	
Gloria in D [R. 589]	14
Kyrie [R. 587]	4
Credo [R. 591]	5
Motets	C

GEORGES BIZET (1838–1875)

Number 38

Georges Bizet wrote music in addition to the opera *Carmen* and undoubtedly would have written much more had he lived past thirty-six, but he is the only composer selected for The List as a result of a single work. No *Carmen*, no Bizet among the Top 50; with *Carmen*, there's no rational way to exclude him.

The sixth-rated of nine Frenchmen on The List, Bizet is one of the thirteen Listed composers in the Middle Romantic period. Most of these thirteen were born in the 1820s and 1830s, and they include such composers as fellow Frenchmen Saint-Saëns and Franck and Russians Borodin and Mussorgsky.

Only two Listed composers lived shorter lives: Schubert, who died at thirty-one, and Mozart, who died at thirty-five. (Mendelssohn lived until thirty-eight and Chopin until thirty-nine.) *Carmen*, Bizet's masterpiece, was first performed in 1875 in Paris, the birthplace and home of the composer, at the Opéra-Comique Theater, three months before he died, probably of a heart attack, following a longtime throat ailment that had weakened him. Stories later circulated that his death came from a broken heart because the public and critics had rejected his opera. In fact, although no smash hit, it was received reasonably well by the critics and had its thirty-third performance the night of his death. One critic praised its fine harmony; another said it "redounded to a musician's credit." Not rave reviews, to be sure, and some people criticized the "immorality" of the libretto, but overall there was not the cruel and devastating kind of reaction that would cause a thirty-six-year-old to despair and give up living. Still, not until three years later did the opera really take off, and then it was performed in Marseilles, Lyons, Bordeaux, St. Petersburg, Naples, Florence, Ghent, Hanover, Mainz . . . and even across the sea in the uncivilized wilderness of New York. One enthusiastic supporter was Tchaikovsky, who wrote to his friend Nadejda von Meck:

To me, this is in every sense a chef d'oeuvre, one of the few pieces which will some day mirror most vividly the musical endeavor of a whole generation. It seems to me that the era we live in differs from the preceding in one way; our composers are *searching*—and first of all, they are searching for pretty and piquant effects—a thing which Mozart and Beethoven and Schubert and Schumann never did . . . and suddenly appears a Frenchman in whose music piquant and spicy passages are not the result of ingenuity but flow freely. They please the ear, but at the same time they touch and trouble. . . . From the beginning to the end it is charming and delightful. In it one finds a number of striking harmonies and entirely new combinations of sound, but these do not exist merely for themselves. Bizet is an artist who pays tribute to modernity, but he is armed by true inspiration. . . . I am convinced that in about ten years "Carmen" will have become the most popular opera in the world.

Bizet, the son of a singing teacher, entered the Paris Conservatory at nine and remained there for nine years, studying piano, organ, and composition. He did well, winning the second pianoforte prize in 1851, the first pianoforte prize in 1852, both the second and first prize for fugue in 1854, and the first prize for organ in 1855. He came in second for the much-prized Prix de Rome in 1856, winning another award for operetta that year, and then won the Prix de Rome (at age eighteen) the next year. After spending three happy years in Italy, he returned to Paris, where he lived until his death. He had written some operas in Italy and concluded that this was the form of music on which he would concentrate.

Back in Paris, things began to get tough for the first time in Bizet's

---

THE MILITARY PEOPLE

Georges Bizet was not really Georges Bizet at all. His proper name was Alexandre-César-Léopold Bizet, a rather strange batch of military choices from a father who taught singing and a mother who came from a professional piano-playing family. The "Georges" was bestowed by a favorite godfather, and stuck.

life. His mother had died when he was en route home, and he also had to make a living. He wanted to compose opera but instead was forced to spend most of his time at common work for someone of his talent— orchestrating dance music, turning orchestral works into piano music, and engaging in almost any other musical activity that would make a franc.

His first completed opera was *Les pêcheurs de perles* (The pearl fishers), set in Ceylon and introduced in Paris in 1863. It received a so-so reaction, some critics accusing Bizet of being a Wagner copycat, but fellow Frenchman Berlioz found in it "a considerable number of fine, expressive packages, full of fire and richly colored." It survived, however, no doubt because it was written by Bizet; it is occasionally performed today, and recordings are available. Three years later Bizet tried again, this time with *La jolie fille de Perth* (The fair maid of Perth), based on a Sir Walter Scott novel. It, too, had a lukewarm reception, but it's also still around, and selections are sometimes heard on classical-music stations. In both cases, the librettos are pretty bad, sort of in the *Jaws III* category. Both of these operas are categorized as "serious" *opéra comique*, while *Carmen* is considered to be a very "tragic" *opéra comique*.

(Technically, in an *opéra comique* the dialogue is spoken, and *Carmen* has often been performed in that mode in Paris. In the U.S., recitative—which *The Harvard Dictionary of Music* defines as "a vocal style designed to imitate and emphasize the natural inflection of speech"—is often used instead of spoken dialogue.) Bizet, not surprisingly given the pre-jet times, had not been to Ceylon—nor, indeed, even to the fair maid's Scotland or Carmen's Spain—but it was not unusual in those days for Romantic composers to select exotic settings for their works.

Saint-Saëns, about the same age as Bizet, was having no greater luck with the audiences at Paris's Opéra-Comique Theater and is reported to have said to Bizet, "Since we are not wanted there, let's take refuge in the concert hall." In short, bag opera and write symphonies. But Bizet would have none of it. "I *must* have a stage," he wrote. "Without it, I am nothing."

What the professionals call "the Greater Bizet" showed up after he was asked to write incidental music for a play entitled *L'Arlésienne* (The woman of Arles) by Alphonse Daudet. The play was first performed in 1872 and barely stayed afloat for a few years, but Bizet's music (he composed twenty-seven numbers) was enjoyed, and he later took four of these numbers and put them into an orchestral suite. A

LINKAGE OF THE ARTS

In a letter home, written when he was in early manhood and living in Rome, Bizet shared some of his developing views:

"I feel my artistic affections growing stronger. Comparison of painters and sculptors with musicians plays a large part. All the arts are connected, or rather there is but one art. Express your thoughts on canvas, in marble or in the theater, it is all one: the thought is the same. I am more than ever convinced that Mozart and Rossini are the two greatest musicians. Admiring Beethoven and [Giacomo] Meyerbeer [unListed German opera composer] with all my faculties, I feel by nature more inclined to art that is pure and easy rather than dramatic and passionate. Thus in painting Raphael is the same as Mozart while Meyerbeer feels as Michelangelo felt. Don't think me too narrow. On the contrary, I have come to recognize Verdi as a genius, but a genius set in the most deplorable path imaginable."

friend combined another four into a second suite, and both are performed today and are frequently heard on the radio.

Bizet wrote two more orchestral pieces, the *Petite* Suite and the

YOU CAN SAY THAT AGAIN

In a letter to a friend, Bizet offered some thoughts on male bonding and women:

"As regards the fair sex I become less and less of the 'chevalier français.' I see nothing in that attitude but a satisfaction of amour propre. I would willingly risk my life for a friend, but should think myself a fool if I lost a hair of my head for a woman. I say all this only to you because, if it got known, it would damage my future chances."

Irreparably, one would surmise. But in time he married Genevieve Halevy, daughter of Jacques Halevy, his professor at the Paris Conservatory and composer of nearly forty operas, the best known of which is *La Juive* (The Jewess).

overture to playwright Victorien Sardou's *Patrie*, both of which were minor successes.

Earlier, as a youth of seventeen, he had composed a four-movement Symphony in C, which much later was adapted into a ballet that was at one time part of the repertory of the New York City Ballet. Again, probably because this is the composer of *Carmen*, it is sometimes heard today, though it ranks only as pleasant and lightweight fare.

Bizet also wrote some piano music, including one piano duet, *Jeux d'enfants* (Children's games). Composed in 1871, it consists of twelve compositions combined into a suite that has been described as a masterpiece of delicacy and wit. (Five of these were arranged into the orchestrated *Petite* Suite.)

STARTER KIT

Included in the Starter Kit are the Symphony in C, the two *L'Ar-lésienne* Suites, *Jeux d' enfants*, and excerpts from *Les pêcheurs de perles*. From there on, it is *Carmen*. It's difficult to find anyone saying anything bad nowadays about *Carmen*, arguably the world's most popular opera. For the record, it is an opera in four acts; the libretto is by Henri Meilhac and Ludovic Halevy; the original short story was by Prosper Merimée. The musicologists advise us that composing it did not come easily to Bizet; some numbers were rewritten fifteen or more times.

Carmen is set in Spain, and the music sounds Spanish, specifically like Spanish folk music. The opera created problems when it was first produced in Paris, but these arose from the plot and characters rather than from the Spanish ambience. The French operagoers initially could not appreciate a bolder and more passionate work than they were accustomed to. The provocative Carmen was a little too much for them. The Opéra-Comique was a family theater, accustomed to the relatively harmless passion found later in early movies. Husbands, wives, and impressionable daughters made up the audience. It was acceptable for figures from history to step out of line, but not real-life contemporary folk. *Carmen* was deemed to have too much realism, too much passion, and too tragic an ending. Some fifty years ago, Paul Henry Lang, Columbia University professor of musicology, described it this way:

> Here we are facing a music-dramatic work of unique force, of poignant *verité dramatique*, the lyrical parts of which disseminate a tender and suave melancholy in which nothing is styl-

OVERHUNG BY FATE

Philosopher Friedrich Nietzsche (1844–1900) was one of *Carmen*'s biggest fans, writing to a friend:

"Yesterday—would you believe it?—I heard Bizet's masterpiece for the twentieth time. Once more I attended with the same gentle reverence. How such a work completes one! . . . The music is wicked, refined, fantastic; and withal remains popular—it possesses the refinement of a race, not of an individual. Have more painful, more tragic accents ever been heard on the stage before? And how are they obtained? Without grimaces! Without counterfeiting of any kind. . . . Fate hangs over this work, its happiness is short, sudden, without reprieve. . . . I envy Bizet for having had the courage of this sensitiveness, which hitherto in the cultured music of Europe has found no means of expression."

ized, everything is presented with almost brutal force and naturalness. Here is folk drama of such concentrated power as was unknown in the grand opera and appeared only a generation later. . . . It was this drama, swift and undisguised in its music, with its overheated southern temperament, dazzling and vital orchestra, wonderful harmonies, inescapable melodies . . . the eternal model of the lyric drama.

The final verdict, more than one hundred years after the first performance: *Carmen* is one of the great creations of the musical stage. If you were to see only one opera, *Carmen* would have to be on the nominating slate.

The most famous numbers include three from Act I, four from Act II, and one from Act III. The Act I arias are the "Habanera" (so called because the rhythm is that of the Cuban *habanera* dance); "L'amour est un oiseau revelle" for mezzo-soprano; the duet for mezzo-soprano and tenor, "Parle-moi de ma mère"; and the *seguidilla* "Près de ramparts de Seville" for mezzo-soprano. From Act II are the Gypsy dance; the "Gypsy Song" for mezzo-soprano; the "Toreador Song" for baritone and chorus, one of the best-known baritone arias in opera; and the tenor's "Flower Song," "La fleur que tu m'avais jetée." From Act III is the "Card Song," "En vain pour éviter."

For orchestral music, the *Carmen* Suite should be in the Starter Kit. One way to include it and stay within five selections would be to add it and count the two *L'Arlésienne* Suites as one piece, but that would be sly manipulation. So I'll leave it off (confident that when you actually buy a compact disc for *L'Arlésienne* Suites you almost certainly will find the *Carmen* Suite on it).

A FAKE?

Despite its enormous popularity as a folk opera, *Carmen* is viewed by the professionals as a "fake": not a fake masterpiece, to be sure, but a fake folk opera. Although the opera makes systematic use of Spanish popular music styles, it is not, of course, Spanish music written by a Spaniard. Smetana's *Bartered Bride* is Bohemian music written by a Bohemian—*that* is true folk opera. *Carmen*, the experts agree, is finer theater. By the same token, Puccini's *Madame Butterfly* is not a Japanese folk opera but rather an Italian opera written about a Japanese subject.

BIZET: THE STARTER KIT

Composition	Recordings Available*
SYMPHONIES:	
No. 1 in C	13
OTHER ORCHESTRAL WORKS:	
L'Arlésienne:	13
Suite No. 1	
Suite No. 2	
Jeux d'enfants (Children's games)	8
VOCAL MUSIC:	
Operas:	
Carmen (complete and excerpts)	11

*Represents the number of recorded releases available of each listed composition as found in a recent issue of the *Schwann/Opus* catalogue. A "C" indicates that a work is only available collected with other compositions.

BIZET: A TOP TEN/A MASTER COLLECTION

Composition	Recordings Available*
SYMPHONIES:	
No. 1 in C	13
OTHER ORCHESTRAL WORKS:	
L'Arlésienne:	13
Suite No. 1	
Suite No. 2	
Carmen Suite No. 1	7
Roma (suite)	1
Patrie (overture)	2
Jeux d'enfants (children's games)	8
VOCAL MUSIC:	
Operas:	
Carmen (complete and excerpts)	11
Les pêcheurs de perles (excerpts)	2
La jolie fille de Perth (excerpts)	2

MODEST MUSSORGSKY (1839–1881)

No. 39

To the tens of millions of televiewers who follow the NCAA basketball tournament each year, the "Big Five" means the starting teams of Georgetown or Louisville or Duke, all thirty-five feet of each. But it was not always so. In Russia in the 1860s, the "Big Five," or the "Mighty Five," wrote music.

Four Russian composers have appeared on The List thus far, but none qualifies as a professional "nationalist." True, Stravinsky described Tchaikovsky as "the most Russian of us all," but that reference was to temperament and emotion. Tchaikovsky's *music* was universal. As for Stravinsky himself, genius that he was, he, along with Prokofiev and Shostakovich, was into the sounds of New Music (or Twentieth-Century Music, or Modern Music, as it was variously referred to in the first half of this century). The Russian heritage was certainly there; one rarely encounters a Russian shorn of his national heritage, after all. But the objective of these other four was not to make "Russian music." Except when the latter two were directed otherwise by the Central Committee, their goal was to make music, period.

Not so the "Mighty Five" of the music world, or the "Kutchka," as they were called at home. These were card-carrying Russian Russians.

This was the group that gathered together in St. Petersburg in the mid-1860s for the stated purpose of creating Russian nationalist music—authentic Russian music, music that was a product of their own heritage rather than music influenced by Italian opera, French ballet, German symphonies, or the like. The "Five" delved into Russian history, collected Russian folk songs, studied Russian folk legends, and, in general, dug deeply into Russian roots. The core of the Russian nationalist school, they dealt with such topics as paganism, the period of the Princes that gave birth to the Cossack regime, the Muscovite Empire, and the reforms of Peter I that struck against Russian nationalist and religious tendencies.

Three of the "Mighty Five" make The List: Modest Mussorgsky, Nikolai Rimsky-Korsakov, and Alexander Borodin. The other two were Honorably Mentioned: César Cui and Mily Balakirev, the leader. Initially, Balakirev was the only one with formal musical training. In time Rimsky-Korsakov became the most trained, skillful, and polished of the "Five," but Mussorgsky showed far more raw power, creativity, and genius.

BORODIN ON MUSSORGSKY

Saddened and distressed by his friend's drinking, Borodin said:

"This is horribly sad! Such a talented man and sinking so low morally. Now he periodically disappears, then reappears, morose, untalkative, which is contrary to his usual habit. After a while he comes to himself again—sweet, gay, amiable and as witty as ever. Devil knows, what a pity!"

What they were into was described a half-century ago by professors Howard D. McKinney and W. R. Anderson:

Perhaps more than is the case with any other people, the Russians have preserved individuality of expression in their folk songs and dances. Folk art of all kinds in Russia is very much alive today, in spite of the colossal regimentation now in force there. A number of features characterize Russian folk and dance tunes and make them sound unusual to Occidental ears: the use of short two-measure phrases and sharply defined animated rhythms; a tonality suggestive of the music of the Greek church; an affinity of style and coloring with the tunes of other Slav countries, together with their love of extravagance, their bravado of expression, and their gift for improvisation. As might be expected in so huge a land, the dances are of widely varying motions. The best-known peasant dance is the gopak, which, starting in a tranquil, melancholy fashion, ends in a tremendous outburst of primitive vitality.

In a short (and alcohol-drenched) career, Mussorgsky became one of the most original of all composers. He wrote *the* Russian nationalist opera, *Boris Godounov*, which is both one of the leading tragic operas of the nineteenth century and one of history's top folk operas. He also produced (1874) one of music's very popular works, *Pictures at an Exhibition* (with help after his death from Maurice Ravel); his intriguing experiments to make music sound like language still fascinate the musicologists; and he is among the nineteenth century's best songwriters.

What appeals most to the experts, perhaps, is his dedication to truth. "The goal of the artist," he wrote, "should be to study the most

---

A WALK IN THE MUSEUM

The music of the suite *Pictures at an Exhibition* is made more interesting by the titles of the paintings—actual paintings by artist Victor Hartmann, a friend of Mussorgsky's who had died, leaving Mussorgsky miserable. The composer said of his loss: "Why should a dog, a horse, a rat have life, and creatures like Hartmann must die? There can and must be no consolation." But later he found some consolation, and from some four hundred Hartmann drawings he selected ten for a solo piano tribute to his friend: "The Gnome," "The Old Castle," "Tuileries (Children at Play)," "Ox Cart," "Ballet of the Chicks," "Two Polish Jews," "Limoges, the Marketplace," "Catacombs," "The Hut on Fowls' Legs," and "The Great Gate of Kiev."

subtle features of human beings and of humanity in the mass. To explore and conquer these unknown regions, and find therein a health-giving pabulum for the minds of all men, that is the duty and joy of joys."

Even among the "Five," Mussorgsky was the most nationalist composer. As a truth-seeker, he was dedicated to truth in Russia, truth in music, truth about the Russian people—and to truthful capturing of their language in music. He called it "reverence . . . for the reproduction of simple human speech." His mission, he said, was "that of setting to music prose straight out of life, of turning out musical prose."

In pursuing the goals of expressing the soul of the Russian people and of expressing their language in music, Mussorgsky—like most zealous innovators—was prepared to break any rule standing in his way. The musicologists say that tradition, public taste, and established forms meant nothing to him—he had no formal musical training to restrain him. He was, by common agreement, the most daring of the "Five" and—in the manner of soul-probers—the most brutal. This is no delicate Frenchman, no Fauré specializing in drawing-room miniatures. Mussorgsky's music is commonly described as crude, rough, savage, realistic, and unpolished.

Members of the "Five" typically worked on one another's manuscripts, and both before and after Mussorgsky's death Rimsky-Korsakov reworked his friend's compositions—restraining, revising, and applying the expertise of his more formal training. With more knowledge—but less genius—than Mussorgsky, he corrected things he viewed as musical mistakes.

True to the code of the "Five," Mussorgsky wrote no symphonies, no sonatas, and no concertos. Those were for the neoclassical reactionaries, not for original-thinking Russian nationalists.

His music is not without melody, but by his own declaration it is his own kind of melody, constructed in his own way. "I foresee a new melody, which will be the melody of life," he once said. And again: "With great pains I have achieved a new type of melody evolved from that of speech. Some day, all of a sudden, the ineffable song will arise, intelligent to one and all. If I succeed, I shall stand as a conqueror in art—and succeed I must."

Born in Karevo in northwestern Russia, the child of down-at-the-heels nobility, Mussorgsky made a poor living as a government bureaucrat in the communications and forestry departments. Like Fellow Fiver Borodin, he was a weekend musician, and in his short life he did not write a great deal of music. In addition to *Boris*, clearly his most outstanding work, he wrote another opera inspired by Russian history, unfinished, called *Khovanshchina* (The times of the Khovanskys). It portrayed early seventeenth-century Russian opposition to the Westernization of religion and politics.

Pictures at an Exhibition, written in 1874 as a piano suite, was transcribed into an orchestral work by Ravel in 1923. Other well-known works include *A Night on Bald Mountain* (1867), a fascinating tone poem of evil, witches, and demons; and the "Introduction and Dance of the Persian Slaves" (subtitled "Dawn on the Moscow River") from *Khovanshchina*.

A NIGHT ON BALD MOUNTAIN

Here is the composer's own program note for his tone poem, commissioned in 1860 when Mussorgsky was twenty-one, written and rewritten by him, revised by Rimsky-Korsakov after Mussorgsky's death in 1881, and first performed under Rimsky-Korsakov's direction in 1886:

"Subterranean sounds of supernatural voices. Appearances of the spirits of darkness, followed by that of Satan himself. Glorification of Satan and celebration of the Black Mass. The Sabbath Revels. At the height of the orgies, the bell of the village church sounding in the distance, disperses the spirits of darkness. Daybreak."

Mussorgsky died of a stroke in a military hospital at the age of forty-two, an alcoholic whose life had disintegrated. His work other than music was unrewarding, and he was always insecure about his raw compositions.

Despite that insecurity, *Boris* gives him a place in history. The opera, which he called a music folk drama, is based on Alexander Pushkin's historical Russian play, written in 1825, which itself is drawn from an eleven-volume work, *The History of the State of Russia* by Nikolai M. Karamzin. Pushkin's drama has been called the "Russian *Macbeth*," because it was inspired by the historical tragedies of Shakespeare and deals with the experience of bloody rulers. The title figure is a Russian czar, Boris Godounov, who, in the 1590s, gains power by murdering an infant and is later tortured by remorse. The chorus represents the heroic Russian people. The powerful music style—critics now say "advanced"—was expressed in the use of harmonies and melodies based on Slavic folk songs rather than the major/minor scales of Western European music.

There are twenty-two scenes in Pushkin's play, some taking no more than a minute. Mussorgsky wrote his own libretto, picking and choosing from Pushkin's work, marrying some scenes, modifying others, and winding up with seven tableaux. His first version took about a year to write, from the fall of 1868 to the winter of 1869–1870. He submitted it to the reading committee of the Imperial Theater in Russia but, a year later, received word that it had been refused. The stated reason was that it did not conform to the usual standards: There was no role for a leading woman, there was no love-torn tenor, and there was no ballet scene. It was also rather tough on czars.

Mussorgsky went back to the drawing board and, in 1872, completed another version, today considered the "original." He took out one tableau and put in three new ones, for a total of nine, losing some continuity in the process. Among his changes was the addition of the role of Marina, a Polish aristocrat who is in love with Grigory, the pretender to Boris's throne.

This version was accepted by the theater, and performances were given in St. Petersburg in 1875, 1876, and 1880, and in 1882, after Mussorgsky's death, in Moscow at the Bolshoi Theater. But it was too strong for the critics and not a smooth piece of work. Not only was the plot scrambled, but the composer's harmonies were too brutal. It needed help; it needed to be made more "accessible." Rimsky-Korsakov took it upon himself to step in and revise. Between 1886 and 1889 he did a new orchestration of the entire score, frequently rewriting the music itself, straightening out the scenes, toning things down, and, in all, creating quite a different opera.

Purists, of course, argue that Rimsky-Korsakov should have done his friend no favors and left it untouched after the composer's death. They cry "shocking disfigurement." But pragmatists respond that it would not have been performed again without Rimsky-Korsakov's work and thus would have dropped out of sight.

This was not the end of the rewriting. Another version was done in 1926 by the Russian Ippolytov-Ivanov, who reorchestrated one tableau, and it was not until 1928 that Mussorgsky's "original" 1872 version was again performed, first in Leningrad and then in Moscow. This is the version that is seen and recorded today.

Of his highly regarded songs, perhaps the most popular are cycles of children's songs called *The Nursery, Songs and Dances of Death,* and

Without Sunlight. One of the best known of many individual songs is "The Song of the Flea."

The words used by the experts for Mussorgsky: "brutally sincere," "steeped in folklore," "uncouth in detail," "painfully bold in harmonies and rhythms," "starkly naked," "overwhelming sincerity," "no artificiality," "bold harmonies," and "a forerunner of modernism." Like most of the outstanding nationalists, he does not often quote actual folk tunes, but their style and sound and makeup are part of his musical nature. There is common agreement among the professionals that in his use of harmony, Mussorgsky was one of the most original and revolutionary of all composers.

FINAL WORDS

In the last year of his life, a terrible alcoholic, Mussorgsky was still trying, or at least was telling himself he was trying:

"My motto remains unchanged. 'Boldly on. Forward to new shores.' To seek untiringly, fearlessly, and without confusion, and to enter with firm step into the promised land—there's a great and beautiful task! One must give oneself wholly to mankind."

STARTER KIT

The first selection is Russia's finest national opera, *Boris Godounov.* What Rimsky-Korsakov and most others viewed earlier as the inexpert composer's crudities are now viewed as signs of his originality and fearlessness.

Kurt Schindler, conductor, composer, and critic who died in 1933, wrote years ago:

With "Boris Godounov," a new type of historical opera was founded. . . . This is a work of simple and compelling logic by a master playwright, in which the great emotional forces, the revolutionizing sentiments of a period, are depicted through the medium of music. Not only was Mussorgsky a wonderful composer, but behind him lay the unexplored musical wealth of the great Slav nation—a mine of rhythmically and melodically unusual folk songs; of Byzantine church chants with their mysterious flavor of the early Christian period; of old bardic tunes, rhapsodical and full of grandeur; of new and violent vocal inflections rooted in the dialect of a rich and varied language. . . . In "Boris Godounov," the people are in the foreground, the great masses are really the principal actor—at first dumb, oppressed, easily swayed; then stirred up, threatening, finally in open revolt and jubilant with warlike spirit. The intense realism of these folk scenes can be compared without blasphemy to such eternal masterpieces as Shakespeare's "Julius Caesar." And in all dramatic music there is nothing so near to Macbeth as the specter scene of "Boris."

It is powerful stuff.

Rounding out the Starter Kit are four orchestral pieces:

• *Pictures at an Exhibition*, one of the most frequently played pieces of music in Maurice Ravel's orchestral transcription, but also available in the original piano version. Mussorgsky wrote it in 1874; Ravel did his thing in 1923.

• *A Night on Bald Mountain*, the nifty witches' brew composed in 1867 and the composer's only symphonic poem. The mountain is Mt. Triglaf, near Kiev, where strange things happen on St. John's Eve each June 23. One critic described it as "starkly naked evil" before Rimsky-Korsakov polished it.

• Two pieces from Mussorgsky's other known opera, *Khovanshchina*, written in 1874: the Prelude and the "Dance of the Persian Slaves," in which a prince is entertained by some Persian lovelies dancing in a provocative way. The opera is set in Moscow in 1682.

This leaves the Starter Kit without any of the songs for which Mussorgsky is highly acclaimed. Here, as elsewhere, we hesitate to recommend a single song in place of a large orchestral work. Well, maybe "As Time Goes By" or, for our southern friends, "Dixie." Also, the Starter Kit is for collectors, and it is not feasible to limit a record, tape, or compact disc to an individual song. Try some anyhow, even if they're not included in the kit. (There should probably be a book for laymen that deals only with the great songs of the great composers.)

MUSSORGSKY: THE STARTER KIT

Composition   *Recordings Available**

ORCHESTRAL MUSIC:

Pictures at an Exhibition (for piano; or orchestrated by Ravel)	30
A Night on Bald Mountain (tone poem)	26
Prelude to Khovanshchina	7
Dance of the Persian Slaves, from Khovanshchina	8

VOCAL MUSIC:
Opera:

Boris Godounov	7

*Represents the number of recorded releases available of each listed composition as found in a recent issue of the *Schwann/Opus* catalogue. A "C" indicates that a work is only available collected with other compositions.

MUSSORGSKY: A TOP TEN/A MASTER COLLECTION

Composition   *Recordings Available**

ORCHESTRAL MUSIC:

Pictures at an Exhibition (for piano; or orchestrated by Ravel)	30
A Night on Bald Mountain (tone poem)	26
Prelude to Khovanshchina	7
Dance of the Persian Slaves, from Khovanshchina	8

OTHER INSTRUMENTAL MUSIC:

Pictures at an Exhibition, piano version	18

VOCAL MUSIC:
Operas:

Boris Godounov	7
Khovanshchina	7

Songs:

The Nursery (song cycle)	2
Songs and Dances of Death (song cycle)	7
Song of the Flea, and other songs	C

JEAN-PHILIPPE RAMEAU (1683–1764)

Number 40

A bold, brainy battler, Jean-Philippe Rameau once boasted that he could put the *Gazette de Hollande* (a newspaper) to music . . . and tried it . . . and failed.

More amateur collectors have not heard of Rameau than have heard of him, although his greatest opera was presented in Paris a few years ago and his keyboard music is available on records and tapes. He was not an insignificant figure in his day, however, and was the center of one of music's most critical wars.

Rameau was
- the top French composer of the eighteenth century;
- an opera reformer who succeeded Monteverdi and foreshadowed Gluck;
- the first modern instrumental colorist;
- second only to Couperin as an early grand master of keyboard composition;
- author of five books on harmony and music theory, including a daring textbook that revised the music world's approach to harmony;
- a creative artist of the first order.

"Rameau," said Voltaire, "has made of music a new art."

Like most original thinkers, he was much abused during his lifetime, but unlike some original composers, he was also a fabulous box-office hit before his death. His greatest opera, *Castor et Pollux*, was given 254 performances in Paris between 1737 and 1785, the statisticians tell us. One Englishman visiting France reported that "although everyone was abusing Rameau's 'horrible' work, it was impossible to get a seat at the opera."

No child genius like Mozart, Mendelssohn, Chopin, or Saint-

A PREMATURE ANNOUNCEMENT

"Music," Rameau wrote some 250 years ago, "is dead." As an author of treatises on composition, he meant that all feasible tonal combinations had been found and tried. Not all twentieth-century composers, including several on The List, would agree. Nor would history.

Saëns, Rameau achieved success the hard way, by study and analysis of musical theory. In 1722 he published *The Treatise on Harmony Reduced to Its Natural Principles*, a "daring" textbook, and for years his "revolutionary" principles of harmony were followed. These principles attacked the traditional theory of harmony on the grounds that the "Ancients"—of the sixteenth century—"based the rules of harmony on melody instead of beginning with harmony, which comes first."

"There are harmonies," he wrote, "that are sad, languishing, tender, agreeable, gay and striking. There are also certain successions of harmonies for the expression of these passions."

And indeed, Rameau's music reflected his theoretical writings. Some fifty years ago, one critic wrote: "He could evoke many varied moods with equal success: . . . languor in 'Tendres plaintes,' . . . animation in 'Feux-Follets' and 'La Joyeuse,' . . . the graceful movement of the dance in 'Tambourin' [a famous piece], 'Rigaudon,' and 'Musette.' He could be lyric and dramatic at turns, pictorially descriptive, on occasion impressionistic, and charmingly witty."

Rameau's problems began with his first opera, *Hippolyte et Aricie*, first performed when he was fifty years old and strongly attacked

AN EMPTY HOUSE?

Rameau had his critics. A French writer who was a contemporary said of him:

"All his mind and all his soul was in his harpsichord and when he had closed that, the house was empty, there was no one at home."

because it was out of the ordinary. Parisian critics found it much too cerebral alongside the light, vocal Italian opera of the day—not melodic enough, overorchestrated, too dissonant. Rameau, a headstrong fellow, vowed never to produce another opera. In fact, he lied and wrote another twenty or so, although few of them are heard today. One exception is *Castor et Pollux*, which is occasionally performed, and a few others have been recorded.

Although the German Gluck, born thirty-one years after Rameau, is generally credited with the final reform of Italian opera, the music people point out that many features of Gluck's operas had been present in French opera from the time of Rameau. These include the comparative subordination of music to drama, the avoidance of mere vocal display, the use of the same kind of style in recitative and aria, and, in general, a more rounded approach to the whole ball of wax. Unfortunately, Rameau never found a libretto that was worth a whole lot, and without one his instincts toward real drama—that is, something more than good singing—were not enough to make contemporary audiences overcome their prejudices against most of his operas.

Professor Lang, our highly respected musicologist and one of Rameau's leading champions, writes of the composer:

> We now arrive at the great enigma of French music, the composer whose inspiration was as typically French as Bach's was German and Scarlatti's Italian, who was the one and only French musician to excel in all fields cherished by French thought—a profound and keen thinker, a great composer, and a superb performer—a man whose theoretical writings became the foundation of modern musical theory, whose works are filled with a wealth of invention seemingly inexhaustible, a born dramatist of the first water, and an artist in whose works nothing is left to the hazards of inspiration, Jean-Philippe Rameau. This greatest and most French of composers remains a man frequently mentioned as a great thinker, occasionally played as a spirited harpsichord composer, and totally ignored as one of the greatest creative artists of the eighteenth century.

The son of an organist of a small church outside of Dijon, Rameau grew up playing the organ, plied this skill in various churches in the south of France, and in 1722 moved to Paris, where he remained for the rest of his life. Composing was less important to Rameau than his intellectual treatises on music theory and harmony. We have seen that

SULKY, BUT GOOD

Rameau was a wanderer in his early years, flitting from France
to Italy and back by circuitous routes. After one brief inter-
lude in Paris, he spent six years as church organist in Clermont, in southern France's Provence region. Rameau tired of
the job, but the directors would not release him. He reacted
by playing as badly as possible one Sunday, messing up the
organ stops and producing horrible-sounding discords. It
worked: a choirboy was sent to him with a message stating that
his services were no longer required, and he stalked out of the
church.

Many years later he was honored by the church—and two
hundred years later his organist chair was still on display at
Clermont.

counterpoint had been the chief textural approach until the seventeenth century, when the needs of Italian opera brought forth single-
melody music, supported by chords. But what to do with the chords,
and what kinds of chords? This was the science of harmony that
Rameau defined.

As a composer, aside from operas, Rameau is famous for his
keyboard work, chiefly the *Pièces de clavecin*—"elegant," "refined,"
and "lucid" works for the harpsichord. They include many works
played today, such as "La poule" and a Gavotte in A Minor.

He published one set of harpsichord pieces in 1705, at age twenty-
two, and another set nineteen years later. The critics speak of their
clarity, their economy, their combination of force and delicacy.
(Music professionals are not unlike wine professionals in the language they choose, understandable given that the problems they face
are similar. One tastes wine or hears music, and the challenge of explaining these senses in words is a mighty one, even for the professionals.)

In sum: Rameau took a giant step toward true drama in opera.
Lang and others suggest that had Rameau been more of a poet and
been able to combine poetry with his musical, theoretical, and intellectual genius, he would have been the true emancipator of French music
drama. As it is, he nonetheless is one of the great musical talents of
France. On The List he trails fellow Frenchmen Berlioz, Debussy,
Saint-Saëns, Ravel, Franck, and Bizet. But all seven fall between Num-

bers 21 and 40, so if you share Professor Lang's position, sneak into your closet and reverse the standings of Berlioz and Rameau, thus making the latter the greatest Frenchman.

NO UNGRACEFUL NOISES ALLOWED

Frenchmen love other Frenchmen, and Rameau had no greater champion 175 years after his death than Debussy, who wrote:

"And what has become of the subtly flowing syllables of our language? We will find them again in 'Hippolyte et Aricie,' the opera of 1733 that the Opera is going to revive, now in 1908. . . . We can be sure that the feeling of the opera has been preserved intact, although perhaps the setting, and something of the pomp of the music, have faded a little. It could never seem 'out of place,' for it is one of those beautiful things that will remain forever so, and despite the neglect of mankind, will never completely die.

"Why have we not followed the advice contained in this piece: to observe nature before we try to copy it? Because we no longer have the time, I suppose. So our music blindly adopts trivialities coming from the direction of Italy, or legendary tales—crumbs fallen from the Wagnerian table d'hôte. . . .

"Rameau was a musician of old-time France, and if he was obliged to concern himself with spectacle [in opera] he felt no need to give up his right to compose real music. That may seem natural enough, but we don't seem able to do it anymore. We have adopted a frenetic way of shaking up the orchestra as if it were a salad, so that any hope of real music must be completely abandoned. . . . I fear that our ears have thus lost the power to listen with the necessary delicacy to the music of Rameau, in which all ungraceful noises are forbidden."

STARTER KIT

Rameau's most famous work is his opera *Hippolyte et Aricie*, based on Racine's *Phèdre*. The work was attacked by critics but well received by the public once audiences got over their early astonishment at its

"radical" nature. An orchestral suite was adapted from it and is recommended as the first Starter Kit selection. Another fine orchestral
suite, from Rameau's last opera, *Les Boréades*, is also recommended.

A third selection is an opera-ballet, *Les Indes galantes*, which includes musical depictions of dancing on an Indian Ocean island, an
erupting volcano, and a storm at sea. It consists of orchestral pieces,
arias, and other numbers, grouped into four suites or "concerts."

A BIG SHAKE

Les Indes gallantes contains what is probably music history's
first orchestral earthquake. The music people tell us that Rameau's orchestration marked a significant step forward in
opera, and he put it to full test by including an earthquake in
this work. The conservatives, of course, found it too noisy
and violent.

Easier to find than the above are Rameau's keyboard pieces, *Pièces
de clavecin*, the most famous of which is "La poule" (The hen). Others
not mentioned earlier include "Le rappel des oiseaux" (The call of the
birds) and "Les trois mains" (The three hands). The recommendation
is for any, though I've singled out "La dauphine" as an example.

The fifth selection is the opera *Castor et Pollux*. For those who do
not want to cope with a three-disc opera, I suggest trying the cantatas
and motets.

RAMEAU: THE STARTER KIT

Composition	Recordings Available*
ORCHESTRAL/ENSEMBLE MUSIC:	
Orchestral Suite from Hippolyte et Aricie (opera)	1
Orchestral Suite from Les Boréades (opera)	1
Les Indes galantes (from ballet)	1
KEYBOARD MUSIC:	
Pièces de clavecin, including:	5
La dauphine	

Composition	Recordings Available*

VOCAL MUSIC:
Opera:
Castor et Pollux   1
(Or: Motets   1)

*Represents the number of recorded releases available of each listed composition as found in a recent issue of the *Schwann/Opus* catalogue. A "C" indicates that a work is only available collected with other compositions.

RAMEAU: A TOP TEN/A MASTER COLLECTION

Composition	Recordings Available*

ORCHESTRAL/ENSEMBLE MUSIC:
Orchestral Suite from Hippolyte et Aricie (opera)   1
Orchestral Suite from Les Boréades (opera)   1
Orchestral Suite from Dardanus (opera)   1
Les Indes galantes (ballet)   1
Pièces de clavecin en concert   6

KEYBOARD MUSIC:
Pièces de clavecin, including: 5
    Tendres plaintes
    Feux-follets
    La joyeuse
    Tambourin
    La poule
    La dauphine
    *Harpsichord suites:
        in A Minor
        in D Minor

VOCAL MUSIC:
Cantatas, including:
    Les amants trahis   1
Motets, including:
    In convertendo   1
    Quam dilecta laboravi   1
Operas and opera-ballets:
    Castor et Pollux   1
    Dardanus   1

GABRIEL FAURÉ (1845–1924)

Number 41

It is improbable that there is a typical Parisian any more than there is a typical Sanduskyite, Toledoan, or Detroiter. But it has often been suggested that Gabriel Fauré is the quintessential Parisian, so let's accept that identification for purposes of convenience.

The music people say this probably means that he was a typical Parisian artist of his day, which indeed he was: civilized, sensitive, elegant, sensible, refined, sophisticated, a musician working chiefly in intimate forms in a rather aristocratic way and with artistic integrity. The professionals speak of the "Hellenic" beauty of his works, of their serenity, and of their balance.

If Rambo is one extreme, Gabriel Fauré is the other.

He wrote no symphonies or concertos and very few other orchestral compositions, preferring piano music, chamber music, and songs—many beautiful songs. He has been called "excellence in miniature" and "a poetic craftsman," and in his quiet way he became one of the most influential musicians of his time. He wrote two operas, *Prométhée* in 1909 and *Penelope* in 1913, neither regarded as a masterwork. Better known is another of his few larger works, incidental music to Maeterlinck's *Pelléas et Mélisande*.

Born in Pamiers, Ariège, France, Fauré had an interest in music said to have begun when he was very young, presumably when he first encountered the town organ. By the time he was eight, he had shown enough musical promise that his father sent him to Paris for study at a famous music school called Ecole Niedermeyer. The director was so impressed by the boy's organ playing—largely self-taught—that he offered him a full scholarship. One of Fauré's teachers was Saint-Saëns, who later became a close friend and had a significant impact on Fauré's life.

THE TEACHING LADDER

Camille Saint-Saëns (1835–1921) taught Gabriel Fauré (1845–1924) who taught Maurice Ravel (1875–1937). Saint-Saëns and Ravel are considerably better known outside of France than is Fauré, perhaps in part because the latter is, by consensus, the most "cultivated" and "cultural" of composers. One latter-day critic described him as "the classic example of a rare, virtually priceless wine that simply refuses to travel."

Fauré stayed at the school until he was twenty, when his professional career began. Over the following several years, he held various appointments as an organist in Rennes and Paris. After service in the Franco-Prussian War, he was introduced by Saint-Saëns to writers such as Flaubert, to musicians such as the unListed Gounod, and to the poetry of Verlaine and Baudelaire. Saint-Saëns also helped him secure the post of choirmaster at the Madeleine Church in Paris, where, in 1896, at age fifty-one, he became the church organist—a position he occupied for many years.

In the 1860s his compositions were mainly songs and in the 1870s mostly church music. His first big work, the *Requiem*, was not written until 1886.

During this time he also taught—first at the Ecole Niedermeyer and, beginning in 1895, at the Paris Conservatory. In 1905 he was named director of the conservatory, a job he kept until poor health and deafness—a condition he attempted to conceal from friends, associates, and authorities for years—caused him to step down in 1920.

Three Frenchmen on The List worked into the 1900s—Debussy, Ravel, and Fauré, although Fauré was fifty-five by the turn of the century and more properly belongs to the late 1800s. In order of rank, he is eighth of The List's nine composers from France, with only Couperin from Baroque days still to come.

Fauré's long life spanned those of composers of various schools and musical styles, from the early radical ideas of Berlioz in his youth to the twentieth-century radicalism of Bartók in his old age. A quiet composer, teacher, choirmaster, and organist, Fauré was not overly moved by any of his rebellious contemporaries. He was a Frenchman through and through, and he and Franck before him had much to do with the revival of French piano music. For years he was almost unknown outside of Paris, although two years before his death in

1924 he was honored with the highest class in the French Legion of Honor.

FAURÉ ON ART

"For me," wrote Fauré, "the essence of art, and especially of music, is to elevate us as high as possible above the mundane."

The magic of Fauré is that he achieved this state by means of intimate music. It is difficult to imagine sounds more different to the ear than those created by Frenchman Berlioz and Frenchman Fauré. But in listening to one of the latter's Sonatas for Violin and Piano—try No. 1, Op. 15—one senses something of power that goes beyond the "calm serenity" usually associated with this composer.

Most of his outstanding piano compositions bear such titles as nocturne, prelude, impromptu, and barcarole. His most recorded orchestral works are an Elégie for Cello and Orchestra, written for piano and cello in 1880 and revised for cello and orchestra in 1901; the orchestral rendition of his Ballade in F-sharp for Piano and Orchestra, composed in 1877–1879 for the piano alone and orchestrated in 1881; and a Pavane for Orchestra and Chorus, written in 1887. Perhaps his most accepted masterpiece is the *Requiem*, published in 1887 and regarded by some as France's finest religious music (Franck's oratorio *Les Béatitudes* is another contender) and by others as one of history's finest choral works.

Fauré really belongs in his own school. The Early Romantics (Mendelssohn, Schuman, Chopin, Berlioz, Wagner, and Liszt) were still alive when he was born. Wagner's music-drama came, peaked, and lost favor during his lifetime. He held steady through the post-Romantic years of Brahms and Mahler, the tone poems of Richard Strauss, the Impressionism of Debussy, two or three of Stravinsky's phases, and the New Music of Prokofiev—and even through his own late deafness.

Aside from the *Requiem*, Fauré is best known for his melodic songs—quiet, gentle, and pure; pleasant listening for any music lover. Of about a hundred songs, the best known include "Clair de lune," "Après un rêve," "L'horizon chimerique," "Les berceux," "Dan les ruines d'une abbaye," and two song cycles, *La bonne chanson* and *La chanson d'Eve*.

THE FRENCH SCHUBERT

Fauré has been called "the French Schubert" because his songs are regarded by the experts as ranking among the greatest in the literature. He produced three volumes of songs, and even the first, composed when he was still quite young, drew this praise from Ravel: "In these pieces, the seductiveness of his melodic contour does not cede to the subtlety of the harmonies."

The critics say that Saint-Saëns, Fauré's friend and teacher, is a composer in the Classical style, while Fauré has more of the Romantic in him (although he far from overflows with Romantic emotionalism). The words and phrases used about him include "subjectivism," "lyrical expressiveness," and "typically French exquisiteness of taste."

Among his highly rated "typically French" works are the Violin Sonata in A, the Piano Trio in D Minor, the Piano Quartet in C Minor, and the Piano Quintet in C Minor.

Fauré is regarded by the French as one of their greatest composers, and, as his impact on a generation of French composers was considerable, his place on The List is deserved.

STARTER KIT

A Fauré Starter Kit should probably consist of chamber music, piano music, songs, and his famous *Requiem*. Because of the popularity of his few larger works, however, I've selected a different mix, beginning with two much-recorded orchestral pieces, his Ballade for Piano and Orchestra and his Elégie for Cello and Orchestra. The former had such a complicated piano part that Liszt—who could play anything and who had a lifelong reputation of helping other composers—returned it to Fauré with a brusque note saying that it was too difficult. (Nothing, of course, was actually too difficult for Liszt himself.)

A third choice is Fauré's beautiful Violin Sonata in A, regarded by some critics as an even finer work than Franck's, which is generally

THE LADY'S SHOULDER STRAPS

Claude Debussy in 1903, writing about a Fauré concert:

"Afterwards, we heard a Ballade for piano and orchestra by the Master of Charms, Gabriel Fauré. It was almost as lovely as Mme. M. Hasselmans herself, who played the piano. She kept having to straighten her shoulder straps as they fell down at every scale that was a little too fast. And she made the most charming movements whenever she performed this little task! I don't know why, but I somehow associated the charm of these gestures with the music of Fauré himself. The play of fleeting curves that is the essence of Fauré's music can be compared to the movements of a beautiful woman without either suffering from the comparison."

held to be one of the most original of all violin sonatas. Passing over the light, whimsical Piano Quartet in C Minor, the final selections are the lovely *Requiem*, regarded today as *the* Fauré composition, and, as a sample of his beautiful and gentle songwriting, the song cycle *La bonne chanson*, written in 1892 to poems of Paul Verlaine. Some argue that these songs give him claim, at least, to being France's greatest songwriter.

One opinion of Fauré's religious masterpiece, which is the centerpiece of the Starter Kit, comes from the great music teacher Nadia Boulanger, who wrote:

"The Requiem" is not only one of the greatest works of Gabriel Fauré, but also one of those which do most honor to music and thought. Nothing purer, clearer in definition, has been written. . . . Certainly it is his musical web, his architecture, his reason and order, that produce his sovereign beauty, as one could demonstrate with a joy, a pride, and a respect for all the minutiae of his workmanship. But it is where these attributes end, admirable as they are, that the real Requiem begins. No exterior effect alters its sober and rather severe expression of grief, no restlessness troubles its deep meditation, no doubt strains its spotless faith, its gentle confidence, its tender and tranquil expectancy. All is truly captivating, and marked with the hand of a master. Everything is usual; but with an alteration, a passing note, some special inflection of which he has the secret, Gabriel Fauré gives a new and inimitable character to what he touches. The end, with its linked chords descending in double measures, strangely recalls an adorable "Agnus Dei" in G major by Claudio Monteverdi.

FAURÉ: THE STARTER KIT

Composition	Recordings Available*
ORCHESTRAL WORKS:	
Ballade in F-sharp for Piano and Orchestra	9
Elégie for Cello and Orchestra	10
OTHER INSTRUMENTAL MUSIC:	
Sonata in A for Violin and Piano	6
VOCAL MUSIC:	
Requiem	8
Songs:	
La bonne chanson (song cycle)	C

*Represents the number of recorded releases available of each listed composition as found in a recent issue of the *Schwann/Opus* catalogue. A "C" indicates that a work is only available collected with other compositions.

FAURÉ: A TOP TEN

Composition	Recordings Available*
ORCHESTRAL WORKS:	
Ballade in F-sharp for Piano and Orchestra	9
Elégie for Cello and Orchestra	10
Dolly (suite for piano duet, turned into ballet)	6
Pavane for Orchestra and Chorus	10
Pelléas and Mélisande: incidental music (suite for orchestra)	5
CHAMBER MUSIC:	
String Quartet in E, Op. 121	3
Piano Quartet in C Minor	3
OTHER INSTRUMENTAL MUSIC:	
Sonata in A for Violin and Piano	6

Composition	Recordings Available*
VOCAL MUSIC:	
Requiem	8
Songs:	
La bonne chanson (song cycle)	C

FAURÉ: A MASTER COLLECTION

Composition	Recordings Available*
ORCHESTRAL WORKS:	
Ballade in F-sharp for Piano and Orchestra	9
Elégie for Cello and Orchestra	10
Dolly (suite for piano duet, turned into ballet)	6
Masques et bergamasques	2
Pavane for Orchestra and Chorus	10
Pelléas and Mélisande: incidental music (suite for orchestra)	5
CHAMBER MUSIC:	
String Quartet in E, Op. 121	3
Piano Quartet in C Minor	3
Piano Quintet in C Minor	2
Piano Trio in D Minor	5
OTHER INSTRUMENTAL MUSIC:	
Nocturnes for Piano (thirteen)	1
Berceuse for Violin and Piano	5
Sonata in A for Violin and Piano	6
Fantaisie for Flute and Piano	5
VOCAL MUSIC:	
Requiem	8
Songs:	
La bonne chanson (song cycle)	C
La chanson d'Eve (song cycle)	C
L'horizon chimerique (song cycle)	C
Clair de lune	C
Dans les ruines d'une abbaye	C
and one hundred songs with piano accompaniment	C

NIKOLAI RIMSKY-KORSAKOV (1844–1908)

Number 42

Nikolai Rimsky-Korsakov is not the most important figure of the "Mighty Five," the group of Russian nationalist composers that banded together in the mid-1860s, but he is the best known to the public, and he wrote the best-known composition—*Scheherazade*, a symphonic suite based on the *Thousand and One Arabian Nights*.

It is an accepted masterpiece as a program work, with its rich interpretation of the legend and its imaginative—the music people say "captivating"—sense of color. "Color" is what its composer was most into, and *Scheherazade* fans say the work has hardly been surpassed in descriptive power. Even the amateur listener will hear and/or sense some extravagant poetry here.

Unfortunately, it has suffered something of the same fate that befalls the four-star restaurant that becomes known as a tourist trap. The tourists all go because the food and ambience are so good. Then the elitists turn up their noses and frequent a little tucked-away restaurant where the food is not as good. So many people have heard and enjoyed *Scheherazade* for so many years, and it has been recorded so often, that now it is thought of as "pop" music. Fifty or sixty years—and several thousand *Scheherazade* performances—ago, critics would have put Rimsky-Korsakov fifteen or so places higher on The List, but today he has slid to a level a little below his fellow nationalist Mussorgsky, a more powerful and much more overwhelming composer, if a less formally trained one. Rimsky-Korsakov composed several operas, none of which stand up against Mussorgsky's profound *Boris Godounov*—although, paradoxically, without Rimsky-Korsakov's professional contributions to *Boris* it might never have made it to the public, and Mussorgsky would be unListed.

Rimsky-Korsakov was born in the Novgorod district on March 18, 1844. He was of a proud, established family that expected him to represent it well. It was decided that he should serve in his country's navy, and for six years he attended the Naval College at St. Petersburg. But his family was also fairly musical, and his own musical talent was evident from an early age. In his autobiography, he writes: "I was not fully two years old when I clearly distinguished all the tunes that my mother sang to me. Later, when three or four years of age, I beat a toy drum in perfect time, while my father played the piano. Often my father would suddenly change the tempo and rhythm on purpose, and I at once followed suit."

As a youth, he played a little piano, dabbled in composition, and after meeting Mily Balakirev, the unListed leader of the "Mighty Five" in St. Petersburg, began dabbling somewhat more seriously—even beginning work on a symphony. Few composers have undertaken a musical work of this dimension with so little formal training. Meanwhile, the navy called, and Rimsky-Korsakov left St. Petersburg for a two-and-a-half-year world cruise in the service of the czar. (The symphony, in E minor, was eventually completed and performed.)

In 1873, the budding composer pulled a Bobby Kennedy—who once said that the way to become U.S. attorney general was to have your brother elected president of the United States. Rimsky-Korsakov was by then quite friendly with the minister of the marine, and he was allowed to drop the rank of lieutenant in the Russian navy and accept the civilian post of inspector of the music bands of the Navy Department. Later he even became an admiral. (The author went from lieutenant [junior grade] in World War II to assistant secretary of defense twenty years later and so is sympathetic to promotions of this nature.)

While still a naval lieutenant, he began working with members of the "Five," and wrote a few songs, some orchestral works based on folk tunes, and composed another symphony, first called *Antar* and later revised as a Symphonic Suite. In these years he also began his first opera, *The Maid of Pskov*, which was finally produced in 1873. Always big on revisions, of both his own work and that of other "Mighty Five" colleagues, in time he rewrote almost everything he had created during the first ten or fifteen years of his composing career.

His first big hit was the tone poem *Sadko*, performed after revisions in 1869. (He later produced an opera by the same name.) The public liked the tone poem, the critics did too, and astonishingly, given his lack of musical expertise, it led to his being offered a job as professor of practical composition and instrumentation at the St. Petersburg Conservatory. The literature suggests that probably no more ignorant a professor ever graced an academy. He wrote by ear.

TCHAIKOVSKY ON THE "MIGHTY FIVE"

"Borodin is a fifty-year-old professor of chemistry at the
Academy of Medicine. Again, a talent—and even an impressive one—but lost because of a lack of knowledge, because
blind fate led him to a chair of chemistry instead of to an
active musical career. However, he has less taste than Cui, and
his technique is so weak he cannot write a line without outside
help. Mussorgsky you very rightly call a has-been. In talent he
perhaps exceeds all the others; but he has a narrow nature and
lacks the need for self-perfection, blindly believing in the ridiculous theories of his circle and in his own genius. Besides,
there's something low about him that loves coarseness, lack of
polish, roughness. He is the direct opposite of his friend Cui,
who is always swimming in the shallows, yet always seemly
and graceful. . . . The most outstanding person of this circle
is Balakirev. But he has grown silent after accomplishing very
little.

"This then, is my honest opinion of these gentlemen.
What a sad thing! With the exception of Korsakov, how many
talents from whom it is hard to await anything serious! And
isn't this generally the way with us in Russia? Tremendous
powers fatally hindered . . . from taking the open field and
joining battle as they should. Nevertheless, these powers exist.
Even a Mussorgsky, by his very lack of discipline, speaks a
new language. It is ugly, but it is fresh. And that is why one
may expect that Russia will one day produce a whole galaxy of
great talents, who will point out new paths for art. Our ugliness is at any rate better than the sorry feebleness (disguised
as serious creative work) of Brahms and the other Germans.
They are hopelessly played out."

But he studied—throughout his life he was industrious and conscien-
tious—and it all worked out famously. Indeed, one of his later pupils
was Stravinsky.

In his autobiography Rimsky-Korsakov acknowledged his early
professorial ignorance:

At the time, I could not harmonize a chorale properly, had
never written a single contrapuntal exercise in my life, and had

only the haziest understanding of strict fugue. I didn't even
know the names of the augmented and diminished intervals or
the chords. . . . In my compositions I strove after correct
part-writing and achieved it by instinct and by ear. My grasp
of musical forms . . . was equally hazy. Although I scored my
compositions colorfully enough, I had no adequate knowledge
of the technique of the strings or of the practical possibilities
of horns, trumpets and trombones."

This from the man who had written the early Symphony in E
Minor, an *Overture on Three Russian Themes*, a *Fantasia on Serbian
Themes*, the symphonic poem *Sadko*, the *Antar* Symphony, a national
opera, and numerous songs. It gives hope to readers of this book: If
Professor Rimsky-Korsakov knew none of this, surely a sound case
exists for us not knowing it.

As part of his professorial learning process, one summer he
plunged into elementary musical studies, turning out sixty-four
fugues. The master Tchaikovsky, writing of Rimsky-Korsakov's transition from natural composer to trained musician, said at the time:
"He is passing through a crisis, and how that crisis will end it is hard
to say. Either a great master will emerge or he will sink definitely into
contrapuntalism."

In the end Rimsky-Korsakov was by far the most musically
learned of the nationalist, enthusiastic, untrained "Mighty Five," and
he spent thousands of hours over the years redoing the work of his
close friends in the group. He became a musical theorist and an author
as well as a fine technician. And he studied each musical instrument
intently, learning the range of its capabilities and analyzing what kinds
of sounds it could produce, a process leading to his eventual mastery
of tone color and orchestration. Some professionals consider him the
"incomparable master of orchestration." He also liked new instruments, a fact known to Tchaikovsky, who, in 1891, found in Paris the
celesta, which he described as a cross between a piano and a glockenspiel. Directing that one be purchased for the first performance of his
Nutcracker ballet, Tchaikovsky also asked that it be sent from Paris to
Russia secretly, because "if Rimsky heard of it he would use it first and
spoil the fun."

Platon Brounoff (1863–1924), pianist and composer, wrote of the
four main traits of Rimsky-Korsakov: "His melodies are of the old
Russian style, entirely original in rhythms and character; his harmony
is brilliant and daring, in which he uses the old Greek scales; he has
an extraordinary talent for instrumentation—dazzling combinations

---

RIMSKY-KORSAKOV ON ORCHESTRATORS

"The post-Wagner age is the age of brilliance and imaginative quality in orchestral tone colouring. Berlioz, Glinka, Liszt, Wagner, modern French composers—Delibes, Bizet and others; those of the new Russian school—Borodin, Balakirev, Glazounov and Tchaikovsky—have brought this side of musical art to its zenith; they have eclipsed, as colourists, their predecessors, Weber, Meyerbeer and Mendelssohn, to whose genius, nevertheless, they are indebted for their own progress."

---

of colors, strong, radiant, and brilliant, and at the same time transparent and clear; finally, qualities which you meet so seldom in the works of other Russian composers—namely, sunshine and warmth."

He wrote more than a dozen operas, some solo piano music, a piano concerto, a concerto for trombone and band, a little chamber music including a Quintet for Piano, Flute, Bassoon, Clarinet, and Horn, and songs and choruses. He is best known, however, for his operas and orchestral works—and, outside of Russia, chiefly for the latter.

He wrote the opera *The Maid of Pskov* in 1872, a third symphony in 1874, and the operas *May Night* and *Snow Maiden* between 1878 and 1881. After a lapse, he entered a period during which much of his best-known work was produced: the *Capriccio Espagnol* in 1887, the *Russian Easter* Overture in 1888, and the famous *Scheherazade*, published in 1889. He completed the opera *Mlada* in 1890; another opera, *Christmas Eve*, in 1894–1895; and his finest opera, *Sadko*, with its "Hindu Chant," in 1896. Five more operas followed: *Mozart and Salieri* in 1897; *The Czar's Bride* in 1898; *Czar Saltan* in 1900; *The Legend of the Invisible City of Kitezh* in 1906; and his most famous opera, *The Golden Cockerel* (Le coq d'or), with its "Hymn to the Sun," in 1907, not long before he died.

One Rimsky-Korsakov work has been heard for more than two decades by televiewers across the country every Saturday night and/or Sunday morning. The theme for the news panel show that was for twenty years called *Agronsky and Company*, and then *Inside Washington*, is the "Procession of the Nobles" from Rimsky-Korsakov's *Mlada*.

Rimsky-Korsakov was only in his mid-sixties when he died of a heart attack in 1908. By then this naval officer turned musician and untrained professor turned music expert had become the Senior Counselor to many Russian composers and the patriarch of Russian nationalist music.

STARTER KIT

The first selection, inevitably, is *Scheherazade*. Rimsky-Korsakov attached to the work's score this description of the legend: "The Sultan Schahriar, convinced of the faithlessness of women, had sworn to put to death each of his wives after the first night. But the Sultana Scheherazade saved her life by diverting him with stories which she told him during a thousand and one nights. The Sultan, conquered by his curiosity, put off from day to day the execution of his wife, and at last renounced entirely his bloody vow. Many wonders were narrated to Schahriar by Scheherazade. For her stories she borrowed the verses of poets and the words of folk songs, and fitted together tales and adventure."

The composer also wrote this program for the work:

> The program I was guided by in composing "Scheherazade" consisted of separate, unconnected episodes and pictures from "The Arabian Nights," scattered through all four movements of my suite; the sea and Sinbad's ship, the fantastic narrative of the Prince Kalendar; the Prince and the Princess, the Bagdad festival, and the ship dashing against the rock with the bronze rider on it. The unifying thread consisted of the brief introductions to Movements I, II, and IV, and the intermezzo in Movement III, written for violin solo and delineating Scheherazade herself as telling her wondrous tales to the stern Sultan. The conclusion of Movement IV serves the same artistic purpose.

The second selection, not as frequently played but still extremely popular, is another one of the most colorfully orchestrated of all classical compositions, the Spanish-sounding *Capriccio Espagnol*, a five-movement piece written in 1887. (Most "capriccios" of the nineteenth century are short piano pieces, written by the likes of Brahms and Mendelssohn.) The fourth movement of this work, called "Scene and Gypsy Song," is particularly praised by the experts.

A third Starter Kit choice is the color-filled *Russian Easter* Overture, based on Greek Orthodox Church themes.

For the final two selections, try the orchestral suites from Rimsky-Korsakov's last operas, *Le coq d'or* and *Czar Saltan*. The former is based on a poem by Pushkin about an ancient monarchy. The latter—also from Russian folk heritage—offers the rich orchestral color for which Rimsky-Korsakov is deservedly famous.

RIMSKY-KORSAKOV: THE STARTER KIT

Composition	Recordings Available*
ORCHESTRAL WORKS:	
Scheherazade (symphonic suite)	31
Capriccio Espagnol	22
Suites from Operas:	
Le coq d'or (The golden cockerel)	7
Czar Saltan	2
Overture:	
Russian Easter	9

*Represents the number of recorded releases available of each listed composition as found in a recent issue of the *Schwann/Opus* catalogue. A "C" indicates that a work is only available collected with other compositions.

RIMSKY-KORSAKOV: A TOP TEN

Composition	Recordings Available*
ORCHESTRAL WORKS:	
Piano Concerto in C-sharp	2
Scheherazade (symphonic suite)	31
Capriccio Espagnol	22
Suites from Operas:	
Le coq d'or (The golden cockerel)	7
Czar Saltan	2
Christmas Eve	2
Sadko	3
Overture:	
Russian Easter	9
CHAMBER MUSIC:	
Quintet in E-flat for Piano, Flute, Clarinet, Bassoon, and Horn	3

Composition	Recordings Available*

VOCAL MUSIC:

Opera:

Le coq d'or   1

RIMSKY-KORSAKOV: A MASTER COLLECTION

Composition	Recordings Available*

SYMPHONIES:

No. 2 (Antar)   3

OTHER ORCHESTRAL WORKS:

Piano Concerto in C-sharp   2
Scheherazade (symphonic suite)   31
Capriccio Espagnol   22
Suites from Operas:
    Le coq d'or (The golden cockerel)   7
    Snow Maiden   1
    Czar Saltan   2
    Christmas Eve   1
    Sadko   3
Overtures:
    May Night   2
    Russian Easter   7

CHAMBER MUSIC:

Quintet in E-flat for Piano, Flute, Clarinet,   2
    Bassoon, and Horn
Trio in C for Cello, Piano, and Violin   1

VOCAL MUSIC:

Operas:
    The Czar's Bride   0
    Legend of the Invisible City of Kitezh   0
    Le coq d'or   1
    Snow Maiden   0
    Czar Saltan   0
    Christmas Eve   0
    Sadko   0

GAETANO DONIZETTI (1797–1848)

Number 43

This is the "fast food" man of music, a fellow who wrote more than seventy operas over a thirty-year career, composed one of his finest in eleven days and a second in six weeks, and produced eight in one three-year stretch. Mendelssohn, a slightly younger contemporary, said of him: "Donizetti finishes an opera in ten days. It may be hissed, to be sure, but that doesn't matter, as it is paid for all the same, and then he can go about having a good time. If in the end his reputation should be endangered, in that case he would have to work real hard, which he would not like. Therefore he sometimes spends as much as three weeks on an opera, taking considerable pains with a couple of arias in it, so that they may please the public, and then he can afford to amuse himself once more, and once more write more trash."

As noted before, three composers dominated Italian opera in the first half of the nineteenth century: Gioacchino Rossini, who died in 1868 after retiring as an opera composer in 1829 at the height of his fame; unListed Vincenzo Bellini, 1801–1835; and Gaetano Donizetti.

Donizetti was another spontaneous melodist, a composer who worked simply, swiftly, and often superficially but sometimes with great talent. He is ranked last of the four nineteenth-century Italian opera composers on The List—trailing the incomparable Verdi (Number 16), the dramatic Puccini (Number 23), and the sparkling Rossini (Number 30). Five years younger than Rossini, he is something of a bridge between that artist and Verdi, born nearly twenty years later. Puccini was more recent, living until 1924.

Donizetti was born in Bergamo, Italy, and died there at about the time of our Gold Rush. His grandfather worked in the textile industry, and his father was a weaver until 1800, when he was named keeper of the municipal pawnshop. His mother was a seamstress.

Young Gaetano showed an early bent toward things musical, and his father hoped that he would become a learned teacher and a church musician, a respectable combination that could lead to a comfortable income. But such a career demanded, among other things, that the boy absorb the principles of counterpoint, and his interests were not in scholarship but in the theater. To succeed there he needed a natural gift for music and experience in achieving theatrical effects. He had the first and acquired the second.

Initially supportive, his father sent him to the Bergamo Conservatory. Later Donizetti attended the Philharmonic Lyceum in Bologna. At Bergamo, the professor of composition was Johann Simon May, a Bavarian musician who had composed not only a number of masses and oratorios, but several successful operas as well. (His best, *Medea in Corinto*, produced in Naples in 1813, is listed in the *Opus* catalogue.) May's entire opera-writing career was spent in Italy, and he is credited with having helped transmit to that country the rich orchestration that Paris and Vienna had long before accepted. His influence on Donizetti, the musicologists say, was significant.

In Bologna, Donizetti, who had earlier encountered the music of Rossini, studied under the same master who had taught that artist, who had become world-famous at age twenty-one with the opera *Tancredi*.

In his first few years of opera composition, Donizetti, understandably, imitated Rossini. Once that phase was behind him, he started doing his own thing and making his own reputation. He wrote five operas in 1828 and another five in 1830.

Meanwhile, in 1828, Simon May had written a letter recommending Donizetti to the directorate of La Scala (Milan's opera house). For the next eight years, the young composer produced two operas a year there. His first international success was *Anna Bolena*, produced in Milan in 1830, in Paris six months later, and then at the King's Theatre in London.

It is almost inevitable that there is some not-very-good music among Donizetti's "fast-food" works. No opera composer was more prolific, for which we may perhaps be thankful. Some of his works were serious, some comic, some semiserious, some semicomic. Although most have long been forgotten, many have not. Recordings in complete form are available today for more than a dozen of his works, and excerpts are available of still more. His most popular operas include two tragedies, *Lucrezia Borgia* (1833) and *Lucia de Lammermoor*

(1835); the semiserious *Linda di Chamounix* (1842); and the comedies *La fille du régiment* (1840), *L'elisir d'amore* (1832), and *Don Pasquale* (1843). All were written over one decade or so, from the early 1830s to the early 1840s, at a time when Donizetti's predecessor Rossini had stopped producing and the great Verdi was just beginning. For this short period, Donizetti and unListed Bellini had the field of Italian opera to themselves.

ITALIAN AUDIENCE

Hector Berlioz gives one account of an early performance he attended in Milan of *L'elisir d'amore*:

"People were talking in normal voices with their backs to the stage. The singers, undeterred, gesticulated and yelled their lungs out in the strictest spirit of rivalry. At least I presumed they did, from their wide-open mouths, but the noise of the audience was such that no sound penetrated except the bass drum. People were gambling, eating supper in their boxes, etc., etc. Consequently, perceiving it was useless to expect to hear anything of the score, which was then new to me, I left."

Although it may not seem so from this report, the opera was a smash hit from the start. Though perhaps a little tough on the performers, it is not all bad to have the attitude toward opera that tens of millions of Americans have toward professional football games. Why not hot dogs in the concert hall?

This was bel canto opera, basically opera that focused on the singers and the singing, the same style in which Rossini had worked. (To refresh the reader's memory, *bel canto* is defined by *The Harvard Dictionary of Music* as "the Italian vocal technique of the eighteenth century, with its emphasis on beauty of sound and brilliance of performance rather than dramatic expression or romantic emotion.") There was a set formula for these works, as there was for *Rocky, Star Wars, Jaws, Dallas*, and other fabulously successful productions of the advanced twentieth century. And if a composer can write *L'elisir d'amore* in eight days and put together the last act of *La favorita* (which recaptured Paris in 1840, just after he had captured it for the first time with *La fille du régiment*) in a few hours, so be it. After all, Mozart composed his three greatest symphonies over a six-week period, so we need not be too elitist about rapid-fire creation.

Opinions differ as to which of Donizetti's operas are the finest, but there is sound support for one comedy and one tragedy, the latter much better known today. It is *Lucia di Lammermoor*, his most ambitious undertaking—although not Donizetti at his best, since comedy rather than tragedy was his real strength. If not an acknowledged masterpiece throughout, masterpiece grades are given *Lucia* for the Sextet in Act II, which has been called one of the finest examples of vocal writing in all of opera.

Don Pasquale, on the other hand, *is* an accepted masterpiece of comic opera. In describing it, the critics use such phrases as "lightness of touch," "frothy humor," "sprightliness," "sparkle," "brilliance," "freshness," "charm," "sauciness," and "comic verve." It is a mixture of tuneful music with light characters and a happy plot, a love story in which love triumphs after unimaginable complexities.

A 1915 ASSESSMENT

Author Arthur Elson wrote of Donizetti three-quarters of a century ago: "The vivacity and charm of the music in these comedies wins high praise even now. No allowance need be made in their favor because of changing standards; they hold their own today with scarcely less vigor then when they were first produced. While the tragedies of the Italian school seem thin and inartistic, the comedies are still models in their particular line."

Donizetti's last years were tragic ones. He lost his wife in 1837, and his health began to decline in 1843 after he wrote the highly successful *Don Pasquale* and its tragic companion piece, *Don Sebastian*. He began experiencing violent headaches, depression, and hallucinations, and in 1845 he collapsed on the floor of his bedroom, partly paralyzed, apparently from a stroke. Shortly thereafter, he entered an insane asylum, where he spent some eighteen months. He was then released to the custody of his brother in Bergamo, where he lived until his death in 1848.

In the asylum, Donizetti was visited by the German poet Heinrich Heine, who was also a prominent journalist and music critic for the Augsburg *Allegemeine Zeitung* in the first half of the nineteenth century. Heine told his readers: "While his magical tunes bring joy to the world, while every one sings them and trills them, he himself sits, a terrible picture of insanity, in a lunatic asylum near Paris. Until some time ago, he had kept a childish consciousness of clothes: he had to be attired carefully every day in full dress, his tail coat decorated with all his orders; and so, from early in the morning until late at night, he sat motionless, his hat in his hand. But even that is over with; he now recognizes no one. Such is the destiny of man."

STARTER KIT

Although Donizetti wrote some eighteen string quartets early in his career (between 1817 and 1821), they are not highly regarded by the professionals, and it makes more sense to confine his Starter Kit to opera. Five complete operas by one composer constitute more of a library than a Starter Kit, however, so I've chosen to recommend some excerpts from a selected five. The entire operas are available, of course, for opera buffs. Three are comic operas, one somewhat more serious, and one a wholly serious tragedy; three are in Italian and two in French.

The tragedy is *Lucia di Lammermoor*, from Sir Walter Scott's novel *The Bride of Lammermoor*. It is about as tragic a tragedy as one could want, replete with violent emotions (love, hate, jealousy), suicide, madness, and murder. Recommended excerpts include "Regnava nel silenzio" and the love duet from Act I; the famous Sextet and the ultrafamous twenty-minute Mad Scene from Act II; and the Tomb Scene from Act III.

The first of the comic operas recommended here is *Don Pasquale*, initially performed in Paris in 1843 and regarded by the professionals as *the* all-around best Donizetti opera. Some experts think it is as good as Rossini's *Barber of Seville*. Here, and in *L'elisir d'amore*, Donizetti is considered to be at his creative best. The plot of *Don Pasquale* is unimportant; the most famous parts include the soprano aria "So anch io la virtu magica" and a duet from Act I; the tenor aria "Chercho lontano terra" from Act II; and, from Act III, the duet for bass and tenor, "Cheti, cheti," the tenor's "Com e gentil," and the soprano-and-bass duet "Tornami a dir che m'ami."

L'elisir d'amore (The elixir of love), in two acts, was first performed in Milan in 1832 and is generally put in the same league as *Don Pasquale*. Its most famous aria—indeed, one of the most famous in all opera—is the tenor aria in Act II, "Una furtiva lagrima," which is as much identified with the famous Enrico Caruso as "Hound Dog" is with Elvis Presley. Other favorites include the bass aria "Udite, udite, o rustici" from Act I, and, from Act II, the duet for tenor and bass, "Veni scudi," and the soprano aria "Prendi, per me sei libero."

La fille du régiment (The daughter of the regiment) opened at the Opéra-Comique in Paris in 1840 and remains a great favorite of coloratura sopranos to this day. It is a lovely mixture of Italian melody and French charm (it's written in French). The best-known numbers are "Chacun le sait" for soprano and chorus and the soprano aria "Il faut partir" from Act I; and four numbers from Act II: the soprano arias "Par le rang et par l'opulence" and "Tyrolienne," the tenor aria "Pour me rapprocher de Marie," and the final "Salut à France."

The fifth selection is *La favorita*, more serious than the other three comic operas, with a quiet, tragic ending, but nothing of the violent tragedy of *Lucia*. The best-known aria is "Spirito gentil," very popular with tenors.

DONIZETTI: THE STARTER KIT

Composition	Recordings Available*
VOCAL MUSIC:	
Operas:	
Don Pasquale	8
Lucia di Lammermoor	20
L'elisir d'amore	9
La fille du régiment	3
La favorita	4

*Represents the number of recorded releases available of each listed composition as found in a recent issue of the *Schwann/Opus* catalogue. A "C" indicates that a work is only available collected with other compositions.

DONIZETTI: A TOP TEN/A MASTER COLLECTION

Composition	Recordings Available*
ORCHESTRAL WORKS:	
Concertino in G for English Horn and Orchestra	1

Composition   *Recordings Available**

OTHER INSTRUMENTAL MUSIC:
Concertino in B-flat for Clarinet and Chamber Orchestra 1

VOCAL MUSIC:
Operas:

Don Pasquale	8
Lucia di Lammermoor	20
L'elisir d'amore	9
La fille du régiment	3
Anna Bolena	6
La favorita	4
Maria Stuarda	5
Maria di Rudenz	1

RALPH VAUGHAN WILLIAMS (1872–1958)

Number 44

Ralph Vaughan Williams is as English as pub darts and the changing of the Palace Guard.

To position him:

Nineteen composers on The List lived in the twentieth century. Nine of them spent most of their working lives in it, some of them working hard to escape from the nineteenth. At least five of these nine at one time or another produced "new," or "modern," or "twentieth-century" music. Three of these were Russian (Stravinsky, Prokofiev, and Shostakovich), one German (Hindemith), and one Hungarian (Bartók). A sixth of the nine was Richard Strauss of Austria, who paved the way for the others, and a seventh was Ravel of France, who created his own different sounds, albeit of a somewhat smoother nature, in the Impressionist style.

The other two looked at nineteenth-century Romanticism, considered it, and made their own, different, new-century choices: Sibelius—screech-and-growl music really doesn't seem to fit with frozen Finland—and Ralph Vaughan Williams of Down Ampney, Gloucestershire.

Vaughan Williams is England's leading nationalist composer, the only Englishman on The List, and, by (my) definition, therefore, the top English composer of music.

It simply isn't done for someone to be born in Down Ampney, grow up as the son of a well-to-do clergyman, attend the Royal College of Music of Cambridge, play the organ at St. Barnabas Church in South Lambeth, London—and then somehow discard all of that and emerge as a composer of the kinds of sounds as peculiar to the day as those produced by a Hungarian Bartók. And basically it *wasn't* done by this most English of all English artists, Ralph Vaughan Williams (not, at least, until late in his career).

FULLY DULL?

Aaron Copland offered this view of Vaughan Williams in 1931:

"It is fairly safe to predict that Vaughan Williams will be the kind of local composer who stands for something great in the musical development of his own country but whose actual musical contributions cannot bear exportation. Besides, he is essentially not modern at all; at any rate no more so than Rimsky-Korsakov. This is of course no fault, but it means that Williams lives in a world that is no longer ours, a condition that results in music unrelated to life as we know it. His is the music of a gentleman-farmer, noble in inspiration but dull."

In 1960, however, Copland amended that earlier sentiment with this comment: "Subsequent works, especially the composer's Symphony No. 4, give the lie to this statement."

Primarily he made melody. But he did a good many other things as well, the most important of which was to become one of the half-dozen top nationalists of music. His music *is* England—English geography, history, literature, spirit, and tradition. An integral part of this, and of his musical career, is English folk music. He looked for it, found it, analyzed it, worked from it, saturated himself in it.

"If the roots of your art are firmly planted in your own soil," he wrote, "you may gain the whole world and not lose your own soul."

He also wrote: "Every composer cannot expect to have a world-wide message, but he may reasonably expect to have a special message for his own people, and many young composers make the mistake of imagining that they can be universal without at first having been local."

And: "Art, like charity, should begin at home. It is because Pales-trina and Verdi are essentially Italian and because Bach, Beethoven and Wagner are essentially German that their message transcends their frontiers. The greatest artist belongs inevitably to his country as much as the humblest singer in a remote village."

Like the other great nationalist composers, out of a combination of folk songs and choral music of the late 1500s Vaughan Williams forged a style uniquely his own. While some of his melodies resemble folk tunes, both he and the musicologists tell us they actually were his own—just as the melodies of the old English composers in Queen Elizabeth I's day were their own.

Vaughan Williams's compositions changed gradually as he be-came increasingly immersed in his country's folk music. In 1907 he wrote three "Norfolk Rhapsodies," which have been described as little more than an orchestral stew of several existing folk airs such as "The Captain's Apprentice" and "A Bold Young Sailor Courted Me." These came from the district of Norfolk. In 1909 he composed the *Fantasia on a Theme by Thomas Tallis*, an orchestral work. The "Norfolk Rhapsodies" exemplify the nationalist approach that takes folk tunes, dresses them up in contemporary orchestral style, and offers them as lovely music. Another approach is for a composer to become so knowledgeable about a nation's folk music that it becomes a catalyst for his own original inspiration and imagination. Some original tunes might still be "quoted," but the work goes far beyond them. In Vaughan Williams's case, he quickly moved to the latter approach. He became a "folk self" . . . and always an English self. He even looked like the sort of pipe-smoking chap you would expect to meet on a narrow road in a lovely little English village such as Castle Combe, chatting with his dog, swinging his walking stick, and dressed in a too-large rough tweed jacket.

Vaughan Williams was much more than folk tunes, however. His supporters say he may one day be recognized as the foremost sympho-nist of the twentieth century. (Sibelius fans say the same thing about Sibelius, another nationalist and another who steeped himself in the folklore and folk songs of his country. And a couple of Russians are among others who would also be in the running.)

After attending the Royal College of Music and spending several years playing the church organ in London, Vaughan Williams became interested in folk music and joined the English Folk-Song Society. Deciding that he was "stodgy" (his word for himself), he went to Paris to study under Ravel, returned to England, and enlisted in the army during World War I despite being forty-two. He picked up his musical

HALF DULL?

Composer-critic Virgil Thomson in 1940 reviewed a performance of the *London* Symphony by the Boston Symphony Orchestra for the *New York Herald Tribune*. Thomson wrote, in
part:

"The sixtieth season of its concerts opened this afternoon
with Vaughan Williams' 'London Symphony.' . . . I remember
hearing the work 20 years ago in that same Symphony Hall,
Pierre Monteux conducting. It is the same piece it was then
too, in spite of some cuts operated by the composer. The first
two movements are long, episodic, disjointed. The third is
short, delicate, neatly sequential, compact, efficacious, charming. The finale is rich and varied. Its musical material is of high
quality, its instrumental organization ample and solid. Also, it
is not without expressive powers. . . . In any case, the last two
of the symphony's four movements are anything but dull,
which the first two are, and more than a little."

life after the war and became a professor of composition at the Royal
College of Music.

Vaughan Williams wrote nearly every type of music: nine symphonies; concertos not only for piano and violin but also for oboe
and, believe it or not, for both tuba and harmonica; other orchestral
works; many vocal works including masses and other religious pieces,
songs, and operas; and, among very short pieces, one that you must
not miss, a romance for violin and orchestra called "The Lark Ascending."

Of the symphonies, written over the course of more than fifty
years, the best known is perhaps his second, the *London* Symphony,
composed in 1913 (and later revised). Music connoisseurs then and
now have described it as a music picture of the city, despite the
composer's insistence that it was not his intention to draw such a
picture.

Symphony No. 1, the *Sea* Symphony, for soprano, baritone,
chorus, and orchestra, based on a text by Walt Whitman and composed between 1903 and 1909, is also a favorite of many. Like
Mahler's Eighth, it contains a lot of vocal music. Also popular is the
Pastoral Symphony, No. 3, written eight years after the *London* and

---

THE COMPOSER ON "A LONDON SYMPHONY"

"A better title," Vaughan Williams wrote of his second symphony, "would be 'Symphony by a Londoner.' That is to say, the life of London (including possibly its sights and sounds) has suggested to the composer an attempt at musical expression, but it would be no help to the hearer to describe these in words. The music is intended to be self-expressive, but must stand or fall as 'absolute music.' Therefore, if listeners recognize suggestions of such things as the Westminster Chimes or 'Lavender's Cry' they are asked to consider these as accidents, not essentials of the music."

Be that as it may, the Thames does flow in the music, Big Ben does chime, and pub music is heard. One musicologist notes that after a revision in 1920 the British Music Society chose this symphony as the most important native musical work produced by an Englishman.

---

described by the composer as "almost entirely quiet and contemplative" in mood.

It was not until some twenty years later, in 1934, that Vaughan Williams produced his fourth, and some say his most dramatic, symphony. Now, finally, some dissonant sounds of the "New Music" are heard. The experts call it "a radical departure" (by now the composer was in his sixties, and it must have been great fun for him to be a little radical). In the eyes of some, this work, the most un-Vaughan Williams-sounding of them all, is his true masterpiece. Glenn Gould, the great pianist who died of a stroke in 1982, once said something about Britannia Waiving the Rules in connection with it. Although the fifth Vaughan Williams symphony went back to the folk sound, it still had more tension than his first three. The final four symphonies were written in 1947, 1952, 1955, and 1957, the last revised shortly before he died at eighty-five.

The critics' words for his symphonies: "Ample," "noble in tone," "fresh," "wholesome," "strong," "honest," "uncluttered," "melodic but reserved," and "English."

Among many nonsymphonic orchestral works, the best known, in addition to the 1914 "Lark Ascending," are the *Fantasia on Greensleeves,* written in 1934; *Flos Campi,* a suite for violin, orchestra, and chorus, of 1925; and his first truly recognized work—and still one of his most successful—*Fantasia on a Theme by Thomas Tallis,* for double string orchestra, composed in 1910. (Tallis was a sixteenth-century Honorable Mention English church composer.) And one should not overlook the Concerto for Tuba and Orchestra, written in 1954!

His best-known vocal music is *On Wenlock Edge* (1909), a cycle of six songs, for tenor, strings, quartet, and piano, to lyrics from A. E. Housman's *Shropshire Lad.* As mentioned above, he also wrote religious music; in fact, parts of his Mass in G Minor were performed for the coronation of Queen Elizabeth II.

STARTER KIT

Two symphonies are included for this composer, who is a nominee as the twentieth century's best symphonist: No. 2, the *London* Symphony, because it is Vaughan Williams and it is London; and No. 5 in D, written twenty-nine years later, when the composer was back in the folk business (even if with more dissonance than earlier) after his "radical" Fourth. On Aaron Copland's recommendation, however, you might want to substitute that Fourth.

THE MELLOW FIFTH

If you like Sibelius, and you should, you'll like Vaughan Williams's Fifth Symphony, first performed shortly after his seventieth birthday in 1942, during World War II, but begun before the war. The two words most often used by reviewers in describing it are "pastoral" and "ingratiating"—in other words, "mellow" and "easy to take." At any rate, it's certainly much easier on the ear than the composer's Fourth Symphony, which is on the biting and abrasive side.

While rural England may not have a great deal in common with rural Finland, this symphony has a distinctly Sibelius-like sound, and in fact, the original dedication read: "Without permission and with the sincerest flattery to Jean Sibelius, whose great example is worthy of imitation."

Two other orchestral works have been selected: "The Lark Ascending" (this represents one of the rare times in the road map when the map maker asserts his own prejudice for fun listening), and the *Fantasia on Greensleeves*, probably his most familiar work. The latter was composed for his opera about Shakespeare's Falstaff, entitled *Sir John in Love*. (In Shakespeare's *Merry Wives of Windsor*, Falstaff says: "Let the skye raine potatoes; let it thunder to the tune of Green-sleeves.") It was later adapted in several ways, including this version for flute, harp, and strings.

The final selection is the song cycle *On Wenlock Edge*.

The professionals would want the *Fantasia on a Theme by Thomas Tallis*, a worthy addition. But one objective here is to identify the best-known works of the great composers. This measuring system obviously gives more weight to public acceptance than to professional critical judgment.

VAUGHAN WILLIAMS: THE STARTER KIT

Composition	Recordings Available*
SYMPHONIES:	
No. 2 (London)	5
No. 5 in D	8
OTHER ORCHESTRAL WORKS:	
Fantasia on Greensleeves	20
The Lark Ascending (romance for violin and orchestra)	14
VOCAL MUSIC:	
On Wenlock Edge (cycle of six songs)	3

*Represents the number of recorded releases available of each listed composition as found in a recent issue of the *Schwann/Opus* catalogue. A "C" indicates that a work is only available collected with other compositions.

VAUGHAN WILLIAMS: A TOP TEN

Composition	Recordings Available*
SYMPHONIES:	
No. 2 (London)	5
No. 4	3
No. 5 in D	8

Composition	Recordings Available*

OTHER ORCHESTRAL WORKS:

Fantasia on a Theme by Thomas Tallis (for double string orchestra)	15
Fantasia on Greensleeves	20
The Lark Ascending (romance for violin and orchestra)	14
Flos Campi (suite for viola, orchestra, and chorus)	4
English Folk Song Suite	6

VOCAL MUSIC:

Mass in G Minor	3
On Wenlock Edge (cycle of six songs)	3

VAUGHAN WILLIAMS: A MASTER COLLECTION

Composition	Recordings Available*

SYMPHONIES:

No. 1 (Sea)	7
No. 2 (London)	5
No. 3 (Pastoral)	3
No. 4	3
No. 5 in D	8
No. 6	5
No. 7 (Sinfonie Antarctica)	3
No. 8	4
No. 9	3

OTHER ORCHESTRAL WORKS:

Fantasia on a Theme by Thomas Tallis (for double string orchestra)	15
Fantasia on Greensleeves	20
In the Fen Country (symphonic impression)	2
Overture to The Wasps	7
The Lark Ascending (romance for violin and orchestra)	14
Flos Campi (suite for viola, orchestra, and chorus)	4
Concerto for Bass Tuba and Orchestra	3
English Folk Song Suite	6

Composition	Recordings Available*
VOCAL MUSIC:	
Mass in G Minor	3
On Wenlock Edge (cycle of six songs)	3
Magnificat	1

BEDŘICH SMETANA (1824–1884)

Number 45

No other composer on The List is the son of a brewmaster. An innkeeper's son, yes, but not a brewmaster's. Bedřich Smetana is the only one. His father, an amateur musician, encouraged his son's violin and piano playing, for fun, but discouraged composition, accurately figuring that more people earned a better living making beer than making music. All good Czechs are glad that young Bedřich persisted. Among those not glad were the Nazis, who banned his patriotic music during their occupation of Czechoslovakia in World War II. (The same thing happened in Poland with Chopin's music.)

Smetana, Number 45, is one of three Czechs on The List. Dvořák, less nationalistic and more highly regarded by the music world, is Number 12, and Janáček, who lived until 1928, Number 48. Smetana encouraged the younger Dvořák, helping particularly to bring him to public attention by conducting his Symphony in E-flat. He is one of thirteen Middle Romantic composers on the list (all were born between 1822 and 1844).

Smetana was both a composer and a music critic, writing for the daily newspaper *Narodny Listy* in Prague—and not at all content with the music life of his city. "The public musical life and activities of our capital are nothing compared to those of great cities abroad," he wrote. Something had to be done about that, and he dedicated himself to doing it. There was no question as to what kind of music he most wanted: Czech music. Once, after leaving Bohemia for a short period, he wrote: "Shall I see these dearly beloved mountains again, and when and with what feelings? When I leave them I am always filled with such longing. Farewell, my beloved country, my beautiful, great unique country. May I rest in your soil. Your earth is sacred to me."

This was the kind of nationalistic sentiment that dominated his symphonic poems and operas—along with the "new" spirit of Liszt and Wagner. The anti-Wagnerites attacked him, but his music became the music of his country—and particularly of the independent Czechoslovakia that was born in 1918.

Smetana was born in Leitomischl, a small Bohemian town in southern Czechoslovakia, then part of Austria. He learned to play the violin and piano very early and fairly well, participating in a string quartet at the age of five to help celebrate his father's name day, and performing a public piano solo at six, but when the family moved to Jindrichuv-Hradec in 1831, Bedřich—the eighth child but the first boy—was still destined to be a brewmaster.

In time, however, he became a patriotic, fervent nationalist and father of the Czech nationalist school; a teacher, composer, virtuoso pianist, and conductor; a founder of modern Bohemian music; the creator of *The Bartered Bride*, the most famous Czech opera, and a set of six Czech-soaked nationalist tone poems, one of which, "The Moldau," is one of the more popular pieces of classical music; a devotee of Czech history, legend, and folk music; and the "guiding beacon" for all future Czech composers.

FOLK MUSIC

You will enjoy the folk idiom of Bedřich Smetana. If folk music appeals particularly to you, you might consider specific exploration of the idiom as expressed by a dozen or so other Listed composers. Strong recommendations include Liszt's *Hungarian Rhapsodies*, Chopin's mazurkas, Grieg's *Peer Gynt* Suites, Sibelius's *Lemminkainen*, Janáček's *Jenufa*, Dvořák's *Slavonic Dances*, Mussorgsky's *Night on Bald Mountain*, Vaughan Williams's "Norfolk Rhapsodies," Weber's *Der Freischütz*, and Bartók's *Dance Suite*.

In a book published in 1915, musicologist Arthur Elson described Smetana as a composer rated a little below the highest standards, who produced "much good music" but did not "quite reach the high level of the greatest masters." And this is about where he comes out on The List. (Interestingly, Elson said the same thing about Dvořák, who some seventy-five years later *is* considered at a level much closer to the top. Dvořák was also the son of an amateur musical tradesman [a butcher] who, like Smetana's father, considered musical talent appropriate for his offspring but, nonetheless, expected his son to follow in the trade.)

In Jindrichuv-Hradec, young Smetana continued to study music as part of his general education, first at primary school and later at the Gymnasium, where his tuition was paid in part by the organist of the church where he sang in the choir. The big move came in 1839 when he was permitted to go on to the Gymnasium in Prague, the music mecca of the day. Although he did not do well at the Gymnasium and soon went to live with a cousin in Plzen, during these years he immersed himself in music—playing in a string quartet, attending concerts, taking piano lessons, improvising dances, and, after a few years, giving lessons to pick up a little money. The senior Smetana finally caved in, providing a few florins and giving his approval of Bedřich's return to Prague to make his own way in music. After a good many fits and starts—including some time spent as music master in the various households of a count for three hundred florins a year plus room and board, and an unsuccessful concert tour—he decided to open his own music school in Prague. Although he had never met Liszt, who was thirteen years his senior, he dedicated his first composition to him, then advising him of that act in a fellow-pianist hard-times letter that asked for Liszt's financial help. It worked: the school was opened and was reasonably successful.

Bedřich was still only in his mid-twenties. He was interested in the "older" music of Beethoven, of course, but also in the "modern" sounds of Schumann, Chopin, Berlioz, and, especially, Liszt. His heart, however, was with the nationalist mazurkas and polonaises of Chopin, in large part because the Austrians were dominating Prague in a fairly heavy-handed way at the time. After the failure of the 1848 Czech independence cause, Prague was not a happy place for the losers, and Smetana believed strongly in independence for his country and freedom for his people. In 1856, still mourning the death of a five-year-old daughter (he had married a pianist named Katerina Kolarova) and distressed by the political conditions, he accepted a conductor's post in Gothenburg, Sweden, to get away from it all.

Although he did well in Gothenburg, becoming a respected figure in the community and beginning some serious composition, five years later he returned to Prague. This was in part because his second wife found the climate in Sweden too harsh and the life too alien for a good Bohemian girl. While in Sweden, he continued to be influenced by the work of his fellow pianist Liszt. Once that influence was solidified, Smetana composed nothing but program music. In a letter to Liszt from Sweden, he wrote: "I cannot describe to you the soul-stirring impression your music has made on me. Art as taught by you has become my credo. Please regard me as one of the most zealous disciples of your artistic school of thought, who will champion its sacred truth in word and deed."

SABOTAGE

Few heroes are perfect. Rimsky-Korsakov suggested in his autobiography that a "dark shadow hung over Smetana" because he deliberately tried to "trip up" the performance of Russian composers' operas when Smetana was opera-house conductor in Prague. The apparent reason seemed to be that Conductor Smetana was either anti-Russian or anti-this-particular-music. According to the Rimsky-Korsakov version, Russia prevailed, despite Smetana's activities.

Upon his return from Sweden in 1861, he helped establish a society dedicated to nationalist music. A provisional theater for Czech music was established, and Smetana promised to write a series of native-language Czech operas for it. The first, in 1862–1863, was something called The Brandenburgers in Bohemia. Neither the music nor the libretto was superior, but it was a new thing for Czechs who wanted to be Czechs, and, when produced in 1866, it was a big public success. During his life he wrote eight operas, all based on Czech themes, including Dalibor, serious and tragic; Two Widows, The Kiss, and The Secret, all lighter; and two even more serious ones, Libusa and The Devil's Wall. But the only one regularly performed outside of his homeland is The Bartered Bride, his second, produced just after The Brandenburgers.

It is a spirited comedy, fun to listen to, filled with Bohemian-sounding polkas and other dance tunes. Though these dances sound like typical folk music, they were actually original creations (Smetena was accused of, and strongly denied, plagiarizing the existing reservoir of Bohemian music).

Like so many other works of so many other composers, *The Bartered Bride* was not an immediate success, despite its warm tone, gay melodies, and spirited polkas. In time, however, it became the single most honored piece of Czech music, and it is still considered one of the greatest of all folk operas.

More frequently heard in the United States is "The Moldau," one of a cycle of six symphonic poems called *Má vlast* (My Fatherland or My Country), born of rural Bohemia, filled with folk legends and with the rhythms of folk songs and dances. You will find the tune familiar. Typical of Romantic program music, it is a "portrait" of the Moldau River, described by Smetana this way:

> Two springs pour forth their streams in the shade of the Bohemia forest, the one warm and gushing, the other cold and tranquil. Their waves, joyfully flowing over their rocky beds, unite and sparkle in the morning sun. The forest brook, rushing on, becomes the River Moldau, which, with its water speeding through Bohemia's valleys, grows into a mighty stream. It flows through dense woods from which come the joyous sounds of the chase, and the notes of the hunter's horn are heard ever nearer and nearer.
>
> It flows through emerald meadows and lowlands where a wedding feast is being celebrated with song and dancing. At night, in its shining waves, wood and water nymphs hold their revels, and in these waves are reflected many a fortress and castle—witness to the bygone splendor of chivalry and to the vanished martial spirit of days that are no more. At the rapids of St. John, the stream speeds on, winding through . . . the rocky chasm into the broad river bed, in which it flows on in majestic calm towards Prague, welcomed by the time-honored Vysherad, to disappear in the far distance from the poet's gaze.

Smetana is also known today for several string quartets, of which his autobiographical Quartet in E Minor is another example of program music. In the composer's words, the first movement "depicts my early love of art and native folk music, my romantic tendencies and unsatisfied yearnings. There is also a warning of future misfortune" (the 1848 revolution which caused him to flee to Sweden).

The second movement, a polka, "recalls memories of my gay life in youth when I used to write dance music and give it away right and left to other young folk, being known myself as an enthusiastic dancer."

The third movement "recalls the bliss of my first love for the girl who afterwards became my faithful wife."

And in the last, "My joy in discovering how to treat Bohemian national elements in my music is expressed; my success, in this direction, until the interruption of the terrible catastrophe, the beginning of deafness; a glimpse into the gloomy future, a slight ray of hope for betterment; painful impressions aroused by the thought of my artistic beginnings."

Smetana, who had contracted syphilis, became deaf in 1874, resigned as conductor of the Prague Opera, continued to compose, gradually lost his health, and finally died in a mental asylum in 1884.

UNFORTUNATE ENDINGS

Smetana is one of the three Listed composers who spent considerable time in a mental institution. He was sixty at the time of his death in one, was deaf, and had many musical enemies, but it is impossible to establish the causes for his mental condition. The two others were Schumann, who died in an asylum near Bonn at age forty-six, two years after attempting suicide, and Donizetti, who died in his home city of Bergamo at fifty-one after many years of depression and eighteen months in an institution. Another who tried suicide was Tchaikovsky, but he survived and eventually died of cholera.

STARTER KIT

Smetana's music is just plain fun to hear. "The Moldau" is the inevitable selection from the six tone poems that make up Má vlast, but you will not regret cheating a little and listening to the other five as well. (They come on one compact disc in any case.)

If there were only one Smetana choice it would have to be *The Bartered Bride*, because it is the most famous Czech opera and is so typically Smetana (and, by definition, typically Bohemian). On the orchestral side, the overture and dances from the opera are recommended. On the vocal side, one can undertake the complete opera or selected arias.

Rounding out the Starter Kit are the best known of Smetana's string quartets, No. 1 in E Minor, subtitled "Out of My Life," and two duets for violin and piano called *From My Homeland.*

SMETANA: THE STARTER KIT

Composition	Recordings Available*
ORCHESTRAL MUSIC:	
The Moldau (from Má vlast)	22
The Bartered Bride (overture and dances)	8
OTHER INSTRUMENTAL MUSIC:	
From My Homeland, Two Duets for Violin and Piano	2
Quartet No. 1 in E Minor (Out of My Life)	3
VOCAL MUSIC:	
Opera:	
The Bartered Bride	4

*Represents the number of recorded releases available of each listed composition as found in a recent issue of the *Schwann/Opus* catalogue. A "C" indicates that a work is only available collected with other compositions.

SMETANA: A TOP TEN/A MASTER COLLECTION

Composition	Recordings Available*
ORCHESTRAL MUSIC:	
Má vlast (six symphonic poems):	
The Moldau	22
Vysehrad	3
Sarka	C
From Bohemia's Meadows and Groves	4
Tabor	C
Blanik	C
The Bartered Bride (overture and dances)	8

Composition   *Recordings Available**

OTHER INSTRUMENTAL MUSIC:
Quartet No. 1 in E Minor (Out of My Life)   3
From My Homeland, Two Duets for Violin   2
   and Piano

VOCAL MUSIC:
Opera:
   The Bartered Bride   4
   Libuse   1

JOHANN STRAUSS (1825–1899)

Number 46

He received 100,000 U.S. dollars in 1872 to conduct one composition fourteen times on a tour of the United States.

When Brahms autographed his wife's fan with a few bars of that same composition, he wrote, "Not by Johannes Brahms . . . unfortunately."

Haydn, Mozart, and Beethoven wrote waltzes. Schubert also wrote a number of them. Weber put a series of them in *Invitation to the Dance*. Berlioz, the Great Rule-Breaker, dared use one as part of his *Symphonie fantastique*. Chopin loved them. Richard Strauss filled *Der Rosenkavalier* with them. Tchaikovsky scattered them in operas and ballets. Ravel tried to revive them.

But in the waltz kingdom, these geniuses were but princelings. The King was Johann Strauss the Younger, son of Johann the Elder, who had already made them the pride of Vienna.

RAVEL ON JOHANN STRAUSS

One of Ravel's best-known pieces is *La valse*, initially intended as a happy symphonic poem with the objective of paying tribute to the Viennese waltz, and particularly to Johann Strauss. "It is not subtle, what I am undertaking at the moment," Ravel wrote to a friend. "It is a Grand Valse, a sort of homage to the memory of the Great Strauss—not Richard, but the other, Johann."

That was before World War I. But the work was put aside and not completed until after the war, in a different political climate. Ravel turned it into a somber ballet, with a Strauss waltz used in the last dance to portray a world that no longer existed.

Strauss biographer Hans Fantel writes: "The universe of the waltz can be epitomized in about fifteen minutes simply by playing 'The Blue Danube.' More eloquently, more concisely than any other work, it embodies the essence of the waltz in form and spirit. . . . When its softly mysterious opening stirs the air with the rich, vibrant pianissimo that only a great orchestra can achieve, if the conductor keeps the tempo a little hesitant and pensive and retains a touch of lassitude even in the more exuberant phases, then the music takes subtle hold of the listener and makes him a living part of a vanished world."

Notwithstanding this later judgment, "The Blue Danube" was one of Johann the Younger's few failures when introduced in Vienna in 1867. Fortunately for the world, the composer dusted it off at Napoleon III's 1867 exhibition in Paris, after he had been presented to the Emperor and Empress Eugénie, and everyone lived happily ever after. As Fantel tells the story, "The Blue Danube" became wildly popular. Every orchestra in Paris took it up, including countless little café ensembles that paid little attention to the symphonic scoring. And, despite the melody's obduracy to the human voice, Parisians insisted on singing it.

"The new waltz," wrote Fantel, "became the musical motif of [Napoleon's] Fair. Foreign visitors returning to their own countries couldn't get it out of their heads. Edward, Prince of Wales, went home humming it. So obsessed was he with the new melody that he asked Strauss to come to London, where Strauss later gave six highly acclaimed concerts at Covent Garden. When he conducted the new waltz as the main feature of the series, even the formidable Queen Victoria nodded her pleasure, as she had once nodded to Strauss's father at her coronation.

"Back in Vienna," writes Fantel, "a crisis developed at the printing plant of Strauss's publisher. The relatively soft copper plates then used for printing music wore out after ten thousand copies. . . . Before the first printing was over, a hundred sets of plates had been worn down, and 'The Blue Danube' had become the most profitable 'property' in the history of music."

RICHARD STRAUSS ON JOHANN THE YOUNGER

Richard Strauss summed up the sentiments of many professionals about his non-kin, Johann the Younger:

"Of all the God-gifted dispensers of joy, Johann Strauss is to me the most endearing. This first, comprehensive statement can serve as a text for everything I feel about this wonderful phenomenon. In particular I respect in Johann Strauss his originality, his innate gift. At a time when the whole world around him was tending towards increased complexity, increased reflectiveness, his natural genius enabled him to create from the 'whole.' He seemed to me the last of those who worked from spontaneous inspiration. Yes, the primary, the original, the proto-melody—that's it."

The once-upon-a-time beginning of this fairy tale took place in a second-rate tavern called the Good Shepherd in a second-rate part of Vienna in 1804, when Johann the Elder was born, son of the innkeeper and his wife. He soon had a toy fiddle, at fourteen was befriended by a professional musician, and at fifteen became a violist in Michael Pamer's famous Vienna dance ensemble. Riverboats brought the three-quarter-time waltz music from outlying country inns, Pamer and others picked it up, and soon Vienna was afflicted by waltz mania. Before long, Johann the Elder joined a man named Josef Lanner and two associates to round out a waltz quartet, and one day, during a busy period, Lanner, out of ideas for new waltz compositions, asked his young associate to write one. Thus the first Strauss waltz was heard.

In time, Lanner and Strauss came to own the city, from the standpoint of musical entertainment. Johann the Elder traveled throughout Europe, composed and conducted, made money, and made children— six with his wife, including Johann the Younger, born in 1825, and five with a mistress. He spent little money on his real family, lots on the mistress, vehemently opposed music training for any of the eleven children, and eventually abandoned the first family for the second. Johann the Younger sneaked lessons anyhow, thanks to others, and in time had much more music training than his father. At nineteen, in part because the Elder supported the Royalists during the 1848 revolution while the Younger backed the rebels, in part because of disagreements over music, and in part because his father was such an ass of a man, Johann the Younger set up shop for himself.

A BIGGER CHIP THAN THE BLOCK

Fed up with his father, Johann, Jr., finally gathered together some musicians, hired a hall, and announced his own insurrection. This was the opening salvo:

ANNOUNCEMENT
INVITATION TO A SOIREE-DANSANT

which will take place on Tuesday, the fifteenth of October 1844, at Dommayer's Casino in Hietzing. Johann Strauss (the son) will have the honor of directing, for the first time, his own orchestra in a program of overtures and opera pieces as well as in a number of original compositions of his own.

Commending himself to the favor of his public,
Johann Strauss, Junior

Tickets available in advance for 30 Kreuzer; at the box office for 50 Kreuzer. It begins at six o'clock.

Despite his own unquestioned success with the waltz, the main composition of Johann the Elder's heard today is the "Radetzky March," written to support Chancellor Metternich. While the father's waltzes *are* played, the "big" Strauss waltzes, the Strauss waltzes that are familiar to everyone, come from the son.

Johann the Younger generously credited Vienna for his genius and success. "If it is true that I have talent," he wrote, "I owe it, above everything else, to my beloved city of Vienna . . . in whose soil is rooted my whole strength, in whose air float the melodies which my ear has caught, my heart has drunk in, and my hand has written down."

Not all things work perfectly for anybody, and the thing that did not work well for Strauss was the operetta. He wrote some sixteen or seventeen or eighteen (depending on how one defines the form), of which only *Die Fledermaus,* an early one, produced in 1874, was a smashing success. It continues to be a smashing success and is an accepted masterpiece, still played in the most prestigious opera halls of the world. Some critics of his day pointed out that, in his operettas, Strauss brought the spirit of the café to the opera house, with none of the affectations one might expect in the work of a café composer turning to more serious efforts. Café composer or not, Strauss imbued *Die Fledermaus* with the movement and poise of the best waltzes, with all the subtle nuances and the exquisite sensitivity, with ironic, glittering humor, and with rich and intoxicating melodies. "He wrote his operetta for the delectation of the masses," said one writer, "and for their entertainment; but, because he was a man of genius, what he touched was often transformed into a work of art."

The second-best operetta of the lot is thought to be *Der Zigeunerbaron,* produced in 1885, but no one puts it in the same league as *Die Fledermaus.*

Strauss died in Vienna on June 4, 1899, never having produced the serious opera he wanted to compose but, as critic Harold Schonberg writes, "as assured of immortality as Beethoven and Brahms."

STARTER KIT

I've gone beyond five in this Starter Kit, as most Strauss works are quite short. *Die Fledermaus* is a certainty; it is available on compact disc as well as on videotape. Some waltzes are also a "must." I've selected "The Blue Danube," "Tales from the Vienna Woods," "Wine, Women, and Song," and "Roses from the South" here; you might want to substitute "Emperor," "Artist's Life," "Wiener Blut," or any others you come across. Then try a few assorted polkas and the overture to *Der Zigeunerbaron* from the Top Ten.

JOHANN STRAUSS: THE STARTER KIT

Composition	Recordings Available*
ORCHESTRAL WORKS:	
Waltzes:	
The Blue Danube	C
Roses from the South	C
Tales from the Vienna Woods	C
Wine, Women, and Song	C
Polkas	C
Overtures:	
Die Fledermaus (The bat)	C
VOCAL WORKS:	
Operetta:	
Die Fledermaus	7

*Represents the number of recorded releases available of each listed composition as found in a recent issue of the *Schwann/Opus* catalogue. A "C" indicates that a work is only available collected with other compositions.

JOHANN STRAUSS: A TOP TEN

Composition	Recordings Available*
ORCHESTRAL WORKS:	
Waltzes:	
The Blue Danube	C
Roses from the South	C
Tales from the Vienna Woods	C
Wiener Blut	C
Wine, Women, and Song	C
Artist's Life	C
Overtures:	
Die Fledermaus (The bat)	C
Der Zigeunerbaron (The Gypsy baron)	C
Ballet:	
Cinderella	C
VOCAL WORKS:	
Operetta:	
Die Fledermaus	7

JOHANN STRAUSS: A MASTER COLLECTION

Composition	Recordings Available*
ORCHESTRAL WORKS:	
Waltzes:	
The Blue Danube	C
Roses from the South	C
Tales from the Vienna Woods	C
Wiener Blut	C
Wine, Women, and Song	C
Artist's Life	C
Emperor	C
Overtures:	
Die Fledermaus (The bat)	C
Der Zigeunerbaron (The Gypsy baron)	C
Eine Nacht in Venedig (A night in Venice)	C
Ballet:	
Cinderella	C
Polkas:	
Neue Pizzicato	C
Auf der Jagd	C
Explosionen	C
Tritsch-Tratsch	C
Unter Donner und Blitz	C
March:	
The Egyptian	C
VOCAL WORKS:	
Operettas:	
Die Fledermaus	5
Der Ziegunerbaron	1
Eine Nacht in Venedig	1

KARL MARIA VON WEBER (1786–1826)

Number 47

Wagner called him the most German of German composers.

Rossini said his masterpiece opera gave him the colic.

Few of his works remain, and most are not mourned.

Yet Karl Maria von Weber, a major precursor of Wagner, was the first German Romantic, the founder of German Romantic opera, a touring virtuoso pianist, an early genius of instrumental color, and one of the first and best "dictator" conductors.

He was also both a skilled lithographer and a cousin of Mozart's wife, though neither fact is of particular significance.

Weber lived to be only thirty-nine, dying in 1826, one year before Beethoven's death, two before Schubert's, and while Wagner, Schumann, Mendelssohn, Chopin, Liszt, and Verdi were in their teens.

Two German composers represent nineteenth-century German opera: Wagner, Demigod and creator of "music-drama," who stands alone; and Weber, who foreshadowed him. Weber produced *Der Freischütz*, the famous folk opera to which Rossini referred, when he was thirty-four and Wagner was only eight, and its enormous success was enough to move the focus of attention in Europe from Italian opera to German.

The most frequently heard of Weber's works is an orchestrated version of a piece for the piano called *Invitation to the Dance,* a lovely combination of several waltz tunes. It was written in 1819, and Berlioz—one of the premier orchestrators of them all—turned it into a work for full orchestra twenty-two years later.

But Weber—like Gluck, and perhaps Monteverdi and one or two others—makes The List not so much for his music itself as for his

BERLIOZ ON DER FREISCHÜTZ

France's all-time best composer, Hector Berlioz (a rebel in his own right), said of *Der Freischütz:*

"It is difficult to find, in searching the new or old school, a score as irreproachable as 'Der Freischütz,' as constantly interesting from beginning to end; whose melody has more freshness in the various shapes it assumes, whose rhythms are more striking, whose harmonic invention is more varied, more forcible, whose use of massed voices and instruments is more energetic without effort, more suave without affectation. From the beginning of the overture to the last chord of the final chorus, it is impossible for me to find a bar the omission or the change of which I would consider desirable. Intelligence, imagination, genius shine everywhere with a radiance, the force of which might dazzle any but eagle eyes, if a sensitiveness, inexhaustible as well as restrained, did not soften its glare, covering the listener with the gentle folds of its veil."

historical contribution to music development. As in the cases of Monteverdi, Gluck, and Weber, that contribution was to opera.

Many critics suggest that most of Weber's works deserve the obscurity into which they have fallen, and that occasional revivals of a forgotten Weber symphony, concerto, or sonata give us pleasant music but not music that should be considered great.

But the music people also stress his historical importance as the founder of German Romantic opera, who filled his scores with echoes of German folk song and dance, and who found texts that used German backgrounds and landscapes. German opera—as distinct from Italian opera—became an established institution with *Der Freischütz.* Thus Weber was to prepare the ground for Wagner. The historians note that he was one of the first to make use of the *leitmotif* (leading motive), a technique that became one of Wagner's basic tools. He is also credited with integrating the recitative into the operatic texture more than earlier composers had, and with using the orchestra more than anyone before him to project atmosphere and heighten dramatic effect. Wagner, incidentally, fully recognized his debt to Weber.

(A reasonable question on the subject of shifting Europe's attention from Italian to German opera might be: "What about Mozart, possibly the greatest opera writer of them all, or certainly one of the three greatest with Wagner and Verdi? He was German." [Actually he was Austrian, but German by the definitions I am using throughout the book.] Mozart, of course, is at least as highly regarded for his operas as for any of the rest of his music, but three of his Big Four operas were written in Italian and the fourth, like Beethoven's *Fidelio*, is not considered "German" in this same sense.)

WEBER MEETS BEETHOVEN

In 1823, at age thirty-six, some four years before Beethoven died, Weber went to Baden.

The main object of the trip, he wrote to his wife, was to see Beethoven. "[He] received me with an affection that was touching; he embraced me in the heartiest way at least 6–7 times and finally exclaimed with great enthusiasm: 'Ah, you're a devil of a fellow, an excellent fellow!' We dined together, very cheerfully and pleasurably. This crude, repelling man really paid me court, served me at table as attentively as if I had been his lady, etc., in short, this day will always be a highly remarkable one for me, as for all those who were present. It quite elated me to see myself being overwhelmed with such affectionate attentions by this great spirit. How depressing is his deafness; one has to write everything down for him."

Pianist, composer, conductor, and director, Weber accomplished his major mission: to lead German music away from the dominance of Italian opera. He was born a year before the death of Gluck, the German composer who had reformed opera but who wrote in Italian and French. In addition to *Der Freischütz*, Weber's operas—written when Rossini's works were sweeping Europe—include *Euryanthe* and *Oberon*. The critics at the time did not think much of *Der Freischütz*, but the public loved it from the start, and so did several fellow composers.

Weber, Number 47 on The List, lowest ranked of all Germans represented, composed a good many other works and excelled in other musical activities. Weber, Mendelssohn, Chopin, and Liszt are regarded as the greatest pianists of their time and Weber, Mendelssohn,

Berlioz, and Wagner as the greatest conductors. Given their other accomplishments, that makes both Weber and Mendelssohn something special. Everyone knows Mendelssohn was special, but Weber needs a public-relations counselor for his contribution.

He was born in Eutin, Oldenburg, the son of a traveling-theater violinist who wanted to cram music down the boy's throat. He studied piano early on and at eleven worked under Franz Joseph Haydn's talented brother, Michael. While studying in Munich, he composed two operas by the age of thirteen. The second of these was performed, but it failed, as did a third. After more study, now in Vienna, he got a job conducting the Breslau Opera, and failed again. Odds and ends in conducting and composition followed, until he spent three years directing the Prague Opera (he was still only twenty-seven) and then moved to Dresden to direct the German Opera. Before long he was commissioned to remain there for life.

It took Weber three years to write *Der Freischütz*, which was first performed in Berlin in 1821. To put this in historical perspective, Weber now was thirty-four, and this was five years after the Italian Rossini had produced *The Barber of Seville* at age twenty-three, and eight years before Rossini's *William Tell*. Berlioz was eighteen. The Romantic age had not yet been truly launched, although Schubert was serving as the bridge between Classicism and Romanticism and the Italian-opera style contribution to Romanticism was under way. Beethoven had six more years to live.

Weber's goal in *Der Freischütz* was to create a German opera for Germans in a German way—in other words, to produce a German folk opera. He found, in a book of ghost stories, one tale he thought might be suitable, and asked a lawyer-turned-writer named Johann Friedrich Kind to turn it into an opera libretto. In the meantime, he began working on the music.

The plot is based on an old legend of a demon who gives hunters magic bullets in exchange for their souls. (With semiautomatic weapons in the forests, demons are no longer so viable.) The demon is named Zamiel, and he has the hunter Kaspar in his power. Kaspar's only out is to find a substitute, and he zeroes in on young Max. Max loves Agatha, daughter of Chief Huntsman Kuno. In a contest to win Agatha, Max falls back on the magic bullets and shoots beautifully. The demon Zamiel directs the last bullet toward Agatha—but a sacred wreath turns it aside and it kills Kaspar instead. Zamiel is satisfied, Max confesses to using the magic bullets, he is forgiven and is allowed to marry Agatha after a year's delay, and it all ends with praise of God's mercy for the pure at heart.

RAPE OF BEAUTY

There is general agreement that Weber's operas *Der Freischütz* and *Euryanthe* are the first wholly Romantic musical works. While the delightful short overture to *Euryanthe* is very popular today and is often heard on classical-music radio stations, it was not always well received. After the first performance in Vienna, one contemporary Sam Donaldson–type wrote:

"The music is horrible. In the great days of Greece, this subversion of all melody, this rape of beauty, would have been punished by the state. Such music is a criminal offense. It would bring forth monsters if it were gradually to achieve universal acceptance. This work can please only fools or idiots or scholars or highway robbers or murderers."

(While many academic "intellectuals" are a little hard to take, one does wonder that "scholars" made it into that select group.)

In short, a boy in danger of losing his girl turns to the powers of darkness for help. He knows he is doing wrong, but the man who has tempted him does not know Good from Evil. The boy is saved because he confesses and thus can receive forgiveness. God, represented by a hermit, intervenes to save him. The man who cannot distinguish between Good and Evil must pay.

The opera is set in a Bohemian forest. In addition to the demonic spirit, it features a fearful Wolf's Glen, eagle feathers and a skull, an eagle's wing, and, in a magic ladle, such goodies as the eyes of a lynx and broken glass from church windows. There are also flapping birds, a black boar, cracking whips, a violent storm, horses' hooves, fiery wheels, thunder and lightning, a Wild Hunt, torrential rain—and, finally, the demon Zamiel himself.

Foreshadowing Wagner, Weber identifies Good with one kind of music, Evil with another, and the simple village-and-hunting life with a third.

The opera was performed fifty times in less than eighteen months. And the young Romantic composers loved it as much as the public did—the legend, the sounds of the hunting horn, the triumph over Evil, the evocation of the past, and the beauty and mystery of the German forest.

Weber's other two successful operas were *Euryanthe*, produced in 1823, and *Oberon*, created in 1826. He considered the latter, written in English by commission from Covent Garden, to be his greatest success, later saying of it: "The emotion produced by such a triumph is more than I can describe. To God alone belongs the glory." But for most others, *Der Freischütz* remains the composer's masterpiece.

Two months after the first *Oberon* performance in London, Weber died. Buried first in London, his body was exhumed eighteen years later and interred again in Dresden at a ceremony presided over by Wagner, who composed an unaccompanied chorus for the occasion—a chorus played at Wagner's own funeral years later.

STARTER KIT

Today, the most highly praised of Weber's works are the overtures to all three operas, *Euryanthe*, *Oberon*, and, particularly, *Der Freischütz*. These three are Starter Kit naturals, along with the popular orchestral version of *Invitation to the Dance*. As a fifth choice, one option would be to go with one of his less-known works, which include two symphonies, *Konzertstück* for piano and orchestra, two piano concertos, two clarinet concertos, a bassoon concerto, a clarinet quintet, a good bit of piano music, and a lot of vocal music. A second option, and the one I have elected, is to recommend *Der Freischütz* in its entirety, in part for historical purposes (although it is still performed regularly in Germany). The opera's most famous single aria is Agathe's prayer, "Leise, leise." (From *Oberon*, as a bonus recommendation, is "Ocean, Thou Mighty Monster.")

Recommended substitutes for the opera, since the overtures can be found on one compact disc, are the clarinet concertos and the clarinet quintet.

WEBER: THE STARTER KIT

Composition	Recordings Available*
ORCHESTRAL WORKS:	
Invitation to the Dance (originally for piano)	11
Overtures:	
Der Freischütz	8
Euryanthe	8
Oberon	8

Composition	Recordings Available*

VOCAL MUSIC:
Opera:
   Der Freischütz (complete and excerpts)   7

AND/OR:

Clarinet Concertos, No. 1 and No. 2	8/7
Clarinet Quintet in B-flat	6

*Represents the number of recorded releases available of each listed composition as found in a recent issue of the *Schwann/Opus* catalogue. A "C" indicates that a work is only available collected with other compositions.

WEBER: A TOP TEN

Composition	Recordings Available*

ORCHESTRAL WORKS:

Concerto No. 1 in F Minor for Clarinet	8
Concerto No. 2 in E-flat for Clarinet	7
Concertino for Clarinet and Orchestra	4
Invitation to the Dance (originally for piano)	11
Overtures:	
Der Freischütz	8
Euryanthe	8
Oberon	8

CHAMBER MUSIC:

Clarinet Quintet in B-flat	6
Grand Duo Concertante for Clarinet and Piano	6

VOCAL MUSIC:
Opera:
   Der Freischütz (complete and excerpts)   7

WEBER: A MASTER COLLECTION

Composition	Recordings Available*

SYMPHONIES:

No. 1 in C	3
No. 2 in C	3

Composition   *Recordings Available**

OTHER ORCHESTRAL WORKS:
Concerto No. 1 in F Minor for Clarinet   8
Concerto No. 2 in E-flat for Clarinet   7
Concerto No. 2 in E-flat for Piano   2
Concerto in F for Bassoon and Orchestra   4
Concertino for Clarinet and Orchestra   4
Concertino in E Minor for Horn and Orchestra   4
Invitation to the Dance (originally for piano)   11
Andante and Rondo in C Minor for Bassoon   4
    and Orchestra
Overtures:
    Der Freischütz   8
    Euryanthe   8
    Oberon   8

CHAMBER MUSIC:
Clarinet Quintet in B-flat   6
Trio in G Minor for Flute, Cello, and Piano   4
Grand Duo Concertante for Clarinet and Piano   6

SOLO PIANO MUSIC:
Piano Sonata No. 2 in A-flat   2

VOCAL MUSIC:
Operas:
    Der Freischütz (complete and excerpts)   7
    Oberon (complete and excerpts)   1
    Euryanthe (complete and excerpts)   1

LEOŠ JANÁČEK (1854–1928)

Number 48

Grim is the word for Leoš Janáček.
Sentimental is not.
Original and bleak are words for him.
Melodic and soothing are not.

If you like the emotional Russian Tchaikovsky, you would probably like the Czech Dvořák. If you prefer the powerful Russian Mussorgsky, you would probably choose the Czech Janáček.

He is the third and last-rated Czech composer on The List, although chronologically the most recent. He created many operas, several of which are in the international repertory. Composer, theorist, conductor, and teacher, he was fascinated by the relationship between language and music. He was also a very late starter who created much discordant music—and he was not a symphonist.

There is one significant difference between Janáček and his two Czech colleagues. He was an organist and teacher in the town of Brno in Moravia, whereas both Smetana, founder of Czech national music, and Dvořák, top Czech composer, were Bohemians who lived and worked in Prague.

Although Janáček was as involved as Smetana and Dvořák in their country's music, his major interest, like the Russian Mussorgsky's, was in his native language and the challenge of developing music related to its inflections and rhythms. The result, for the long-lived, unconventional Janáček, was music that straddled the two centuries in which he worked—more experimental, more daring, and more original than the melodious sounds of Smetana or Dvořák, but not as dissonant or progressive as those of Stravinsky or Hindemith (although the older he got, the more discordant his music became).

Mussorgsky talked about "living prose in music," about "reverence for the language of humanity," about "reproduction of simple human speech," about having "characters speak on the stage exactly as people do in real life, without exaggeration or distortion." His goal was "to turn out musical prose." Janáček's music is also built around speech patterns. He collected and studied Moravian folk music some twenty years before Bartók and a colleague undertook similar work in Hungary and the Balkans. He believed that "all of the melodic and rhythmic mysteries of music can be explained in reference to the melody and rhythm of the musical motives of the spoken language." Indeed, some picture Janáček as sort of a twentieth-century Czech Mussorgsky, nearly as realistic and powerful as the Russian, who was a generation older, but with dissonant "New Music" overtones reflecting the early twentieth-century influences Mussorgsky never experienced.

Given his preoccupation with "song speech" or "speech melody," it is not surprising that Janáček is best known for vocal music—chiefly opera, but also a large and famous mass. Given characters who "talk" more than "sing," it is also not surprising that what melody is found in Janáček's operas is carried by the orchestra. And given the unusual rhythm of Czech speech, it is not surprising that Janáček's music has an original sound, unlike any other.

LONG-LIVED SINGER

Janáček wrote four operas in the decade before his death at seventy-four, three of which were based on some of the more peculiar subjects in the history of opera. *The Cunning Little Vixen* has a cast of birds, insects, and animals as well as humans; *From the House of the Dead* is set in a prison camp; and *The Makropulos Affair* (or "Case" or "Matter") deals with a woman who is 337 years old. His eighth and next-to-last opera, it was based on a play by Karel Capek.

When Janáček asked for permission to use the story, the playwright responded: "I've too high an opinion of music—and especially of yours—to imagine it linked to such a conversational, highly unpoetical and garrulous play as my 'Makropulos Case.' . . . [But] I don't regard the fiction of an internal, or 300-year-old, person as my literary property, and therefore won't stand in the way of your using it as you think fit."

Janáček was born in 1854 in a schoolhouse in the village of Hukvaldy, the son of a schoolmaster and the ninth of thirteen children. He sang in the church choir with interest and talent, and when he was ten his father took him to a monastery in the town of Brno for an audition with the choirmaster there. He was accepted and spent the next several years as a pupil there, with music becoming increasingly important to him. During those years he learned to play the organ, developed into a fine pianist, participated in choral activities, and began to do a little composing.

The next steps in his musical education were stints in Prague at the College of Organists and then at the State Teachers' Training College, from which he obtained his teaching certificate in 1878. For the next several years he traveled a good bit—a less kind assessment might be "drifted"—in and out of the major European musical cities of St. Petersburg, Leipzig, and Vienna. Although this all added to his musical knowledge, in 1882, at age twenty-eight, he returned to Brno and helped organize a College of Organists there. For the next thirty-seven years, until after World War I, he was the leading teacher in Brno, which became the center of Moravian musical education.

Jenufa, his first important opera, was written between 1894 and

1903, when he was in his forties, and premiered in Brno in 1904. Although the opera was Janáček's first successful work, it was another twelve years before it was produced in more sophisticated Prague. Even then, it did not become widely known until a poet named Max Brod translated it into German for production in Vienna. Despite the fact that Janáček composed for a quarter of a century thereafter, *Jenufa* is still his most famous work. While the plot involves the murder of an illegitimate baby—scarcely a typical Romantic theme—the music is considerably more conventional than that of his later folk operas: *Katya Kabanova* (1921), *The Makropulos Affair* (1925), and *From the House of the Dead* (1928).

These "speech melody" works tend to capture the attention of the critics, but the earlier and more conventional *Jenufa* has remained the popular favorite. However, *the* Czech national opera continues to be Smetana's *Bartered Bride*.

Janáček's other works include a *Sinfonietta* (a minisymphony), written in 1926; a Concertino for Piano and Chamber Orchestra in 1925; a tone poem (*Taras Bulba*) in 1918; and, much earlier in his career (1893), some fun folk-tune works called *Lachian Dances*.

The musicologists note that Janáček's nationalism is more like Bartók's than like the fervent patriotism of a Grieg or a Smetana—or a Sibelius with his *Finlandia*—in that he systematically incorporated the folk music and rhythms of his country into his music (as did the English Vaughan Williams). This is a different brand of identification-with-country than that associated with emotional, patriotic music.

STARTER KIT

Although Janáček's best-known works are his operas (including a lovable animal-story opera, *The Cunning Little Vixen*), for a Starter Kit one opera, and/or excerpts from it, is enough to handle. The obvious selection is *Jenufa*. It is supplemented by two orchestral works, an orchestral/chamber blend, and his big *Slavonic* Mass.

One orchestral recommendation is the *Sinfonietta*, which Janáček chose to compose in five movements, paying little or no attention to the old Classical structure. The second orchestral work is the tone poem *Taras Bulba*, based on a war between the Poles and the Cossacks (Taras is the central figure). Janáček, again veering from the norm, made it one of the few three-movement tone poems (most being in one movement). The first deals with the death of one son, the second with the death of another son, and the last with the capture and execution

A VERY LATE BLOOMER

One of the slowest starters on The List, Janáček was virtually an unknown at age fifty, in the early 1900s. Fifty years ago, when he had been dead for more than a decade, he still rated only a paragraph or so in most books about classical composers.

The music gurus said then that he had delved deeper than Dvořák into folk music but was receiving little recognition, in part because he experimented with harmonies fairly extreme for his day. It was also agreed that he took little or no pains to write music that was comprehensible outside his own country, one critic commenting that he kept "to his peculiarly naive style, writing with an exuberance that to foreigners appears childish and making no concessions to a possible market and its demands for 'tunefulness.' "

In more recent years he has been viewed considerably more favorably, as an artist of real significance, and his nine operas get more attention each year.

of Taras himself. Another selection is his offbeat Concertino for Piano and Orchestra, scored for solo piano plus a chamber orchestra of a half-dozen instruments rather than a large modern orchestra.

FOR THE CZECH MILITARY

Janáček's *Sinfonietta* is not a miniwork as the title suggests but rather a substantial composition, more than twenty minutes long, written in five movements and employing a big, multi-trumpet orchestra.

Janáček dedicated the work in 1926 to the armed forces of Czechoslovakia, saying that it expressed "the contemporary free man, his spiritual beauty and joy, his strength, his courage, and his determination to fight for victory." A sound message for the post-Communist era as free people struggle in Eastern Europe with courage and determination.

The final Starter Kit choice is one of the composer's most stirring pieces, his *Slavonic* Mass, also called *Glagolitic* Mass (*Glagolitic* refers to an old Slavonic alphabet, and the words are in archaic old Slav). A large work for orchestra, chorus, and soloists, it was composed in 1926 when Janáček was past seventy. One critic has said that it puts the listener into "a primitive Slavonic world." The composer said that it was meant to "express the atmosphere" of Kyrill and Methodius, two Greek apostles of the ninth century. It includes a rather wild organ solo. This is a work for Slav peasants, not elegant Parisians.

JANÁČEK: THE STARTER KIT

Composition	Recordings Available*
ORCHESTRAL WORKS:	
Sinfonietta (suite in five movements)	10
Taras Bulba (tone poem)	7
CHAMBER MUSIC:	
String Quartet No. 1 (Kreutzer)	9
VOCAL MUSIC:	
Opera:	
Jenufa	3
Mass:	
Slavonic (or Glagolitic) Mass	7

*Represents the number of recorded releases available of each listed composition as found in a recent issue of the *Schwann/Opus* catalogue. A "C" indicates that a work is only available collected with other compositions.

JANÁČEK: A TOP TEN

Composition	Recordings Available*
ORCHESTRAL WORKS:	
Sinfonietta (suite in five movements)	10
Taras Bulba (tone poem)	7
Concertino for Piano and Orchestra	4
CHAMBER MUSIC:	
String Quartet No. 1 (Kreutzer)	9

Composition	Recordings Available*

PIANO MUSIC:

| In the Mist | 12 |
| Capriccio for Piano (for left hand) | 4 |

OTHER INSTRUMENTAL MUSIC:

| Sonata for Violin and Piano | 7 |

VOCAL MUSIC:

Opera:

| Jenufa | 3 |
| The Cunning Little Vixen | 2 |

Mass:

| Slavonic (or Glagolitic) Mass | 7 |

JANÁČEK: A MASTER COLLECTION

Composition	Recordings Available*

ORCHESTRAL WORKS:

Sinfonietta (suite in five movements)	10
Suite for String Orchestra	1
Taras Bulba (tone poem)	7
Concertino for Piano and Orchestra	4
Idyll for String Orchestra	2
The Cunning Little Vixen (opera suite)	2

PIANO MUSIC:

In the Mist	12
Capriccio for Piano (for left hand)	4
Sonata for Piano ("Oct. 1, 1905")	1

OTHER INSTRUMENTAL MUSIC:

| Sonata for Violin and Piano | 7 |

CHAMBER MUSIC:

Sextet for Wind Instruments	4
String Quartet No. 1 (Kreutzer)	9
String Quartet No. 2 (Intimate Pages)	11

Composition	Recordings Available*
VOCAL MUSIC:	
Operas:	
Jenufa	3
The Cunning Little Vixen	2
The Makropulos Affair	1
From the House of the Dead	2
Katya Kabanova	1
Mass:	
Slavonic (or Glagolitic) Mass	7
Song Cycle:	
The Diary of One Who Disappeared	2

FRANÇOIS COUPERIN (1668–1733)

Number 49

Ordinaire de la musique de la chambre du roi and *organiste du roi*.

When you are both of those things—both main music man for the king and the king's organist—you've got it made. If the king is King Louis XIV of France, no minor figure in history, and if things are not going well for him, either politically or on the battlefield, and if he therefore turns, in his Versailles Palace, to his music man for comfort and solace, you'd better produce.

François Couperin—Le Grand Couperin, to distinguish him from other members of his very musical family, which was a more powerful dynasty in French music for two centuries than the Kennedy clan threatened to be in recent American politics (although Kennedys still do loom on the horizon)—produced a great deal. His works include four books of harpsichord pieces (some 230 in all); more than forty organ pieces; some religious vocal music; and a fair bit of chamber music, including four *Concerts royaux* written to please his monarch.

To conjure up a mental picture of this composer, consider female mud wrestling on the one hand and François Couperin, "galant instrumentalist," on the other. (*Galant* is not quite modern-English *gallant*, but close: Well-bred. That which strives to please. Affable, correct in its setting and in its bearing.)

Le Grand Couperin, "galant instrumentalist," was, more specifically, the father of French keyboard music; the greatest of French harpsichordists (called *clavecinists* in France); and a major Baroque artist, one of two French Baroque musicians on The List. He was honored as a near saint two centuries after his birth by fellow French composers Debussy and Ravel and hailed by them and others as the "purest and most characteristic expression of the French temperament in music."

There is nothing passionate, unrestrained, powerful, or brutal about Couperin. The usual words for him are "courtly," "gentle," "polished," "delicate," "poetic," and "decorative." What sets him apart is that he did what he did almost flawlessly, with virtually perfect balance. The naysayers call him light, delightful, and charming; his fans see a polished gem.

King Louis XIV liked Couperin. And so do many esteemed musicologists, who advise us that the great German masters regarded Couperin's art with amazement. Bach and Handel studied and copied him. So did Telemann. A sensible fellow, Couperin knew precisely the limits of his art and, the experts say, never strayed beyond them.

DEBUSSY ON COUPERIN

Writing in 1908, Claude Debussy commented:

"Why do we not regret the loss of these charming ways in which music was formerly written, so lost that it is now impossible to find the least trace of Couperin's influence? His music was never superfluous, and he had great wit—something we hardly dare show these days, considering it to lack grandeur. But grandeur is something that often stifles us without our ever achieving it."

And in 1913:

"Why are we so indifferent toward our own great Rameau? . . . And to Couperin, the most poetic of our harpsichordists, whose tender melancholy is like that enchanting echo that emanates from the depths of a Watteau landscape, filled with plaintive figures? When we compare ourselves to other countries—so mindful of the glories of their pasts—we realize that there is no excuse for our indifference. The impression with which we are left is that we scarcely care at all for our fame, for not one of these people is ever to be seen on our programs, even at this time of the year [the Christmas holiday season] when we make a point of coming closer to our distant relatives."

Before *this* Couperin there were musical Couperins in France by the fistful: brothers, cousins, and uncles, serving their kings and otherwise making music as court composers, organists, singers, violinists, and clavecinists. But the most famous of the flock was Le Grand himself, for forty-four years the organist at St. Gervais Church in Paris, and Superintendent of court chamber music and royal instructor to both Louis XIV and Louis XV. In his early years he wrote some organ masses and some sonatas. In 1693 he entered the service of the king as one of four organists in the king's chapel, and from then on his professional career was made.

Twenty years later he published his first *Livre de clavecin* (book of music for harpsichord). Three others followed. Each was divided into a half-dozen sets of pieces that Couperin called *ordres*. Some of the compositions in the first book were dance suites (a typical form of the day), conglomerations of dances including:

Pavane—A slow and stately Spanish-Italian court dance. For the dance-minded, if you find yourself in a time warp, you should take two single and one double steps forward, followed by two single and one double backward.

Galliard—A gay, lively, and frolicking dance, usually in triple time, in contrast to the slow pavane.

Courante—There is a French *courante* and an Italian *corrente*, but they are not the same dance. Since this is Couperin, we'll stick with the French, which was in moderate time, with frequent shifts from one tempo to another. This produced an unstable rhythm, which, the experts say, is typical of the dance. Bach used it, as well as Couperin.

Saraband—Experts today say it probably came from Mexico, appearing in Spain in the early sixteenth century. It is uncertain how a dance "lascivious" enough to "inflame very honest people" (as it was described in a Spanish treatise dealing with "public amusement") wound up as a slow dance of dignified style, "usually without upbeat." In the seventeenth century, it became a standard part of a suite.

Minuet—King Louis XIV is said to have danced the first minuet in 1653, which would have been fifteen years before Couperin was born. Everyone liked it, or nearly everyone, and it quickly took the place of the courante and the pavane. King Louis XIV adopted it as the official dance of his court. The ones we know from court dances in the movies are graceful, dignified, and in moderate tempo. Later, in the symphonies of Mozart and Haydn, the minuet became faster and faster, and then humorous—until, the music people say, it gradually led to the whimsical scherzo. It is the only one of the Baroque dance types that survived after the dance suite went out of vogue, which was about 1750.

Gavotte—A French dance, in moderate tempo, which became popular in the middle of the seventeenth century. Like many of these dances, it changed from time to time over the years, now without upbeats, and now with upbeats. Dancers performing it sometimes kissed, which is commendable and which may account for its popularity. Bach, like Couperin, used the gavotte in his suites.

Gigue—As the name suggests, this evolved from the English or Irish sixteenth-century jig, although it developed differently in Italy and in France, and so it was very double-time lively. In the instrumental compositions of the suites that were popular between 1650 and 1750—Couperin's time—the gigue usually was the final dance movement of the composition.

Allemande—German in origin, moderate in speed, and serious in character—but not heavy, the experts tell us. The allemande usually was the first movement of these dance suites of the seventeenth and early eighteenth centuries. The standard order was: allemande, courante, saraband, and gigue.

In addition to the dance-suite compositions that employed these dances, Couperin's *ordres* for the harpsichord included the small solo pieces for which he is best known. He called them "portraits," and they are considered to be the forerunners of works called "character pieces" in the nineteenth century. Couperin gave them fanciful and/or descriptive titles, and, like the program music of the Romantic period, they were sometimes designed to present pictures in music. An example, from the sixth *ordre* of his *Pièces de clavecin*, is "Les barricades mysterieuses." A good many harpsichord pieces by Rameau are similar in nature. Examples of the nineteenth-century solo-piano character pieces which were to follow are Schumann's "Der dichter spricht" (The poet speaks) and Ravel's *Jeux d'eau* (Water games).

More than two hundred years after his birth, not only Debussy but also Ravel acknowledged Couperin both as the greatest French clavecinist and as one of the greatest of all masters of the French musical style. Ravel, in fact, wrote a piece in his honor.

Like other composers of his day, Couperin also wrote religious music, considered intimate and spiritual.

Couperin was a Frenchman, and his music is quintessentially French in style: graceful, tender, ironic, discreet, sensible, and delicate.

STARTER KIT

Since Couperin is primarily a harpsichord composer, readers are advised to try any of his many compositions for this instrument. "La

---

SERENE, SAUCY, AND SATIRICAL

Alec Robertson, in *The Music Masters*, offers us details about Couperin's famous harpsichord character pieces:

"The titles of his pieces are more often convincingly illustrated in his music than some of his critics have allowed, and insufficient attention has been given to his harmonic and rhythmic variety, which is considerable. To take a few examples, how different is the serene portrait of 'Soeur Monique' from the sauciness of 'La Pateline,' the grace of the dance of 'La Princesse Marie' from the grotesque hops of 'L'Arlequine,' distant ancestor of Petrouchka. Illustrating another side of his genius, there is, in the eleventh 'Ordre,' the brilliant satire of the lampoon directed against the 'Incorporated Society of fiddlers' ('Les Fastes de la grande et ancienne Menestrandise') who wished to force the organists and clavecinists to join their union."

---

favorite" is one option; a Passacaglia in B Minor another. Also recommended are "Les jongleurs," "Le tendre Nanette," "La dangereuse," and "Les baccanales." (Note: Couperin's music, like Bach's and Handel's, sounds better on the instrument for which it was intended than on the modern piano, and there is no problem today in finding harpsichord recordings.)

Couperin had an explanation (of sorts) for the titles:

I have always had in view different incidents that guided me in their composition; hence, the titles correspond to ideas that I had. I may be excused from rendering an account of them. Nevertheless, as there are among these titles some that appear to flatter me, it is well to state that the pieces bearing them are, in a manner, portraits which, under my fingers, have sometimes taken on the guise of good likenesses and that the majority of these opportune titles are applicable rather to amiable originals that I desired to represent than to copies I made of them.

Other Starter Kit recommendations are any two of the *Concerts royaux*, which are ensemble works, plus an orchestral piece for cello and strings, and one of his beautiful organ masses. But the harpsichord compositions are the "musts."

COUPERIN: THE STARTER KIT

Composition	Recordings Available*
CHAMBER/ORCHESTRAL WORKS:	
Concerts royaux (instrumental ensemble with harpsichord)	4
Pièces en concert for Cello and Strings	5
KEYBOARD MUSIC:	
For harpsichord:	
Pièces de clavecin (four volumes), including:	16
La favorite (chaconne)	
For organ:	
Pièces d'orgue consistantes en deux messes, including:	3
No. 1 (A l'usage ordinaire des paroisses)	4

*Represents the number of recorded releases available of each listed composition as found in a recent issue of the *Schwann/Opus* catalogue. A "C" indicates that a work is only available collected with other compositions.

COUPERIN: A TOP TEN/A MASTER COLLECTION

Composition	Recordings Available*
CHAMBER/ORCHESTRAL WORKS:	
Concerts royaux (instrumental ensemble with harpsichord)	4
Pièces en concert for Cello and Strings	5
Sonatas:	
La steinquerque	2
La sultane	3
Les nations	5
L'apothéose de Corelli	2
KEYBOARD MUSIC:	
For harpsichord:	
Pièces de clavecin (four volumes), including:	16
La favorite (chaconne)	
Passacaglia in B Minor	

Composition	*Recordings Available**
For organ:	
Pièces d'orgue consistantes en deux messes, including:	3
No. 1 (A l'usage ordinaire des paroisses)	4
No. 2 (Propre pour les couvents)	4

ALEXANDER BORODIN (1834–1887)

Number 50

Is "Stranger in Paradise" a typical piece of classical music? What about "And This Is My Beloved"? Everyone is familiar with the first by name and sound, and about as many with the second, by sound if not by name. If you know those two pieces, you should recognize a string quartet and a section of an opera.

To hear "Stranger in Paradise," listen to Alexander Borodin's opera, *Prince Igor,* introduced in St. Petersburg in 1890 after the composer's death, especially the "Polovtsian Dances" section. To hear "And This Is My Beloved," play his String Quartet No. 2 in D, of 1881. And for more of Borodin in bits and pieces, go back to the Broadway musical show *Kismet* and its lovely tunes. A fellow could make a Broadway living from Borodin, and some have.

A POSTHUMOUS TONY

Compared to the number of theatergoers, not a lot of people are acquainted with Borodin's Second String Quartet—certainly not as many as are acquainted with the Broadway musical *Kismet,* produced in 1954. So popular was the song hit "And This Is My Beloved," stolen blatantly from the Quartet music, that Borodin received a Tony Award for it, sixty-seven years after his death. No more popular piece of chamber music has come out of Russia.

Borodin was another of the amateur musicians of the "Mighty Five," the group represented earlier on The List by Mussorgsky at Number 39 and Rimsky-Korsakov at Number 42. He was a professional scientist—a chemist and professor of chemistry, a researcher in the field of solidifying aldehydes, a graduate doctor, a known lecturer outside of Russia—and only a weekend composer. His mentor/professor once told him: "I count on you to succeed me but you think of nothing but music. You make a mistake hunting two hares at once."

Not too much of a mistake, however, inasmuch as Borodin came close enough to pulling it off to be considered among classical music's greatest composers. He wrote slowly, taking years to complete a work—and not writing a great deal and not completing some that he began. But most of what he did write survives. All of the "Mighty Five" were nationalists, and he was the first Russian nationalist to win international recognition.

Borodin was a melody man. His melodies can be heard not only in his eleven beautiful songs but in every piece he ever wrote, most of which reflect the Eastern, Oriental part of his Russian heritage. Like Rimsky-Korsakov he was also strong in the use of orchestral tone color, in part because, again like Rimsky-Korsakov, he gradually acquired a superb knowledge of what each instrument could do. But he was without formal training and consistently needed help from his friends of the "Five" to perfect and complete his works. It took him twenty years to write *Prince Igor*, the opera for which he is famous, and even then it was seriously edited by the more trained, red-pencil-always-available Rimsky-Korsakov—and finally completed by Rimsky-Korsakov and unListed Alexander Glazunov, an Honorable Mention composer.

WEAK TECHNIQUE

Borodin's doctoral thesis was entitled "On the Analogy of Arsenical with Phosphoric Acid." Tchaikovsky indicated he thought Borodin should have kept entirely to his scientific career, once describing the composer-scientist this way: "Borodin is a fifty-year-old professor of chemistry at the Academy of Medicine. Again a talent—even an impressive one—he has less taste than [César] Cui [career army officer and one of the "Mighty Five"] and his technique is so weak that he cannot write a line without outside help."

Claude Debussy had a different view; it was he who called Borodin's B Minor Symphony "the best of all Russian symphonic works."

Borodin was the illegitimate son of Prince Luke Gedianishuili and the wife of a physician. According to custom, he was given the name of one of the prince's serfs, Porfiry Borodin, and, also according to custom, he was raised by a governess and with private tutors, as befitted the son of a Prince. Music was an early interest; he wrote a polka at nine and a concerto at fourteen, after mingling with band musicians and attending orchestral concerts. But this was fun and games compared with his serious dedication to science. He was a brilliant student at the Academy of Medicine and Surgery, became an assistant professor of pathology, received a medical degree, and was sent to Heidelberg for graduate study in chemistry. There he met, and later married, Ekaterina Protopopova, a pianist, who shared his love of music.

EKATERINA AND CLARA

Q. What did Alexander Borodin and Robert Schumann have in common?

A. Both were married to outstanding pianists—the former to Ekaterina Protopopova and the latter to Clara Wieck, daughter of Friedrich Wieck, one of the leading pedagogues of his day. Ekaterina led her chemist husband away from the music of Mendelssohn, an early hero, and toward the works of three other composers: Schumann, Liszt, and Chopin. Twenty years after they became engaged, Borodin dedicated his famous String Quartet No. 2 to his Ekaterina.

After returning to St. Petersburg he continued working with laboratory burners with one hand and musical notes with the other, in time becoming the fifth member of the "Mighty Five." Under the influence of those colleagues, he wrote music on weekends until his death of a burst aneurism during a carnival dance in 1887.

Critics quarrel over whether his masterpiece is *Prince Igor* or a short tone poem, *In the Steppes of Central Asia*, written in 1880 and called by the professionals "an exquisitely perfect miniature" and "an ideal blend of his heritage: the Oriental noble father and the Slavic mother." The composer described it this way:

Through the silence of the steppes of Central Asia is heard the strain of a peaceful Russian song. Sounds of horses and

AN AMIABLE CHAOS

The music researchers commonly speak of the chaos—some call it the amiable chaos—of Borodin's household, as he spent 85 percent of his time on his scientific career and another 40 percent on his music. The fact that these numbers add up to more than 100 percent is what caused the chaos. One historian, Richard Anthony Leonard, described the scene this way:

"People swarmed through [the apartment] at all hours of the day. . . . When all the beds were taken, they slept on couches or on the floor or dozed in chairs; not infrequently they took Borodin's bed. The apartment itself was usually a litter of disorder and disarray. Five years after they moved in, the Borodins still picked their way around piles of books and music, half unpacked trunks and suitcases. . . .

"Since Borodin never seemed to remember whether or not he had eaten, meals were fantastically irregular, with dinner often begun as late as eleven o'clock at night. Along with the transient guests, relatives and partial strangers, the Borodins shared their meals with a colony of cats . . . which walked on the tables, leaped onto the backs of the diners, and in general treated the Borodin ménage as a feline liberty hall."

camels come from the distance, approaching ever nearer, and with them the strains of a haunting Eastern melody. A caravan is crossing the desert escorted by Russian soldiers. It progresses on its long journey confident in the protection afforded it by the soldiers. The caravan disappears into the distant horizon. The song of the Russians blends with that of the Orientals in a common harmony, until both fade away from the plains.

With that program before you, listen to the music. The "peaceful Russian song" is heard in the solo clarinet. Plucked strings are the steps of horses and camels. The "haunting Eastern melody" comes from an English horn. As the soldiers come into view, the Russian song is repeated by two horns and, as they near, by the full orchestra. Other instruments—clarinets and cellos, then the strings—repeat the

Eastern melody. The blending of the Russian and Oriental themes is soon heard—the Russian theme in violins and flutes, the Oriental one in bassoons and horns. And they fade away.

Borodin is also known for what a few writers consider to be Russia's most beautiful symphony (Tchaikovsky fans, among others, dissent), his Symphony No. 2 in B Minor, completed in 1877. He also wrote two other symphonies.

In the chamber-music field, the favorite is his 1881 String Quartet No. 2 in D. The third movement, the Nocturne, is especially beautiful and famous, with many recording artists concentrating on it rather than on the entire quartet.

A FULL PLATTER

It's not easy being chemist, researcher, lecturer, professor, and composer. Borodin wrote:

"In winter, I can compose only when I am too unwell to give my lectures. So my friends, reversing the usual custom, never say to me, 'I hope you are well,' but, 'I do hope you are ill.' "

STARTER KIT

The lovely and melodious music of Borodin is heard in all five Starter Kit choices—the "Polovtsian Dances" from *Prince Igor*, Symphony No. 2 in B Minor, the String Quartet No. 2 in D, the *Steppes* tone poem, and the overture to *Prince Igor*. Listeners unfamiliar with Borodin will enjoy him, full-time chemist and untrained weekend composer though he was. Tuning in on his compositions is a good way to sneak up on classical music, and new collectors should ignore the fact that some erudite critics put the "Polovtsian Dances" in a "light" class with Brahms's "Lullaby," Dvořák's *Humoresques*, Grieg's "Last Spring," Liszt's *Liebesträume* set, Mendelssohn's "Spring Song," Rimsky-Korsakov's "Flight of the Bumblebee," and Sibelius's "Valse triste."

Prince Igor is not as powerful as Mussorgsky's *Boris Godounov, the Russian opera*, nor was Borodin as talented (or as *Russian*) as Mussorgsky, but the descendants of Alexander Borodin may justifiably feel that the world benefits more from his music—a blend of Oriental sensuality and Russian fierceness—than from his genuine expertise and writings in chemistry.

When Borodin turned to string quartets he incurred the frowns of some of the "Mighty Five." Chamber music was not their thing; it was not an accepted route to nationalist music. Borodin enjoyed the work, however, and composed our Starter Kit choice in just two months—for him, record time.

BORODIN: THE STARTER KIT

Composition	Recordings Available*
SYMPHONIES:	
No. 2 in B Minor (Valiant)	9
OTHER ORCHESTRAL WORKS:	
In the Steppes of Central Asia (tone poem)	18
Polovtsian Dances (from Prince Igor)	29
Overture:	
Prince Igor	8
CHAMBER MUSIC:	
String Quartet No. 2 in D	13

*Represents the number of recorded releases available of each listed composition as found in a recent issue of the *Schwann/Opus* catalogue. A "C" indicates that a work is only available collected with other compositions.

BORODIN: A TOP TEN/A MASTER COLLECTION

Composition	Recordings Available*
SYMPHONIES:	
No. 2 in B Minor (Valiant)	9
No. 3 in A Minor	2
OTHER ORCHESTRAL WORKS:	
In the Steppes of Central Asia (tone poem)	18
Polovtsian Dances (from Prince Igor)	29
Overture:	
Prince Igor	8
Nocturne for String Orchestra (from String Quartet No. 2 in D)	7

Composition	Recordings Available*

CHAMBER MUSIC:
String Quartet No. 2 in D   13

OTHER INSTRUMENTAL MUSIC:
Petite Suite for Piano (orchestrated by Glazunov)   3

VOCAL MUSIC:
Opera:
    Prince Igor   2

SONGS:
Song Collection   C

CHAPTER V

The Orchestra

A symphony orchestra consists largely of various kinds and sizes of fiddles. Anyone who has ever been to a county fair knows that these are stringed instruments played with bows.

This chapter is for those who know a little more than that, but not a great deal—who recognize a trombone and a clarinet but are a little shaky about a bassoon, an oboe, and an English horn. It is also for those who are familiar with an oboe on a first-name basis but are uncertain how many to expect in a symphony orchestra.

I'll identify some major current symphony orchestras, including those that do a lot of recording of classical music, and there will be a little orchestral history—but this is not a textbook, and I'll chiefly link that history to our Listed composers, or them with it. I'll talk a bit about orchestration—the art of composing for a symphony orchestra—and then about the instruments, one by one.

Some are considerably more complicated than others, in that some—like the woodwinds—have all kinds of sisters, cousins, and aunts, while others—like the brass—have fewer close relatives.

A sound place to start (no pun intended) is with the symphony itself, the composition written for a symphony orchestra. Symphonies traditionally have tunes, or themes, or melodies in them (easier to find in some symphonies than in others), and traditionally they are divided into four movements, or sections. The word *symphony* comes from the Greek: *syn* (together) and *phōnē* (voice or sound). Sound together. Symphony.

The simplest definition of a symphony orchestra is a large group of musical instruments that plays symphonic works. And there are a lot of them in the United States. A recent count by their trade association showed more than seventeen hundred. Some are of amateur status in small villages and colleges, and some are commonly called "major." But if you want to lose friends, tell them that the symphony orchestra they hear on July Fourth is not a "major" one.

Still, the reputations of some orchestras surpass those of others. Five symphony orchestras in America are commonly considered "top drawer." In alphabetical order, they are

> Boston Symphony Orchestra, founded in 1881
> Chicago Symphony Orchestra, founded in 1891
> Cleveland Orchestra, founded in 1918
> New York Philharmonic Orchestra, founded in 1842
> Philadelphia Orchestra, founded in 1900

This is a dangerous game, because reputations do not always tell the whole story and new conductors, new money, new leadership, and new community interest can move an orchestra from one drawer to another in short order.

A breath later are several others, including two in Canada:

> Detroit Symphony Orchestra, 1914
> Los Angeles Philharmonic Orchestra, 1919
> Minnesota Orchestra, 1903
> National Symphony Orchestra, Washington, D.C., 1931
> Pittsburgh Symphony Orchestra, 1927
> Saint Louis Symphony Orchestra, 1880
> San Francisco Symphony Orchestra, 1909
> Montreal Symphony Orchestra, 1934
> Toronto Symphony Orchestra, 1918

A few more of the finest symphonies in the United States include

> Atlanta Symphony Orchestra, 1933
> Baltimore Symphony Orchestra, 1916
> Cincinnati Symphony Orchestra, 1895
> Dallas Symphony Orchestra, 1900
> Houston Symphony Orchestra, 1913
> Indianapolis Symphony Orchestra, 1930
> Milwaukee Symphony Orchestra, 1959

But an injustice would be done if we were to leave out important orchestras in Birmingham, Buffalo, Columbus, Edmonton, Tampa, Orlando, Honolulu, Kansas City, Louisville, Ottawa, Newark, Portland (Oregon), Fort Lauderdale, Phoenix, Rochester, Seattle, Syra-

cuse, St. Paul, San Antonio, San Diego, Vancouver, Winnipeg, and
other cities.

The most famous orchestras in Europe include

Amsterdam Concertgebouw Orchestra
Bavarian Radio Symphony Orchestra (Munich)
Berlin Philharmonic Orchestra
Czech Philharmonic Orchestra
Orchestre de Paris
Philharmonia Orchestra (London)
St. Petersburg Philharmonic Orchestra
Vienna Philharmonic Orchestra

Among other strong European orchestras that record, some of
them frequently, are

Academy of St. Martin-in-the-Fields (London)
BBC Symphony Orchestra (London)
Berlin Radio Symphony Orchestra
City of Birmingham Symphony Orchestra (England)
Dresden Philharmonic
Frankfurt Radio Symphony
Hallé Orchestra (Manchester, England)
Krakow Philharmonic
Lyons Orchestra (France)
Monte Carlo Philharmonic Orchestra
Munich Philharmonic Orchestra
Royal Philharmonic Orchestra (London)
Spanish National Orchestra (Madrid)
Toulouse Orchestra (France)
Warsaw Philharmonic Orchestra
Zürich Tonhalle Orchestra

Orchestras have distinct personalities. For years, the Chicago
Symphony under Sir Georg Solti had a big, bold, Chicago-like "brass"
sound. Chicago is the kind of city that likes horns, trumpets, and other
brass instruments. The Philadelphia Orchestra under Eugene Ormandy was known for a lush string sound (Philadelphia and the
Cricket Club, you know). The Cleveland Orchestra traditionally has
favored woodwinds, which has more to do with its longtime genius
conductor, George Szell, than with Lake Erie or the Cuyahoga River.

Thus, under Solti, Chicago favored Bruckner, Wagner, Mahler,
and the powerful German sound; Cleveland, under Szell, favored the

smaller, more controlled sounds of Haydn and Mozart. That's what they favored, but both played all sorts of things. The woodwind sound of the Cleveland Orchestra persists after Szell, but the lush string sound of the Philadelphia Orchestra has not been the same since Ormandy's time. The New York Philharmonic is what one would expect from New Yorkers—tough and aggressive musicians who want to do their own thing, much as New York taxi drivers want to do *their* own thing. "Nearly all of them think of themselves as soloists," said one orchestra insider, "the ones who should and the ones who shouldn't." He added: "Members of the New York Philharmonic can play like angels when inspired, but God help the conductor who turns them off. This is true to some extent anywhere, but nowhere as much as in New York." For all of this, it is a first-rate orchestra, almost worth enduring the indignity of New York to hear.

The Boston Symphony has been extremely influential in the orchestra world. This is partly because of its home in civilized Boston, partly because it was founded more than one hundred years ago, and partly because of the orchestra's famous summer home in Tanglewood, Massachusetts, with its long tradition of music performance and instruction. The quality of its conductors and performers, and its practice of searching out and giving opportunity to young talent, especially young American talent, also contributes to Boston's reputation.

Officials of the National Football League like to say that on any given Sunday any team in the league can beat any other team. It all depends on individual and group performance. The same thing is true for the top orchestras. Performance depends on what they are playing and on the chemistry—between the conductor and the orchestra, between one section and another, or among musicians in one particular section. Also, as in football and the theater, the quality of the performance can depend on the relationship between the players and the spectators.

An eloquent description of a living orchestra comes from Aaron Copland, who wrote:

> This disparate conglomeration of personalities and talents is
> truly an entity like a nation; it is a living thing that breathes
> and moves in ways peculiar to its own being. At its head is a
> leader who, through bodily gestures and facial expressivity,
> acts out the music's progress. There are subtle understandings
> between leader and instrumentalists, psychological adjust-
> ments between player and player, or section and section, all

intent on achieving a single goal—the illumination of the composer's thought.

Before moving into history, let's take a preliminary look at the symphony-orchestra instruments. To keep it simple, consider only four groups: strings, woodwinds, brass, and percussion. The first three consist of only four basic instruments each, and the fourth of drums, cymbals, and such.

The primary strings are the violin, viola, cello, and double bass. The four woodwinds are the flute, oboe, clarinet, and bassoon. Basic brass instruments are the French horn (usually called simply the horn), trumpet, trombone, and tuba. The percussion system consists of a batch of different kinds of drums plus a lot of other instruments that are hit, rubbed, or shaken.

At the concert hall or when watching TV, try keeping your eyes on those four sections and the dozen or so instruments in them. If you do that, a few related big brothers and kissing cousins fall easily into place—the small flute, or piccolo (*piccolo* is Italian for small); the big contrabassoon, which is the deep-voiced version of the bassoon; the English horn, or *cor anglais*, an inbred cousin of the oboe; and the scores of percussion instruments, including triangles, cymbals, gongs, and xylophones.

There is no set number of performers in each instrumental section or in the complete orchestra. A major orchestra today may have 90 to 105 musicians, although a community orchestra might be half that size. The composition of a big orchestra would be something like this:

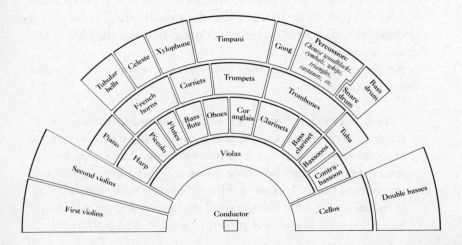

STRINGS

12–16 first violins
12–16 second violins
8–12 violas
6–10 cellos
4–9 double basses

BRASS

2–8 French horns
2–4 trumpets
2–3 trombones
1–2 tubas

WOODWINDS

2–4 flutes and piccolo
2–4 oboes and English horn
2–4 clarinets
2–4 bassoons

PERCUSSION

2–5 timpani (one player)
Cymbals, triangle, snare drum,
   brass drum, gongs, xylophone,
   etc. (one to three players)

OTHER

One or two harps, a piano, and on various occasions a saxophone, harpsichord, celesta, Wagner tuba, guitar, various electronic instruments, and on and on.

ORCHESTRATION

Orchestration is writing music for an orchestra, which means assigning parts to the various instruments. As mentioned in chapter 2, the orchestrator must consider the ranges of those instruments, their timbre or tone color, whether they are to play loudly or softly, and even their technical ability to play rapidly.

Before the Baroque period (Bach and Handel's time), most composers did not leave instructions on their scores about which instruments were to play what notes. What the assembled musicians saw before them was what they *all* were to play. And even in Baroque times, when assignments were made, it was common practice for some instruments to be interchanged with others—flutes could play parts written for the violin, for example, and vice versa.

Sometimes one comes across the term *instrumentation*, which is defined as the art of using instruments in a composition by assigning specific ones to play specific parts of that composition. It would appear to the uninitiated that once the composer has completed all of his instrumentation he has, in fact, orchestrated.

Tone color, one of our earlier building blocks, is perhaps the most discussed tool of the orchestrator. All of us know that a note sounded by the cello does not sound like the same note sounded by the piccolo. When you take the tone color of each, and add the tone color of a bassoon, and make some decisions about loudness and softness, you are beginning to orchestrate.

If you want to be light and graceful, you probably do not want to write a lot of parts for cellos, double basses, trombones, and tubas— and not many for trumpets. If you want a march rhythm, you probably want to turn to clarinets, horns, and trumpets. If you want to have a conversation within the orchestra, a common technique is to have woodwinds talk to strings.

Christoph Gluck from The List was an early devotee of tone color. "Instruments ought to be employed not according to the dexterity of the players," he said, "but according to the dramatic propriety of their tone." Like most composers, Gluck had his favorite instruments and showed his favoritism in his work. Adam Carse, in *The Orchestra from Beethoven to Berlioz*, gives one example: "To the viola, the Cinderella of the string orchestra, Gluck was the fairy godmother who rescued the instrument from a mean position and made it not only independent and indispensable, but discovered in it individuality which was quite its own." On the other hand, we are told that Gluck was wary of the clarinet—although he was big with the trombone.

Among his many other contributions to orchestration (recall that he wrote a still-famous book about it), Hector Berlioz "freed" the harp. (The music people are very big about "rescuing" and "freeing" and "emancipating" individual instruments. But their terms make sense.) The harp had been around for a long time, doing very well for itself. But Berlioz was one of the first to write special parts for the harp—two harps, in fact, in his *Symphonie fantastique*. Berlioz also did good things for the trombone, giving it important themes to carry in that symphony.

The composer is the artist, seeing (and hearing) the finished product in his imagination, choosing his colors, blending and contrasting, fashioning melody against background, establishing patterns of rhythm, deciding whether to bluster and shout or plead and caress.

Orchestral music is conceived as orchestral music; it is not written for one instrument and then arranged for the orchestra. Arrangements *are* made, of course; a Ravel can take a piano piece by a Mussorgsky and turn it into *Pictures at an Exhibition*. Mr. Bach's organ pieces were made into orchestral works and played magnificently by the Philadelphia Orchestra. Routinely, however, although the orchestral composer may have a piano at hand to help him, he does not first write for the piano and then orchestrate.

Nikolai Rimsky-Korsakov, who wrote a two-hundred-page treatise on orchestration and was professor of orchestration at the St. Petersburg Conservatory, gave very specific instructions to his students. For example: "Though far less flexible than the woodwinds, brass instruments heighten the effect of other orchestral groups by their powerful resonance. Trumpets, trombones and tubas are about equal in strength; cornets [then more in use than now] have not quite the same force; horns, in 'forte' [loud] passages are about onehalf as strong, but 'piano' [quiet] they have the same weight as other brass instruments played softly."

To obtain the proper balance in loud passages, the professor told his classes, two horns are needed to one trumpet or one trombone. I've picked Rimsky-Korsakov as our Designated Orchestration Expert (D.O.E.), and I'll quote him concerning individual instruments, beginning with the following advice on some woodwinds:

The following combination of two different woodwind instruments in unison yields the following tone qualities:

Flute + oboe. A quality fuller than that of the flute, sweeter than that of the oboe. Played softly, the flute will predominate in the low, the oboe in the upper, registry.

Flute + clarinet. A quality fuller than that of the flute, duller than that of the clarinet. The flute will predominate in the lower, the clarinet in the higher registry.

Oboe + clarinet. A fuller quality than that of either instrument heard separately. The dark nasal tone of the oboe will prevail in the low register, the bright "chest" quality of the clarinet in the high compass. . . .

Bassoon + clarinet. Very full quality. The gloomy character of the clarinet prevails in the lower register, the sickly quality of the bassoon in the higher. . . .

Bassoon + oboe + clarinet + flute. This combination is extremely rare. The color is rich and difficult to describe in words. The tone of each instrument will be separated from the others more or less in the manner detailed above.

And that's what orchestration is about.

DEVELOPMENT OF THE ORCHESTRA

When was the modern symphony orchestra born? A common answer is the eighteenth century. In addition, Listed Monteverdi, 1567–1643, was a master of an early form of "orchestral" instrumentation—this part for the oboes, that part for the trumpets, and so on. It's impossible to pinpoint a specific date (which would not be particularly helpful to us in any case), in part because history is not that clear and in part because of conflicting definitions concerning the difference between a batch of musicians playing together and the same batch playing as an orchestra.

In and around 1700, European orchestras typically consisted of about twenty performers and played mainly in churches, theaters, and the homes of noblemen. For example, Bach, born in 1685, had an eighteen-musician orchestra when he was working for Prince Leopold in Cothen early in the 1700s. Most of the instruments were strings, grouped around a central harpsichord, but at different times this orchestra also had oboes, bassoons, trumpets, horns, drums, and the occasional flute. In works of more than one movement, Bach would use different instruments in different movements for variety—and, as today's musicians point out, to give the wind musicians a rest. The Bach orchestra remained basically unchanged for the first half of the eighteenth century.

Public concerts increased during Haydn's lifetime (1732–1809). When he was in the service of Count Esterhazy (beginning in 1761), his court orchestra had twenty-five members, although on his trips to London in the early 1790s he was astounded to find as many as forty musicians onstage. By this time, although most European courts had their own orchestras, there were also more orchestras not connected with the court, a mixture of professionals, semipros, and amateurs, playing for the fun of it when they were not making a living elsewhere.

In Haydn's eighteenth century, the strings and harpsichord remained the backbone of orchestral compositions, but both oboes and bassoons became permanent members of the orchestra. The flute initially appeared as a substitute for the oboe but later joined up on its own. In the mid-1700s, clarinets were added. By 1750 almost every European orchestra also had a pair of horns, providing "middle" sounds (between the ranges of the high and low instruments).

There is general agreement on the importance of one early group, the Mannheim Orchestra. It was assembled in the mid-1700s by a school of composers in Mannheim, Germany, who operated at the court of the Elector Palatine. In 1741, the Elector recruited a Bohemian violin virtuoso named Johann Stamitz, who became concertmaster and put together an orchestra consisting chiefly of fellow composers. There in Mannheim—and simultaneously in Paris—clarinets and horns were added to the flutes, oboes, bassoons, and string instruments that were already playing together.

Veering away from the Baroque counterpoint of Bach and Handel, the Mannheim composers got into a lot of single-melody-plus-chords music, with the violins generally carrying that melody. The music people tell us that the composers also used dynamic devices and orchestral effects that became the foundation for the symphonic style of the Vienna Classical school. Thus, there is a direct link between the Mannheim work and the compositions created by the future genius (who was only nine years old in 1741) Franz Joseph Haydn, called fondly (but erroneously) the father of the symphony.

The Mannheim Orchestra looked like this:

16 violins	2 double basses	2 clarinets
4 violas	3 flutes	4 bassoons
2 cellos	3 oboes	5 horns

It also borrowed military drums and trumpets as needed.

This came to around forty performers, on good days when everyone could be gathered together. Note that even then nearly two-thirds of the instruments were strings, and two-thirds of the strings were violins. When drums were called for, all four of the modern instrumental families were represented: woodwinds, brass, strings, and percussion, with parts for each.

By the first half of the nineteenth century, the orchestra had grown to between sixty and eighty musicians. Many new instruments had been added and many old ones modified and redesigned. As the orchestra grew in size, the sound volume went way up. This had an important impact: the orchestra had now outgrown the homes of noblemen and moved into the theater and concert hall. For the date-minded, the first public concerts are believed to have been given in London in 1672, but the first concert hall was not built until much later, in 1748, in Oxford. The idea of a structure devoted to orchestral music then spread to the Continent. Not everyone considered this to be progress; some felt that the more intimate sounds of Haydn and Mozart were lost in the bigger halls. But the ticket marketers no doubt were looking for more seats—and Beethoven was soon to follow. His symphonies could not be contained in a music salon.

Seeking more tone color, Beethoven (1770–1827) brought in trombones, added the piccolo and the contrabassoon to the woodwinds, increased the number of horns, gave more time to the timpani, and demanded still more violins. Then the orchestra-minded Berlioz (1803–1869) wrote his book on how to compose for the orchestra and dreamed up new ways of playing existing instruments, such as muting the horns and hitting the cymbals with a drumstick. Always a Big Thinker, he proclaimed that the "ideal" orchestra should have 240 strings, 30 pianos, 30 harps, and a correspondingly large number of wind and percussion instruments.

During the nineteenth century, composers like Berlioz, Liszt, Wagner, and Richard Strauss increasingly focused on instrumental tone color and the ways in which the sounds of different instruments blended together—again, not to everyone's satisfaction. "Color for the sake of color" was the charge of some critics. Meanwhile, still more instruments were being invented and older ones perfected—valve systems were developed in the brass family and keywork in the woodwind family. As composers experimented, instrument making progressed; conversely, as instruments developed, composers became more imaginative.

Composers in the late 1800s sought to do more and more things. Bigger was better. Wagner (1813–1883) was a leading exponent of this trend (he was especially deep into brass). The *Ring* operas, for example, are scored for fifteen woodwind instruments and twenty-one brass, plus harps, percussion, sixteen first and sixteen second violins, twelve violas, twelve cellos, and eight double basses. Mahler (1869–1911) also broke some records; his Eighth Symphony is scored for a piccolo, four flutes, four oboes, an English horn, an E-flat clarinet, four bassoons, a contrabassoon, eight horns, four trumpets, four trombones, a tuba, timpani, a bass drum, cymbals, a tam-tam, a triangle, chimes, a glockenspiel, a celesta, a piano, a harmonium, an organ, two harps, a mandolin, four fanfare trumpets, three fanfare trombones, seven vocal soloists, two mixed choruses, a boys' choir, and all the first and second violins, violas, cellos, and double basses. It is called the *Symphony of a Thousand*, and it caused many composers to think things were starting to get out of hand. It was also a long way from Messrs. Haydn and Mozart.

No wonder that the music people later talked about "Romantic excesses," the emotional binges that encouraged production of this type. One of the first composers to start scaling back the orchestra was Impressionist Debussy (1862–1913), who chose his instruments carefully for their particular tone colors. Since about 1910, major symphony orchestras—although still using one hundred or so musicians—have been smaller than those of Romantic days.

To get a feeling for the development of the orchestra from the Classical period into the twentieth century, try listening to the following four compositions (better still to see and hear all four on videotape):

Haydn's Symphony No. 104 (*London*), 1795
    2 flutes, 2 oboes, 2 clarinets, 2 bassoons
    2 horns, 2 trumpets
    2 timpani
    first and second violins, violas, cellos, basses

Beethoven's Symphony No. 9 (*Chorale*), 1823
    1 piccolo, 2 flutes, 2 oboes, 2 clarinets, 2 bassoons
    4 horns, 2 trumpets, 3 trombones
    2 timpani, bass drum, cymbals, triangle
    first and second violins, violas, cellos, basses
    chorus and four solo voices

Wagner's *Götterdämmerung* (opera), 1872
    1 piccolo, 3 flutes, 3 oboes, 1 English horn, 3 clarinets, 1 bass
        clarinet, 3 bassoons
    4 timpani, cymbals, tenor drum, triangle, bells
    16 first violins, 16 second violins, 12 violas, 12 cellos, 8 basses
    13 solo voices

Ravel's *Daphnis et Chloé* (ballet), 1911
    2 piccolos, 2 flutes, 1 alto flute, 1 English horn, 2 clarinets, 1
        E-flat clarinet, 1 bass clarinet, 3 bassoons, 1 contrabassoon
    4 horns, 4 trumpets, 3 trombones, 1 tuba
    4 timpani, bass drum, cymbals, snare drum, triangle, tambourine, castanets, antique cymbals, gong, glockenspiel, celesta
    first and second violins, violas, cellos, basses
    chorus

Haydn, Beethoven, and Ravel, following custom, do not spell out the number of strings. Most likely there would be eight first violins and six second, as opposed to the larger numbers called for by Wagner.

THE INSTRUMENTS

A brief technical note (and a mite bit of history) might be helpful before we launch into the descriptions of the individual instruments. Pitch—not Bob Feller's or Nolan Ryan's kind—is the highness or lowness of musical tone and is a function of the frequency of the number of vibrations per second caused by the vibrating string, the column of air, or whatever is producing the sound. Some woodwind and brass instruments are commonly identified by the fundamental tone produced by their entire air columns. Thus, a clarinet might be "pitched" in B-flat or in E-flat. These would be two separate instruments, with the fundamental tone of the former higher than that of the latter. One does not have just a plain old ordinary clarinet, like a plain old ordinary violin. It has to be pitched somewhere.

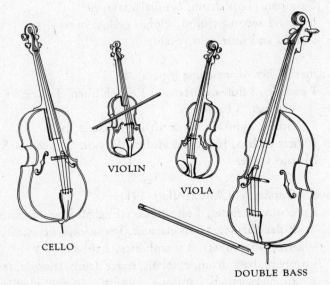

VIOLIN

VIOLA

CELLO

DOUBLE BASS

Bowed Strings

BOWED STRINGS

As noted earlier, and as evident at first glance, stringed instruments constitute about two-thirds of a major symphony orchestra. Violins are divided into two groups: first violins and second violins. The first all play the same part; the second sometimes play that same part but usually play another. Each of the other groups of strings plays parts written specifically for that group: one part for all the violas, another for all the cellos, and yet another for all the double basses. (This is *not* the case for woodwinds and brasses, where each individual instrument can expect a part of its own: first horn, second horn, third horn, for example.)

Today's orchestral string instruments are very much of one family. Most of us know that the violin, viola, and cello all have the same shape; the shape of the double bass differs slightly with its sloping shoulders and flat back. All have four strings. The violin and viola are held under the chin; the bigger cello rests on the floor with an end pin; and the much bigger double bass also sits on the floor, with the musician usually standing.

These four form a voicelike choir, although the analogies with vocal parts are not precise because most instruments have a larger range than most singers.

Violin—Soprano: clear and sharp

Viola—Alto: mellower, like Marian Anderson; warmer than the violin

Cello—Tenor or baritone: rich, deeper, and more masculine than the violin and viola

Bass viol (or double bass)—Bullfrog; music's lowest voice

Rimsky-Korsakov, our Designated Orchestration Expert, emphasized to his students that stringed instruments have more ways of producing sound than any other orchestral group, passing from one shade of expression to another better than other instruments.

Violin: The violin, with its strings stretched across a hollow wooden box, is the smallest of the four stringed instruments, plays the highest notes, is unquestionably the orchestra's most important member, and is its primary source of melody. The strings are made of pig gut, sheep gut, steel, or nylon—generally steel or nylon today, although most professionals use sheep gut. The strings are of different thicknesses; the sound comes from their vibrations as they are stroked with a horsehair stretched along a wooden bow. To achieve a given note, the player presses a finger against a string, changing its effective length. A short string produces a higher note than a longer one, as any twanger of rubber bands knows. No instrument is more flexible; the violinist can produce a greater variety of sounds than any other musician in the orchestra.

Second violinists aren't happy about being called "second fiddle," a term suggesting that their talent is inferior to that of first fiddlers. This is no longer the case in major symphony orchestras, although it was at one time. First violins are grouped to the left of the conductor and customarily carry much of the melody; second violins are on the conductor's right and generally provide the accompaniment.

My lists of composers' works include many violin concertos, including works by Bartók, Beethoven, Brahms, Dvořák, Mendelssohn, Mozart, Sibelius, and Tchaikovsky, as well as Haydn, Hindemith, Prokofiev, Saint-Saëns, Schumann, Shostakovich, and Stravinsky—plus, in different form from the later concerto, Vivaldi and Bach.

Many listed composers also wrote violin sonatas, including Mozart (who composed forty-two), Bach, Beethoven, Mendelssohn, Franck, Brahms, Fauré, Schumann, Grieg, Debussy, Bartók, and Prokofiev.

An example of a favorite symphonic segment for violinists is the fourth movement of Mahler's Fifth Symphony.

Viola: The viola's sound has more warmth and less sparkle than the violin's and is richer and deeper-bodied. For many years composers relegated it to standby roles. Until the mid-1700s it was heard only in the orchestra, but later it became important to chamber music (and vital to the string quartet). Before this century there were no virtuoso viola performers, and it still is not generally regarded as a solo instrument.

Among the best-known works for the viola are Mozart's *Sinfonia concertante* (K. 364) for violin, viola, and orchestra; Berlioz's *Harold in Italy* for viola and orchestra; Debussy's Sonata No. 2 for Flute, Viola, and Harp; Hindemith's *Der Schwanendreher* for viola and orchestra; several Hindemith viola sonatas (he was a viola virtuoso); and Bartók's Concerto for Viola and Orchestra. Hindemith also wrote both a sonata and a concerto for the older *viola d'amore*, which was a popular instrument in the Baroque era.

Cello: Next in size is the resonant, majestic violoncello, called simply the cello. Because its strings are longer and thicker than the viola's, its notes are an octave deeper. For years it strengthened the bass section of church choirs. Since the early days of the string quartet it has played the bass role there, rarely being given the melody— though it can and sometimes does take on that job. Cello aficionados hold that it is one of the most expressive of all symphony instruments—all twenty-two pounds of it—now equally effective in an accompanying or solo capacity.

Famous cello concertos have been written by Listed Brahms (double concerto for cello and violin), Dvořák, Haydn, Hindemith, Prokofiev, Saint-Saëns, Schumann, and Shostakovich. (Another dozen or so well-known cello concertos are available from unListed composers). Other popular cello works include several sonatas by Saint-Saëns; five by Beethoven; two each by Fauré, Hindemith, Brahms, and Mendelssohn; and one each by Debussy, Prokofiev, Grieg, and Richard Strauss. Also an Elégie for Cello and Orchestra by Fauré, *Podhaka* by Janáček, a sonata for violin and cello by Ravel, *Funf Stücke im Volkston* by Schumann, *Variations on a Rococo Theme* by Tchaikovsky, and six famous Bach suites for the unaccompanied cello.

Bass: This big baby goes by many names: bass viol, double bass, contrabass, string bass, or just plain bass. Also, bull fiddle. Its strings are as thick as ropes, its tone is the lowest of the stringed instruments, and it is frequently plucked (as opposed to bowed).

Double-bass players are indebted to Beethoven (as is the entire civilized world), who did great things for their instrument in his Fifth Symphony, pairing a double bass with the cello section in a strong third-movement melody. It *does* make listening more fun if you keep your ears open for that combination, just for fun's sake. From that time on, the story goes, double-bass players have deemed themselves largely responsible for the loudness or softness of the entire orchestra. While this may not be a wholly objective assessment, given the source, the bass is indeed capable of being timid or aggressive—and when it is aggressive, the rest of the orchestra must take note.

Every major symphony orchestra has a double bass, but few outstanding solo parts have been written for it. One famous exception is the "role" of the elephant in Saint-Saëns's *Carnival of the Animals*. While not often used in chamber music, exceptions include Schubert's *Trout* Quintet for violin, viola, cello, double bass, and piano, and Dvořák's Quintet in G for two violins, viola, cello, and double bass. Since there are so few double-bass compositions we'll break a rule: two unListed double-bass players who wrote specifically for it were Domenico Dragonetti (1763–1846) and Giovanni Bottesini (1821–1889). Stravinsky used the double bass as one of eight instruments in *L'histoire du soldat*, Verdi gave it a dramatic part in the last act of *Otello*, Schubert put it to work with cellos in the opening melody of his *Unfinished* Symphony, and Beethoven paid considerable attention to it in his Fourth and Ninth Symphonies as well as the Fifth.

The entire violin family sprung from the viol clan, popular during the Renaissance. That group consisted of treble, tenor, bass, and great bass instruments. The viols were invented in the fifteenth century, peaked in the sixteenth, and were on their way out in the seventeenth, replaced by the violins that had been challenging them since the 1500s.

Dance music, more than anything else, helped do in the viol family, whose tones were too soft and delicate for the dance band. By 1685, the birth year of Bach and Handel, the violin, viola, and cello had been perfected by the Amati, Guarneri, and Stradivari families in Italy—with Antonio Stradivari (1644–1737) being the accepted master of all violin makers. The violin has changed very little in the last 350 years.

As the twentieth century began, however, some composers were moving away from the violin, the other strings in its family, and the emotionalism of Romantic music in general. Stravinsky, with his intellectual, antisentimental approach, did not have any strings at all in *Les noces*, his Wind Symphonies, or his *Symphony of Psalms*. But despite such twentieth-century exceptions, there is, as we have seen here, a wealth of stringed music by composers on The List, from Monteverdi to Handel, from Mozart to Beethoven, from Mendelssohn to Tchaikovsky, and into our times.

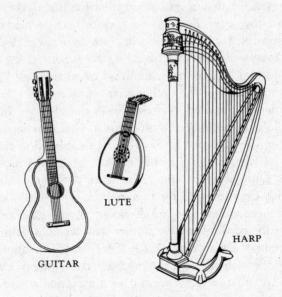

LUTE

GUITAR

HARP

Plucked String Family

PLUCKED STRINGS

Harp: The big harp is usually considered apart from the bowed string family. Initially an offshoot of the hunter's bow, it stands sixty-eight inches tall in a triangular frame and is played by plucking its strings. Although one of the oldest of all instruments, mentioned in the Bible and played by heavenly Hollywood angels, it has been part of the orchestra for only about 150 years. Its forty-seven strings differ in length and in thickness and provide a total range of six and one-half octaves, just short of the piano's seven. Seven pedals can alter the pitch of the strings.

The modern triangular harp first appeared in Europe in the twelfth century, although that version had no pedals. It has been basically unchanged for a thousand years, unlike other early plucked instruments such as those in the lyre family, whose offspring include not only the lute and the guitar, but also the clavichord, harpsichord, and piano. In today's symphony orchestra, it is used mostly as a solo instrument, less frequently for accompaniment.

The most familiar special effect of the harp is the *glissando*, the rippling sound caused by sliding fingers rapidly over the strings. Some experts call it one of the most overworked platitudes of music, but acknowledge it is nonetheless effective.

Monteverdi was among the first to write for the harp, using it in his opera *L'Orfeo*, and Debussy was commissioned to compose his *Danses sacrée et profane* for it. Handel wrote harp parts for some of his oratorios and also composed harp concerti grossi (in F and B-flat). In the mid-1700s the harp was popular in musical salons and a great deal of music was written for it. Liszt later asked harpists to play transcriptions of his piano music. Berlioz, always looking for extra tone color, included harps in his orchestral works, most notably in the *Symphonie fantastique*, where he startled his audience by using two harps. Impressionists Debussy and Ravel almost always included a harp in their scores: Debussy's *La mer* is one good example; his Sonata No. 2 for Flute, Viola, and Harp is another. Ravel wrote an "Introduction and Allegro" for string quartet, flute, clarinet, and harp; Mozart a Concerto for Flute and Harp (K. 299). Wagner included the harp in his orchestral scores; Hindemith composed a harp sonata; and an unListed composer, François Boieldieu (1775–1834), wrote a lovely harp concerto.

Lute and Guitar: Now a few hundred years past its peak, the lute has too much history to pass over, even for us novices. We can, and will, ignore the heraphone, the heng chok, and the hibernicon, but the lute rates a little attention—in part because it first appeared in Mesopotamia about 2000 B.C. The classical lute is mentioned in French literature from 1270 on and in English literature beginning in 1395. It originally had four pairs of strings, which increased to five in the fourteenth century, six during the Renaissance, and thirteen by Baroque times—and these numbers differed from country to country.

The lute is shaped something like a half-pear, with the stalk representing a finger board. There is no bridge, and each string is duplicated. The fingers of the right hand do the plucking while the left stops the strings to set the pitch.

Of Listed composers, Bach and Couperin wrote extensively for the lute, with Bach (naturally) being considered a lute giant. It is fair to say that he was the last great lute composer, having written five suites, a prelude, and a fugue for it. When the orchestra expanded and private concerts gave way to public ones, the lute was too delicate to compete. It disappeared from the orchestra, although some attempts are being made today on both sides of the Atlantic to revive lute music. At one time in Britain it was the most serious solo instrument and also was commonly used for accompanying songs. It still is used by some Arabs.

Another plucked-string instrument is the guitar, which has six strings. While known as a Spanish instrument, it was actually played by the Egyptians five thousand years ago and brought to Spain by the Romans. By 1500 it was Spain's national instrument. Later, Berlioz, Schubert, and Weber all wrote for it—Schubert a cantata for men's voices and guitar, and Weber some thirty songs with guitar accompaniment. Today the guitar appears with the symphony orchestra only in featured roles. Several famous unListed Spanish and Brazilian composers have produced beautiful works for it, including Honorable Mentioners Manuel de Falla and Heitor Villa-Lobos.

A guitar-type instrument called the banjar, or banjo, was brought by slaves to the United States from Africa. Its music was imitated by Debussy in a piano prelude called *Minstrels*.

WOODWINDS

The term *woodwind* comes from the fact that most of the original family members were made from wood. Today, traditional woodwinds have been overtaken by technology. Modern flutes and piccolos are metal; so are many clarinets. Oboes and clarinets are sometimes made of ebonite—rubber hardened by the addition of sulphur. Some modern flute tubes are even made of gold, and ivory clarinets can be found. And plastics are here as they are everywhere. But the name remains woodwinds—and indeed a good bit of wood is still found in professional symphony orchestras.

In several cases, such as the clarinet, different versions of an instrument exist. These include such far-out offshoots as the bass flute, which is a little like a woolly-mammoth hummingbird.

Like the violin family, although not quite as tidily, the woodwinds form a choir including soprano, alto, tenor (or baritone), and bass "voices." But before getting into them, we should recall that an octave is all eight tones of any major or minor scale and that middle C is the pitch located near the center of a piano keyboard. Another important technicality: the vibrations in woodwinds are triggered in different ways. In the flute family, the player blows a stream of air against a sharp edge at one end of the instrument. All clarinets have a single reed, a shaped piece of cane fastened to the mouthpiece. When air is blown through the space between the reed and the mouthpiece, the thin tip of the reed vibrates, triggering a column of air inside the tube. The oboe, the bassoon, the contrabassoon, and the English horn have double reeds instead of a single one.

Given that background, here is the woodwind order, from high to low pitch, including not only the basic flute, oboe, clarinet, and bassoon, but also their cousins:

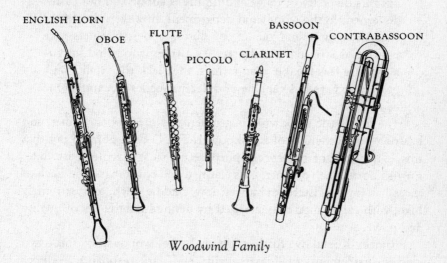

Woodwind Family

• Piccolo. A half-sized flute, with tones an octave higher. The high soprano voice; the highest-pitched orchestral instrument.

• Flute. From just above middle C up three octaves. The soprano voice of the woodwind family.

• Oboe. From just above middle C up two octaves. The soprano of the double-reed woodwinds.

• English horn. An oboe-and-a-half in size. From just below middle C up two octaves. The alto voice.

• Clarinet. The standard (B-flat) clarinet reaches from just below middle C on the low end to an octave below a flute of the same size on the high end. The alto clarinet is lower, and the bass clarinet still lower by another octave. (There has also been a basset horn, a sort of tenor clarinet, an octave below middle C, which is to the clarinet what the English horn is to the oboe.)

• Bassoon. From two octaves below middle C to almost an octave above it. The bass of the woodwind family.

• Contrabassoon. Big brother of the bassoon, and an octave lower. The deepest instrument in the orchestra, only a half-tone above the lowest note on the piano.

In comparing string and woodwind sections, Designated Orchestration Expert Rimsky-Korsakov commented:

> Considering the instruments it comprises, the string group offers a fair variety of color, and contrast in compass, but this diversity of range and timbre is subtle and not easily discerned. In the woodwind department, however, the difference in register and quality of flutes, oboes, clarinets and bassoon is striking to a degree. As a rule, woodwind instruments are less flexible than strings; they lack the vitality and power, and are less capable of different shades of expression.

The four basic woodwind instruments—flute, oboe, clarinet, and bassoon—are generally of equal power. The D.O.E. pointed out that this is not true of the special-purpose cousins: piccolo, bass flute, English horn, small clarinet, bass clarinet, and contrabassoon. Each of these has four registers, or ranges: low, middle, high, and extremely high, with each range characterized by definite differences of quality and power.

Rimsky-Korsakov further divided the woodwinds into two classes: instruments of "nasal quality and dark resonance"—oboes and bassoons (and English horns and contrabassoons)—and instruments of "chest quality and bright tone"—flutes and clarinets (and piccolos, bass flutes, small clarinets, and bass clarinets).

"Flutes and clarinets are the most flexible woodwind instruments, the flutes in particular," said the D.O.E., "but for expressive power and subtlety in nuances the clarinet supersedes them; this instrument can reduce volume of tone to a mere breath."

One of the distinctive qualities of woodwinds is the fact that they have different tone color in their high and low registers. Rimsky-Korsakov wrote about the different impressions he got from each of the basic woodwinds when played in the extreme registers: very low and very high. In the very low register, he heard the flute as "dull and cold," the oboe as "wild," the clarinet as "ringing and threatening," and the bassoon as "sinister." In the very high register, he heard the flute as "brilliant," the oboe as "hard and dry," the clarinet as "piercing," and the bassoon as "tense."

Flute: The flute is the most sweet-toned of all instruments, sounding birdlike in higher ranges. Today's flute, a stepchild of the once-popular instrument called the recorder, is twenty-seven inches long and is held sideways (in earlier times it was blown straight-on, like the recorder). The sound comes from blowing against the sharp edge of a flanged hole drilled in the side of the tube near one end. Popular for the entire period covered by The List, the "common" flute is made of wood or silver, although, as mentioned earlier, there has been a great deal of experimentation with different kinds of metals by symphony-level flutists. (In *Season with Solti*, William Barry Furlong described the favorite instrument of the Chicago Symphony's principal flutist some years ago. The main body and the head joint were platinum. The chimney—the hole into which the air goes—was gold. The foot joint—the small third section—was silver.)

The flute family normally has neither tenor nor bass members—just the high-soprano (or coloraturo) piccolo and the soprano flute.

Telemann wrote concertos and sonatas for the flute. Vivaldi composed six concertos for flute, strings, and continuo. Handel wrote numerous flute sonatas. Bach featured the instrument in his Orchestral Suite No. 2. Gluck used it in two operas, *Orfeo ed Euridice* and *Alceste*. Mozart gave it eternal fame in his opera *The Magic Flute* and also wrote four flute quartets and two flute concertos. Haydn composed the well-known Sonata in G for flute and piano; Beethoven a trio for flute, violin, and viola. Schubert wrote Variations in E Minor for flute and piano. Mendelssohn featured the flute in *A Midsummer Night's Dream*, Brahms in his Fourth Symphony, Bizet in *Carmen*, Debussy in *The Afternoon of a Faun*, Ravel in "La flute enchantée" from his *Sheherazade*, and Tchaikovsky in the *Nutcracker* Suite.

In the twentieth century the flute has seen more solo action than ever, with sonatas by Hindemith and unaccompanied pieces by Debussy, among many others. Debussy's *Syrinx* is perhaps his best-known work for solo flute; he also composed a sonata for flute, viola, and harp. Prokofiev wrote a sonata for flute and piano. Two flautists (or flutists)—James Galway and Jean-Pierre Rampal—are as well known today as any performing classical musicians, even to the lay person.

Oboe: The standard orchestral oboe looks much like a clarinet, with a slightly shorter tube—twenty-three inches compared with twenty-six—and a conical shape that gets wider toward the bell (the flared end). While it can make sharp and lively music, its real thing is to be melancholy, mysterious, and sad. It customarily is not a life-of-the-party instrument. As noted, the oboe—like the bassoon and unlike the clarinet—is a double-reed creation. The most common oboe is a treble or soprano, although the family also includes an instrument in the alto range (the oboe d'amore), a tenor (the English horn), and a bass or baritone. All are descendants of instruments played in seventeenth-century France; the word *oboe* comes from the French *hautbois*—*haut* (high) plus *bois* (wood).

In the smallish orchestras of the 1700s, a pair of oboes usually served as the main soprano woodwinds. There was a well-known Parisian band called "The Twelve Great Oboes of the King," and—rather typically of the yearning-to-be-difficult French—it consisted of ten oboes and two bassoons.

Although a favorite over the centuries, the oboe has lost some stardom since the more versatile clarinet joined the orchestra. The clarinet has a larger range, is less tiring to play, and is less prone to malfunctions. The double reeds of the oboe are exceedingly tricky, and part of being a superior oboist is being a superior reed maker, shaving reeds to the thinness and narrowness of choice. The best oboists say it takes years to learn to make them properly; symphony-orchestra oboists always have several spares on hand during concerts, frequently changing reeds during the program. Wicked rumors used to circulate in symphony orchestras that playing the oboe would drive musicians insane. Good oboists scoff at this heresy. The truth, they say, is that one has to be insane to take up the oboe in the first place.

Few orchestral compositions since the 1700s have excluded the oboe. Bach, Handel, Mozart, and Beethoven all wrote for the original wood version. Among well-known List compositions featuring this instrument are Bach's Double Concerto in C for Violin and Oboe, Handel's two concertos for oboe and strings, Telemann's Concerto in F Minor, Mozart's Concerto in C (K. 314) and Quartet in F for Oboe and Strings (K. 370), Schumann's *Three Romances*, Hindemith's Oboe Sonata, Vaughan Williams's Concerto for Oboe and Strings, and Richard Strauss's Concerto for Oboe. Rossini featured the oboe in his overtures. Mozart and Vivaldi were among many others who gave it important parts, even when not featuring it. Some of the best-known oboe parts in symphonies are those in Tchaikovsky's Fourth and Beethoven's Third.

Clarinet: The youngest orchestral woodwind is the versatile clarinet, an orchestra favorite since the 1900s. It is twenty-six inches long with eighteen side holes, six of which are covered by fingers and the rest by keys. The highness or lowness of the tone is determined by the specific holes stopped. Few (except understandably prejudiced musicians who specialize in other woodwinds) dispute that it is the most important woodwind in the orchestra. Its range is wide, and it is almost as "expressive" as the violin, able to play very quietly and to modulate quickly from loud to soft. In military-band music—where there are no violins—it takes the violin parts. Some thirteen clarinets exist today, the six most common, from highest- to lowest-pitched, being the E-flat, B-flat, A, alto, bass, and contrabass. The B-flat and the A are the ones most often used in the symphony orchestra and are typically played by the same performer. A full symphony orchestra usually includes three clarinetists, with the third shifting to an E-flat version when needed. The alto, bass, and contrabass clarinets all have upturned metal bells and look not unlike saxophones, not surprising since the bass clarinet was perfected by the inventor of the saxophone, Antoine Joseph Sax (1814–1894). In pitch, the bass clarinet is the equivalent of the stringed cello.

Mozart had a lot to do with making the clarinet dignified and respectable, and three of his works are still a basic part of the clarinet repertoire: his Concerto in A for Clarinet (K. 622), Quintet in A for Clarinet and Strings (K. 581), and Trio in E-flat for Clarinet, Viola, and Piano (K. 498).

Weber wrote two well-known clarinet concertos, a clarinet concertino, and a famous clarinet quintet, and he featured the instrument in many other compositions as well. Schumann and Brahms both composed solo pieces for it; Brahms also wrote a Quintet for Clarinet and Strings. Bartók wrote *Contrasts* for violin, piano, and clarinet. Stravinsky, who was particularly interested in (and influenced by) the work of jazz clarinetists, featured the instrument in his *Ebony* Concerto. A fellow named Benny Goodman, not on The List, also did some special things with it. Woody Herman wasn't far behind.

A close relative of the clarinet is the basset horn, built first in the 1770s. An alto voice, it was used by Mozart in *La clemenza di Tito*, in other operas, and in his *Requiem* Mass. Richard Strauss included it in several operas, Beethoven in *Prometheus*, and Mendelssohn in two pieces for clarinet, piano, and basset horn.

Bassoon: The fourth primary orchestral woodwind, and the biggest, is the bassoon, another instrument that dates back at least to the seventeenth century. Stretched out, it would be nine feet long, but it is doubled up, for convenience and to preserve the eyesight of neighboring musicians. Like the oboe, it has a crook on one end (called a *bocal*) that leads to a double reed; on the other end the tube leads to a bell that is turned upward. Heavy enough so that players must support it with a sling, the bassoon is the multipurpose bass of the woodwind family, comparable to the cello of the strings. Its deep, low, nasal voice is often used as the orchestral clown, although it can also be solemn if the composer wants it to be. Someone once said it sounds like a baritone with a bad cold. It is the most expensive of the woodwinds, excepting special flutes made of abnormally precious metals.

Mozart, Vivaldi, and Weber each wrote a concerto for the bassoon. Beethoven and Berlioz experimented considerably with it. Tchaikovsky wrote a bassoon melody into his Fifth Symphony, and Stravinsky used it at its highest register at the opening of *The Rite of Spring*. Hindemith and Saint-Saëns both wrote sonatas for bassoon and piano, Prokofiev composed "Humorous Scherzo" for four bassoons, and Grieg featured one in "In the Hall of the Mountain King" from his *Peer Gynt* Suite No. 1.

There is also a double bassoon, or contrabassoon, about twice as long and an octave lower, and not too frequently used. It doubles back on itself four times and rests on the floor. One place to hear it is at the beginning of Brahms's First Symphony. Beethoven used it to portray the hollowness of the dungeon in his opera *Fidelio*. Mahler also wrote a good many near-solo parts for it.

Odds and Ends: In 1904, after some twenty-four years of work, Wilhelm Heckel produced a heckelphone, which looks like a big oboe. His work was done in part at the request of Wagner, who wanted a baritone voice with the characteristics of the oboe but with a more powerful tone. Richard Strauss put it in *Salome,* and it sometimes appears nowadays in large orchestras. Hindemith wrote a trio for viola, piano, and heckelphone. It is the kind of instrument that gives orchestra managers fits, since not every orchestral closet has a heckelphone in storage when it is called for.

In 1842 the aforementioned Antoine Joseph Sax invented the saxophone, and today a whole family of them exists, used more in military and jazz bands than in symphony orchestras. Soprano saxophones are straight; the deeper-toned versions have a bent crook and an upturned bell. Saxophones are not normally found in classical music, though Bizet included one in his *L'Arlésienne* Suites, as did Richard Strauss in *Symphonia domestica* and Vaughan Williams in his Sixth Symphony. Debussy wrote a *Rapsodie* for saxophone and piano, and Ravel featured it in *Boléro*. Hindemith, who composed for so many instruments, wrote a saxophone sonata.

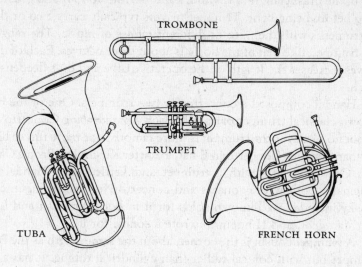

Brass Family

BRASS

Brass instruments are no more—or not much more—than brass tubes, often with lots of bends and three, or sometimes four, valves. The sounds come from the vibration of the air in the tube, which in turn is caused by what the player is doing with his lips. The trick to it all is the *embouchure*—the manner in which the mouthpiece and lips meet. Valves give the player the option of choosing different lengths of tube: the longer the tube, the lower the fundamental tone.

Four primary brass instruments, all with offshoots, are found in the modern orchestra: trumpets, horns, trombones, and tubas. Rimsky-Korsakov, D.O.E., believed that brass instruments were so similar in register and timbre—that is, in range and tone quality/ resonance—that the student-composer needed no detailed discussion of these qualities. Recall that he had a very different view about woodwinds.

Trumpet: The trumpet has been around for a long time. Natural trumpets—straight, with no valves, finger holes, or slides—were played in ancient Rome, Egypt, and the Orient. A few hundred years later the trumpet makers began to bend it, chiefly because its length was becoming unmanageable. Back in Bach's day (the eighteenth century), it was seven or eight feet long in prebent configuration, and had no valves. They weren't developed until the early 1800s.

Equipped now with valves, today's trumpet is the soprano member of the brass clan. It is a cylindrical tube, four to four and a half feet long before being bent. Trumpet players typically carry two or three instruments with them, to fit different ranges of music. The range of the trumpet, like that of the horn, is about three octaves. Each of three valves increases the length of the operative tube and thus deepens the pitch.

Handel composed a concerto for two trumpets. One of the best-known classical trumpet parts is in Bach's *Brandenburg* Concerto No. 2. But no piece for the trumpet is more famous, nor more fun to listen to, than Haydn's Concerto in E-flat, a Starter Kit choice. Bach's *Christmas* Oratorio starts with a trumpet and kettledrums. Handel and Telemann both wrote sonatas and concertos for the trumpet. Stravinsky included well-known solos for it in both *Petrushka* and *L'histoire du soldat*, and Hindemith wrote a sonata for it.

A trumpet cousin is the cornet, about the same length as the B-flat trumpet but with conical rather than cylindrical tubing. It has a less brilliant, more mellow tone, most noticeably in the higher register. Found more often in bands than in symphony orchestras, it is a flexible instrument, and some say it is to the brass band what the violin is to the orchestra. (You may recall that some say the same thing about the clarinet.) French composers at one time tried scoring their music for both trumpets and cornets without much success.

Another member of the brass family is the flugelhorn, which is fuller in tone than either the trumpet or the cornet.

Horn: The horn was blown on stag hunts in France several hundred years ago. A long time before that, men—and women too, perhaps—were blowing into hollowed animal tusks. By 1650 the horn was sixteen feet of coiled brass tube, with a wide bell. The coil was big enough so that the hunter—or the hunter's man—could carry it over his shoulder when it was not being played. Eventually, rotary and piston valves were invented, making the instrument more versatile. With the horn, as with other brass instruments, valve technology has been critical to development. All of this leads to today's orchestral French horn, a conical-shaped, coiled, eleven-foot tube with a funnel-shaped mouthpiece. The player supports it with his or her right hand in the bell. Today, many musicians prefer a double instrument, twice-coiled and four feet longer, with an extra (fourth) valve. The tube circles around in front of the player, with the large bell ending up between the right shoulder and right hip. It is the instrument that looks as though it should be accompanied by a plumber. (It's fortunate that it doesn't need one, since a good plumber is hard to find nowadays.)

The horn sound blends with those of the woodwinds and strings as well as with those of its brass cousins, one of the reasons for the instrument's orchestral popularity since the 1700s. In skilled hands its sound is mellow and rich in the middle register—and in unskilled hands it's sort of a cracked-note disaster. One of the more difficult instruments in the orchestra to play, it is affected significantly by heat and humidity, and sometimes even the experts have trouble. The highest notes are brassy, the lowest solemn and rather noble.

The highest-pitched of the dozen members of the horn family is the C-alto horn, little used today. The lowest in pitch is eighteen feet long. The family also includes the post horn, a straight tube four feet in length.

Vivaldi, Bach in the *Brandenburg* Concerto No. 1, and Handel in *Water Music* and *Julius Caesar* featured the horn. Haydn used horns in his early symphonies and wrote two concertos for horn, the first of them (in D) ranked in excellence with four horn concertos by Mozart (K. 412, 417, 447, and 495). Haydn, Mozart, and Beethoven used the horn extensively in orchestral work. The latter also wrote a sextet for two horns and strings (Op. 81b).

Schumann composed his *Konzertstücke* for four horns and starred the horn in his Adagio and Allegro (Op. 70). Brahms wrote a trio for horn, violin, and piano (Op. 40); Richard Strauss composed two well-known horn concertos; Hindemith, who wrote for almost every instrument you can name, produced sonatas for horn and piano in 1939 and 1943.

Trombone: *Tromba* is Italian for trumpet; a *trombone* is thus a "big trumpet." It is an old instrument, dating back at least to 200 A.D., and was the first of the brasses to be perfected. In the 1400s it was frequently used in church music and in so-called tower music, which was performed in clock towers by bands. They played music to signal the time and also to entertain the town folk. In those days there were four sizes of trombone, one for each singing voice, but over the years the soprano and alto gradually disappeared, leaving a mellow tenor and a noble-sounding bass. The one most used in orchestras is the tenor version, constructed in three sections, including a U-shaped slide, all totaling some nine feet of brass. It used to be called the *sackbut*, from a couple of French words that translated as "push-pull." The trombone usually has no valves or keys; the tones change as the musician moves the slide to seven basic positions. Many notes are attained not by slide shifting, however, but by the musician's breath and his or her lip movement.

Today's symphony orchestras usually have two tenor trombones and one bass. Like other brasses, trombones are sometimes muted and, as everyone knows, can also produce amusing *glissando* (sliding) sounds, which are a result of the musician blowing and moving the slide at the same time.

Jack Teagarden and others helped make the trombone a big jazz instrument. Hindemith and several unListed classical artists wrote solo works for it, but not a lot of classical solo trombone music has been composed.

Composers started putting trombones into their work around 1600. The first Listed artist to use them was Monteverdi, who had five working as an accompaniment to his chorus of underworld spirits in his opera *L'Orfeo*. The instrument went out of fashion during the Baroque era and was revived by post-Baroque/Classical Gluck for his *Orfeo* and for the opera *Alceste*. Mozart jumped aboard and used three trombones in the graveyard scene of the second act of *Don Giovanni*. Beethoven put three in the finale of his Fifth Symphony; Brahms, Wagner, and Richard Strauss all employed it; Stravinsky wrote *In Memoriam Dylan Thomas* for tenor, string quartet, and four trombones; and Rimsky-Korsakov composed a trombone concerto.

Tuba: The tuba family consists of at least six basic tubas, with several more offshoots. The core group includes soprano, alto, tenor, baritone, bass, and contrabass versions, but a principal tuba player in one symphony orchestra owns thirteen instruments and forty-odd mouthpieces. A true tuba specialist will change mouthpieces according to the particular music, to help keep his sounds in balance with the different instrumental sections of the orchestra. One mouthpiece might be best for lighter Berlioz music, for example, another for the organlike sounds of Bruckner, and still another for the unique tone color of Mahler. The tuba is the youngest, biggest, and lowest-pitched of the brasses. It wasn't invented until the 1820s and 1830s and wasn't brought into the orchestra until still later. Its tube is twelve to sixteen coiled feet long and is equipped with three to five valves. In the United States, the main orchestra tube is keyed in B-flat, with a range of about two octaves, all below middle C. The deepest of the family is the bass tuba, once called the bombardon, which starts a hair above the bottom of the piano keyboard and has a range of two and one-half octaves. The baritone tuba is sometimes called the baritone horn, and the tenor tuba, whose sound is similar to a tenor trombone's, is known also as the euphonium. John Philip Sousa thought it would be a good idea for marching-band purposes to make the big bell a removable part of the tuba, and his resulting creation is called the sousaphone. Its coiled body is round, rather than oval like the orchestral tuba, with an open center that allows the musician to play it while carrying it on his or her shoulder.

The tuba's sound, like that of the other brass instruments, comes from the vibration of the lips against the mouthpiece. The very wide conical tube flares out into a very large bell, which points straight up.

Musicologist Arthur Elson had this to say about the tuba back in 1915:

> Wagner gave an impetus to the use of tubas, calling for five in his Trilogy. Here the two bass tubas are in F instead of E-flat. The tuba has been used as bass for three trombones in four-part harmony. It often takes the bass part of the brass group, sometimes in unison with the deeper trombones; and it has even been employed as a bass for strings.
>
> The tuba has not the smooth quality of the trombone, but its gruff harshness can be made very effective. Wagner employed this tone color in the first act of "Die Walküre" to picture the fierce character of Hunding. The weary Siegmund, driven by storm and pursuit, has taken refuge in Hunding's forest hut. Soon the footsteps of the returning warrior are heard outside; and just as he enters the door, the four tubas play the short, pregnant motive that represents him in the music. The effect of these tubas by themselves is impressively savage. In [Wagner's opera] "Siegfried," when the hero has found the lair of the dragon, that redoubtable monster utters many dragonine curses on the tubas, before meeting a well-merited death.

Most symphony orchestras have one tuba, which often plays with its mellow equal, the bass trombone. One can hear this in Tchaikovsky's Fourth Symphony (Tchaikovsky also uses a tuba to end the first movement of his Sixth Symphony). Wagner, as Elson suggests, was a big tuba fellow, giving it a part in the overture to Die Meistersinger as well as in other works. In fact, he mated a tuba and a French horn to produce what is still known as the Wagner tuba—although actually it is closer to a French horn. Bruckner and Richard Strauss both wrote for this new Wagner toy, Strauss giving it solos in Don Quixote.

Wagner's influence on behalf of the tuba was not lost. In 1969, there was a ski instructor and part-time jug-band musician in Aspen, Colorado, who sometimes played Wagner's music on the tuba while

skiing. His full name, so far as anyone knew, was Jerry Tuba. Despite
their mutual appreciation of the tuba, Jerry was a much nicer fellow
than Wagner.

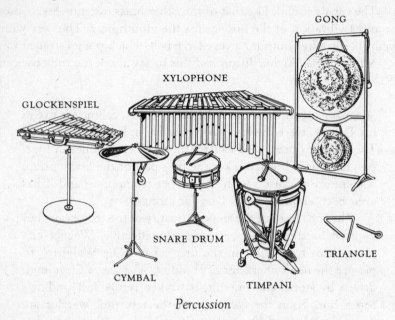

Percussion

PERCUSSION

Percussion instruments are devices that are banged, shaken, or tapped.
There are two kinds of percussion instruments—those just for banging (untuned percussion) and those that have definite notes (tuned
percussion). The old bass drum is an example of the former, the
xylophone an example of the latter. They startle, arouse, incite, and
awaken.

Perhaps surprisingly, the simple drum is actually not the first
percussion instrument, by several thousand years; banging a stone
with a stick came much earlier. So did notched sticks, rattles, and
hollowed log drums. Musical stones go back to 2300 B.C., which is way
before Rolling ones. Mesopotamians had a rattle called a sistrum.
Cymbals, in contrast, are relatively recent, dating perhaps to 1000 B.C.
The percussion family includes ancient hourglass-shaped talking
drums, modern metal oil drums, chains jerked in and out of boxes,
half coconut shells banged together, washboards, cowbells, wind-bells,
thunder sheets, and even brake drums.

Lots of percussion instruments do not make the average symphony orchestra. But lots do. Real anvils are used in Wagner's *Die
Meistersinger*. In Mahler's Sixth Symphony a wooden box is hit with

a large mallet. Vaughan Williams calls for a wind machine in *Sinfonia Antarctica*.

TUNED PERCUSSION

Timpani: Timpani is a good enough word, often used, but non-musicians may be more familiar with the alternate term kettledrums. These are the most important orchestral percussion instruments—with all respect to Mr. Mahler and his hammered box and to Herr Wagner's anvils. A kettledrum is a large copper (or now sometimes fiber glass) bowl with a skin stretched over one end and devices for tightening it to change the tuning. (Screws around the head are used to tighten for fine tuning, and a foot pedal is used to change the pitch during a performance.)

The drummer uses fourteen-inch wooden sticks with both hard and soft heads. Earlier versions of the drum were flatter than today's and were slung on both sides of a horse so that a mounted player could beat them while riding. Turkish armies used them when fighting Crusaders in 1300. Nowadays, however, one rarely sees a horse at such concert halls as the Kennedy Center in Washington or Lincoln Center in New York. Perhaps out West in Los Angeles. More likely, even there the timpanist stands or sits on a chair surrounded by five different-sized kettledrums arranged in a semicircle, the instruments resting in cradles of crossed sticks or on metal frames. A timpanist needs to be a perfectionist. One mistake, and the whole audience knows it.

Handel and Bach rarely used timpani. Haydn, Mozart, and Schubert occasionally called for a pair of them. One of the early solo timpani parts was in Haydn's Symphony No. 103, nicknamed the *Drum Roll* Symphony. Beethoven was the first to employ them fully; there are fine timpani passages in his Sixth, Seventh, and Ninth Symphonies and in his Violin Concerto, Piano Concerto No. 5, Mass in D, and *Fidelio*. Berlioz put two pairs in *Symphonie fantastique* and wrote in another work for sixteen pairs—typical of his extravagant style of orchestration. Mahler has good timpani action in many of his compositions, as does Stravinsky in *The Rite of Spring* and Bartók in his Concerto for Orchestra.

Xylophone and Marimba: The xylophone is a familiar instrument, made of strips of hard wood, each tuned to a note, assembled like a piano keyboard. The player taps them with wooden or hard rubber xylophone tappers. Today's model is not too different from those in use hundreds of years ago. One of the most famous xylophone passages is the "skeleton bones" section of Saint-Saëns's *Danse macabre*. Saint-Saëns also used it in *Carnival of the Animals*, Mahler in his Sixth

Symphony, Shostakovich in his Fifth, Stravinsky in *The Firebird*, and Bartók in Music for Strings, Percussion, and Celesta.

The marimba is a deeper-toned xylophone, popular in Mexico and Central America, where there are whole marimba orchestras.

Glockenspiel: The history of the glockenspiel is uncertain. The word, in German, means "play of bell," and the instrument probably is an offshoot of a bell lyre used in military marching bands. One type looks like a xylophone with metal bars instead of wooden ones; it has been in the orchestra in this form since the late 1700s. Another has pianolike keys, although not many of these are used today. Mozart wrote the key-type into *The Magic Flute* (it is played by the character Papageno). Ravel used a glockenspiel in *Daphnis et Chloé*, Handel in his oratorio *Saul*, Wagner in *Die Meistersinger*, and Richard Strauss in *Don Juan*.

Cimbalom: The cimbalom is a sibling of the old dulcimer, which originated in western Asia in the Middle Ages and came to Europe in the twelfth century. For centuries it was a basic instrument of Gypsy music. It is stringed, trapezoid-shaped, and played with light hand-held hammers. Bartók used one in his First Rhapsody for Violin and Orchestra, Stravinsky in *Renard*.

UNTUNED PERCUSSION

Snare Drum: The snare drum came to the orchestra in the 1700s from the army, where it was slung at a band player's side. It is still used this way in marching bands; in the orchestra, it sits on a stand. It has two drumheads (unlike the kettledrum), with long, thin strings of metal, called snares, stretched across the lower one. The player hits the top skin, the air hits the bottom skin, the skin hits the snares, and out of it all comes a rattling noise. Gluck borrowed it from the military for his operas; Rossini gave it a solo role in his overture to *La gazza ladra* (The thieving magpie) in 1817; Berlioz used it in *Symphonie fantastique*. Rimsky-Korsakov, Shostakovich, and Ravel all liked it, and it plays a major part in Ravel's *Boléro*.

Tenor Drum: This is a cylindrical drum without snares—just a plain drum, between the bass and snare drum in size. Berlioz, not surprisingly, had six in his *Te Deum*. Wagner put them in his operas; Richard Strauss and Stravinsky also used them.

Tambourin de Provence: This is a double-headed drum with a single snare over the upper head. Bizet employed one in his *L'Arlésienne* Suites.

Bass Drum: The bass drum is the largest orchestral drum—or nonorchestral drum, for that matter. When it has only one head, as is common in England, it is called a gong drum, but not many of these are found in American orchestras. The bass drum also came from the military band and probably originated in Turkey. Of Listed composers, the first to use it was Gluck. Mozart put one in *Abduction from the Seraglio* in 1782; Haydn in his Symphony No. 100, the *Military*; Beethoven in his Ninth Symphony; Stravinsky in *The Rite of Spring*; Puccini in *Madame Butterfly*; Tchaikovsky in the *1812* Overture; and Prokofiev in *Lieutenant Kijé*. Verdi, in his wonderful *Requiem*, called for the largest bass drum available. Many composers use the bass drum for funeral marches.

Cymbals: Cymbals are two thin plates of brass, which can be clashed together or brushed lightly. Alternatively, one can be held and hit with a stick or mounted on a stand and hit with two sticks. Bartók used a suspended cymbal in his Sonata for Two Pianos and Percussion; Stravinsky favored a cymbal struck by a triangle. Mozart included them in *Abduction from the Seraglio*, Debussy in *Fêtes*, and Berlioz in his "Queen Mab" scherzo.

Triangle: A metal rod, bent in the shape of a seven-inch equilateral triangle, and struck with a thin steel rod, the triangle is suspended from a stand or from the player's hand. A famous, albeit small, triangle role can be found in Liszt's Piano Concerto in E-flat. Rossini (in the overture to *The Thieving Magpie*) and Wagner (in *Siegfried* and *Die Meistersinger*) helped get it into the orchestral club.

Tambourine: A very small, one-headed drum with metal discs around the side, the tambourine is commonly thought of as coming from Spain but actually had its origins in ancient Mesopotamia. It can be shaken, hit with a hand, banged against a knee, or rubbed with a thumb. In *Petrushka*, Stravinsky had one dropped on the floor. Karl Maria von Weber is credited with giving it orchestral status.

Castanets: Castanets are technically concussion rather than percussion instruments, since they are two similar objects—hollowed pieces of wood—banged together. In the orchestra, they are usually mounted on a stick and are used to give a Spanish flavor to music. One example of orchestral use is in Prokofiev's Piano Concerto No. 3.

Chinese Wood Block: A Chinese wood block is simply that: a wood block, usually a teak rectangle six inches or so long, partly hollow, and struck with a drumstick. Prokofiev put it in both his Fifth and Sixth Symphonies.

Tam-tam: This is basically another name for the gong, though purists make some distinctions between the two. Ravel's *Daphnis et Chloé* has not only a tam-tam but almost every other percussion instrument.

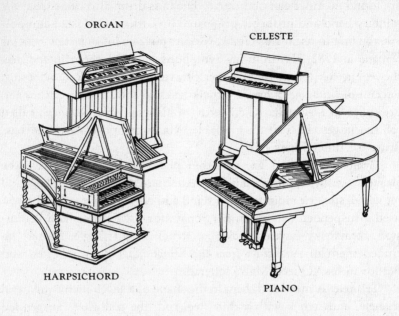

ORGAN

CELESTE

HARPSICHORD

PIANO

Keyboard Family

KEYBOARD INSTRUMENTS

Piano, Harpsichord, and Clavichord: The piano, invented in Florence in the early 1700s, was originally known as the *pianoforte*, Italian for "soft-loud." The keys control a mechanism that culminates in little hammers hitting strings. A combination of three foot pedals and dampers controls whether the strings continue to vibrate once hit or are stilled. As everyone knows, the range of sound over the keyboard is wide, from very low to very high. Mozart had a piano—rather than a harpsichord (more on this below)—but the piano of his time was quite different from that used by Liszt, which by then (the mid-1800s) had a cast-iron frame and much thicker strings. Writing for the Mozart piano was not the same as writing for the Liszt piano, but closer to it than writing for the harpsichord.

The piano is used infrequently as an orchestral instrument, though Stravinsky included it in *Petrushka*, Bartók in his *Dance Suite*, and Saint-Saëns in *Carnival of the Animals*. And, of course, there are myriad piano concertos.

Before Mozart, in Baroque days, there were three important keyboard instruments: the organ, the clavichord, and the harpsichord.

The harpsichord had two keyboards instead of one, and its strings were plucked by quills instead of hit with hammers. As works of many Listed composers illustrate, it was a very popular solo instrument in its time and has enjoyed a big revival in the recent movement back to original-instrument music. The harpsichord's sound is bright—some say "silvery," some "tinny"—but cannot be sustained like the piano's. There is just one brief "ping," of the same softness or loudness regardless of how lightly or heavily the key is struck. The harpsichord cannot produce the rising crescendo and falling decrescendo of the pianos used by Mozart, Beethoven, or Liszt.

In the 1600s and 1700s, it was more common for the average home to have the smaller and much less expensive clavichord. Basically a rectangular box with a keyboard along one long side, the clavichord combined keyboard and strings. It produced a small, gentle sound, good for a small room but not for a concert hall or as part of an orchestra. In one sense it was more like the piano than the harpsichord in that the string was hit (albeit with a small blade rather than a hammer) instead of plucked. A great deal of clavichord music was written before the instrument was replaced by the piano in the late 1700s.

Of Listed composers, Haydn was the first to compose for the piano, with Mozart just behind him. They were into études, sonatas, and concertos. Beethoven is famous not only for sonatas and concertos, but also for short pieces such as his "bagatelles" that foreshadowed the brief works called character pieces (under many individual names) by later composers.

Chopin, who wrote almost entirely for the piano, used such terms as "impromptus" and "preludes" for his works; Schumann's piano compositions included pieces called *Papillons* and *Kinderscenen*, and Schubert's included *Moments Musicaux*. Brahms wrote "nocturnes," Liszt "études" and "rhapsodies," and Mendelssohn (and others) pieces known as "capriccios" or "caprices." As we have seen, Grieg and Dvořák were famous piano composers, as were Debussy, Ravel, Stravinsky, and Fauré. Later came Bartók and Hindemith.

Famous piano concertos noted earlier include three by Bartók; five by Beethoven; No. 1 and No. 2 by Brahms; No. 1 and No. 2 by Chopin; one by Grieg; two by Mendelssohn; many exciting ones by Mozart, including but not limited to K. 271, 450, 453, 459, 466, 488, 491, 503, 537, and 595; Nos. 1, 2, and 3 by Prokofiev; one for the left hand in D and another in G by Ravel; No. 4 (and others) by Saint-Saëns; one by Schumann; No. 1 by Shostakovich; and at least No. 1 by Tchaikovsky.

Haydn wrote sixty piano sonatas, Mozart seventeen, Beethoven thirty-two, Schubert ten or so, Brahms three, and Liszt his very famous B Minor sonata. Ravel composed a piano "sonatine" and Debussy a famous sonata for violin and piano.

The most famous harpsichord composer is Bach. Others on The List include Handel, Rameau, and the great French master Couperin. Though the harpsichord was replaced by the piano in the late eighteenth century, in the late nineteenth and twentieth a back-to-the-original movement arose. A great deal of harpsichord music is available today.

Celesta: Invented in 1886, the celesta is similar to a keyboard glockenspiel and looks like a miniature piano, with black and white keys which operate hammers that in turn strike metal plates. It produces a soft, silvery sound, ranging from middle C to the highest notes of the piano. Tchaikovsky heard about one and was perhaps the first Listed composer to use it, putting it in the "Dance of the Sugar Plum Fairy" in the *Nutcracker* Suite. It earned a title spot in Bartók's *Music for Strings, Percussion, and Celesta.*

Organ: Every churchgoer knows that the organ is a keyboard instrument in which keyboards and pedals force air into a series of pipes, causing them to sound. The big difference between it and the other keyboard instruments is that pipes, rather than strings, are the operative sound-makers. Organs have been around for a couple of thousand years, and organ music peaked, as one might suspect, with Bach in the first half of the eighteenth century. The organ of Bach's time was quite a different instrument from the one used during the Romantic period, although in the twentieth century there has been a return to the Baroque version.

The organ is not put to work in most symphonic music, but it is used occasionally, in part because so many Listed composers were organ virtuosos. Saint-Saëns's Symphony No. 3 in C Minor, known as the *Organ* Symphony, is the leading example. Liszt and Franck wrote organ compositions, and Hindemith, who composed for everything, as we have seen, wrote a concerto for organ and orchestra as well as other organ-and-chamber-orchestra works.

CHAPTER VI

Compact-Disc Discography

A discography is a descriptive list of recordings grouped by category, composer, performer, or date of release. This particular one is related to the fifty Starter Kits and is designed to help lead readers toward the best record-shop selections of those 250 compositions.

It recommends only compact discs—in today's market, the best way to go. The sound quality of CDs is superior to that of LPs or cassettes, and because CDs are read by laser beam, there is no wear or deterioration in use. Unless your dog eats it, or you beat it with a hammer or smear peanut butter on it, a compact disc should outlast you.

For readers who aren't into compact discs and don't want to be, because of the cost of equipment and recordings, this discography should still be useful. Record-store people and catalogues can quickly tell you whether cassettes of these CD recommendations are available. In many cases the same performances will be on cassette, and most of the time the cassette version would still be a recommended choice for the Starter Kit composition. And in all cases the CD recommendation provides a sound point for beginning your search.

Unfortunately, since the Starter Kits are across-the-board representations of the composers, they will rarely match up perfectly with compact discs. The Beethoven Starter Kit, for example, calls for one symphony, one piano concerto, one (his only) violin concerto, one piano sonata, and one string quartet—a little of everything except vocal music. But compact discs are not put together that way. No single disc has an orchestra playing a symphony, a star pianist working with an orchestra on a piano concerto, a violin virtuoso and orchestra performing a violin concerto, a piano soloist alone offering a sonata, and a string quartet.

As a result, in nearly all cases you must buy four or five compact discs for each composer to satisfy the Starter Kit requirements. This can become expensive. Having purchased almost every disc recommended in this chapter, I have the weakened bank account to prove it. The good news is that all who take this route will find themselves not only with the 250 Starter Kit selections but with perhaps twice that number of compositions—a lifetime collection of wonderful music from these fifty fine composers (and occasionally from other artists, although I have tried to limit that).

Here is an example of how it will work:

One Starter Kit selection for Beethoven is his Fifth Symphony. Our discography recommendation for the Fifth is the version by Herbert von Karajan and the Berlin Philharmonic—a disc which, however, also includes the Eighth Symphony and the *Fidelio* Overture, two non-Starter Kit compositions. Similarly, the Starter Kit calls for Beethoven's Piano Sonata No. 23 (*Appassionata*). Our recommendation is a recording by Vladimir Ashkenazy—and on this disc he also plays Sonatas No. 8 (*Pathétique*) and No. 14 (*Moonlight*). An extra string quartet comes with the Beethoven Starter Kit selection of his Quartet No. 13 in B-flat, Op. 130. But the designated piano concerto, No. 5 in E-flat, is long enough to fill a disc by itself, as is the violin concerto. The final scorecard: five compact discs to cover the five Starter Kit recommendations for Beethoven, yielding ten of his most famous compositions.

Rarely are more than five discs needed per composer. The few exceptions are in cases where a composition is long enough to take up two or three discs, as sometimes happens with operas, oratorios, and masses. Examples include Handel's *Messiah*, Haydn's *Creation*, and Bach's Mass in B Minor. In most cases, highlights or excerpts of these long compositions are available on one disc, which still provides an hour or so of that work. Pocketbook and personal taste must rule; with rare exceptions, whether the Starter Kit recommendation is for excerpts or full productions, the record stores will also have the other version by the same musicians.

Warning: No discography can be up to date, as new discs come out, and others are taken off the market, daily. Some of these soon reappear, sometimes with different prices, and some seem to fade away into the Great Disc Store in the Sky. Record stores may have on their shelves items that have left the catalogues, and obviously no store can stock all catalogue listings. It is an imperfect world. My guess is that a dozen or more recommendations here will have vanished by the time you look for them. Do not despair; in 99 percent of the cases, viable substitutes exist of the same selection, and in the other one percent your needs can be filled with a choice from the Top Ten. By definition, the Starter Kit nominees are the war-horses, the compositions that have been performed and recorded by the greatest artists of the last several decades. Some few classic recommendations, in fact, although not many, go back before stereophonic sound. Several of the superstar conductors and some of the superstar soloists in this discography are now dead, yet their performances remain unequaled. It is improbable that many new discs arriving in the record stores tomorrow will have better renditions than those now on the market of a Beethoven concerto or a Bach cantata. New music all-stars will emerge, of course— only yesterday there was no Anne-Sophie Mutter on the violin, and an unknown George Szell is inevitably standing in the wings—but the older members of the Hall of Fame will not then be cast into darkness.

In any event, beginning collectors should not be overly concerned about scrupulous adherence to the recommendations in this chapter. My purpose will have been accomplished if a reader is led first to Mozart, then to his symphonies as part of that genius's most famous works, then to the best-known of those symphonies, and finally to Nos. 39, 40, and 41 as the supreme examples. Of secondary importance to the average beginner is whether the Mozart Symphony No. 40 he owns is the Karl Boehm and the Berlin Philharmonic version, the Sir Neville Marriner and the Academy of St.-Martin-in-the-Fields version, or the Sir Charles Mackerras and the London Philharmonic version.

This is not to suggest that all of those sound the same; even an untrained ear can hear differences—as an untrained palate can taste differences in wines without being able to describe them as the professional wine tasters do. But no second-rate orchestras or conductors are cited above, and most of us amateurs would be as happy with a Boehm as with a Mackerras. Also, in rare cases the recommendation is for the *only* rendition of that work.

Still, the recommendations shoot for the best. Like the rest of the book, they reflect research into expert opinion rather than personal appraisal. Sources include books, magazines, personal interviews, newspaper reviews, and commentary on classical-music radio stations. Bill Parker's *Building a Classical Record Library*, published by Minnesota Public Radio, Inc. and recommended to the author by Robert Aubrey Davis, classical-music superexpert on Washington, D.C.'s public-radio and TV station WETA, was particularly helpful. And Parker notes that *his* recommendations are a distillation of material from *High Fidelity*, *Stereo Review*, *Musical America*, *Ovation*, and *Fanfare* magazines, plus selected reviews from *Gramophone*, *American Rec-*

ord Guide, Opera News, and Canada's *Magic Flute.* Another source was *The Record Shelf Guide to the Classical Repertoire* (Prima) by another knowledgeable public-radio commentator, Jim Svejda of KUSC in Los Angeles. A third was *Discovering Great Music* by Roy Hemming (New-market Press).

The greatest help, perhaps, came from several editions of *The Penguin Guide to Compact Discs, Cassettes and LPs,* published by the Penguin Group in London. All who want to buy recordings should equip themselves with the latest copy of *Penguin,* which rates record-ings on a one-, two-, and three-star system, awards a rosette in ex-traspecial cases, identifies a few real bargains, and, most useful of all, offers a critical narrative review of each selection. Some translating to American labels is necessary when dealing with this British publica-tion—for example, if shopping in the United States you must think *Angel* when you see *HMV* (for His Master's Voice)—but a little work with a *Penguin Guide* in one hand and the mandatory *Opus* catalogue in the other (plus a friendly record-store professional if needed) will easily bridge these British/American difficulties.

As in all matters, tastes differ and people sometimes have sharply different views on orchestras, conductors, and individual perform-ances. Parker gives the example of a Wagner opera on Deutsche Gram-mophon chosen as one of the hundred most inspired recordings of all time by one group of editors, while the opinion of another veteran reviewer was that in twenty years of listening to music no record had left him so perplexed and disheartened.

To limit the number of discs and avoid duplication while still presenting the most outstanding performances, some compromising was necessary. I have taken the middle ground, concentrating on excel-lence, accepting a minimum of repetition, and also considering the pocketbook.

Even with the best intentions, some duplication is inevitable to fill Starter Kit requirements, especially when they contain several short works. For example, in the case of Ravel it is essential to have his *Boléro,* which is only seventeen minutes long. But it is currently impos-sible to get his other Starter Kit compositions on available CDs with-out duplicating a *Boléro.*

There is a totally different and relatively cheap route toward a wonderful sound library, complete with expert commentary, if you are fortunate enough to live in an area served by one or more good classical-music radio stations. Buy an inexpensive tape deck and a couple hundred blank ninety-minute cassette tapes, from discount stores or on sale. With patience—a lot of patience—and listening—a lot of listening—in three or four years you will be able to record almost all of the compositions recommended in the Starter Kits (plus hundreds from the Master Collection and Top Ten lists). It is easier if the radio stations in your area offer a monthly program guide so that you can plan in advance, but it can be done in any case for those prepared to substitute classical-music listening for television viewing. The radio listener obviously must take what he or she gets in the way of conductors and orchestras, but the station programmers are apt to choose only the best artists, except for some occasional experimenting, and before long a persevering home recorder will have two or three versions of many Starter Kit recommendations. In time, he or she is guaranteed 90 percent of the 250. Although the sound is unlikely to equal that of a CD played on a more expensive home system, this record-it-yourself process is an excellent way to get started with classical music. And if a novice is fortunate enough to have commentators of high caliber, he or she can learn a great deal while collecting.

One trick, if you have a VCR, and especially a VCR with stereo sound, is to hook it up to an FM radio and record the radio music on a six-hour videotape. This enables you to do a lot of recording when not at home, or when busy with other things. At your leisure, the sound from the videotape can be edited onto shorter blank cassette tapes. Some sound quality will be lost, but there is no cheaper way to create a magnificent classical library. And it's an enjoyable treasure hunt. One serious disadvantage is that when playing cassettes—store-bought or home-recorded—you don't have the instant access to individual compositions or parts of them that you get with a CD.

Enjoy.

1. JOHANN SEBASTIAN BACH

The Starter Kit calls for only one *Brandenburg* Concerto—just enough to get the taste of these six ultrafamous compositions, which still place as high as third or fourth in audience surveys conducted by classical-music radio stations. It is almost impossible to find one alone on a compact disc; in any case this is Bach, and little attention should be paid the rules. The recommendation here is for all six, on two discs. This is typical of the difficulties in marrying Starter Kit choices to compact discs. Similarly, while the Starter Kit proposes Bach's Concerto for Two Violins, S. 1043, the recommended compact disc also carries two more violin concertos. There is no way to have too much

Bach, and here, because of the *Brandenburg* Concertos and the length of the Mass in B Minor, you will want seven CDs as a starter.

Violin Concertos No. 1 in A Minor, S. 1041, and No. 2 in E, S. 1042,
      and Double Violin Concerto, S. 1043
Angel CD 47005
Mutter, English Chamber Orchestra, Accardo

Brandenburg Concertos (six), S. 1046–51
Philips 400076 (two discs)
Academy of St. Martin-in-the-Fields, Marriner

Organ collection, including Toccata and Fugue in D Minor
London 417 711
Hurford, organist

Cantatas No. 80, Ein' feste Burg ist unser Gott, and No. 140, Wachet
      auf, ruft uns die Stimme
London 414 045-2
Fontana and other soloists, Hymnus Boys' Choir, Stuttgart Chamber
      Orchestra, Munchinger

Mass in B Minor
Deutsche Grammophon Archiv 415 514 (two discs)
Argenta and other soloists, English Baroque Soloists, Monteverdi
      Chorus, Gardiner

2. WOLFGANG AMADEUS MOZART

You need a lot of Mozart symphonies, a lot of his piano concertos, a sampling of other compositions, and highlights (at least) of one or more of his operas. Fortunately, there is a good way to get there with four discs. You can also choose to buy five, if you want more symphonies, and six if you remember and enjoyed the movie *Amadeus* and want the memorable *Requiem* Mass that was featured in it.

Symphonies No. 40 in G Minor and No. 41 in C (Jupiter)
Telarc CD 80139
Prague Chamber Orchestra, Mackerras

Piano Concertos No. 15 in B-flat and No. 21 in C
Philips 400 018
Brendel, Academy of St. Martin-in-the-Fields, Brendel, Marriner

Serenade No. 13 (Eine kleine Nachtmusik), K. 525; Divertimento for
 Strings No. 1 (K. 136); A Musical Joke, K. 522
Philips 412 269
Academy of St. Martin-in-the-Fields Chamber Ensemble, Marriner

The Magic Flute (highlights)
Angel CDC 47008
Popp, Bavarian Radio Symphony and Chorus, Haitink

BONUSES

Symphonies Nos. 38 in D and 39 in E-flat
Philips 426 283-2
Gardiner, English Baroque Soloists

Requiem Mass (No. 19) in D Minor, K. 626
Philips 411 420-2
Price, Dresden State Orchestra, Schreier

3. LUDWIG VAN BEETHOVEN

While the five listed discs constitute a wealth of Beethoven music, a little later on it is mandatory for you to pick up Symphonies Nos. 3, 6, 7, and 9, supplementing No. 5. Outstanding choices for Beethoven symphonies include Karajan and the Berlin Philharmonic, Boehm and the Vienna Philharmonic, Solti and the Chicago Symphony, and various performances by Bernstein and Marriner. The professionals find significant differences among these, some of which can be recognized by those of us who are less initiated. When dealing with conductors and orchestras of this caliber, individual taste clearly comes into play.

Symphonies No. 5 in C Minor and No. 8 in F; Overture to Fidelio
Deutsche Grammophon 419 051
Berlin Philharmonic Orchestra, Karajan

Violin Concerto in D
Angel CDC 47002
Perlman, Philharmonia Orchestra, Giulini

String Quartets No. 13 in B-flat, Op. 130; No. 8 in E Minor, Op. 59,
    No. 1
Calliope CAL 9637
Talich Quartet

Piano Concerto No. 5 in E-flat (Emperor)
Philips 416 215
Arrau, Dresden State Orchestra, Sir Colin Davis

Piano Sonatas Nos. 8 (Pathétique), 14 (Moonlight), and 23 (Appas-
    sionata)
London 410 260
Ashkenazy

4. RICHARD WAGNER

Satisfying the Starter Kit requirement for the *Siegfried Idyll* is simple
enough; the problem then is what to do about operas. Not everyone
wants a zillion hours of a heard-but-not-seen *Ring* cycle, even if those
four operas are the most representative of Wagner. Complete renditions of the *Ring* operas and six or seven others are available, of
course, but there are several other options—collections of orchestral
excerpts, collections of arias from different operas, and, in some cases,
highlights of one opera. I recommend a Wagner stew, without complete versions of any single opera, exhibiting personal prejudice
against unseen opera for the amateur collector. Wagner buffs will not
concur.

Siegfried Idyll and opera orchestral and choral excerpts, including:
    Der fliegende Holländer: Overture; Lohengrin: Prelude to Act I
    and The Bridal Chorus; Die Meistersinger: Prelude; Tannhäuser:
    Overture; Tristan und Isold; Prelude and Liebestod; Die Walkure:
    Ride of the Valkyries; Parsifal: Prelude and Good Friday Music
Deutsche Grammophon 413 849 4 (four discs)
Berlin Philharmonic Orchestra, Kubelik; Bayreuth Festival Orchestra,
    Böhm, Gerdes, Karajan

Vocal collections: Selections from Götterdämmerung, Lohengrin, Tannhäuser, Tristan und Isolde
Chandos CHAN 8930
Jones, Cologne Symphony Orchestra

5. FRANZ JOSEPH HAYDN

Five Haydn discs provide a wonderful Haydn collection. Many splendid options exist for the symphonies, including Walter and the Columbia Symphony, Sir Colin Davis and the Concertgebouw, Solti and the London Philharmonic, Hogwood and the Academy of Ancient Music, Dorati and the Philharmonia Hungarica, Karajan and the Berlin Philharmonic, Bernstein and the Vienna Philharmonic, and Tate and the English Chamber Orchestra. You cannot go wrong with any of these. The choice below is based on excellence plus cost-effectiveness. For the *Creation*, other fine choices include Karajan and the Berlin Philharmonic and Marriner with the Academy of St. Martin-in-the-Fields. The string-quartet recommendation includes both the *Emperor* and *Sunrise* movements.

Symphonies Nos. 94 in G (Surprise), 96 in D (Miracle), and 100 in G (Military)
London 417 718
Philharmonia Hungarica, Dorati

Symphonies No. 103 in E-flat (Drum Roll) and No. 104 in D (London)
Deutsche Grammophon 410517-2
Berlin Philharmonic Orchestra, Karajan
English Chamber Orchestra, Tate

Horn Concertos No. 1 and No. 2; Trumpet Concerto in E-flat; Divertimento à trois in E-flat
Nimbus NIM 5010
Thompson, Wallace, Philharmonia Orchestra, Warren-Green

String Quartets Opus 33, No. 3; Opus 76, Nos. 3 and 4
Intercord CD 820729
Melos Quartet

The Creation (Die Schopfung)
Deutsche Grammophon 43103S
Blegen, etc., Bavarian Radio Chorus and Symphony Orchestra, Bern-
stein

6. JOHANNES BRAHMS

Wilhelm Furtwängler's live 1952 performance of Brahms's First Symphony, in mono sound, is one classic. Bruno Walter's recording with
the CBS Symphony Orchestra is another. And there are many more
recent excellent choices. For history's sake, even though it is not
stereo, the recommendation here is for Furtwängler.

Symphony No. 1; Variations on a Theme of Haydn
Deutsche Grammophon 427 402 (mono)
Berlin Philharmonic Orchestra, Furtwängler

Piano Concerto No. 2 in B-flat; Haydn Variations
RCA 60536
Gilels, Chicago Symphony Orchestra, Reiner

Violin Concerto in D; Beethoven violin concerto
RCA RCD1 5402
Heifetz, Chicago Symphony Orchestra, Reiner

Clarinet Quintet in B Minor; Mozart Quintet
EM1 CDM7 63116
de Peyer, Melos Ensemble

Piano miniatures: Intermezzi, Op. 117; 6 Pieces, Op. 118; Variations
on a Theme by Paganini, Op. 35
Deutsche Grammophon 431 123-2
Zilberstein

7. FRANZ SCHUBERT

Although it is only one of many, Bruno Walter's rendition of Schubert's famous Unfinished Symphony is generally accepted as special.
Another top-rated version is Sir Neville Marriner's on Philips. If you

want to add a fifth disc to those given here, a strong recommendation is Wilhelm Furtwängler's rendition of Schubert's Symphony No. 9 in C (the Great), on Deutsche Grammophon with the Berlin Philharmonic. Recorded in the early 1950s, this is a classic. One excellent set of all Schubert symphonies is Claudio Abbado's with the Chamber Orchestra of Europe on Deutsche Grammophon.

Symphony No. 8 in B Minor (Unfinished)
Odyssey YT 30314
Columbia Symphony, Walter

Piano Quintet in A (Trout); String Quartet No. 14 (Death and the maiden)
London 417 459
Curzon, Vienna Octet, Vienna Philharmonic Orchestra Quartet

Fantasia in C (Wanderer); Impromptus No. 3 and No. 4; Piano Sonata No. 21 in B-flat
RCA 6527
Rubinstein

Die schöne Müllerin (song cycle)
Deutsche Grammophon 415 186
Fischer-Dieskau, Moore

8. ROBERT SCHUMANN

If you want to go beyond the Starter Kit into all four Schumann symphonies, try the set by Bernard Haitink on the Philips label with the Amsterdam Concertgebouw Orchestra. The Starter Kit proposes No. 1 and No. 4.

Symphonies No. 1 in B-flat (Spring) and No. 4 in D Minor
Deutsche Grammophon 415 274
Vienna Philharmonic Orchestra, Bernstein

Piano Concerto in A Minor; Weber's Konzertstück
Philips 412 251
Brendel, London Symphony Orchestra, Abbado

Piano Quartet in E-flat, Op. 47; Piano Quintet in E-flat, Op. 44
Philips 420 791
Beaux Arts Trio, Rhodes, Bettelheim

Fantasia in C, Fantasiestücke
Philips 411 049
Brendel

Dichterliebe (song cycle); Liederkreis (song cycle)
Deutsche Grammophon 415 190
Fischer-Dieskau, Eschenbach

9. GEORGE FRIDERIC HANDEL

A choice to be made here is what to do about the *Messiah*—whether
to buy a complete version, consisting of two or three compact discs
(depending on the label) and lasting for the afternoon, or to settle for
one disc of highlights. In either case, several sound options are available. Another decision is whether you want authentic period instruments or modern ones. In the last few years there has been a big trend
toward using "original" instruments for Baroque music, even though
our ears are less accustomed to them. Good choices for the *Messiah*
include (but are not limited to) Harry Christophers, Sir Georg Solti,
Sir Colin Davis, Andrew Davis, Christopher Hogwood, Nicklaus Har-
noncourt, and Sir Neville Marriner. While the recommendation here
is for Solti's highlights, once you have completed the Starter Kit shelf
you may want to come back to the *Messiah* and supplement with a full
version by someone else.

Water Music: Suites Nos. 1, 2, and 3 (complete)
Deutsche Grammophon 410 525
English Concert, Pinnock

Music for the Royal Fireworks; Handel concertos
Deutsche Grammophon Archiv 415 129
English Concert, Pinnock

Twelve concerti grossi, Op. 6, Nos. 1–12
Philips 410 048 (three discs)
Academy of St. Martin-in-the-Fields, Brown

(Or settle for one disc with Pinnock and the English Concert with four concertos, Op. 6, Nos. 5–8, Deutsche Grammophon 410-898-2.)

Trio Sonatas (for flute and violin), Op. 2, No. 1; (for violins), Op. 2, No. 3; Op. 5, No. 2 and No. 4; Violin Sonata in A, Op. 1, No. 3; Sonata for Two Violins in G Minor
Deutsche Grammophon Archiv 415 497
English Concert, Pinnock

Messiah (highlights) ·
London 417449
Chicago Symphony and Chorus, Solti

10. PETER ILYITCH TCHAIKOVSKY

Cheating is approved under the right circumstances, and circumstances provide the three big Tchaikovsky symphonies, Nos. 4, 5, and 6, in one excellent Russian two-disc set. Buy it, even if it does go beyond the Starter Kit. From there on, the issue is whether you want excerpts or full ballets, and whether you choose to limit your library to *Swan Lake*, the Starter Kit choice, or to add the *Nutcracker* and *Sleeping Beauty*. Complete ballets, suites, and excerpts all are available.

Symphonies Nos. 4, 5, and 6
Deutsche Grammophon 419 745 (two discs)
Leningrad Philharmonic Orchestra, Mravinsky

Piano Concerto No. 1 in B-flat Minor; Rachmaninoff Concerto No. 2
RCA 5912
Van Cliburn, RCA Symphony Orchestra, Kondrashin

Violin Concerto in D; Mendelssohn violin concerto
London 410 011
Chung, Montreal Symphony Orchestra, Dutoit

Romeo and Juliet (Fantasy Overture); Berlioz's Roméo et Juliette
Deutsche Grammophon 423 068
San Francisco Symphony Orchestra, Ozawa

Swan Lake (highlights)
Philips 420 872
London Symphony Orchestra, Monteux

11. FELIX MENDELSSOHN

Among choices bypassed for the famous Mendelssohn violin concerto are performances by Kyung-Wha Chung and the Montreal Symphony under Charles Dutoit, Cho-Liang Lin and the Philharmonia Orchestra under Michael Tilson Thomas, Sir Yehudi Menhuin and the Philharmonia under Kurtz, and a 1954 mono classic of Menhuin and Wilhelm Furtwängler's Berlin Philharmonic. You would enjoy any of these talented artists, orchestras, and conductors. Also, an outstanding set of Mendelssohn's five symphonies is Ernst von Dohnányi's with the Vienna Philharmonic on the London label. Another set is Abbado's with the London Symphony, one disc of which is chosen here for Symphonies No. 4 and 5.

Symphonies No. 4 in A (Italian) and No. 5 in D (Reformation)
Deutsche Grammophon 415-974
London Symphony Orchestra, Abbado

Violin Concerto in E Minor; Bruch Violin Concerto
Deutsche Grammophon 400 031
Mutter, Berlin Philharmonic Orchestra, Karajan

A Midsummer Night's Dream: Overture and incidental music
Angel CDC 47163
London Symphony Orchestra and Chorus, Previn

Overtures: Calm Sea and a Prosperous Voyage; Fair Melusina; The
    Hebrides (Fingal's Cave); A Midsummer Night's Dream; Ruy Blas;
    Trumpet Overture; Overture for Wind Instruments
Deutsche Grammophon 423 104
London Symphony Orchestra, Abbado

Octet in E-flat for Strings; String Quintet No. 2
Philips 420 400
Academy of St. Martin-in-the-Fields Chamber Ensemble

12. ANTONIN DVOŘÁK

In addition to the recommended choice for the *New World* Symphony, other outstanding performances are available on compact disc from Fritz Reiner and the Chicago Symphony, Christopher Dohnányi and the Cleveland Orchestra, and Klaus Tennstedt and the Berlin Philharmonic. And, since this is one of the most recorded of all symphonies, there are many more fine productions. Beyond the Starter Kit, a good bet is also Symphony No. 8 in G. Neeme Järvi and the Scottish National Orchestra have done all Dvořák's symphonies on Chandos discs, and their rendition of the Eighth is especially recommended.

Symphony No. 9 in E Minor (From the New World); American Suite
London 430702
Vienna Philharmonic Orchestra, Kondrashin

Cello Concerto in B Minor; Tchaikovsky's Rococo Variations
Deutsche Grammophon 413 819
Rostropovich, Berlin Philharmonic Orchestra, Karajan

Overtures: Carnaval, Op. 92; In Nature's Realm, Op. 91; Othello, Op.
  93; and Scherzo capriccioso
Chandos CHAN 8453
Ulster Orchestra, Handley

String Quartets No. 11 in C and No. 12 in F (American)
Calliope CAL 9617
Talich Quartet

Slavonic Dances
London 430 735
Royal Philharmonic Orchestra, Dorati

13. FRANZ LISZT

One option is both orchestrated and solo piano versions of some of Liszt's famous *Hungarian Rhapsodies*. If you feel this is too much rhapsody, substitute the composer's *Faust* Symphony, preferably by Sir Thomas Beecham and the Royal Philharmonia Orchestra on

Angel. The selections bypass Liszt's famous and familiar *Liebesträume*
music, which you can have by substituting a Jorge Bolet piano sonata
on London for the Brendel sonata listed below.

Piano Concertos No. 1 in E-flat and No. 2 in A
Deutsche Grammophon 423 571
Zimerman, Boston Symphony Orchestra, Ozawa

Les préludes, Tasso and other tone poems
London 417 513
London Philharmonic Orchestra, Solti

Hungarian Rhapsodies Nos. 1–6
Philips 412 724
Leipzig Gewandhaus Orchestra, Masur

Piano Sonata in B Minor; Deux légendes; La lugubre gondola
Philips 410 040
Brendel

Hungarian Rhapsodies, complete
Deutsche Grammophon 423 925 (two discs)
Szidon, pianist

14. FRÉDÉRIC CHOPIN

Arthur Rubinstein is the acknowledged master interpreter of Chopin's solo piano music—ballade, scherzo, sonata, polonaise, waltz, or
whatever. An excellent substitute for all fourteen waltzes is Dinu
Lipatti on EMI.

Piano Concertos No. 1 in E Minor and No. 2 in F Minor
Deutsche Grammophon 415 970
Zimmerman, Los Angeles Philharmonic Orchestra, Giulini

Ballades Nos. 1–4; Scherzi Nos. 1–4
RCA RCD 7156
Rubinstein

Sonatas No. 2 and No. 3; Fantaisie in F Minor
RCA 5616
Rubinstein

Polonaises Nos. 1–7
RCA 5615
Rubinstein

Waltzes Nos. 1–14
RCA RCD1-5492
Rubinstein

15. IGOR STRAVINSKY

While the opera-oratorio *Oedipus Rex* is important enough to be included in the Starter Kit and while representative of the composer's full works, it really is not nearly as much fun to listen to as the *Firebird* ballet, offered here as a substitute.

Symphony of Psalms; works by Poulenc and Bernstein
CBS MK 44710
English Bach Festival Chorus, London Symphony Orchestra, Bernstein

Symphony in C; Symphony in Three Movements
London 414 272
Suisse Romande Orchestra, Dutoit

Oedipus Rex
Orfeo C-07183
Bavarian Radio Symphony and Chorus, Davis

Firebird (complete ballet)
Philips 400 074
Concertgebouw Orchestra, Davis

Rite of Spring; Petrushka
CBS MK 42433
Columbia Symphony Orchestra, Stravinsky

Soldier's Tale
Nimbus NIM 5063
Lee, Scottish Chamber Orchestra, Friend

16. GIUSEPPE VERDI

As in the case of other opera composers, the main choice here is between highlights recorded on a single disc for each opera and complete operas, each taking three discs. The discs listed below are for highlights, but in each instance complete operas also are available by the same performers. From a budget standpoint, one compromise is to turn to full operas on cassettes, considerably less expensive than compact discs. Another option, and my preferred one for opera, is to substitute videotapes—new ones, or your own taped from television.

Aida (highlights)
London 417 763
Tebaldi, etc., Vienna Philharmonic Orchestra, Karajan

Rigoletto (highlights)
London 421 303
Milnes, etc., London Symphony Orchestra, Bonynge

La traviata (highlights)
London 400 057
Sutherland, etc., National Philharmonic Orchestra, Bonynge

Il trovatore (highlights)
Deutsche Grammophon 415 285
Plowright, etc., St. Cecelia Orchestra, Giulini

Requiem Mass
Telarc CD 80152 (two discs)
Dunn, etc., Atlanta Symphony Orchestra, Shaw

17. GUSTAV MAHLER

Symphonies are one of the two things Mahler is about, and there are scads of good recordings of them. Beyond the recommendations below, options include recordings by Solti and the Chicago Symphony, Muti and the Philadelphia Orchestra, Walter and the Columbia Symphony, Ozawa and the Boston Symphony, Karajan and the Berlin Philharmonic, and Inbal and the Frankfurt Radio Symphony Orchestra. Songs are the other Mahler thing, and, in addition to the recommended discs featuring Dame Janet Baker, there are out-standing performances by several other singers including Kirsten Flagstad and Jessye Norman.

Symphony No. 1 (Titan)
London 417 701
London Symphony Orchestra, Solti

Symphony No. 4 in G
CBS MDK-44908
Battle, Vienna Philharmonic Orchestra, Maazel

Das Lied von der Erde
London 414 194
Ferrier, Vienna Philharmonic Orchestra, Walter

Des Knaben Wunderhorn
Nimbus NI 5084
Baker, Evans, London Philharmonic Orchestra, Morris

Lieder eine fahrenden Gesellen; Lieder und Gesange; Im Lenz; Winter-
   lied
Hyperion CDA 66100
Baker, Parsons

18. SERGEI PROKOFIEV

Both Starter Kit symphonies can be found on one compact disc with the Los Angeles Philharmonic. Other choices for excellent perform-ances of these symphonies, but on separate discs, are Bernstein and the New York Philharmonic and Järvi and the Scottish National Orches-tra for the First Symphony; and Bernstein and the Israel Philharmonic, Slatkin and the Saint Louis Orchestra, and Janson and the Leningrad (St. Peterburg) for the Fifth. As noted earlier, there also are many good *Peter and the Wolf* options, including André Previn on Telarc and Dudley Moore with the Boston Pops Orchestra on Philips.

Symphonies No. 1 in D (Classical) and No. 5 in B-flat
Philips 420 172
Los Angeles Philharmonic Orchestra, Previn

Piano Concerto No. 3 in C; Bartók piano concerto
London 411 969
Ashkenazy, London Symphony Orchestra, Previn

Lieutenant Kijé (suite); Love of Three Oranges (suite)
Sony Classical MDK 46502
Maazel, Orchestre Nationale de France

Peter and the Wolf; Cinderella (ballet), Suites No. 1 and No. 2
Chandos CHAN 8511
Lina Prokofiev, Scottish National Orchestra, Järvi

19. DMITRI SHOSTAKOVICH

At this writing, the only way to get the *Age of Gold* Suite is in combination with one or more of the composer's symphonies. The recommendations will give you five Shostakovich symphonies—the first, the second, the third, the fifth, and the ninth. The early ones were written when he was in his early twenties and are not considered his finest work. However, he wrote fifteen in all and is viewed as one of the twentieth century's best symphonists, so not to worry.

Symphonies No. 1 in F Minor and No. 9 in E-flat
London 414 677
London Philharmonic Orchestra, Haitink

Symphony No. 5 in D Minor
London 410 017
Royal Concertgebouw, Haitink

Piano Quintet, Op. 57; Piano Trio No. 2
Chandos CHAN 8342
Zweig, Borodin Trio, Horner

Symphonies No. 2 (October Revolution) and No. 3 (First of May); Age
  of Gold Suite
London 421 131
London Philharmonic Orchestra and Chorus, Haitink

Concerto No. 1 for Piano and Trumpet; Concerto No. 1 for Cello;
  Concerto No. 2 for Piano

CBS Masterworks ("Portrait Series") MPK-44850
Previn, New York Philharmonic Orchestra, Bernstein

20. RICHARD STRAUSS

In this case, outstanding renditions of the recommended discs for the Starter Kit provide bonuses. Inasmuch as Starter Kit selections are based on the composer's music, not on available compact discs, this happy circumstance does not always exist and does not permanently endure.

Death and Transfiguration; Till Eulenspiegel; Salome: Salome's Dance
Seraphim 4XG 60297
Dresden State Orchestra, Kempe

Ein Heldenleben; Four Last Songs
Chandos CHAN 8518
Scottish National Orchestra, Järvi

Der Rosenkavalier (excerpts)
Deutsche Grammophon 415 284
Tomowa-Sintow, Vienna Philharmonic Orchestra and State Opera
    Chorus, Karajan

21. HECTOR BERLIOZ

The complete version of Solti's *Damnation of Faust* is available on a two-disc set for those who want that much of that long work, which the composer called a "dramatic legend" and which is known also as a concert-opera. Here, the recommendation is for the highlights. On another point, do not miss the combination of Dame Janet Baker and Sir John Barbirolli for *Les nuits d'été*. It is considered to be a special treat as a recorded song cycle.

Symphonie fantastique
Philips 411 425
Concertgebouw Orchestra, Davis

Roméo et Juliette
See Tchaikovsky

La damnation de Faust (highlights)
London 410 181
Riegel, etc., Chicago Chorus and Symphony Orchestra, Solti

Overtures: Le carnaval Romain; Harold in Italy
Deutsche Grammophon 415 109
Berlin Philharmonic Orchestra, Maazel

Les nuits d'été; Songs from La mort de Cléopâtre and Les Troyens
Angel CDM 7 69544
Baker, New Philharmonia Orchestra, Barbirolli

22. CLAUDE DEBUSSY

Inasmuch as most of Debussy's works are short, a good many compositions can be packed into four compact discs. As in all cases, we have tried to restrict the choices to the Listed composer, although to avoid repetition one recommendation does include some Ravel. With this collection, you will have the best of Debussy: orchestra, piano, and song.

Jeux; Nocturnes
Philips 400 023
Concertgebouw Orchestra, Haitink

La mer; Prélude à l'après-midi d'un faune; Ravel's Boléro and his
    Daphnis et Chloé Suite
Deutsche Grammophon 413 154
Berlin Philharmonic Orchestra, Karajan

Arabesques No. 1 and No. 2; Ballade; Images, Book I; L'isle joyeuse;
    La plus que lente; Rêverie; Suite bergamasque
Conifer CDCF 148
Stott

Chansons de Bilitis. Recitation with musical accompaniment
Deutsche Grammophon 429738
Deneuve, Ensemble Wien-Berlin

23. GIACOMO PUCCINI

Although it took a while, highlights are available on compact disc of all five Starter Kit operas—*Madame Butterfly, Tosca, La Bohème, Turandot,* and *Manon Lescaut.* Complete operas of all can be found. One option is to collect the highlight discs plus a collection of Puccini arias and duets; a second is to go for as many two-disc full operas as you want; a third is to fall back on cassettes . . . or videotapes. And check the record stores to see what came out yesterday.

Madame Butterfly (highlights)
London 417 733
Tebaldi, etc., St. Cecelia Academy Orchestra and Chorus, Serafin

Tosca (highlights)
Deutsche Grammophon 423 113
Ricciarelli, etc., German Opera Chorus, Berlin Philharmonic Orchestra, Karajan

La Bohème (scenes and arias)
London 421 301
Tebaldi, etc., St. Cecelia Academy Orchestra and Chorus, Serafin

Arias from La Bohème, Gianni Schicchi, Madame Butterfly, Manon Lescaut, La Rondine, Tosca, Turandot, Le Villi
Angel CDC 47841
Caballé, London Symphony Orchestra, Mackerras

Turandot (highlights)
London 421 320
Sutherland, Pavarotti, etc., London Philharmonic Orchestra, Mehta

Manon Lescaut (selections)
Myto Records 1 MCD 904.21
Olivero, Domingo, Arena di Verona Orchestra and Chorus

24. GIOVANNI DA PALESTRINA

For historical reasons, it is mandatory to have *Missa Papae Marcelli* in your collection, and good to have a sampling of motets. While there are not a lot of compact disc choices of Palestrina, enough are available for a starter library. Aside from *Missa Papae Marcelli*, this is one of those cases where it is wise to begin by accepting what your record stores carry rather than undertaking a laborious search.

Missa brevis; Missa nasce la gioia mia; Primavera madrigal
Gimell CDGIM 008
Tallis Scholars, Phillips

Missa Papae Marcelli; Stabat mater
IMP Classics PCD 863
Pro Cantione Antigua, Brown

Motet and Mass: Tu es Petrus
Argo 410 149
Kings College Choir, Cleobury

Missa, Aeterna Christi Munera; Magnificat Primi
Toni; Motets, etc.
Hyperion CDA 66490
Choir of Westminster Cathedral, O'Donnell

Missa de Beata Virgine
Hungaroton HCD-12921
Jeunesses Musicales Chorus, Ugrin

25. ANTON BRUCKNER

Bruckner's symphonies are so long that the disc makers figure they don't have to give you much else on a CD. For the four Starter Kit symphonies, four different conductors and orchestras have been selected, for comparison and variety. Some believe that the most famous interpreter of Bruckner is Wilhelm Furtwängler, available for some symphonies.

Symphony No. 4 in E-flat
Deutsche Grammophon 415 277
Berlin Philharmonic Orchestra, Karajan

Symphony No. 7 in E
London 414 290
Berlin Radio Symphony Orchestra, Chailly

Symphony No. 8 in C Minor; Wagner's Siegfried Idyll
Philips 412 465
Concertgebouw Orchestra, Haitink

Symphony No. 9 in D Minor
Odyssey MBK-44825
Columbia Symphony Orchestra, Walter

Te Deum; Brahms's German Requiem
Deutsche Grammophon 410 521
Vienna Philharmonic Orchestra, Karajan

26. GEORG TELEMANN

Telemann's works are short, so it is more prudent to recommend the best all-around discs than to try to single out specific Starter Kit choices. To be fair to Telemann fans, three discs are identified and recommended. You may decide that they all sound so much alike that you might cheat, buy one, invite friends over for an evening of Telemann, and play the same disc four times. That works with Vivaldi, too.

Concerto for Flute, Oboe D'Amore, and Viola D'Amore in E; Concerto polonois; Double Concerto for Recorder and Flute in E Minor; Triple Trumpet Concerto in D; Quadro in B-flat
Oiseau-Lyre 411 949
Soloists, Academy of Ancient Music, Hogwood

Concerto for Trumpet and Orchestra
Philips 420 954
Soloists, Academy of St. Martin-in-the-Fields

Water Music (Hamburg Ebb and Flow); Concertos in A Minor, B-flat, and F
Deutsche Grammophon 413 788
Cologne Musica Antiqua, Goebel

27. CAMILLE SAINT-SAËNS

If you want to try a more irreverent version of *Carnival of the Animals* than the one recommended below, a good choice is one recited by Hermione Gingold, with verses by Ogden Nash, on Deutsche Grammophon. The music is by Boehm and the Vienna Philharmonic, and it is coupled with Prokofiev's *Peter and the Wolf*. But the recommended disc also is delightful. My grandchildren like any version of *Carnival of the Animals* and *Peter and the Wolf*, even though I had some trouble convincing one four-year-old that Peter's grandfather and *his* grandfather were different people.

Symphony No. 3 in C Minor (Organ); Danse macabre; Le déluge: Prelude; Samson et Dalila: Bacchanale
Deutsche Grammophon 415 847
Litaize, Chicago Symphony Orchestra, Barenboim

Carnival of the Animals; Ravel's Mother Goose
Philips 400 016
V. & P. Jennings, Pittsburgh Symphony Orchestra, Previn

Piano Concertos No. 2 in G Minor and No. 4 in C Minor
Angel CDC 47816
Collard, Royal Philharmonic Orchestra, Previn

Cello Concerto No. 1 in A Minor; Schumann cello concerto
London 410 019
Harrell, Cleveland Orchestra, Marriner

28. JEAN SIBELIUS

Among artists who have recorded all seven Sibelius symphonies are Ashkenazy and the Philharmonic Orchestra on London (the best bargain, with four midpriced discs) and Sir Colin Davis and the Boston Symphony Orchestra on Philips. Fine discs of the First Symphony also offer Järvi and the Gothenburg Symphony Orchestra on BIS, Karajan and the Berlin Philharmonic on Angel, Rattle and the Birmingham (England) Orchestra on Angel, Berglund and the Helsinki Symphony on Angel, Gibson and the Scottish National Orchestra on Chandos, George Szell, and others. Unless you are an elitist—for whom this book is not—any of them will do just fine. Sibelius is for common folk-music lovers.

Symphony No. 1 in E Minor; Karelia Suite
London 414 534
Philharmonia Orchestra, Ashkenazy

Symphony No. 2 in D
BIS CD 252
Gothenburg Symphony Orchestra, Järvi

Violin Concerto in D Minor; Glazunov and Prokofiev concertos
RCA RCD1 7019
Heifetz, Chicago Symphony Orchestra, Hendl

Kalevalá: Four Legends
BIS CD 294
Gothenburg Symphony Orchestra, Järvi

En Saga, Op. 9; Finlandia, Op. 26; Legend, The Swan of Tuonela, Op. 22/2; Tapiola, Op. 112
Angel 69017
Berlin Philharmonic Orchestra, Karajan

29. MAURICE RAVEL

This is the only time in the discography when the recommendation is for one conductor/orchestra combination for all Starter Kit selections. Charles Dutoit and the Montreal Orchestra—the French connection—have become world-known for their interpretations of Frenchman Ravel and are enthusiastically recommended in one four-disc midpriced set. One Starter Kit choice, "Pièce en forme de Habanera" for violin and piano, cannot be found on CD without incurring considerable duplication, but it is only three minutes long, and enough music is in this set to make up for its absence.

Alborada del gracioso; Une barque sur l'ocean; Boléro; Piano Concerto in G; Piano Concerto for the Left Hand; Daphnis et Chloé (complete ballet); L'eventail de Jeanne: Fanfare; Menuet antique; Ma mère l'oye (complete); Pavane pour une infante défunte; Rap-

sodie Espagnole; Le tombeau de Couperin; La valse; Valse nobles
et sentimentales
London 421 458 (four discs)
Montreal Symphony Orchestra with Chorus and pianist Roge, Dutoit

30. GIOACCHINO ROSSINI

The best way for beginning collectors to handle Rossini may be with
a combination of highlights, a complete opera, some overtures, and a
group of arias. For those who want them, a dozen complete operas are
available.

Il barbiere di Siviglia (Barber of Seville) (highlights)
Philips 412 266-2
Baltsa, Allen, etc., Academy of St. Martin-in-the-Fields, Marriner

Guglielmo Tell (William Tell) (complete)
London 417 154 (four discs)
Pavarotti, Freni, etc., Ambrosian Opera Chorus, National Philhar-
monic Orchestra, Chailly

Overtures: Il barbiere di Siviglia, La cener entola, La gazza ladra,
L'Italiana in Algeri, Otello, La scala di seta, Semiramide, William
Tell
Philips 412 893
Academy of St. Martin-in-the-Fields, Marriner

Collection of arias from several operas
London 421 306
Horne, Ambrosia Opera Chorus, Royal Philharmonic Orchestra,
Henry Lewis

31. EDVARD GRIEG

His Peer Gynt music is by far Grieg's most popular work, and many
renditions of it are on the market. The best known of them over recent
years have been interpretations by Sir Thomas Beecham and the Beecham Choral Society, Herbert Blomstedt and the San Francisco

Chorus and Symphony Orchestra, Herbert von Karajan and the Berlin Philharmonic, and Neemi Järvi and the Gothenburg Chorus and Symphony Orchestra. The choice here is for Sir Neville Marriner, but I would reemphasize that the whole idea is to help readers become more familiar with excellent performances of these compositions. No rule bars appropriate substitutions.

Piano Concerto in A Minor; Schumann concerto
London 417 728
Lupo, London Symphony Orchestra, Previn

Peer Gynt (extended excerpts)
Angel CDC7 47003
Popp, Academy of St. Martin-in-the-Fields, Marriner

Holberg Suite; Lyric Pieces from Op. 12, 38, 43, 47, 54, 57, 67, 68;
    Norwegian Dance No. 2, Op. 35; Peer Gynt: Morning
Teldec ZK 42925
Cyprien Katsaris

Holberg Suite; Two Elegiac Melodies; Lullaby, Op. 68/5; Two Melo-
    dies, Op. 53; Two Melodies, Op. 56
BIS CD 147
Norwegian Chamber Orchestra, Tonnessen

Songs (with orchestra), including Ich liebe Dich
Arkadia 2 CD-576 (two discs)
Flagstad, BBC Symphony Orchestra, Sargent

32. CHRISTOPH GLUCK

Four of the five Starter Kit choices are in the catalogues and the fifth—Suite der Divertissement from *Iphigénie en Aulide*—undoubtedly will reappear. The complete *Iphigénie en Aulide* opera is available in two-disc sets on Erato and Eurodisc labels, but inasmuch as *Orfeo ed Euridice* already is in the Starter Kit it is unlikely that many readers will want two Gluck operas in their beginning collections. For those who do become dedicated Gluckians, complete operas of *Alceste* and of *Echo et Narcisse* can be found. A suggested substitute for the *Aulide* music is the ballet, *Don Juan*.

Orfeo ed Euridice (complete)
London 417 410 (two discs)
Horne, Lorengar, etc., Orchestra and Chorus of the Royal Opera
    House, Solti

Iphigénie en Aulide: Overture
Koch Legacy 3 7119 2
Berlin Philharmonic Orchestra, Strauss

Concerto in G for Flute and Orchestra
Jacklin 506-2
Graf, Zürich Camerata, Tschupp

Overture: Alceste
Koch International Classics, Legacy Scenes 3-7011-2
Royal Concertgebouw Orchestra, Mengelberg

Don Juan (ballet)
Bayer BR 100 016
Arcata Ensemble Stuttgart, Strub

33. PAUL HINDEMITH

Hindemith's popularity has not quite happened, despite the high professional assessment of his music. But in the compact disc field, a
considerable amount is available to provide a strong Hindemith section for your music library.

Requiem: When Lilacs Last in the Dooryard Bloom'd
Telarc CD 80132
DeGaetani, Atlanta Chorus and Symphony Orchestra, Shaw

Concert Music for Strings and Brass; Symphonic Metamorphosis of
    Themes by Weber; Mathis der Maler
Deutsche Grammophon 429 404
Israel Philharmonic Orchestra, Bernstein

Kleine Kammermusik No. 2 for Wind Quintet
Bis CD-291
Bergen Wind Quintet

Sonata for Trumpet and Piano
Crystal CD-663
Plog, Davis

Das Marienleben, Op. 27
Jecklin 574-2
Janowitz, Gage

34. CLAUDIO MONTEVERDI

The trick here is how best to combine some opera, some madrigals, some masses, and some vespers in order to capture an honest Monteverdi. Compact disc producers do not offer clean-cut choices that are in sync with the Starter Kit. Five discs are needed to satisfy Starter Kit requirements, although after studying them you may decide that you can do with fewer in your early collection days.

Solo vocal music: Ab aeterno ordinata sum; Confitebor tibi, Domine
    (three settings); Deus tuorum militum sors et corona; Iste confessor Domini sacratus; Laudate Dominum, O omnes gentes; La
    Maddalena Prologue: Su le penne de venti; Nisi Dominus
    aedificaverit domum
Hyperion CDA 66021
Kirby, Partridge, Thomas, Parley of Instruments

Lamento d'Arianna
EMI (Deutsche Halmonia Mundi) CDCB 49414
Consort of Musicke, Anthony Rooley

Madrigals: Book No. 4
Oiseau-Lyre 414 148
Consort of Musicke, Anthony Rooley

Masses: Missa de cappella a four; Missa de cappella a six; Motets
Hyperion CDA 66214
The 16, Harry Christophers; M. Phillips

Vespers: Vespro della Beata Vergine
London 414572
Tear, Palmer, Gardiner, etc. Philip Jones Brass Ensemble;
Monteverdi Orchestra and Chorus

35. BÉLA BARTÓK

The most popular Bartók orchestral work is his Concerto for Orchestra. Among many outstanding renditions are those by Solti and the Chicago Symphony on London, Karajan and the Berlin Philharmonic on Deutsche Grammophon, and Boulez with the New York Philharmonic on CBS. While Dorati and the Concertgebouw are recommended here, that is in part because this disc includes other Bartók music. If you don't mind another rendition of Mussorgsky's *Pictures at an Exhibition*, you might choose Solti instead.

Concerto for Orchestra; Two Images, Op. 10
Philips 411 132
Concertgebouw Orchestra, Dorati

Music for Strings, Percussion, and Celesta
See Hindemith

Miraculous Mandarin (complete ballet); Two Portraits, Op. 5; Prokofiev's Scythian Suite
Deutsche Grammophon 410 598
Ambrosian Singers, London Symphony Orchestra, Abbado

String Quartets No. 3, No. 4, No. 5
Chandos CHAN-8634
Chilingirian String Quartet

Hungarian Peasant Songs; Dance Suite; Three Rondos on Folk Tunes; Rumanian Dances
Denon C37-7092
Schiff, piano

36. CÉSAR FRANCK

Many consider that the best rendition of the Symphony in D Minor is one by Pierre Monteux with the Chicago Symphony Orchestra on RCA. But that one is coupled with two other composers, and the recommendation here by Karajan is combined with another Starter Kit choice. No guilt is felt in saving you a few dollars.

Symphony in D Minor; Symphonic Variations
Angel CDM 69008
Weissenberg, Berlin Philharmonic Orchestra, Karajan

Violin Sonata in A
Deutsche Grammophon 415 683
Mintz, Bronfman

Piano Quintet in F Minor; Dvořák quintet
London 421 153
Curzon, Vienna Philharmonic Orchestra Quartet

Three Chorales for organ, with other organ works
REM 311095
Clerc

37. ANTONIO VIVALDI

Everyone but Lawrence Welk and Kay Kaiser has done *The Four Seasons*—Marriner and the Academy of St. Martin-in-the-Fields, Pinnock and the English Concert, the Drottingholm Baroque Ensemble, Mehta and the Israel Philharmonic, Perlman and the London Philharmonic, I Musici, the Scottish Chamber Orchestra, Abbado and the London Symphony, Hogwood and the Chamber Orchestra of Europe, the St. Paul Chamber Orchestra with Zukerman, the Israel Philharmonic with Perlman, the Virtuosi of England, Munchinger and the Stuttgart Chamber Orchestra, Karajan and the Berlin Philharmonic, Karajan with Mutter and the Vienna Philharmonic, Schwartz and the Los Angeles Chamber Orchestra, the trio at the national headquarters of Goodwill Industries, and the Washington Redskins Marching Band. In recent years it was more recorded than any other piece of classical music. We have chosen Sir Neville Marriner's version.

The Four Seasons
Argo 414486
Loveday, Academy of St. Martin-in-the-Fields, Marriner

Gloria in D (RV 588); Gloria in D (RV 589)
Argo 410 018
Russell, St. John's College Cambridge Choir, Guest

Concerto in C for Two Trumpets and Strings, with oboe, oboe-violin
    and violin-cello concertos.
Chandos CHAN 8651
Thompson, Early, Turovsky. I Musici de Montreal

Concerto for Guitar and Orchestra
London 417617-2
Fernandez, English Chamber Orchestra

Concerto in C for Mandolin and Orchestra
Suphraphon CO-2306
Mislivecek, Prague Chamber Orchestra

38. GEORGES BIZET

Since Bizet is on The List only because of *Carmen*, we'll break a house
rule and recommend the entire opera rather than excerpts. The symphony he wrote at seventeen is combined here with the two *L'Arlésienne* Suites. Rarely heard, but available for Bizet buffs from EMI
with the Toulouse Orchestra, is the rest of the *L'Arlésienne* incidental
music. The two suites constitute only about half of it. To avoid duplication, we'll bypass *Jeux d'enfants*.

Symphony in C; L'Arlésienne Suites 1 and 2
Angel CDC7 47794
French National Radio Orchestra, Beecham

Carmen Suites No. 1 and No. 2; Grieg's Peer Gynt music
Telarc CD 80048
Saint Louis Symphony Orchestra, Slatkin

Carmen (complete)
Deutsche Grammophon 410 088 (three discs)
Ricciarelli, etc., Paris Opera Chorus, Berlin Philharmonic Orchestra,
    Karajan

39. MODEST MUSSORGSKY

Some fun music is missing in the recommendations below because of no current compact disc recording of the "Dance of the Persian Slaves" from the opera *Khovanshchina*. Also, some Starter Kit repetition is necessary since not a lot of Mussorgsky is available on compact disc. One recording that should not be missed is the Cleveland Orchestra rendition of two of his most famous compositions. And one that you might bypass on the grounds of length and expense is a three-disc set of his famous opera, *Boris Godounov*—although sooner or later you have to get into that powerful work.

Pictures at an Exhibition (orch. by Ravel); Night on Bald Mountain
Telarc CD 80042
Cleveland Orchestra, Maazel

Night on Bald (or the bare) Mountain; Khovanshchina: Prelude; Borodin's Prince Igor: Overture and Polovtsian dances; Glinka's Russian Overture
London 417 689
London Symphony Orchestra, Solti

Boris Godounov
London 411 862 (three discs)
Ghiaurov, Vienna Philharmonic Orchestra, Karajan

Pictures at an Exhibition for piano, with other piano music
Calliope CAL 9687
Rudy

40. JEAN-PHILIPPE RAMEAU

Six compact discs are required to meet Starter Kit recommendations, giving you more Rameau than your library needs at this time. This is another place where you might want to settle for a smaller sample of orchestral music, harpsichord works, and vocal compositions.

Les Boréades: Orchestral Suite; Dardanus: Orchestral Suite
Philips 420 240
Orchestra of the Eighteenth Century, Bruggen

Hippolyte et Aricie: Orchestral Suite
Editio Classics 7700a
La Petite Bande, Kuijken

Les Indes galantes: excerpts (harpsichord)
Harmonia Mundi HMC 901028
Gilbert

Pièces de clavecin en concert (Five suites for harpsichord and strings)
Sony SK 45 868
Rampal, Stech, Ritter

Motets: In convertendo
Harmonia Mundi HMC 901078
Herreweghe, Chapelle Royal Choir, Ghent Collegium Vocale

Castor et Pollux (orchestral music)
Philips 426 714-2
F. Brügen, Orchestra of the Eighteenth Century

41. GABRIEL FAURÉ

The amount of music on a compact disc makes it possible to have several other Fauré songs along with the Starter Kit selection of *La bonne chanson*.

Ballade in F-sharp for Piano and Orchestra; Fantasie in G for Piano
    and Orchestra, Op. 111; Ravel's Piano Concerto in G
Pro Arte CDD-313
Varsano, Philharmonic Orchestra, Davis

Elegie for Cello and Orchestra, Op. 24; Aprés un rêve; Dolly; Pavane;
    Pelleás
Deutsche Grammophon 423 089
Eskin, Boston Symphony Orchestra, Ozawa

Sonata in A for Violin and Piano, Op. 13
Deutsche Grammophon 423 065-2
Mintz, Bronfman

La bonne chanson, Op. 61; Poème d'un jour, Op. 21; Les berceux; La
    chanson d'Eve; Eau vivante; O mort, poussiere d'étoiles; Le hori-
    zon chimerique; Le jardin clos: Exaucement; Je me poserai sur ton
    coeur; Cinq mélodies de Venise; Mirages
Philips 420 775
Gerard Souzay, Dalton Baldwin

Requiem; Pavane, Op. 50
Angel CDM 69038
Armstrong, Fischer-Dieskau, Edinburgh Festival Chorus, Orchestre
    de Paris, Barenboim

42. NIKOLAI RIMSKY-KORSAKOV

It is not possible on compact discs to complete the Rimsky-Korsakov
Starter Kit without having some repetition. The recommended selections keep that repetition to a minimum while still providing outstanding performances. And it is okay to hear two renditions of pieces like
the *May Night* Overture and the *Snow Maiden* Suite, especially with
the Scottish National Orchestra playing Russian music. Also, one of
the wonderful things about compact discs is that by pushing a button
you can pass right over a composition if you want to.

Scheherazade; Borodin's Polovtsian Dances
Angel 47717
Royal Philharmonic Orchestra, Beecham

Capriccio Espagnol; May Night Overture; Sadko, Op. 15; The Snow
    Maiden Suite
Philips 411 446
Rotterdam Philharmonic Orchestra, Zinman

Christmas Eve (suite); Le coq d'or (suite); Legend of the Invisible City
    of Kitezh (suite); May Night Overture; Mlada (suite); The Snow
    Maiden (suite); The Tale of the Tsar Saltan (suite)
Chandos CHAN 8327-9
Scottish National Orchestra, Järvi

Russian Easter Overture; Capriccio Espagnol; Tchaikovsky's Ca-
    priccio Italien and Marche Slav

Odyssey MBK 42248
Philadelphia Orchestra, Ormandy

43. GAETANO DONIZETTI

Three recommendations here are for excerpts from individual operas, and the fourth is a selection of arias from several different operas. With all respect to the dedication of Texaco and its long history of Saturday afternoon broadcasts of the Metropolitan Opera, this reflects my own prejudice against heard-but-not-seen opera. Complete versions of Donizetti's major operas are available on compact discs (two or three discs per opera) for those who prefer them.

Don Pasquale (selections)
Nuova Era 6766
Sera, Dara, Teatro Regio di Torino Orchestra and Chorus, Campanella

L'elisir d'Amore (excerpts)
London 2-A 414461-2
Sutherland, Pavarotti, English Chamber Orchestra, Bonynge

Lucia di Lammermoor (selections)
Angel CDM-63934
Callas, Casellato, Philharmonia Orchestra, Serafin

Arias from Don Pasquale; Don Sebastiano; Il Duca d'Alba; L'elisir d'amore; La favorita; La fille du régiment; Lucia di Lammermoor; Maria Stuarda
London 417 638
Pavarotti, with various orchestras

44. RALPH VAUGHAN WILLIAMS

A house rule is that beginning collectors cannot have too much Bach, Schubert, Smetana, Sibelius, Mozart, Beethoven, Haydn, and Vaughan Williams. The best set of Vaughan Williams symphonies, all in a seven-disc box, is Sir Adrian Boult's on EMI with the London Philharmonic, first out at full price and then at midprice. To handle the

Starter Kit, the recommendation here is for the Boult rendition of the Second Symphony and another version of the Fifth.

Symphony No. 2 (London); Fantasia on a Theme by Thomas Tallis
Angel CDM 64017
London Philharmonic Orchestra, Boult

Symphony No. 5 in D; The Lark Ascending
Chandos CHAN 8554
London Symphony Orchestra, Thomson

English Folk Songs Suite; Fantasia on Greensleeves; The Lark Ascending; Norfolk Rhapsody No. 1; Serenade to Music
Angel CDCM 64022
London Symphony Orchestra, Boult

On Wenlock Edge
Opal CD 9844
Elwes, Kiddle, London String Quartet

45. BEDŘICH SMETANA

Curiously, three of the four available discs of *The Bartered Bride*, the most famous Czech opera, are sung in German. But there is also a complete opera in Czech, on the Supraphon label, plus excerpts of it.

Mà vlast (complete); The Bartered Bride: Overture and Dances
Deutsche Grammophon 419 768
Vienna Philharmonic Orchestra, Levine

From My Homeland (two duets for violin and piano); works by Dvořák and Janáček
Panton 81 1202
Sniti, Hála

String Quartets No. 1 in E Minor (Out of [or From] My Life) and No. 2 in D Minor
Denon C37 7339
Smetana Quartet

The Bartered Bride (in Czech)
Supraphon 10 3511-2 (three discs)

Benackova, Dvorsky, Novak, etc. Czech Philharmonic Orchestra and
Chorus, Kosler

46. JOHANN STRAUSS

Some (not all) elitists may advise that you ignore these Johann Strauss
recordings, on the grounds that he should not be Listed in the first
place. Just agree, and never tell them you have bought the discs. A
zillion collections are available. I would spend little time tracking
down these particular ones. One optional route is to collect separate
CDs for waltzes, polkas, and overtures.

Waltzes: The Blue Danube; Tales from the Vienna Woods; Roses
from the South; Kaiser Waltz; Wine, Women and Song
London 417 706
Vienna Philharmonic Orchestra, Boskovsky

New Year's Concert 1990 in Vienna: Overtures, Polkas, Waltzes,
Marches, by Strauss senior and Strauss junior
Sony Classical SK 45808
Vienna Philharmonic Orchestra, Mehta

Die Fledermaus
Angel CDHB 69531 (two discs)
Schwarzkopf, etc., Philharmonia Chorus and Orchestra, Karajan

47. KARL MARIA VON WEBER

Another strong choice for the Clarinet Concerto is Stolzman on RCA
with the Mostly Mozart Festival. Benny Goodman also weighs in on
Musicmasters.

Overtures: Oberon; Euryanthe; Abu Hassan; Der Freischütz; Ruler of
the Spirits; Invitation to the Dance
Nimbus N1 5154
The Hanover Band, Goodman

Clarinet Concertos No. 1 in F Minor and No. 2 in E-flat; Concertino
in C Minor

Chandos CHAN 8305
Hilton, City of Birmingham Symphony Orchestra, Järvi

Clarinet Quintet in B-flat; with Mozart Quintet
Deutsche Grammophon 419600
Brunner, Hagen Quartet

Der Freischütz (complete)
Deutsche Grammophon 415 432 (two discs)
Janowitz, Leipzig Radio Chorus, Dresden State Orchestra, Kleiber

48. LEOŠ JANÁČEK

The fit between Starter Kit recommendations and available compact
discs is a good one here, with all five recommendations found on four
fine CDs. "Powerful emotion" may not be the first thing that leaps
into mind at the first mention of the City of Birmingham (England)
Symphony Orchestra, but the CD reviewers use such phrases as "Slavonic passion," in discussing that fine symphony's interpretation of
Janáček's *Glagolitic* Mass. Because *Jenufa* is regarded as *the* Czech
opera, both a complete version and another of excerpts are listed for
your choice.

Sinfonietta; Taras Bulba
London 410138
Vienna Philharmonic Orchestra, Mackerras

Glagolitic Mass
Angel CDC 47504
City of Birmingham Symphony Orchestra and Chorus, Rattle

String Quartets No. 1 (Kreutzer Sonata) and No. 2 (Intimate Pages)
Denon C37-7545
Smetana Quartet

Jenufa (complete)
London 414 483 (two discs)
Söderström, Vienna Philharmonic Orchestra, Mackerras
                                   or
Jenufa (excerpts)
Myto 2 MCD 904.22
Hillebrecht, Bavarian State Opera Orchestra and Chorus, Kubclik

49. FRANÇOIS COUPERIN

Choices are limited, but three discs should satisfy the Couperin desires of a healthy percentage of readers. Here, as in other cases of less well-known composers, more CDs become available as more time passes.

Concerts royaux Nos. 1 in G; 2 in D; 3 in A; 4 in E Minor
Harmonia Mundi HMC 901151
Claire, Csee, Moroney, Ter Linden

Pièces de clavecin (harpsichord suites), Orders 7 and 8
Denon CO 1719
Dreyfus, harpsichord

Pièces d'orgue No. 1 (Messe a l'usage ordinaire des paroisses)
Harmonia Mundi HMC 90714
Chapuis, organist

50. ALEXANDER BORODIN

Two compact discs handle Starter Kit recommendations, since the *Prince Igor* Overture is on a Mussorgsky recording.

Symphony No. 2 in B Minor; In the Steppes of Central Asia; Prince
    Igor: Polovtsian Dances
RCA 60535
National Philharmonic Orchestra of London, Tjeknavorian

String Quartets No. 1 in A and No. 2 in D
Angel CDC 47795
Borodin Quartet

Index

ABOUT THE AUTHOR

Phil Goulding was born in San Francisco in 1921, grew up in Cleveland, attended Hamilton College in upstate New York, and spent World War II in the navy. He has lived in Washington, D.C., since 1950, as a newspaper reporter, an assistant secretary of defense, and a petroleum-industry executive. Twenty years ago he wrote *Confirm or Deny*, a book about the Pentagon, the press, and the public. He says that was a subject he knew something about. With his wife Miriam and their two furry children, he now divides his time between Washington and a Chateaugay Lake cabin in the Adirondacks. He also has five two-legged children and a growing gaggle of grandchildren.